SURVIVAL DESPITE THE PEOPLE:
DEMOCRATIC DESTRUCTION OR SUSTAINABLE MERITOCRACY
DIDEM AYDURMUS
COVER: ANDRE FRITZ
COVER INSPIRED BY ILLUMINATE ALTERNATIVE CREATIONS

ISBN-13:978-1537678689
ISBN-10:153767868X

This book is self-published. The reasons are simple. I wanted it to be available as soon as possible and to anyone who wants to read it.

With small changes, the following text was submitted to the Graduate School of Social Sciences of Istanbul Bilgi University in partial fulfilment of the requirements for the degree of Doctor of Philosophy at the Department of International Relations. It is a dissertation. Critique is welcome. Contact me via email.

Dedicated to Meghan Rose as a placeholder for all the brave people who invest their lives so others can have a chance. Humanity is truly in debt to you.

Acknowledgements

I would like to thank my parents for their unlimited support, but even more for their idealism. Both have committed their lives to helping others and I cannot express how much I admire their efforts to make this world a better place against all odds. Being raised by those two wonderful people alone inspired my choice of topic, which revolves around social justice and equity at its core. My deep appreciation goes to Beate Fröhlich-Ilenburg, my grandparents and my siblings: Ahmet Aydurmus, Aysegül Kirman, Sinem Bücker, Nuri Bücker and Suna Bücker. Among the many friends that I am grateful for I can only mention a few. I express my gratitude to Jörg Hornung, Kira Schmidt Stiegenroth, Thomas Traub, Henrik Wesselmann and Katharina Wex for showing me how to be a better person. I also want to thank Robert Bitsch, Eris Celikel, Shazad Chaudhary, Sean Cox, Katrien Desimpelaere, Meike Dolkemeier, Manel Ebrahim, Amelie Eichmann, Vanessa Elges, Jim Mason, Aaron Finkbeiner, Josephine Gehlhar, Ilka Grunwald, Rebecca Grohnfeldt, Michalis Hadjikakou, Dan Halper, Karl Hideyo, Serdar Kadioglu, Özkan Kizilkan, Albert Lehrman, Liu Huying, Hendrik Lönngren, Sebastian Noethlichs, Elif Sandal Önal, Özgün Özcer; Sezin T. Özsakinc, Karin Polit, Andrea Reyes Elizondo, Martin Robson, Jody Sabral, Sonia Seidel, Hendrina Francis van Schalkwyk, Pavel Senderak, Sarah Thöle, Tobias Varennes, Borja Vazquez, Frank Waibel and Saira Zuberi for their academic help, carrying books across continents, trust in me, and especially for their friendship.

Good teachers should never be forgotten, therefore I would like to especially thank three of my high school teachers: Klaus Höfig, whose stickmen drawings of Plato's cave will remain in my memory forever; Kurt Reißner for his hope to enlighten all his students; and Helmut Remus for providing his students with an understanding of history and politics, even against their will. I would also like to thank my co-advisors, Alper Akyuz and Ilay Romain Örs, and the other members of my PhD jury Fikret Adaman, Murat Ergin and Sezai Ozan Zeybek. There are countless others to whom I am very grateful, and you are all in my heart. This includes the food delivery service personnel sent by yemeksepeti.com, which most certainly contributed to my personal carbon footprint; as well as the staff of the Atatürk library; YouTube, for providing me with countless hours of music; and the TYT network for reporting on various incorporated issues. To all suffering animals, I am sorry.

Last, but not least I would like to thank my supervisor, Bogac Erozan, who is one of those people who are always committed to helping others. I was very fortunate that he agreed to work with me.

TABLE OF CONTENT

1. INTRODUCTION

> "Humanity is conducting an unintended, uncontrolled, globally pervasive experiment whose ultimate consequences could be second only to a global nuclear war" (World Meteorological Organization 1988).

This experiment made the 21st century the century of unprecedented mass extinction. While Earth has experienced mass extinctions before, this extinction has a unique quality. It is caused by human behaviour (EPI 2012). Despite all controversy about the starting date, calling the planet's current phase Anthroposcene appears appropriate.[1] Human beings and their contemporary habitus have a significant impact on Earth's ecosystems. Technological advances gave mankind the power to severely damage life support systems for millennia to come.[2] This means that "for the first time ever, geological time scales must now figure in our moral calculations of the costs and consequences of our actions" (Ball 2006:140; Jonas 1984).[3] Concerned scientists have been pointing out for years that "[t]he environmental crisis is real", and not mere alarmism (Buell and DeLuca 1996:xii; Höffe 2009:138). The worst case scenario of devastating the planet until it becomes uninhabitable for humans cannot be excluded.[4] Survival is at stake.

Despite the widely acknowledged criticality, governments refrain from taking serious action. The political response in the majority of cases remains limited to symbolic actions.[5] What is more, climate change occurs faster than expected. Large-scale changes can already be observed. Not only the total meltdown of the North Pole in summer could be expected within the next couple of decades, but many other events will put human and animal life at unparalleled risk. "The reluctant conclusion of the most eminent climate scientists is that the world is now on a path to a

---

[1] The concept has to be understood as a geological epoch. Not every human being on Earth is actually responsible.

[2] "The IPCC [Intergovernmental Panel on Climate Change] is right to think that it will take thousands of years to undo the harm that we have done and that in our terms there is no going back" (Lovelock 2009:Loc. 61). Loc. stands for location used by the Amazon Kindle book format. Some of Amazon's own editions do not provide any other possible

[2] "The IPCC [Intergovernmental Panel on Climate Change] is right to think that it will take thousands of years to undo the harm that we have done and that in our terms there is no going back" (Lovelock 2009:Loc. 61). Loc. stands for location used by the Amazon Kindle book format. Some of Amazon's own editions do not provide any other possible format of reference. Since references always depend on the edition, there is no qualitative difference compared to traditional page numbers.

[3] "We accept responsibility for events in our own world, but not for what occurs in the natural one. Its storms, droughts, and floods are "acts of God," free of human control and exempt from our responsibility" (Commoner 1992:3).

[4] "The Future of Humanity Institute conducted a poll of academic experts on global risks. They gave an estimate of 19 percent probability that the human species will go extinct before the end of this century. The Stern Review: The Economics of Climate Change factored a 9.5 percent risk of extinction within the next century into its calculations" (Marshall 2014:Loc. 3494). Political commentator Hartmann titled his recent book *The Last Hours of Humanity Warming the World to Extinction* (2013).

[5] "We now have the certain knowledge that the Kyoto Protocol, which entered into force as recently as 2005, is wholly inadequate to the challenge" (Burnell 2009:4). In addition to the agreed reductions being insufficient, trends show that emissions are still rising. CO_2 emissions among others still increase dramatically (International Energy Agency 2012; Olivier et al. 2013). "The Kyoto Protocol committed the advanced economies to greenhouse gas emission reductions equivalent to about 5 percent over 1990 levels by 2010. [...] Globally, emissions have risen by 40 per cent since 1990" (Jackson 2012:Loc. 524-26).

very unpleasant future and it is too late to stop it" (Hamilton 2010:vii). The question today is not about whether it is happening but about the speed of climate change and the level of preparedness. Scholar after scholar has declared that business as usual will make the planet uninhabitable (Meadows et al. 2004; Jackson 2012; Randers 2012; Hohensee 2013). About two decades have passed since scientists, such as Goodland and Daly, stated that "[t]he transition to sustainability is urgent because the deterioration of global life support systems – the environment – imposes a time limit" (1996:1004). Without fast and determined policies, the future could witness a change in global temperature of 4-6° degrees Celsius leading to conditions similar to those found "today only in tiny and frowsty submarines" (Leggewie and Welzer 2009:10; my translation).[6] Political science cannot ignore this fact as it is likely to affect all politics and dominate the coming decades (Burnell 2009; Beeson 2010; Ehrlich and Ehrlich 2014; Schüttemeyer 2011; Tremmel 2011).[7] It should be the central scheme of all considerations. Yet, "[i]t would be an astonishing revelation to those outside the discipline that when political scientists contribute to questions related to the environment, they do so *despite their discipline*" (Agawal and Lemos 2009:69; my emphasis).

This consideration takes environmental sustainability as the most fundamental issue for politics and political science.[8] The security of breathable air, clean water, and food has to be taken as the necessary priority of politics. Their absolute importance to human life is indisputable. Any government today has to take the anthropogenous effect on the biosphere and the responsibility of entering the Anthroposcene into account. Everything else is irresponsible.[9] Coping with (the problem of) limited natural resources should be of uttermost concern. Any government then could be judged by its capability and actual performance regarding the achievement of sustainability as a priority. While this judgment is not value-free, it is certainly not value-laden. Survival as a motif is nearly a universal. Crafty politics questions what kind of conditions and circumstances are probable in the future and what kind of impact politics can have on these (Höffe 2009:24). So far, cases of crafty politics in the 21st century can hardly be found. New problems proverbially need new ways of thinking. Instead of trying the very ways that caused the problem, one needs new approaches. Humanity is facing a problem, a serious threat, and the search for solutions entails radically different thinking (Leggewie and Welzer 2009:199; Latour

---

[6] When asked if 4°C degree warming is alarmist or realist, many scientists agree that it is realistic. The question was asked at a conference in Oxford and "[t]he answer was unambiguous: in a show of hands everyone indicated they believed four degrees is realistic rather than alarmist" (Hamilton 2010:192).

[7] "The impacts of climate change will dramatically affect human health, water resources, agriculture, and ecosystems" (EPI 2012:53).

[8] For a comprehensive definition of environmental sustainability (see Goodland and Daly 1996:1008f.).

[9] For Hamilton "in the climate change debate the true moral questions do not concern what kind of actions should be taken, but why those who should act to avert calamity have not done so" (2014:341).

2007). Facing all possibilities, it is important to look at politics unapologetically and diagnose problems and shortcomings. A theory of good green governance "has to still emerge in a coherent form" (Connelly et al. 2012:281). Political science needs to define good green governance. This inquiry seeks to explore factors of good governance and policies that attribute significant attention to the 'health' of the biosphere. The urgency of taking measures against environmental degradation is critical in this context. Political science must identify and challenge widely held beliefs and dismantle them for what they are. Not only truth claims must be analysed, but also alternatives need to be elaborated. With respect to this task, this work is committed to Carr's statement that "[p]olitical science is the science not only of what is, but of what ought to be" (2001:6).[10]

Although the threat is known for at least four decades, instead of avoiding deterioration, natural resources have been overexploited and this overexploitation has only been expanded and accelerated (Anderson 2012).[11] One reason is the acceptance of potentially conflicting ideals and values. Prominently, every age has its predominant ideals. They are predominant in that they often stay unopposed and will not be questioned, but taken as universal truth. As internalised ideas, people understand them as natural, even though they are born out of a specific historical context and their validity remains questionable (Bourdieu 1977). Democracy is such an ideal.

> "The superiority of democracy over all other forms of government is so deeply ingrained in our way of thinking that alternatives such as meritocracy (government by the most able) or plutocracy (government by those with the largest social stake) say, can be declared imperfect without argument or evidence, as though they were all primitive forms of tribalism or manifestations of class-ridden inequalities. In this way, very often, democracy wins by default because it is deemed to have no real contenders" (Graham 2013:Loc. 343-47).

But democracy has not proven to be sustainable. While claiming superiority and neutrality, democracy allows practices that lead to considerable destruction.[12] Therefore, the first part of

---

[10] This is in accordance with climatologist and geophysicist Mann stating that "it is no longer acceptable for scientists to remain on the sidelines" (2014). Natural as well as social scientists can be found arguing for the acceptance of responsibility. "People who like "realism" in their theories often want not only standards that have a good chance of being met, but also specific (and nonhopeless) prescriptions for institutions. They sometimes want the theory to say what we should do, now, given the way people actually do act" (Estlund 2009:Loc. 3833-34).

[11] Though relatively common, nature should not be understood as a pristine world apart from human activity. The term 'nature' has to be understood not in opposition to culture as in modernist thought, but as subject of contemporary natural science which takes human culture as factor into account. As such it will neither be understood as purely constructed. The meaning of nature or the environment itself is not neutral. The term 'environment' is relatively new. De-Shalit sees a "little-noticed philosophical trap" in the belief that "a non-political view of nature, or the 'environment', which should inspire our politics, in fact we tend to interpret nature in a normative and political way such that it enhances and sustains the political views to which we are already committed. Even so-called scientific notions of nature and the environment presuppose certain normative commitments. The 'environment' is itself a tricky notion" (2006b:87f.).

[12] Environmental annihilation could be an outcome of "the dominance of particularistic and short-term interests, short electoral cycles and, more recently, to the dominance of neoliberal ideology (also referred to as the ideology of 'laissez-faire' or 'market fundamentalism') with its emphasis on the 'free market', a minimal role for governments and distaste for planning" (Bührs 2012:413).

this work questions the prospects of one of the most salient doctrines of our age, democracy, which was regarded as "the only game [left] in town" (Dahl 1989:203).[13] Whilst the fruits of 'progress' are excessively consumed, the responsibility that comes with power is forgotten in the light of modern freedom and 'consumer democracy'. Democracies by and large allow individual citizen to 'freely act' and consume what they can pay for. Individuals decide themselves which car to drive and how much fuel to burn. Meanwhile, the recognition that the consumption pattern of the industrialised nations needs to be changed in order to solve the serious threats of contemporary ecological reality, can be found in agreements such as the Agenda 21 (see Kuckartz 2008). Indeed, the correlation between temperature and CO_2 emissions, as well as GDP and CO_2 emissions, is overt (Burnell 2009; Granados and Carpintero 2009; Lane 2011a; EPI 2012),[14] but the economic growth paradigm remains dominant. Whereas capitalism is standardly presented as the main cause for unsustainability, a critique of democracy reveals factors beyond economics and sheds light on issues which can be overlooked otherwise. Many liberal thinkers believe that the state should and can be neutral regarding different lifestyle or even the good and thereby foster unsustainable practices.[15] Consequentially, not only eco-friendly consciousness, but also voluntary actions are crucial for change within democracies.

The first research question is whether democracy could be sustainable. The assumed superiority of democracy needs to be evaluated for the case of devising and implementing environmentally sound politics. Ideas of freedom and free choice will not only be discussed as potentially harmful, they will also be presented as rather insignificant, if change does not occur in a timely manner. If means for the implementation of eco-friendly policies are not sufficient, the burden of pollution will have a totalitarian quality as it will deeply penetrate people's whole lives. In a pessimistic scenario where the vast majority of humanity will not have access to non-hazardous air, thousands of years of discussions on freedom and choice will lose their significance.[16] Thus, state interference could become fundamental. It is necessary to consider whether and why people still believe in democracy, whether people want this freedom, and if it does contribute to the common

---

[13] The discussions assume a minimum familiarity with the canon of political theory.

[14] CO_2 emissions and GDP per capita do not follow a Kuznets curve, a U-inverted curve. The hypothesis that pollution decreases after a certain point is false. The relation between CO_2 emissions and GDP is more likely to be N-curved (Granados and Carpintero 2009).

[15] "Our freedom of body and mind, and the abundance of materialism, offer a pleasant life that can be rejected only with difficulty, for what is the alternative? Thus democracy has to be defended and those not with us are against us in our quest to maintain our lifestyle. Those attacking or even criticizing democracy will be seen as enemies, for the benefits of materialism are at stake" (Shearman and Smith 2007:2).

[16] "In any event, the human animal is psychosocially ill-equipped for a life of crowded deprivation, whether in a disease-ridden city or in the emerging global village. Even without the unprecedented population and environmental pressures to come, political tensions in the twentieth century spawned two world wars, and we seem congenitally condemned to carry on genocidal regional conflicts all over the planet. What is the prognosis for civil society and global peace if material growth falters from resource scarcity or accelerating global ecological change?" (Miller and Rees 2013:Loc. 132).

good (Brown 2012:70f.). Importantly, as Nussbaum in an inquiry into the basis of 'humanness' pointed out any definition of freedom will include a concept of a good life, although in varying degrees (1992). This must not only be understood vice versa, but also as inalienably interconnected. Anybody who grasps at least parts of the problem, will independently get to recognise the similarities of today's world with the fate of the Easter islands: Today's world, too, is based on unsustainable practices that people think they need, but that might cost us the chance for survival.

Any defiance of democracy or simple inquiry provokes a powerful opposition and stands against a large group of politicians, scholars and people alike. There is an enormous accumulation of literature on democracy from more than a couple thousand years. Ideas of democracies vary greatly through centuries and the political spectrum. Notably, including the majority of the subjects, and therefore making them active citizens, is a relatively new approach to governance. Many protagonists of democracy throughout the ages highlighted the importance of knowledge and expertise (Mill 1901; Dahl 1989). A significant number understood moral virtue and an orientation towards the common good as indispensable. Still to argue not just about democracies, but to call it into question might be met with aggressive reactions in many parts of the world including academia. It looks like a difficult enterprise and one is most likely to be dismissed as a lunatic or an elitist, or simply both, especially when proposing alternatives.[17] Forms of elitism vary greatly. Any time one makes claims about humanity he can find himself in a position of being accused of arrogance.[18] Blühdorn highlights that doubt about the sustainability of democracy is a taboo (2011:2).[19] In accordance with this, Meyer writes describing 'the story of environmentalist thinking' that "[u]nlike earlier authors, today we find almost no one who identifies their own theory as anti-democratic; the position has become one attributed to theories by critics" (2006:783).

---

[17] "Elitism follows from perfectionism if one supposes that society should be arranged so as to promote the human good, that human good is a rare and fine achievement, and that only a few people are capable of leading lives that achieve any human good" (Arneson 2000:38).

[18] I understand a vague idea of happiness as the ultimate aim of politics, but security of resources for basic needs must be understood as the basis for everything else. Saying something about our whole race and defending some idea of a greater good valid for everybody will always be an easy target for notions of arrogance. Remaining silent, on the other hand, is a secure haven and extreme relativism may be for many people a philosophy, which excuses their non-involvement and often selfish behaviour. The 'noble modesty' of declaring not to know what is good for other people lifts responsibility, which might come with the bold claim that one actually thinks to know better. Especially, regarding the environment a sense of responsibility is indispensable, since here individualistic rationality and collective rationality oppose each other as will be elaborated later. Individualistic ethics emphasizing freedom ignore the fundamental interrelations of all human beings and the difficulty of human beings to comprehend this relatedness.

[19] Some authors would probably be unhappy being cited in a context that legitimizes nondemocratic means. Many do not support my argument and therefore might see some of the references taken and thoughts borrowed as displaced or castrated. As in accordance with the standard academic code of conduct, I did not however purposefully 'adjust' their contributions.

The second research question is if and how a sustainable alternative to democracy can be imagined. In spite of its unpopularity, the second part and third part seek to discuss meritocracy as an alternative principle. So called 'ecoauthoritarian' views are seldom discussed fairly.[20] Meritocracy is usually their suggested alternative, which can be defined as

> "a political order with a constitution that vests ultimate sovereignty in a ruling group *solely* on the grounds that that group has relevant competence and virtue. The only constitutional requirement on the method by which members of the group are selected is that it should be defensible as leading to selection on merit" (Skoruspski 2013:116; my emphasis).

Advocates of meritocracy assume that politicians chosen for their expertise, competence and virtue will produce better politics. Here, it is imprecise to classify everyone without a formal scientific training as layman. A farmer with a lifetime of experience cannot plausibly be described as 'layman'. Moreover, expertise by definition is restricted to a specific area. Meritocracy is a form of elitism. However, it should not to be confused with elitism based on racism nor does it have to lead to declaring unequal worth and dignity. The underlying idea of the latter parts of this work is that although people are typically made to believe that democracy is the 'best solution' to human life, the security of the Earth's future may be in better hands, if the public does not decide freely and policies do not depend on the probability to ensure future election.[21] Correspondingly, this work will explicitly deliberate whether another form of government can be considered at least as legitimate as democracy in ensuring the necessary conditions for life today and in the future.

1.1. TERMINOLOGY

First and foremost, environment and nature will be used synonymously and utilised in a fashion that resembles everyday practice.[22] Sustainability will be taken literally as the ability to 'sustain' activities indefinitely. In ecological footprint terms, this requires living like there is only one earth.[23] Although there are different kinds of sustainability, including social sustainability, environmental sustainability will be taken as the precondition of other forms of sustainability. This is the case, because the collapse of our global ecosystems would affect all parts of life. A

---

[20] Simplified: ecoauthoritarians believe in the inadequacy of democracy to cope with environmental problems and therefore alternatively propose authoritarian solutions.

[21] "Will the world really be stupid enough not to do what is perfectly doable, namely, to allocate enough money and manpower up front to solve the climate crisis as it emerges over the next several decades? I am sad to say that my answer is yes, I believe the world will be sufficiently stupid to postpone meaningful action. Simply because it is in the short-term interest of those that run the world—democratic majorities and the capitalist system" (Randers 2012:Loc. 4795-98).

[22] Both concepts are not neutral and are often wrongfully perceived as beyond the human realm. Nevertheless, it is useful for the topic of this book to use the terms in their common-sense meaning, if not signified otherwise. If not for any other reason, it is more convenient for the reader.

[23] Environmental sustainability can be defined as keeping consumption below the amount of the natural resources that can be replaced in the same amount of time. This could also be understood as equilibrium between consumption and replacement.

discourse over sustainability always includes a normative dimension, since resources can be distributed according to different rationales (e.g. Aristotle 2009). Lane explains:

> "Sustainability is not about maintaining the status quo ad infinitum into the future. It is about reconfiguring society within the limits of the earth so that over time, society will be ever more able to realize and instantiate the good. What is unsustainable is what undermines the ability of society to develop in this way, or leads it to backslide in its ability to realize and instantiate what is valuable. Sustainability, then, has ethics as much as science at its heart" (2011b:19).

Besides sustainability, other terminology needs clarification. This involves explanations of 'purely' scientific terms as well as those who are politically charged. Natural science terminology has the advantage of being less ambiguous and subject to dispute.

Global warming and climate change will be used interchangeably. They both describe the same process in the long run with the latter being more sensible with respect to short-term processes as well as regional difference. Tipping point or threshold event roughly describe the point where a development is accelerated possibly triggering other events, which lead to the effects growing exponentially. Such threshold events could be for example the release of large amounts of methane gas currently captured in permafrost, the total absence of Arctic Sea ice in summer or Amazon rainforest dieback. Calculations of such tipping points are subject to extreme difficulties given many unknowns and complex processes, like positive feedback loops, where one event causes extreme acceleration as well as possibly triggering other events. Leggewie and Welzer do not exaggerate when describing tipping points as a threat only known in catastrophe movies (2009:101).

The politics of nature or environmental politics, used synonymously throughout the text, possesses a distinct terminology. While some authors carve out neat definitions, meanings can be blurred in public discourses as well as academic texts (Dobson 2007). Most environmentalism can be found somewhere between ecocentrism and anthropocentrism (Vincent 1998:446f.). This book is mainly written from an anthropocentric viewpoint. Anthropocentrism in contrast to ecocentrism focuses on 'human animals' as the centre of concern and source of meaning. "Anthropocentrism [...] is the view that the nonhuman world has value only because, and insofar as, it directly or indirectly serves human interests" (McShane 2007:170). Ecocentrism not only adds the concern for non-human animals, but includes all parts of the ecosystems and a duty to care for nature. An ecocentric framework could mean that "ethical actions will be those that promote all life on Earth" (Bell et al. 2001:30). Though the author's ethical position tends to be rather ecocentric, for the purpose of clarity, it appears unnecessary to complicate issues by expanding the framework of moral considerations to cover ecocentric arguments (for a discussion see Sagoff 2002 or Light and De-Shalit 2003a).[24] Taking a mainly anthropocentric position is more familiar to the language of politics and policies (McShane 2007). Where the difference seems inconsequential, whether the point of protecting nature is ecocentric or anthropocentric, the latter position is chosen in order to improve accessibility of the arguments. An exception is made when animals are explicitly considered. [25] In any case, even for those who classify the intrinsic value of nature debate as deprived or fringe are likely to attribute non-instrumental value to parts of nature in their daily practices (Butler and Acott 2007). People marvel at beautiful natural sceneries beyond the recreational value which they assign to the view. The fate of the polar bear touches most people, although his existence does not have a direct effect on our lives. Either way, environmental protection can be taken as an aim independent of the source of value.

Porrit differentiates environmentalism and ecology listing it as a difference between politics of industrialization and politics of ecology (1985:216f.). However, his binary listing involves extreme dichotomization. The term 'ecology' by itself is interpreted differently and "applies to a number of heterogeneous ideologies, theoretical perspectives, and political practices" (Gimenez 2000:292). Although some authors insist on a difference between environmentalism and ecology, varying in their commitment to sustainability between weak/strong or shallow/deep (Burchell 2002; Dobson 2007), this work does not use this distinction. Since 'weak sustainability' is not sustainable, it will not be counted as sustainable.[26] Respectively, environmentalism can only mean a commitment to 'strong sustainability'. In distinction, ecology might refer to a commitment to sustainability paired with an ecocentric view, whereas environmentalism encompasses anthropocentrism as well.[27] If environmental and ecological integrity require sustainability the possible theoretical distinction is irrelevant for the discussions of governance forms here. This also means that environmental integrity and ecological integrity are often used interchangeably.[28] Thence, these distinctions are mostly insignificant for the arguments elaborated. When employing the concept of integrity, it is useful

---

[24] I agree with Eckersley, when she calls anthropocentrism into question and labels it "human chauvinism" (1992:50; see also Baxter 2005). The idea that other sentient beings do not deserve representation is to say that their suffering cannot possibly matter (see Singer 1975, 2006; Zamir 2007; cf. Leahy 2005). Note that ecocentrism does not necessarily lead to environmentally sound management.

[25] This is not to deny that other ethical approaches are manifest in cognition and emotion.

[26] Standardly in economics, strong sustainability refers to maintaining the same amount of 'natural capital'. Weak sustainability in contrast counts human-made capital as substitutable for natural capital. Weak sustainability describes the sustaining of the total capital: human-made and natural. Various problems with the latter will be become apparent throughout this book. Additional problems arise from categorizing life support systems as capital and from the complexity of the subject including uncertainty. For a more comprehensive discussion of the concepts see Holland (2002).

[27] 'Deep ecologies' reject a nature/culture dichotomy (see Escobar 1998), but so does a significant percentage of social scientists in general.

[28] Ecologically sound and eco-friendly will be used interchangeable with sustainable.

to be reminded of its Latin origins. The related Latin word *integritas* can be translated to chastity, honourableness, soundness, purity, selflessness, and even mental vigour (PONS 1999:521). As with the English term it has a strong moral tone and is more positively connoted than the relatively neutral concept of sustainability. The label 'green' in contrast to sustainability will be used in a looser fashion following common practice including perception and self-descriptions. The term 'sustainable development' is subject to much criticism, which will be discussed in the context of growth ideologies.[29] The adjective 'renewable' will also be used in its common-sense interpretation. It should be noted though that it "is used as a human value judgment: it has no basis in science" (Lovelock 2009:Loc. 1354).[30] Technically fossil fuels are renewable over long epochs. Environmental discourses are laden with metaphors, such as the Spaceship Earth, Mother Nature and Gaia (Dryzek 2005). This book will try to avoid such a terminology, since they are essentially ideological and try to appeal to emotions rather than reason. Finally, one

> "can define climate change as an economic problem, a technological problem, a moral problem, a human rights problem, an energy problem, a social justice problem, a land use problem, a governance problem, an ideological battle between left and right worldviews, or a lack of respect for God's creation. Each approach will generate different responses, different ways to share the costs, and, especially, different language with which to justify action" (Marshall 2014:Loc. 1617).

Seeing it as a political problem can include all of these perceptions.

1.2. METHODOLOGY

Dryzek, among others, observes that the traditional schools of thought such as liberalism, conservatism, socialism, and fascism can appear to be the same from an environmental perspective, given their commitment to industrialism (2005:13; see also Gorz 1980). In view of that, Talshir writes that

> "the environment was instrumental in challenging the boundary of the political as the environment was, par excellence, the non-political issue. The Enlightenment ethos of progress, dependent on the exploitation of nature and advancement of science and technology, was rarely challenged before on these grounds. Nature was never a subject in the moral or political sense. The realization that natural problems are political, that economic growth — advocated by left and right alike — encroaches upon Earth's limited resources, and that national systems can hardly address ecological issues, challenged the underlying assumption concerning the political arena" (2004:Loc. 854-58).

Ecological thought is not only challenging but also comparatively new within political science, which gives works in the field the chance of originality (Humphrey 2007:Loc. 3536). In other

---

[29] "Sustainable development, as that term is commonly used and understood, means making continued economic and social development more resource efficient and less detrimental to the environment. But making development more sustainable, while highly desirable, is not the same thing as actually achieving sustainability" (Sustainable World Initiative 2014).

[30] I tried to exclude nuclear energy as an issue from the discussions. My lack of technical expertise in the field means that I am not qualified to classify nuclear energy as negative or positive in environmental politics (e.g. Hansen 2015 vs. Connelly et al. 2012). Anyhow, I recognize that nuclear power is a highly politicized issue that is typically a part of green party programs and political mobilisation.

words: "If the environmental predicament is unprecedented, so too is the political theory needed to grasp it" (Whiteside 2006:89; see Jonas 1984).[31] Many mechanisms need further investigation.

Taking the environment as a core concern of political theory promises knowledge gains in both, political theory in general and green political theory in particular. This book approaches sustainability of life support systems as an objective common good.[32] In this sense it follows a perfectionist tradition. While human nature and nurture are factors central to reaching this good, the discussions will not claim an objective good in regard to human nature itself. This approach has the advantage that it goes beyond particularistic approaches and eurocentrism. The development of a framework for an evaluation of governance independent from the idea of what is commonly understood as democratic participation is part of the following elaborations. Given the centrality of life support systems, the widespread insistence on the importance of a self-determined life in a democracy, and the very concept of autonomous decision making, need to be questioned. Instead of questioning democracy on its normative grounds, the quality under examination is its prospective sustainability. Connelly et al. highlight that greens need to recognise "that authoritarian solutions are lurking in the background" (2012:62).[33] Whereas the maintenance of life support systems is *sine quo non,* maintaining it (or not) as subject to democratic practice, has irreversible consequences. Given the urgency of environmental protection, it might not be efficient to discuss the means in parliaments for instance. After all, projects and innovative ideas are often put back years and stopped by representatives. If environmental protection cannot be a matter of choice, it must be the dictation of our time. According to Randers

> "there are only two ways out of overshoot: managed decline or natural collapse. Currently humanity is seeking the first alternative, a planned and orderly program of reductions of greenhouse gas emissions, in time to keep global warming below plus 2°C" (2012:Loc. 3033-38).

However, he judges the continuation of climate change in an accelerated form much more likely given that attempts remain insignificant. In regard to environmental politics it is fair to speak of worldwide state failures (Maier 2008:135). Here, Duit poses essential questions that are yet to be answered: "Why are some countries so much better at addressing environmental problems than others? Are different environmental policy regimes evolving in different political systems, how

---

[31] Jonas points at the proceeded idea that the best state is also the best state for and in the future (1984:42; e.g. Plato 1982).

[32] Though in a different context it could make sense to differentiate between public, collective and common good, the terms will be used interchangeably.

[33] "The prospect of runaway climate change challenges our technological hubris, our Enlightenment faith in reason and the whole modernist project" (Hamilton 2010:31). Dryzek warns against the potential for a revival of authoritarian discourse, which "may yet find vindication if, for example, the global greenhouse effects comes to the worst" (2005:50).

do they compare?" (2014a:8). Many factors and mechanisms are poorly understood. There is a clear need for additional perspectives, since "despite a fairly substantial number of studies on [environmental performance], a coherent understanding of what causes better environmental performance is yet to emerge" (2014a:15). Aiming at a better understanding, this book includes an exploration against prevailing ideas and covers both, the empirical and the normative dimension of political science. Thereby, the purpose of this work is not to point at the malaises in democracy; it is to contribute to an evaluation and improvement of the quality of environmental politics in general. The objective is the identification of governance systems capable of sustaining human life.34 Accordingly, environmental sustainability will be taken as a non-negotiable priority.

The importance of sustainability suggests an outcome orientation.

> "Governance is not an end in itself. We seek to create governance systems and to operate them effectively and efficiently in order to steer human societies toward advantageous outcomes and away from harmful developments. It follows that it is always important to evaluate the performance of governance systems in instrumental terms and in the context of specific challenges. Is a given governance system solving or alleviating the problem(s) that led to its creation? Is it doing so in a manner that keeps transaction costs under control and that avoids the occurrence of costly side effects or unintended consequences? Do the results conform, at least roughly, to widely shared conceptions of fairness or justice?" (Young 2009:30).35

This work can be categorised as instrumentalist, although it does not merely look at means to ends. In this it employs an extended utilitarianism. Because of its consequentialist nature a utilitarian approach greatly benefits this work. The apparent premise is that politics needs to ensure basic opportunities for survival; thus, that human life is valuable in itself and needs to be protected (see Jonas 1984).36 The approach will further be (strategically) positivist. It is metaphysical essentialist, even if in a minimalist manner, as it focuses on life support systems as the foundation for human life. In this context, strategic positivism means that it is based on the admission of limited resources as well as a limited carrying capacity of Earth, while at the same time acknowledging the fallibility of science and expertise. The emphasis will lie on interrelations, since understanding nature as interrelated lies at the heart of ecological integrity. The approach is also system functionalist to the extent that it asks how democratic systems

---

34 "Climate activists have long insisted that science should guide policymaking. Yet over the years it has become ever clearer that the biggest challenge for humanity may not be to master the intricacies of climate science but rather to answer the much more vexing questions of how political systems operate and why they are so resistant to heeding science's alarm bells. It is a deadly irony that three U.S. presidential debates took place in 2012 without the word "climate" being uttered even once, swiftly followed by nature's "last word" in the form of the devastating Superstorm Sandy that hit the eastern United States, a storm that likely was made worse by the gathering pace of climate change. If we fail to learn how to make our political systems pay attention to climate challenges, we will have to learn how to deal with massive population displacements in coming decades" (Renner 2013:Loc. 7661-67).

35 "Systems of governance should be assessed by their consequences; any individual has a moral right to exercise political power just to the extent that the granting of this right is productive of best consequences overall" (Arneson 2004:40).

36 See Arneson's discussion of "Perfectionism and Politics" (2000).

produce (un)sustainability and which regime functions best for environmental integrity as an end.

Since the objective is to analyse and elaborate the prospects of sustainable governance, the discussions are based on meta-analysis covering a vast array of research. Suggested principles are not purely deductively chosen, but build on and corroborated by empirical studies. Some are second order principles derived from practice in the sense Westra construes them (see Westra 1998). Although environmental degradation is a global problem, this text is concerned with the state level. The nation state, although relatively new in human history (Hobsbawm 2004, Jenkins 2008), will probably persist for at least the next couple of decades that are critical for climate politics.[37] The overrepresentation of some countries in the following discussions is related to the general lack of comprehensive research on less prominent cases (see Beeson 2015). It poses a restriction for the application of theory however one can argue that these countries play such a significant role in the global destruction that from a more pragmatic point of view, it is fair to state that especially relevant cases are included.[38] Given the scope of the subject, works from different disciplines will have to be employed and set into a common framework.[39] The selected literature was combined in two steps. First, I selected the standard works in democracy and green theory. Second, I added works that are especially useful for comprehending good green governance or lack thereof. This led to a diverse selection of authors and works.[40] Although green thought has compilations, the combination of the outcomes of the existing research is rare.

The scope of the general discussion is exceptional, so is its openness to nondemocratic means. The particular form of engagement with the ethical aspects and empirical reality in the realm of sustainable governance is unique. Especially the third part covers an understudied area. Above all, contemporary political theory rarely shows due interest in meritocracy (see Bell 2015). In practice, meritocracies are hard to find. Green states do not exist. This poses a serious limitation for this work. It means that claims in regard to the viability and feasibility of ecologically

---

[37] International cooperation and a comprehensive global climate regime are highly desirable. "Ensure Environmental Sustainability" is one of the lesser known Millennium Development Goals that was not accomplished (un.org). Developments show that they are for various reasons unlikely to work (Giddens 2009:91ff.).

[38] Although a central issue in many green parties, gender will not play a role in this work. Neither the relationship between the state and minorities nor class will receive specific attention. Though possibly beneficial such analysis is beyond the scope of this work and comes with its own set of problem. For instance, class as a category itself is highly problematic in today's world. Politicians of green parties are not singled out either. Their impact appears minimal in the overall context of this book's main concern.

[39] Marshall warns that scholars "who take ownership of climate change consistently attempt to shape it in their own image, defined by their own discipline. Climate change, though, requires a much more creative and flexible approach that also considers what is not known or not said" (2014:Loc. 1453).

[40] "Few other policy areas can match it for sheer complexity. Nor are failures in most other policy areas likely to be as catastrophic or irredeemable as those affecting the environment, especially if the more pessimistic harbingers of environmental doom are correct" (Carter 2007:171).

sustainable meritocratic states, hereafter called ecomeritocratic, will remain theoretical. Hence, suggestions about meritocracy have to be theoretically convincing and might only be falsified, if states decided to act in accordance with its suggestions. In answering ontological question 'what is?' political science can utilise empirical findings. Looking at the normative question 'what should', however, always involves a degree of speculation.[41] Though much of scientific discovery involves speculation – the term alone seems so suspicious to those involved in academia – it is seldom admitted. The higher the stakes the more important becomes a broader evaluation of potential problems and strategies of governance. Too often, "rational political argument is terminated long before it even started" (Levy 2004:59). Instead of advancing a deeply penetrating regulation of life and constituting a perfect state and instead of drawing an alternative society, this work proposes the adaption of principles for sustainability. To state the obvious: there is no second Earth to experiment or gamble with.

1.3. STRUCTURE

The book is divided into three parts and two separate hypotheses. The first part and third part include a hypothesis, while the second part suggests principles.

Hypothesis 1 of the first part: Democracy is incapable of ecologically sound governance.

Hypothesis 2 of the third part: A meritocracy with focus on ecologically sound governance is feasible.[42]

The first part puts democracy under scrutiny in a manner that addresses the underlying causes of its unsustainability. The lengthy elaboration of democracy's sustainability constitutes an important critique. The dominance of democracy advocacy among green thinkers demands a serious engagement. The treatment lays grounds for the other two parts. Following an extensive critique of democracy, the second part provides grounds for a revision of good governance taking sustainability as the most pressing concern of politics. It revises a framework for good governance within political theory. The third part will deepen the examination of meritocracy and nondemocratic environmental governance in more practical terms. It constitutes a practical engagement with the question of autocracy and meritocracy in regard to the environment.

---

[41] This covers two sides: 1. Polluting practices 2. Solution policies.

[42] Commonly, visions are proposals that mark possible worlds, while utopia is used for unrealistic worlds. If sustainable democracy has to be classified as utopia, alternatively visions of sustainable governance need to be formulated. Bookchin judged: "Either we will create an ecotopia based on ecological principles, or we will simply go under as a species. In my view this is not apocalyptic ranting – it is a scientific judgement that is validated daily by the very law of life of the prevailing society" (1980:71). Here an important differentiation needs to be made between vision and ideology. Criticizing capitalism in particular, Heilbroner stresses that "ideology is readily enough identifiable either by its indifference to generally recognized facts of economic or social or political life, its manifestly weak or question-begging logic, or by its reckless overstatement" (1988:189). Visions for him are not falsifiable.

Many green theorists argue that a green democracy is needed. The criteria differ and often include strengthening democracy in the sense of developing more inclusive institutions. Yet, citizens do not normally use the chance to green their democracies. **Chapter 2.1.** tackles general assumptions of democratic theory, democracy in practice and its effect on the environment. Democracy's legitimacy often rests on means, but sustainability is an end. Democratic theorists typically believe in a direct correlation between fair procedures and the enhancement of the common good. Both are understood to be intimately related. However, a green synergy has failed to emerge. The voter himself often lacks knowledge about political issues and when his vote's impact is seen as part of an aggregate of individual interests, such ignorance is rational. Assumptions about his reasonability and rationality need to be questioned. Democratic feedback mechanisms, far from keeping waste in check, rather appear to enable unsustainable politics. Elections frequently enhance short-term thinking and interest groups tend to lead conversations. Green parties got established, but failed to attract enough support. While other issues have priority, green parties remain largely unpopular and environmental literacy of politicians overall is not to be expected. Public opinion, at the same time, is neither precisely measurable nor a good benchmark for achieving sustainability. **Chapter 2.2.** probes the relevance of sustainability. It highlights that nature and nurture do not equip people to deal with environmental degradation. Above all, human beings are less consistent than many theories assume. The link between behavioural change and change in values is stronger than vice versa. Hence the requisite ecological citizen is unlikely to rise up from education only. The capacity to overcome cognitive dissonance and rationalise one's behaviour suggests rather the contrary. Here, individualism as a rationale and its impact are explored. It is shown that due to its division between private and public sphere, liberalism cannot produce green citizens, but necessitates green citizenry, if sustainability is to be achieved. Neither the concept of a green citizen nor the concept of the green consumer is convincing. In practice, sustainability is condoned to be a matter of choice. Furthermore, the chapter exposes the idea of green growth and with it ecological modernisation theory as a culprit and not as a solution to environmental destruction. In particular the future is discounted in the process, whereas sustainability is inherently future-orientated. Overall, the chapter shows that the dominant mind-set is incompatible with the reality of interrelatedness in a limited world. In view of these factors, **chapter 2.3.** discusses the widespread demand for more democracy as a solution to environmental ills and its effects. At this point, the proposed postdemocratic tendency, where democracy has become a mere management of values instead of a ground for arguing about competing values, is examined. While the claim itself is eurocentric, the debate exemplifies that the nature of nature as a subject is inherently political and therefore necessitates political centrality. Environmentally sound politics cannot abandon truth claims. For that matter, the impact of more participative approaches proves to be ambiguous. Research does not substantiate the assumption that participation has a positive impact. Often, affectedness, far from being helpful, is a barrier to better policies, while hierarchy is regularly reproduced, hence even deliberative democracy does not succeed in levelling playing fields. Even more disconcerting, the belief in the power of the greener argument needs to be renounced. More involvement can mean stronger resentment and the externalisation of costs. Consensus as a benchmark favours politics of the smallest common denominator. Besides, sizing the unit for participation is especially problematic. Decisively, participative approaches can neither overcome nor disguise the fact that throughout time, space, and species, democracy is always a minority government. After integrating the proposal for overcoming problems raised in the first two chapters, this chapter concludes with an assessment of democracy's adaptability. Especially through the multiplication of veto players the propensity for change decreases. Democracy's status quo bias and the urgency of climate change with its catastrophic potential lead to serious doubts about the future of democracy. However one spins democratic participation, the practice does not leave much room for optimism. When a country witnessed successful green politics, more often than not it is despite and not because of democracy. Evidence indicates not just state failure but system failure.

What is more, when decisions become irreversible, the affected community is extended, so democratic government cannot be justified as self-determination. After classifying democracy as a minority government, democracy loses its ledge in legitimacy. When the rationale of legitimation is either applied consistently or shifted, democracy would have to be sustainable in order to be legitimate. If democracy is about self-determination, it cannot destroy the livelihood of those excluded from having a voice. If democracy is about substantive performance, it cannot destroy life support systems. So far, it revealed clear incompetence in the protection of nature. That is why the second part of this book proposes an alternative ethical framework. It attempts to revise the concept of good governance focusing on sustainability as an outcome.[43] Building on the prior assessment of democracy's deficiencies, ecoauthoritarian proposals become ecologically worthwhile. **Chapter 3.1.** begins with the discourse following *The Limits to Growth* (Meadows et al. 1972). It puts the original findings into historical perspective. The recognition of the physical limits is the basis for the assumption that a different system is required and for the ecoauthoritarian legitimation of firmer state interference. The demand for expert planning is plausible, when accounting for the complexities and urgency of climate change. Revising good

---

[43] Macedo writes that it "often seems that instituting competent authorities to deal with mounting problems requires technocratic and bureaucratic institutions constituted on the basis of expertise or merit, insulated from democratic accountability" (2013:233).

government means giving the environment priority. Therefore, **chapter 3.2**. reverts to the role of the state as the protector of the common good. The purpose of the state is repeatedly understood as mitigating conflict and ensuring the common good. While many scholars problematise good as subjective, setting ecological sustainability as the central aim overcomes such charges. **Chapter 3.3**. explores ethics and principles inferred from the acceptance and acknowledgement of life support systems as *sine quo non* and in consequence their protection as non-negotiable. Given this kind of outcome orientation, it shows the usefulness of consequentialism. It further suggests that a harm principle combined with a capped capabilities approach is not only desirable for justice advocates, but proves easily applicable to environmental dilemmas despite their complexities and interrelatedness. Mill did not see the advent of modern technology, so anyone applying the harm principle today must update it. It has to fit the new circumstances as described by Jonas (1984). Consequentialism is inherently holistic and this can be understood as ideal for an ethics for environmental protection, which is highly dependent on the recognition of interrelation. Emancipating science from being a voice among others could mean changing the narrative (of destruction). Accepting the limits of science, while proactively implementing solutions, calls for a strategic positivism. The framework for green politics roughly comprises the harm principle as an approach to ethics, the capped capability approach as a refinement of an approach to ethics in a limited world and strategic positivism as an approach to knowledge. Throughout the chapter, it is illustrated why experts are more inclined to fulfil the criteria of such ecological integrity-oriented ethics by applying the advanced principles to different contexts. In sum, this foundation for a nondemocratic government underpins that legitimacy can and must be found beyond a contemporary idea of political equality (if such is likely to preclude sustainability).

Following the second part, the third part constitutes a more practical evaluation. The revision of good governance demonstrates what sustainability as a non-negotiable should entail. **Chapter 4.1**. looks at reservations against autocracy's potential for environmentally sound politics. It places preconceptions into the revised governance framework and shows that many lack substance. Notably, the category of autocracy is commonly made to include all failed states, which produces many misleading statistics. The chapter establishes that a general unsustainability of autocracy is not supported by evidence. Instead there are grounds for assuming that autocracies have greater potential given fewer veto players, typically stronger control over resources and infrastructure. Stereotypically they can mobilise the state apparatus more efficiently, so aims are often achieved, increasing the prospects. They conceivably consider longer time frames. The subsequent **chapter 4.2**. deepens the good governance discussion by coming back to an essential point of ecoauthoritarianism. Employing Bell's books about China and political meritocracy, it discusses the practicality of meritocracy and its limitations. The chapter also considers the possibility of mixing systems. Meritocratisation as a tool of improving democracy's sustainability is subject to various problems. For instance "[t]he slippery slope to full electoral democracy may be impossible to stop once some central government leaders are chosen by means of one person, one vote" (Bell 2013:10). Also, once the practice of 'one person, one vote' is introduced, people are not willing to give up the idea (Bell 2015). Competition between differently selected authorities is an obstacle to the meritocratisation of democracy as well. The chapter ends with briefly looking at the PRC's environmental record and speculating about the future. **Chapter 4.3.** combines the ecoauthoritarian debate, the ethical discussion and the more practical aspects of meritocracy. It proposes a synergy of meritocratic procedures and greener outcomes while sketching ecological integrity via meritocracy. Based on the fact that the majority wishes for competent government and that setting standards is a common place in most areas of life, it stresses the quiescent acceptability of meritocracy. The chapter refines some aspects of an ecomeritocracy. Lastly, **chapter 4.4.** enters a policy debate. Hereby, it spotlights the advantages of strong state interference against the main drivers of environmental destruction. Putting Earth first is meant to ensure broader protection. The practical implications are far reaching. Because consumption is unlikely to drop significantly and people have loss aversion, limiting the headcount is a central part of the equation. Moreover, population growth can be exponential, but food production could follow the opposite path. Ecoauthoritarians recognised this threat and thus advocated for birth control as more humane. Being able to control population growth has monumental effects on the share of resources that can be distributed. Footprint budgeting equals a fair share for everybody. It is policy proven to achieve reduction while protecting the poor in the past. Such a policy in the meantime perfectly fits the rationale of a capped capabilities approach. It leaves room for choice and preferences, while respecting the physical realities of a limited world.

This part examines democratic theory and practice in the context of environmental politics directed towards sustainability.[44] It attempts to cover all relevant issues within the broad concept of democracy. To critically review assumptions about the compatibility of democracy and environmental sustainability is its main focus. Taken as a main pillar for green political theory, the possibility of a mismatch between sustainability and democracy appears to lack comprehensive inquiries. The following discussions therefore aim to widen the discourse by discussing democracy's sustainability while allowing explicitly for democracy's general unsustainability as an option. This broad setting adds to the ubiquitous and potentially misplaced questions of how, the questions of whether and if democracy can be sustainable. Many millennial old objections as well as praises of democracy have to be readdressed in the light of their effects on the natural life support systems.

The term 'democracy' can mean anything and nothing, it is "not so much a term of restricted and specific meaning as a vague endorsement of a popular idea" (Dahl 1989:2). Democracy is not a new idea and it is probable that democratic elements existed in prehistoric times (Dahl 2000). The fact that some forms of democratic practice have probably existed long before Athenian democracy should not restrain social scientists from placing democracy under scrutiny. Science has long passed the classical functionalist idea that endurance must indicate something to be 'positive' or 'natural'. According to Dahl, democratic systems come into existence when a significant percentage of members of a group sees each other as "equally qualified to rule" (2000:10; 1989:30ff.). Spread through time and space what is commonly called democracy changes with its context. Aristotle's typology of regimes and systems paid attention to the number of people participating in governance (one, some, all) and the purpose of governance (self-interest vs. 'common good') (2009). He already pointed out that there is not only one democracy, but many. Historically, the debate about political regimes has always been a major place of disagreement, yet the discourse of the last 25 years made it look otherwise. Even the term itself has never been value-neutral. In Athens, *demos* was also used in a pejorative fashion for the common people (Dahl 2000:12; Pfetsch 2003:70) and democracy remained to be understood in a negative way even in the early 20th century (Przeworski 2010:4). Critics often say that democracy means 'the rule of the average man' or 'the ignorant masses'.

There are myriad definitions and interpretations of what constitutes a democracy. The history of ancient Athens, for example, does not just include elections but lotteries as well. There is hardly

---

[44] Hypothesis 1: Democracy is incapable of ecologically sound governance.

any consensus in political science on the exact characteristics that make up a democracy and its many variations have led to the common practice of democracies with adjectives. Literally 'the rule of the people', democracy is understood as 'the rule of the many' or 'rule of the majority' in contrast to other political regimes such as aristocracy, autocracy, monarchy or dictatorship (Aristotle 2009). One answer Dahl gives to the question 'what is democracy?' is that it provides opportunities for effective participation, equality in voting, gaining enlightened understanding, exercising final control over the agenda, and includes the whole adult population (2000:38; Dasgupta and Maskin 1999:69). Estlund answers rather pragmatically that "democracy is the actual collective authorisation of laws and policies by the people subject to them" (2009:Loc. 594-95). Modern democracies are signified by three connected elements that in themselves lead to tensions: protection, participation and inclusion (Schultze 2004). Firstly, the democratic state needs to protect its citizen from arbitrary usage of state power, most importantly it needs to institute civil rights and constitute the rule of law. Secondly, a democracy needs to ensure effective participation i.e. provide its citizens with the opportunity to form their 'own' preferences as well as the chance to voice those preferences and have them included in the decision-making process. Thirdly, inclusion means that the sovereignty lies with the people and that this is independent of gender, race, religion etc. A division into three different models of democracy – liberal, republican and deliberative – is common among political theorists. Schultze characterises them as follows: Liberal democracy is realistic in comparison to deliberative democracy. It is based on the protection of individual rights and interests with an instrumental understanding. Liberal democracy dominates the politics of mass democracies. Republican and deliberative democracies, on the other hand, are closely related and less realistic and practical in their interpretation (2004:152).[45] They are interested in a common good (e.g. Kant 1999; Pettit 2012) and believe in the possibility of finding it via communication that is directed towards building a consensus. Democracies can also be divided into different systems or subtypes. Different factors typically play a role in classification (Schultze 2004):

1. The conception of a society as pluralistic/heterogeneous vs. homogeneous.

2. The modus of participation as direct vs. representative.

3. The degree of participation as weak vs. strong i.e. many areas of participation

4. The pattern of decision making as consensus-based vs. majoritarian

5. The style of politics as competitive vs. proportional.

---

[45] Given their higher standards they are more difficult to achieve.

From 'strong democracy' over cosmopolitan democracy to defect democracy, many theorists have their own classification and ideals (Lauth 2010; Przeworski 2010).[46] There has not been and will probably never be a unified theory of democracy.

Still strikingly, as Graham asserts, good government and democratic government are identified as synonyms, though they should not mean the same thing. Since if they did have the same meaning it is to make "the merits of democracy tautological – true by definition" (Graham 2013:Loc.335-38; see also Przeworski 2010). This identification seems to hold true regardless of the specific interpretation of democracy theorists. Dahl points out that the term 'democracy' is used for the ideal as well as for actual governments (2000:26). This is a focal point of any discussion. While democracy is often discussed in its ideal form (Dahl 1989:84; Roemer 1999:56f.; Kagan 2008:111f; Przeworski 2010), autocracy is rather viewed in terms of its real life occurrences.[47] While the latter is associated with Hitler, Mao, or Stalin, the former is typically associated with abstract concepts like freedom and equality. A comparison between different regimes is neither new nor can it be conclusive. It naturally has to involve multiple layers of comparison and therefore points of reference. An analysis of democracy's sustainability has to be as holistic as possible, examining theory and practice and their consistency in regard to environmental realities. Part of the evaluation also involves the question of human nature and how democracy incorporates human tendencies. If democracy is appropriate to handle (for instance) environmental problems, it must have working mechanisms that take human nature (regardless of being understood as essentialist or not) and its different dimensions into account. This attempt necessarily encompasses different theories within democratic theory as well as an interdisciplinary approach. Various claims of democratic and green thought need to be addressed and contrasted with each other theoretically and empirically.[48] In a nutshell, sustainability is taken as the litmus test for democracy.

Liberal democracy builds on a deep trust in education and therefore on the 'convertibility' of human beings. Most green theorists share this trust in education as a main component for an environmentally friendly performance. They therefore not only share the assumption of a citizen

---

[46] For the concept of strong democracy see for example Barber (1984).
[47] Many works on democracy set strict qualifications. If specific conditions are "all fulfilled can one speak of a democracy, whereas in the other case we are dealing with an autocracy" (Wurster 2013:83). But if all 'defect' systems are categorized as non-democracy and therefore fall into the autocracy category, the latter category will always include too many failed states to enable any meaningful comparison.
[48] Since green thought compromises a diverse field, Meyer questions that it can be subsumed as one ideology (2006). It should rather be understood as a category similar to political as well as democratic thought.

who can be 'enlightened' with classical liberalism, they also see it as the key to a green state. Ball points out that a green state

> "requires a civically (and environmentally) educated and engaged citizenry whose members have what Mill called 'active characters'. Such active and attentive citizens demand accountability from their government and their representatives" (2006:145; Mills and Kind 2004 and Carter 2007:65ff.).

One of the questions to be posed consequentially is whether such citizenry is possible or utopian. An early critique was that the dependency on the character of the citizen "would limit the effectiveness and efficiency of government: the ecological crisis calls for drastic, unpopular measures, the good of which will only be visible in the long term" (Wissenburg 2006:21; Ophuls 1977; Stephens 2001b; Radcliffe 2002:25ff.). This investigation of green democracy then must include the connected questions of responsibility taking, since responsibility and the lack of responsibility are central factors of a sustainable engagement. Noteworthy, many democracy supporters do have a critical view on democracy and its requirements. Dahl famously states that 'real' democracy does not exist anywhere, but that instead actual systems can be classified only as polyarchies i.e. rule of the many. Thus, he would agree that democracy is a romantic notion. But even his polyarchy cannot exist everywhere. Instead the type of society that tends to polyarchy can be labelled "liberal, capitalist, bourgeois, middle-class, business, modern (and postmodern), competitive, market-oriented, open" (Dahl 1989:251). Chiefly, most of these characteristics can be clearly associated with undesirable impacts on the environment.

On the one hand, high living standards cause waste and pollution. Consumption is the main driver of environmental devastation. On the other hand, climate change renders these living standards obsolete. The result of its urgency and the finiteness of natural resources is enormous (time) pressure on institutions (Leggewie and Welzer 2011:35). It is important to realise that climate change challenges these standards in a dual way. The lesser acknowledged (or maybe purposely overlooked challenge) is that the impact of climate change itself has a strong effect on global food production, health etc. The other challenge that seems to be more overt is the actual conditions and efforts i.e. cutting back on consumption today that climate change mitigation needs.[49] Eckersley summarises a central part of the issue as follows:

> "Ecological problems persist because they are generated by the same economic, scientific, and political institutions that are called upon to solve them. While the state cannot but acknowledge the ecological crisis, it nonetheless continues to function as if it were not present by denying, downplaying, and naturalizing ecological problems and declining to connect such problems with the basic structure and dynamics of economic and bureaucratic rationality" (2004:Loc. 1118-21).

---

[49] The fact that economic growth and job creation are taken as more important is an indicator of this non-observance.

Eckersley makes a strong point when she emphasizes the need for looking outside the box (2004). One should not employ the same mechanisms with the same characteristics that were causal to environmental degradation in the first place.[50] Radical rethinking is a necessity, since efforts within the existing systems have not been shown to be sufficiently effective.[51] It is clear that sustainability needs to be a holistic effort.

> "Increasingly, sustainability politics must connect bottom-up with top-down and be concerned not just with the allocation of material resources, ecological space, status, and authority but also with *who* defines the future and what perspectives and experiences matter" (Leach 2013:Loc. 5295-97; my emphasis).

The question of who defines the future also determines means and ends. Democracy could be understood as the most inclusive approach to participation including diverse viewpoints. Whether it is necessarily a reliable or even the only potential answer to environmental issues needs to be studied.

Empirically, many factors that are independent of the political system play a role in its performance (Croissant 2010:124ff.; Muno 2010; Tong 2011; Wurster 2013). This is especially the case for environmental politics, since the approach to nature is dependent on the natural resources of a country (i.e. its chances to exploit and therefore pollute), its culture and level of industrialisation. Oil productions, for example, lead to a huge ecological footprint.[52] Consequently autocracies with oil reserves do have a significantly higher footprint than other countries, but so do oil-rich democracies (Ward 2008).[53] Many scholars believe that liberal democracies are better for the environment. "Democracy and individual freedom are cornerstones of mainstream green ideology" (Pepper 1996:44). But the belief is often based on mere assumption. In general, scientific findings regarding the relationship between democracy, 'development' and freedom are presented as more definite than evidence suggests (Petersen 2009:3; see Carter 2006).[54] Clear evidence for a causal relationship between 'the quality of a democracy' and successful environmental performance is needed (Leggewie 2011:27ff.; see also Burnell 2009 and Rawls 2011:Loc. 354-62). The question here is not about the degree to which democracies are and can actually be democratic, but about the effect of the attribute 'democratic' i.e. the relationship of 'democraticness' in theory and practice in relation to environmental

---

[50] Not everybody agrees on the necessity of radical change, Connelly states: "We must work with institution that we have" (2012:383).

[51] This idea is represented for example by the slogan of the global climate change movement "Don't change the climate, change the system".

[52] This work employs the concept of (ecological) footprint in general terms meaning the usage of natural resources, including nature as a sink.

[53] On the other hand, scarcity of fossil fuels and the connected reliance on imports can be a decisive factor in the advance of renewable energy. Lee, for example, comes to the conclusion that this was a major factor in South Korea's politics (2013).

[54] 'Development' and freedom independent of definition are inseparably connected to environmental integrity.

22

integrity. Thus, this involves two points of reference. Differences in classification[55] will only be pointed out in so far as they influence the politics of nature.[56] One can make theoretical arguments in favour of various regime types' potential eco-friendliness and they deserve discussion. Some arguments that are typically made in favour of democracy may have negative consequences in regard to the environment. For instance, "[p]roperty rights allow for security of contract and capital, but property rights also lead to rapid economic growth and decreased environmental sustainability" (Whitford and Wong 2009:193). Analogous to economic growth democracies are said to be connected to higher living standards, but higher living standards in return are likely to lead to greater environmental depletion as mentioned above.[57] Property rights are often understood as comprehensive rights (Stephens 2001a). They typically include the right to exploit connected resources and they limit the state's ability to interfere in environmentally destructive behaviour. A green democracy, it is argued, must therefore redefine property rights (Eckersley 2004; Meyer 2011).

Democracy theories' approaches, analyses and results have not been sufficiently studied in the context of their effects on the environment. Such a study maintains that the conflicts that arise from the ecological reality and its mitigation need to become a major part of the democracy discourse (see Martin 2013). "[P]hilosophical treatments of democracy's value have often tried to explain why politics should be democratic even though democracy has no particular tendency to produce good decisions" (Estlund 2009:Loc.55-56). The intrinsic value debate fills libraries and there are reasons to believe that democracy has value in itself. However, any attempt to save it might be rendered useless in a world characterised by natural catastrophes, disease, famine and therefore conflict.[58] A re-evaluation is inevitably required.

> "Socio-environmental conflict [...], should not be subsumed under the homogenizing mantle of a populist environmentalist-sustainability discourse, but should be legitimized as constitutive of democratic order. This, of course, turns the climate question into a question of democracy and its meaning" (Swyngedeouw 2011:78).

Although scarcely acknowledged, the viability of contemporary democracies has become intrinsically tied to its environmental performance. The discussion needs to resolve the tension

---

[55] Differences in degree and focus: somewhat democratic, fully democratic, in transition, consolidated etc. and structural differences: presidential, semi-presidential, representative, federal etc. (see Lauth 2010a and Merkel 1999).
[56] Empirical studies that point at the differences between different democratic systems' environmental performance are restricted and suffer not only a small-N problem, but also have to cope with a multiplicity of related and independent factors (Whitford and Wong 2009; Muno 2010:365f,; Wurster 2013; Duit et al. 2014).
[57] Judging a state by its living standards was already misapprehension for Rousseau (Pfetsch 2003). Ecological modernisation theory will be discussed later.
[58] Huxley was concerned about population pressure on finite resource in 1958: "Unsolved, that problem will render insoluble all our other problems. Worse still, it will create conditions in which individual freedom and the social decencies of the democratic way of life will become impossible, almost unthinkable. Not all dictatorships arise in the same way" (2000:29f.). Today even the head of the World Bank openly shows concern that the world will experience battles for food in the future (Elliot 2014).

between means and ends, between instruments and consequences as the environment is not simply another issue area (Plumwood 2006; Carter 2007; Muno 2010). The question is after all, whether democracy can cope with the challenges of environmental destruction. Accordingly, a substantial share of the following discussion can be seen in the light of Goodin's reflection that

> "[t]o advocate democracy is to advocate procedures, to advocate environmentalism is to advocate substantive outcomes: what guarantee can we have that the former procedures will yield the latter sorts of outcomes?" (2013:Loc. 3723-28; Meyer 2006; Connelly et al. 2012).

Liberal democracy is open about the outcome of democratic procedures. Consequentially its engagement with ethics is restricted.

Politics cannot be separated from moral considerations and the nature of politics involves critical engagement with its content. This is even more important for the politics of nature.[59] If democracy results in politics divorced from actual engagement in ethical questions, it becomes mere management of interests and as such might not be able to ever become 'truly green'. The ideal of liberal neutrality only emphasizes procedures, "whereas ecologism defends a substantive ideal, demanding definite results" (Wissenburg 2006:22).[60] If procedures, such as the ones that are supposed to produce an 'overlapping consensus', are more important than the outcome for democracy, it could indicate that chances for sound environmental politics are nil (see Humphrey 2007:117).[61] Most severely, there is the possibility that ensuring environmentally sound governance needs radical steps, while politics that focus on consensus are only able to produce 'politics of lowest common denominator'. This would seriously temper democracies' ability for effective and efficient environmental policy making.

---

[59] Further discussions of the relationship between politics and morals can be found throughout this book.
[60] "Political liberalism [...] aims for a political conception of justice as a freestanding view. It offers no specific metaphysical or epistemological doctrine beyond what is implied by the political conception itself" (Rawls 2011:Loc. 888-89).
[61] Huemer criticizes Rawls, since even a "basic level of agreement seems unattainable" (Huemer 2013:Loc. 1600).

2.1. The Logic of Democracy and its General Effects on the Environment

Since the next couple of decades are essential to alter the course of climate change, democracy's general effects, effectiveness and efficiency become pivotal. "In theoretical and policy debates alike, the pressing nature of the environmental challenge has drawn attention to the classic dilemma of democracy versus effectiveness, procedure versus outcome" (Bäckstrand et al. 2010a:6). To talk about the effects and efficiency of a regime type is a way to avoid normative disputes. From a functionalist perspective structures and procedures of a political system are studied independently from their specific purpose in regard to their contribution to find solutions (Saretzki 2011:58). In order to evaluate democracy's environmental performance, it is imperative to ask about its competence and 'productivity'. The question is not only what democracy can accomplish when referring to its procedural legitimacy, content, and effectiveness, but also if sustainability can be achieved in a timely manner. It is useful to define performance in environmental matters as the conversation of life support systems and the delivery of goods in a sustainable mode of distribution. This chapter involves the inquiry whether democracy can actually achieve good environmental performance and which mechanisms favour such performance.[62] The considerations of this first chapter can be broadly understood as matters of inherent logic and general effects.

In *The politics of the earth: environmental discourse*, Dryzek expresses the concern about democratic politics writing that the "limits of effectiveness [are] increasingly apparent" (2005:120; see also Dahl 2000:2). Schmidt expresses similar concerns about democracy in general listing the gap between high expectations in combination with relatively small means of control by democratically legitimised politics as a weakness of democracy (2010:464).[63] Nominally, democracy enjoys great legitimacy, but this has positive and negative consequences. The logic of democracy leads not only to advantages but also to disadvantages. Democracy depends on the citizens' ability to process information. It further depends on feedback of its citizens, which commonly is understood as one of democracy's main checks and balances. Recognising these dependencies is the key to an analysis of environmental politics. One of the main components herein is the often debated autonomy of the individual which is said to either strengthen or reduce efficiency. The former is supported by green political theorists who think that the liberal state is "suffering too many democratic deficits to be able to respond to ecological

---

[62] Even if Habermas is right that "the pursuit of efficiency colonizes the lifeworld" (Elling 2008:261), the abandonment of efficiency, as a general aim, favours delayed action.

[63] "Legitimate policies do not necessarily make the governance arrangements environmentally effective in terms of reducing the problem of depletion of the stratospheric ozone layer or climate change impacts, to take two examples. The environmental impact of specific modes of governance is a methodologically complex issue, left unanswered by political scientists. The predominant approach in political science and environmental politics is to conceptualize effectiveness in terms of policy, institutional or compliance effectiveness" (Kronsell and Bäckstrand 2010:42).

problems in a reflexive and concerted manner" (Eckersley 2004:Loc. 227-28; Bührs 2012; cf. Humphrey and Stears 2007; Leggewie and Welzer 2011:174ff.). The latter is evident in Hobbes' *Leviathan* where "liberty, rather than being understood as expanding the boundaries of participation is seen as a restrictive dynamic on the effectiveness of a rule" (Glass 2006:734; see Hobbes 2007). Whereas Eckersley points at the deficits, the opposite could be the case and

> "success of the democratic and liberal political institutions may hinge on the ability of leaders and their constituencies to see beyond fears, to reject paranoid resolutions of political conflict, and to build coalitions for whom trust is rooted in a collective self-interest" (Glass 2006:746).[64]

Green democracy depends on many variables and it needs enormous change in the course towards sustainability. Eckersley argues that

> "the likelihood of this trajectory ever being realized is crucially dependent on the degree to which states can be made more democratically accountable in terms of a distinctly green rather than liberal conception of democratic state governance" (2004:Loc. 244-245).

But this attempt to tribute more importance to "distinctly green" is only half-hearted. In his work *Green Political Theory*, Goodin shows that greens are strongly committed to agency and share a significant amount of values with liberalism (2013; Blühdorn 2011). Green theorists, therefore, need to give an explicit framework to green political theory that contrasts it concretely to the liberal side in practice (e.g. Eckersley 2001; 2004).[65] If differences cannot be made out, it is fair to question democracy's ability to produce sustainability. Further, the "more democratically accountable in terms of a distinctly green" conception presupposes that the public values environmental integrity sufficiently. Humphrey summarises the problem as follows:

> "Ecocentrism, or even an environmentally enlightened anthropocentrism does not come easily, and without such a change in values democracy's ability to deliver ecologically sustainable outcomes remains in serious question" (2007:29; see Eckersley 2004:Loc. 1159).

But even where the public holds green values, valuing it without acting upon it is a common tendency in Western democracies. Different interests typically have the upper hand in citizen's behaviour. Green democratic theory needs to show how to overcome these discrepancies. If liberties are to be given up, green democratic theory has to express clearly which ones and how this will be decided.

Another important factor for effectiveness and efficiency is compromise. Democratic practices are often signified by compromises between different standpoints. Dahl values compromise as an

---

[64] Collective self-interest, though already a problematic notion, is either an oxymoron; self-interest vs. collective interest or redundant since the common good of protecting the environment is in the collective interest/self-interest. In contrast to the Rousseau's terms 'sum of all will' and 'general will' (2008), it is likely to be an expression of a rational choice thinking.

[65] Providing a normative framework and adding 'the excluded' is not enough. It needs to be clear how it ensures actual environmental protection. This will be further discussed in regard to deliberative democracy.

art which citizens and leaders in a democracy learn (2000:58). Yet, truly green politics cannot be anything but a sustainability package (Goodin 2013:Loc. 380-85; Wurster 2013), since compromising regularly means 'green washing'.[66] Sound environmental politics cannot afford weak measures and "since compromise is central to democratic politics, many radical environmentalists are deeply suspicious of, if not hostile to, conventional democratic politics" (Ball 2006:133). Sustainable democracy would need committed politics that includes citizen and politicians alike and therefore poses a high threshold of qualifications. Former Prime Minister Blair openly stated that sustainable living involves too drastic cuts and stagnation, and consequentially will not be agreed upon (Davis 2007:199; Shearman and Smith 2007:xv; Maniates and Meyer 2010a; cf. Eckersley 2004:Loc. 706-7). Still 'new modes of governance', which meant to be more inclusive, are regularly seen as means to 'salvation' in mainstream green political theory, although recent studies show that these great expectations in "new modes of environmental governance as regards their legitimacy and effectiveness can only partly be fulfilled", which makes Hogl et al. suggest them "as two genuine acid test criteria for these modes" (2012a:9; Duit et al. 2014). In sum, green political theory generally assumes that democracy can effectively and efficiently lead to sustainability, but such a claim needs to be assessed.

2.1.1. LEGITIMACY, LEGITIMATION AND PERFORMANCE

Legitimacy and Legitimation are essential to any discussion of governance types.[67] Huemer defines the legitimacy of a political system as

> "a matter of the permissibility of imposing that system on all the members of a given society. It is, in part, a matter of the permissibility of intentionally, coercively harming those who disobey the rules produced by the system" (2013:Loc. 1621).

Legitimacy is a core component of ruling. "Leaders must not only ask for sacrifices, but must also possess the moral authority to make this call seem legitimate" (Peterson 2010:114; see also Jasanoff 2012).[68] Thus, any form of legitimacy is ultimately dependent on a specific value system. Political ecologists believe that rules and regulations have to be accepted by the populace in order to achieve sustainability (Dobson 2006:224). Accordingly, perceived legitimacy is a necessity for green aims, although it does not necessarily lead to the acceptance of rules and regulations, it serves as a facilitator.

---

[66] Compromise and consensus will be subject in the later discussion.
[67] Thus, Pettit criticizes utilitarian and contractualist thinking for their lack of engagement with legitimacy and points out that it is important "how people actually relate to the regime" (2012:144); problems of state legitimacy in regard to globalization will not be part of the discussion, since this is beyond the scope of this book. For an elaboration of globalization concerning ecological problems see Hurrell (2006:176ff.).
[68] Similarly, Huemer defines political authority as "the hypothesized moral property in virtue of which governments may coerce people in certain ways not permitted to anyone else and in virtue of which citizens must obey governments in situations in which they would not be obligated to obey anyone else" (2013:Loc. 849).

Today "the word 'democratic' has such a powerful positive connotation that questioning it is like questioning the desirability of social justice or a healthy life-style" (Graham 2013:Loc. 48-49). People do not only assign intrinsic value to it, but also do not question it. It is understood as desirable beyond doubt i.e. has 'legitimacy beyond doubt'. Democracy as an ultimate good is internalised in most political discourses globally. "[T]he legitimacy of the democratic State is deeply embedded in our ways of thinking. It pervades almost all that is said and thought and done in contemporary political life" (2013:Loc. 46-47). In consequence, one might argue that its wide acceptance makes it the most powerful source of legitimacy. But legitimacy can be derived from democracy without green aims and can even serve as a barrier to sustainability depending on the terms in which it is defined.

Legality, justification and consent are three interconnected dimensions of legitimacy.[69] Respectively, legitimacy can mean an objective criterion of a political system based on the legality of a rule i.e. a purely descriptive criterion, but it can also be understood as based on normative criteria autonomous of a specific system (Nohlen 2004:487). While the judgment of endogenous legality is relatively easy, anything beyond an evaluation of lawfulness has significant limitations. The legitimacy belief, according to Weber, signifies internal (not necessarily active) consensus and approval of a given system (2014). He famously characterises three forms of legitimate rule: traditional, charismatic and bureaucratic rule. Contemporary governments derive legitimacy from all three sources to varying degrees, since these are better understood as ideal types. Referring to either higher guidance, though still frequently in use, order or rationality is not sufficient alone (Przeworski 2010:165; Tong 2011). Meanwhile, legitimacy is actively influenced by any given political system. It therefore needs to be characterised as a rather empirical and dynamic than a normative and static concept (Nohlen 2004; Tong 2011; see also Doherty and Wolak 2012:302).[70] These characteristics mean that the concept is highly contextual. Differences in values and norms play a huge role empirically. The sociologist Luhmann describes legitimacy as the factual belief in the rightfulness and value of a specific 'should' in legitimation by procedures (1983; Petersen 2009:7). His conception focuses on the perception, but includes the substantive as well as procedural dimension. Though power can be a result of legitimacy, legitimacy signifies forms of authority that are beyond the compliance as a result of force (see Weber 2014). Still, legitimate authority can exist without

---

[69] Note that I agree with the claim that a social contract technically cannot exist due to various reasons, but particularly due to the problem of exit (see Huemer 2007). This work, therefore, does not assume that people in democracies 'voluntarily' chose their political system.
[70] Any description will necessarily utilise normative elements.

everybody accepting the rationale of a rule. If this was not the case, legitimate authority would be impossible. Undoubtedly, legitimacy cannot require universal consensus. Respectively, Estlund asks: "Why should the objection of someone who is, say, crazy or vicious carry that much moral weight-enough to defeat a justification even if it is acceptable to everyone who is not crazy or vicious?" (2009:Loc. 94-96). Though not meant in such a way, his rhetorical question indicates an argument that undermines democracy in environmental matters as will be further elaborated in later discussions.[71]

While procedural legitimacy refers to the process of government elections and decision making, substantive legitimacy refers to the content of the governance. Hereby, the latter can encompass both intention and consequence, whereas the former may vary as well. Contemporary political discourses differentiate clearly between means and ends (Graham 2013:Loc.458-59) and the democratic process is routinely treated as an end in itself. The distinction runs along the lines of procedural vs. substantive, procedural vs. epistemic, participatory vs. result-orientated, voluntarist vs. cognitivist, means vs. ends, input vs. output.[72] The tension that these dichotomies create is essential for the discussion here. The elaboration will therefore make a theoretical differentiation between procedural and substantive legitimacy as well. It will also try to point out where such a distinction is mistakenly blurred. The core of the problem lies in the fact that to advocate democracy is, first and foremost, to concentrate on the procedure, but environmental integrity is substantive (Goodin 2013; Wissenburg 2001a; Wissenburg 2006:23f.; Connelly et al. 2012:80).

> "In other words, on pain of inconsistency, greens, who advocate ecological stability and integrity, natural authenticity, animal rights, or any other environmental cause, can never make an ultimate commitment to democracy itself. That is, they cannot be committed to the idea that the outcomes of the political process can be good if they are actually agreed upon, regardless of their content. Strictly speaking, the moral value of democracy cannot underpin a genuine green conception of the good society" (Levy 2004:53).

Critical advocates of democracy could deny this by pointing at the premises which their concept of democracy encompasses, but these advocates thereby demark the limitations of democracy itself rather than providing a solution.[73] Meanwhile, most scholars who advocate green politics see democracy as a precondition for a more sustainable future. But as Estlund argues "[p]rocedural fairness is about the retreat from substance, and the question is when to retreat

---

[71] Depending on the framework contemporary societies might fall not necessarily within the spectrum of mental diseases, but fulfil the criteria to be classified as 'addicted' to unsustainable lifestyles.

[72] There are two different usages of the term 'output legitimacy'. One refers to the legitimacy that the output gains from the process (see Newig and Kvarda 2012) and the other to the legitimacy that is denoted by the substance of the output itself, which means for this work, whether a given policy has positive effects on the preservation of nature or not. If not noted otherwise I will use the latter interpretation, since the former understanding is misleading and is much better described as procedural legitimacy. Hence output includes the actualization of policies.

[73] This could be the case if a stable environment is recognized as an ultimate precondition of any democratic rights.

and when to hold our ground" (2009:Loc. 1242). The following three sections will elaborate the differences between both forms of legitimacy as well as their relation within the context of the environment with the last section discussing a possible synergy for greener politics.

2.1.1.1. REFLECTIONS ON PROCEDURE-BASED LEGITIMACY

"Should we say that the fairness of the procedure is the explanation of democracy's moral importance" (Estlund 2009:Loc.128-129)? This would implicate that the fact that everybody gets one vote is core of its value. Procedural legitimacy is regularly expressed as rule by the people. There is an increasing global consensus that democratic elections are the only valid basis for legitimate government.[74] Schmidt believes that there is no alternative that is empirically more cogent and theoretically more respectable than the rationale and legitimation of collectively binding decision making by the empirical will of the voter (2010:453-471).[75] Politicians aim to gain control through elections, which if successful leads to the claim i.e. justification, authority and power to use resources at their will (Graham 2013:Loc. 39-42). Procedural legitimacy takes such a prominent position that elected leaders routinely justify their actions by declaring it 'the will of the people'. The fact that the people elect their representatives themselves is often understood as a ledge in legitimation and can be used to neglect reasonable objection that are based on substance such as environmental assessments.

Perceived fair elections are part of the minimal requirements for all democracies, though they may survive with significant lacks in legitimacy or acceptance (Gilley 2009). If a political process seems unfair on the one hand, the government does lose legitimacy and a change of system becomes more likely. On the other hand, if people perceive political institutions as legitimate and have confidence in them, they are likely to judge the procedures as fair (Doherty and Wolak 2012:302ff.; Newig 2012:54f.). It also means that procedures that are perceived as fair, regardless of their outcome, increase the willingness of the citizenry to support policy outputs. Liberal theorists like Rawls (2011), who to their defence believe in an immediate connection between fair procedures and 'good outcomes', assume that people will commit to any result of deliberation (Connelly et al. 2012:39; see also Elling 2008:31ff.).[76] Their theoretical arguments

---

[74] Participation in elections may also be understood as "implicit consent" to a political system (Huemer 2013:Loc. 1248); elections as a factor will be covered later.

[75] Petersen, on the other hand, emphasizes that democracy cannot count as an end in itself, because democracy is neither an inevitable consequence of individual self-determination nor can individual and collective self-determination be equated (2009:32).

[76] Deliberation as an ideal is highly problematic and will be discussed in detail in the last chapter.

routinely sound not just hard to fulfil, but even utopian (e.g. Rawls 2011:Loc. 3074-80).[77] Though fair procedures are expected to produce better politics, Estlund argues that the legitimacy itself and therefore authority of an outcome needs to be independent of the question whether it "actually got the right answer" (2009:Loc. 146-48; see Christman 2005:84 for the differentiation between voluntarist and cognitivist).[78] Especially in countries with sizable social divisions, it is said to be critical that the citizens believe in the fairness of the democratic process, since the opposition is likely to ascribe their belief in the government's legitimacy on the procedures. Whilst politicians' popularity is subject to change and may depend on the policy output, the legitimacy of state institutions rather depends on the processes (Doherty and Wolak 2012). Doherty and Wolak find that people are not biased in their evaluation of procedural justice as long as they are clearly fair or unfair, but will use their prejudgments if the lines are blurred.[79] Legitimacy derived from the process is sometimes described as 'output legitimacy'. In that case the term 'output legitimacy' refers to the legitimacy that the output gains from the process. Much confusion between the two ways in which output legitimacy can be signified might arise from the widely shared belief that procedural fairness i.e. output legitimacy in the non-substantive version leads to better outcomes, including eco-friendlier policies. This would mean that one form of output legitimacy inevitably leads to the other and therefore makes a differentiation redundant. But the Condorcet's Jury Theorem (meaning that the greater the number of decision makers the higher the competence in decision making) cannot be taken as a case for greener outcomes. It cannot support epistemic value claims, since if the jury is negatively biased in any sense, the process is likely to have a worse outcome than a coin flip (Estlund 2009; see also Taber 2003 and Huemer 2013).[80] This weakens the argument for collective decision making which rests on the fact that individuals are better than random in choosing the right answer. Indeed, the wisdom of the crowd exists already in relatively small groups and needs only a minimum of 51% of people with the right answer. In any case, environmental matters involve complex issues that may affect people directly. Green politics involve the acceptance of ecological soundness as a higher standard, they therefore set high qualifications.

---

[77] "Though these theorists exert considerable effort to describe the conditions that they believe would establish the legitimacy of a political system, they make no serious effort to show that any political system satisfies those conditions. One possible explanation for this omission is that, in fact, no government satisfies the conditions for legitimacy" (Huemer 2013:Loc.1556).

[78] See 'The paradox of democracy' (Graham 2013:Loc. 548-50).

[79] Environmental politics in general are difficult to judge and lines therefore seldom clear. Examples are the problem to single out 'affected' from 'non-affected' or the setting of 'acceptable' limits of chemical concentrations and exposure levels.

[80] "Individual voters might indeed be better than random, but this is not obvious. Factual errors, prejudice, and other factors could, for all we know, outweigh the average voter's margin of better-than-random competence, at least on matters that are sufficiently contested that they end up being settled by a vote" (Estlund 2009:Loc. 3273-74).

In contrast, "[i]f fair proceduralism succeeds, it allows us to avoid potentially messy questions about which independent standards should be used to judge outcomes" (Estlund 2009:Loc. 985-86). Yet while procedural legitimacy links the establishment of norms and values to the process, it disguises the fact that the process itself presupposes norms and values such as equality (Petersen 2009:9f.; Stephens 2001a).[81] It is necessary to recognise that procedures are not morally neutral and that "the democratic process is itself a form of justice" (Dahl 1989:164; Eckersley 2004:Loc. 1695-98; Schmitt 2004, Estlund 2009).[82] For instance, if procedural fairness serves as the justification for democracy, rolling dice has the same legitimacy. Democracy can take various forms and if one wanted to ensure formal fairness and equality, choosing by lot, though not morally neutral either, could be understood as the fairest procedure. Nevertheless, any form of democracy is based on 'enlightened' beliefs.

> "[T]he idea and practice of democracy are justified by the values of freedom, human development, and the protection and advancement of shared human interests, the idea and practice of democracy also presuppose three kinds of equality: the intrinsic moral equality of all persons; the equality expressed by the presumption that adult persons are entitled to personal autonomy in determining what is best for themselves; and following from these, political equality among citizens" (Dahl 1989:311).

All three kinds of equality are critical in determining democracy's place in environmental politics. Not only are they prerequisite for the belief in its legitimacy, but as assumptions they also have consequences. Only the postulation of a strong principle of equality can justify a democratic process of one vote per person (1989:97; Rawls 2011; cf. Roemer 1999:67). One needs to assume that everybody has the potential to make reasonable decisions. However, a strong principle of equality might be "as absurd as Plato's royal lie", which includes the consideration that "if ordinary citizen don't understand their own interests, you would concede that like children they are morally unqualified to rule themselves" (Dahl 1989:58f.; see Plato 1982).[83] Knowledge of the problems and willingness to recognise these problems as such is a precondition to understanding your own interests and making reasonable decisions. But knowledge and power is shared unevenly in all democracies (Dahl 1990). Przeworski comments: "We called the founders' bluff about political equality" (2010:169). Notably, political equality also includes moral equality. The presumption of intrinsic moral equality may have evolved into

---

[81] See the debate concerning green liberalism between Wissenburg and Stephens as discussed below (Wissenburg 2001b:27; Stephens 2001a, 2001b).

[82] "But when one perfects this substantively indifferent and neutral process even more and takes it to the absurdity of only a mathematical-statistical majority determination—a substantive principle of justice will nevertheless always still have to be presupposed, if one wishes to keep the entire system of legality from collapsing immediately: the principle that there is an unconditional equal chance for all conceivable opinions, tendencies, and movements to achieve a majority. Without this principle, majority calculus would be a grotesque game, not merely because of its indifference toward every substantive result. The concept of legality derived from this principle would also be a shameless mockery of all justice" (Schmitt 2004:Loc. 993-98).

[83] But "[t]he very method of choosing representatives through elections, rather than by lot, is based on the belief that all people are not equally qualified to rule" (Przeworski 2010:73).

a main obstacle for a greener world. Hence, democracy needs to be reviewed, even without procedural consideration such as the Condorcet or Ostrogorsky Paradox (e.g. Dahl 1989:154 and Arrow 1970).[84]

Foremost, the tyranny of the majority "stands over individuals in the way a master stands over a slave or subject" (Pettit 1999:175). There can be doubt about the moral unambiguity of majority decision making in particular, because this, as famously put, could also mean that two wolves and a sheep get to decide about dinner choices (see Schmitt 2004).[85] Some people must submit against their interests, which makes voting also the imposition of a will over another will (Przeworski 1999:47). This includes the fact that

> "however arbitrary the collective majoritarian will may be on any issue, it is a will which we may have real discursive difficulty in challenging and criticizing. If you oppose that will, after all, you expose yourself to the charge of being elitist and of not having faith in the wisdom of the ordinary people" (Pettit 1999:177f.).

Thus, discontent with democratic decisions is often disregarded.[86] But Shapiro and Hacker-Cordon highlight that majoritarian principles themselves are easily captured by a self-interested but skilled elite (1999a:14). A well-organised minority can have more influence than a heterogeneous majority (Mosca 1950; Gilens and Page 2014). Interest groups with specific issues have disproportionate power. Accordingly, Leggewie and Welzer do not find the inaction with regards to environmental protection surprising, since it is based on particular interests (2009:48, see Plehwe 2011; Krysmanski 2011; Madden 2014). The main barrier for sustainability might be an unwilling majority as well as a well-organised minority that has huge profit margins from polluting industries.[87] The consequence for environmental politics within a democratic framework would be devastating.

Part of the reason could be the fact that the procedures themselves follow the rationale of one vote per person and it is possible that even if democratic voting does not openly advertise individualist thinking in the form of egoistic thinking, internalisation of individual voting might

---

[84] The additional challenge regarding the representation of non-humans that would be necessary for a non-anthropocentric green politics will not be discussed extensively. The paradoxes describe how different ways of counting (or tweaking) will lead to different winners.

[85] "By a curious irony, the language of egalitarian respect for ordinary people gives a sort of moral immunity to a force that may represent the most serious threat of all to the freedom as non-domination of certain individuals" (Pettit 1999:178).

[86] Westra comments that the problem is "our belief that the choices and preferences of the majority in democratic, affluent countries are and should be viewed as absolute, beyond discussion" (1998a:3; see also Conly 2013).

[87] Eckersley points out that even an eco-efficiency effort "demands more ecologically sensitive accounting techniques and management practices, tighter policy coordination and integration, and some modest realignment in state goals and practices to bring environmental concerns to the fore in fiscal and industry policy. To coordinate the changes, governments would face some tough battles with industries that have been beneficiaries of ecologically damaging subsidies (e.g., agricultural subsidies or low-energy charges relative to other industries) or other government assistance" (2004:Loc. 941-45).

produce a cognitive framework that strengthens self-interest more than collective interests. These possible negative effects of democratic procedures in particular will be subject to discussion throughout the whole chapter. Fairness of individual voting can be understood as an advantage of democracy in abstract moral terms (Estlund 2009), but if this advantage indirectly leads to a disadvantage for the environment, priority setting needs to be considered. So called 'procedural fairness', contrary to the belief that it will necessarily produce better outcomes, is ambiguous in its effect on substance. Procedural legitimacy does not inevitably translate into substantive legitimacy.

2.1.1.2. REFLECTIONS ON PERFORMANCE-BASED LEGITIMACY

Substantive legitimacy asks for the result 'for the people'. The people in this dimension could be understood as the recipient of governance. It seems common sense that fair procedures produce fair outcomes. Interestingly, this kind of belief in fairness is habitually maintained and defended against contradicting evidence. US Americans for example not only value meritocracy, but despite the facts believe that they actually live in a meritocracy (McNamee and Miller 2009:14). Political philosophers have long been interested in the substantive aspects of governance, measuring the performance on the basis of the approximation of a higher good. If Machiavelli's prince succeeds he has substantive legitimacy. Machiavelli prioritizes ends over means, which is often misinterpreted as sanctifying any means (2009; Pfetsch 2003:100ff.).

Substantive legitimacy covers at least two different sides. Though both judge the legitimacy of an action by the outcome, they approach the problem from two different directions. Taken to its extreme, the first form of substantive legitimacy judges the action 'only' by the intention of the actor, while the second judges the action 'only' by the outcome i.e. consequences. Still both ask for substance and not procedure hence ends. Simplified, this means an action is good if the intentions are good as for Kant or an action is good if the result is positive as for Mill. The proverb that "The road to hell is paved with good intentions" hints at the difficulty that arises from the former interpretation, particularly when it comes to environmentally sound politics. For the purpose of an analysis of environmental politics, it does not make sense to focus on the question, whether the actors have inferior motives or not. The presumption that some people follow 'evil' motives has little analytical value. However, since politics always mean a prioritisation of goals, it is indispensable to ask for the hierarchy of these goals. Whether policies were well-intended or not becomes secondary if survival is at stake.[88] This does not mean to exclude intentions or policy directives from the analysis or to exclude the normative dimension.

---

[88] Externalities are particularly important.

If politics were only to be analysed in regard to their actual outcome, analysis would be restricted to the retrospective. Eckersley comments comparing democratic systems that

> "[at] the end of the day, the relative merits of liberal versus ecological democracy ought to be judged not simply in terms of their procedures but also in terms of the ultimate values they seek to serve and uphold" (2004:Loc. 1695-98).

Eckersley also writes that

> "a minimum a good state would uphold the rule of law and the separation of powers, be free of corruption, and uphold those civil and political rights that are essential to the practice of ecological citizenship" (2004:Loc. 38-39).

Her description involves substantive as well as procedural criteria for 'good' which might have to be weighed against each other. A consequentialist approach in environmental politics has the advantage that 'good governance' can be judged by substantive outcome. In contrast to liberal neutrality, the expected output of governance is implicitly presupposed. This means that government actions can be evaluated by their impact on environmental integrity i.e. their effectiveness and efficiency to conserve nature. Substantive legitimacy, in its latter form then, derives from the results of a decision-making process and depends on the question of whether goals and values are satisfied (Petersen 2009:9). The question is whether and how much sustainability can be achieved within green democratic theory and practice (Barry 2001:59f.).[89]

Climate politics hint at output orientation as a general problem for democracy theory (Saretzki 2011:59). Generally, when autocracies show spectacular outputs, "[d]emocracy's international supporters tend to deem such 'output legitimacy' inferior both in moral terms and as a strategy for regime survival" (Burnell 2010:7). Though

> "[c]ritics, not only the adversaries but those who are sympathetic to the "rule by the people," contend that a process of collective decision-making, no matter how "democratic," cannot be justified unless it produces – or at least tends to produce – desirable results" (Dahl 1989:5).

The process then cannot constitute the sole legitimation of a democratic system. Even if perfect fairness and clarity could be attained, it would not be sufficient. Moreover, Gilley states "[l]egitimacy requires that there be such a thing as widely acknowledged common good that is no mere aggregate of individual interests but something that transcends those interests" (2009:4). In a similar fashion Höffe understands 'content' legitimation as only having the potential for universal approval, if it benefits every individual and additionally the whole society (2009:79). In a sense, voting needs to result in positive externalities i.e. be a form of merit good for all.[90] Thus,

---

[89] Baxter applying Kymlicka's cosmopolitanism classifies ecologism as consequentialist, since "ecologism espouses the 'intuitions' that (1) the well-being of all life-forms matters (2) moral rules must be tested for their consequences on the welfare of life-forms" (1999:148).

[90] Economics calls the cost that one does not pay or does not pay directly externalities.

Przeworski counts governments as "representative if they do what is best for the people, act in the best interest of at least the majority of citizens" and thereby declares that securing representation in this sense is not a distinctive feature of democracy (1999:31f.; 2010:165f.; Tong 2011). But as already pointed out above, there is a firm tendency to believe that democracy actually delivers, since

> "[a]lmost all normatively desirable aspects of political, and sometimes even of social and economic, life are credited to democracy: representation, accountability, equality, participation, justice, dignity, rationality, security, freedom, ..., the list goes on" (Przeworski 1999:24).

If this is legitimately the case, it would be a striking argument for democracy. Whilst the confusion between correlation and causation is a topic of undergraduate classes, many of these assumptions still lack definite proof and are part of continuing debates.[91] The empirical evidence on the connection between democratic regime and development shows that claims are hard to prove. The literature also tends to be unpersuasive due to serious methodological shortcomings (Bradhan 1999:93). This is relevant because ecological modernisation theorists argue that development is the condition for sustainability. Besides, there is not even a necessary correlation between democracy, rule of law and human rights records either (Petersen 2009:37).[92]

Democracy's capacity to solve environmental problems is certainly far from desirable and

> "positing a necessary relationship between green politics and democracy is mistaken, and constitutes an example of wishful thinking on the part of ecological political theorists" (Humphrey 2004:116; de Geus 2004; Ball 2006:132; Saretzki 2011; cf. Eckersley 2004:Loc. 2916-18).

Despite environmental protection laws democracy's performance is "not better than in places of civil disorder or autocracy" (Shearman and Smith 2007:70). There is no proven relation between the way a state is constituted and the effectiveness in its policy outputs regarding internal security, welfare and environmental protection (Leggewie 2011:29), where all of which play a role for environmental integrity. In theory democracies are expected to cooperate better regarding climate mitigation, but practice does not support this hypothesis (Betz 2013:22). Environmentally friendly politics can be found in stable democracies, but stable autocracies could prove to be better in implementing such policies than most democracies. Democracies typically also have free market economies, which through the logic of growth have huge impacts

---

[91] E.g. Roemer attributes the high degree of redistribution in Nordic countries to homogeneity of values and not the democratic regime itself (1999:65); "There are good reasons to doubt that majoritarian politics converge on common interests in modern polities, that politicians in any meaningful sense are constrained by elections to represent the voters' interests, or that they even pursue policies – such as egalitarian redistribution – that would benefit an unambiguous majority of citizenry" (Shapiro and Hacker-Cordon 1999a:3).

[92] Note that in some definitions rule of law and human rights protection are a necessary condition in order to classify as democracy.

on the management of and approach to natural resources. Yet, Saretzki points out that if democracy's preference for environmentally destructive economic systems (with overexploitation of resources as well as irreversible damages) is not inevitable, the system does not have to be rejected on principle (2011:53).

Some qualities assigned to democracy are not only proven to have conflicting effects, but most certainly play a negative role in environmental politics. Schmidt sees democracy as providing the guarantee of political equality and security of material conditions of freedom within legitimate governance (2010:453-471). "Security of material conditions of freedom" is vague enough to avoid the conflict between political equality and economic freedom. Hence, such phrasing avoids the tension between the values of equality and freedom, which both appear in the list of attributes above. Still, given future prospects of contemporary politics, security of material conditions of freedom is currently not ensured in any democracy (Reiber and Zelli 2011). Freedom as a central notion of democracy is highly problematic for environmental integrity. Pettit understands the duty of a state as

> "treating its citizens as equals, the state ought to be guided by the idea of promoting such freedom, putting in place the resources and protections that can guard people against domination" (2012:73).

Schmidt likewise counts the protection against tyranny and guarantee of a 'weak leviathan' as a further advantage particularly in constitutional democracies (2010:453-471). But given continuous environmental degradation the conflict between domination, necessity, and freedom becomes overt. If a certain degree of freedom now undermines the fulfilment of basic needs in the future, it becomes questionable in how far and whether the state can be "guided by the idea of promoting such freedom" and protect against domination at the same time; both seem the same only at first glance. Equally troubling is the reality of citizens' severe inequality. McNamee and Miller show that

> "[i]n a substantial sense, the upper class in America is also a ruling class. Despite the ideology of democracy in which everyone has an equal say in deciding what happens, the reality is that those who have the most economic resources wield the most power" (2009:84; Gilens and Page 2014).

As mentioned earlier, small powerful minorities can effectively occupy public discourses. The findings suggest that one of the biggest democracies has strong veto players that gain from exploitation of natural resources, while being better protected against its effects. The interests of veto players might be more relevant for environmental politics than the form of the regime (see Leggewie 2011:29 and Madden 2014).[93]

---

[93] They enjoy relative freedoms while being a cause of domination.

Less ambitious is a justification of democracy on the basis of its performance regarding 'primary evils'. The democratic decision-making process might avoid "war, famine, economic collapse, political collapse, epidemic, and genocide" (Estlund 2009:Loc. 2362-70). If democracies tend to do better regarding primary evils, it would make sense to assume that this is applicable to other goods as well (2009:Loc. 2469-70). But even if democracy has in fact performed better on the related issues, it is fair to question this tendency for the future. Respect for ecosystems is a premise for the avoidance of all these primary evils. Rather than counting environmental destruction as just another evil, it is imperative to understand the connected tension between their opposites i.e. 'primary goods' and a minimum of environmental integrity as a basic prerequisite, thus sine qua non. Human beings want "survival, food, love, shelter, health, respect, security, satisfying work, friends, family, leisure" (Dahl 2000:52; Nussbaum 1992). Looking at it from a Maslowian angle, the material conditions are a premise for further satisfaction. As for example argued by Beeson, environmental destruction is likely to threaten democracies globally (2010; see also Tilly 2003).[94] Most significantly, climate change "threatens to render all human political projects irrelevant" (Kingsnorth 2009:37). Westra, who is commonly classified as 'ecoauthoritarian', writes that "nothing can be moral that is in conflict with the physical realties of our existence" (1998a:11; see Humphrey 2007:20).

2.1.1.3. IS A GREEN SYNERGY OF PROCEDURE AND PERFORMANCE POSSIBLE?

If green procedures, meaning inclusive and fair procedures, actually produced greener outcomes, procedural and substantive legitimacy would not be in tension. A summary of this apparent shortcoming in most of green thought can be seen in Humphrey's observation that

> "an understandable desire to pursue two political goods simultaneously has resulted in an attempt to forge a non-contingent link between these two goods when such a link is neither necessary nor plausible. In that sense it constitutes an example of (attempted) wish fulfilment, placing the cart of substantive outcome before the horse of analytical enquiry" (2004:116).

When it comes to substantive green output, democracy suffers from a legitimacy deficit that is also often overlooked because of other priorities.[95] A focus on and trust in procedures may lead to neglecting results.

---

[94] "From the standpoint of legitimacy, the reason that democratic failure is rare is that democracy, when it is actually working, generates supportive and effective feedback from society that keeps the state performing optimally. To explain democratic failure in terms of legitimacy, then, implies one of two possibilities: either social values change in an undemocratic direction (perhaps aided by the influence of antidemocratic social or political elites), or democracy is seen as *contributing to a broader performance failure* by the state" (Gilley 2009:189; my emphasis; see also Hausknost 2011).

[95] Arneson ends a chapter on the question of just democracy concluding that he "has searched without any success for sound arguments for the claim that there is a non-instrumental moral right to a democratic say" (2004:58). But if it fails to produce good outcomes, it also lacks an instrumental legitimation.

Mainstream greens must show that without participatory democracy,[96] non-violence, and egalitarianism

> "an ecologically sustainable society is unattainable. If they cannot do so, then perhaps greens must either drop their radical political and moral agenda, or concede that environmental outcomes are less important to them than doing things the 'right' way" (Carter 2007:52; Mills and Kind 2004; Goodin 2013:Loc. 3194-97; cf. Schmitt 2004 and Saretzki 2011).[97]

In line with the latter Arias-Maldonado writes "[h]opeless as it might sound, greens can only wait until sustainability becomes a generalizable interest, thus opening itself to collective definition and democratic institutionalization" (2007:248; Buell and De Luca 1996).[98] He, thereby, indicates that nature has no primacy, despite the green label. Greens want to be as inclusive as possible i.e. advance the public's engagement, although neither democracy nor environmental governance might directly affect legitimacy in the public's perception. It could be argued that in comparison to an autocratic leader, the elected politician's legitimation is actually less dependent on his performance, since he derives significant legitimacy from elections. Still, many politicians are inclined to act in a way that their performance is perceived positively, but in environmental matters it often leads to policies that could be labelled 'cosmetic surgery' (Maier 2008; Assadourian 2013:Loc. 6386-88; Leonard 2013:Loc. 5345-48).[99] In a comparison between different regime types between 1990 and 2005, Wurster finds that the average democracy scores higher on 'weak sustainability', while the average autocracy scores higher on 'strong sustainability' (2013).[100] Reelection and party politics self-evidently play a role. Mandates are given on the subjective basis of voter's preference and their perception of the performance. A major problem is that "people may be poor judges of their own interest, and politicians, knowing what is best for the public, may still act in ways that citizens do not appreciate" (Przeworski 1999:32). As with procedures, the public judges performance on a subjective basis and not by objective criteria (Petersen 2009:33).

---

[96] "Regarding legitimacy, the claim that participatory processes increase legitimacy as compared to less participatory procedures can be put into question too. The challenge lies in ensuring an adequate representation of legitimate interests" (Newig and Kvarda 2012:38). In accord, Randers speculates about 2052 that "you will be much poorer than you would have been in 2052 if a benevolent dictator took control in 2012 and forced through the necessary investments to keep everyone employed and global warming below plus 2°C" (2012:Loc. 4860-61).

[97] The insistence on non-violence and grassroots democracy is rooted in the birth and generation of green ideology within other movements (see Carter 2007).

[98] "[G]reens have placed considerable emphasis on the importance of maintaining consistency between ends and means" (Eckersley 2001:321). They may tend to overlook a possible conflict.

[99] "To date, although sustainable development has been almost universally adopted as the policy paradigm driving strategies to protect the environment, no country has yet got anywhere close to achieving even the very weakest forms of sustainability" (Carter 2007:356).

[100] As explained in the Introduction, 'weak sustainability' can technically not be classified as sustainable.

Any discussion of legitimacy and legitimation has to acknowledge that it is practically impossible to measure content with a system (2009:7).[101] This does not mean that estimations are not useful, but rather that they have to be critically assessed. As stated above citizens' approval typically consists of a mixture of procedural and substantive legitimacy. In his study of state legitimacy, Gilley looks at legitimacy sources by correlation and finds that citizens themselves do not appear to grant democracy or rights a preeminent role (2009:44).

Factor	Correlation
General governance	0,73
Income level	0,69
Gender equality	0,69
Welfare level	0,68
Economic governance	0,67
National happiness	0,65
Liberal rights	0,39
Private ownership	0,39
Environmental governance	0,24

Table 1 Impact of Different Issues on Perception of Government Legitimacy

Factors that have a particularly high positive correlation with perceived legitimacy are general and economic governance, the income and welfare level, gender equality, and national happiness. All of these could be understood in substantive terms. Despite the difficulty to measure factors such as happiness, it is interesting that anti-authoritarian attitudes as well as democracy/democratic rights both ranked on the same place behind the other factors, thus take only a medium position. Still a factor of 0.6 or higher in Gilley's research means that individually they could predict at least a third of the difference in legitimacy. Liberal rights and private ownership, on the other hand, seem insignificant in comparison, while environmental governance ranks even lower. These numbers show that supporters of liberal procedural legitimacy overestimate the acceptance and effects, because those rights are not valued more than some others (Gilley 2009:44f.).[102] These numbers also show that waiting for an environmental consciousness is probably 'hopeless'. Meanwhile, elected governments have few incentives to focus on sound protection policies. Still, there is much confusion about environmental politics by the public and greens alike.

---

[101] E.g. the Mubarak regime enjoyed relatively high legitimacy in Gilley's calculations (2009).
[102] The subchapter on Input and Feedback Mechanisms will look at issue prioritisation more closely and include further studies. The environment tends to be mentioned last in various studies (e.g. Buck 2013).

As mentioned above, greens entertain the idea that all dimensions of their thought are not only justified and compatible but even inseparable. At the heart, one can find a diffusion of means and ends, in which democracy is seen not only as an end in itself, but as a means to environmental integrity as an end. Carter summarises Goodin's position writing

> "that the significance greens attribute to the theory of agency – the means of getting there – is wrongheaded. Instead, the green theory of value, which underpins the case for sustainability, should take priority [...]. It may be desirable that Good actions coincide with Right actions – that democratic, non-violent methods achieve the sustainable society – but it is not essential. Put simply (and simplistically), green ends justify the means" (Carter 2007:52; see Goodin 2013).

Priority-setting could resolve the contradiction in case both dimensions of mainstream green political theory are not irreconcilable.[103] Schmitt's solution to the possible collision of formal rules, namely establishing a framework that is not subject to democratic disposition, could be applied by green theorists. Whence the conflict might be solved

> "by admitting that there are preconstitutional and prelegal substantive values or concrete decisions to which appeals might be directed when the formal rules of a liberal- or socialdemocratic regime collide or appear vulnerable. If such substantive criteria indeed prove available, then these, and not the law itself, as liberals hope, are the source of the regime's legitimacy" (McCormick. 2004:Loc. 129-32; Schmitt 2004).

In this case, the substantive value that takes priority could be ecological integrity, but greens could equally declare participation as a "prelegal" substantive right, thus the clash between green theory of value and green theory of agency remains for which "greens themselves fail to provide any guidance as to how we should go about resolving such a conflict" (Goodin 2013:Loc. 2879-83; cf. Stephens 2001a and Wissenburg 2001b). However, Goodin believes that green theorists in fact set their priority on the outcomes in case values collide.

> "The green theory of agency is a theory about how best to pursue the Good and the valuable, according to a distinctively green analysis of what is good and valuable. Some theories of agency might elevate right action, regardless of consequences, to an art form in and of itself. Green theory is not among them. It aims first and foremost at producing good green consequences" (2013:Loc. 421-23).

Therefore, the preference should be clear. Green political theory and activists, alike, need to focus on environmental sustainability first and need to trade off some aspects of the 'green package'.[104] Waiting as Arias-Maldonado suggested poses a tremendous risk.

---

[103] "If we accept Robert Goodin's contention that there is no set relationship between democratic process and environmental outcome (a view that I would broadly endorse), then thinking about how such outcomes relate to such processes, and what may make these outcomes more or less likely, or what interference into the process we may have to tolerate to achieve outcomes that 'we' desire, remains an important task" (Humphrey 2007:4).

[104] "There is simply no place for moral preciousness and keeping one's green credentials clean when the fate of the earth hangs in the balance" (Goodin 2013:Loc. 4105-13).

"Questions of ecological sustainability must therefore be constitutional essentials, even in an ideal theory. A theory of justice does not work without an environmentalist perspective of one kind or another" (Horstkötter 2004:Loc. 4130-31).

Further considerations of green political theory need to not only prove that this admission of a hierarchy of values is necessary, but also show to what extent foresaid compromise of green theory is feasible. Here, it is essential to understand the limits of agency in itself as well as the limits of agency for the implementation of 'real' green politics. The assumption of unity between good procedures and substance rests to significant part on the belief in the enlightened citizenship.

2.1.2. THE RELATIVE IGNORANCE OF THE VOTER

"One natural hypothesis about why we actually want people's views taken account of by the process is that we expect people's views to be intelligent-maybe not to any high standard, but better than a coin flip. This introduces an epistemic dimension, and it is important to see what this would and would not commit us to" (Estlund 2009:Loc. 136-138).

In other words, a key assumption is that people are capable of making reasonable decisions, though evidence shows that this is too simplistic. The assumption that people are ignorant and therefore are not able to make rational or even reasonable decisions cannot be easily dismissed.[105] It stands against the liberal hypothesis that individuals themselves know their interests best or at least that other people do not know it better. Theories that claim the contrary are often regarded as elitist. However, it cannot be denied that convoluted issues such as climate change are beyond the comprehension of 'many'. Most certainly people with superior knowledge do exist in all areas (2009:Loc. 141-44), but in environmental matters which involve complex interrelationships it is inevitable.[106] When discussing relative ignorance it has to be acknowledged that it is not a trait distinctive to democracy alone, but that it is likely to have a bigger influence within a democracy than in other political regimes that rely less directly on the citizen's participation.[107] Rationality requires not just the ability to reason, but also knowledge as a basis for such reasoning. Following Habermas, Elling states that "a fundamental point for any environmental assessment must be the belief that knowledge can transform a situation, and that the knowledge about risks allows everyone to avoid them" (Elling 2008:7). In this sense, knowledge becomes the central criterion, which is often believed to change preferences and behaviour.

---

[105] Lying will not be addressed separately.

[106] "The survival of democracy depends on the ability of large numbers of people to make realistic choices in the light of adequate information" (Huxley 2000:105).

[107] Taber comments: "The American voter, as revealed in public opinion research over the past half-century, is a wretched caricature of the noble citizen of normative democratic theory. Uninterested in politics, poorly informed on public matters, intolerant of diversity, ideologically unsophisticated – it seems a miracle that any system dependent on such a creature could have survived, let alone prospered" (2003:455).

The principle of political equality suggests that if means for deliberation, learning and discussion are given, all the members of a political community are equally well-qualified to participate in decisions (Dahl 2000:39; see communicative reason in Elling 2008:258; cf. Ophuls 1977:209ff.). While it appears ethically desirable that all people are equally qualified, even well-qualified, the principle of political equality is extremely idealistic. As an ideal or as a benchmark it is likely to distract from the empirical evidence. This is symptomatic for most ideas based on liberalism, which not only builds on an optimistic view of an individual's moral autonomy, but also depends on a vague idea of 'reasonableness'. In his work on political liberalism Rawls lists four requirements (2011:Loc. 1855-59):

1. "The two moral powers, the capacity for a sense of justice and the capacity for a conception of the good. "

2. "The intellectual powers of judgment, thought, and inference."

3. "A determinate conception of the good interpreted in the light of a (reasonable) comprehensive view."

4. "The requisite capacities and abilities to be normal and cooperating members of society over a complete life."

Theories that build on these requirements have to find a balanced interpretation, since these elements could not only represent unworkable expectations, but could as well be meaningless, if only a minimum is utilised to classify the population as inhabiting these traits. In general, they suffer from vagueness and ambiguity. Rawls' struggle mirrors the tension of green theory described above. On the one hand, he declares that

> "a conception of objectivity must specify an order of reasons as given by its principles and criteria, and it must assign these reasons to agents, whether individual or corporate, as reasons they are to weigh and be guided by in certain circumstances. They are to act from these reasons, whether moved by them or not; and so these assigned reasons may override the reasons agents have, or think they have, from their own point of view" (2011:Loc. 2267-70).

On the other hand, he insists that

> "political liberalism takes for granted not simply pluralism but the fact of reasonable pluralism; and beyond this, it supposes that of the main existing reasonable comprehensive doctrines, some are religious" (2011:Loc. 201-5).

Rawls avoids some criticism by distinguishing between reasonable and rational.[108] Still, it is hard to imagine anything but a minimum overlapping consensus.[109] Notwithstanding, Rawls' whole philosophy depends on reason as a universal faculty. He writes that

> "our exercise of political power is fully proper only when it is exercised in accordance with a constitution the essentials of which all citizens as free and equal may reasonably be expected to endorse in the light of principles and ideals acceptable to *their common human reason*. This is the liberal principle of legitimacy" (Rawls 2011:Loc. 2579-81; my emphasis).

Following this definition of legitimacy, it also difficult to imagine how this can lead to a theory of justice that can be the basis of/for action. Anyhow, Rawls argues that

> "the status of the natural world and our proper relation to it is not a constitutional essential or a basic question of justice [...]. It is a matter in regard to which citizens can vote their nonpolitical values and try to convince other citizens accordingly. The limits of public reason do not apply" (2011:Loc. 4026-51; see Humphrey 2006).

Here, he grossly underestimates the all-encompassing nature of the politics of nature. Differences in reason and rationality might be too great to be overcome.[110] The welcoming of climate change by some fundamental Christian groups as the step towards Judgment Day is logically consistent with their doctrine. Within this belief system, speeding up the process by polluting more instead of less is perfectly rational, even reasonable.

While a strong principle of equality can justify one vote per person, differences in "motivation, ability, and opportunity", Althaus explains, lead to an uneven distribution of knowledge among the citizens (2003:15; Huemer 2013:Loc.4583). The preferences of voters are not informed equally either. This is increasingly evident: For example, in Fishkin's study only a little more than half of the people knew who was in control of the US Senate offices (1997:8ff.). Dahl admits that

> "political beliefs of most people everywhere are likely to be rather rudimentary. [...] Knowledge of a variety of aspects of political life, including the rules of the game, is likely to be markedly greater among leaders and activists than among the general population of a country and certainly far greater than among the politically apathetic inhabitants" (1989:261).

---

[108] "As rational we have to balance our various ends and estimate their appropriate place in our way of life; and doing this confronts us with grave difficulties in making correct judgments of rationality. On the other hand, as reasonable we must assess the strength of peoples' claims, not only against our claims, but against one another, or on our common practices and institutions, all this giving rise to difficulties in our making sound reasonable judgments" (Rawls 2011:Loc. 1421-23). Rawls understands the ability of being reasonable and rational as moral powers.

[109] There is a lack of "evidence or reasoning to show that some particular political system would be agreed upon by all reasonable persons" (Huemer 2013:Loc. 1555). Shapiro makes an even stronger statement on this idea: "Certainly none of these appealers to consensus has engaged in what a social scientist would regard as empirical study of the values in question" (1999:13).

[110] For a discussion of the problem of radically different ontologies in regard to the environment and public reason as well as the problem with novel views in Rawls see Humphrey (2007).

Choosing Plato as an opponent, Dahl suggests that Plato does not comprehensively explain why only a minority is capable of ruling and that Plato fails to support such view (Dahl 1989:65f.).[111] Though Plato not only emphasizes the diversity of people, he likewise discusses the difficulty of virtue and the temptation that material goods pose for the majority of a population (1982). He explicitly problematises material goods as an inferior pleasure as well as a characteristic of an inferior regime type, most notably oligarchy. Plato prominently sees a tension between wealth and virtue. He makes a strong point characterising people as different i.e. exhibiting diverse traits and strength.

Meanwhile, mechanisms of exclusion and therefore factors are not alien to democracies. Not just foreigners remain excluded. People that are classified as "incapable of attending to their own basic interests" remain controlled by "a paternalistic authority" (Dahl 1989:181). While Aristotle, Locke, Mill, Rousseau and others spoke in universal terms, they still did not plea for universal inclusion (Dahl 1989:96; see also Bowles and Gintis 1986). It would be dishonest to claim that measurements that classify people as 'incapable' are not necessary and not somehow arbitrary at the same time. After all, democracies exclude children from voting and set a relatively random age of inclusion. This exclusion shows that democracy declares some people as 'unqualified to vote'. The democratic logic links maturity and reason to age mainly. Democracy must assume that by the time children reach the voting age, they attained reason. This again leads back to the dangerous consequences of accepting multiple comprehensive worldviews under the banner of liberal neutrality and the tension between a green theory of agency and a green theory of value. Political liberalism cannot be indifferent and reasonable at the same time. Commoner criticised democracy and capitalism on this very basis (1992). For ecological integrity, there can only be one guideline and that is rational scientific principles based on understanding nature and not on the idea of capital accumulation.

In turn Elling's Habermasian approach problematises instrumental reasoning while labelling the "environmental problematic" as "exclusively modern", where following only "cognitive instrumental rationality reflects back to everyday life in a singular manner, whereas the moral-practical and the aesthetic-expressive rationality are suppressed by instrumental dominance" (2008:63f.; Macauley 1996a:17f.; Eckersley 1999 and Wehling 2002). In other words, he understands the problem as one of a discourse that is focused on instrumental rationality.

---

[111] Plato's argument is typically employed by ecoauthoritarians.

Instrumental rationality itself cannot be devoid of ethical consideration though.[112] This observation resembles the question of substantive vs. procedural legitimacy, in which it was pointed out that a value framework also underlies procedural measures. It follows that instrumental reasoning itself is not problematic as long as the ends are clearly defined as green, if the outcome is prioritized. The problem, then, is rather than being one of instrumental reasoning itself, a society that allows socially undesirable rationality or ends to be equally valid. Elling states that contemporary practices of "reflexivity leads to purposive rationality without ethical or aesthetic rationales" (2008:19, see Mauss 1990:157ff. and Gimenez 2000:299), but he understands environmental assessment that involves multiple actors and therefore other rationales as improvement. His strong belief in communicative reasoning thereby equally blinds him to the fact that allowing for a diversity of rationales might be a central part of the problem. At the same time, Elling wants "reasoned compromises" (2008:257) and hopes that "concern for the environment is internalized in reason" (2008:26). That "it is often argued that environmental destruction is irrational" (2008:30), should make one suspicious about such hopes, since rather than being stopped, destruction has only been facilitated. The idea of reasonableness could be a prominent mistake.

> "Rawls assumes that, once all particular inclinations and all individual characteristics (or knowledge thereof) are excised, all reasonable and rational people will be convinced by the same arguments. This assumption rests on a particular diagnosis of the phenomenon of widespread intellectual disagreement: that such disagreement is due entirely to such factors as ignorance, irrationality, and biases created by knowledge of one's individual characteristics" (Huemer 2013:Loc. 1712).

Distrusting this capability, Plato criticises democracy for being an irrational form of government, because he sees a conflict between democracy and rationality (1982; Graham 2013:Loc. 406-7). He, in contrast, does not believe that people can simply age into rational citizens even with proper education.

Further aggravating in this context is the fact that green democracy asks for more understanding from a rational citizen than ancient Greece. There is a constant information deficit especially in regard to environmental problems that involve complex systems. But

> "[a] green democratic constitution would [...] require the flourishing of its own kind of public reason – in this case, critical ecological reason – that recognizes, protects, and rewards ecologically responsible social, economic and political interactions among individuals, firms and communities" (Eckersley 2004:Loc. 1706-9).

---

[112] Gimenez points at this limited understanding of rationality since "what is decried today as Western or male rationality is actually capitalist instrumental rationality, which reduces people and nature to means for profit maximization and capital accumulation" (2000:298; see also Heilbroner 1988).

Critical ecological reason is the premise for Eckersley's green state (2004). While a green democratic state would be ideal, it remains that to expect rational citizens to be in the majority is unrealistic. Not only may people lack the capability to understand as well as willingness to engage with political issues but agreement on "principles all rational people might accept" seems equally problematic (Eckersley 2006:94; Huemer 2013). Eckersley may hint unwillingly at a different problem. Namely that the democratic ideal might need a concept of rationality that is too inclusive.[113] In a similar note Elling believes that it becomes "more and more apparent that [universally acceptable] rationales do not exit" (2008:6). Yet, the acceptance and tolerance of diverse rationales lead to 'environmental nihilism'. In contrast to other forms of nihilism, this trend has irreversible effects. Sustainability as a complex issue makes expert solutions a exigency, to claim otherwise is either based on a naïve belief in the rationality of the crowd or an equally naïve constructivism that negates the factuality of environmental destruction itself and makes it a matter of a discourse mainly (Luhmann 1986; Diekmann and Preisendörfer 2001; Latour 2007; Blühdorn 2012). Nonetheless, the issue is further complicated by powerful climate change deniers that question science itself, which in turn leads to

> "the frustration of scientists, who see an astonishing decoupling of scientific consensus and public belief, as well as, in some cases, an inverse correlation between the amount people know about climate change and the political will to act. Indeed, scientists have heroically expanded knowledge and explained it to the public on the assumption that if people only, then they would act" (Hohensee 2013:Loc. 4939-41).[114]

Relativism in this instance can be particularly damaging. Many participatory approaches assume that the contribution of local knowledge will lead to better output, but even "public authorities suffer from an information deficit, especially because many decisions in environmental governance are highly technical in nature and thus call for expert knowledge instead of lay contributions" (Newig 2012:52; Milic and Rosselot 2011).[115]

The results of the politics of nature influence all areas of politics and economics, which lead to even more complexity and means that issues cannot be solved in traditional ways. "Ecological problems hence conflate with the basic intuitions of how politics and economics work and require a sophisticated understanding of interrelated and gradual processes" (Talshir 2004:14; Diekmann and Preisendörfer 2001; Huemer 2013). Shapiro and Hacker-Cordon accentuate that

---

[113] "Political liberalism assumes that, for political purposes, a plurality of reasonable yet incompatible comprehensive doctrines is the normal result of the exercise of human reason within the framework of the free institutions of a constitutional democratic regime. Political liberalism also supposes that a reasonable comprehensive doctrine does not reject the essentials of a democratic regime" (Rawls 2011:Loc. 174-77).

[114] "The anecdotal associations, especially when they are amplified as a story by the media, are so powerful that they cause people to ignore contrary scientific evidence" (Lovelock 2009:Loc. 874).

[115] Elling sees problem in distancing sciences through specialization from mainstream traditions (2008:45). He extensively discusses the concept of 'reflexive modernity' in the context of the environment. Newig and Fritsch found no evidence that the integration of local knowledge or the social learning is actually enhanced by participation (2011).

"[d]emocracies find sustenance in prejudice as often as in reason" (1999a:1). By assuming the majority to be rational, democracy not only opened the doors for "demagoguery", but also encourages "inexpert action" (Graham 2013:416-17). Democracies undermine expert decision making, since as Dahl points out, citizens have the option "not to listen to experts" (2000:71). One connected issue is the naïve belief in technology as a solution to environmental problems. Particularly in matters of survival the principle of equality risks diverting the attention from focusing on actual expertise to the point where important actions are not taken. Accordingly, Schmidt ranks the abstract equality without regard to the qualifications of the citizens as a constitutional weakness of democracy (2010:464). Even if all citizens were equally able to comprehend political issues, the scope of today's issues and their interdependence impede the citizen's decision. Adding to the problem is the fact that politicians in democracies are rather "mediocre managerial staff" than meritocrats (2010:464; my translation), who often lack the time and prior knowledge to comprehend scientific findings. Again the Condorcet Jury Theorem cannot play a positive role, since it presupposes that a significant percentage of the decision makers are able to understand the issue at hand. Recognising a (common) self-interest is not as certain as the idea of reason suggests.

2.1.2.1. THE ENVIRONMENT AS SELF-INTEREST

Wise leaders need to acknowledge the difference between collective and individual rationality. Environmental degradation poses a huge challenge, since what seems rational to many individuals, leads to collective irrationality.[116] Nonetheless it is easy to accept that environmental integrity is not only in the collective, but also in everyone's individual interest, if reasonableness is presupposed. This discussion includes the idea that sound environmental politics is in the self-interest of every rational person. It should be a matter all reasonable people can agree on, assuming nothing more than self-interest. In this case collective and individual rationality could be the same (see Mill 1901).

In *Democracy and its critics*, Dahl uses dialogues between protagonist and antagonist in order to clarify his points (1989). In one dialogue the antagonist of democracy reflects on the assumption that everybody is qualified to rule. The crucial point of his argument is that many people may not understand their own basic needs, interests or good. In fact, he says people try to find happiness in consumption despite most religious suggestions to the contrary and the severe

---

[116] Randers notes: "I am a biologist, and the trajectories humanity has followed over the past twenty-five years, despite very clear warnings, makes me wonder about human rationality. To be more precise, I wonder about the apparent victory of our selfish, evolutionarily short-sighted reasoning that maximizes personal goods at present over the intellectual or moral rationality that would have been able to avoid the crisis" (2012:Loc. 2659-6).

impact on global life support systems. The United States are an obvious example for such tendencies. Dahl observes that

> "for three centuries the Americans avidly collaborated in the destruction of their natural environment, indifferent in the main to its importance to their well-being. [...] Yet a few people were enlightened enough to foresee the consequences" (1989:60).

Dahl presented this argument more than a quarter of a century ago and the development ever since has only accelerated. Undeterred by the visibility of destruction today, people consume ever more, which strengthens the antagonist's objection further. If people knew about their own basic needs, interests or good (cf. Mill 1901), this development was paradoxical.[117] The antagonist in his critique offers a causal explanation. Here, lack of better knowledge serves as the explanation not unwillingness itself.[118] Nature suffers, because people do not know or are unaware that they need an intact ecosystem more than a BMW. Ignorance then can simply be interpreted as 'misled priorities'. By the same token anthropocentric environmentalists argue that people are ill-informed and short-sighted about their 'true' interests (McShane 2007:17). This dilemma was already apparent to Cicero who expressed his concern that "citizens because they are also humans have pronounced tendencies to forget their own wider and common interests" (Baehr 2008:14; see also Cicero 1979). If this could be observed during the Roman Empire, the complexities of the contemporary worlds and the more inclusive citizenry can only mean that these tendencies are amplified. A healthy environment is sacrificed to narrower self-interests, namely immediate consumption. This overlaps with Plato's criticism of democracy (1982).

> "The modern equivalent of the Platonic democratic citizen is the stereotyped 'ungreen' consumer, who runs the kids to school in the 4 × 4 before returning to a house full of electronic gadgets, and buzzes around Europe during the holidays with cheap flights on Ryan Air or EasyJet" (Humphrey 2007:22).

But what does it entail for democratic systems? In democratic theory, a person's interest or good is defined by his choice, if he had an enlightened understanding. That means if he had the fullest attainable understanding and choices (Dahl 1989:180f.). In practice, it is hard to uphold that a majority in any democratic country currently approximates an enlightened understanding concerning nature. This is a rather self-evident observation. While "[c]ommon sense dictates special preparation to avert these apocalyptic threats", environmental politics is signified by inaction (Davis 2007:2; see also Carter 2007). Even with issues of high personal importance, the average knowledge is insufficiently low. Estlund points out that if parents do poorly on

---

[117] The impact of individualism will be subject of later discussions. It needs to be acknowledged that a logical consistent application of a rational choice approach may also see this vocation of self-interest as problematic, since in its perspective "rational self-interest is subject to the well-known free-rider and prisoner's dilemma syndromes, and cannot avert, but on the contrary will always promote, 'the tragedy of the commons'" (Scruton 2006:13).

[118] The relationship between knowledge and behaviour is essential throughout this book and will be discussed further.

questionnaires "about important matters pertaining to raising healthy and educated children", how can competence be expected from the voter (2009:Loc. 230-32; see Taber 2003)? While he maintains that doing badly on these questions does not necessarily mean that they are not capable of making good decisions, it is essential to note that it is fair to derive at the conclusion that they are less likely to make good decisions. If one accepts that citizens are not qualified to make specific decisions, how can they be expected to be qualified to make general ones, since the complexity rather rises with the level of abstraction?[119]

2.1.2.2. GENERAL EFFECTS OF THE MEDIA

A focal way in which these issues are simplified for the population and brought to their attention is through media. The media therefore partly determines citizens' environmental (in)competence. Environmental sociologist Hannigan describes clearly how the media and its structure contributes to the information deficit (2006:80-92). Particularly the attempt at neutrality leads to overrepresentation of climate change deniers (Worcester 1997:160, Hannigan 2006; Shearman and Smith 2007:27ff.; Höffe 2009:266ff.; Karmasin 2011). Neutrality and objectivity are routinely confused. Shows often consist of an 'expert opinion' for both sides, despite the fact that more than 97% of climate scientists subscribe to the theory of anthropogenic global warming (Cook et al. 2013).[120] If experts disagree or seemingly disagree on facts, how can ordinary citizen be expected to have "privileged information? Given the conflicting testimony of experts, it would seem that the typical citizen cannot reasonably reject any proposed policy" (Roemer 1999:61; see Maier 2008:134ff.).[121] The viewer on the other side might gain the impression of the issue being much less conclusive and undecided than it actually is and therefore is likely to support inaction until definite results are presented. The media often shapes the way people view an issue. Their framing tells the viewer about the relevance of a topic, the responsible actors and as importantly, what actions are necessary. Giving an equal platform to climate change deniers is an active contribution to failed climate policies.

Further worsening the situation, mainstream media operates with news packages that are produced under pressure in relatively short time (Hannigan 2006). Journalists focus mainly on discrete events and look for responsible people or corporations and therefore do not normally

---

[119] Critics say that democracy "is the rule of the average men; and the average men, it is held, is plainly an irrational and incompetent man. He is, indeed almost by definition, a mediocrity, and such cannot be expected to judge wisely of the numerous and complex affairs of state" (Spitz 1965:36). Many people already have difficulties to differentiate between weather and climate.

[120] In an exceptional step the BBC decided in July 2014 "not to insert 'false balance' into stories when issues were non-contentious" (Knapton 2014).

[121] Especially terms like 'certainty' are paramount in understanding the International Panel on Climate Change reports and similar findings, but here scientific language deviates substantially from common sense understanding.

present the bigger picture (Hannigan 2006). News packages portray problems as singular and mono-causal, rather than the outcome of institutional problems and social developments. The framework of today's news where they have to be fast and entertaining does not leave room for explanation of complicated issues. Even if people understand the issue the news circle helps to push uncomfortable matters out of people's consciousness. The attention of the media does not follow the objective conditions of climate change, but spikes with events like the Copenhagen Climate Summit. Issue attention circles fail to represent actual conditions and advancement of climate science. Much of the environmental catastrophe so far occurs in relatively slow processes and therefore does not make it into the news. Even in 'developing' countries with more dramatic events, the environment as a topic vanishes quickly from the political discourse, media and most importantly from democracy's cognition (Mayr 2009:101f.; see also Pralle 2009).

Thus, the environment becomes just another policy area, which is put within the discourse of business opportunities. In accordance, reports often blame protesters for an interruption of commerce. The public eye has the tendency to shift the attention from actual quality to marketing campaigns and policy issues then become parts of a show of 'political brands' (Crouch 2008:131; Schmidt 2010:453-471; Leif 2011). The majority may be more interested in symbols than actual news anyway (Edelman 2005). People are "only incidental bystander" in policy debates and not the informed citizen that can get involved (Hannigan 2006:91). Furthermore, journalists are themselves not sufficiently informed about science to report on it. Press statements of companies are often uncritically repeated (Leif 2011).[122] But complex environmental issues are also too complicated for presentation. This invokes the question, if free media in environmental issues even matters. The public's actual awareness of environmental problems remains extremely low. This is especially concerning, since information effects can have a significant impact on public opinion and political knowledge matters according to Althaus (2003:143).

Importantly, editors are subject to a power structure that has to cave in for pressures of status quo players. They regularly reproduce the dominant mainstream view. Many media outlets are owned by or depend on the advertisement revenue of powerful corporations that have their own agenda, hence are likely to present a perspective that is in their interest (Karmasin 2011). Freedom of speech allows them to also present their angle of the issue with dangerous consequences for the political discourse. Althaus, for example, finds that knowledgeable

---

[122] "Misleading information rarely comes with a warning label. People usually cannot recognize that a piece of information is incorrect until they receive a correction or retraction" (Lewandowsky et al. 2012:111). Furthermore Lewandowsky et al. stress that correcting misinformation is harder than commonly acknowledged.

members of a group may misrepresent the group's interests after following a specific media channel (2003:141). Most parliamentarians informed themselves on technological developments "almost exclusively from mass media" (Beck 1997:25), despite the introduction of new communication tools, it is reasonable to assume that this could be still the case. Though independent media exists and the internet is a place of a multiplicity of sources of information, drastic changes that produce informed citizens are unlikely. The diversity of sources makes it difficult for the user to understand validity and reliability of information presented.[123] Businesses have huge incentives to provide blogs etc. that present their practices as environmentally friendly. Information and entertainment have become indistinguishable to the extent that even traditional media outlets fall into the trap to mistake satire for reality. But more concerning is the fact that the internet is also home to 'a million distractions', so ignorance becomes more rational in the sense that information costs rise. Different information and entertainment channels compete for the user's attention. In a sense ignorance is more rational than knowledge.

2.1.2.3. THE LOGIC OF RATIONAL IGNORANCE

Countless studies show that large parts of the population are for example even ignorant about the meaning of the abbreviation of political parties. Rousseau clearly understands rights and obligations as different sides of the same coin, but what if one side remains unfulfilled. This is especially crucial for sustainable living (Etzioni 1998). The right to vote includes the duty to obtain information. While this is logically coherent in theory, what this means in practice cannot be narrowed down clearly. The complexity of the world does not allow for a neat definition of practical obligations of a citizen. It is impossible to set a benchmark for a minimum on time a citizen needs to invest as well as to set a minimum level of information he has to obtain.

> "The low levels and uneven distribution of political knowledge can be dismissed as a normative problem in only two ideal situations: when information costs as well as opportunities to become informed are the same for all members of a population, or when a population has common interests and all members give opinions in accordance with those interests" (Althaus 2003:275).

Whereas "all members" should agree to protect the environment as a common interest, opinions conflict with this interest. The ideal of political equality, then, clashes with a reality of ignorance. Ignorance seen from a rational choice perspective is multidimensional: there is a lack of information, it is not rational for the voter to get informed and the current structure does not support it. The result is that the voter is unlikely to know and/or comprehend his interests fully,

---

[123] E.g. *Frankfurter Allgemeine Zeitung* journalist Müller-Jung writes, commenting on the huge demonstrations in New York in September 2014, about progress and states that the Brazilian rainforest deforestation has been reduced by 75 % since 2004 (2014). 2004 saw de facto the worst deforestation and is therefore a disputable baseline. Deforestation declined dramatically in comparison. Yet, 2013 saw a rise in deforestation from 2012 and the quality of existing rainforest is said to be deteriorating (Carrington 2013; Laurance et al. 2014; see Forsyth 2003:31ff.).

especially regarding complex issues. The difficulty is that rationality is highly contextual. The rational approach has to consider that "what people believe and care about need to be factored" (Osborn 1997:131; Diekmann and Preisendörfer 2001; Caplan 2006; Petersen 2009:51f.). This was already evident for many political thinkers and can be found in Aristotle and Hobbes for example, since admitting "that man is naturally social and/or political would be to shut the door to the attainment of pure rationality" (Hale 1966:83; Hobbes 2007; Aristotle 2009). Neither beast, nor god, man is entangled in social relationships as is his worldview. An employable green political theory needs to acknowledge this (Stephens 2001a, Stephens 2001b). The methodological individualism of rational choice theory, therefore, often remains too reductionist.

Though game theory comes with many analytical shortcomings, it is nevertheless worthwhile to consider the additional dimension that a rational choice theory approach provides. While the assumption of rationality is problematic in general, it is a valuable exercise to assume rationality and explore the implications (Johnson 2010). Hence, the rationalist approach is a tool not a solution in environmental policy (Osborn 1997:136; see Diekmann and Preisendörfer 2001; cf. Simmons 2011). Rationality in rational choice theory is rather defined by the choice of means and not the choice of ends and that is true regarding decision about nature as well (Downs 1985, Connelly et al. 2012:144). Again, this leads back to the tension between procedures and substance. Rationality does not depend on what is to be achieved, but the instruments used to reach the goal. The assumption of the voter as a *homo oeconomicus,* i.e. a self-interested utility maximiser, then undermines democracy in many dimensions.[124] There are conceptual problems with the idea of the self-interested utility maximiser which are partly taken up in other discussions in this book. They can be summarised under the umbrella of the ever lurking question of priorities of individualist freedom. For instance, when ignoring the question of intellectual competence of comprehension assuming an 'enlightened citizen' the conflict between short-term and long-term benefits in the distant future remains.[125]

Nevertheless, the angle sheds light at a fundamental problem viz. rational ignorance. If the aim of voting is to have an influence in politics, the means of voting are unsuitable. The effective

---

[124] Some authors use the concept of *homo politicus,* but since a rational choice approach advocates argue that people follow the same logic for economic decision as for political decisions this differentiation is superfluous (see Simmons 2011 and Downs 1985).
[125] It is a choice between ends and not means (see Ophuls 2012:Loc. 411).

influence that a single vote has is minuscule. It therefore is not rational for the voter to invest time in getting informed about politics (Downs 1985; Caplan 2006).[126] Consequentially,

> "[c]reating social circumstances that facilitate democratic rule also mean, for example, that the decision units should be small enough for people to comprehend the issues facing the polity, preferably from first hand experience. (That gives rise to green proposals for decentralization, workplace democracy, and suchlike.) It also means, more importantly still, that there must be at least rough socioeconomic equality within the decision units. For then and only then will people have the sort of rationally well-grounded sense of political efficacy that is required for them to bother participating at all" (Goodin 2013:Loc. 3049-54 [sic!]).

Hence, the costs of getting informed outweigh the benefits within the contemporary systems. Political knowledge is rarely beneficial except for impressing friends (Althaus 2003:14). While people may still get informed about their own narrow interests, the information costs of gaining knowledge about other people's interest are even higher (Dahl 1989:61; cf. Rawls 2011). Dahl feared that the greater availability of information will not lead to greater voting competence, instead it possibly means a "higher demand for comprehension" (2000:187). More information needs more sophisticated citizens, who need to put forth greater effort. If it was not possible to produce enlightened citizens *en masse* in the past, it is illogical to assume that despite increasing complexity it will be possible in the future. The citizen needs to be able to grasp an issue in order to make a decision. But complexity is also a problem because biases increase with complexity and lack of clear evidence. Meanwhile, careful evaluation of evidence is replaced by "partisan reasoning", if information cannot be easily processed (Doherty and Wolak 2012:305). The reason why minors are excluded from democracy is the assumption that they are not yet able to comprehend a minimum of information necessary to make decisions. This is a focal point because, "if the criterion of competency overrides a claim based on rights, then the argument for democracy rests on mushy grounds" (Dahl 1989:126; Mill 1879; Höntzsch 2010).[127] Environmental integrity depends on complex systems analyses and issues "often need to be highlighted for the public and decision-makers by scientists and experts in order for the issues to be effectively set on the agenda" (Hogl et al. 2012a:3; Radcliffe 2002:37f.; Pralle 2009; Aklin and Urpelainen 2014).[128] Relative and rational ignorance illustrate a weakness of democratic theory neatly. Rational choice theory claims that it does not make sense to attain sophistication in politics. Democratic theory is particularly vague about qualifications, while sustainable measures depend on specific knowledge. When layman and expert are both classified as 'equally qualified', the differentiation between knowledge and ignorance becomes irrelevant. Not only is the

---

[126] "They are also likely to make errors in decisions that are unimportant to them, where they do not care to devote sufficient thought to identify the best option" (Huemer 2013:Loc. 4568).

[127] Climate change "brings together two areas over which people are likely to be both ignorant and irrational – politics and science" (Humphrey 2009:158).

[128] Long-term planning will be discussed in later chapters.

principle of equality problematic, but a majority of voters and politicians might also be arguably unqualified 'to participate in governing'.

The above discussion showed that assumptions of democratic theory clash with the necessity of good environmental governance. Both may not even speak the same language.[129] The required expertise is based on comprehensive knowledge that does not only take other people into account, but also involves the dimension of long-term planning. Thus, environmental politics questions basic assumptions of democratic theory.[130] How the input of the citizens as electorate and potential voter effects politics needs to be put under scrutiny in theory and practice.

2.1.3. INPUT AND FEEDBACK MECHANISMS

Given that input and feedback mechanisms are understood to be a major advantage of democracy, asking about its impact on sustainability is a vital part of the question whether democracies are and can in fact be sustainable. Diverse mechanisms as checks and balances are said to play a role in democratic societies. Accountability to the public is seen as a superior feature. Citizen's input accordingly characterises democracy. Schmidt among others describes democracy as a relatively effective method of articulation and congregation of individual preferences that ensures a relatively secure mediation between politics and society, which includes feedback systems that function as a warning system (2010:459; see also Dahl 1989). This means that democracy is believed to have effective input and feedback mechanisms that do not only serve as an indicator of public support, but also help to correct errors.[131] Checks and balances allegedly "keep gross abuses and wastes under control" (Bradhan 1999:102). The presupposed self-correcting effects are often praised, though debates about the actual in- and output continue as presented throughout this chapter. Hereby a discussion of perceived checks and balances needs to include four interrelated questions: What feedback channels are idiosyncratic to democracy?[132] Does the feedback matter? If so, how does it matter? Is the feedback 'reliable' and 'valid'?

Schmidt additionally sees a general advantage in democracy as a relatively open and adaptive political regime with huge potential to respect different interests (2010). Responsiveness to

---

[129] An obvious example is the opposition between democratic choice and environmental necessity.

[130] "There are of course comprehensive doctrines that either are not, or possibly cannot be, adhered to in a way that is reasonable in [Rawlsian] sense, but just because they are so they do not form part of the 'overlapping consensus' of reasonable doctrines. Doctrines that, for example, 'reject one or more democratic freedoms' must be contained" (Humphrey 2007:120; Mouffe 2002).

[131] This evaluation includes multiple channels, since "only by narrow political science conventions do we confine discussion of political representation to parliamentary politics and electoral processes" (Saward 2006:185).

[132] Deliberation and participation will be discussed as characteristics of a strong democracy.

preferences then is seen as particular advantage of democracies, but this does not mean that nondemocratic systems do not take people's wishes into account. The Chinese Communist Party for example is "found quite responsive to needs" locally in many instances (Bradhan 1999:104). Though responsiveness is understood as positive in general, this needs to result in a better outcome for nature to support green theory's claims.[133] Comparing different systems and their actual environmental record, Ward observes that while other constitutional structures might have an impact, "there is little to suggest that openness of the system to the green message helps" (2008:401; Hayward 2001).[134] While Schmidt counts responsiveness as strength, he, yet, lists that the will of the people is fictional, fallible, and seducible as a weakness of democracy (2010:459ff., Rousseau 2008). People are easily deceived. Not only unsustainable preferences by themselves, but populism pose an additional danger. Nationalist as well as class struggle rhetoric can be easily employed in favour of a polluting industry. Consequentially, the question is to what extent responsiveness can be advantageous. In a sense, the fickleness of the many is added to the fickleness of human nature (Schmidt 2010:464). As a theorist of deliberative democracy Dryzek puts his hope nonetheless into democracy's input mechanisms. Discussing greener politics he calls for a Popperian attitude towards public policy and politics and claims that this is only possible in a liberal democracy for its capability for open feedback (Dryzek 2005:111f.).[135] However, such attitude would demand not only enlightened feedback, but also clear policy lines that can be neatly identified and changed by the population. The central obstacle for his call is the dependence of democracies on the quality and channel of feedback. While green democratic thought builds on the possibility of ecological citizenship (e.g. Jennings 2010), de Geus believes that "[p]oliticians understand better than ever before that the majority of the population is primarily interested in a secure, comfortable and convenient existence" (2004:Loc. 2534-35). If he is right, it means that people are likely to measure governance looking at security, comfort and convenience. Such findings do not leave much room for optimism. Here, environmental politics clearly show the tensions between these three ends (e.g. Mitchell 2011). Notwithstanding, they are also in contradiction with themselves in regard to short-term vs. long-term rationality. The provision of security, comfort and convenience today risks their provision in the future. Importantly, politicians are not judged by their effect on the future, but by what they are perceived to cater today. Politicians are therefore likely to follow a rationale directed towards immediate returns. It follows that these ends as feedback for greener means and ends

---

[133] For a theoretical discussion of the epistemic value of responsiveness see Petersen (2009).

[134] This observation is based on a concept of 'weak sustainability'.

[135] Wurster speculates that "[d]ue to their higher implementation and information processing capacities, increased political competition (high error-correction, innovation and problem-solving capacities) and wider inclusiveness in favour of present public goods democracies should perform better with regard to weak ecological sustainability than autocracies" (2013:80).

are amiss. They mean a prioritisation of aims that are often incompatible with sustainability such as GDP growth. A connected reservation against Dryzek's suggestion is the fact that the correction of errors, abuse and waste is only possible given reversibility, whereas many aspects of environmental degradation are not reversible. Extensive use of fossil fuels for today's convenience for example will have a damaging impact in the future that cannot be reversed. Hence, if the public's input reflects de Geus' observation the case for sustainable democracy rests on shaky grounds. Furthermore preferences, interests and needs in general should not be understood as synonymous. The feedback governments get from the population does not have to reflect actual privation, but can also simply be based on tastes and is highly dependent on cultural expectations.

> "The appeal to 'needs' seeks a kind of philosophical bedrock. It is often thought that while we disagree about wants, human needs are self-evident: water, food, shelter, and so on. But in fact, philosophers and historians have long pointed out how even these most 'basic needs' are always interpreted within social contexts and conceptions of the good" (Lane 2011b:19; Nussbaum 1992).

Still it is a common imprecision. In one article, for example, eco-feminist Plumwood is very careful to dismantle many common dichotomies, but she does not reflect upon the question of wants and needs nor does she effectively engage in the tension of individual vs. collective rights that lies at the heart of the ecological challenge (2006:51-74).

A further difficulty for democracy arises from the difference between individual rationality and collective rationality (Arrow 1970; see Lane 2011b). Respect for ecosystems is necessary to ensure 'the common good' and is often in conflict with individual preferences, it is therefore questionable to which degree a better articulation and congregation is supportive rather than the opposite. It can result in what "Hardin and Barry called 'rational man, irrational society'" (Humphrey 2007:13). This is exceedingly apparent in the politics of nature. What seems rational on the individual level can be destructive for society. In many ways the enlightened citizen is expected to think for the common good, thus transcend the distinction between individual preferences and societal needs. Again, high expectations are dependent on the aggregated input of individual choices. Yet, one "cannot expect [the individual] to have as much sympathy with other people's sectional interests as with his own" (Thompson 1966a:98; Rousseau 2008). The idea that if everybody decides in their own interest and in consequence all interests are cared for is particularly problematic given the difference between individual and collective rationality and the perceived negligibility of the individual's action. It is suggested that deciding in your own interest in elections adds a dimension of fairness yet the outcome then cannot be more than the sum of all wills (Thompson 1966a; see also Stephens 2001a). Radical political change needs support of the population. Sustainability does not only need radical change, but change that is collectively rational. The idea of green citizenship acknowledges this and judges citizens as capable. However, industrialised countries in the meantime cannot overcome the fact that current unsustainable practices of production and consumption are not only accepted but democratically legitimised (Brand and Wissen 2011:104). When affected by a policy, citizens are in fact less likely to vote in the general interest as if they believe they are not affected (Roemer 1999:62). This has ample consequences. "In theory, democracy is bulwark against socially harmful policies, but in practice it gives them a safe harbour" (Caplan 2006:1).[136] Radical change in favour of sustainability would affect most citizens. Again, if the public feedback is taken seriously, democracy's performance strongly depends on the content of the input.

The enlightened voter is not in the majority. Notably, political judgments "are often a mixture of hard evidence, soft evidence, no evidence and uncertainty" (Dahl 2000:28). This is in particular the case, if elections decide. The average voter forms his judgment on this basis. It is sensible to reflect the capability of a system based on this mixture. In the first half of the last century, Schumpeter not only indicated that the issues at hand are too complicated for most voters, but – and this is crucial for the environment – that what follows is a disconnection of democracy, the voter's interest and a common good (2003:256f.; Shapiro Hacker-Cordon 1999a:4).[137] Democratic systems do not formally require the citizen to get informed, nor do they establish it as a moral duty.[138] A realistic judgment about elections acknowledges that the average voter may not understand the issue on the agenda and as importantly be aware of the issues that are not on the agenda. Correspondingly, democracy does not primarily derive its value from substantive legitimacy, but it can rather be described as the imposition of rule "derived from counting of heads, the sheer force of numbers, not from the validity of reasons" (Przeworski 1999:48).[139] Dependence on the citizen's input may pose a serious barrier, since it means that the content of it determines the direction. This means that the feedback itself then does not necessarily control waste. To conclude, democracy becomes a problem for environmental integrity if its subjects are

---

[136] Caplan may disagree with the kind of policies declared a harmful in this work.

[137] The concept of interest itself is problematic. Etymologically it derives from the Latin word 'interesse' meaning 'to take part in', which leads back to being affected in a sense.

[138] There is some evidence for a decline of voters' interest in political matters except for what affects their wallet. A decline in numbers voting and an increase in distrust in politicians can be witnessed in many western democracies (Shearman and Smith 2007:90; Crouch 2008). Following rational choice theory as elaborated above, it does not make sense for the voter to get informed as the costs are much higher than the benefits.

[139] "It is natural to object that democratic arrangements, by placing important and difficult decisions in the hands of the masses, are deprived of any substantial epistemic resources. The ignorant may well outvote the enlightened few with regularity. Thus, either democratic politics lacks authority and legitimacy, or I am wrong to claim that these depend on the system's having epistemic value" (Estlund 2009:Loc. 2423-25).

representatives of an unsustainable system (see Blühdorn 2011:24).[140] With voting as an essential part of democracy's legitimacy, elections are at the very least seen as an indicator of citizen's generalised approval. The discussion on feedback mechanisms focuses on elections as a policy instrument and public opinion, since they can be interpreted as central input in a democracy.

2.1.3.1. ELECTIONS AS POLICY INFLUENCE

"Democracy, the authorization of laws collectively by the people who are subject to them, is inseparable from voting" (Estlund 2009:Loc. 969-70). Elections need to be considered as a potential key factor of democratic performance. The idea of elections presupposes competition of ideas and therefore competing policies. In a democracy anybody is understood to have the opportunity to express ideas and interests and to compete for support (Dahl 1989). This includes freedom of information, which paradoxically also includes freedom of misinformation. If the people's will is fictional, fallible and seducible, attributes like open and adaptive could be dangerous. Respect for different interests includes respect for particular interests that might cause harm especially if these interests are dominant. McBay, co-founder of the Deep Green Resistance, a group that declares mainstream environmentalism as ineffective, summarises a focal point of his experience in one sentence: "The majority will never be on our side" (2011). If he is right, democratic politics have only a little chance to avoid environmental collapse. Elections serve as a means for citizens to, even if only in a limited fashion, express what is commonly understood as their 'will' or 'side'. It is important to question not only McBay's claim, but to also investigate the role that elections play for the politics of nature. Elections as an institution are understood to have a core influence on democratic politics. This includes different aspects. The implications of voting on the political personnel, on the individual level as well as the structural level and the general effect of both on the substance and therefore the sustainability need to be subject of an inquiry. Given the interconnected nature of these levels, arguments will overlap. As for other parts it necessarily involves theoretical arguments regarding democratic elections as well as examples. Although election systems are diverse, it should be nonetheless attempted to raise the most pressing issues for green political theory.

Seemingly self-evidently, the core of elections is deciding about the leadership. The question 'who actually rules?' is regularly ignored in democratic theory.[141] Shearman and Smith judge rather harshly that "[t]he democratic system itself attracts to politics people who are the most unsuitable for government" (2007:132). If politicians were pure interest-maximisers of rational

---

[140] "Whether or not feedback is impaired depends on values of the people" (Dryzek 2005:112).
[141] Höffe points out that there are good reasons for Plato's vow for property-less and family-less politicians (2009:240).

choice theory, it would mean that they are not elected to pass legislation, but pass legislation in order to get elected (Simmons 2012; Przeworski 1999:32). Politicians sometimes do everything to get elected while taking bribes or acting contrary to public opinion. Assuming a self-interested politician, Simmons asks why politicians should even work for the common good and finds such inclination rather suspicious (2012; cf. Jonas 198:181ff.). The voter in contrast will vote for the person whom he perceives as most qualified to implement his preferences. Yet for election many criteria play a role that cannot be directly understood as contributing to political literacy or competency. On the contrary, Fishkin says that representatives that openly state that they decide on the basis of reason and deliberation risk being voted out of office (1997:33).[142] Studies show that not just money, but height and attractiveness play a significant role in broad electoral success (Jacobs 1997b:49; e.g. Rosar, Klein and Beckers 2008; e.g. Verhulst, Lodge and Lavine 2010). Furthermore, incumbents are more likely to win government positions (Przeworski 2010). Even rain on Election Day seems to be a factor beyond electoral turnout (Bassi 2013; Henderson and Brookes 2014). The candidate with the better election campaign is also more likely to win. Meanwhile, the commercialisation of politicians, who become 'advertisement technicians', is a serious problem in electoral systems (Schmidt 2010). Many of the elected are rich in comparison to the general population. Wealth does not necessarily lead to a shift away from the values of consumer culture. Depending on the political culture a huge part of a politician's appeal to the public might be drawn from charisma. This does not mean that the elected has to necessarily be politically impotent, but it diminishes the probability for a candidate who is environmentally literate, irrespective of the fact that talking of sacrifices i.e. restrictions already impairs his ability to be perceived positively. Given deficiencies such as "the generally modest level of scientific literacy characteristic of elected officials" strong environmental politics are unlikely (Orr 2009:7). One severe problem is also that the positions in environmental ministries are typically low profile and that other ministries with more senior politicians are in particular enabled to interfere into environmental affairs (Connelly et al. 2012:318).[143] In the meantime calls from climate scientists for brave politicians with a willingness to act contrary to public opinion and risk their chances for reelection become louder (e.g. Hamilton 2010). The constituency itself normally only asks for actions in reaction to a problem.

---

[142] Such findings are diametrical to Rawls' demands of citizens "to repudiate government officials and candidates for public office who *violate public reason* [...]. Thus citizens fulfil their duty of civility and support the idea of public reason by doing what they can to hold government officials to it. This duty, like other political rights and duties, is an intrinsically moral duty" (2011:Loc. 6792-6800, my emphasis). The specific cultural context is likely to play a huge role in the evaluation of what counts as appropriate forms of reasoning.

[143] "George W. Bush placed fundamentalists in positions of authority throughout the federal government, including departments and agencies administering federal lands and environmental laws, and these appointees were not shy about amending scientific reports"(Orr 2009:131).

De Geus therefore calls liberal democracy "reactive" towards the environment where "proactive" would be necessary (2001:21; Blühdorn 2011).

Furthermore, active leadership is not the only factor for good environmental governance. Environmental protection is a unique issue that might be beyond comprehension until issues become too apparent. Sustainability needs decision makers equipped with the agency and expertise to implement sound policies. An experiment in policy management involving multiple factors comparing students and managers showed that managers were more successful in designing policies in a complex situation (Diekmann and Preisendörfer 2001:46). Instead of making each decision, they collected information first and then made block decisions.[144] The experiment showed that successful policy decisions need to be assessed in a holistic way and that such decision making needs schooling. Hence a specific training is necessary. Interestingly many participants delayed decisions and believed to be in a good condition even immediately before a catastrophe. Some green parties have burdened themselves with some structural restrictions that may affect the quality of their politics. Macintyre writes in 1966 that "[p]arties become in-groups, elections become occasions when rival minorities solicit the electorate, and the electorate plays a passive rather than an active role in its choices" (1966:186).[145] To counter this green parties often have term limits, which although giving chances to less senior members of a party and ensuring rotation, it could also negatively influence the party's abilities[146]. Many skills are only learned during office, while networking can be a core part of politics. Though meant as a barrier to nepotism and power concentration, this internal mechanism may practically restrict external power as well. Whereas such restrictions are neither the monopoly of green parties nor inevitable, they derive from the commitment to a green theory of agency. After all, they are meant to make participation more inclusive and ensure the primacy of content over individual politicians. Whether they achieve such aim is questionable. Overall these structures and procedures of democracies do not systematically support the rise of environmentally sound decision makers.

The extent to which the content of democratic practice is affected by the modalities of leadership selection is essential to the evaluation of its potential for sustainability. Gilens and Page's study shows at least for the US that despite the belief of many scholars the median-voters' preferences

---

[144] Block decision is qualitatively different from issue aggregation and logrolling.
[145] For a discussion of oligarchical tendencies inherent in party politics see for example Bender and Wiesendahl (2011).
[146] In contrast, Singapore's ministers are carefully selected and are "expected to stay at least three to five terms in office because, as Lee Kuan Yew puts it, it takes about two terms in office for a minister to become good at his job," which in the current terms means good "long-term (mainly) economic planning" (Bell 2013:19).

do not play a role for the outcome of political decision making (2014).[147] Gilens and Page's research is exceptional not only in its results, but in its possible falsification of many assumptions. The following discussion will nevertheless reflect on the content utilising the assumption that the voter does play a role at least in a minimal sense in determining the content of politics. While asking the question how the voter played a role, it might be possible to further investigate the question of whether he is relevant. Regardless of if it is the case or not, the main point here is the effect of elections as an institution on the content of environmental politics. The question remains how elections play a role for the content of politics (even if the voter himself does not matter): whether and how they play a role in environmental politics.

The voter is said to determine the content by voting parties into office that represent his interests. If the majority dislikes a government's politics they may democratically dispose the government. Hence, one of the outstanding strengths of democracy is the peaceful transition of governments via elections (Schmidt 2010).[148] Such transition is even understood as a strong signal for the consolidation of a democracy. People can vote governments in and out of office and governments can change rather smoothly. Foremost, the procedures ensure a majority's will. Unpopular governments are said to risk losing elections. While this can be seen as an important part of checks and balances, it is limited.[149] In the context of environmental politics, this idea comes with further reservations that need exploration. In order to understand the implications, it is useful to assume environmental politics was the only issue on the agenda. Though self-evidently environmental protection is not the only issue on the agenda given the scope that interference into people's lives would have to have, it could overshadow all other issues, especially due to its interconnectedness. Assumed it was the only issue, if environmental protection was popular and a government did not act accordingly, they would be voted out of office. Similarly, if it was unpopular a government that implemented protection policies would be voted out of office. Following this logic, democracies' likelihood to pursue eco-friendly policies depends on the population's will, since the procedure of elections is neutral to the contended content. Preventing climate catastrophes is 'unpopular', since real environmental protection involves sacrifices and it is typically low on the agenda. *Ergo*, this strength cannot count in a context of environmental politics.[150] Even if parties want to implement policies for the environment, upcoming elections may discourage it (Dryzek 2005:119f.). This is in particular the

---

[147] Zizek cynically describes free elections as a matter of courtesy of the powerful (2012:117). The powerful politely pretend not to be in power and ask the people to freely decide, whether they want to give the power to the powerful.
[148] Such peaceful transitions of governments are rarer than common sense would assume (Przeworski 2010).
[149] This is not only the case because incumbent parties have significantly higher chances.
[150] Przeworski judges: "[A] bad government cares about being re-elected and caters to voter's myopia, while a good government valiantly goes to defeat by turning the country into a national park" (1999:32).

case, because the social benefits are long-term, while the costs are immediate. Put differently, since it would involve considerable restrictions on consumption "governments are reluctant to implement such unpopular policies because an angry electorate might vote them out of office" (Carter 2007:54). Protective policies are likely to get punished (see Stretton 1976). Describing a specific instance of missed environmental protection policies Davis writes: "Gore decided to do nothing. The election was coming nearer and he did not want to have a controversy with one of his core support groups" (2007:196). Electoral competition regularly interferes with the introduction of policies. Short-term strategies of power maintenance are dominant in democracies and election circles play a significant role (Leggewie and Welzer 2011:158f.; see also Arrow 1970).[151]

This can lead to delays, discontinuities and incoherencies. If a government fell out of favour because of its environmentalism, the next government could also reverse the policies (Baxter 2005:159). Democracy, particularly regarding long-term strategies, undermines planning reliability (Petersen 2009:25). This is particularly problematic, since environmental protection needs not only unpopular steps, but also solid long-term planning and strategies. Giddens underlines that climate change mitigation needs a consensus transcending party lines and urges that "beyond the rhetoric of immediate party politics, there has to be agreement that the issue is so important and all-encompassing that the usual party conflicts should be suspended or muted" (2009:114).[152] It is not possible to determine the actual role of fear of the constituency in upcoming elections. Multiparty politics often make punishing governments for unpopular decisions more difficult.[153] Even if the majority has a clear understanding of an issue, multiparty systems and the practice of coalition building can mean that the voters can neither easily identify who is responsible nor withdraw support completely (Schüttemeyer 2011a:17).[154] Parties also aggregate different issues and representatives engage in logrolling. Hence, the voter is not only expected to be informed and look beyond rhetoric but also decide on different issue's importance (see Buchanan and Tullock 2001). Vote aggregation and packaging can result in inconsistent

---

[151] Moreover, following Edelman, Schmidt problematises "politics as ritual" and "politics as extravaganza", since continuous campaigning led to feverish conditions (see Edelman 2005; Schmidt 2010:464). Along, the importance of economic elite preference should not be forgotten (Gilens and Page 2014).

[152] The problem of calling for transcending cooperation will be discussed in the context of consensus-building.

[153] Politicians may fear electoral loss anyway.

[154] A further problem that can hinder representation in multiparty systems is the fact that while in some countries unstable coalitions are formed between parties with huge disparities, coalitions between similar parties are frequently excluded in other countries. The former has been the case in Nepal where a coalition between the Marxist-Leninists and the right-wing governed, while the latter case is typical for Germany, where the social democrats are unwilling to form coalitions with the left party. Multiparty governments were actually found to have a smaller range of policies, but more political stability than single-party government (Colomer 2011).

policies overall, even if representatives engaged in deliberations (Pettit 2012:246). Parties and their representatives themselves also assign priorities to different interests.

> "Liberal democratic systems [...] treat environmental movements as just another special interest group and environmental interests as tradable off against other kinds of benefits, a position that fails to reflect the intrinsic value of nature and the fundamental enabling services it provides" (Plumwood 2006:71).

Meanwhile issue aggregation does not only lead to less visibility of environmental policies because of more prominent issues. It also increases the likelihood of popular policies being not implemented despite their popularity because they are bundled with other policies or traded.[155] Majorities for example regularly poll in favour of forest protection but this is typically an insignificant issue for most parties (Shearman and Smith 2007:82). Overall, sound environmental politics are hampered by structural barriers.

Decisively, a polled "'demand' for strong national standards does not translate into a vote" (Humphrey 2009:149; Duit 2014b:337).[156] Anecdotal evidence for the dichotomy between abstract and concrete is provided by the German Green Party's struggle. When they called for an increase of the petrol price to 5 DM/litre (≈2.5 €) in the 90s for example, their demand was based on solid reasoning aimed at the enlightened citizen and his collective rationality. But it meant loss of the electoral support and the initiative failed. Prominently, social democrat Steinmeier commented that whoever attacks the car industry is not "close to the people" (Leggewie and Welzer 2011:120). His statement is symbolic for a general problem that occurs, when a policy is understood to prescribe personal sacrifice. Eco-taxes for example have shown to be particularly unpopular amongst the public (Carter 2007:340).[157] At large, few politicians are willing to call for the necessary changes. A majority of people is affected, so the political costs are perceived as too high. Here, Hamilton sees a particular dishonesty in climate change mitigation.

> "These costs loom so large in the political calculations that no government seems willing to do what is needed, which is to speak to their citizens as adults, explaining that we face an emergency, one that can be met only at some cost and inconvenience. Sadly, the national and international political institutions that must bring about the changes are too slow, too compromised and too dominated by old thinking to mandate the energy revolution we must have to guarantee our survival" (Hamilton 2010:173).

Citizens and governments seem unable to arrive at collective rationality. Neither does the citizen overcome the problem of transcendence nor does the politician.

---

[155] But this does not necessarily increase the likelihood of unpopular policies.

[156] The question if party politics are a barrier to the implementation of policies such as national forest protection (despite popular demand) needs further investigation.

[157] Eco-taxation is defined as the "use of economic, and in particular fiscal, instruments for environmental protection" (Markandya et al. 2002:87f.). Environmentally hazardous goods or services can be taxed in order to internalize formally external costs. The most prominent example is the carbon tax. Taxes as an instrument will be discussed as a market mechanism.

The rational choice theory's assumption is that if it promises votes, the environment will be part of the agenda (Mayr 2009:107; Downs 1985). Despite the partially refuted argument about democratic peace, involvement in a war can also secure electoral support (which by itself it interesting since it present a high cost activity involving sacrifices as well). If the war is popular, the bellicose party is likely to have electoral success. Incumbent parties might gain from the rhetoric of an external threat. War itself is not only human suffering, but means excessive waste of natural resources and pollution (see Sanders 2009). It is therefore imperative to mention war within this discussion. Connected emissions are not publicly accessible and are not fully accounted for in the calculated consumption of most countries.[158] The spending on its military industrial complex of the United States alone dwarfs all other countries (UN 2014). The sheer amount of financial gains creates large incentives for the weapon and weapon-related industry to mobilise publics in favour of war (se Mitchell 2011).[159] Given that many so called 'advanced democracies' have huge military industries politicians have incentives for continuation. Politics that promote peace and cut military spending may directly influence the country's overall economic performance and employment rate. Though the connection between this industry and democracy might have significance for environmental politics, an investigation is beyond the scope of this book. In any case, to the extent in which involved interest and interest groups have a proven effect on democracy, they are likely to have an effect on emissions as well. Again, from a purely profit-maximising position, it can be argued that parties only profit from political offices, hence the political content is not relevant. Yet, even such a reductionist position needs to include multiple factors such as competing interest groups.

Although 92% of the German electorate, for example, declared that the initiation of a greener economy was part of their voting decision, environmental politics were not a dominant part of the election campaigns in 2009 (Schüttemeyer 2011a:12).[160] At first sight, this seems a surprising result from a rational choice point of view, since it does not match the declared preference. If electoral support was the main incentive, it must mean that other issues had ranked higher or appeared strategically more useful for parties and campaigners. One major weaknesses of democracy is, in fact, that gaining and preservation of power tend to be prioritized over relevant

---

[158] Reisch and Kretzmann for example attempted to calculate the impact of the Iraq war between spring 2003 and fall 2007 (2008). They point out that the calculated emissions are greater than the emissions of 60% of all countries. Particularly important, they highlight: "The emissions associated with the war in Iraq are literally unreported. Military emissions abroad are not captured in the national greenhouse gas inventories that all industrialized nations, including the United States, report under the United Nations Framework Convention on Climate Change" (2008:4).

[159] Note that interestingly stocks for companies in the weapon industry are a relatively stable investment (e.g. Levitt 2013).

[160] The environment was not a topic of election campaigns in the UK either (Jacobs 1997b). It remains a widely ignored topic. It barely got mentioned during the American primary debates in 2016.

(*sachgerecht*) politics (Schmidt 2010:464). A content analysis shows quickly that even in Europe, "electoral politics remain dominated by traditional materialist issues, such as the state of the economy, taxation, public order and welfare policy" (Carter 2007:2). The environment does not have a real electoral basis as signified by only marginal support. In the meantime, political parties will not take a position that is far away from the preference of their voters and in particular, large parties are unlikely to take a stance that diverts from the majority opinion (de Geus 2001:21; Przeworski 2010).[161] Competition between parties often means that the actual spectrum of choices for the voter is very limited. Parties tailor their message to appeal to a majority, but since "nature is not merely one 'interest group' among many; its interests are not on a par with those of (say) corporate polluters and should not be viewed as negotiable" (Ball 2006:133; Baber and Bartlett 2005). Yet given the centrality of the economic performance incumbent parties are regularly driven to weigh producer's interest disproportionately in order to ensure reelection (Carter 2007:184). Importantly, weak minorities might hinder climate mitigation policies, when parties and political elites set their strategy regarding the next legislation period.

Green parties cannot be understood as fully excluded from these tendencies. Notably, not all environmental claims reach an audience for the reason that some "are perceived as being too extreme, misanthropic or too complex" (Hannigan 2006:75f.; Maniates and Meyer 2010). Especially the quest for acceptability by a broader public seems to be a major drive in the 'deradicalisation' that makes most contemporary green party politics follow only a policy directive of 'weak sustainability'.[162] The greens of the 70s and 80s, even before nature's destruction became as excessive and overt, have openly stated that strong policies are necessary. But today's greens are "tamed" (Kingsnorth 2009:38; Callaghan 2000; Burchell 2002; de Geus 2004:Loc. 2432-35). Democratic integration is likely to be a cause, since radicalness is lost through institutionalisation. "[A]n important underlying theme is that many green theorists and activists have increasingly come to accept that liberal democracy is here to stay, so ecologism needs strategies for reforming it" (Carter 2007:79). As indicated this could mean that green politics are reformed by liberal democracy to the point where measures are too weak to guarantee environmentally sound politics. This is an aspect, where the differentiation between environmentalism and ecology might appear useful to many. For instance, Dobson differentiates between environmentalism and ecology on the basis of a commitment to sustainability (2007).

---

[161] These tendencies can be observed despite reasonable criticism of public choice theory and the Median-Voter Theorem.

[162] Inescapably, green parties are subject to a specific context, hence they do not all follow the same party program or strategy. Some countries have a variety of parties who would fall under the umbrella term 'green party'. However, given their limited success, this is negligible in the wider context.

But if environmentalism signifies only a weak commitment to sustainability it is meaningless. Eckersley points at a commitment to 'strong sustainability' as a defining feature of green thought (2001). But if defined in Eckersley's terms the question is whether 'tamed' green parties can still be understood as adhering to green thought. In Germany, whose greens are often characterised as the leading example of a green party, the result of the people's feedback, Leggewie and Welzer say, is that they lack the courage to ask for minor changes such as the introduction of a speed limit (2009). Even the introduction of a mandatory 'Veggieday', a meat-free day, in public canteens, caused a public outcry. After getting a lot of critique for interfering in people's private choices the policy idea was dropped.[163]

In spite of becoming more established and some visible progress being made, green parties are still the exception and given the urgency attract a relatively small number of voters. European politics have witnessed the rise of green parties and in reaction all parties now make use of 'green rhetoric', but the actual bearing on policies so far is small (Callaghan 2000; Carter 2007:355; Ward 2008; Gilbert and Littler 2009:131ff. Humphrey 2009).[164] While at its height in 1998 part of the coalition government the German Green party only had a relatively small impact.[165] They in spite of the higher visibility of climate change failed to mobilise increasing electoral support ever since.[166]

---

[163] In 2014, a key topic of the German Greens was food in general (Die Grünen 2014). Maybe they chose this topic, since it seems rather uncontroversial. Food is an issue that can engage people on a personal level, when it comes to their own consumption.

[164] "The presence of green parties obviously goes some way toward providing more systematic representation of environmental concerns, but green parties are typically poorly resourced and still politically marginal when compared to mainstream parties backed by wealthy and vested producer interests (i.e., capital, and to a diminishing extent, organized labor)" (Eckersley 2004:Loc. 1645-47).

[165] Blühdorn judges that "they had reached this position of potential influence, they suddenly had to realise that, under contemporary conditions, the classical green views and projects find less public support than ever. Even a moderate ecological tax reform or the very gradual phasing out of nuclear energy were almost impossible to implement" (2012:25; see also Carter 2013:222).

[166]

Year	1998	2002	2005	2009	2013
Votes	3.424.315	4.110.355	3.838.326	4.643.272	3.694.057

Table 2 Total Votes for the Green Party in Germany (bundeswahlleiter.de).

European parties in general do not show significant increases. Table 3 indicates the relatively marginal backing green parties have mobilised in national elections.

	1980s	1990s	2000-2006	2007-2011	2012-2015
Finland	2.8	6.9	8.0	8.5/7.3	8.5
France	1.1	7.2	4.4	3.3	5.5
Germany	5.1	6.3	8.4	10.7	8.4
Italy	2.5	2.7	2.1	***[167]	***
Netherlands	-	5.0	5.6	8.0*	4.2*
Norway	<0.5	<0.5	<0.5	<0.5	2.8
Spain	0.9	**	**	**	**
Sweden	2.9	4.3	4.9	7.3	6.9
Switzerland	7.1	5.5	7.4	11.0/13.8	11.7
UK	0.3	0.5	0.9	1.0	3.8

Table 3 General Election Percentages for Green Parties in Europe's Ten Largest Economies[168]

Not only are other values and norms still prominent, green political issues are even in decline. In many countries, the environment became less an object of public concern. In Great Britain concern for the environment fell drastically between 1989 and 1990 (Worcester 1997). During the 90s, there was still substantial support for environmental policies and green consumption. Yet despite it being an issue with huge potential none of the Britain's two major parties used it (Worcester 1997; see also Callaghan 2000). By the time of the 1997 general elections, the environment ranked far behind "unemployment, health care, law and order and education" (Worcester 1997:163). Similar developments can be seen in other countries (Diekmann and Preisendörfer 2001:96f.). The 2015 British elections left the Green Party itself with only one seat. When election results have high percentages for green parties it is usually due to "extremely low electoral turnouts, the disastrous shape of the competing parties and/or the abandonment of green demands for radical change in favour of market-friendly eco-policies" (Blühdorn 2012:25). Greens have, as suggested earlier, not only been 'tamed' by the integration into the traditional party spectrum, green issues are also incorporated by dominant interests and blemished. There

---

[167] *Combined results of different green parties **Several green parties with percentages under 0.5% ***Shared lists but without significant gains.
[168] In general, such lists can only show tendencies and are necessarily a simplification due to differences in systems. They further take results out of context and therefore should not be overinterpreted. There might be a Fukushima effect i.e. green parties with elections in 2011, could have benefited from the catastrophe. Results before 2007 are averages in case of more than one election. Table 3 combines data from Alvarez-Rivera 2015, Bundesamt für Statistik 2015, Bundesministerium für Inneres 2015, Carter 2007:89 and House of Commons Library 2015.

is a huge gap between the logic of party politics which might lead to all parties claiming green topics and real commitment.

Recent studies show that over the last several years, particularly since the global economic crisis, concerns regarding the environment have been in decline throughout the Western world (Ratter, Phillipp and von Storch 2012; Scruggs and Benegal 2012).[169] Environmental protection is still not taken seriously enough, despite the fact that many countries have now established green parties and that numerous parties entertain a general language of sustainability. Different issues also play a more important role in election campaigns than the environment.[170] Generally, economic performance, unemployment rates, national strength etc. are given priority (Commoner 1992; Shearman and Smith 2007; Hadler and Haller 2011; Scruggs and Benegal 2012; Harms 2013; Duit 2014a).[171]. Opponents of climate change mitigation often argue that it is expensive, leads to economic decline, and therefore loss of jobs. The actual effect of an unemployment rate on electoral success is unclear. The question, whether green policies causing unemployment would have a negative effect on political parties, remains theoretical. Delayed action could be 'justified' by fear of loss of votes after all. Whether this is actually the case is still debated. Carlsen observes a tendency of punishing right-wing governments for high unemployment in Australia, Canada, the UK and the US (2000).[172] Wright's analysis of US politics shows Democrats always having an advantage from higher unemployment rates (2012). Colomer notes a tendency in Europe to punish incumbent governments when the electorate perceives the economy as bad (2012). Studying Swedish general elections, Elinder finds a correlation between a decrease in unemployment and an increase in support for the incumbent government (2010). How unemployment rates and electoral success relate must be understood as highly contextual. Still, the latest decline in public concern over climate change in the US and Europe, according to Scruggs and Benegal, is best explained by unemployment rates and not by Climategate and the

---

[169] Effects are highly contextual. It should be noted that Bainchini and Revelli find, studying Italy, that, though ranking behind party affiliation and fiscal conservatism, urban environmental performance can have influence on the popularity of the local government if citizens are properly informed (2013). Urban environmental performance is more immediate.

[170] "Democratically elected governments cannot be expected to make the rational economic choice: electoral competition drives politicians to promise increase in welfare now. Poor people living harsh lives in poor countries and especially where average life expectancy is short can be expected to 'overdiscount' the promise of enhanced future benefits. The politicians make a politically rational response" (Burnell 2009:8). Giddens proposes that all political parties should agree on keeping climate change on top of the agenda (2009:93). This idea is not only utopian, but also in a sense undemocratic, since it restricts 'the democratic will'.

[171] It should be clear though that each of the issues needs sustainability in the long term. Still even politicians, who should have an understanding of the gravity of the situation like Merkel who holds a PhD in physics, do not act accordingly either. Though climate scientist and government advisor Schnellnhuber told her "to form a coalition of the willing" she denied by referring to other priorities (Spiegel Online 2012).

[172] Results for left-wing governments were less conclusive.

media or the weather (2012; see also Stadelmann-Steffen 2011).[173] However, weighing the environment against economic growth etc. derives from a categorical mistake that does not only try to capture the value of nature in monetary terms. It also underestimates the holistic cost of destruction, in particular, its consequences.[174] Often, but not always, there is not only a tension between issues given priority and environmental protection, but they can be mutually exclusive. This is a huge problem since given the fight against unemployment, its preeminence over the environment effectively means to measure unemployment rates against 'the future' (Leggewie and Welzer 2009:18).[175]

In regard to ignorance, the voter lacks a comprehensive understanding of "the implications of living in a world damaged by global warming" and "he seems unable to grasp what the loss of millions of species of plants and animals will mean to people in the year 2100" (Randers 2012:Loc. 1100-1105). Given the degrees of separation and abstraction, the question is whether it is reasonable to expect the general public to look beyond their own experience and what this means in regard to electoral support. Hence, majority support for sustainability seems fantastic. As explained previously, classical rational choice theory, on one hand, assumes that "when citizens do come to take political action within a democracy, they will be motivated by a narrow conception of their interests, and will possess only a very rough understanding of how to promote them through the ballot box" (Humphrey 2007:13). This is said to be even more the case because while the consumer has to pay the bill if he is mistaken about a product, the costs of his mistakes in politics are dispersed over the population (Caplan2006:14; Simmons 2011).[176] Following this logic, citizen's beliefs, even when mistaken, do not create significant personal costs. Taber, on the other hand, writes that

> "citizens do not seem especially sensitive to their own material interests when making political decisions. Unless the material outcomes from a public policy or issue are very clear, very large, and very imminent [...], self-interest does not determine opinion or action" (2003:44).

In his research two main problems for environmental politics, short-term thinking and material self-interests, "turn out to have little to do with public opinion on a wide range of political issues" (Taber 2003:44). Caplan similarly thinks that citizens do in fact direct their attention to their

---

[173] The controversy over the content of leaked emails between leading climate scientists is known as Climategate. Climate change deniers used and still use passages out of context to allege manipulation of data.

[174] "Part of the damage of any pollutant often is the loss of human life" (Buell and De Luca 1996:34).

[175] If sound environmental policies would actually lead to an increase in unemployment or have other negative effect cannot be easily determined. Germany for example as a country with a substantial car and chemical industry has more jobs in environmental protection than in both other areas combined (Jacob 2008:35).

[176] Rational choice theory correspondingly concludes that a democracy therefore will produce more public goods than necessary, but this is only logical, if the costs are externalized and spread. While the petrol example shows the opposite air as a public good is dispersed, while the costs of filling the car (carbon taxes) are not. It also depends on a citizen/consumer distinction.

perception of a general interest (2006:19). Many advocates of democracy think "public opinion in democratic countries tends to move toward an ever more inclusive commitment to ideas like intrinsic equality and equal consideration" (Dahl 1989:179; cf. Stadelmann-Steffen 2011). Still, citizens might report that they do not vote in their self-interest, meaning in favour of their own bank account etc. but for the overall economy, yet such statements can hardly be tested. It is difficult to evaluate related claims, including the question whether a degree of self-deception could be involved.[177] Though environmentally friendly behaviour can be based on reason, people have a significant stake.[178] Even if Taber is right, costs of environmental politics can be clear and immediate.

Equally optimistic, Jacobs sees a chance for green politics in appealing to the public as citizens and not as consumers (1997b:51). While it might be favourable if humans were able to rationally differentiate between different roles, it is likely that particularly in an intricate world such neat distinctions do not exist. Meanwhile, "any theory that simply assumes that political actors are benign" and that is based on the assumption "that self-interested consumers become citizens concerned with the public good, that politicians express the values of citizens in public law, and that bureaucrats quite neutrally administer that legal expression of public values" needs to be placed under scrutiny, even if one does not believe in the dominance of *homo oeconomicus* (O'Neill 2006:163). The constituency, though not as narrowly as rational choice theory suggests, has a tendency to see the impact of their vote in terms of their own life and consumption (Hamilton 2010; Simmons 2011 cf. Caplan 2006). Stadelmann-Steffen's research into determinants for environmentally friendly voting behaviour in Switzerland supports the rational choice assumption that private costs have a substantial impact on the voter's choice (2011). Voters even favour bans and regulations instead of market mechanisms. The reason is assumed to be that the former's costs are less visible. Stadelmann-Steffen's findings strongly suggest that in environmental matters, self-interest directs voting behaviour. Additionally, Jacobs' suggestion includes a second flaw. The differentiation between private and public sphere cannot be upheld when private consumption has global effects. Above all consumption is political (in a sense) under current conditions. In both cases, an enlightened citizen that sees beyond his own immediate needs is a condition.

---

[177] There is also speculation that the negligible influence of a single vote makes the voter more likely to vote in accordance with his values than his direct interests. Though there does not necessarily need to be a difference. In a similar light Pettit writes that "there are grounds for arguing that in a large-scale, secret election or referendum, the most rational stance for a voter to take is to use the vote for the pleasure of expressive satisfaction" (1999:176).

[178] It can be observed that "self-reporting environmentalists often vote for environmentally abusive candidates. On the question of whether these espoused preferences are simulative or merely weak, it is interesting to note that respondents often opt for very strongly worded environmental commitments" (Humphrey 2009:150).

"The conceptual dichotomy between consumer and citizen fails to register the ways in which – in everything we do, public and private – we are either producing sustainably and so reproducing sustainability itself, or we are producing unsustainably and so reproducing unsustainability itself. We are not negligible individuals lost in the mass and entitled by our liberty to act indifferently to our effects [...] So while we sometimes buy as consumers (idiots, singular, for the Athenians), sometimes vote as citizens (polits, singular), we cannot sever those identities from each other completely" (Lane 2011b:125f.; Callero 2009:29).

Consequentially, a sustainable society needs its public to act as citizens in each case. But since politics could actively interfere in consumption by the means of rules and regulation, a sustainable democracy depends more on the actual electoral support than on what is sometimes understood as 'consumer democracy'. Here it depends on the particular political culture and the place market freedom takes up in people's value systems.[179]

Unique characteristics hinder the environment from benefitting from popular support and democratic feedback mechanisms. Since environmental degradation is a relatively slow process in comparison to people's daily lives, it often fails to attract a sense of urgency.[180] As suggested environmental integrity is a complex issue, consequentially, it also lacks obvious solutions. As such, Giddens remarks it is also less likely to 'make it' on the agenda (2009:112; Pralle 2009:785). Easier to grasp economic growth is still sine qua non of every government, despite the fact that unlimited growth is contrary to any concept of sustainability. Improvements in the environment are harder to illustrate and harder to use for mobilisation of a voter basis. It is hard to argue that, when the environment does not even play a significant role in the national elections of countries that are understood as particularly vulnerable to climate change, environmental politics does have a real chance to have an impact in elections anywhere. Notably, the Dutch elections after the economic crisis of 2008/2009 have experienced how environmental politics stands in the shadow of economic politics (Lekakis and Kakous 2013:4). The Netherlands in the meantime is seriously threatened by the rise of the sea-level due to its geographical location. Many parts of the country are below sea-level. Looking at the widespread inaction, Leggewie and Welzer ask the disturbing question, how irresponsible one can be to prefer electoral success to long-term success and chances of survival (2009:92).[181] Without a shift in norms and values the voters' preferences do not support truly green policies (see Buck

---

[179] "Not only do proponents of public choice theory fail to distinguish between different kinds of association, but they make a corresponding failure to distinguish between the different goods or interests an individual may have as a member of an association" (O'Neill 2006:171).
[180] Cognition processes will be discussed in the following chapter.
[181] Yet, if the people themselves are in favour of the continuation of destructive behaviour, a responsible government would have to rule despite the people. Deciding against the majority's will could be understood as patronizing. While representatives have no imperative mandate, diverting from this will cannot be labelled as rule by the people, but only for the people.

2013).[182] Defying Inglehart's theory on postmaterialist values, many industrialised countries entered an age of hyperconsumption (see for example Luke 1999). Inglehart probably misjudged people's inclination to accumulate and to integrate commodities into people's daily lives. From a Maslowian (and eurocentric) perspective, it appears logical that basic needs need to be accommodated before people can have postmaterialist attitudes, but the scope of basic needs has been extended massively during the last century.[183] Inglehart underestimated consumer culture and its propensity to manufacture ever more needs. Many past luxury goods are essentials today, so the bar for minimum living standards rises continuously, even if citizens utter support for non-materialist values. Previously non-existent goods like e-book reader or iPad have become required gadgets for many within half a decade. Here, Carter points out that greater affluence only results in greater future expectations and that green parties are mainly 'successful' in Europe, where consumption rates are high (2007:97ff.). Whereas this seems to support Inglehart, drops in consumption are still to come. Whereas greens routinely argue that protecting nature leads to higher quality in life (Holsworth 1979), affiliated arguments are not very effective in election campaigns. They lack concreteness and immediacy.

Jacobs points out that an additional problem for sound environmental politics is that long-term environmental policy mandates a lot of trust in the government and that this trust, listing Britain as an example, cannot be taken as a given (1997b). Again, effects of policies aiming to improve the quality of life are often neither immediate nor can they be easily measured, while the costs are felt directly. "The [quality of life] argument effectively offers a gamble: exchanging the certainty of reduced private consumption for the uncertain benefits of public expenditure and regulation. It is a gamble many voters may reasonably reject" (1997b:56; see also Blühdorn 2007). Parties that promise abundance and a bright future today can capture votes easier than parties asking for restrictions in favour of a future that 'is not that bad'. This is a well-known impediment, since

> "the prospects of re-election are going to depend most saliently on the experience of voters in the present, so that there is going to be a powerful incentive for politicians to make that experience sweet and to downplay future costs, where these are costs that electors may be presumed to care about, but to be easily led into ignoring" (Pettit 2012:232).

---

[182] Stephens' discussion of Wissenburg's green liberalism expounds the problem of unsustainable preferences and the necessity of studying preference formation (2001a).

[183] Defying the assumption of postmaterialist values, Shum's research shows that "[o]utside of the advanced industrialized countries, one cannot assume that citizens of richer countries have systematically more positive attitudes towards environmental protection policies than citizens of poorer countries" (2009:287; see also Singer 1994:59ff.). Even in industrialized countries, there is no necessary correlation between wealth and environmental concern. Careful analysis shows that wealthier households in California for example tend to give less support to state-wide environmental propositions (Wu and Cutter 2011).

Emphasising the same development Shearman and Smith write under the title "Plato's savage beast" that

> "elections have become the promise of largesse to the voter. This is the fundamental reason why important decisions on true sustainability are not made today. [...] [U]nless liberal (democracy can successfully address this issue, there is no rationale for its existence" (2007:76; Ophuls 2012:Loc. 1615).[184]

As long as the voter expects and candidates promise fast returns without any costs, democracy cannot cope with the protection of nature. Thus, radical changes may not be implemented for the fear of losing electoral support. Politicians' fear of asking for sacrifices is one explanation for the broad support for ecological modernisation theory, which optimistically proposes the compatibility of economic growth and environmental protection.[185]

Still, Simmons points out that people are easier scared by bad images than captured by positive images (2011). But if this is the case the question is why greens were not able to use this tendency to their full advantage. Any discourse that understands environmental integrity as a postmaterialist value ignores the obvious. The environment is matter (Talshir 2004:Loc. 609-12). 'Rebranding' nature, as a core matter, might create the opportunity to implement better policies before the problems of environmental destruction materialise in a way that cannot be ignored.[186] If Simmons is right, apocalyptic images may actually help green parties to gain momentum. On the other hand, oppositions can invoke negative images of immediate costs. In rational choice approaches, politicians are said to compete for votes following similar principles as the free market. In that case, perceived attractiveness of a product is vital. In fact, political parties do effectively use people's emotions for their advantage in some areas. But it seems to mean that instead of comprehensive environmental protection small issues are chosen to present the candidate or party as green. Here, Maier points out that it is ethically but also instrumentally questionable in regard to biodiversity why not all animals deserve protection and why instead 'sexy' animals like the polar bear or tiger are chosen for campaigns (2008:134; Gilbert and Littler 2009; see Pettit 2012:200).[187] Small fixes are not only naïve but dangerous because they distract from implementing 'real' solutions (McLaughlin 1995; Pralle 2009). Inaction will lead to the occurrence of more dramatic weather events and disasters with higher frequency. Public choice theory explains for the meantime that because of the high information costs of climate politics, it

---

[184] "Society will be far more inclined to continue deferring its debt to nature unless the majority of citizens are assured that they will not be unfairly and excessively burdened by this agenda" (Buell and De Luca 1996:56).

[185] Ecological modernization theory will be discussed later.

[186] Social fact will be a central concept, when analysing cognition and behaviour.

[187] Huxley comments on contemporary politics in 1958: "Democratic institutions can be made to work only if all concerned do their best to impart knowledge and to encourage rationality. But today, in the world's most powerful democracy, the politicians and their propagandists prefer to make nonsense of democratic procedures by appealing almost exclusively to the ignorance and irrationality of the electors" (2000:123f.).

is actually rational for politicians to 'sell' small-scale individual acts in favour of well-organised interest groups that ensure a maximum of publicity (Mayr 2009:75). Hence, protection campaigns are generally short-sighted and only limited in effectiveness. Randers, a professor of climate strategy, describes the prospects as follows:

> "Each event will lead to public outrage and create fear for the future. But in most cases the short-term costs of action will be seen as unacceptably high and lead to a "well-considered" decision to postpone significant action. Only very slowly will the unending sequence of extreme weather events create a political majority in favor of real action. Only after decades will society vote in favor of the extra voluntary investment that is necessary to cut emissions significantly" (2012:Loc. 2589-93; see also Marshall 2014).

This conclusively means that action in electoral systems cannot be expected until threshold events have been surpassed.

However, the majority of greens maintains that more involvement of the public i.e. the stronger integration of citizens into policy making is substantial for sustainable politics. Though, if this assumption is valid, democratic input and feedback mechanisms must prove to have a positive impact on ecological integrity. Yet the public's stronger involvement might repeatedly be an obstacle to sustainability. As a general problem, Bradhan points out that multiple veto systems tend "to reject too many good proposals" (1999:103). Here, this is particularly problematic in two ways. First, environmental degradation needs to be stopped in a timely manner. Multiplying the number of actors involved necessarily leads to longer timeframes. Change is halted until a proposal is found that finds enough support. Second, resource conflicts typically involve various interests groups that have vast interests in the continuation of exploitation, since most costs are externalised while the benefits remain aggregated and benefits for the interest group simply outweigh their costs.[188] Moreover, Zeller speculates that parliamentary liberal democracy might represent the capital disproportionately and that it cannot be isolated from property relationships (2011:108). Truly green politics pose an extreme challenge to all property relationships and their use. In each instance democratic veto mechanisms are likely to be employed against any policies that would change the status quo against the interests of powerful players. When considering the reason for the better outcome of European politics in comparison to the United States, Davis states:

> "The policymaking systems of the European countries are not open to public scrutiny as the American system. Industry is brought into the government discussions at an early stage, the number of scientists is smaller, they are less likely to raise objections publicly, and the

---

[188] In the case of car usage fumes are dispersed globally (and additionally accumulate over time).

> European parliaments do not have the American tradition of free-wheeling investigations and exposés" (Davis 2007:207).[189]

Davis understands less feedback, i.e. fewer veto systems and conflict parties, as the reason for better results.[190] Rather corporatist countries are said to have better environmental records, but such findings might be restricted to earlier studies (Duit 2014a:14). Studying air pollution shows that

> "[t]he goal-oriented, accommodative, co-operative and consensual style of corporatist policy-making results in lower emissions of traditional air pollutants than the process-oriented, competitive and disjointed form of pluralist interest representation" (Crepaz 2006:268).[191]

In addition, multiplying checks and balances does not always work in the positive sense as many democratic theorists would hope for. A link between multi-layered involvement and participation of the public and better environmental records has not been proven. Importantly,

> "what makes corporatism so effective – its centralised, hierarchical, character – also makes it very susceptible to corruption, moral hazard and agency loss. There are reasons to believe that, while the corporatist system of interest representation may be effective, it may not be very democratic" (2006:270).

Studies of the effects of veto player's support Davis's suspicion (Poloni-Staudinger 2008; Dryzek, Norgaard and Schlosberg 2013:Loc. 499; Madden 2014). The existence of multiple veto players generally affects environmental policies negatively.[192]

Even where the citizen can 'directly' determine the policy choice, greener choices are not automatically made. Typically, green political theory favours direct democracy. But 'direct engagement' with an issue does not necessarily lead to green outcomes. Though the limited data does not allow for a generalisation, even direct democracy seems to undermine many claims. The Swiss direct democracy shows that actual popular initiatives for positive environmental policies are seldom successful. Milic and Rosselot find that only 12-17% of sound policy suggestions pass, while more than half of the decisions against environmental soundness pass (2011). While proposals with weak measures that are supported by the political elite are relatively successful, stronger measures tend to be softened in a consensus-building process (Stadelmann-Steffen

---

[189] Note that it is not proven, that industry is not brought in at an early stage in the US, so Davis' claim can only be understood as a tendency. It is also important to mention that European democratic systems are diverse and further differentiations must include an elaboration on the achieved degree of sustainability.

[190] "Their potentially greater ability to reform, combined with a lower number of veto players, could give the parliamentary and the presidential systems advantages over semi-presidential systems" (Wurster 2013:80). But in fact parliamentary and semi-presidential systems show mixed result (2013:85).

[191] The question of the impact of consensus building mechanisms will be discussed in the context of strong democracy.

[192] Writing an encyclopaedia entry on autocracy Waskey uses this point as an example for its advantages: "Even today autocratic governments exist in many places. Arab sheikdoms of the Persian Gulf region can be described as autocratic; although their rule often appears to be benign, it is still very strong. This can have administrative advantages because decisions can often be achieved without having to engage in exhausting battles with interest groups or opposition parties that exist in democratic states. Thus, a decision to adopt green technology can be made by the ruler even if other interests are hurt" (2011:106).

2011).[193] Hence, Swiss citizens do not show the enlightened voting behaviour desired by the majority of green theorists. On the contrary, Swiss and Californian experiences with direct democracy have shown that the outcome regularly favours economic elites and the already dominant white educated male tends to be overrepresented (Merkel 2011). Neoliberal or conservative fiscal politics often win. Not only does the direct democracy in Switzerland show right-wing populism and discrimination, the empirical study of direct democracy additionally shows a preference of particular interest instead of the common good, which amounts to exactly the opposite of an enlightened green citizenship.[194]

2.1.3.2. PUBLIC OPINION AS DEMOCRATIC INPUT

Besides periodic elections, public opinion polls might be interpreted as a ubiquitous measurement of support or disapproval. Although public opinion is often defined by opinion polls and presented as something that is manifested, it is dynamic and politicians can only have a vague idea of it. Politicians and the media alike tend to reify public opinion. It may sound counterintuitive; however, polling as the most common way to get an impression appears to be a deeply flawed method. Again among others, fickleness can be a problem. Green theorists, on the one hand, argue that a supportive civil society is quintessential to environmental integrity. Randers, on the other hand, fears that communication technology will enable continuous polling of a self-interested public opinion that will hamper sound decision making and lead to the 'cheapest solution' (2012:Loc. 3651-56). Still, the standing of the public on issues cannot be ignored regardless of how faulty it may appear from a scientific point of view.[195]

> "The opinion of a rationally irrational public may have no bearing on the question of how much climate change abatement we, as a society, should pursue; but it may have a bearing on how much will be tolerated, and in what form. For this reason public attitudes to climate change have to be taken seriously" (Humphrey 2009:166).[196]

Public opinion cannot be ignored in its entirety.[197] Self-evidently it cannot have an effect on scientific facts themselves. Though it does not necessarily provide normative guidelines either, it might show what can be implemented. Hamilton comments even on China that "[d]espite the government's recognition of the dangers of global warming, it would sacrifice its political

---

[193] The percentage depends on the stringency of the classification.
[194] It should be noted that California and Switzerland offer first-rate education.
[195] "Concern about public opinion is understandable as it is an important factor in policy change: while the earth's climate may not react to what people think about the climate, elected politicians often do" (Scruggs and Benegal 2012:505).
[196] Many scholars do believe that the degree, i.e. 'the should', should be part of public deliberations (see Gillroy and Bowersox 2002).
[197] "Any one governing agent or agency may be tempted to challenge popular feeling and to face down popular resistance. But the very fact that the state acts only when its component bodies all come into alignment – and that it is forced to act under the constraints of a rule of law – means that the government as a whole is less likely to be disposed to display such bravado. That government will not be as ready as any individual part might be to ignore or push back against popular resistance" (Pettit 2012:223).

legitimacy if it pushed through the sorts of measures required by the science" (Hamilton 2010:94). Effective governance needs at least minimal support of the population. If too many citizens oppose policies, governments cannot count on compliance.

Public opinion needs to be understood as in constant fluctuation, although many norms are relatively stable, extreme shifts can occur within a decade. An example for the possibility of rapid change is the seismic transformation in public attitude toward gay rights in the US. Supported by massive lobbying efforts, including the entertainment industry as a strong cultural influence, significant gains in acceptance were made within the last decade. Today many people identify themselves as tolerant towards homosexuals and support equal rights. Generally, collective identities and therefore culture play a decisive role in the formation of public opinion (Taber 2003:448). Differentiation consequently is a determinant. The identification with a certain 'class' can lead political behaviour (Campbell et al. 1980). This can have a huge negative impact, if a group defines itself to a significant degree through the use of status symbols directly connected to hyperconsumption.[198] Such a consumer class then is unlikely to support concrete restrictions on the behaviour that contributes to their identity. Particularly economic interests, but also cultural and social factors remain important even in the absence of controversy over causalities of climate change (Diekmann and Preisendörfer 2001:54). Questioning certain practices can indirectly be understood as questioning somebody's identity. Besides the cultural context, opinions are also subject to environmental conditions. During times of extreme weather for example people are more likely to perceive climate change as a threat. Donner and Daniels prove a significant correlation between temperature and public opinion about climate change in the US (2013; Scruggs and Benegal 2012). There might also be seasonal variations (Althaus 2003:239). Framing of polls therefore is crucial.[199] A majority of surveys might not give the interviewed the chance to think. The literature in psychology on the effects of context and manipulation grows continuously. In many situations it makes sense to speak of the mood of the public rather than of the opinion. The Fukushima disaster impressively showed the influence of external events.

One cannot create an instrument for exact measurements of the public's interests. Rather than mathematical equations, representations of public interests need interpretation. They are

---

[198] The lifestyle of Amish communities shows the opposite case.
[199] Looking at different polls regarding climate change Scruggs and Benegal find that there seems to be no difference in results caused by difference in wording (2012). Yet, a new American study found that even 'climate change' and 'global warming' trigger different responses (Leiserowitz et al. 2014).

neither fixed nor clear. Meaning is attributed in processes that involve multiple actors, channels and directions. Using the language of symbolic interactionism, Saward describes this as follows:

> "If for example an electoral constituency's interests were transparent, then a representative could simply 'read off' those interests and act on them. But the signified, or the object, is not the same as the collection of people who make up the constituency (the referent). It is a picture, a portrait, an image of that electorate. The 'interests' of a constituency have to be 'read in' via a subject or signifier, not 'read off'. This is an active, creative process, not one of passive reception of signals from below. The business of political figures, parties, lobby groups and social movements is aesthetic because it is political" (2006:186).

Public opinion is not a direct reflection of public interest. Both cannot be simply understood as a given or natural.

> "The creations are theoretical, but they are also political in a deep way: they involve particular claims about what interests are, how they need to be construed. And those particular claims play their role in making a new potential political constituency visible, of defining it through representation" (Saward 2006:187; see also Fishkin 1997 and 2009).

To a large degree the processes then involve formation and regrouping or simply manipulation. Therefore, public interest and opinion can never be understood as autonomous or independent, but only as contextual as illustrated in the quotations above.

The validity of public opinion should be made an object of investigation. Despite the question whether public opinion matters or not, the invocation of public opinion itself can be problematic. Facts are not a matter of public debate. Public opinion can include normative judgment and also encompasses worldviews. Each can interfere with the public's perception of facts. Though Rawls employs the idea of 'burdens of judgment' (2011), many people in fact have absolute ideas about morality and are therefore convinced about the truthfulness (Humphrey 2007:123). Public opinion encompasses facts, morals, beliefs and counterfactual beliefs. Yet many areas that fall within the reign of a democratic public are not subject to dispute. Science is relatively reliable making valid 'truth claims' in the form of scientific facts, though it cannot tell what is morally right.[200] History shows examples that may be judged as wrong by contemporaries, but are not in conflict with facts. Whereas people might doubt the wisdom of the crowds condemning Jesus and Socrates to death, neither case contains a scientific error.[201] These are matters of opinion and the question of validity does not apply to this area of public opinion. However if public opinion i.e. a majority says that there were weapons of mass destruction in Iraq, the Earth is flat or that global warming is a hoax, public opinion errs.

---

[200] "Do not suppose that conventional wisdom among scientists is similar to consensus among politicians or lawyers. Science is about the truth and should be wholly indifferent to fairness or political expediency" (Lovelock 2009:Loc. 11).
[201] Note that for this point it is irrelevant, if Jesus was an actual historical figure.

One important aspect of this is the question of public clamour (Simmons 2011; see also Fishkin 1997:47f.). Crazy people are said to drown people with common sense, since they tend to be more passionate. Town hall meetings etc. therefore cannot be understood as a representative sample of public opinion even if they were more representative of the social strata. Opinion polls do not provide a neutral picture either, but instead are largely "mobilization of bias" (Connelly et al. 2012:157). The Condorcet Jury Theorem is not effective in practice, but also not necessarily in theory. Running simulations Althaus comes to the conclusion that the debate "over the wisdom of collective preferences [is] far from resolved" (2003:31). In fact he even questions the validity of collective rationality models. Reason for his doubt is the fact that ill-informed responses cannot cancel each other out, since they are not equally distributed. Whether aggregation produces collective rationality depends on "the ratio of noise to signal" (2003:55). Althaus' results suggest that "any emergent information-pooling properties of majority decisions are largely determined by the distribution of ill-informed opinion" (2003:55). He lists serious flaws in opinion polling. First, they often overrepresent the knowledgeable demographic group. Second the preferences of the least informed are "amplified in collective preferences because ill-informed people tend to give similar responses to survey questions" (2003:93). They do not tell if the participants are right or wrong about something, bad or well informed and give a distorted view (2003:311; Fishkin 1997:38ff.). Gaps between surveyed and fully informed opinion "are often substantial" (Althaus 2003:194). Third, collective opinion should often fail to represent the full range, as touched by Saward's comment in the previous section (Althaus 2003:92; Saward 2006). One of the problems with strong democracy is the high expectation in its citizens. They need to be "thoughtful citizens" (Orr 2013:Loc. 6154-56; Lewandowsky et al. 2012). More citizen involvement is seen as a solution to many problems and citizens are understood as "subjects of a supressed authentic reason" (Blühdorn 2011:23).[202] Since this is not experienced empirically, the citizen is frequently described as misled by an oppressive structure. The citizen's emancipation is typically narrated as an overcoming of this structural constraints followed by gaining unique agency and reason (see Bowles and Gintis 1986). Though unclear how this emancipation comes about, the outcome is seen optimistically. Blühdorn suggests that in order to participate in the opinion formation and policy making within secular and liberal democracies rational discourse is a premise (2012). Beliefs and behaviour have to be taken into account in order to establish space of ecologically sound politics, because elections, decisions and consumer preferences do not only follow rational argumentation. The change of economic conditions might have even led to an

---

[202] "Collective opinion may at times appear rational, but this result is neither inevitable nor even likely" (Althaus 2003:92).

increased likeliness of denial of "various facts" (Scruggs and Benegal 2012:508). Good environmental governance needs to build on actual material conditions.

Acknowledging democratic outcomes and recognising actual material conditions can at times be difficult. Graham sees the paradox of democracy as a real problem for democratic theory. He emphasises that the will of the majority is at times in opposition to rational judgment, hence they cannot both have the same normative force (2013:Loc. 548-50). Where opinions differ, voting is an option, but while it carries normative weight from the process, it cannot establish facts.[203] Facts about the environment are not subject to discussion, but ground in factuality (see Latour 2004 vs. Latour 2007; Blühdorn 2012). Physical truth is a matter of advanced science and not popular decision. Only an extreme relativism would deny a difference. Latour picks climate change in particular to point at a dangerous tendency (2007). A relatively new development added to the dangers of a naïve trust in ideologies is an "excessive distrust" in science (2007:10). Here, the argument of social construction is used against scientific evidence which might 'save our planet'. While contemporary discourses are often deprived of facts, Latour explains that his constructivism tried to renew empiricism not abolish it; it is therefore time to turn to a realistic position. His criticism was not meant to support an anti-science stance, but instead to lead to a better understanding of sciences. Here positivism as well as anti-positivism can be employed to direct public opinion into inaction. Climate change mitigation faces two major obstacles, on one side many people have a naïve trust and in a sense modern trust in the superiority and possible subjugation of science over nature, on the other hand, critiques of science are employed to negate certainty. Again, public opinion as a whole has similar strengths and weaknesses to the individual.[204] Democracy may in fact encourage misinformation (Lippmann 1998).[205] Hereby a difference between relying on wrong information and ignorance "as the absence of relevant knowledge" needs to be made (Lewandowsky et al. 2012:107). Climate change deniers are more dangerous than those who simply do not know.

Latour highlights that environmental politics are largely matters of fact and not matters of public opinion (2007). While many people continue to hold false beliefs about science, the climate crisis further unfolds. Shearman and Smith use the metaphor of a patient in intensive care with multiple organ failure to explain one of the key points (2007:7). It is clear that an expert has to lead the operation and that the treatment cannot be found by opinion polls. The expert accordingly does not explore opinion polls in order to save the patient. If the environment is

---

[203] Science itself largely drives its value from the process – the scientific method.
[204] See the examination of cognitive dissonance.
[205] "Demagoguery is the winning strategy as long as the electorate is prejudiced and credulous" (Caplan 2006:19).

equated with the treatment of a patient in intensive care, public opinion as a guide for action appears less reasonable. Yet, democracy treats the opinion of a baker the same as the knowledge of the scientist. Graham puts this problem as follows:

> "Like the belief in the superiority of democracy, the belief that politics is a matter of opinion rather than knowledge is very deeply ingrained in contemporary culture. The two ideas can be connected, of course, because if there are no political experts – no political equivalents of knowledgeable physicians – then everybody's opinion is equally good. But how can this be? Surely both the analysis of political problems and the devising of effective solutions to them are matters requiring extensive knowledge and expertise?" (2013:Loc. 444-47).

The problem of comprehension is robust. Citizens also "often don't know if conditions are good or bad because of government obscuring" (Przeworski 1999:37; Pralle 2008).[206] Anderson notes: "A prerequisite of responding to the climate challenge is exposing the void between the rhetoric and the reality around efforts to reduce emissions (mitigation)" (2012:17). In general people tend to hold false beliefs (Taber 2003). Depending on the area the effect can vary between inconsequential to extremely dangerous. It probably makes no difference for somebody's life if he believes the sky is pink or green. Believing that one can fly, on the other hand, might lead to premature death. Climate change belongs to the latter category and issues connected to it have real influence and are often irreversible, hence comprehension is a must. Lewandowsky et al. note that opinion and belief formation are especially of public interest "if major streams of beliefs persist that are in opposition to established facts" (2012:107). Whereby individual error might lead to suboptimal outcomes for the individual, a majority that believes in misinformation can produce harmful political decisions.[207]

Thompson's discussion of populism in the Philippines highlights the preeminence of the people's perception for electoral success (2014). The person with the strongest narrative gets elected, while the substantive reality is overshadowed by the narrative. Strong narratives can catch people's imagination, especially if they involve national strength. Unfortunately, as seen in the failure of the Kyoto negotiations, nationalism is a huge obstacle to climate mitigation globally and locally. International climate change negotiations are impeded by the focus on national interests, customarily in form of claims to economic growth. Though nationalist populism can occur anywhere, propaganda might be more important in a free society (Lippmann 1998). Populism is marked by a frontier and the claim to speak against the status quo in favour of the people (Laclau 2005). Emotions are evoked by the creation of a threat. Environmental policies

---

[206] "Despite assurances by public opinion researchers that the public's low levels and uneven social distribution of political knowledge are relatively benign to the functioning of democracy, the mass public is often unable to make up for its attentiveness" (Althaus 2003:311).

[207] "[S]eemingly systematic efforts to misinform" about climate change can be proven and while the public is aware of ideologically motivated misinformation, they may not be able to recognize *false information* (Lewandowsky et al. 2012:109).

can be stalled by simple images of an 'other'. There are not just the other polluting nations, but those that begrudge the nation's success. Populism can be used to unite against an outside threat or to polarise. There are enemies from within that are parts of the populist othering. Environmentalists, but in particular vegetarians, can be drawn as 'enemies of freedom'.[208] The example of the Koch brothers and their powerful climate denial narrative is exceptional in its scope.[209] Populist politics

> "evacuate dissent through the formation of a particular regime of environmental governance that revolves around consensus, agreement, participatory negotiation of different interests, and technocratic expert management in the context of a non-disputed management of market-based socio-economic organization" (Swyngedeouw 2011:77).[210]

Populism accordingly can negatively affect the environment in multiple ways. It can direct people's attention away from actual threats. It can be used to silence dissent from within. It can be used to belittle dissent and lead the discourse into other directions. Last it can be employed in favour of powerful interest groups. It needs to be noted that it could equally be utilised by conservation movements. This could be reminiscent of the 19th century Romantic Movement.

Intriguingly, the question whether public opinion on issues actually matters is still moot. Caplan claims that politicians do listen to the public and that the power of interest groups is in fact overestimated (2006:20). He thinks that politicians only divert from public opinion in favour of interests groups if the public itself does not take a strong stance on the matter. Leggewie problematises polls as a "monthly dictate" (2011:25), whereas newer empirical research suggests that politicians are far less influenced by the 'voter's will' in their actual decision making than common sense, or scholars like Caplan and Leggewie would suggest. Arguments about the voter's ignorance lose momentum if public opinion actually does not matter, but so do arguments that tie legitimacy to representing the public will. If public opinion does not matter, it does not matter if the voter is informed and if public opinion does not matter in democratic systems their legitimacy cannot be derived from representing the public. In regard to their environmental records, Ward tried to examine autocracies and democracies, which is difficult due to inconsistent and missing data. He finds that public opinion in support of environmental policies in democracies does not seem to impact the outcomes of decision making (2008:405). Shum finds supportive data for median-voter preference and the importance of public opinion

---

[208] Cunningly describing this form of mobilizing Huxley writes that it utilises "the impulses that are below self-interest offers false, garbled or incomplete evidence, avoids logical argument and seeks to influence its victims by the mere repetition of catchwords, by the furious denunciation of foreign or domestic scapegoats, and by cunningly associating the lowest passions with the highest ideals, so that atrocities come to be perpetrated in the name of God and the most cynical kind of Realpolitik is treated as a matter of religious principle and patriotic duty" (2000:75f.).

[209] The Koch brothers own large companies including some in fossil fuel industries. They prominently give huge campaign contributions and support institutions involved in climate change denial.

[210] The second chapter includes the predicament of market-based approaches.

regarding air pollution, but not for climate change (Shums 2009).[211] He speculates that for the latter public opinion is insignificant due to global collective action problems. The recent study by Gilens and Page focusing on the United States draws a rather grim picture and stands contrary to all positive attributes democracy theorists like to assign (2014). It also questions Shum's confirmation of median-voter model of environmental policy making by questioning the voter's influence in general. Gilens and Page show analysing quantitative data from more than 30 years that in fact the average voter's preference did not matter (2014; see also Mayr 2009:104).[212] They conclude that

> "[w]hen the preferences of economic elites and the stands of organized interest groups are controlled for, the preferences of the average American appear to have only a minuscule, near-zero, statistically non-significant impact upon public policy" (Gilens and Page 2014:575).[213]

This would mean that actual politics are not influenced by the voter's opinion, which at the same time might mean that the ignorance discussed above is insignificant. At odds with these newer findings, Caplan states:

> "In the naïve public-interest view, democracy works because it does what voters want. In the view of most democracy sceptics, it fails because it does not do what voters want. In my view, democracy fails because it does what voters want" (2006:3).[214]

Caplan points out that elected politicians often shared the same worldview with the majority of voters and that this worldview is not "hijacked by special interests", instead people simply held wrong beliefs (2006:21f.; cf. Przeworski 2010:88).

But Gilens and Page's impressive research takes multiple factors into account. They also conclude that decisions are regularly made in line with the majority and assure that "preferences of average citizens are positively and fairly highly correlated, across issues, with the preferences of economic elites" (2014:570; see also Taber 2003:458).[215] This seemingly leads to a chicken and egg question without clear causation, which Gilens and Page see as the reason

> "why serious scholars might keep adhering to both the Majoritarian Electoral Democracy and the Economic Elite Domination theoretical traditions, even if one of them may be dead wrong in terms of causal impact. Ordinary citizens, for example, might often be observed to "win" (that is, to get their preferred policy outcomes) even if they had no independent effect

---

[211] Air pollution is recurrently a local problem that has more immediate solution and whose costs are more visible.

[212] Gilens and Page studied 1,779 cases.

[213] "Policy failure at this scale certainly reflects the stranglehold of coal and oil money on public policy. And the magnitude of failure has been multiplied by the wasted treasure and time spent chasing the neoconservative mirage of U.S. global domination" (Orr 2009:7).

[214] At least for the United States this view is questionable (Gilens and Page 2014:17).

[215] "The fly in the ointment is that none of this evidence allows for, or explicitly assesses, the impact of such variables as the preferences of wealthy individuals, or the preferences and actions of organized interest groups, which may independently influence public policy while perhaps being positively associated with public opinion – thereby producing a spurious statistical relationship between opinion and policy" (Gilens and Page 2014:565).

whatsoever on policy making, if elites (with whom they often agree) actually prevail" (Gilens and Page 2014:570).

Does this mean that at least for the US 'the fear of the ignorant masses' can be partly rejected? The fact that the average citizen does not have influence on policies does not necessarily mean that his ignorance does not have an effect and therefore is inconsequential. It can be argued that exactly his ignorance enables such policies, hence popular support can be mobilised by minorities to draw the public to one side. Multiple actors, channels and directions contribute to complexity, but also leave opportunities for active directing. If campaigning for a position is unsuccessful, the proposed ignorance can enable policies that are contrary to the preferences of the majority of the public counting on their lack of comprehension and interest, hence silent consent. Edelman assumes an elite manipulation as probable, when he describes 'politics as ritual' (2005, see also Crouch 2008).[216] This would mean that the ledge in legitimation of democratic rule, rule by the people, cannot count as such, since the people might follow 'mistaken beliefs' introduced by a minority. Their beliefs then could not count as genuine, but would have to be understood as manufactured. Correspondingly, 'fickleness' could serve as a facilitator for elite manipulation. The data is unclear at this point. Gilens and Page's

> "results speak less clearly to the "third face" of power: the ability of elites to shape the public's preferences. We know that interest groups and policy makers themselves often devote considerable effort to shaping opinion. If they are successful, this might help explain the high correlation we find between elite and mass preferences. But it cannot have greatly inflated our estimate of average citizens' influence on policy making, which is near zero" (2014:576).

It could also follow that if citizens express abstract preferences for climate change mitigation while not showing interest or support for concrete measures, these preferences could be an outcome of elite power in opinion formation. Simultaneously it enables interest groups to delay action.[217]

Californian Proposition 37 for GM labelling is an interesting example (see Zilberman et al. 2013). The proposition would have introduced mandatory labelling for products containing genetically modified organisms. Though the proposition enjoyed large support at the beginning, it ultimately lost at the ballot box. Opponents would argue that in the end the voter was swayed by 'solid' argumentations (such as the food products being allegedly safe and the possibility of rising food prices as a consequence of labelling). Still, the fact stands out that the opposition invested $45.6 million while supporters spent $8.7 million (2013:15, see also Merkel 2011). Given the numbers and the outcome of the ballot this example speaks in favour of interest group

---

[216] "Mass democracy is also in large part a sham. To be meaningful, democracy requires settings that allow direct knowledge of persons and issues" (Ophuls 2012:Loc. 1615).
[217] Note that opinion formation is a complex issue. As highly contextual it cannot be mono-causal.

manipulation. After all, the majority was initially in favour of labelling. Corresponding with Gilens and Page, Hamilton views elected governments not as representing the people's will and interests, but instead the economic interests of particular groups. For him "[c]limate change represents a failure of modern politics" (Hamilton 2010:223). At that juncture this implicitly suggests that people have wills and interests prior to politics, but that they have false consciousness.[218] Classifying one will as a genuine will of an enlightened citizen involves a normative dimension that is in tension with democracy.

Part of democracy is the acceptance of an expressed will.[219] People express abstract support for the environment, but not for concrete policies that are connected to cost in their private lives.[220] But this means that the disparity between the voiced preference and the actual will to commit to real change is part of the failure of climate change politics. The failure cannot be simply misrepresentation by elected governments. One possible explanation suggests

> "the existence of a 'post-ecologist' turn, represented by, above all, a move away from 'authentic' demands for environmental change and sustainable social and economic practices, towards demands that are made inauthentically (although still presented with all due seriousness) between the making of apparently strong environmental demands on the one hand, and a reluctance to back them up with a 'willingness to pay' on the other, on the part of western publics" (Humphrey 2009:147).

Studies find that citizens declare their willingness to pay in the abstract, but discontent with concrete measures. Following Blühdorn, Humphrey suggests that politics have moved even beyond symbolic politics to what can be called "simulative eco-politics" (2009:152; see Blühdorn 2012). Madden even finds a negative correlation between government advocacy for the environment and policy implementation (2014:581). At least in this area, politics reveals itself to be mere theatre deprived of any substance. It indicates that politicians will continue to make promises about the environment, while the democratic public seems uninterested in holding them accountable.[221] A central aspect of the politics of nature is often a performance, in which public and politicians alike make claims and demands, but despite articulated criticism appear uninterested in actual policy changes. While Humphrey jokingly suggests that this seeming paradox could be explained if one assumes that polled citizens preferred an unlisted policy, the paradox can be equally explained by a gap between abstract values and willingness to act in

---

[218] The idea of 'true interests' touches various problems including questions of nature vs nurture as well as autonomy and the possibility of paternalism. The existence of survival as a 'true interest' was established as premise of this work in the introduction.

[219] The democratic premise of an enlightened citizen again conflicts with actuality.

[220] In the example the anti-labelling campaign suggested that food prices would rise with mandatory labels. "Public enthusiasm for solving problems helps to get issues on agendas initially, but subsequent cynicism, unwillingness to sacrifice, or lack of understanding may lead to a decline in attention and agenda status" (Pralle 2009:787).

[221] A majority of climate activists can be observed supporting politicians by applauding them to talk about the significance of climate change and sharing their quotes on social media.

accordance (2009:148ff.). Another option is to assume that the demands simply lack authenticity. Since knowledge is largely present, this finding can only be explained by the capability to overcome cognitive dissonance.[222] If public opinion and public reason are not understood as synonymous, the disparity is not automatically a paradox. Though public opinion can be based on reason, reason is only one aspect among many.

---

[222] Knowledge is restricted to knowing the problem, but cannot be understood as *verstehen* i.e. understanding.

2.2. The Irrelevance of Sustainability for the Citizen Consumer

The first chapter of this examination looked at the logic of democracy and its effects on the environment in a broader sense. This included its legitimacy in regard to both substantive as well as procedural terms. It further elaborated on the subject of individual ignorance in regard to (political) knowledge in general and its effects on environmental politics. It, in particular, looked at input and feedback mechanisms and their impact on sustainability. The chapter's central point is relevance or lack of relevance i.e. irrelevance. The question whether the environment has relevance in democracies was touched, but needs to be studied more specifically. Looking at the relevance of environmental sustainability for the citizen and consumer also largely avoids normative claims. Whether and how nature has and can have relevance in democratic politics is directly connected to the question, if democracy can be sustainable. What is more, to answer the question of relevance the assessment needs to differentiate between two dimensions of political action: reality and simulation (Edelman 2005; see also Baudrillard 2010). The focus is social construction, cognition and behaviour.

The chapter begins with focal findings from different sciences on cognition and shows how the politics of nature pose a genuine challenge to human nature and culture. Not just the general public misses the full scope of environmental degradation, "even with indicators, focusing events and feedback, issues do not come to the attention of policymakers as 'objective' problems whose meaning is established and uncontested" (Pralle 2009:785). Furthermore in science as in politics, ecological problems are compartmentalised and therefore spread across different disciplines and responsibilities (Connelly et al. 2012:165; Oreskes and Conway 2014). It is essential to elaborate the questions whether and how the status quo and human cognition enable sustainable democratic politics. Accordingly, this chapter will also address individualism, liberalism and capitalism as dominant and interconnected ideologies. Individualism as a rationale, and with it the possibility of greening liberalism, need to be reviewed. This includes a reflection of the dichotomy between pluralism, the connected relativism and the necessity of focusing on the environment. The tension between priorities of working life support systems, in contrast to individualism's prioritisation of the individual, needs to be examined.[223] If something is not a priority, it self-evidently has less relevance. As suggested earlier liberal democracy is a particularly forceful idea. The environment can either become relevant within liberal democracy and its focus on freedoms or sustainability is not possible. Here, opinions differ between liberals and the majority of green thinkers whether individualism and market economics can lead to

---

[223] The environment is regularly downgraded to irrelevance as it is ordinarily perceived as a third order Maslowian factor (see Worcester 1997:164).

green politics. Accordingly, a consideration of economic 'solutions' to environmental problems which appear to have gained hegemonic status will follow. The chapter concludes by highlighting the typical role of the future in democratic politics and delineating how discounting the future is systemic (including a cognitive challenge).

2.2.1. COGNITIVELY CHALLENGED CITIZENS

In order to fully understand why democratic politics struggle with sustainability and whether democracy can succeed in establishing environmentally sound politics, people's cognitive processes should be taken into account with respect to their influence on politics. A fundamental query is the contrast between the importance of environmental integrity and the irrelevance it appears to have in practice. The political inertia to the problem of environmental destruction is to be explained partially by the cognition process and therefore by the way humans give meaning to the world. Understanding climate change, recognising the gravity of the situation as well as acting in accordance to this knowledge poses a huge cognitive challenge to contemporary man.[224] Human nature and nurture are barriers to environmental integrity.[225] Perceptions are constituting factors to environmental degradation. Research suggests that not only is the human biological background not primed to apprehend (*verstehen*) problems of this scope, a global consumer class is also socialised into a lifestyle that runs contrary to such cognition and possible solutions. Those parts of the global population that are not part of this class are routinely 'made to aspire' becoming part of it (Ehrlich and Ehrlich 2013). Much of contemporary cultural representation celebrates material culture and glorifies consumption. Environmental protection often falls into a niche area and has little relevance in people's perception. Thus, social construction plays a significant role. Social construction means "societies or individuals do not necessarily react to the problems as they "really are", but as they are described by science, by politics, by social movements, by mass media, and so on" (Wehling 2002:162; Edelman 2005; Pralle 2009; Thaler and Sunstein 2009; Conly 2013; Moloney et al. 2014). Moreover, the inherent difficulty of many environmental problems undermines the effectiveness of communication because there is a mismatch between the "usual modes of understanding" and what is needed to grasp the essence of the problem (Aklin and Urpelainen 2014:173). While the earlier inquiry was concerned with ignorance and lack of information, the focus here is on particular obstacles in the realm of cognition. It covers information processing from the point of

---

[224] Marshall for example sees climate change "not as a media battle of science versus vested interests or truth versus fiction, but as the ultimate challenge to our ability to make sense of the world around us" (2014:Loc. 71).

[225] Caldwell lists five "prejudicial behavioral obstacles to an operational concept of sustainability": excessive growth of human population; disclination to foresee or forbear; short-term assessment of opportunity; failure to respect natural systems and over-reliance on technological ingenuity (1998:4). The obstacles are all, to different degrees, connected to cognition. Not only is the future tense absent in some languages, even European languages like German did not have a future tense until modern times (Welzer 2011).

view of comprehension. Full comprehension is defined here as accompanied by appropriate behavioural change or at least willingness for this change. One of the main concerns is the gap between knowledge, comprehension and behaviour, which is sometimes called the 'value-action gap' (e.g. Barr 2006). While information, knowledge and rationality were the focal points of earlier discussions, the elaboration here focuses on the irrelevance of climate change in daily lives, which has a significant effect on democratic politics. Cognition is a barrier to green citizenry, but also the premise of a green democratic state. A distinction between literacy in form of knowledge and understanding, which means that environmental degradation becomes a part of a person's cognition, helps to illuminate the problem. Literacy here only relates to knowledge about nature.[226] Despite the possibility of theoretical distinction, the steps from knowledge to comprehension to action are neither inevitable nor a one way road (e.g. Dryzek, Norgaard and Schlosberg 2013). The way humans process the world cannot be reduced to such a simple equation.

The absence of real action clearly hints at a lack of comprehension. Notably,

> "difficulties are seen not as symptoms of impending collapse but, rather, as problems to be solved by better policies and personnel. In other words, the populace does not yet understand that the civilization has reached an impasse" (Ophuls 2012:Loc.1430).

Simple observations on humans and contemporary culture allow for this claim.[227] People may not fully comprehend that emerging problems cannot be fixed easily and that their actions contribute to environmental destruction. An actual grasp would make the tradeoff too overt. Nobody, for example, would "willingly give up drinkable water or breathable air, but we do so every day" (Peterson 2010:93). It is clear that a, for a democracy critical, 'critical mass' lacks comprehension. At least a substantial minority would have to understand and therefore support good environmental governance in order to set the necessary change into motion. However, most people are unlikely to reflect on the true costs and benefits of their habitus. Here, "our cognitive limitations to understanding environmental degradation seriously compromises our emotional engagement and our willingness to act" (Kollmuss and Agyeman 2002:254). It is a necessity to acknowledge that "despite our pretensions to rationality, scientific facts are fighting

---

[226] "One is 'environmentally literate' when one knows about the greenhouse effect, the ozone layer, biodiversity, and the like. Literacy does not necessarily imply that this information carries with it any particular moral implication" (De-Shalit 2006b:86).

[227] Contemporary culture as a singular is meant to signify, but not reify, a globally overlapping culture. This work, in general, follows Geertz' definition of culture as a 'web of meaning' (1994:9). In this case contemporary culture describes a widely shared web of meaning in particular with regards to consumer culture. While national cultures might differ, SUV and iPad have successfully penetrated many markets internationally.

against more powerful forces" (Hamilton 2010:ix).[228] A green democracy is particularly handicapped by these forces.[229] Attention and motivations seem to follow drives, not enlightened rationality. As noted earlier, democracies rely on a minimum of enlightenment of their citizens and this is especially apparent in the green theory of agency.

> "A basic faith in the intelligence and perceptiveness of the common person pervades democratic thinking. And this can potentially mitigate attitudes that lead to destructive relationships between humans and nature" (Jennings 2010:227).

But practice does not follow this logic. Instead denial and avoidance seem to be common practice. Real action appears unnecessary. Human intelligence and perceptiveness are not employed and maybe not employable in huge numbers in the fashion that the green theory of agency advocates.

Above all science, technology and human rationality have not developed at the same speed. Additionally, the gap between laymen and experts continuously widens. Hence, humanity struggles with enormous technological advancement at its use. The development of advanced technology has given risks a new dimension as discussed by Jonas (1984) and Beck (1997). Humans become, in a sense, more powerful and therefore are able to cause much greater damage but becoming more powerful does not automatically mean that they mastered or fully comprehend the technology that is currently in use. The average citizen cannot fully understand the repercussion of his actions, but has powerful tools at his disposal. Intermittently, the risks can even be unclear to scientists. The debate about genetically modified organisms (GMOs) shows this clearly.[230] With greater power, humanity is facing risks with new attributes. The new risks are regularly global, irreversible, invisible, build on causal interpretation and are, as a result, open to interpretation (Diekmann and Preisendörfer 2001:26; Marshall 2014).

Labelling something as risk, threat, or danger can already signify a certain mode of thinking and action. While danger is often perceived as something external, risk is something that is self-inflicted.[231] Interestingly humans are less sensible to risks. Self-infliction distorts an evaluation of the threat. Meanwhile, attitudes towards the source of pollution also affect the perception (Bell

---

[228] Showing valuable insights into human behaviour, Huxley writes: "The power to respond to reason and truth exists in all of us. But so, unfortunately, does the tendency to respond to unreason and falsehood — particularly in those cases where the falsehood evokes some enjoyable emotion, or where the appeal to unreason strikes some answering chord in the primitive, subhuman depths of our being" (2000:77).

[229] "[T]here is little reason to expect that a society obsessed with celebrities and shopping will suddenly change direction and start making choices solely on the basis of new, post-materialist values" (Hannigan 2006:25).

[230] Many consequences of GMO usage cannot be predicted, since GMOs interact with a complex environment (see for example Westra 1998a:123ff.; Forsyth 2003:125ff. or Whiteside 2006).

[231] See Bell et al. for the difference between 'self-induced risk' (smoking) and external risks i.e. dangers (a shark attack) (2001:472).

et al. 2001:240). The typical consumer is unlikely to critically assess the true costs of his consumption. A racing fan is less likely to see car combustion as a source of resentment. A particular obstruction with risk is also that humans are notoriously inept when it comes to judging the likelihood of certain events. They tend to fear improbable events like airplane crashes more than common occurrences like cancer from smoking. Risks are constantly under- and overestimated. Narrowly defined, climate change itself is not a risk since it is already happening. Environmental destruction is real and people are and will be affected with certainty. Still, the issue fails to be recognised for the threat it poses. Randers derives from the experience of the last forty years that "[o]nly a sudden and highly visible resource collapse or climate crisis will be able to kick the public and key politicians into believing in the need for strong action" (2012:Loc. 2052-54). Nature's degradation is already visible, and regardless of threshold events is very probable to accelerate. The existence of feedbacks is well established in climate science but so far largely ignored in the political discourse. Furthermore, the majority of people lacks the ability to understand exponential functions (Ophuls 2012:Loc.317). Hence, action has already been delayed and is likely to be delayed until the effects are felt more severely. The degree of climate change and its effects ranging from the consequences of a 2°C degree to the catastrophic implications of a 6°C degree change in global average temperature justify speaking of risks, though the talk of risks in the public discourse might well be a hindrance for action as it leaves a gap for wishful thinking.[232] In sum, daily habits and the difficulty to make people accept risks as 'real' disable change (Giddens 2009:230; Conly 2013).

Prominently, the acceptance of anthropogenic climate change and the means to mitigate its dangers pose a cognitive challenge. Natural and social sciences emphasize the slow process of evolution as an obstacle to comprehend the gravity of the problem as well as to act in accordance. They point out that, in evolutionary terms, the relatively short time span since the Palaeolithic means that human brains give priority to short-term gains, immediate events, the local environment and small spaces (e.g. Shearman and Smith 2007). Until now there was no reason for humans to develop cognitive functions beyond, since other capabilities did not make humans 'fitter' in a Darwinian sense.

> "The forces of genetic and cultural selection were not creating brains or institutions capable of looking generations ahead; there would have been no selection pressures in that direction. Indeed, quite the opposite, selection probably favoured mechanisms to keep perception of the environmental background steady so that rapid changes (e.g. leopard approaching) would be obvious. But now slow changes in that background are the most lethal threats. Societies have a long history of mobilizing efforts, making sacrifices and changes, to defeat an enemy at the gates, or even just to compete more successfully with a rival. But there is not much evidence

---

[232] Though extreme changes of 8°C degree are unlikely, it is nevertheless important to ensure that they do not become reality. In other areas such as fire insurance etc. humans constantly take the worst case into consideration.

of societies mobilizing and making sacrifices to meet gradually worsening conditions that threaten real disaster for future generations. Yet that is exactly the sort of mobilization that we believe is required to avoid a collapse" (Ehrlich and Ehrlich 2013; see also Bell et al. 2001:67f. and Marshall 2014).

In short, nature has not equipped humans to grasp the challenges of the 21st century. Environmental destruction is a slow process, although threshold events can lead to dramatic changes. It happens over vast spaces and its mitigation requires recognising interconnectedness and causalities. Ecology and climate science are subjects focused on interrelations. Understanding environmental conditions demands comprehending abstract processes, whereas the conditions in which humans developed for most of the time mean "that human beings excel at concrete perception but are much less adept at abstraction (Ophuls 2012:Loc.398). Hence, many problems are beyond cognition and need specific training to comprehend. Processes are often slow compared to human perception. Humans are much more susceptible to risk when they perceive the risk as pressing within a strictly limited time frame. Hamilton puts this as follows: "One hurdle to recognising the threat posed by global warming is the fact that humans have evolved to assess and respond to risk through immediate feelings rather than cognitive processing" (2010:119). This lack of immediacy should be understood in two connected ways. Neither immediacy of time and space nor immediacy in regard to emotional susceptibility is pronounced.

On the one hand, "reliance on secondary information about environmental destruction removes us emotionally from the issue" (Kollmuss and Agyeman 2002:253).[233] Immediate reactions, on the other hand, can be quite vigorous in particular when they are fuelled by apocalyptic images. For instance the baby boomer generation in Germany was warned and acted against Waldsterben.[234] Its exaggeration and the immediacy of the threat probably caused people to force environmental action that largely benefited German forests. Emotional engagement mobilised a sufficient percentage of the population and protective measures were implemented. Again, suddenly dying forests are easier to grasp than climate change. Slowly encroaching degradation escapes recognition. Despite the protection efforts, 70% of the German forests in 2007 had visible damage (Leggewie and Welzer 2011:43f.) and only 38% showed no crown defoliation in 2013 (BMEL 2013).[235] Yet the absence of large-scale visible Waldsterben on the national level, rather than only being a success for environmental movements, might in fact hinder these since

---

[233] Interviewing victims of extreme weather events Marshall notices that those affected are even less likely to fear climate change (2014). Emotional and direct engagement, accordingly, may not lead to an understanding either, since coping mechanisms suppress full cognition.
[234] Waldsterben literally means 'forest dying'.
[235] Note that Northern Europe is comparatively unaffected so far. Effects of precaution cannot be accounted for and remain hypothetical.

the same generation now perceives the warning as false alarms, similar to the reception of the *Limits to Growth* on the international level (Meadows et al. 1972). The book was initially a bestseller that shocked a global audience. Thence, many scientists in particular economists, tried to debunk its predictions (e.g. Simon 1983). It was a prediction and not a problem itself (Davis 2007:43). What had followed was a general dissecting of the predictions. The warning of the *Limits to Growth*, were routinely dismissed on behalf of drawing an overly pessimistic picture, which made action 'avoidable'. Both cases accentuate the importance of perception and reception. While the environment has steadily deteriorated, the relatively slow pace of the deterioration made it easy to lose sight of the destruction. Though natural resources are not exhausted as the simulations suggested, large parts of the predictions can be observed nevertheless (Meadows, Meadows and Randers 2004; Turner 2008; Randers 2012). Still, critiques managed to depreciate concern by calling the book and its authors 'alarmists', which is a label that is still in use today and helps to ignore otherwise reputable scientists (see Barry 2004). Changes in the predicted direction of the 1972 models are spread over more than 40 years and therefore easily overlooked. It is ironic that because slow processes do not seem alarming, respectable scientists are called 'alarmist' even after many predictions have actualised. A barrier to recognition is also that of perceiving change of different degrees. It is harder to register the step from already polluted to even more polluted (Bell et al. 2001:67) or similarly from infested to more infested forests. Gradual environmental degradation may escape cognition. In regard to global warming, people typically employ the metaphor of the slowly boiling frog. The slow changes in temperature make it impossible for the frog to recognise the threat. To take the metaphor further, one could say that although experts are frogs too, they are frogs with clip boards and thermometers. This makes them more adept to recognise climate change and pollution.

2.2.1.1. THE PUBLIC VS. THE SCIENCES VS. CLIMATE CHANGE

Democratic environmental politics face two major problems connected to science. The first problem is that the public may not understand environmental science due to its complexity and the fact that the public and scientists employ different languages, methods and often worldviews. The second problem is that, though not a general phenomenon, some societies experience a growing distrust in sciences. Even Latour, as a famous sociologist of science, admits that the questioning of science in contemporary discourses has produced new dangers (2007). Many narratives are in conflict with science. These can have severe consequences when scientific findings are denied and ignored. Both problems have multiple layers and can influence each other.

Support for solving environmental issues is also dependent on the public's perception of scientific consent. Aklin and Urpelainen find that in their experiments people in general do trust in the accuracy of scientific information regarding the environment, but support depends strongly on unison (2014). When 98% are said to agree, problem solving is largely supported. But when 80%, a great majority, are said to agree, "a substantively large and statistically significant drop" of support occurs (2014:174; see also Marshall 2014). Moreover, scientific language and discourses deviate greatly from everyday language. Not just the different usages of concepts like uncertainty hamper communication, the difference between beliefs and facts can remain unnoticed.[236] Precise probabilities are customarily understood as misleading by climate scientists, but terms like 'certain' or 'virtually certain' are subject to interpretation outside the realm of science. The Intergovernmental Panel on Climate Change (IPCC) uses the term 'virtually certain' for percentages higher than 99% and 'very likely' for percentages between 90-99% (Shearman and Smith 2007:22). The usage is not in accord with the public's ideas about probability. There are also large differences in the interpretation of probabilities between people and "probability terms are susceptible to self-serving interpretations" (Budescu et al. 2014:508). Often verbally communicated, probabilities seem weaker. If both findings are taken together, chances for public support for saving the environment appear small. Hence, preventive measures remain unlikely. Worcester claims that most people actually do not believe what scientists say in environmental matters (1997:160). Given Aklin and Urpelainen's study the difference between not believing, as Worcester claims, or believing, as their test participants claim, might be inconsequential unless scientific consent is not only established but also recognised by the population. In the usage of terms like 'uncertainty', Shearman and Smith see the chance for governments to excuse inaction (2007:22). Confusion is enough to justify political inertia. Research shows that ambiguity in symbolism elevates the difficulty in understanding which has a direct effect on behaviour (Bell et al. 2001:127). This might contribute to explaining the fact that snow storms can be perceived as falsification of global warming. Generally, climate scientists encounter a vast array of nonsensical arguments that are often meant to seed distrust and confusion (see MacCracken 2011).[237] Freedom of speech allows for all sides to make claims. Yet, opinions do not matter in science, what matters are the results of the application of scientific methods. In liberal democracies, truth and therefore facts are in one dimension open to democratic discussion and everybody's interpretation. However, scientific facts are not products

---

[236] "For laypeople, the magnitude of uncertainty does not matter much as long as it is believed to be meaningful" (Lewandowsky et al. 2012:124).
[237] E.g. snow storms staged as proof that global warming is a hoax.

of debate. There is an important ontological argument here: climate change is objective truth.[238] Still, ambiguity can be found in the way scientists represent science. Public debates with climate scientists are problematic, since the stereotypical climate scientist does not exhibit traits that are typical for good public speaking (Marshall 2014:Loc. 1210). Confident posture and strong rhetoric are essential for the recipient of a message. Accordingly, the opposing side commonly employs cunning public speakers that give the impression of strength and certainty.[239]

Liberal democracy's freedom of expression is playground for ignorance and elections may in effect be an incentive to foster opposing ideas (Lippmann 1998; see also Lewandowsky et al. 2012). If resources are at stake, stake-holders can be interested in supporting contradicting narratives such as global warming being a hoax. Meanwhile, a sober look at sciences tells that there is no further capacity for emissions left and that the 2°C degree aim, meant "lights off" yesterday (Anderson 2012:32). "The prevailing orthodoxy that informs policy-makers is couched in a 'can-do' language, far removed from the reality we are facing" (2012:32; Jackson 2012). Narratives are problematic if they are wrong and they have negative consequences for the environment. While not stating 'untruths', many articles involve extensive cherry picking. Depending on the level of sophistication such claims can be politically powerful. Though deniers were certainly taking part in the process, Hamilton sees "the strategies routinely used by the public to avoid or downplay the scientific warnings" as having more influence on governments' actions (2010:119). A decline in belief in climate change can be observed in diverse places (Ratter, Phillipp and von Storch 2012; Scruggs and Benegal 2012). Repetition of false beliefs is thereby a strong predictor of the acceptance of a belief (Lewandowsky et al. 2012:113). Continuous denial eventually leads to firmer beliefs. Emission superpowers, the US, Canada and Australia, are fertile grounds for deniers and even scepticism towards ecological modernisation (Dryzek, Norgaard and Schlossberg 2013:Loc. 1462). Science struggles with strong cognitive forces which seem to run contrary to rationality, but are in line with the human ability to rationalise. Hamilton writes:

> "As in all instances where an understanding of a complex issue requires advanced expertise, those without training must decide not what to believe but who to believe. In this case we are obliged to accept the verdict of those most qualified to deliver it, that is, those recognized within the community of scientists as the experts with the best knowledge and insight"(2014:337).

---

[238] "Denial requires a willful misreading of the science, a romantic view of the ability of political institutions to respond, or faith in divine intervention" (Hamilton 2010:xii).
[239] In *Gorgias*, Plato warns that "the rhetorician qua rhetorician has no advice to give at all. Rather, rhetorical power is entirely parasitic upon real knowledge. And in like fashion, Plato supposes, rhetorical power in the forum is equally parasitic on genuine political wisdom" (Graham 2013:436-39; Plato 2009).

Though Hamilton's words seem clear and even common sense, they are not. Not just puzzling but highly problematic is the fact that it seems that addressees of information do not discriminate between studies sponsored by a group of their peers or multinational companies (Lewandowsky et al. 2012:113). Even more devastating for the standing of expert knowledge is a new study that suggests that internet users are more prone to believe unknown commentators than actual experts (Kareklas, Muehling and Weber 2015). Popular fiction around climate change that pretends to be an actual representation of reality actively influences people who are hardly able to discern facts from fiction (Lewandowsky et al. 2012). Besides, Scruggs and Benegal find that not only do "people's priorities shift with the economic conditions, but that their beliefs about basic climate facts and their trust in climate science also appear to change" (2012:508). Even the perception of facts and the recognition is embedded in a wider context and subjects to change. Climate change is a highly politicised issue, which means that information is subject to biases from "additional social meaning and becomes a marker of group identity" (Marshall 2014:Loc. 386).

The fact that climate science often fails to make clear predictions due to complexity should not mean to

> "abandon science altogether. Rather, it indicates that the domain of legitimate science must be extended. The mechanical paradigm provided an adequate first approximation of reality for simple systems in simpler times. But new science is needed to interpret reality as humans force nature into domains of unfamiliar and unpredictable behavior. For sustainability, society will have to live with, and adapt to, the increasing uncertainty that this implies. Perhaps the most important adjustment will be the replacement of arrogant certainty with precautionary restraint in our relationship with nature" (Miller and Rees 2013:Loc. 208).

The potential for a sustainable democracy depends on the possibility of public support for precaution in particular when its scientific understanding remains limited. At this junction, an additional idiosyncrasy of contemporary science hinders environmentally sound politics. Scientists are reluctant of so called 'type II errors'. Type I errors are preferred over a type II errors.[240] A type I error means not acknowledging or accepting that something exists that actually exists. A type II error is the opposite, acceptance of something that in fact does not exist (Lemons 1998; Oreskes and Conway 2014). Science has set an arbitrary line of 95% certainty as a default line. Scientists are essentially trained to be conservative. This means that in order to establish that, for example, a chemical has a negative impact on the environment, 94% certainty is not enough. Sustainability needs the precaution that follows the opposite logic. Carter, among

---

[240] Induction is typically explained as the assumption that all swans are white until a black swan is proven to exist.

others, enhances the idea that science and scientific knowledge is essential (Carter 2007:177).[241] Yet, democracy provides no guarantees that this knowledge will be taken into account, either by the public or politicians.

2.2.1.2. COGNITIVE DISSONANCE OR DOUBLETHINK?

The social-psychological dimension of environmental protection or rather destruction appears to be underestimated and largely unexplored (Busch 2011:81; see Marshall 2014).[242] One of the most puzzling developments is that while the threat grows and becomes better observable every year, emissions actually keep rising (Leggewie and Welzer 2011:78; Anderson 2012).[243] Practice not only diverges in spite of the knowledge about environmental degradation, it seems to even take a diametrically opposed path. While science can predict the negative consequences with growing certainty, global consumption rises. Important reasons for destructive behaviour are their habituation, comfort-seeking and the tension between putative norms and personal interests (see Kollmuss and Agyeman 2002:250). The lack of action is not necessarily caused by lack of knowledge as mentioned earlier. Instead there is the huge disparity between knowledge, values and behaviour that demands attention. This disparity should result in cognitive dissonance (Leggewie and Welzer 2011:78).[244] Cognition can be either consonant or dissonant. Cognitive dissonance occurs when perception, thoughts, opinions or wishes are incompatible with each other and they are experienced as such.[245] Not acting in accordance with beliefs can cause distress, whereas relief can be found in change of perspective, distraction or blame shifting.[246]

---

[241] Leggewie and Welzer see two illusions: 1. The problem and process are already understood. 2. Conventional strategies of observation, moderation and correction can be used to solve it (2009:101).

[242] "There are three kinds of actors in this process of subversion: those who tell the lies, those who repeat the lies, and those who allow themselves to be seduced by the lies" (Hamilton 2014:336).

[243] These trends can even be observed in the European Union. "In 2012, increased coal consumption was observed in the United Kingdom (+24%; the highest consumption level since 2006), Spain (+24%; the second year with an increase after two years of decreasing consumption), Germany (+4%) and France (+20%), versus decreases in Poland (4%) and the Czech Republic (8%) (Olivier et al. 2013:43).

[244] An Australian study for example found that "despite two decades of environmental education, young people are both more likely to engage in wasteful consumption and less likely to feel guilty about it" (Hamilton 2010:76).

[245] Mill describes the longing for consonance as follows: "The deeply-rooted conception which every individual even now has of himself as a social being, tends to make him feel it one of his natural wants that there should be harmony between his feelings and aims and those of his fellow creatures. If differences of opinion and of mental culture make it impossible for him to share many of their actual feelings-perhaps make him denounce and defy those feelings-he still needs to be conscious that his real aim and theirs do not conflict; that he is not opposing himself to what they really wish for, namely, their own good, but is, on the contrary, promoting it" (1879:52). Mill assumes that the individual follows the common good because of a naturally inherent feeling and the consciousness of the interconnectedness (Höntzsch 2010:35). He misjudges people's ability to identify with other people, in particular if there are more degrees of separation.

[246] "Blame-shifting is a useful, if often indefensible, means of denying guilt. It is a form of moral disengagement whereby we disavow our responsibility for the problem or the solution" (Hamilton 2010:127).

Cognitive dissonance can also be relativised by denouncing or avoiding information.[247] Only a small percentage of information on environmental destruction is actually noticed (Leggewie and Welzer 2011:81).[248] Humans in general tend to selectively believe what benefits them.[249] The multiplicity of media offered supports this proclivity. Though there is a larger variety, people usually consume not a broader but a narrower range of information (Lewandowsky et al. 2012:111). In spite of greater connectivity and availability of information, people live in their 'own bubbles'.[250] Confirmation and optimism bias are well established in psychology. Not only do humans privilege confirmative information, they tend to see things positively. Both mechanisms impact the evaluation of ecosystem degradation (Marshall 2014). For instance, people optimistically think that their own environment is less polluted than other places (Bell et al. 2001:241). Information about their regions being especially polluted is recurrently overlooked. The data on global ecosystems shows alarming trends. Yet, human beings rely more often on anecdotes than on data (Marshall 2014). Again, they rely more on the concrete and particular than abstracts. As discussed earlier, opinions on climate change not only vary with the weather or personal experience of extreme weather events but can also be influenced by simple things such as the presence of a dead plant in the same room as the survey participant. Studying human cognition shows multiple factors that influence acceptance of anthropogenic climate change.[251] It also illuminates weaknesses that can be exploited by various interests.

Anderson notes that "policy-makers (along with many academics and climate specialists) repeatedly make statements, emphasising the importance of staying below 2°C whilst at the same time proposing policies that imply a very high chance of exceeding 2°C" (2012:18). The focus on possibly meaningless long-term targets, the trust in technology and ignorance about cumulative emissions, while huge changes in lifestyle would be necessary "are tailored to cater for our cognitive dissonance" (2012:21).[252] Edelman divided political action into two dimensions: orchestration and reality (2005). While climate politics seem to be sophisticatedly orchestrated, solutions are neither in line with reality nor sufficiently realised. Some scholars declare that, even with the most optimistic assumptions, the 2 °C target is not possible (Hamilton 2014:336).

---

[247] Anderson sees cognitive dissonance as "an academic disguise for hypocrisy – sticking our head in the sand and, despite the science and data, convincing ourselves everything is going to be all right" (2012:16).

[248] "Challenging information can create an uncomfortable cognitive dissonance, such that people endeavour to limit exposure to that which is incongruent with the beliefs they hold" (Doherty and Wolak 2012:305).

[249] A differentiation between knowledge and belief is a subject of psychology but not of specific concern here.

[250] Customization of search engines etc. further magnifies this process. The role of free media as a facilitator of enlightened citizenship needs to be radically rethought.

[251] "[A]ccepting climate change requires far more than reading the right books, watching the right documentaries, or ticking off a checklist of well-meaning behaviors: It requires conviction, and this is difficult to form and even harder to maintain" (Marshall 2014:Loc. 91).

[252] The belief in ecological modernization serves as dissonance redactor.

Hamilton insists that it is not confusion that is the worriment, but lack of moral courage (2010). There is silence around the reality (Marshall 2014). Climate conferences can be seen as a good example for Edelman's orchestration. Representatives pledge commitment to the issues, just like many citizens, while consumption practices remain unchallenged. Questioning the effectiveness of the promises that are made in regular intervals remains the exception. Since acceptance of reality might be too much to cope, denial and avoidance of contradicting facts are possibly at play simultaneously. In his Gifford Lecture series, Latour suggests correspondingly that everybody is a climate sceptic in a sense and that the fact that one cannot save his own children may also lead to denial (2013). The widely accepted unsustainable habitus then is paired with the putative impotence of the individual. Notably, people are "less likely to worry about problems when they feel there is nothing to be done about them" (Pralle 2009:786). This is not in contradiction with climate change as a self-inflicted risk. While humanity collectively destroys the environment, the individual responsibility and therefore agency is ordinarily regarded as negligible (Lane 2011b). This stands in stark contrast to the agency democracy promises in theory and mainstream environmentalism propagates.

The impact of the sum of individual actions is the problem, while most people see their impact as negligible. The focal problem is the contemporary habitus in many parts of the world and the connected cognition (Leggewie and Welzer 2011:49). It is a lifestyle that feels natural to 'the agent' and as a result remains unquestioned (Bourdieu und Wacquant 2006). Habitus and internalisation enable dangerous practice. Discussing habitus Bourdieu points out that especially through repetition and integration into people's lives, actions are often not only unconscious but also appear rational (1977; Bourdieu und Wacquant 2006:161). Accordingly cognitive dissonance might not even be felt. Furthermore, contemporary lifestyle has created not only denial, but the assumption that one deserves what he has (Leggewie and Welzer 2011:49; Shearman and Smith 2007).[253] Cognition or awareness can be influenced by campaigns. There is ample evidence for the limited responsiveness to awareness campaigns though (Bell et al. 2001; Kollmuss and Agyeman 2002; Reuscher et al. 2011:30). Part of the problem is one of deep internalisation.[254] In environmental campaigns even people with strong commitments eventually stopped following the eco-friendly behaviour. While many projects still focus on informing global publics (e.g. Gore's Climate Reality), a lack of information is not the core of the problem. Just as Socrates in the Platonic dialogues, liberals and deliberative democrats alike assume that knowledge will lead people to the 'right' direction. In a sense, they believe that people do not act against their own

---

[253] Another cognitive bias involved is the just-world hypothesis or just-world fallacy (see Lerner 1980). In a sense this is a further status quo bias.
[254] Lane points at the etymological joint origin of ethics and ethos (2011b).

knowledge, but this is a leap of faith. Lane discusses the fallacy that rationality is more powerful than desire clearly:

> "Will the person who knows about climate change actually always, and thereby, do the right thing, or do we not sometimes act against what we know to be right? This is the classical problem which Aristotle baptized *akrasia*, often referred to as 'weakness of will', and describing the phenomenon of someone seeming to know or have decided that it is best to act in a certain way, yet acting otherwise [...] Socrates denied the possibility of *akrasia*, holding that people only act against what they know to be best 'by reason of ignorance', as if there were no other psychic motive forces other than knowledge or ignorance" (2011b:117).[255]

Many people still hope that humanity can escape the consequences of human actions (Hamilton 2010). Hope defies knowledge. Psychology shows that complicated mechanisms of processing further aggravate recognition. A study of a sect even showed that when cognitive dissonance occurs in groups in form of a disconfirmation it can lead to a stronger belief and commitment to persuade outsiders (Harmon-Jones and Mills 2009a:6f.).[256] This could mean that those feeling dissonance might try harder to convince others of their belief.

Lack of recognition can be in the interest of others and externally induced and/or supported, but might as well be caused endogenously.[257] Lane neatly illustrates the dilemma by writing about the contemporary Platonic cave and its inhabitants:

> "Their career paths to power and prestige lead to public damage, not to public service. What they take to be solid facts are dangerous illusions. The technologies and infrastructure and assumptions in which they have invested their time and money and belief are fraudulent; the glare of reality would expose these as wishful delusions. The newcomer is likely to be shunned at best, stoned at worst. How could anyone be expected to tolerate such arrogant insults to their whole way of life? Pull back the camera on this scene, however, and it appears in a new light. The busy self-righteousness of this political order is indeed, in reality, built on foundations of sand. The prizes they strive for are made of smoke and mirrors; success in their competitions is self-undermining. In fact, powerful figures, invested in the maintenance of this existing delusional social order, parade the objects and languages in which the people believe, denying that any external challenge to them could be valid. Denial of the external perspective looks from this higher vantage point like keeping one's head in the sand, refusing to face what is obvious and valid" (2011b:3).

The challenge of cognition involves not only understanding slow, large scale and complex processes; it also involves questioning a social reality that is ubiquitous. Full awareness consequentially questions the self and its identity, since it is involved in destructive practices. The idea then undermines many people's positive self-understanding fundamentally.[258] Like Lane, Anderson calls out 'modern' man:

---

[255] In Hall's opinion akrasia is better translated as powerlessness than lack/weakness of will or self-control (2010:72).
[256] "People who are unconvinced about climate change will say it's been colder" (Marshall 2014:Loc. 264).
[257] Gifford and Heath found a negative correlation between the belief in the free market and climate science (2006). The more people believed in the market, the less they believed in climate science. In contrast to science, economics actually act in a way, people believe. If many people believe in the value of a particular stock, it will eventually rise.
[258] "The idea of man-made global warming has been such an idea, greeted with as much hostility and ridicule as Plato's cave denizens mustered for their unwelcome messengers from the outside world" (Lane 2011b:5).

"The belief that it is possible to endlessly pursue [...] growth of everything and that the human species is somehow clever enough to defy the laws of science and physics betrays a certain arrogance in our collective imagination" (Anderson 2012:22; see also Hamilton 2010).

This is essential for the question of democracy's sustainability as it depends on the dominant narrative. The unlimited progress discourse that embarks on the current social reality is deeply ingrained. Politicians and public have internalised discourses of economic growth and consumerism and maintain the system by playing according to its rules. Those who best internalised the system can profit from its maintenance and are more willing to deny evidence. The Judeo-Christian idea of dominance over nature in particular has been criticised by ecologists for its destructive potential in forming a general framework of legitimate exploitation of natural resources that spread well beyond the borders of Western countries. Troublesome for enlightened citizenship is that internalisation can fully or partly block any reflection. Economic growth and materialism appear as obsessions that override the reality of environmental destruction.

Human beings tend to have loss aversion. Paired with optimism bias they are less likely to believe in a negative future. Lovelock draws a grim picture on this overall proclivity which extends to scientists as follows:

"above all, humans hate any conspicuous change in their daily way of life and view of the future [...]. Business as usual is unfortunately how most of science is done, even though we know that it has no place in science's probabilistic world" (2009:Loc. 67).

Besides widespread habituation, loss aversion is an additional factor for denial rather than enabling strong policies. Change is seldom perceived as something positive and scientists are often too removed from the political reality to actively pursue change. Active engagement would mean pointing at false optimism (Hamilton 2010). In "Post-environmentalism: an internal critique" Buck calls for a new approach (2013). He characterises today as an "era of insecure affluence demands", which he writes makes the public less sensitive to images and facts about climate change than before, "when post-material values thrived and people were primarily worried about pollution" (2013:888). Yet, his critique disguises two points. First, postmaterialism failed to manifest itself as popular form of living as discussed earlier. Even as a part of an avant-garde culture, it was merely a simulation. Green consumerism gives the impression of a call for less consumption, but the majority of self-declared greens do not exhibit modesty. Second, it is not the poor who are mainly responsible for environmental degradation. Those who do consume the majority of resources are not faced with the question whether to save the planet or to eat. Sustainability needs to call 'affluence demands' into question. Buck's critique implies that economic concerns led people to make less sustainable life choices and that earlier approaches had actual resonance, where they in fact had rather marginal impacts. Buck welcomes a postenvironmentalist narrative of sustainability that does not alarm in order to lower living standards but that portrays it as opportunity for "greater economic security and prosperity" (2013:884). But such departure is problematic. Again, it sounds like an environmentalist narrative has been dominant. And it draws a rather harmless picture and lacks the moral courage that Hamilton emphasizes.[259] It leaves too much room for delay. Strong policies would mean that living standards have to be lowered. Greater responsibility in climate change could be interpreted as an argument for huge cuts in emissions. Instead the responsibility in terms of historic justice is recurrently overlooked.

Pointing fingers at other's polluting practices is very common. Blameshifting is a routine practice. One form of distraction can be to shift blame to others and another can be to avoid reflection on one's own practices. Typically both mechanisms are simultaneously at work. A common form of blame shifting is directing the responsibility toward other countries whose gross pollution is higher.

> "Delegation is a means to remove feelings of guilt. The person who delegates refuses to accept any personal responsibility and blames others for environmental destruction (e.g. the industries, the multi-nationals, the political establishment). People who delegate are unlikely to take any pro-environmental behavior that asks for personal sacrifices" (Kollmuss and Agyeman 2002:255; see Marshall 2014).

Pointing at other people's wasteful behaviour can be a negation of social responsibility that disables positive change. Shared responsibility in the meantime can lead to the bystander effect (Marshall 2014:Loc. 440). Here, each person assigns responsibility to another person who could act, so he does not feel responsible to interfere.

Responsibility and feelings of guilt are transferred in many instances. As identified by Swyngedeouw, the discourse over CO2 is an exemplary scapegoat (2011:70ff.). Focusing on CO2 is not only a reductionism that includes reification and commodification of the threat. The discourse around carbon stylises the people not as "heterogeneous political subjects, but as universal victims, suffering from processes beyond their control" (Swyngedeouw 2011:71). Citizens and consumers' actions are not identified as the cause of destruction. Therein the nature/culture dichotomy enables externalising a "fetishized enemy" in the form of CO2 and allows shifting blame (Swyngedeouw 2011:72). The forces of physics are separated from the human realm. The cause of the problem is to be found outside society, which is typical for

---

[259] "Affluent societies are generally unwilling to make sacrifices which are commensurate with the part they have played in causing environmental degradation" (Linklater 2006:110).

populist politics. Buell hints that this human mechanism of externalising allows enjoying consumption of single use products while uttering disgust towards recycling offenders (1995:65). Studying Norway as a country with a significant level of policy commitment as well as public concern, Norgaard discovers mechanisms that hamper the transformation of knowledge into practice (2006; Dryzek, Norgaard and Schlosberg 2013:Loc. 453). As citizens of a big oil exporter Norwegians in effect benefit immensely from polluting industries. While voices of concern are typical in the country, export of crude oil and emissions have grown beyond the provisions of the Kyoto Protocol (Marshall 2014:Loc. 1401).

Hamilton finds that most striking about human reflexivity is the decision not to reflect (2008; 2010 and 2014). Active reflection would uncover cognitive dissonance. The existence of cognitive dissonance and its moderation is a challenging objection to the assumptions of rational choice approaches, hence public choice theory, but also to Rawls' public reason for example. While rational choice approaches build on the ability for consistent action, the disparity between knowledge and action cannot be easily explained. It defies even the idea of minimal rationality or embedded rationality, since means and ends are not consonant. Such inconsistency is not just found on the individual level but is endemic. Incoherent behaviour and deception is not the exception. "No matter how ambitious or idealistic our stances as citizens, once we act as consumers, most of us will have considerable difficulty complying with our own civic ideals" (Hausknost 2014:367; Rostboll 2005). Denial and avoidance means that intelligence and perceptiveness are rather used for opposite purposes. Orr comments on the manifest shortcomings in fighting environmental degradation:

> "Perhaps we really are not so much a rational species as we are exceedingly clever rationalizers. Again, the evidence cannot be lightly dismissed. The sources of irrationality are many, starting with the still small voice of our genes that moves us to do their bidding and extending through our ineptitude at seeing patterns and systems and acting accordingly. Perhaps our evolutionary career has hardwired us to myopic tribal loyalties. Maybe we are just sinful and fallen, deserving of death excepting the redeemed, as fundamentalists would have it. Having multiplied extravagantly and extended our dominion over the air, seas, and lands and into the depths of the atom and gene beyond any rational limit, we are too successful for our own good" (2009:139).

The skill for rationalising is paired with increasing power through scientific progress. Instead of taking responsibility the individual engages in self-deception. Pollution is a field where many people do have agency after all, even if limited to their own private consumption and social circles (Marshall 2014:Loc. 3242).[260] The capacity for this deception and its effects should not be underestimated. When people behave environmentally friendly in one area, they are actually

---

[260] Unfortunately for environmental politics "the most pervasive narrative of all is the one that is not voiced: the collective social norm of silence" (Marshall 2014:Loc. 88).

likely to feel free to waste more in another area (2014:Loc. 3319). People may save more electricity but at the same time increase their water consumption. Human beings have a limited amount of will power, the concentration on one issue leads to less attention on another (Hausknost 2014:368).[261]

Whereas information is often understood as a condition for behavioural change, evidence seems to hint that the causal chain is the opposite (Hadler and Haller 2011). Behavioural change can be followed by a change in norms and values. Again, this process can be understood as a means to reduce dissonance. Psychology knows this phenomenon as cognitive rationalisation.

> "On this view, our identity is continually reshaped by inference from the evidence of our actions; it is not so much sheer habit, but the unconscious or partly conscious drive for consistency, which shapes future conduct. One experiment designed to test this theory found that people primed by having been asked, and who agreed, to make a small commitment illustrating a new value (putting a tiny card in their window in favour of safer driving) were subsequently far more likely than the control group to allow a large unsightly sign to the same effect to be erected in their front yards. Once people have formed a commitment to a certain kind of behaviour, they reshape their conception of their own identity, and from there identity reshapes their reasons, making new reasons become salient to them" (Lane 2011b:169).

Preferences cannot be understood as a priori. Induced behavioural change then leads to change in consciousness of the public as a whole, even for elements that were previously unsupportive (Hadler and Haller 2011). As long as the behaviour did not change, awareness might also be suppressed as a mean to a dissonance reduction, hence people are enabled to ignore dissonance. If knowledge led to more environmentally friendly lifestyles, one would assume that more information is a key solution. Although countries with a majority that identifies as protestant score higher on 'environmental consciousness', countries with a catholic majority or mixed countries show better results in environmental action (2011). When questioned, the publics in all industrialised countries are sensitive towards climate change, if literacy is taken as a measurement. Yet, there is only a weak connection between environmental consciousness and actual behaviour (Diekmann and Preisendörfer 2001:94ff.).[262] Several studies show that "general attitudes toward the environment are not predictive of eventual behaviour" (Bell et al. 2001:481f.; Kollmuss and Agyeman 2002). A more environmentally conscious person "probably does engage in more pro-environmental behaviour" (Bell et al. 2001:33). Yet behaviour is marked by inconsistency through different dimensions. Diekmann and Preisendörfer present

---

[261] Human psychology is affected by small things so much that even being freshly showered can have a negative impact on social behaviour.
[262] See for example Micheletti, Stolle and Berlin (2014).

research which demonstrates too much concentration on smaller things such as the avoidance of plastic bags (2001:105ff.).[263]

People buy new iPhones every other year, despite recurring news about cutting rainforests and bad working conditions. The bystander effect coupled with the social norm also means that everybody buying a new phone on a regular basis is used as an excuse for one's own behaviour. The next car will be more powerful and bigger in spite of environmental literacy.[264] Again, a differentiation between consumer and citizen is highly problematic. The environmentalist using his Apple device in order to get his message across may appear 'preposterous'. Yet, this dissonance is symbolic for the wider population and is typical for the politics of simulation. Ingolfur describes it as

> "a societal strategy of societal self-deception [that] entails, first, the reflexive redefinition of the core values of modernity; second, the cultivation of reformist discourses such as those on ecological modernization, democratic renewal, and social inclusion; and third, the implementation of policy programmes designed for the cost-effective management of the unavoidable side-effects of contemporary self-realization" (2004:45).

None of these discourses involves real commitment and sufficient change (Carter 2013). They support the idea that current political systems are able to cope with ecological problems. Optimism reigns. The ubiquity of the deception in environmental matters led to the concept of 'green washing'. Green washing is a process in which a thing or an action is presented as environmentally friendly or at least less destructive.[265] Whole green product lines and brands satisfy the costumer's limited willingness to pay (see Humphrey 2009), while not having to give up anything the green customer can green wash his conscience. Intentionality is taken as more important than the outcome, when people judge actions (Marshall 2014:Loc. 3101; see Linklater 2006). Green products help to show the intention of the consumer to protect the environment, so he is able to claim less responsibility. Responsibility in modern life is, at the same time as it is individualised, also transferred. Politics and economics alike engage in simulation.[266]

Inventing the term 'doublethink', Orwell describes the possibility of holding two contradictory beliefs simultaneously without feeling uncomfortable because of their dissonance. Doublethink means, though mutually exclusive thoughts and beliefs are making up the agent's reality, he

---

[263] The drive to convenience as a factor will be discussed under low cost thesis in the following chapter.
[264] The car can be understood as symbolic for individualised omnipotence and greatness and is often experienced as such (Busch 2011:91). Cars are representative for many problems that environmental protection faces.
[265] "With the widening of the ecological debate there developed a feeling that humanity could make a reasoned decision between alternative futures" (Radcliffe 2002:3f.).
[266] "Cooperate executives, union heads, political leaders, grassroots activists, and consumers all pledge their allegiance to "green" values" (Buell and De Luca 1996:xi).

remains unaware of their contradiction.[267] Environmental problems are not mute in daily lives, politics or the economy, but people prefer to ignore them and even more, people have become insensible towards social and ecological challenges (Busch 2011:81ff.). A process of dissociation, where the consciousness for examples disintegrates memory, cognition and identity that are normally connected, can also be a reaction to the dissonance. Not just slow changes remain unnoticed, but human beings also have selective memories.[268] Busch points at a psychological "double life", where emotions are suppressed and the self is split, similarly to the process doctors in the Third Reich as well the builders of the nuclear bomb were likely to have experienced (2011:87). The consciousness of risky consumption practices is suppressed and authorship, therefore responsibility ignored. This is most apparent in the fact that supporters of green parties fly more than others (see Diekmann and Preisendörfer 2001:115).[269] Blühdorn points at postmodern individuality as one of the factors that enable far reaching dissonance. The multiplicity offered means that citizens are more tolerant towards internal inconsistencies and contradictions (Blühdorn 2011:24).[270] Thus doublethink becomes easier. It can be argued that the omnipresence of unsustainable practices within and across societies additionally lessen sensibility to cognitive dissonance. It follows that the sums of these individual and societal shortcomings make it unlikely that there will be a bottom-up demand for sustainability. "[E]nvironmental policy research has shown clearly that the mere provision of information will never be sufficient to bring about decisive change. Governments will have to initiate" (de Geus 2004:Loc. 2624-25). Consciousness is more likely to follow change in behaviour. Widespread preferences for greener politics and concrete demands may develop after behavioural change.

2.2.1.3. ENVIRONMENTAL DEGRADATION AS A (TOTAL) SOCIAL FACT

"Most importantly, we have to stop pretending that there is any possible way back to that lush, comfortable, and beautiful Earth we left behind sometime in the twentieth century. The further we go along the path of business as usual, the more we are lost" (Lovelock 2009:Loc. 68).

While climate change and large environmental damage are scientific facts, they can hardly be described as social fact. Social facts exert external constraints on the individual and society as a whole. Social facts typically manifest a constraint in the form of laws, beliefs, values and morality

---

[267] Analogously, Jackson asks: "Are we really committed to eradicating poverty? Are we serious about reducing carbon emissions? Do we genuinely care about resource scarcity, deforestation, biodiversity loss? Or are we so blinded by conventional wisdom that we daren't do the sums for fear of revealing the truth?" (2012:Loc. 1638-41; see also Forsyth 2003).

[268] "A drought of several years may soon be forgotten with relief at a few weeks of rain, as experienced recently in some parts of Australia" (Spash 2007:143).

[269] This seems reminiscent of a classical experiment in psychology, where the forbidden toy is likely to appear more attractive (Harmon-Jones and Mills 2009a).

[270] In a sense, it could be argued that it is the opposite of the uniform society in '1984' but this leads to a discussion of 'postmodern identity' that is irrelevant to the argument.

but also in customs (Durkheim 1982; Mauss 1990). If climate change had established itself as a social fact, people could not ignore the constraints that it would create within society.[271] Ecological citizenship as suggested by green democratic theorists would be possible. So far, it has failed to become a social fact. People are 'apocalypse blind' given that there is little doubt that many societies will face climate induced collapse (Leggewie and Welzer 2011:98f.).[272] It is still socially acceptable to own a private jet, drive an SUV or fly to exotic places. The individual and society do not determine it immoral. An extra dimension is given by the fact that in many cases people had to work for those things. Studies show that if somebody puts more effort into something, he is more likely to evaluate it positively (Harmon-Jones and Mills 2009a:8). Hence, driving an expensive car or living in a huge home are accepted and valued. Though one could argue that modesty takes such an effort as well, modesty lacks the social status to be aspired (see More 1992).[273]

Democratic systems do not get the necessary input to transform into green democratic states as wished for by Eckersley and others (2004). This objection holds true in particular for Wissenburg's green liberalism (2006). A green state demands the recognition of physical limits. It demands a reinterpretation of lifestyle choices. Green politics and sustainability "need not only social capital, correct knowledge, and good leadership, but also shifts in cultural perspectives and values, including a reconception of both pleasure and necessity" (Peterson 2010:110; Carter 2007:65, Hamilton 2010; Bührs 2012). Priming is possible, putting issues such as paternalism aside, but studies show that the magnitude is relatively small (Bell et al. 2001:486). In other words, environmental degradation and therefore soundness would have to become a social fact. Yet, this is hardly possible under current conditions in many democracies.

> "Liberal-democratic governments are designed to 'manage' an existing 'independent' reality, not to design and create one anew. According to this logic, liberal democratic governments might only start to react and 'manage' the situation when our reality becomes crisis-ridden and when it will be too late to avert dangerous climate change" (Hausknost 2014:371).

Again democracies prove to be rather reactionary than proactive. Whereas increased consumption there and again is understood as a legitimate solution to a weaker economy, environmentalism asks for reductions (Peterson 2010). Since environmental degradation does

---

[271] "[W]e scan the people around us for social cues to guide our own response: looking for evidence of what they do, what they say, and, conversely, what they do not do and do not say. These cues can also be codified into rules that define the behaviors that are expected or are inappropriate—the social norm. If we see that other people are alarmed or taking action, we may follow them. If they are indifferent or inactive, we will follow that cue" (Marshall 2014:Loc. 450). Social conformity and peer pressure are well-studied phenomena.
[272] "If we are not honest about the situation we will continue to do nothing substantive" (Anderson 2012:16).
[273] "Once we get rid of that dominant conception of the good life, we can again bring to the centre of the stage questions about the preservation of the planet's ecology, and about global justice" (Singer 1994:20f.).

not have the necessary priority, proposed change can be perceived as too onerous.[274] Freedom to consume as long as it is within one's budget seems to be part of the contemporary social consensus. "It would be difficult to formulate a proposition further from the political mainstream" than cutting consumption (Jacobs 1997:47). Jacobs' statement appears still valid today. Significant reduction in consumption is an unaccepted necessity. What happens when respect for ecosystems becomes a social fact and therefore includes a strong moral dimension is shown by the 2011 tsunami in Japan. Though citizens of Tokyo had long before been asked to save energy, pleas had not impacted overall consumption. But when it became a "morally charged choice" demand dropped by 20% in peak hours (Marshall 2014:Loc. 1157).

Peterson points out that the processes of privatisation and individualisation can have a negative effect on the willingness to make sacrifices and commitments (2010:101ff.). North Americans for example are unwilling to give up private cars, cheap animal products etc. and they thereby fail to recognise that they sacrifice basic goods such as clean air and water and destroy biodiversity. Here politics that aim for sustainability must challenge ideas "how things are and must be" (Peterson 2010:105). The former goods are demerit goods that are often seen as part of basic rights. The fact that many consumer goods serve as status symbols and as identity further complicates the issue (Zavestoski 2003; Harris 2013). Commodities are even acquired by using credit and seek to generate social recognition. Hamilton expresses this aspect clearly:

> "When we ask affluent consumers to change their consumption behaviour we are asking of them much more than we realise. The purpose of the shift in marketing from promoting the qualities, real or imagined, of a product to promoting brands as a lifestyle choice was to exploit the modern need to construct a sense of self. If we have constructed a personal identity in large part through our consumption activity, and consuming is how we sustain ourselves psychologically from day to day, a demand to change what we consume becomes a demand to change who we are. If, in order to solve climate change, we are asked to change the way we consume, then we are being asked to give up our identities—to experience a sort of death. So firmly do many of us cling to our manufactured selves that we unconsciously fear relinquishing them more than we fear the consequences of climate change. So the campaign to maintain a liveable climate is in this sense a war against our own sense of who we are" (2010:74f.; see also Jackson 2012:Loc. 967-68).

This identification has become so pervasive that those who do not participate in consumerism not seldom self-define by the very act of abstaining i.e. they claim the identity of the other. It has become the identity of a significant part of humanity to live beyond their monetary means and most importantly beyond the planetary means. These identification processes are deeply

---

[274] "The normalcy of sacrifice in some aspects of our lives is not paralleled by acceptance of sacrifice in environmental discourse and practice. Even though the logic of sacrifice is woven into major aspects of most people's lives, in other words, environmentally motivated sacrifices — such as changing eating or driving habits — seem to many an impossible barrier" (Peterson 2010:93).

engraved in many contemporary cultures.[275] Yet, a sustainable society demands the opposite, the penetration of environmentally friendly thinking and actions throughout all dimensions of life.

> "Even if a democratic government decides against people's will, mitigation is improbable, since [r]egulation which fails to engage with the habits, ideas, passions, and appetites of the people being regulated is unlikely to work very well" (Lane 2011b:10; Marshall 2014).

Hence, an evolution of social norms is indispensable.[276] If care for the environment was a social fact, unsustainable practices would become unacceptable (see Latinis 2000; see also Ehrlich and Ehrlich 1990:231 and More 1992). So far, green parties have not achieved to establish norms of sustainability in any democracy.

Grassroots movements and the majority of greens insist on voluntariness. Peterson points out that

> "changes can emerge, at least in a democratic society, only as a result of a widespread political consensus, which requires leadership, organizing, and ultimately, personal commitments not just to a movement, but to the kind of identity and actions it demands" (2010:112).

One main barrier is to establish this respect for ecosystems as the dominant discourse. Political theorists though

> "are very optimistic about the possibility of people taking responsibility and developing an attitude of care to the environment, so long as they are allowed to and encouraged to participate in decision making about the environment and in environment-friendly projects such as preservation" (De-Shalit 2006b:94).

More than 40 years of delayed action should lead to a more realistic approach to environmental politics. Political theorists as human beings suffer from an optimism bias too, in particular if they invested their careers into optimism about democratic publics (see Lane 2011b). While optimism is not negative per se, in this case it is dangerous. Hamilton makes a crucial point

> "arguing that the evidence that large scale climate change is unavoidable has now become so strong that healthy illusion is becoming unhealthy delusion. Hoping that a major disruption to the Earth's climate can be avoided is a delusion. Optimism sustained against the facts, including unfounded beliefs in the power of consumer action or in technological rescue, risks turning hopes into fantasies" (2010:132).

He clearly sees the acceptance of climate change as a precondition for any form of adaption. This acceptance needs to deeply penetrate society. Mauss differentiates between social facts and total social facts. Total social facts in some cases hold whole societies and institutions together and in other cases hold a significant amount of institutions together (1990:176). They can function as

---

[275] "Consumer goods provide a symbolic language in which we communicate continually with each other, not just about raw stuff, but about what really matters to us: family, friendship, sense of belonging, community, identity, social status, meaning and purpose in life" (Jackson 2012:Loc. 1144-48; Cannavo 2010:228).
[276] Ecologists frequently say: "Sustainable living requires a re-education of society based upon consuming less and producing for basic need on a self-sufficiency basis" (Burchell 2002:13).

the engine. Mitigating the climate crisis presupposes a radical restructuring of contemporary life. Given the scope, ecological integrity presupposes sound environmental thinking to become a total social fact. In some cases social facts are obligatory. Sustainable living as an obligation would solve most dilemma associated with environmental degradation. It seems unlikely that this is possible within a democratic framework, especially when individual freedom is emphasized.

2.2.2. INDIVIDUALISM AS RATIONALE

For an understanding of environmental governance, a reflection on the connection between individualism, democracy and sustainability is indispensable. The impact of individualism on the politics of nature as well as the relationship between individualism and democracy are central. Pepper claims that "non-aggressive individualism is a cornerstone of radical green political ideology" and that "individual self-fulfilment is also vital – for respect and love for others, and for nature, must be funded in self-respect" (1996:17). Such a claim of necessity is unfounded. The idea that the individual must care for itself first before it can care for others including nature is not grounded in sociological research about the environment (Kollmuss and Agyeman 2002). In fact individualism, in any form, could be incompatible with sustainability. It is central to investigate whether it can be consistent with green outcomes, since it builds on individual rationality and the individual as a point of departure. Metaphysically, it is to be located at the opposite of ecology, since ecology emphasizes interrelatedness.[277] The acceptance of interrelatedness is the core of sustainable living.[278] Yet, individualism as an ideology and self-interest as a legitimate claim remain widespread. Callero summarises:

> "Individualism is a belief system that privileges the individual over the group, private life over public life, and personal expression over social experience; it is a worldview where autonomy, independence, and self-reliance are highly valued and thought to be natural; and it is an ideology based on self-determination, where free actors are assumed to make choices that have direct consequences for their own unique destiny" (2009:17).

Free choice, autonomy and independence are central to this belief system and stand in opposition to interrelatedness of not only ecology but also science in general (see Carter 2013).[279] It facilitates atomistic thinking that is contrary to the fact that individual choices have direct consequences on others. If greens do support individualism this could be inconsistent with green outcomes. As touched upon earlier the gap between individual and collective rationality is not

---

[277] This contrast between individualism as a dominant discourse and ecology leads Carter to label the latter as "subversive" (2013:82; see also Porrit 1985:216 and Arias-Maldonado 2007:241).
[278] Nature cannot be neatly separated into parts.
[279] The first two so called "Laws of Ecology" are "Everything is connected to everything else" and "Everything has to go somewhere" (Commoner 1979:16ff.).

only particularly overt in environmental politics, it is also dangerous.[280] Prioritizing individual interest runs contrary to the public good in particular in regard to future generations. While arguments about interrelatedness can be made to point at the individual's interest in the wellbeing of others who currently live, the connection can hardly be established in regard to the future. What Graham points out for democracy in general, is outstandingly problematic for environmental politics: "If everyone looks rationally to his own interests, then the interests of all are sacrificed" (2013:Loc. 302-3). While it is sometimes argued that in this way all people are cared for and the affected knows best (Mill 1901; Dahl 1989:296), caring beyond oneself is an exigency for the environment. The common good is not simply a by-product of self-interested actions.[281] Enlightened and ecological citizenship are typically signified by seeing beyond one's own interests.[282] This in a sense contrasts with individualism which often includes the idea of the human individual having "ultimate value and dignity" (Rapport 2006:298).[283]

In sum, the commensurability, of a common good and the prioritisation of the individual, is highly questionable.[284] Individualism, then, inherent to liberal democracy but also significant in other forms of democracy, is a major obstacle to sound environmental politics. A discussion of sustainable politics needs to take this into account. Hence, an assessment of the potential of democracy for sustainability has to include the discussion of individualism, because "democracy, at least in its Enlightenment form, is inherently individualistic" (Taber 2003:435). The contemporary democratic rationale of 'one person, one vote' manifests individualism. The citizen is systematically encouraged to think in his own interest. Many moral philosophers problematise the tension and sometimes irreconcilability of individual and collective good that is normally neglected in political discourse. When choices are understood as autonomous and freedom of choice is valued higher than other values, the common good can easily be sacrificed. Correspondingly, liberal democracy can advance free choices that are not only socially harmful, but set the course for catastrophe (Humphrey 2007:Loc. 690; Randers 2012). The tension between the individual's particular interest and collective good is particularly strong in Singer's

---

[280] Elections are unlikely to deliver socially 'desirable' politics. "Majority voting ensures that the corporate judgements are responsive to the judgements of individuals, as seems appropriate, and the problem is that such individual responsiveness makes it difficult to achieve collective rationality" (Pettit 2012:192).

[281] "The democratic process is a gamble on the possibilities that a people, in acting autonomously, will learn how to act rightly" (Dahl 1989:192).

[282] For example "[t]he Rousseauian democratic form of [a social] covenant requires something much more difficult, but perhaps more lasting – it requires a transvaluation of values; an expansion of the moral and the civic imagination, and, in short, civic virtue" (Jennings 2010:225; see also Dryzek 2005:115ff.).

[283] Mill solves this problem by identifying individual and collective good with each other (1879, 1901).

[284] Commenting on Mill, Watkins warns: "We should not make a religion of individuality" (1966:163).

works. He understands self-interest as a rival viewpoint to ethics (Singer 1994:5).[285] Coming from a scholar who has been interested in a wider good for decades this judgment should not be taken lightly.

Before discussing in further detail it is useful to list essential characteristics of individualism. Individualism as a rationale for decision making suffers from five complementary problems:

1. It presupposes autonomy.[286] The assumption of autonomy does not only make preferences black boxes, it also sanctifies these preferences. They are valued as authentic parts of the individual and therefore remain unquestioned (see Stephens 2001b). Although ubiquitous active interference (shaping of choices), is often understood negatively (Hamilton 2008; 2010).

2. It prioritizes the individual.[287] The individual's preferences are prioritized before those of society or the 'natural' world. Actions in favour of society will be understood as sacrifices and not as a norm (see Maniates and Meyer 2010).

3. It cannot cope with collective action problems. While the individual's impact is negligible, the impact of the sum of all individual actions is not (Lane 2011b). Driving to work every day is rational at the individual but not the collective level. Each individual has an incentive to continue harmful behaviour from a narrow rational choice point of view (Hardin 1968).

4. It underestimates the individual's effect on others. Individualism ignores interrelatedness (Carter 2013; see also Mill 1901).[288] The idea of independence also enables the individual to act without considering a moral obligation towards others. As long as the link is not emphasized, harmful acts cannot be considered morally wrong.

5. In its extreme, it devalues sciences by making facts a matter of individual opinion. With its potential for atomism, it respects competing views. Thence, scientific evidence is 'managed' with other worldviews (Blühdorn 2011:22f.).

---

[285] Though successful businessmen are often used as inspirations, contemporary cultures still define heroism differently. Heroes are understood as those who sacrifice their own good for the sake of others. They do not define themselves as ends.

[286] The question of accepting choices as free, both ontologically and epistemologically, and as valuable, is central. There is no unanimous definition of autonomy. Autonomy, independence, freedom and liberty may be defined differently, but often lack clear distinctions from each other. The idea of autonomy always involves a minimum of reason and is generally understood as an outcome of processes of emancipation (see Christman 2005). If one states that the individual acted autonomously, independently or freely, the question should be 'from what' or 'of what'. Freedom is often defined as the ability to do or not to do 'what one wants' (Dahrendorf 2006:50ff.). Epistemologically, Cartesian philosophy asserts that there is nothing else one can be sure of than his own existence. The furthest application of logic leads to the individual, oneself, as the only absolute. This atomism cannot be falsified and remains logically valid, but is scientifically as well as socially not very fruitful.

[287] For the ancient philosophers justice had priority (e.g. Dahrendorf 2006).

[288] "Individualism implies both equality and liberty" (Dumont 1992:76). Early 20th century liberal theorists understood freedom as more important than equality though (Dahrendorf 2006:48f.).

Sustainable politics are in conflict with each of these tendencies in many ways. Climate change and natural destruction can be the consequence. Wapner's description of environmentalism sheds light on some of the conflicts:

> "Environmentalism is, at bottom, a moral movement. It seeks to extend moral consideration to our fellow humans, to those who will come after us, and to the wider more-than-human world of which we are a part and which deserves support independent of its contributions to our lives" (2010:56).

Environmentalism and ecology are based on a particular worldview that stands in contradiction to individualism. In Wapner's description environmentalism even enters an intrinsic value debate that extends rights well beyond humans, whereas the beliefs in the legitimacy of individual choices and the subsequent consumerism have a strong role in limiting the rights of the 'more-than-human world'. As a moral movement it is related to a different worldview: for a shift from *homo oeconomicus* to *homo sustinens* (or the ecological citizen), individualism needs to be overcome. The simultaneous emergence of mass production, individualisation and environmental destruction is not merely coincidental. "Individualisation created the social conditions for the flourishing of modern consumerism by providing the opportunity for the marketers of goods to step in and satisfy the desire to find and express a self" (Hamilton 2010:70). Sustainability needs a reversal of these developments. Consistent green political theory acknowledges this. Despite this acknowledgement, reversal is unlikely as long as individualism remains the dominant discourse.[289] Even green theorists like Jacobs state that it is unclear whether the majority identifies their own wellbeing with the general conditions and that in fact "[t]he promotion of neo-liberal ideology in recent years would appear to have undermined" such identification (1997:59).

2.2.2.1. (GREEN) LIBERALISM AND THE PRIORITISATION OF THE AUTONOMOUS INDIVIDUAL

The question whether democracy produces a more individualist culture is difficult to answer. Although not all democracies are based on individualist cultures, the rationale of individual vote may lead to more self-regarding decision making and therefore even practices. Durkheim accounts to Christianity and enlightenment the implementation of individualism as a social fact (see Rapport 2006). Classifying it as a social fact on the one hand shows that it is something not natural, but merely constructed, and on the other hand attributes it as 'valued' by society. Following this train of thought, individualism evolved from particular historic circumstances and

---

[289] This discourse is global. Jenkins writes that "China in the modern era seems no more immune than other countries with non-Western cultural traditions from the seemingly irresistible attractions of modern materialistic individualism with its environmental and social problems" (1998:155). Today, it is evident that consumerism has attracted a large Chinese upper and middle class. China is not immune, but it needs to be examined how this 'disease' is created and can be cured.

cannot be understood as a universal (Rapport 2006:298ff.).[290] The idea of non-interference premises on autonomy or "the myth of individualism" (Callero 2009:31), whereas empirical sciences proves interrelatedness.[291] Mauss describes a societal evolution beginning with a tribal stage of personage, where the being is only in relation to others (1990). What individualism fails to recognise is that this is the very basis of humanity. Today's ties are seldom as apparent as those of Mauss' subjects of research, but human beings do not have an identity independent of others (see Fay 2003). Many ideas of freedom are counterfactual and serve as ideologies. Normatively negative freedom is repeatedly supported and individual freedom celebrated regardless of facts.[292] Hamilton does not only expound the problem of hope, he also reflects on an exaggerated concept of agency symbolised in the American dream of upward mobility (2010:129f.). Individualism builds on the idea that the individual is able to autonomously achieve success regardless of initial circumstance.[293] Without a minimum belief in freedom the idea of self-determination and therefore democracy are paradoxical. Accordingly the problem of dependency was subject to discussions throughout history. For instance, in debates about voting in England in the 17th century it was suggested to exclude "servants, wage earners, and beggars, on the ground that such people were not in fact free to exercise their right, as they depended on somebody who had to be pleased" (Dumont 1992:80). While this example shows direct dependency, it nonetheless hints at dependence as a constant variable. In environmental matters, direct self-interest is likely to affect a significant amount of voters who see their livelihood dependent on private cars or polluting industries. Direct dependency is the most visible form of dependency. Individualism negates dependency.

De Geus understands liberalism as an umbrella for prioritizing the individual (2001). In general modernism refers to the individual as the basic unit of society. Historically liberalism developed in opposition to absolutist societies which in fact could be understood as attributing less

---

[290] The question whether the idea of individualism as natural is ethnocentric is not central to the discussion here.

[291] Seeing such autonomy as counterfactual did not just occur with modern neuroscience and related fields. Schumpeter for example criticizes "attributing to the will of the *individual* an independence and a rational quality that are altogether unrealistic" (2003:253).

[292] In this interpretation real freedom means that restrictions for the individual are minimal and fewer limitations mean more freedom. Thus negative freedom is seen as the highest value, which conclusively means that freedom is not justice (Dahrendorf 2006:51). According to Dahrendorf, Berlin's interpretation of positive freedom is not freedom, but 'un-freedom' and merely what Plato or Hegel would understand as freedom (2006:53f.). Freedom here is independent of the wishes of the people to actually use it. However, the perception of many people differs greatly from liberal theory. In a study, "most devalued freedom in favor of money and power. Freedom is not about being left alone by others. Nor is freedom about such effete rights as free speech. Most disparaged the concept-partly because they took it for granted, but also because it doesn't matter if you can say what you want if you can't do what you want" (Alford 2003:152).

[293] This is relevant because the perception of autonomous preferences and the connected hope can set the frame for environmental politics.

importance to the individual.[294] The interrelatedness and importance of the collective in ecology hence stands in stark contrast to an ideology that believes in autonomy, where self-determination and freedom from interference play a particularly significant role. Many green theorists who attach importance to the individual's autonomy and responsibility believe in the potential of human nature to improve as touched upon earlier. In the tradition of Locke in particular, 'good' laws and education are assumed to eventually lead to a good society.[295] Before the 18th century education was available only to the privileged few, so given that universal education was a popular utopia, it could easily be assumed to be a panacea to mankind's malaises. The belief that universal education makes the individual more rational and that it would use its reason to direct its actions towards a general good, was commonly spread among intellectuals, especially utilitarians. Rationalism is at the core of liberalism. The belief in rational consensus is problematic as the basis of liberalism, since politics in itself is a place for value conflicts (Mouffe 2011:5). The belief in the dominance of reason and its inevitability blinds liberalism to actual practice.

A fundamental dispute between liberalism and ecology concerns ontology. There is a difference whether ontology is *a priori* to reasoning and therefore 'prior to politics' or if reasoning can be understood in any sense as autonomous (Humphrey 2007:Loc. 3112-3116; Mouffe 2002; see also Brown 2012).[296] Nussbaum importantly points at liberal hypocrisy in regard to their critique of essentialism. While their "objection is that by determining in advance what elements of human life have most importance, the essentialist is failing to respect the right of people to choose", they are "essentialist about the central importance of human freedom and autonomy " (1992:208). Justifications as to why freedom and autonomy is a condition for humans flourish are typically avoided. Humphrey highlights that it is seldom clear why autonomous living is given priority normatively (2007:Loc. 2247-2258). He attests a similar problem in Eckersley's delineation of a green state. He stresses that for Eckersley, autonomy is defined as having the chance to live according to a species' nature (Humphrey 2007:Loc. 2356; see Eckersley 2004). Subsequently, Humphrey suggests several shortcomings. The justification for democracy is linked to a particular interpretation of autonomy that hence has to be revised in Eckersley's green state. In a

---

[294] Enlightenment "thinkers lionized personal liberty in contrast to control by unjust, arbitrary, and often incompetent despots. At a time when some political leaders were imagining alternatives to despotic monarchy, many viewed the elevation of individual rights as a necessary response" (Oreskes and Conway 2014:Loc. 515). The difference between polyarchy and earlier governments is "the astounding expansion of individual rights" (Dahl 1989:219).

[295] Rawls states that "citizens are regarded as having a certain natural political virtue without which the hopes for a regime of liberty may be unrealistic" (2011:Loc. 5833-43).

[296] Hadler and Haller find that the national context has less impact on positioning towards the environment than gender, age and education (2011). Age, on the other hand, does not appear to play a big role in concern (Micheletti, Stolle and Berlin 2014:222).

sense similar, it leads back to the widespread insistence on the dependency of human flourishing on some form of autonomy. Trying to encompass non-human animals her theory lacks "an explanation as to why democracy is justified by the need to 'live a species life'" (Humphrey 2007:Loc. 2392).[297] Humphrey further problematises Eckersley's suggestion that autonomy is exigent, but not sufficient for flourishing and wellbeing. His point is that it is unclear if an autonomous life itself has priority or if the higher goal is human flourishing for which autonomy is seen as a premise.[298] A possible argument could be that it "may only be a necessary and not sufficient condition for flourishing, but it confers dignity upon existence in and of itself" (Humphrey 2007:Loc. 2294; see Graham 2013).

While attempting to develop a green liberalism Wissenburg admits that liberalism is often understood as incompatible with respect for ecosystems:

> "Whatever liberalism is taken to mean, it has a bad name when it comes to matters of ecology and the environment. Liberalism values individual freedom, particularly freedom of thought and religion, freedom of lifestyle, the freedom to live the life of one's choosing. Care for the environment is usually seen as interfering in the genesis of individual preferences, which seems taboo for liberalism – their development is a purely private affair" (2001a:192).

Although ubiquitous in practice, "interfering in the genesis of individual preferences" is seen as unjustified paternalism. The question of the status of different concepts of the good and expressed preferences is central for contemporary liberalism and in a sense for democracy.[299] The idea of self-determination is closely related to the idea that individuals have their own choices. Preferences hence have to be understood as a central component of 'democratic choice'. Decisively, preferences and needs are routinely equated, since liberalism typically refrains from questioning preferences and instead treats them as black boxes.[300] Though today political liberalism is interpreted as tolerance towards different concepts of the good (and it often appears to be a consequence of a 'postmodern denial of truth'), classical liberalism was less relativistic. Here contemporary liberalism struggles with consistency. While it has a strenuous trust in reason and rationality, it nonetheless seemingly supports a multiplicity of viewpoints.

---

[297] Though compatible with liberalism at first sight, this definition at the same time has mutinous potential. Imagining a bee's autonomy in playing its role in a hive seems absurd. However, judging it, as absurd and a caricature of autonomy, is specieism. Hither, ecologists point at an arbitrary distinction between human and non-human animals. The flourishing of the bee is a good example on how ecologist thought challenges individualism.

[298] Eckersley herself highlights the difficulty of state neutrality and the focus on autonomy stating that "[t]o uphold its ultimate ideal [...] of individual autonomy, liberalism needs not only a liberal political system but also a liberal social matrix that recognizes, protects, and rewards the rational, autonomous self in ways that make it "normal"" (2004:Loc. 1308-11). Yet, Eckersley's definition of autonomy equally assumes normality. To live in accordance with nature is essentialism.

[299] "A crucial assumption of liberalism is that equal citizens have different and indeed incommensurable and irreconcilable conceptions of the good" (Rawls 2011:Loc. 4823-42).

[300] Sen notes that "it is traditional in social choice theory to make the empirical assumption that individual choices will, in fact be entirely based on individual preference" (1993:13). It is noteworthy that methodological individualism underestimates interrelationships (Carter 2013:68ff).

Wissenburg sees one advantage of black-boxing preferences in making a concept of human nature unnecessary (2001b).[301] As remarked earlier, liberalism's neutrality inevitably builds on a specific idea. At this juncture it promotes individualism. Since this is the case, Wissenburg's claim that liberalism avoids a concept of human nature is false.[302] Stephens criticises Lockean reason as "identifiably utilitarian egoism" (2001a:8).[303] He further underlines that Wissenburg's green liberalism is following a similar notion of agency which by employing preferences as black boxes is misguided. Stephens rejects Wissenburg's conceptualisation of agency as too instrumental and depending on unquestioned premises (2001a:19). He sees in this liberal characterisation of virtue and value the hindrance to civic virtues that would be necessary for green citizenry. Stephens specifically stresses economic freedoms which are commonly unsustainable. Treating preferences as given avoids the question of origin or their formation. But it at the same time sanctifies unsustainable preferences since they remain unquestioned. Wissenburg acknowledges in a direct response to Stephen's critique that liberalism always includes

> "a substantive common good and a substantive view of human nature. Neutrality, in particular, is seen as a good because it is good for someone, and it is good for someone because it promotes the individual's 'flourishing' in some way" (Wissenburg 2001b:27; see Nussbaum 1992).

The idea of choice as a means to human flourishing indicates a clear understanding of human nature as freedom-seeking. Without such an understanding it would not be relevant which capabilities are supported by a state. Meyer regards green liberals' attempt to theoretically establish a need for liberalism in environmental theory as unconvincing, stating that they fail to show the desirability of "liberal commitments" and therefore as being "persuasive only to those who share these commitments" (2011:358; see also Brown 2012).[304] Regardless of the indicated openness to content, liberals clearly limit restrictions that could be compatible with/or conditional for human flourishing. This is clear without even invoking provocative extremes such as the possibility of 'happy slaves' who flourish in their submissive role. In fact more pressing issues like trading environmental freedom against economic freedoms show the limitation of liberalism.[305] Priority setting and corresponding restrictions could appear crucial in practice.

---

[301] Locke in contrast was convinced that truth in fact can be found via the application of reason (Stephens 2001a:6; Locke 2008). He openly followed a particular interpretation of human nature and reason. Note that some scholars argue that green political theory often misrepresents Locke by ignoring essential writings on morality (Gillroy and Bowersox 2002).

[302] Self-determination becomes the essence of humanness (Brown 2012).

[303] "The moral key for Locke is to acquire the right desires, training acquisitiveness to economically productive impact whilst restraining desires that would violate Christian natural law" (Stephens 2001a:9).

[304] For Meyer, the question should be "when and how environmental concerns might resonate with citizens" and not the compatibility of liberalism and sustainability (2011:357).

[305] E.g. clean air, which can be formulated into a positive freedom as a right to clean air and a negative freedom as the right to be free from pollution is in tension with the economic freedom to produce cars.

Whereas Wissenburg counts it as strength, avoiding a targeted discussion of human nature can lead liberalism to have a crucial blind spot. Discussing social justice, Nussbaum stresses that "desires and subjective preference are not always reliable indices of what a person really needs, of what would really be required to make that life a flourishing one" (1992:230; Conly 2013; see also Sen 1993:28ff. and Harris 2013). Some unsustainable tendencies derive from specific human inclinations as suggested in debates about cognition. Yet, non-interference as a priority takes them as reliable and given.

Following this thought, the state should not interfere in the preference formation, because liberty is understood as not privileging a specific concept of the good (Wissenburg 2001b; Stephens 2001a).[306] Respectively, Wissenburg acknowledges that green liberalism cannot guarantee green citizens.[307]

> "Liberalism only cares about (and may interfere with) personal convictions if they harm others, if they illegitimately infringe on their freedoms and lives, and convictions cannot do that unless they are translated into practice "(2001b:36).[308]

The tolerance towards different concepts of the good takes priority. Wissenburg's assertion reflects the typical neglect of interrelation. Harm is mostly interpreted in a narrow sense as if individuals were mostly unconnected, which could be due to the focus on autonomy. The actual focus then is autonomy more than harm. Understanding oneself as autonomous regardless of the origins of this understanding has consequences i.e. is translated into practice.

> "The refusal to recognise the way others contribute to or support our lives has many political and ethical aspects: political because it encourages us to dispossess the other and to starve them of resources rather than to share, justice aspects because we fail to give others their due, and ethical aspects because we fail in care, consideration and attention" (Plumwood 2006:64).

Convictions are never mere convictions. It is not a coincidence that green thought shares significant parts of its outlook with communitarianism, since it typically understands humans as

---

[306] Rostboll puts forward a definition of autonomy as "to be continually open to learn-ing, to revise one's views in the light of new arguments" (2005:377). Though his definition seems to escape the independency question, given well-established phenomena like the confirmation bias, the chances of this form of autonomy seem small.

[307] Correspondingly, in ecoauthoritarian thought "the liberal protection of individual freedoms stand condemned along with the 'facile' reliance on the democratic preferences of the majority in the liberal-democratic formula" (Humphrey 2007:Loc. 1872).

[308] Wissenburg sees two reasons why liberalism conflicts with the vision of a deep green state:

1. "it requires the prescription of a deep-green life and the explicit elimination and prohibition of all others, which is by definition incompatible with the liberal ideal of dignity and emancipation through freedom of lifestyle and equality of opportunity."

2. "the deep-green life risks self-effacement by denying what liberalism seeks to regulate: the existence of rogue elements in society who willingly or unwillingly sabotage social harmony" (2006:32).

social animals who carry responsibilities.[309] The tension between prevention of harm and minimum interference is a common difficulty in liberalism. Though mentioning harm as a restricting principle, only a thin interpretation of a harm principle is applied.[310] If sustainability is not achieved, harm will not be prevented. A consistent application of the harm principle would lead liberalism to become more protective and radical (see Barry 2001:69f. and Meyer 2011). The precautionary principle, which could be understood as a part of a strict version of the harm principle, is for example in conflict with liberal neutrality. A consistent application would recognise the inner tensions and tradeoffs.[311]

Whereas some preferences could actually be modified in practice, Wissenburg's idea of freedom from authority does not leave such an option. He effectively leaves no room for interference claiming that

> "allowing a state to influence the development of personal convictions is to move back to dark pre-democratic ages [...] The most that can be demanded is that people consider arguments for particular green ideologies and respect those living accordingly" (2001b:36f.).

Such a claim is inconsistent with democratic reality since any public education is involved in shaping convictions. States engage in campaigns trying to foster an interpretation of a public good. To believe in autonomous preference formation is to assume that it is possible to deprive the individual of all prior history and social context, and so to take everything away that basically was part of his socialisation and hence identity. This understanding of preference formation disregards the entire field of social psychology. Pressing for non-interference is further problematic because black-boxing preferences

> "especially where developmental visions are unavoidable (for example, education), simply leave the field clear for dominant economic interests to 'intervene' in 'preference formation' with their ideals, promoting consumption over creative questioning – as is happening" (Stephens 2001b:46; Brown 2012:66f.).

Businesses do not typically question the sustainability of the demands they create and their interpretation of the good focuses on economic growth and expansion. In fact Wissenburg acknowledges the privileging of the free market:

---

[309] Connelly et al. remark that "the individualism which lies at the heart of liberalism, whether in its political expression (the insistence on rights and liberties) or its economic expression (the insistence on markets) creates a problem for environmentalists who are attempting to develop new forms of community and political participation relevant to a sustainable society" (2012:64).

[310] The close relatedness of conviction or worldview and behaviour is not subject here, but cannot be easily dismissed.

[311] There are different versions of the precautionary principle. A precautionary principle as a guiding principle will be discussed in the second part of this book. In general the precautionary principle holds that in case of scientific uncertainty and potential danger 'carefulness', however vaguely defined should be the rationale for action.

Writing from the perspective of the future, Oreskes and Conway judge that "[t]he ultimate paradox was that neoliberalism, meant to ensure individual freedom above all, led eventually to a situation that necessitated large-scale government intervention" (2014:Loc. 629).

"The free market is an indispensable part of liberalism; it would not bathe same without. Setting the economic sphere apart, black-boxing it, so today, does indeed make it easier to claim that liberalism can be green" (Wissenburg 2001b:39).

While here he admits to avoiding questions of supply and demand creation, he also indirectly points at a connected more pressing issue. If liberalism's existence is dependent on a free market, liberalism's sustainability also depends on the possibility of a free market being green. If a free market cannot be green, according to his logic, liberalism cannot either. Meyer summarised positions that dismiss liberalism and the idea that it could be compatible with sustainability.

"Privileging private preferences expressed in the marketplace, liberalism is characterised as promoting possessive individualism and unbridled consumerism. In the name of state neutrality, it precludes meaningful restraints upon the ownership or use of private property, excludes collectively defined conceptions of the good, and devalues citizen virtue or public-regarding action" (2011:362).

Meyer writes that critics of liberalism do not see a difference within the liberal tradition. The critiques reject Stephens' and Wissenburg's position. Both would object to some aspects of this characterisation.

Noteworthy, an extreme liberalism and idea of tolerance towards different lifestyles even restricts democratic publics to make decisions that favour the environment. A crucial issue is the scope of decision making and hence legitimate interference and where to draw the line of state neutrality. Full neutrality leaves the state not only powerless, but makes state and democracy superfluous. A democracy would have literally nothing to decide and consequentially rule. As pointed out liberal positions appear in tension with themselves and partly inconsistent. The chance for sustainability depends on the question whether neutrality and the sanctity of abstract choice have to been maintained (Meyer 2011:364; Blühdorn 2011:7).[312] Wissenburg answers the question positively stating "that ecologically destructive lifestyles cannot be excluded on grounds of principle: neutrality prohibits judgments on the ethical worth of different lifestyles" (2006:22). In regard to the missing guarantees, Stephens calls Wissenburg's green liberalism liberal first and green second (Stephens 2001a:2; see also Dahl 1989:170f.). 'Green' is used as an attribute for liberalism, yet it depends on the preferences of the society. The attribute 'green' can only be accomplished if the citizens actively support green values. Sustainability correspondingly could be understood as a matter of chance. Again, responsible green citizenry is a premise and

---

[312] Here contrasts in statements are stark. Arias-Maldonado posits that "the natural space for moral duties and obligations towards nature is outside the political system" (2007:241). He therefore must see a potential for sustainability in voluntary actions, whereas Hausknost suggests that "choice is no reliable ally in our struggle for sustainability, as sustainability is but one of many goals we pursue as consumers, and usually not the most important one" (2014:369).

not a necessary consequence of such attempts at green liberalism. Departing significantly from Wissenburg's interpretation of liberalism and pointing at this flaw in the conception, Stephens believes in the possibility of a green liberalism as long as it is 'social liberalism'.[313] He sees this space created by

> "rethinking some Enlightenment assumptions about agency, rationality and property [and] evaluating the worth of particular liberties, criteria for which will generate a broad regulative ideal of the human agent" (Stephens 2001b:45).

Stephens finds it necessary to use an idea of the good, though not an all-encompassing one, as a benchmark. While Wissenburg believes that the differences are minor (2001b), Stephens claims to be green first and liberal second (2001b).

Generally, it is useful to avoid judging environmental concerns among other concerns (such as religion, sexual orientation etc.) which remain private concerns even with a thicker application of the harm principle (Meyer 2011:371).[314] In one later elaboration of green liberalism Wissenburg clarifies that negative liberty "can no longer be seen as the supreme criterion of a good society" (2006:31). He thereby seemingly departs from prior elaborations. The non-interference of the state in people's 'private' lives and choices then has lost priority. To conclude, if it is not possible to melt 'liberal' freedoms into sustainable practices, liberalism in general has to be disregarded as an (ecologically) unsustainable ideology.

2.2.2.2. PUBLIC, PRIVATE AND AUTONOMOUS CHOICES

Liberalism entails no or minimum interference. The propagation of minimum interference also means a division into private and public spheres. Democracy is often understood as a regime with a division between public and private, while totalitarianism is said to dissolve those lines (Lauth 2010a:103). Yet, one can argue that the division line can never exist in the first place, since people, society and the political are always intertwined.[315] Divisions between what is demarked as public and what is understood as private are purely arbitrary (Bowles and Gintis 1986).[316] Such a separation is not only based on a binary opposition, it also fails to acknowledge interrelatedness. The attempts to draw a line between citizen and consumer are a good example. Hybrids like citizen consumer, consumer sovereignty or consumer democracy compel a rethinking of the pure forms anyway. The private and public distinction underestimates interrelations by default. In the crowded ecologically stressed world of today most actions have

---

[313] Barry believes that social liberalism may allow for a greening since it is open to state intervention (2001).
[314] It is understood that ideally "personal rights provide a way of ensuring for everyone some free space that cannot be easily violated by ordinary political decisions" (Dahl 1989:220).
[315] A definition of 'the political' is part of a later discussion.
[316] One major topic of dispute in this work is whether reproduction is solely a private right.

effects on others and they therefore cannot be considered as private and a matter of personal choice only.

Individualism wishes to limit interference into the individual's so called 'private choices', but choices regularly interfere with other people's lives. The extent to which these choices have an effect is especially eminent in the realm of environmental protection. Carter importantly emphasises that

> "liberal democracy nurtures an atomised individualistic focus on the private sphere, which makes it a poor breeding ground for the ecological consciousness and responsible citizenship needed to bring about a sustainable society" (2007:56).

The idea of an independent space creates a realm where the individual is not perceived to be liable for his actions beyond himself. But choices of the individual (from the point of sustainability) can only be understood as private in the sense that they do not interfere with others in an unlimited world. Once scarcity as a factor is introduced, one's choice limits another person. Orr calls it "paradoxically" that

> "one of the weaknesses of liberal democracy may be not that it asks too much of its citizens but that it asks too little. Having mostly handed off all responsibility for assessing issues and setting policy to elected politicians, voters are free to indulge themselves in narrow and virulently asserted positions rather than having to come together, work to perceive the common good" (2013:Loc. 6183-86).

Clearly, he criticises the lack of duty to think for a common good and to get engaged as citizens.[317] The private realm in liberalism is detached from the public sphere. Such a worldview is likely to have consequences. Dahrendorf explicitly mentions that there were only a few liberals who actively engaged in the resistance against fascism (2006:126). The correlation between liberalism in theory and taking responsibility in practice i.e. resistance would be an interesting field of study. The liberal paradox of tolerance towards illiberal lifestyles may be subject of such an elaboration. If greening states needs more than individual change, liberalism is not the right ideology for its promotion.[318] While the state is meant to leave its interference into the private sphere at a minimum, the private individual's impact is neglected.[319] The harm principle is not

---

[317] The quandary of more participation is discussed elsewhere. Many liberals have a theoretical trust in the wisdom of democratic citizenry that might lead to a confirmation bias empirically. Josephson writes about the distinction between democratic and autocratic regimes that "[a]ny balance that exists in democratic regimes between the private and public sectors, which permits careful weighing of individual rights versus the social good, is absent in authoritarian regimes. The authorities in those regimes assume that *they* should determine what balance, if any, is achieved" (2005:23). While the latter part of his statement might hold true, the environmental and equity record of many democracies leads to the question of the meaning of balance and further if the word 'balance' can even be meaningful in some cases.

[318] Greening i.e. making states ecologically sustainable.

[319] Young emphasizes an essential point that only libertarianism seems to avoid, namely that "the demand for governance arises from the existence of interdependencies between human actors. If the actions of individual members of a group had no implications – positive or negative – for the other members of the group, there would be no demand for governance" (2009:18).

uniformly applied. Lane hints that interestingly Plato's republic took "the individual more seriously than do most modern liberals" with their

"insistence on the separation between public law and private morality as a political axiom – no matter what the consequences of that which unfolds in the private realm. Insofar as moderns tend to insist that people should be left free to do what they like (within the limits of the harm principle), and fail to consider the consequences if what people like to do undermines the survival of the polity or society itself, it is actually the modern pundit – not Plato – who is manifesting a belief that the individual does not matter. Somehow, the modern society is supposed to be immune to the habits and characters of individuals. Or to put it another way, indifference to individuals' choices is underwritten by the belief that those individuals are negligible from the standpoint of society. What they do, don't do, care about, desire, and believe is negligible to the career of society and can be safely neglected and left alone" (2011b:94).

The fact that those individuals and their behaviour make up a society seems self-evident, but appears occasionally forgotten. It is the disconnection that the private and public distinction creates that enables ignorance to the consequences of individual actions. While individual freedom is prioritized, the effects of this freedom remain unconsidered. In contrast to political philosophy of top-down approaches

"moderns tend to think that however people choose to live privately will have no bearing on the maintenance of the polity. Plato, on the other hand, thinks that how people live privately has massive significance for whether or not the polity can be maintained" (2011b:97).[320]

Convictions accordingly matter. Making worldviews and lifestyles purely private effectively means banning the political. It renders environmental politics meaningless overlooking that the private realm, however neatly defined, does not exist in a vacuum. Environmental degradation is ultimately the result of aggregated individual actions (even if people were not connected and though not everybody participates).

Although the private/public distinction is characteristic for liberalism the size of the supposed realms varies widely. Libertarianism as an extreme individualist position is an enormous challenge to environmental integrity. On the liberal spectrum it is located on the opposite of social liberalism. An extreme expansion of the private realm is seen as enhancing the private good. This can be understood as enhancement of a collective good if and only if the collective good is the sum of all individual goods and there is no tradeoff between different individual goods. Again, scarcity as a factor should change assumptions radically. The question of state interference and scope of liberties is essential in environmental politics, since the answer lays the grounds for legitimate means. Rawls as one of the most prominent contemporary political theorists believes that people should be able to pursue their own ways to fully participate in life

---

[320] This is not necessarily the case in classical liberalism. Kantian morals, for example, specifically integrate private and public realm. While he differentiates between private and public use of reason his imperatives avoid collective action problems by including generalizability as a condition.

(2011). Capacity development for him depends on liberties. He understands political liberty as a condition to develop a sense of justice. While libertarian Tomasi interprets Rawls' theory of justice as including economic freedom, meaning the liberty to decide about wealth, occupation and working condition, this is debatable (2013). Rawls leaves room for the state to restrict economic liberties. People do vote collectively on the conditions after all.[321] The possibility of economic restrictions is overt in the "Two Principles of Justice" (2011). Additionally the conflict between economic and political freedom speaks against Tomasi's interpretation. Without state interference in a free market society, choices, although understood as the choices of individuals, are likely to be the person's with most economic means. The private and public sphere distinction has cognitive and institutional consequences. The means of effective governance depend on the question of legitimate interference of the state. Hence, the smaller the private realm the greater power the state has to direct and implement sustainable policies. In line with this, Commoner believes that a major reason Americans have not been able to combine ecology and economics is "the social belief that technology choices should be made by the private firm rather than by public authority" (Buell and De Luca 1996:59; Commoner 1992). For him, "substantial environmental improvement can occur only when the choice of production technology is open to social intervention" (1992:217; see also Gurr 1985). Sustainability necessitates more integrative approaches.

> "Whereas liberal democratic theory enables the "privatization of good" (to borrow Alasdair Macyntyre's formulation), green democratic theory seeks the politicization of the private good as well as the repoliticization of the public good" (Eckersley 2004:Loc. 1193-96 see also Leonard 2013:Loc. 5370-75).[322]

Recognising the interconnectedness, green political theory has to consequentially reformulate and reintroduce the good as inherently political.

While Dahrendorf honours early 20th century representatives of negative freedom, he concedingly develops the thesis that they are not resistance fighters (2006:150f.). Those valuing negative freedom as the highest good will not actively fight for freedom. At the end fascism was defeated, but what does it mean for liberalism, if its intellectual protagonists are not willing to defend it in practice? The reluctance with which green liberalism opposes discussing tradeoffs of different freedoms seems to mirror the unwillingness to get involved in actuality. Individualism as a rationale depoliticises issues while providing a specific definition of freedom that undermines the capability of people to search for freedom anywhere else than in individuality. Notably, it is simultaneously relativistic and therefore makes worldview and behaviour a matter

---

[321] Note that this argument could also be made for voting on the restriction of political freedoms.
[322] Wissenburg's green liberalism does not fit this call for a repolitisation of the good.

of personal choice.[323] The relatively dominant rational choice theory functions at the same time as it tries to explain behaviour as an ideology and is therefore self-reinforcing. If it declares self-interest as a natural form of behaviour, it at the same time legitimises it (see Heilbroner 1988:25ff.). Individualism fosters an egoistic outlook on the world. It allows for self-interest as a rational choice, if not the most central one.[324] It claims autonomy of this interest and denies interconnectedness as well as effects on others largely. Rational choice theory and its game theory variations are fundamentally individualistic, since their basis is the individual as a rational and self-interest maximising unit. Thus, policies are judged by the possible benefits for the individual and not society at large. The individual is then unwilling to pay a price he does not benefit from. Appealing to sustainability as self-interest does not suffice since the collective action problems would remain. Simmons, advocating public choice theory, tries to assess people's political behaviour analogous to their presupposed economic behaviour (2011). Voting in his interpretation is an irrational behaviour, but can be an expressive act similar to cheering in front of a television at a football match. Whereas a bad decision in a market is directly felt by the agent, a bad political decision is usually not. This does not only make ignorance rational. People may also be able to look for personal benefits while costs are externalised. Opportunity costs in politics are not easily recognised as real. According to public choice theory the state therefore is spending too much money, since the costs are not carried by the individual (Tullock and Buchanan 2001). Due to the multiplicity of government spending this kind of judgment is hard to evaluate. Most certainly efforts and spending for environmental sustainability are insufficient. While rational choice theory is reductionist the arguments about the opportunity costs in regard to the environment might be fruitful.

Framing in democratic politics encourages "voters to think of themselves as choosing between alternative objects of desire – better public services or lower personal taxation" (Graham 2013:Loc. 459-460). In particular, framing environmental policies in an individualist manner such as opportunity costs can have negative effects. Language is repeatedly used in a personalising fashion and therefore does not support, but rather undermines thinking for a greater good. Conditioning and priming is of high relevance regarding the range of behaviour between altruism and egoism. Experiments suggest that the choice of words can already influence responses in either direction, which means that the social environment is fundamental

---

[323] Dahrendorf contrasts Thomas More's bravery to the liberals' and describes him as loyal to the institutions. He hints that resistance is not rational (2006). Rational man may opt for the smaller evil for himself and therefore be potentially hindering for resistance.
[324] The "Kleines Wörterbuch der Marxistisch-Leninistischen Philosophie", for instance, regards the function of the "Ideology of Individualism" as "legitimation of exploitation, drive for profit and egoism" (Buhr and Kosing 1974:142; my translation).

(Hamilton 2010:156). Hence a context that encourages independence and individualism is likely to lead to less socially desirable behaviour. Environmental common goods will be negatively impacted. Studying such priming shows that it can even undermine cultural norms and

> "that they indicate that if the objective is to motivate people to act on climate change we should not be reinforcing their independent self-concept but seeking to remind them of and activate their cooperative, pro-social side" (Hamilton 2010:157).

The fostering of pro-environmental attitudes is likely to occur in rather cooperative settings, while individualism is counterproductive. Norms ultimately are a matter of habitus and highly dependent on the 'field' (Bourdieu 1977). Comparing ethical standards between private employees and employers to workers in a traditional type of firm in China, Lam and Shi find that unethical behaviour had higher acceptability among the former (and younger people in general) and therefore suggest that collectives "may cultivate altruistic spirits to a certain extent" (2008:476).[325]

Studies show that people are unlikely to voluntarily lower their living standards (see for example Cox 2013). Leading scholars believe that even deep psychological awareness of environmental destruction will not be sufficient for sacrificing one's high standard of living now (Marshall 2014:Loc. 968). Such dominance of self-interest means "prioritizing the things that affect us, here and now, and disregarding those that affect others" (2014:Loc. 985). Despite political discussions, many citizens favour policies on the basis of self-interest evaluations and not in regard to a common good (Roemer 1999:61). Since polled majorities in Great Britain and the US in the meantime do not assume that they will be affected themselves (Marshall 2014:Loc. 982), the focus on self-interest is not only an obstacle, but the major barrier to more sustainability. For many Americans, who think the government's main task is to protect self-interests of the citizens, actual steps towards environmental protection are understood to curtail personal freedom illegitimately (Hohensee 2013:Loc. 5004-10; see also Heintel 2011; Cox 2013). At the same time,

> "many democratic theorists think that standards of political legitimacy should not depend on citizens doing much more than looking out for their own interests in a pretty casual way, and they often think this precisely because they think that is how people are likely to act" (Estlund 2009:Loc. 223-24).

That means self-interest is taken as the norm within the system and political legitimacy must therefore be able to cope with input that could be purely a product of self-interested individuals.

---

[325] "When technologies, infrastructures, institutions and social norms reward self-enhancement and novelty, then selfish sensation-seeking behaviours prevail over more considered, altruistic ones. Where social structures favour altruism and tradition, self-transcending behaviours are rewarded and selfish behaviour may even be penalized" (Jackson 2012:Loc. 3007-9).

Shearman and Smith understand self-interest as a central driving force in democracies stating that "[d]emocracy has become the playground for self-interest and probably always was" (2007:75). The consequence for a potential for better environmental politics is calamitous if sustainability does not appear to be in the self-interest. Democracy in this case is seen as a system that 'aggregates' and does not question interests and therefore cannot lead to a common good.[326] Such a suspicion has been voiced from the beginning of the environmental movement. Thus, democracy "was the first defining trait of liberalism to be criticised in the 1970s" by those that became known as ecoauthoritarians, since "it would promote the expression of short-term individual (human) preferences, discouraging reflection on the formation and sensibility of those preferences" (Wissenburg 2006:21; Radcliffe 2002:25ff.; e.g. Ophuls 1977). By the logic that the state is there to satisfy individual needs, it cannot arrive at collective preferences. To believe otherwise is the same as believing in Smith's invisible hand. What is relevant is that the opportunity costs for the citizen are in fact (rather) unreal. The negative effects of environmentally bad behaviour are distributed among everybody. The environmental costs of driving an SUV therefore is minuscule for the agent, hence supporting a party that wishes to reduce the ecological footprint by measures such as engine size regulation or taxes would be irrational within a self-centred worldview. According to prominent green theorists

> "liberal democracies reveal a systematic bias against the protection of public environmental interests and in favor of certain private interests. In other words, the liberal democratic state (and the liberal culture that it both reflects and shapes) is not impartial in the way it prioritizes certain freedoms over others. The upshot is that the liberal democratic state can only guarantee formal rather than substantive freedom for all to determine their own conception of the good" (Eckersley 2004:Loc. 1211-139).

The liberal democratic state values these ideas of freedom and choice greatly. An ideology that says it is 'reasonable' to disagree with others, even if one's position causes significant environmental destruction, cannot be sustainable. While Eckersley values the liberal democratic state for its supposed freedom of self-determination in regard to a conception of the good, this includes the freedom to engage in destructive behaviour.

High-carbon lifestyles are viewed as legitimate as long as priorities do not change. Individualistic attitudes are likely to produce observable negative impacts on the environment. Accordingly, Randers writes pessimistically: "We will remain stuck too long in the ideal that individual rights have priority over the common good, a view that will be increasingly unhelpful in an ever more crowded world" (2012:Loc. 1002-3).[327] Wurster notes that democracy has a negative effect on

---

[326] "One's desire is a good reason for choosing in one's own personal sphere, but less compelling for choosing in other people's personal sphere or even in public spheres" (Sen 1993:23).
[327] Jacobs supposes that the dominance of individualism made consumption "the highest political good" (1997b:50).

CO2 emissions and energy consumption in general (2013). A consumerist lifestyle is likely to be causal. Restricting consumption can be understood as a direct interference and conflicting with a liberal interpretation of rights and choice.[328] Jacobs wrote in 1997 that the "[p]romotion of private wellbeing" is a "dominant feature of contemporary politics" (1997:59). In many countries this feature has only been further pronounced. Shearman and Smith judge similarly, saying that the

> "institution of liberal democracy fails to adequately address the challenges of the environmental crisis, and by giving an even greater license to greed and individual self-satisfaction, it is potentially a more environmentally destructive system than most other systems under which humans have lived" (2007:55).

Wissenburg concedes that "the set of admissible 'green' lifestyles excludes much of what liberalism allows, and vice versa, liberalism does not seem to offer a healthy environment for the flourishing of green lifestyles" (2004:64).[329] In many democratic countries affluence and comfort have become a norm that is not probable to be voluntarily sacrificed (Orr 2013:Loc. 6226-29). Accordingly, most green theorists judge it implausible that sustainability will be possible through the sum of individual actions. Buell and De Luca for example write: "Humans, left to their own devices, always want more" (1996:xi). More than 15 years ago Barry assumed that it could be possible that liberal democracy will have to handle overconsumption (2001:78). Today it should be clear that this is not tentative anymore, but that the overexploitation has become untenable. However, if democracy is understood as emancipatory and "directed towards the improvement of living standards and rights", it might be limitable to any kind of form that achieves sustainability (Blühdorn 2011:22ff.).

If autonomy of choice is taken as a central point for human flourishing, imposing limitations on energy usage for example can be interpreted as 'highly paternalistic'. Liberalism does not in fact avoid a moral discussion, but instead only mutes critical considerations. There are great differences between choice- and interest-based approaches to human rights. If dignity depends on choosing ends and means freely and rights therefore are understood to be located in the

---

[328] "Personal consumption has become a dominant, even a defining feature of contemporary society, and its promotion probably the single most important objective of modern politics, more or less unquestioned right across the political spectrum" (Jacobs 1997b:47).

[329] "Democracy provides the freedom of action, the liberalism, for each individual not only to fulfil all material needs but to accumulate unlimited wealth and the commercial power it confers – at least in principle" (Shearman and Smith 2007:11).

capacity for autonomy, environmental governance is impaired.[330] If valuable life is seen as dependent on freedom of choice, paternalism is rejected as undermining. Again, arguments centred on free choices by and large underestimate interconnectedness and therefore are blind to tradeoffs.[331] Whereas choice-centred approaches to human dignity cannot logically cope with mentally impaired human beings other than declaring them as lesser humans, interest-based approaches can. The question here is not whether collective cognitive dissonance counts as a mental impairment. This could be arguably the case as implicated in terms like 'fossil fuel addiction'.[332] Choice can be understood as procedural, while interest-protection overtly preludes content. If dignity, instead of being grounded in choice, means that someone has interests, it does not only allow for paternalism for the protection of interests, it also allows for animal rights.[333] To achieve sustainability within a choice-focused system environmentally responsible citizens are essential.

Still, environmental destruction feeds the assumption that people are not morally responsible beings.[334] It is widely believed that "to hold down mass consumption will need government force to back it up" (Heartfield 2009:46). Yet, political liberalism does not provide the justification for governments to do so. Consequentially environmentalists are sometimes disregarded as 'fascists' interfering into people's so defined 'private realm' (see Litfin 2010:118). Green politics are often judged as belonging to the private realm. Some scholars problematise this tendency.

> "Consumption and lifestyle choices are seen as belonging to the domain of the individual in which the state must, in principle, not be involved. For this reason, in a world with an ever more individualistic and materialist culture, society's support for restrictive consumption measures will not be impressive. In these circumstances the individual's freedom to act will generally be preferred in importance to an unpolluted environment" (de Geus 2004:Loc. 2595-98).

Eckersley criticises that the liberal democratic state places the environment and green living into the realm of private preferences and worldviews, which makes them private matters and places

---

[330] The fact that such choice-based ethics cannot incorporate people who are mentally impaired is important. Depending dignity on autonomy is controversial. Interesting along with this is the consistent vagueness of democratic theory on the question of minimum capabilities. Making autonomy a priority is problematic in particular since malnourishment has been shown to result in lesser mental faculties. If dignity depends on non-interference and choice, not only does that assign less dignity to mentally impaired people, but a consistent acknowledgement must recognize tradeoffs between rich and poor. The boundary has to be set somewhere as capability approaches for example recognize (e.g. Holland 2008).

[331] The choice to drive SUVs etc. is in conflict with sustainable living and therefore a direct interference in other's lives.

[332] The concept of individual self-determination is subject to many challenges. Listing them is beyond the scope of this chapter.

[333] While one might not think that animals have choices, most people agree that animals have interests.

[334] "At a very fundamental level, what is wrong with climate politics boils down to selfishness of governments, selfishness of politicians, selfishness of businesses, selfishness of special interests, and, at least among those of us who are affluent, selfishness of individuals" (Harris 2013:Loc. 53).Conjointly, Badiou describes how democracy leads to a hedonistic mentality in accordance with Plato (2012:19ff.). Plato foresees a total catastrophe resulting from the lack of discipline (1982). Whether one agrees with Plato's causation or not, the disastrous exploitation of natural resources is undeniable.

them outside the rights that get priority (Eckersley 2004:Loc. 1238-42; Meyer 2006:773f.). Evaluating the potential sustainability of democracy, Höffe states that politics has limited responsibility and should mainly create incentives, because it has to accept the autonomy of the citizen and his self-actualisation (2009:116). In that he explains politics cannot require three-litre cars or restrict reproduction. This leads to a strict dependency on individual choices. Consequentially this does not leave much room for effective politics.[335] Green consumerism and self-centred eco-friendly behaviour cannot logically transcend much further than the individual actually practicing it. Impacts depend on the interference in the practice of others. For example,

> "if someone really wants to work on reducing household waste, civic organizing to get a mandatory curbside recycling and composting program is a far more effective way to increase recycling and reduce waste than trying to maintain an eco-perfect household" (Leonard 2013:Loc. 5366-68).

Change has to occur on the societal level, but tendencies to locate drivers of change at the grassroots level are widespread. This could derive from choice-based interpretations of society and the ethical rejection of top-down impositions. When asked, almost 75% of German parliamentarians for example locate the responsibility for environmental and climate protection and societal change at the individual level (Alemann, Klewes and Rauh 2011:30; cf. Pepper 1996:29). This includes 48% of Green parliamentarians who understand the burden of change and innovation as individual responsibility (Alemann, Klewes and Rauh 2011:31). Contrarily, some scholars argue that the individual is not responsible for destructive practices. Hale writes: "Simply because oil consumers effectively endorse the consumption of oil does not commit those consumers to the acceptance of risks associated with extracting that oil" (2014:156). But lack of the ability to fully comprehend the costs that are connected with oil consumption cannot be used as an excuse. If it is an excuse then the consumer has to be also judged as incompetent to participate in governance. Information about oil extraction is easily accessible. If the individual is equipped with choice, responsibility inevitably follows. Car usage can be avoided. Costs might vary, but the recognition of the environmental and ethical costs of consumption is habitually avoided. Here, those who believe in choice and see the individual as responsible are consistent. Embracing responsibility and duty Singer is especially concerned with animal welfare. For him the case appears clear. "Consumers have an ethical responsibility to be aware of how their food is produced" (Singer 2013).

---

[335] "Some greens emphasize the ecological equivalent of 'clean hands' (personal actions, appropriate lifestyles and suchlike) at the expense of political action that might carry far greater ecological consequences. Those who do, though, are in effect giving considerations of agency priority over considerations of value and consequences. That, I think, is an error" (Goodin 2013:Loc. 2916-19; see Hobson 2013:61).

2.2.2.3. THE CONSUMER CHOOSES 'LOW COSTS'

Part of the problem enhanced by liberalism and the focus on the individual is acceptance of property as an innate right. Locke's liberalism declares property as a property of humanness. If property makes people human, it necessarily appears impeccable for the state. The freedom to 'belongings' correspondingly is a requirement. The freedom of the individual is time and again equated with the freedom of the market (Heintel 2011; Cox 2013). In *Sustainable Democracy. Individuality in The Politics of the Environment*, Buell and De Luca write that "[h]owever problematic excessive consumption is for the environment and for equity, consumerism remains a realm in which many citizen have carved out a space for some freedom" (1996:142). The statement places freedom within the realm of the market.[336] It fails to account for the costs of production. Neither environmental nor human costs are attributed to this 'freedom', though costs can be uncovered. The statement foremost masks dangerous assumptions about individual liberties behind a loose concept of freedom. Here it is hasty and misses that the carving out of one's freedom lying in consumption of material undoubtedly is carving somebody else's freedom. Consumer democracy signifies the idea of decision making with the pocket book. Its celebration shows its wide legitimacy and acceptance. Notwithstanding that so called 'consumer choices' are limited to those who have the means to actually consume (see Barth 1997 and Stretton 1976:174ff.). The division line in consequence not only runs between those with and without green values, but also between the have and have-nots. The dimension of social injustice is particularly overt if consumption is counted as a political act. Counting consumption as a political act shrinks the scope of government power. Eckersley correspondingly excoriates liberal democracy for depoliticising decisions about investment, production and consumption and making them essentially private as long as they have no clear victim (2004:Loc. 2920-26; see Schlosberg 2003). Hither, further social injustice is disguised, since leaving these issues a matter of individual choices detaches them from their cultural context. Not only do the marginalised have less (now openly counted as political) purchasing power, the costs of consumer choices are also easily transferred onto them. Tradeoffs between different groups' freedoms are easily overlooked.[337]

---

[336] "Without gifts, community is lost; without the individuality and anonymity of the market, freedom can be lost" (Litfin 2010:130).

[337] "The world's affluent consumers are essentially taking away the right of all people to a sustainable and livable environment. People have obligations based on their contributions to climate change (through their pollution), their responsibility for it (through their consumption choices and connections to those affected) and their capabilities (to act and to aid). Affluent individuals are not entitled to behave frivolously in ways that violate the fundamental rights of others, including people far away, to enjoy a stable climate" (Harris 2013:Loc. 1892).

Furthermore there are cultural drawbacks enhanced by the idea of consumer sovereignty. It implies not only that consumption is an act of freedom, it also makes restricting consumption from the political side less feasible (Meyer and Maniates 2010b:88). Calling consumption 'freedom' is a form of materialism that disables sustainable policies. De Geus formulates this contemporary dilemma clearly:

> "[C]itizens mainly assert their individuality by means of accumulating property, buying consumer goods and following their desires, without accepting limits to their freedom. According to this Lockean credo, liberalism is principally a defense of the individual's right to inequality in possessions, expanding property and human desires, rather than a defense of the purposes of society as a whole-for instance – a clean environment and nature conservation" (2001:29).

If freedom is to be found in the accumulation of material wealth, government restrictions on such consumption can be interpreted as a direct attack on one's individual rights and individuality. Furthermore, Jacobs warns against "the neo-liberal assumption that the consumer is a sovereign individual, making autonomous choices in the free market" (1997:50). Consumption is part of the social context and has become part of a person's identity as elaborated earlier.[338] About two decades ago, Jacobs already described the difficulties that radical greens, who see consumption as a moral matter, encounter when they ask individuals to consume less (Jacobs 1997:51). To cope with sustainability it is "surely useless to ask the individual to reduce their consumption voluntarily or to see as better off if they do not play the comparative game" (1997:51; Harris 2013:Loc. 1733). Similarly to the term 'relative deprivation', it makes sense to speak of 'relative abundance'. Relative deprivation is typically used to explain felt deprivation that is not caused by an absolute lack of resources, but by comparison. It describes a psychological mechanism. One effect of relative deprivation could be 'relative abundance'.[339] Though people may not be rich as an absolute, their lifestyles exceed the carrying capacity of ecosystems, hence the relationship is abundance. People may still feel relative deprivation while consuming abundantly. The promotion of these feeling is strengthened by liberalism as a discourse.

Scruton believes that it is "not uncommon to point to liberalism as the evil genius behind the ecological crisis" (2006:20). Such a position is evident in this paragraph by de Geus:

> "Western liberal democracies have always stressed that the freedom to consume keeps the capitalist economic system going and constitutes an inalienable right of the individual citizen: the freedom to consume can be seen as the basic expression of the Lockean creed of valuing 'life, liberty and the pursuit of happiness'. In this liberal ideology the role of the government is

---

[338] "Group pressure towards conformity" undermines ideas of autonomy and should not be underestimated (Hannigan 2006:140).
[339] Not to be confused with the term in biology.

certainly not to restrict consumer behaviour or to re-evaluate personal lifestyle choices in the light of sustainable development" (de Geus 2004:Loc. 2551-55).

Whereas the former discussion on cognition clearly shows that environmental destruction is a cultural problem, governments fail to recognise this as de Geus points out (2004:Loc. 2493-96; Hobson 2013:62). Humphrey locates the problem of environmental destruction not necessarily at the level of the political system, but at the values and choices (2006:314). Delinking a political system from value and choice is problematic in itself. A political system that encourages individualism is less likely to have a green outcome than a system that is orientated towards a common or collective. The individual is in a way freed of responsibility towards the common good and hence the environment and can concentrate on pure self-actualisation (Blühdorn 2011). Here, Eckersley sees the strength of critical ecology in contrast to liberal democracy, since "[t]he function of liberal democratic politics is to mediate and contain the struggle among self-interested players to pursue their private interests" (2004:1205). In case of a consumer democracy buying green suffices.

The priority of convenience for the individual is mispriced as touched upon earlier. Comfort and convenience are momentous for ecocide (Hadler and Haller 2011; Mayr 2009:100). While lack of knowledge plays a role, informing people does not "ordinarily produce rapid changes in institutional or individual behaviour" (Ehrlich and Ehrlich 2014; Barr 2006). The low cost thesis developed by Diekmann and Preisendörfer points at the dilemma that self-centred behaviour poses to the environment. It states that people act eco-friendly only if the costs are low. Recycling and waste avoidance for example are often a matter of convenience (Barr 2006). People will not sacrifice comfort, despite better knowledge. Consequently, one can find many practices which are overtly hypocritical. Awareness of personal inconsistencies is not only avoided, but also not criticised by others. Inaction about climate change is the norm. The fact that everyday life is seen as a matter of personal choice supports this hypocrisy.[340]

Kingsnorth points out that "[t]he challenge today is to keep that original deep green version against shallow green who make it look idealistic, naïve, misanthropic or simply old fashioned" (2009:39; Dryzek 2005:47). Yet the chances for such a challenge could be bleak. Scholars like Wissenburg disregard such original deep version. Even more, he implies that the vision is contrary to human nature:

"Issues relating to the ideals of the deeper, ecological version of environmentalism require a change of heart that seems too fundamental to be communicable, not to mention ill-suited to

---

[340] "To support a radical politics is, for many, more a lifestyle choice in keeping with a consumer identity than a risky personal transformation" (Martin 2009:120).

be translated into political action (i.e., policy). It involves [...] one or more of the following elements: a rejection of progress as a goal; a modest lifestyle; controlling the instinct for self-protection and survival expressed in 'gathering' goods; 'intrinsically' or impersonally valuing nature where we cannot shed a tear about a million Tutsis viciously slaughtered, and so forth" (Wissenburg 2004:65).[341]

Thus sustainability as a social fact would appear implausible to Wissenburg.[342] Here, the distinction between citizen and consumer might be useful as the individual is said to have two preferences (Dryzek 2005:113). Green voters are often green consumers but not necessarily green citizens as defined in a deep sense. Contemporary greens are sometimes identified as 'bourgeois'.[343] Green consumerism, despite being fashionable and therefore appearing pervasive, is not a widespread phenomenon (Carter 2007:232). In fact, green consumerism tends to build on a highly individualistic culture and a high-end lifestyle that is not marked by modesty and not available to a majority. These greens consume green goods but are unlikely to have a low ecological footprint.[344] They vote for green parties, but their demands, as discussed by Humphrey, are merely abstract. "People are prepared to hold strong views on environmental matters for as long as those views are costless" (Humphrey 2009:160; Smith 2004). Just as rational choice theory judges the information costs too high for the general population, other eco-friendly behaviour in general comes with higher costs than most people are willing to accept (Diekmann and Preisendörfer 2001:71ff.). This is exemplified in the common notion that taking public transportation instead of using a private car appears too inconvenient.

Again, there is a value-action gap as discussed earlier in this chapter.[345] Despite better knowledge people are unwilling to sacrifice their personal interests for a greater good, even when the sacrifice does not appear as major from an external point of view. Cognition makes it possible to avoid understanding the real costs and feeling the costs of environmentally sound behaviour as higher. Individualism socially sanctifies it as choice. Consciousness is much less important in

---

[341] Blühdorn judges that ecologists' reliance on the individual had to fail, "also because increasingly complex life-world contexts make ever more excessive demands on individuals, and render the belief in an ecological morality ever more unsuitable" (2012:162).

[342] It should be noted that this statement explicitly refers to a human nature. This statement is hardly compatible with the green liberalism laid out earlier.

[343] Some socialist theorists may rightfully criticize greens as 'petit bourgeoisie' (as well as theoretically naïve) (Carter 2013:199). The difficulty of green consumerism has already been pointed out two decades ago (for example. McLaughlin 1995:274). McLaughlin writes that greens should never built alliances with the wealthy, because of capitalism's inherently distractive relationship to nature.

[344] "The sustainable consumption movement capitalizes (often literally) on consumerism to promote environmental sustainability, although in the process it may not prevent unnecessary consumption" (Harris 2013:Loc. 2999).

[345] "As far as environmental knowledge and literacy is concerned, the populations of contemporary liberal democracies are perhaps the most environmentally aware, with public opinion indicating a large degree of sympathy towards environmental issues. But we have to recognise that the relationship between existence of this sympathy and actual policy making is not simple" (Connelly et al. 2012:150). Many green theorists enthusiastically assumed not only spreading of environmental values, but also overestimated their impact on actual politics. For a discussion about Eckersley see Meyer (2006:776f.).

environmental behaviour although it is more controversially debated than the simple fact that a greener action is perceived as less convenient (Diekmann and Preisendörfer 2001; see also Stadelmann-Steffen 2011:501). Occasionally people make small changes in their life and free their conscience. But many practices need to be classified as indulgence. While any step is a step, given a consumerist lifestyle small changes are insufficient. Worsening the negative impact, these indulgences often free the individual of the feeling of guilt and encourage wasteful behaviour in other areas.[346] They follow green values when it does not mean sacrifices in their personal lives. They recycle, might drive smaller cars, but they are equally and often more involved in high carbon activities such as exotic family vacations. Green voters claim to understand the necessity of limitations, yet their cooperation is restricted to small acts (Muno 2010:354). The green citizen has a sticker with a pro-environmental message on his car (see Dryzek 2005:113). Moreover, today mere watching can be perceived as active participation (Leggewie and Welzer 2011:147). So called 'clicktivism' is symbolic for this phenomenon. The individual shows its support by clicking the 'like button' or even sharing the message, but he does not cooperate on a larger scale, when it comes to paying higher costs. Micheletti, Stolle and Berlin describe political consumerism as seemingly gaining importance with "buycotting" being more important than boycotting (2014:213). However, they underline the gap between proclaimed political consumerism and actual consumption exemplified in the generally low amount of fair trade coffee purchases (2014:214ff.).[347] In fact it looks like "the actual percentage of people claiming to participate in political consumerism is far higher than the actual market share" (2014:216; see also TransFair e.V. 2015). Generally, the 'green citizen' might even be involved in environmental protest, but he does not avoid the plastic lid for his coffee. In a sense, most people who identify as 'green' are low cost greens.

> "Where relatively inexpensive fix is not possible and solutions may require major behavioural change and/or social or economic restructuring, political will and public interest begins to wane. At this point there may be acceptance of a simple amelioration of effects, or symbolic action, rather than the elimination of causes" (Connelly et al. 2012:150).

The low cost problem is even a global one and it is a major obstacle in climate negotiations and the discussion about common but differentiated responsibility. A majority of citizens globally are in support of climate change mitigation on the national as well as international level "as long as these initiatives do not demand a significant alteration of lifestyle" (Giddens 2009:101). People do not engage and fight for reforms that they theoretically say that they wish (Leggewie and Welzer 2013). The low cost thesis hints at the fact that green behaviour should be a matter of

---

[346] Public choice theory understands engagement in environmentalism as indulgence (Mayr 2009:93).
[347] Coffee can be indicative for general consumption since it is a widespread good with high availability of fair trade and organic options. Fair-trade coffee generally enjoys a symbolic status; percentages therefore should be seen as the upper benchmark.

morality and not price. It points at the barrier to collective action. For collective action problems "often it seems, paradoxically, that cooperation is least likely where those involved stand to lose most" (Connelly et al. 2012:143). Shearman and Smith warn that the democratic will influenced by individualism typically "treats the environment as a resource" (2007:82). The environment as a resource stands in competition with other resources.

While denying that sustainability will be achieved on the individual level, Jacobs believed that nonetheless the democratic public will come to terms with scarcity. He states that "environmentally sustainable consumption will not come about through individual choices, but through regulatory policies collectively decided and imposed by the state" (Jacobs 1997:51). The low cost thesis shows that even with fertile grounds for sustainability i.e. the existence of green consciousness actual sustainability is improbable.[348] Chances of sustainable democracy depend on green citizens, yet not even green voters show such traits.

2.2.3. ECONOMIC 'SOLUTIONS' TO ENVIRONMENTAL PROBLEMS

Given the centrality of the market advanced by green liberalism the suitability of economic 'solutions' has to be discussed more comprehensively. Though widely propagated as a solution to scarcity and physical limitedness of the world, market mechanisms have not managed to show to lead to sustainability in any meaningful sense. 'Green capitalism' would need a drastic transformation, in which goods and services become emission-neutral. For many ecologists it is hard to imagine a free market inciting such transformation (Westra 1998:198f.).[349] The accumulation of capital and the aim of unlimited growth contradict a philosophy of modesty that is necessary to remain within planetary boundaries (see More 1998).[350] The critique of money and wealth as a driving force in politics has a long tradition. Lane points at Socrates problematising the love for money and comments that today "love of money is rooted in and reinforced by the general way in which current financial and economic models operate" (Lane 2011b:120; see Plato 1982). Prominently, the term 'sustainable' capitalism can be presented as

---

[348] Whereas some problems can be solved by individuals "[c]limate change is a collective problem that demands collective solutions. In other words, it needs good, strong policies enforced by governments" (Hamilton 2010:80).

[349] On the contrary, the introduction of (initially) cheap biotech agriculture for example can lead to its spread within an unregulated market.

[350] "If consumption stimulated greater productivity, then greed was not only permissible but even (albeit with concern) enjoined. *Pleonexia* [≈greed] went from being viewed as a signal vice, to a tolerated evil, to an accepted and sometimes even celebrated pathway from individual to social good – and now, with the erosion of any notion of voluntary moderation, it has come full circle to become a threat to social stability, health, and indeed sustainability once again. The complexity of our political world today is that, while religious fanaticism remains a threat, we can no longer afford to indulge in greed as the lesser evil. To recover the language in which to explain greed as a vice, and articulate the social context of self-discipline as a virtue, it is natural to begin by exploring their original contours in the ancient Greek political imagination" (Lane 2011b:40). In contrast to Lane, who writes that greed is accepted as lesser evil in society, Singer says about capitalism that it leads to an understanding "of acquisition for its own sake as an *ethically sanctioned* way of life" (1994:66; my emphasis). Either way capitalism then is a clear obstacle to moderation.

an oxymoron (Harvey 2014, cf. Jackson and Victor 2015).[351] Sustainable growth as well as sustainable development may have to be equally judged as useless concepts given the fact that the current economic activities already exhaust more than the planet's natural capacity and so called 'absolute decoupling', i.e. complete decoupling of GDP and CO2, has not been achieved anywhere.[352] Economic growth and sustainability are in contradiction. Economic circles cannot expand indefinitely and much of the destruction is caused by the attempt to monetise the global natural resources, on which life on Earth depends. Yet, "[t]he liberal democratic free enterprise society that Fukuyama proposes as the ultimate outcome of all history is built on the idea that we can keep doing this forever" (Singer 1994:16). Nevertheless, free market environmentalism remains popular, in particular for economists and politicians. This subchapter will discuss the various dimensions and attempts in which the projects of green growth and proposed market mechanisms to sustainability have failed and are doomed to fail in the future.[353] It will show that, although progress has been made, the inherent logic of capitalism makes sustainability unattainable and even serves as a counterforce (Eckersley 2004, Shearman and Smith 2007; Carter 2013).

The economy, which to a great extent as a concept is a product of capitalism, regularly gets priority over sustainability (e.g. Connelly et al. 2012:151).[354] Lukes' third face of power gives an explanation why it is so difficult to promote radical accounts of a sustainable life (see Lukes 1998). Sustainability is in competition with "a societal 'consensus around the value of a market economy", which is the reason for the popularity of ecological modernisation (Connelly et al. 2012:159; see also Heilbroner 1988). Economics take a leading role in the construction of

---

[351] Here, a Marxist point of view suggests that "[t]he greater the destructive effects of the free market on nature, the more obvious the need for its antithesis (i.e., prevention, regulation, and planning)" (Gimenez 2000:302).

[352] "Urgently needed are demonstrably workable models of development that are both environmentally benign and relatively equitable, in terms of their distribution of costs and rewards even within generations" (Schrecker 1998:229). There is a huge gap between theory and practice. Connelly et al. warn that economic instruments need to be tested in practice (2012:200).

[353] "The strength of the economistic models is that they disaggregate complexity and point to a few, simple, determined connections between variables that can be manipulated: i.e. they provide a recipe for what can be done, as well as forceful, dynamic models that are intellectually satisfying. The drawback is that such models decouple that which they depict from all other contexts, and thereby leave out numerous cultural factors and human factors, and vital prerequisites and consequences" (Barth 1997:241).

[354] The dependency on the economy for state revenue often leads to this focus (Carter 2013:206ff.). Leggewie and Welzer point at a truism, which people easily forget when prioritizing the economy especially during a financial crisis: A bank can start functioning again somehow, the sea level cannot be dropped (2009:19). Young partially self-contradicting writes that "[e]conomic growth that ignores impacts on the environment is no longer acceptable. Environmental protection that is insensitive to the social and cultural concerns of those living on the land is not adequate. Hanging on to social or cultural practices in ways that sacrifice the environment or result in economic stagnation is a recipe for failure. Accordingly, political leaders now strive to organize societies in ways that lead simultaneously to economic, social, and environmental progress. But this is a tall order. It is always hard to maximize with respect to two or more evaluative dimensions; a challenge intensified by the lack of a common metric for evaluating tradeoffs between or among them" (2009:19). For instance, hanging on sharing practices would be good for the environment, but successfully propagating them could lead to stagnation in GDP terms.

popular culture, cognition and government decision making.[355] The 2008/2009 economic crisis for example was followed by many governments implementing special polices to set their economies 'back on track'. Instead of enacting policies that benefit the environment, policies typically were rather destructive. Examples can be found in the stimulus packages of countries like France and Germany, where the governments even subsidized new car ownership (Lekakis and Kousis 2013). In situations of economic crisis, states repeatedly privatize public goods and transfer power to the free market and corporations. This has serious consequences. Property relations matter. Here, public and private sphere, if ever separable in the past overlap clearly. Neoliberalism, despite reiteration of the line in theory, has practically blurred the boundaries of economy and politics even further (Crouch 2008).[356] At many instances it is not possible to neatly separate politics and economics. Central decisions can be in the hands of 'non-political' actors having other interests than the common good, which has historically led to environmental destruction. Commoner concludes:

> "The current environmental crisis is the unanticipated outcome of the ways in which corporations that are entrusted with these decisions have chosen to provide us with transportation, food, and power" (1992:ix).

He attributes the core of the problem to the economic system where he also locates part of the solution while others more pessimistically include democracy.

Importantly, if one answers the question whether democracy can exist without capitalism negatively, this alone is likely to undermine the idea of sustainable democracy.[357] Though political science still debates the prospects of democracy without capitalism, it is important to note, that in practice democracy without capitalism cannot be found. De Geus understands liberal democracy and the market economy as Siamese twins who are hard to separate (2001). Dahl also approaches the question whether democracy needs a different economic system (326ff.). A decentralised system of market socialism, according to him, would be consistent with democracy. One might imagine a democratic society without free markets as an abstract, yet it is hard to imagine it in the concrete. This is additionally problematic since capitalism and its

---

[355] Referring to the impact of the famous Stern Review Jackson writes: "It's telling that it took an economist commissioned by a government treasury to alert the world to things climate scientists – most notably the Intergovernmental Panel on Climate Change (IPCC) – had been saying for years. This is partly a testament to the power of economists" (2012:Loc. 519-21).

[356] Such a differentiation in regard to nature is neither possible nor desirable, since it is overly reductionist. It can be argued that a division into two distinct spheres is not only an illusion, but always has been an illusion (e.g. Mitchell 2011). A broad understanding of economy sees it as the social process of the provision and distribution of human beings with goods in the interplay of overall context. Limited resources are utilised for the satisfaction of competing needs (Firth 2012). In contrast to classical economics, Polanyi prominently centralises the institutional embeddedness of production, distribution and consumption (1977; see also Heilbroner 1988).

[357] Shearman and Smith think that "even if liberal capitalism ceased to exist there would still be the potential for an environmental crisis because of the destructive tendencies within the heart of democracy itself" (2007:4).

economic freedoms regularly undermine democracy and its political freedoms. Though political and economic freedoms are in tension and economic inequality causes political inequality, it is hard to imagine one without the other. Most crucially, to talk about democracy without considering economic power is void (Latouche 2005). Economic power is of considerable importance in democratic systems.[358] Some see citizens' involvement in politics as insignificant in comparison to companies in today's democracies, where "[v]oters do little, even, to set political agendas" (Shapiro and Hacker-Cordon 1999a:3). As demonstrated by Gilens and Page, economic power plays a central role in political decision making (2014). Environmental politics are no exception to this. The often evoked agreement on chlorofluorocarbons (CFCs) is, as an example of global environmental action and political negotiations, in fact further proof (Dryzek 2005; Davis 2007). The (late) breakthrough was only achieved when industry had cheap substitutes. Similar to the reduction of lead, rather than successful deliberation the cause was economical. In both cases gains for the environment did not come through politics, but through the market. Politics were subordinated to economic rationality. Hence, it could be argued that free market solved the problem. Yet, improvements for the environment were side effects of developments of the market rather than incentive for it. The economic growth in many democracies might be a consequence of the free market economy and property rights and not democracy itself, while the fact that only autocracies manage enormous GDP growth over time suggests that democracy may hinder growth (Petersen 2009:34ff.; see also Dahl 1989:229 and Dahl 2000:58).[359] In his historical description, Mitchell attributes many democratic movements to carbon as concentrated power (2011). Variations in dependency on the free flow of energy enabled or disabled successful opposition to nondemocratic rule. The connection between fossil fuels as a concentrated energy and economic prosperity is self-evident. If Mitchell is right, carbon has enabled exponential economic growth, while simultaneously allowing democratic movements, because of the dependency of this growth on carbon.[360] This is in accord with the findings that democracy is more often a consequence of economic growth than vice versa (e.g. Kurtz and Schrank 2007).

Wissenburg highlights that the free market is an inseparable part of liberalism (2001b:39). He openly admits that greening it depends on the preferences of the consumers and producers.

---

[358] It is remarkable that while democracies do not allow for political power to be inherited, they do allow economic power to stay in the same family. The fact that economic power is inherited but political is not, should make one sceptical about the former and both. In many cases economic power has shown to be easily translated into political power and vice versa.

[359] This does not mean that wealth is equally distributed.

[360] The democratisation could be interpreted as a democratisation by chance. The dependency on coal meant that workers could successfully block its circulation and therefore use (the threat of) standstill as bargaining power (controlling means of production).

While he also argues that preference formation should be a realm of non-interference in theory, he acknowledges that this is problematic in practice. Non-interference in practice can have negative consequences.[361] Free trade agreements may put pressure on environmental protection by prohibiting governments to interfere. Public choice theory assumes that market failures are determined to happen in politics as well. But this would only be the case if politics follows the same logic as the market. In the case of the market, the systematic lack of sustainability may be the biggest market failure yet to fully materialise. Capitalism tends to undermine itself in the long run.

> "Examples of capitalist accumulation impairing or destroying capital's own conditions hence threatening its own profits and capacity to produce and accumulate more capital are well-known. The warming of the atmosphere will inevitably destroy people, places, and profits, not to speak of other species life. Acid rain destroys forests and lakes and buildings and profits alike" (O'Connor 1988:22).[362]

It is commonplace to counter arguments about limits to growth with the outcome of the famous bet between Simon and Ehrlich.[363] Jackson criticises measuring scarcity with the help of commodity prices, which he declares to be "just too volatile to offer reliable information" (2012:Loc.499; Buell and De Luca 1999:50).[364] The fact that many resources have become cheaper in the last 40 years is often taken as a proof for (ecological) modernisation theory and as a counterargument against limits to growth. Withal, scarcity by itself has no meaning. It is a product of human action (Helfrich 2011:139; see also Buell and De Luca 1996). In comparison to other disciplines the object of economics, economies react to the opinion of experts. If they think the stock is good, the price actually goes up. The 'facts' generated by the market appear to be independent and objective (Hausknost 2011:129).

---

[361] Government interference is essential since "that we can count on spontaneous processes to solve problems of governance of the sort we face today is just as far-fetched as the idea that we can count on the invisible hand to solve problems of economic coordination. Not only are difficulties arising from ignorance and high transaction costs likely to prevent progress in this realm, but also any such hopes would run full-tilt into a massive free-rider problem" (Young 2009:20). Notably, "people in liberalized market economies tend to have higher per capita carbon emissions, higher infant mortality, higher teenage pregnancies and a greater percentage of people reporting that they 'feel like an outsider' (Jackson 2012:Loc. 3041-43).

[362] "As early as the 1970s, neo-Marxist theorists drew attention to the "fiscal crisis" of the welfare state stemming from the state's contradictory imperatives to facilitate capital accumulation, on the one hand, and to iron out the harmful social and ecological consequences of capital accumulation by providing an expanding menu of protective welfare (and environmental) services, on the other hand. Now, in the new millennium, the growing intensity of economic regionalization and globalization is making it increasingly difficult for governments to solve a range of social and ecological problems within their territory and beyond" (Eckersley 2004:Loc. 684-87).

[363] The scholars famously bet on the prices of commodities in the future, since a higher price is interpreted as a sign of scarcity. Ehrlich lost. Despite his strong language he misjudged the 'progressiveness' of the capacity to exploit.

[364] Prices for fish for example often rise after resources are nearly depleted (Carter 2013:31). "The ideological view that the market is the best way for people to maximise aggregate public utility depends crucially on the adequacy of market prices as an index of utility. But this belief may represent the deepest level of mystification produced by our economic institutions" (Barth 1997:238). It needs to be remarked that despite the term 'renewable resource' renewable resources like water or soil are not unlimited.

Most crucially, environmental friendliness simply appears to be irrational within its logic unless it pays. A significant percentage of consumption is luxury consumption way beyond necessity. The industry sells "consumers things they didn't realize they wanted, creating the demand as well as creating the product" (Lawlor 2014:408).[365] Hamilton contrasts that whereas those who believe in the freedom of the market talk about free choice the marketing industry openly admits that they use people's insecurities (2008). Advocates of green consumerism and liberalism are mostly silent on this matter. Lawlor believes that it might be possible to encourage people to buy less and to bring people to make ethical choices in general (2014:415). However, Shearman and Smith conclude using Brazil as an example that while liberal democratic governments allow for opposition, "democracy allows for greater economic freedom that leads to deforestation", hence is unable to protect public goods (2007:70).[366] As mentioned earlier, barriers to sustainability are cognitive frameworks that connect freedom with consumption as symptomised in terms like 'consumer sovereignty'.[367] Advocating market mechanisms and consumer sovereignty are intimately connected. Additional to the social justice aspect and the fact that it makes reductions look like sacrifices, it indeed gives the consumer the false impression of agency according to Princen (2010:145ff.). He understands it as a myth that shifts responsibility "absolving those who truly have market power and who write the rules of the game and who benefit the most" (2010:146). Framing in the market place is meant to increase, not decrease consumption. Even environmentally conscious consumers for example buy a new phone every two years, since it is made to appear obsolete (see Lawlor 2014:418). While inventive capitalists introduced planned obsolescence, the opposite should be reinforced. Products should be made to last. Self-evidently products that do not need replacement, lead to lower demand. This is unlikely to be in the interest of companies whose businesses are built on sales. Thus, if the economic system builds on more consumption as a main driver, it does not respect limits that lie outside its 'belief system'. Accordingly, De-Shalit accentuates that some scholars believe that the market is "the best and most efficient mechanism to ruin the entire universe" (2001:392).

2.2.3.1. THE GROWTH IDEOLOGY AND ECOLOGICAL MODERNISATION THEORY

Dominant political ideologies take a necessity for growth for granted. This might "render most political theories of the past and the present quite irrelevant as they currently stand" (Carter 2013:23). The economic growth 'obsession' has been unsuccessfully questioned by

---

[365] Many goods derive their value from the status that they provide (Paech 2012:5). Goods merely serve the function of improving the owner's societal standing.

[366] Crouch highlights that if the citizens trust that cooperation but not politics can solve problems, governments lose control (2008:138f.).

[367] "Citizenship is expressed when the sovereign buys according to belief, to values, and not just to price (e.g., a fuel-efficient car, sweatshop-free shoes, or eco-friendly cleansers)" (Princen 2010:152).

environmentalists for decades (Singer 1994:57).[368] The growth narrative remains powerful and is a main obstacle to sustainable visions.

> "The trouble is, economic growth is a belief system and set of practices that aims to achieve— every day—ever more goods and services, forever. [...] Green growth like many other environmental initiatives in our struggle towards reining in the human endeavour, still falls under the umbrella of growth" (Martin 2015).

Economic growth has become not only an overarching aim of governments. Presented as a necessity it is seen as a gauge of governance. Economic growth is commonly taken as the single most important factor for a country's success. Interest rates as the orientation for judging something as economical mean that an investment needs to earn interests and profits (Kennedy 2012; see also Jackson 2012). Hence, it is commonly – and maybe falsely – argued that a capitalist economy necessarily has to achieve exponential growth (Jackson and Victor 2015).

While growth is fetishised, it is seen as synonymous of not only economic progress, but social progress as well.[369] Growth and a high GDP appear to have 'sacred powers' for which lesser goods can be sacrificed (Hamilton 2010:64; Princen 2010). Growth is an ideology so deeply ingrained in contemporary societies that questioning it is not only rare, but appears irrational.[370]

> "Economic growth has become a staple of our individual and collective experience. To the degree that sacrifice calls for rejecting material prosperity, it is out of sync with the momentum of contemporary society and its values" (Wapner 2010:34).

Thereafter success is measured as annual GDP increase. Economic decline, on the other hand, becomes a spectre that captures the population's fear. Looking at the European Union it is "likely that countries with high GDP per capita may be less willing to adopt significant changes to the status quo because of uncertain outcomes" (Madden 2014:581). At the same time, poverty and

---

[368] Prominently, ecological modernists are inherently optimistic. Limits "have all been overcome by the exercise of human ingenuity just as the doom was being prophesied with the deployment of steam engines to greatly improve agricultural efficiency, and the discoveries of oil and of fracking oil and gas, respectively, for the three examples given. It is incumbent on those who would continue to predict gloom to learn from history and make a comprehensive review of human progress before coming to their conclusions" (Kelly 2013:1; cf. Gorz 1980:24ff.). Using such a strong language, Kelly overtly ignores the well-known pollution problems of fossil fuel industry. For instance, fracking not only tends to pollute groundwater, it can also lead to earthquakes with increased frequency (McGarr 2016). Calling such invention "ingenuity" is euphemistic.

[369] "The idea of progress implies that something more or better is created; and if so, there can be no moral basis on which to dismiss the requirement that those whose lives have been shattered by induced changes should be the first to receive shares from that 'progress dividend'" (Barth 1997:242). It might be helpful to define "progress in terms of working hours" (Hamilton 2010:87f.). Not more material abundance, but fairer distribution and more time freed for leisure could be a benchmark for a greener definition of progress.

[370] Gorz writes in 1980: "All production is also destruction. This fact can be overlooked as long as production does not irreversibly deplete natural resources" (1980:20). Today some forms of production may cause minimal destruction. Software is a good example of such a good, however even the production of software is dependent on hardware and therefore resource destruction. Put differently: "Our economy is like a giant happiness machine. Dredgelike, it sucks in resources at the front end and spews out wastes at the back, all the while leaking emissions into air, water, and soil. Natural resource industries and agriculture lie at the front end and waste disposal at the back. An outside view of the economy looks at these operations and their leakage and concludes that the economic dredge is a generator of harmful global changes, unsustainable in its operations and progressively destructive of ecological integrity" (Miller and Rees 2013:Loc. 323).

generally unstable economic situations equally hinder sustainability by making the accommodation of businesses a priority (Buell and De Luca 1996:73). Special economic zones can be introduced to attract industry, besides tax cuts, fewer labour and environmental regulations are regularly part of the offer. Spending money on the military industrial complex increases the GDP, while in the meantime being an extremely polluting business sector. If the enlargement of military can count as societal progress is questionable. Independent of the answer, the impact for the environment is negative.

Beyond the often presented problems of GDP as a measurement of societal progress lie particular ones for the environment. The planet is finite. Jackson points at this problem stating that "[e]conomists have to be able to answer the question of how a continually growing economic system can fit within a finite ecological system" (2012:Loc. 570-71; see also Arrow et al. 2004). Advocates of degrowth find support in the simple statement that infinite growth within a finite system is impossible. They believe in a revision of economical paradigms.

> "Any consumption that is based on the depletion of natural capital should not be counted as income. Prevailing models of economic analysis tend to treat consumption of natural capital as income, and therefore tend to promote patterns of economic activity that are unsustainable" (Goodland and Daly 1996:1005).

Many models do not differentiate between quantitative and qualitative growth. As a matter of fact GDP counts all economic activity indiscriminately. The costs of degradation further economic growth. Jackson explains that

> "all kinds of things are included in the GDP – the costs of congestion, oil spills and clearing up after car accidents, for example – which don't really contribute additionally to human well-being [and that] to count both sets of activities as contributing meaningfully to economic welfare seems perverse" (2012:Loc. 2356-62).

Capitalism manages to profit from environmental destruction while it is a major driving force. Not only is a large part of the accumulation of capital produced with the exploitation of natural resources, large sums are also made by the mitigation of this destruction. For instance, the treatment of new, revived and expatiated diseases could mean increased profits for the pharmaceutical industry. In an ironical fashion environmental pollution can positively affect the GDP, whence even 'been taken' as societal progress, while impairing human capabilities. Controversial figures like Lomborg maintain that the benefits of economic growth outweigh the costs in the future and that it is in fact better in monetary terms (lomborg.com; Humphrey 2007:Loc. 3213). Jackson and other economists, as presented in the Stern Review, instead point at the marginal costs of environmental protection today in comparison to the future (Jackson 2012; Stern et al. 2006; Hamilton 2010). Different ways to discount the future as well as other uncertainties are subject to prolonged debates. Meanwhile the "logic of capital accumulation is rarely challenged" (Connelly et al. 2012:280). Most debates remain within the discourse of conventional economics and largely ignore ethical dimensions (see Spash 1998). While it becomes clearer that Earth is defined by finite resources, the growth ideology seems to boldly ignore this fact unless gains for the economy can be made by invoking scarcity. Here, a whole green industry means that "sustaining and nurturing apocalyptic imaginaries is an integral and vital part of the new cultural politics of capitalism" (Swyngedeouw 2011:69).

Most popular among those who believe in greening industries and green growth is the ecological modernisation theory. Carter describes ecological modernisation as "[a] policy strategy which aims to restructure capitalist political economy along more environmentally benign lines based on the assumption that economic growth and environmental protection can be reconciled" (2007:xix). Ecological modernisation theory suggests that economical including technological development is a condition for better environmental management (e.g. Asafu-Adjaye et al. 2015).[371] Ecological modernists assume that once economies have grown, resources and knowhow for sustainability can be easily developed and measures to protect the environment will be introduced. These developments are said to simultaneously increase international competitiveness. Decoupling is central to ecological modernisation (Eckersley 2004:Loc. 904-5). An uncritical look at local emissions in 'advanced' democracies presents a rosy picture as Monbiot points out (2013). Yet, ecological modernisation theory has been largely proven invalid (e.g. Caradonna et al. 2015). The assumption that once a certain level of wealth is achieved, emission levels will plummet is based on false premises.[372] More development does not lead to less pollution. In fact, the relation between income and pollution is more linear than expected (Lane 2011a; Seidl and Zahrnt 2012:10f.; Knill, Shikano and Tosun 2014:66ff.). Rich and stable democracies have the means to "privilege the environment at the expense of economic growth without putting the regime at risk (although governments might pay an electoral price)" (Burnell 2009:12). Despite the favourable conditions, reality shows that countries like Australia, Canada, Japan and the US as well as Western European countries have huge ecological footprints instead. Additionally, increasing levels of income do not lead to more regulations.

---

[371] Höffe writes that it is more important to improve education, since improvement of financial conditions could lead to more consumption and weaken the interest in the common good (2009:84). As typical for democracy advocates Dahl assumes that democracy fosters knowledge (2000:59). However as mentioned earlier, knowledge is insufficient.
[372] Some environmentally friendly behaviour is a result of scarce resources/household means. People may not have the monetary means to have a huge footprint.

Despite the empirical evidence that ecological modernisation is a misnomer the theory remains particularly popular among policy makers.[373] The concept "offers ecological soundness and economic success, a win-win scenario that avoids having to make impossible demands of voters; it offers a democracy-friendly way of being green" and most importantly it

> "holds out some prospect that democratic processes and ecological outcomes can be brought together, as self interested citizens in liberal democracies become convinced that 'green growth' is good for them; it does not require large scale value change, nor the imposition of hair-shirt environmentalism" (Humphrey 2007:Loc. 2140-2156).

It appeals because it does not necessitate actual change and in most cases legitimises further economic growth. Ehrlich and Ehrlich comment that politicians "think the disease is the cure" (2014; Ehrlich and Ehrlich 1990:162; see also Eckersley 2004; Hausknost 2014).[374] Admittedly, some sustainable technologies need significant investments and this means that governments must have the means to assign proper funding etc.[375] However, ecological modernisation theory has to also quietly presuppose "the political will to effectively institutionalise these principles and instruments" (Connelly et al. 2012:201). The development of new technologies is expensive. The price of advanced technology could be used as an objection to ecological modernisation theory. Maintaining lower consumption and not growing, only to then cut back appears to be more prudent. Instead of developing new techniques, cutting back on overall consumption is cheaper. There is an additional bias within ecological modernisation theory. Studies tend to focus on "cutting edge businesses and best practices" and ecological modernisation theorists overestimate the force of greener production (Hannigan 2006:28).[376] In the best case scenario, realised by some Western European countries, 'weak sustainability' policies are implemented. Hence the kind of reformism introduced does not lead to respect for ecosystems (see Carter 2013). Barry writes that "ecological modernization can be viewed as an account of how existing political and economic institutions within liberal democracies have responded to public pressure to 'do something' about environmental problems" (2001:61, see also Ingolfur 2004:36f.). So far, politics, as predicted by critiques of ecological modernisation theory, have failed to introduce structural change (Blühdorn 2011). One could assume that structural change and decoupling

---

[373] An "Ecomodernist Manifesto" for example has been recently published (Asafu-Adjaye et al. 2015). Its optimistic content includes "factually incorrect statements, deficient and contradictory argumentation, dubious environmental claims, and shocking omissions" (Caradonna et al. 2015:4).

[374] See Wapner's discussion of the issue calling it "Promethean environmentalism" (2010).

[375] Kelly writes that "it is only civilizations backed by strong economies that are in a position to do the research and make the necessary scientific, engineering and technological advances to offset environmental threats. Scientific views that undermine economic progress are a threat in themselves, and need a careful and robust justification before they are widely propagated" (2013:3; cf. Nicholson 2013).

[376] In "Commodity Potential: An Approach to Understanding the Ecological Consequences of Markets", Manno accurately describes problems of commoditisation: "Since high commodity intensity solutions receive by far the greater amount of research and development (R&D), they invariably appear to be more advanced and competitive. It is then logically compelling to utilize these solutions and apparently irresponsible to suggest the adoption of lesser-developed alternatives. Communal solutions therefore always appear less capable of meeting human needs" (Manno 2013:Loc. 6775). Best practice should additionally not be misinterpreted as best possible practices.

from industrialist to service-centred society happen by itself (Diekmann and Preisendörfer 2001:29). After all postmaterialist values might flourish once basic needs are satisfied, but that does not necessarily correlate with lower consumption rates as discussed comprehensively above.[377] New needs are regularly created and the value-action gap remains pressing. Notably, Lekakis and Kousis highlight that green economy practices further stress the environment (2013). Given the widespread urge to remain within a growth paradigm, the lack of structural change is to be expected, while rhetorical dominance of the discourse therefore is not surprising (Connelly et al. 2012:166ff.; Kenis and Lievens 2014). Interpretations of the ecological modernisation theory vary. Nonetheless, economic growth always means higher emissions, since absolute decoupling could not be achieved anywhere (e.g. Lane 2011a). The magic point, where real economies start decreasing emissions without economic decline, has not been found.

Decoupling is a much lauded concept, but it has yet to prove its realisability. Empirically, economic decline has shown to be the most effective cause for a decrease in pollution.

> "There is overwhelming evidence linking economic growth with CO2 emissions. Therefore, recessions are "good news" in terms of prevention of global warming. The severe drops in industrial activity, transportation, and consumption of fuels that have occurred worldwide from the fall of 2007 will immediately translate into smaller emissions, providing temporary relief in terms of reducing the high speed at which humanity is approaching a climate crisis due to greenhouse gases [...] the observed acceleration of emissions during the 1990s and the present century throws major doubts on the effectiveness of carbon trading schemes now in place in a number of countries to supposedly cut emissions in a business-friendly manner" (Granados and Carpintero 2009:16).

In sum, green growth remains an illusion. The limits of sustainability have been passed, so even if the green sector grows, sustainability cannot be advanced without economic decline (Seidl and Zahrnt 2012:10f.; Rees 2013).[378] There are various reasons for decoupling to be extremely difficult. The rebound effect is well known: saved energy is often used otherwise and not actually saved. But in addition to the difficulty of actual savings, the future energy return, in comparison to the energy invested is also in decline (Seidl and Zahrnt 2012). The difference for example between oil pumped and oil made from tar sands is enormous. Furthermore, gains in the green sector do not remain purely sustainable. To measure reduction only by pollution per GDP unit is clearly misleading (Scruggs 2009).

---

[377] "It is claimed that higher national income due to more growth provides more resources to devote to environmental protection. Of course, this does not answer the question of whether those resources will in fact be devoted to climate protection or spent by households upgrading their home entertainment systems. As people become wealthier do they become more benevolent or more greedy?" (Hamilton 2010:39). Much of the avoided pollution is immediately compensated. "Buying a slightly more efficient car or improving the performance of supermarket refrigerators has nothing to do with solutions to climate change if we subsequently drive further or chill more of our food" (Anderson 2012:17).
[378] "Ecological footprint analysis shows that our species, using prevailing technologies, has already exceeded global carrying capacity by one-third. This means that we currently maintain our consumer lifestyles and economies, in part, by degrading and liquidating natural capital" (Westra et al. 2013:Loc. 680).

"The efficiency with which the global economy uses fossil resources and generates carbon dioxide emissions is improving in some places. But overall we are making faltering progress at best. To make matters worse, relative decoupling is barely half the story. It measures only the resource use (or emissions) per unit of economic output. For decoupling to offer a way out of the dilemma of growth, resource efficiencies must increase at least as fast as economic output does" (Jackson 2012:Loc. 1446-51).

Evidence for a sustainable growth economy has not been found, especially since the aim of economic growth means trying to externalise costs for profits (Kingsnorth 2009:41).[379] Non-profit green businesses cannot lead to zero waste as long as they are primed towards growth. The employees of green businesses will not spend 100% of their income in sustainable manner. More purchasing power is likely to lead to purchases that fall outside the range of sustainable consumption.[380] Even if a customer buys organic t-shirts, buying ten t-shirts, while rising the income of green business cannot be understood as a sustainable practice. Those who praise economic growth combined with decoupling ignore this. So far, it has not shown any success, but the

"fact that in the real world almost every promise of the so-called 'uncoupling' of economic growth and pollution levels, and win-win strategies have turned out to be untenable does not seem to change the opinions of politicians, bureaucrats, corporations and citizens: they are all too eager to continue believing in the profoundly optimistic assumptions of modern win—win/technocratic policy-making" (de Geus 2004:Loc. 2429-32; Jenkins 1998).

GDP and pollution remain inseparable.[381] The relationship is so strong that GDP "is also the best statistical index we have of the aggregate of pollution, depletion, congestion, and loss of biodiversity" (Randers 2012:Loc. 1694-97).

First and foremost, ecological modernisation theory and the growth ideology ignore external costs. Given the silent outsourcing of dirty industries Carter asks whether "ecological modernisation requires a large periphery of poor countries to act as a waste tip for the polluting activities of a rich core of nations" (2007:23; see also Lekakis and Kousis 2013). Neglecting these realities, ecological modernisation theory advertises the compatibility of not just status quo maintenance, but growth in material wealth and ecological sustainability. In contrast, degrowth is likely to mean less working hours, but also less material wealth (Schrecker 1998:219). Hence, such a vision is hard to sell democratically. As argued earlier promoting voluntary reductions in

---

[379] "Green is the new red and red is green, because of the relationship between protection and common property i.e. non-property markets can be just as autistic, if in different ways. Obviously, they respond only to human, consumer preferences that can be couched in monetary terms. Any market actor trying to take non-pecuniary factors into account is going to have its profitability, and so survival chances, damaged (this is not to gainsay the possibility of green consumerism)" (Dryzek 1996:24).

[380] "The market economy controls the populace by the cult of consumerism" (Shearman and Smith 2007:95). Employees of green business are hardly excluded.

[381] "While it is always possible to improve eco-efficiency, it is not possible to achieve 100 percent eco-efficiency and as world production, trade, and population continue to increase in absolute terms, overall environmental degradation will inevitably continue to rise" (Eckersley 2004:Loc. 953-55).

consumption has historically been unsuccessful, while introducing mandatory reductions may not be politically viable within a democratic system. Planning degrowth could be inevitable in order to avoid chaos (Anderson 2012; Sakrar 2012). This may include nationalisation of means of production. Typically, connected approaches remain understudied in comparison to market mechanisms, which thus far show limited success.

2.2.3.2. (GREEN) MARKET MECHANISMS

A wide view of market mechanisms includes variations of taxes, setting limits, offsetting, tradable pollution permits, and non-interference.[382] Except for the latter, each case means government involvement although to differing degrees. They can all be categorised as a form of regulation and are not mutually exclusive, but can be combined.[383] Whereas Hamilton understands social preferences as part of the democratic process, free market economists see interference as illegitimate (2010:59). Regulations can be framed as a competitive disadvantage (Dryzek 2005).[384] One argument is that investors will relocate, if they dislike antipollution policies. It is also argued that eco-friendly standards restrict markets' productivity and "structured in this way, the environment usually loses" (Buell and De Luca 1996:57). However, other factors certainly play a role. Given the multiplicity of factors, it needs to be studied, in which cases such policies are decisive.[385] This does not touch the question of priorities for governments: a better local environment or potentially more income.[386] Fear of cooperate flight could equally be taken as an argument for the nationalisation of companies. State enterprises necessarily are bound to the local territory and law. Höffe sees an obstacle for a socialist state for setting the environment as a priority arguing that it would not be economically competitive (2009:302). Yet, such critique remains within the same logic of growth, increased production and consumption as central themes. Decisively, market rationality also means that companies will invest in projects with fast and considerable returns, while

> "public goods projects impose costs in the present but benefits over the long run, and because the benefits spill over beyond the immediate users, they are not the kind of projects that capital and equity markets fund at optimal levels" (Wallack 2004:Loc. 4346-48).

At the same time the free market is likely to forego essential services such as supplying water to rural communities leaving unprofitable services to the state (Dobner 2010). A review of business

---

[382] Different ways of setting baselines such as runner up etc. will not be subject of the discussion here.

[383] "The issue of reclaiming the commons and protecting the natural environment from cooperate plunder is also intimately connected to the issue of the regulation of corporate power" (Shearman and Smith 2007:154; see also Dryzek 2005).

[384] Governments may equally interfere by using incentives. Subsidies for filtering equipment for example have shown to be effective means in China (Shin 2013:920).

[385] For instance stability of policies can have a strong effect if long-term investments are required. One reason why the US lags behind Germany renewable energy politics is that the latter had more stable policy (Karapin 2014:120).

[386] If the area actually benefits also depends on the costs of the pollution for the population.

management literature shows that while it was attempted to show that businesses as well as the environment can simultaneously profit, it is mainly proven that greening business can be an advantage in some cases (King and Toffel 2009). The literature did not demonstrate that "win/win opportunities will be sufficient to bring about meaningful environmental improvements" (2009:98). Instead it seems that free enterprises will not make the changes that could ensure sustainability. This appears especially self-evident, when seen from a degrowth perspective.

Instead of accepting that the free market and market rationality are part of the problem its advocates categorise the nature of the problem as ethical and political (Princen 2010:148). In the meantime, the market is presented as moral-free and value-free. However, the fact is that "the operation of markets is a dynamic that changes over time so that those markets accepted today may be seen as unacceptable tomorrow, and those of yesterday are often unaccepted today" (Spash 1998:49).[387] Failing to rationally trade one commodity for another violates basic economic assumptions, but the citizen may sell his house but not his children (1998:60). While it is unacceptable today to sell children, it is acceptable to buy private jets that may jeopardize future generations. To insist on a division of market and politics deprives the market of important correctives. It legitimises unsustainable practices. Economics tends to be falsely presented as an ethically neutral subject. "Rather than remove the ethical and political from the study of economics [...] these aspects need to be reintroduced" (Spash 1998:49).

Introductions to economics explain that aggregate demand does not only depend on the willingness to pay for a product. It is not defined by the number of people who want or need something, but includes the ability to pay.[388] This means that large percentages of populations are regularly excluded from market calculations, since they by definition are not part of the market. As touched upon earlier, lacking purchasing power the poor cannot demand environmental integrity from the market therefore they are effectively disenfranchised (Przeworski 1993:220; Barth 1997; Carter 2013). The market instead answers to the demand of the wealthy, since they have the means to appropriate goods. Many luxury goods in the meantime are disproportionately bad for the environment. Yachts, private planes and expensive cars, but also comparatively cheap mass products like electronic gadgets are in demand in

---

[387] 'All societies' know things that are unacceptable to trade. Societies may even differentiate between different categories of goods in terms of their 'tradability' or 'convertibility' into forms of wealth. See for example Ferguson (1992).

[388] "The economy that much of the world has come to accept as a determinant of human choices has no necessary relationship with human need, as market choices are based on access to money" (Mellor 2006:43).

economic terms and the market therefore supplies. Przeworski describes this inequality, as in a sense, acceptable in today's democracy, stating that

> "[t]he only limits to economic and social equality that are acceptable today are those that result from the fact that democracies function, and will continue to function, in market economies, not those that reflect political inequality" (2010:169).

However, those forms are interconnected and inequalities that are accepted in practice could lead to the questioning of equality as a general aim in many democracies. Either one assumes that equity is not an aim or one has to judge democratic governance as a failure in substantial terms, given that the gap between rich and poor does not become smaller in most countries. Such a statement further disguises the already touched upon conflict.

> "Increased economic freedom can raise income equality by widening income-earning opportunities, and it can lower equality by reducing income redistribution toward the poor. [...] Given this assortment of estimates, observers who value income equality highly might conclude that the tradeoff is considerable. Others for whom economic freedom is paramount might instead judge the tradeoff to be small. Thus, any assessment of the substantive significance of the tradeoff is subjective" (Carter 2006:175).

This set of problems bears relevance for the sustainability of democracy. On the one hand, countries with higher economic inequality have larger footprints (Wilkinson and Pikett 2011; worldbank.org). On the other hand, economic inequality is also reflected in different consumption patterns. Pairing the negative consequences of economic inequality with the uneven vulnerability of environmental damage, the global poor are affected disproportionately. Disadvantages are exaggerated. A judgment about the suitability of market mechanisms depends on whether one agrees with Jackson that "[p]rosperity for the few founded on ecological destruction and persistent social injustice is no foundation for a civilized society" (2012:Loc. 587-88; see also Schlosberg 2003).[389] In spite of the initial reservations against market mechanisms, contemporary greens support such mechanisms, "underlining their readiness to accept the capitalist economic system, just as their entry into national parliaments and then into government declared their willingness to work within liberal democracy" (Carter 2007:351).

---

[389] "Living in harmony with nature does not necessarily require egalitarian communities of the standardly green sort, for example. One of the paradigm cases discussed earlier – the medieval English village – was characterized by great disparities of status and wealth between lords and peasants" (Goodin 2013:Loc. 2862-64). Although it is sometimes argued that pollution is democratic in that it affects everyone equally, this is a misunderstanding. Gated communities etc. already show the difference between rich and poor in environmental conditions (Schrecker 1998:229). Wealth enables the recreation of an environment with trees in spite of other places becoming concrete deserts. Miller and Rees conclude: "On first reading, one might simply say that progress in improving human welfare globally is incomplete; we have a moral duty to extend the benefits of liberal-democratic, free-market, knowledge-based societies to impoverished people everywhere. Indeed, we are morally compelled to do so. But this mainstream interpretation, however compelling in its humanitarian urgency, is itself incomplete. It ignores the crumbling biophysical stage upon which the human drama is being played out. Certainly concerns for human well-being, justice, and equity remain, but these are too often abstracted from the deteriorating state of the planet. Rather late in the play, we are beginning to recognize that a necessary prerequisite for both economic security and social justice is ecological stability. We have no choice but to ensure that economic growth does not further imperil the structural integrity and functional health of the ecosphere" (2013:Loc. 138).

Again, the question arises whether this tamed version of green politics can go beyond a weak form of sustainability i.e. non-sustainability.[390]

In the meantime, voluntary changes by corporations largely depend on cost-benefit calculations (Lemos and Agawal 2009:76f.; see also Carter 2007 and Reuscher et al. 2011). Hence the demand for green products has to be in place before changes from the supply side are to be expected. Of course green consumerism needs supply as well as demand.[391] Yet, the incentive for green products, unless created by the government, is dependent on at least an expected market. Voluntary eco-labelling can be seen as a market mechanism, but labels are normally introduced as an instrument. The idea of buycotting was discussed earlier. Companies and consumers, if they concentrate on appearances only, can be satisfied with tactics of 'green washing'.[392] Comparing about 30.000 companies in the US, Darnall and Sides even found that companies participating in the four biggest voluntary programs had a worse record than non-participating (2008).[393] Delmas highlights that information on effects of "disclosure programs, such as eco-labels, is still thin" (2009:231). He also summarises potential difficulties of studying these effects. This goes beyond the value-action gap. For green liberalism to work, green demand is needed. Volkswagen produced a 3 litre car from 1998-2005, but finally stopped production due to lack of demand (Lamparter 2011). Six years before Volkswagen started to sell these efficient cars, Commoner wrote that a car is "produced solely as a salable object – a commodity– with little regard for how well it fits into either sphere: the system of transportation or the environment" (1992:8 [sic!]). Here, in contrast to many other economists Commoner does not propose an 'innocence of corporations', but instead declares that they are aware of the outcome of their work.

Concurrently, Beckerman points out economists are not interested in the elimination of pollution, but in finding an 'optimum level' (1972:330).[394] Yet, the optimum in pollution from a common sense point of view, does not involve calculations of a tradeoff between clean air, water,

---

[390] There are socialists sceptical towards greens for this reason, since they only attempt to "ameliorate the ecological impact of capitalism" instead of aiming at a system transformation (Connelly et al. 2012:65).

[391] "In the marketplace ends are treated as wants, and no judgement of their moral rightness is allowed to enter criteria of choice" (Lövbrand and Khan 2010:58).

[392] Orr finds harsh words: "We define ourselves as consumers, a word originally designating disease. But what we consume is the planet's primary productivity, on which other species also depend. We think of ourselves as little more than rational players in an economic system conceived along with the industrial revolution 250 years ago—an infinitesimal slice of the 3.8 billion years of evolving life" (2009:139).

[393] Note that the strictness of a program is likely to have a direct effect on the numbers of participants.

[394] On the opposing side, Commoner's critique of capitalism is explicitly visible in his stance against standard levels of pollution and for its total eradication (1992). He supplementary asks how a human life can be calculated and writes that "the apparently "objective" cost-benefit approach is quickly engulfed in deep moral and political issues: Should society try to mitigate all human suffering regardless of the cost? On the other hand, since social resources are limited, is it not reasonable to alleviate suffering in keeping with some measure of effectiveness?" (1992:67).

and soil and economic growth. Any line of pollution is subject to arbitrariness and involves constructing a line. The common sense answer would be that the optimum is zero pollution. Still boundaries are often set for what can be labelled 'acceptable'. Even in the cases where the limits are not passed and set at a reasonable level, meaning that they do not pose a greater risk to a healthy adult, the standard line is a healthy adult (see Gilley and Bowersox 2002). Children and elderly as well as people with weaker constitutions are at risk at much lower levels. Setting standards for allowing pollution is difficult. Repeatedly "decision makers appear to be seduced by the apparent technical simplicity of economic calculations" (Connelly et al. 2012:238).[395] One huge hurdle with market mechanisms, in particular with monetary instruments such as taxes, or even fines, is the blindness for the ethical dimension.[396] Notably, cost-benefit analysis effectively ignores the question of why pollution is produced at all (Dryzek 2005:86). This seems obvious, when one is asked to put a price on the value of a human's or 'only' a pet's life. If the costs of nature's exploitation are internalised using measurements like emissions permits, the economic value remains an abstract and barely represents other forms of value (see for example Connelly et al. 2012). Money becomes the rationale of decision making, hence moral concerns are muted.

2.2.3.3. MONETISING NATURE AND ITS DESTRUCTION

There is an essential difference between assigning intrinsic value to nature and merely monetary value. The likelihood of protection of the environment rises with the attribution of value in itself (Barr 2006:44; see also Sagoff 2002). Making nature a commodity and assigning monetary value means that it becomes an interchangeable i.e. tradable good. It enables considerations that are purely in terms of profits (Norton 2002). The decision to cut trees is deprived of its moral dimension. Whereas norms are used to direct behaviour, once resource usage is translated into

---

[395] There are many critical scholars on the other hand. Shearman and Smith use particularly strong words stating that the secular version of divine rights are "the market forces that in many ways now rule our lives more oppressively and totally than any king or dictator in the premodern world" (2007:13). Today, "human populations are forced to live in a global habitat that contains an enduring, growing residue of the consequences of their economic activities in the form of accumulating waste and pollution. Our 'Vote' in the market on what should be produced, i.e. our input in shaping public policy, is a judgement that focuses entirely on the utility of the commodity to us, and cannot, through the market price mechanism, take all the other enduring consequences of such a policy of production into account. Some of those consequences may be very much opposed to our utilities – yet market prices mystify their existence and lead us eagerly to support activities that produce dis-utilities" (Barth 1997:238). Bell and De Luca write: "The use of market-based monetary value of human life to determine the strictness of environmental and safety standards removes from politics the question of the importance society places on material growth. It displaces the question of how much preservation of life really means to us and if we are willing to adjust present growth patterns or future scenarios to fulfil this meaning" (1996:35).

[396] "A more persuasive ethical objection concerns their potential inequity, or regressive impact. By raising the price of some environmentally sensitive goods such as water or energy, eco-taxes discriminate against lower income groups because a larger share of their disposable income goes on these basic needs than is spent by higher income groups" (Carter 2007:339; see also Stretton 1976:214ff.). If not well planned ecotaxes can be regressive taxes putting an extra burden on the poor.

monetary terms, ethical reservations can be overcome or forgotten.[397] A fundamental part of a critique of emissions trading should be that the concept reduces the atmosphere from a common good to tradable pollution rights (Leggewie and Welzer 2011:109). In addition, privatisation often causes its own problems. The privatisation of recycling in some cases leads to more illegal disposal for example (Baker and Eckerberg 2014:196). Equally important, it fails to encourage reductions, since as Baker and Eckerberg point out trash becomes a commodity.

Again, the anthropological study of three different groups' handling of the forest as a resource shows how classical economics' assumptions conflict with practice. The general economic assumption is that the attribution of monetary value can serve as protective measure. But of the three groups, the one that "considered cash value a high priority" acted least sustainable (Atran et al. 2002). The Itza, whose resource management can be described as 'forest ecosystem management', had a culture that was interwoven with the forest.[398] Believing that spirits have preferences and that they may punish violations against their preferences was mentioned as a motivation (in interviews).[399] A worldview that is based on interrelations, similar to 'Western ecocentrism', is possibly the core of the Itza's sustainable behaviour. Their observations lead Atran et al. to highlight that

> "[t]o date, rational-decision and game-theoretic accounts involving human use of nonhuman resources have not considered the possibility of resources' (e.g., species') having their own measures of "utility" or resources' and humans' being "players" in the same game. Prima facie, this idea is implausible, because species are assumed not to have motives, desires, beliefs, or strategies for cooperation or deception that would be sensitive and systematically responsive to corresponding aspects of human intention" (2002:439).

In this case study the protection of the forest is based on a different rationality than an economic one. Culture producing social facts takes a leading role in the question of sustainability i.e. the management of the common pool. In a study in China, Lam and Shi found that the older cohorts who had been raised before the market liberalisation had "a higher standard on social responsibility" (2008:470).[400] Market economies do not promote responsibility. Anderson and Huggins recognise not only the importance of cost-benefit analysis in free market environmentalism but assume it is a general driving force and write:

---

[397] There are clear warnings suggesting that "to make all the values involved in the environment commensurable through the medium of money is illegitimately to push economic rationality beyond its proper disciplinary boundaries into domains where this method will lead us astray" (Ward 2006:289; Elling 2008:26ff.; see also Commoner 1992).
[398] Forest ecosystem management means the management of a forest with regard to sustainability concerns.
[399] It is hard to differentiate between fear and respect. A discussion of the difference between fear and respect as a motivation goes beyond the scope of the book. It is enough to underscore that the forest has a meaning beyond its monetary value.
[400] Research shows that politically left-leaning people tend to be more interested in environmental politics (Diekmann and Preisendörfer 2001:110ff.). They are at the same time more inclined to sustainable citizenship in practice (Micheletti, Stolle and Berlin 2014:222).

"None of us are willing to take on significant costs today without some possibility of a return on our investment. So why invest trillions of dollars now to reduce carbon if we cannot expect a return in the next hundred years? Even the most liberal policy analyst must wonder whether emission reduction policies make good economic sense" (2008:9).

The line of thought is posed within a cognitive scheme that is deprived of all other than monetary values. While it is reductionist, it is at the same time dangerous due to the reinforcement of self-interest as a driving force and not social responsibility.[401] At the same time defenders of liberalism repeatedly underline that the free market is not the cause of the destruction but "environmentally harmful preferences" (Wissenburg 2001a:194; cf. Commoner 1990 and Luke 1999:64ff.). Among other things, consumers regularly look for the cheapest product independent of who supplies (Höffe 2009:93). Similar objections raised against the possibility of green liberalism earlier apply here. A (voluntary) green market has green citizens/consumers as a premise (and not a product).[402]

Lyon accentuates that voluntary agreements tend to fail when the government does not pose a serious threat of regulation (2009:62; see also Reuscher et al. 2011). Corporations can in the meantime influence governance in both directions. Lyon's research shows that while a combination of carbon tax and subsidies for research and developments most probable to improve environmental governance, carbon tax as a single policy is more effective than the latter (2009:50). For companies changes might not be a consequence of taxes, if they have an interest keeping the technology running (Buell and De Luca 1999:52). It could be cheaper to pay taxes than to invest in new technology for example. Carbon tax and offsetting are modern day indulgences.[403] In each case a price is paid as an *indemnification*. They are not real reparations in so far as they cannot nullify an action. Taxes are imposed by governments and are in a sense a form of compensation, sometimes even understood as punishment. The government may use taxes for offsetting, but that is not a given. Offsetting means that a polluting action is 'paid off' by supporting a greener action or project. In the case of offsetting, the damage is 'intentionally' and knowingly generated, with the understanding that it will be offset (Driver 2013:170). Both represent distorted mechanisms of value. Driver notes that compensation is typically paid, when one "harms others unintentionally, and the compensation is the best that can be done after the fact" (2014:170). In case of consumption and the widely spread understanding of the issue of

---

[401] "Market societies, of course, are premised on, justified by, and encourage each of us to get some piece of action" (Buell and De Luca 1996:12).

[402] A vast array of green thought is based on the wish that people eventually will become fond of nature and that it will "transform their modes of action" (Radcliffe 2002:43).

[403] Connelly et al. underscore that scholars such as Goodin describe market environmentalism as indulgence, which signifies selling what cannot be sold (2012). Note that the idea of indulgences is individualistic too. A price is paid to God for a soul. This includes that those harmed are not compensated, but one is protecting oneself from hell or purgatory.

pollution, it is difficult to demark the line between unintentionally and intentionally. The agent usually prioritizes. In case of meat consumption for example, it seems absurd to say that the consumer unintentionally caused the death of an animal. Speaking of intention in these matters does not make sense. Something might not be intended, but the action is taken despite unintended effects. Thus, offsetting cannot be understood as compensation in the sense Driver noted. Marshall describes the morally unconvincing logic of offsetting by the example of power plants:

> "A new coal-fired power plant in Europe can "offset" its emissions by buying carbon credits from another new coal-fired power plant in India. This seems to be not so much robbing Peter to pay Paul as robbing everyone to pay them both off" (Marshall 2014:Loc. 2811).

There are two objections to such action. The first objection is that typically those suffering from the pollution are not the ones compensated. This could be alleviated by changing forms of compensation and/or the recipient. However, the second objection is more severe. Polluting is not a neutral act. It has to be recognised as a morally bad act giving the consequences. The action remains bad even if the compensation was fairer. Offsets are like beating one's child, but then making sure that someone else does not beat his (Carter 2013). Ensuring that another child does not get a beating cannot equalise the fact that a beating took place. Neither can one murder someone innocent and then save somebody's life or many lives to make up for the first action. Hence, wasting precious resources cannot become morally acceptable by paying, yet market solutions disguise this (Connelly et al. 2012:193). To date, politics mostly focuses on end of the pipe solutions, instead of avoiding the creation of environmental harms in the first place (Marshall 2014:Loc. 2846). Commoner criticises emission trading writing that

> "unlike the conventional marketplace, which deals in goods – things that serve a useful purpose – this scheme creates a marketplaces in "bads" – things that are not only useless but often deadly. Apart from the issue of morality, it should be noted that such a scheme cannot operate unless the right to produce pollutants is exercised – hardly an inducement to eliminating them" (1992:15f.).

Emission certificates have not been proven to be effective (Leggewie and Welzer 2011:109). One reason could be the absence of the moral dimension. Another might also be their cheap price (see sandbag.org.uk).

Raising the costs for polluting acts can lead to better behaviour. Taxes can be effective. The average EU citizen used 191 plastic bags in 2010 and only 6% of them were recycled, according to the EU, but when Ireland introduced mandatory pricing for single-use plastic bags in 2002, their use was reduced by 90% within a year (Neslen 2014). Also looking at study on bag consumption, Kollmuss and Agyeman conclude that economic factors prove to be of major importance in the "new policies and strategies that are meant to influence and change people's behavior"

(2002:249). Nevertheless in both cases, outcomes are not generally applicable to all environmental harms. One factor for instance is the fact that people are willing to act environmentally friendly, if it involves low costs. In the case of disposable bags, the effort to bring a bag is miniscule in comparison to many other issues. Again, eco-taxes themselves do not enjoy much support (Carter 2007:340). Also reframing taxes within the economic discourse does not necessarily make them more popular either. Gunster examines if the involvement of economists employed within the same discourse can enable politicians to convince the public (2010:192). She discusses a case in British Columbia where an eco-tax was attempted to be propagated as tax shift and not as a rise. Voters were also informed that the taxes should not lead to economic decline and job losses, hence, the arguments stayed within the same logic and merely countered those by critics. Ultimately in this case it did not work. Staying within the same discourse may counter some arguments, but also leaves out the moral dimension that provides additional support. Gunster states:

> "The possibility that the contradiction of using tax cuts (with their emphasis on personal self-interest) to sell environmental policy (which requires more expansive forms of moral reasoning that take the well-being of others into account) might have been a mistake was never considered" (2010:195).

Value priming and framing and the emotional dimension play a much underappreciated role. For the majority, social facts have greater importance than rational arguments.[404] Arguments about the indispensability of private vehicles for commuting may lose their power, at least in regard to a moral justifiability, if contrasted with the deadly impact of the pollution they cause (Gunster 2010:200ff.). Once car usage is reframed as an egoistic and harmful act, it may lose some support. Leaving issues like this within the frame of monetary value undermines the more pressing moral dimension. Thence framing can be an effective means of achieving sustainability and disregarding sustainability as an intrinsic value can turn against it.[405]

2.2.3.4. THE HOLY GRAIL OF PRIVATE PROPERTY

Darwin assumed that certain kinds of possessive behaviour are natural (Buell and De Luca 1996:38). Once something is categorised as natural, it typically escapes scrutiny. Different conceptions of property have consequences for environmental politics. Whether natural or not, the conceptions vary from property as a solution to property as a problem. In general property rights tend to be more secure in democracies (Dahl 2000:59). Here, the question could be asked whether secure property rights do not mainly favour the rich. If property rights are the solution,

---

[404] Short-term self-interest can be a social fact however when broadly acknowledged as a legitimate.
[405] "Arguments that renewable energy brings greater energy security encourage the expansion of domestic fossil fuels. Arguments that the low-carbon economy will bring jobs become vulnerable to evidence that the high-carbon economy might bring more job" (Marshall 2014:Loc. 3975).

privatisation is the key process to a healthy environment. If property is the root of environmental harms, "some form of communism" must be the solution (Carter 2013:34; see also More 1992:201).

> "Certainly we need to appropriate in order to survive. But if the form that the appropriation takes itself threatens life – as the institution of private property can thus to be argued to – then it cannot be justified. And neither can any political philosophy (such as liberalism) which is premised upon it" (Carter 2013:33).

Locke's idea of humans naturally having a right to life, liberty and property actually proves to be an extremely dangerous idea in today's world. First, this interpretation of human nature implicates that those without property are not actualising their humanness and therefore are lesser humans.[406] Second, it gives property an extraordinary status. Hence the idea that property is part of human nature, especially paired with individualism, has troubling effects. While Locke pointed out that one should not take more than one can use, so food would not spoil for example, he did at the same time propagate Calvinist ideals. Locke also employed the idea of unlimited resources and the legitimate appropriation of nature by man through labour.[407] Together with Calvinist or Protestant ethics (Weber 2009) and capital accumulation as a sign of dignity these ideas are ultimately able to cause irreparable destruction. While those ideas in Locke's times meant a disqualification of some humans as non-human, today they have even worse consequences. Whereas Rousseau saw particular interest as something which needs to be integrated into the general will, Locke is a champion of individual interest. His philosophy supports developments that today mean that resources are depleted, natural sinks exhausted; while climate change is an eminent threat people still defend their rights to own what they want and even reinterpreted Locke's natural liberty rights to a right to pollute (see Gillroy and Bowersox 2002). While Locke could have not foreseen today's scarcity and disliked waste, the status of property as a status enhancer can be derived from his thought.[408]

As epitomised in the division between anthropocentric and ecocentric worldviews, differing values can lead to different cognition and behaviour. Whitford and Wong hypothesised about a

---

[406] Note that properties moreover does not only mean belongings, but also for qualities (the properties of sth./sb.).

[407] Wissenburg defends Locke and judges his morality wrongly applied: "The proviso is flawed because it assumes infinite resources: my taking the last breath of fresh air would be illegitimate because someone else took the last but one breath, leaving too little for me, and so on" (2006:29; Locke 2008:21ff.). Again, it is not clear, if Locke assumed infinite resources. Maybe Locke and his contemporaries were less blind about potential scarcity and included the problem, but they could certainly not have imagined the powerful tools of 'modern' man. The usefulness of Locke for green thought remains disputable.

[408] "In the formation of the new patterns of identity construction, the dynamics of the capitalist system has an important role to play. Economic thinking and the logic of the market have invaded all societal sub-systems, and marginalized all alternative ways of thinking. The permeation of all social relations and activities by the code of payment and profitability implies that identity formation becomes a primarily economic matter, and takes first and foremost the form of material accumulation and consumption. The increasingly one-dimensional pattern of identity construction and self-experience fuels competition for scarce resources and opportunities" (Ingolfur 2004:39).

connection between English traditions and worse environmental records given that they build on a particular interpretation of private property and focus on economic growth (2009). A representative Australian survey even suggests that climate change scepticism is "associated with a radical conception of private-property rights" (Lo 2014:550ff.). A worldview with a focus on private property has a negative effect on environmental protection.

> "A modern reader cannot help being struck by the difference in the attitudes of Rousseau and Smith to the forests and nature generally. Since the world has followed Smith, rather than Rousseau, the continuing destruction of our forests is not surprising. But now it is time to stop and ask: why are we *still* following Smith rather than Rousseau?" (Singer 1994:48).

The question if humans have a natural tendency for appropriation is only relevant, if 'natural' is either understood as something good or/and inevitable. Despite the synonymousness, property is not universally understood as a good. In Plato's republic only the lower classes own property (1982). In More's utopia where hunger and excess are unknown, gold is worn by slaves, children play with gems and people habitually change houses (1992). Indeed, Rousseau's expressed his opinion particularly briskly.

> "The first man, who after enclosing a piece of ground, took it into his head to say, this is mine, and found people simple enough to believe him, was the real founder of civil society. How many crimes, how many wars, how many murders, how many misfortunes and horrors, would that man have saved the human species, who pulling up the stakes or filling up the ditches should have cried to his fellows: Beware of listening to this impostor; you are lost, if you forget that the fruits of the earth belong equally to us all, and the earth itself to nobody!" (Rousseau 2002:113).[409]

In contrast advocates of free market environmentalism often employ the argument that 'nobody washes a rental car' (e.g. Anderson and Huggins 2008).[410] Free market environmentalism sees privatisation of public goods as key. It is argued that people take care of their own property.

> "At the heart of [free market environmentalism] is a system of property rights to natural resources that, whether held by individuals or a group, create inherent incentives for resource users because the wealth of the owner is at stake if bad decisions are made. In short, free market environmentalists strive to transform environmental problems into assets" (Anderson and Huggins 2008:7).

To compare the environment to a rental car is problematic. People pay for the use of a rental car. Its use involves a contract that is very limited and based on a money exchange. The user acquires a right that can be measured in monetary terms. The relationship is purely instrumental. It is fair to assume that people do wash their own cars not because it is a necessity, but because they value having a clean car. The responsibility lies in their hands. It might therefore be not about ownership per se, but about responsibility. If one borrows a car from the neighbour, one is likely to return it clean, since it is a social norm. Thus, protecting the environment has to be

---

[409] Read 'civilized' society.
[410] Free market environmentalism is regularly recognized as oxymoronic.

understood as everybody's responsibility in form of a social norm. Using the comparison of a rental car is a reductionism that negates the social dimension. The 'solutions' of free market environmentalism depend on private property rights. They therefore rather weaken social ties by relying on self-interests instead of encouraging collective responsibility. If somebody does not wash his car, it is his own choice. Property in a sense makes it people's 'own business' and means a deprivation of the social relationship. Establishing a community of trust is taken as a focal process for green democracy. But as mentioned earlier such developments need huge efforts. In some cases the environment does have similar properties as commodities. They

> "are not simply used, they are used up. And when they are used and used up, this is understood to be an act of individuated appropriation. To the extent that you consume a commodity, someone else cannot. The concept of a commodity fits naturally in a situation of natural or artificial scarcity where resources are to be broken into discrete units and distributed across the members of a group or population for consumption. A commodity is something that ceases to exist as it is consumed" (Jennings 2010:228).[411]

Ironically, if the environment was valued for its intrinsic value rather than in monetary means, beautiful forests could be saved via privatisation. The owner then might take care of it as if it was a Picasso. Empirical evidence does not support the claims that property rights are particularly useful for sustainability, but instead shows significant problems regarding social suggestion (e.g. Sjöstedt 2014).

The logic of privatisation is connected to the idea of nature as separable from humans (see Hamilton 2010). Even if privatisation was an effective means for environmental protection, it would still contradict the philosophy of interrelatedness in ecology. Precisely, the ignorance of interconnectedness may render privatisation an insufficient means.[412] Nature is foremost a web of interrelations. The recognition of interconnectedness further renders privatisation morally dubious.

> "Investment decisions – decisions to withhold a part of society's resources from current consumption and to allocate them to replace or augment the instruments of production – have an impact that is both general and long-lasting, that is, public. Yet the very institution of private property implies that they are a private prerogative. Control over investment is the central political issue under capitalism precisely because no other privately made decisions have such a profound impact" (Przeworski 1993:218).[413]

---

[411] Wissenburg admits difficulties here stating that "there are also two problems associated with property rights that are typically liberal. Private property, or more precisely legitimate ownership, implies that owners are free to use their property in any way they like, even to destroy it or use it to their own advantage, to the disadvantage of the community. Thus nature, landscapes, animals and natural resources are prima facie unprotected; the onus of proof is on those who would argue for a need to restrict property rights" (2006:22; see Heilbroner 1988).

[412] Property marks not only a relationship to a resource, but a relationship to the owners' environment that will be effected if the owner changes the resource.

[413] Here Przeworski points at a general tension between democracy and private property: "The combination of private property of the means of production with universal suffrage is a compromise, and this compromise implies that the logic of accumulation is not exclusively the logic of private actors" (1993:219).

For sustainability "the decommodification of nature through political interventions in consumption and production process" is key (Duit 2014b:322; see also Griffith 2003:140).[414] It would be consistent for the camp wishing more democracy to also question property, since a radical change to an ecologically sustainable life would make it necessary (Zeller 2011). Carter points out that while its complexity clearly means that free market environmentalism cannot achieve sustainability and while complexity makes planning a necessity, it also leaves some matters to chance (2007:224). Market rationality usually discounts the future.

2.2.4. THE FUTURE DISCOUNT[415]

Sustainability is inherently future-oriented. Considering 'the future' adds manifold problems to politics. The cognitive problem is only one among many.[416] The future is a conundrum for democratic theory. It gives another dimension to the question of democratic inclusion and accountability of the now (and generally of the living). Democracies systematically disregard the future (Leggewie and Welzer 2011:159). This discount is larger in practice than in theory. Considerations about the future are another area where norms and values are in a significant discord with witnessed behaviour. When asked, people do accept the interests of future generations as holding significance, but as discussed earlier their actions do not show such a consideration. Further, if democracy derives its value from inclusion, the fact that the majority is excluded from decision making that clearly affects their livelihoods poses a serious problem to the legitimacy of democracy. The contrast between elite decision making as a government of a minority and democracy as a system with greater inclusion becomes irrelevant, when the potential future population is included as an excluded group.

Dahl's discussion of democracy shows the difficulty 'future people' mean for democratic theory. Corresponding with his observations, sustainable politics are improbable because "an exclusive demos is unlikely to protect the interests of those who are excluded" (Dahl 1989:129). Current pollution is likely to affect the Earth's climate for thousands of years. So future generations will be negatively influenced by unsustainable laws, but "laws and rules imposed by an outsider would violate the self-determination of all those subject to the laws" (1989:108). Self-determination is argued to be fundamental to the value of democracy. Thus, the scope of

---

[414] "Property rights are not sacrosanct for liberals: particularly the Millian tradition of social liberalism has embraced the notion of a welfare state" (Wissenburg 2006:23). Though Wissenburg underlines this, he prefers Locke.

[415] Discounting the future in economics for example is defined as follows: "Discounting is the practice of placing progressively lower numerical values on future benefits and costs the further into the future they occur. The practice of discounting arises because individuals attach less weight to a benefit or cost in the future than they do to a benefit or cost now" (Markandya et al. 2001:60f.).

[416] Ontologically, it is clear that the present has more actuality than the future which only has potentiality (Höffe 2009:36).

democratic decision making cannot legitimately jeopardize the future. Within normative democratic theory, it has been a long standing objection that a majority cannot make decisions that are fundamental and irreversible if they affect either territorially or temporally excluded groups (Leggewie 2011:26).[417] Despite such an understanding this point is seldom taken seriously and explored with its full repercussions. A sustainability discussion has to include two different future discounts: firstly, the way humans discount the future in general (e.g. Hume 2013:Book III); secondly, the discounting of the future as a practical and normative challenge for democratic theory (e.g. Dahl 1989). The former discount directly influences the latter.

De Geus affirms how only the contemporary is interesting in democratic debates and as an example he points out how the discussion in the Netherlands focuses on energy efficiency etc. and economic growth without paying attention to intergenerational justice (2001:27). Though the deterioration of the environment has actual consequences today, the vast majority of the costs will be transferred to future generations. Since not all environmental harms have a long time horizon though, they are not equally discounted. In fact, pollution that is perceived as more immediate and experienced stronger locally follows a different logic (Shum 2009:290). The *demos* is directly affected in this case, in contrast to general ecosystem deterioration and climate change where costs cannot be easily calculated or understood. Given the existence of tipping points it is very likely that the coming generations will not pay the debts in monetary terms, but suffer physical harm including loss of lives (Tremmel 2011:148).

Stressing the normative dimension, Höffe assumes that future generations are entitled to restrictions today, because the climate is an intergenerational public good (2009:174; Connelly et al. 2012:40ff.; cf. Wissenburg 2006:27). The climate as an intergenerational public good gives rise to the moral question: how much climate protection can future generations expect from us? (Leggewie and Welzer 2011:57). The moral question is followed by the question of ability: are democracies able to avoid discounting the future or able to remain stable? Already Cicero wrote that every state needs prudent planning in order to last (1979:132ff.). Ironically, the Roman Empire by some accounts, collapsed for similar reasons civilisations today are under stress (Ophuls 2012). Thence the utilisation of resources has to be prudent. Politics that prepare for the future will avoid 'unhealthy' developments and instead foster positive ones (Höffe 2009:15ff.). Here, the concept of ecological health is more practical than the broad concept of sustainability.

---

[417] For this matter, long-term problems, even if reversible should be included, since they can have significant effects. Sprinz defines that a "long-term problem exists only if the mechanism creating it leads to substantial adverse effects for at least a human generation of 25 years or if the remedy would take an equally substantial amount of time" (2009:2).

Westra employs Karr's definition for ecological health and uses two criteria (Westra 2013:Loc. 668). An activity is ecologically healthy when neither degradation occurs that hinders future productivity nor it produces externalities in form of pollution. Ensuring future productivity involves precaution. Particularly because of the difficulty in predicting tipping points the precaution becomes fundamental and there is nearly full consensus among ethicists that the protection of future generations demands a precautionary principle as a guideline (Tremmel 2011:146f.).[418] The ethical dimension cannot be underestimated. Litfin writes in this regard:

> "Though it might sound odd to speak of a debt to posterity, consumer society is utterly dependent on a transfer of wealth from the future; the involuntary character of that transfer, however, makes it more a theft than a gift"(2010:133).

Since future generations have not and cannot agree to unsustainable practices, overexploitation cannot be understood as 'morally neutral'. They are not just excluded from decision making. They are also likely to be deprived of fair chances. Intergenerational justice does not allow mortgages without guarantees (Höffe 2009:231). Even in the 21st century, the environment determines chances for life.

Here, some technological optimists point at the difficulty of understanding future needs as well as at the fact that material wealth and living conditions, so far, have improved during the last centuries. They further point out that one cannot know what people in the future will find valuable. The dominant understanding of intergenerational justice involves the equal shares of resources. Habib suggests that this inevitably means offsetting, since finite resources would otherwise diminish (2014:137f.). He also elaborates the fact that resources do not have the same value to every generation due to inventions etc. This leads him to emphasize that "[i]f the things claimed are valueless, then people don't have anything at stake, and we don't feel the need to arbitrate to avoid unfair losses" (2014:140). But such an argument is based on a fallacy. It grossly underestimates the physical limits to growth. It is likely that technology will further improve and that some resources find adequate replacement. But not taking an appropriate degree of precaution and assuming that humanity will be able to make up for past errors is technological optimism that is not grounded in science (see Anderson 2012). To depict the idea of protecting breathable air as paternalism seems absurd, yet is implicit in some optimists' argumentation. A minimum bar needs to be the protection of resources for basic needs (see Gillroy and Bowersox 2002). Furthermore, the exact opposite argument can be made. Because one is ignorant about the interests of future generations, one should apply a higher degree of protective measures

---

[418] Machiavelli in a sense can be counted as predecessor of such a principle, since he made the inclusion of uncertainty i.e. *fortuna* an imperative of wise statesmanship (2009).

(Scholtes 2010). That is why from a standpoint of intergenerational justice a precautionary principle should be applied to ensure ecological health. At a minimum, future generations will want working life support systems (see Jensen, McBay and Keith 2011:Loc. 81-89). Cutting consumption is an inevitable option and becomes more significant, the longer action is delayed (Litfin 2010). As affirmed earlier, time sensitivity is critical. For the majority, it is hard to imagine that it might be too late to act or that one will not have the agency to act in a couple decades and precaution runs counterfeit to the human approach to time and the propensity to value short-term benefits (Leggewie and Welzer 2011).

Humphrey points out that ecoauthoritarians share their reservations towards democracy with Plato since they have a similar view of humans "as creatures of appetite, unless they are ennobled by philosophical reflection sufficiently well to appreciate where the human good 'truly' lies" (2007:Loc. 695; see Plato 1982). Ecoauthoritarians equally understand human nature as inclined to disregard long-term interests. The discounting of the future is even greater in politics since it does not only involve oneself, but concerns of others as well (Höffe 2009:35).[419] Though self-interested decision making is less common in smaller social circles, and people do for instance pay into pension funds, such tendencies cannot be extended to politics.[420] Consequentially, democracy suffers from the tendency for short-sighted politics that yields to the present and is blind regarding future (Schmidt 2010:464).

> "The issue is whether in the long run a democratic process is likely to do less harm to the fundamental rights and interests of its citizens than any nondemocratic alternative" (Dahl 2000:48).

Central to this book is to consider the scope of liberty in a multidimensional way, which means the inclusion of future generations. Shearman and Smith "present a case against democracy, showing how freedom and liberalism have the potential to propagate environmental tyranny far greater than any threat posed by the former Soviet Union" (2007:2). Democratic short-sightedness could possibly impel a significant decline in liberty as well as diminished capabilities in the future (see for example Randers 2012). Hence, an evaluation of democracy's sustainability may uncover that democratic systems in sum provide less rights. The comparison between autocracy and democracy leads to the consideration whether the ledge in legitimacy is too costly in regard to sustainability (Höffe 2009:13). This is especially the case since this ledge is only

---

[419] Where it concerns appetites and rewards for oneself people are still tempted to disregard a healthier body later for the cake now.
[420] De-Shalit describes nationalism as a powerful force to overcome the future discount through identification (2006a:80). Yet, nationalism often leads to reproduction and economic growth campaigns that stand in stark contrast to the proposed necessity of limiting population. Nationalism has also been used as a force to downplay intranational inequality (Aydurmus 2009). Neither population and economic growth, nor inequality, has positive impacts on the environment.

valid for present voting population. Additionally there is said to be a demographic problem in some democracies. The population is ageing and older people are a powerful group with enormous voting power. If rational choice theory's self-interested voting logic applies, the future becomes even less important in politics. Consequentially, policies directed towards the future would be even less attractive and likely (Höffe 2009:213ff.). Yet, research does not show that older people are less likely to live sustainably, rather to the contrary (see Wurster 2013; Micheletti, Stolle and Berlin 2014). Independent of the question whether older people support sustainability or not, the fact that they decide about politics whose negative consequences will not affect them raises question about affectedness and legitimate representation.

One speculation, on the other hand, assumes that autocracies have shorter time horizons than democracies, because the median voter is assumed to have less "incentives to maximize rents and exploitation of natural resources" than an autocrat (Shum 2009:289). Two difficulties with this speculation were discussed extensively. First, the median voter's preference is not necessarily the main driver of political decision making (see Gilens and Page 2014). Second, political competition and election cycle significantly impair chances for future planning, in particular when it comes to immediate costs and long-term benefits. In fact studies have shown that "policy propositions that involve long-term behaviour changes and costs will be subject to voters' opposition" (Stadelmann-Steffen 2011:490). Policies and therefore sustainability are limited by the voter (Höffe 2009:246). Other problems are added. Although a list here cannot be comprehensive, it is important to name some other barriers. As previously discussed, the voter's ignorance has to be accounted for. But ignorance does not stand alone as a matter of lack of knowledge long-term developments may also be cognitively challenging for the human brain. Importantly, the effect of individualism on morals and values should also not be underestimated as pointed out earlier. Given these factors, Wurster expects no difference between democratic and nondemocratic regimes in regard to 'strong sustainability' (2013).

Politicians need agency in order to take the necessary steps towards a sustainable future, but given the unpredictability of the future it is easy to criticise action (Höffe 2009:241). Giddens sees long-term planning and stronger states as a matter of 'fashion' (2009:94ff.). He marks the counterrevolutions of the 1980s as a turning point and advances a solution to democratic short sightedness in planning "reconciled with democratic freedoms, some of which should be actively extended, rather than reduced, in relation to the demands of climate change" (2009:96). This for him also means "a return to greater state interventionism, a conclusion that is reinforced by the failure of deregulation" (Giddens 2009:96). He meanwhile suggests planning with a scope beyond environmental policies that overcomes short-termism and uses strong institutions. While he hints at a specific vision as part of this project and altering public attitude as a key, the question remains what if the electorate does not support such a vision: How can altering the attitudes towards more cautions approaches be legitimised? After all, liberalism does not demand a consideration of intergenerational justice (Wissenburg 2006; see also Horstkötter 2004:Loc. 4027-29). So far, precaution has in fact not been the mode of action. Politics gamble with the future. The light-heartedness in the general approach to the future can be observed in many climate negotiations and in particular in the discussion about reduction of emissions.

> "Policy goals 40-50 years in advance are at best meaningless because they express only an intention; at worst, they are a substitute for immediate measures to cut emissions. They allow governments, and their publics, to feel good because their intentions reflect their values without committing to the difficult and dissonant task of putting those values into practice" (Hamilton 2010:123).

In a sense, it is expected that politics copes with the future and thereby takes responsibility (Höffe 2009:9). Yet, such an expectation is reminiscent of the gap between abstract demands of voters as well as politicians and actually sustainable policies. There is an immanent tension between democracy continually communicating problems to keep them alive, while in the meantime postponing solutions (Leggewie 2011:26). Similarly, major reformation is typically postponed in Western democracies. Discounting the future is far more likely than precaution.[421]

Höffe sees the condition of democracy's sustainability in the incorporation of the common good, the application of collective wisdom in regard to tasks of the future as well as in the prudence to value long-term interests in contrast to short-term interests (2009:238). But he leaves the question whether democracy could be able to achieve this form of prudence unanswered. The fact that governance is limited by time periods in all democracies means that long-term planning and respect for ecosystems are less likely (Schmidt 2010:464). Randers writes, summarising the last forty years, that society and especially a democratic one "indeed tends to choose the cheapest solution" (2012:Loc. 3443-44). His judgment is based on hard data showing the continuous rise of emissions. Actual achievements of environmental politics lag far behind what is rationally possible, since "short-termism in democracy and capitalism will limit the extra investment that is necessary for a rapid transition from fossils to renewables" (Randers 2012:Loc. 2465-66). As an example of short-termism Shearman and Smith list the excessive use of water reservoirs, where "democratic decisions to use these resources are made ad hoc without long-term planning or sustainability requirements" (2007:44). Moreover, civil society's active participation also

---

[421] "Society—in both democratic and authoritarian regimes—is rather blind to long-term advantages. Humanity is blatantly short-term, and hence organized redistribution before needs become critical has been rare" (Randers 2012:Loc. 3435-36).

means that protest can mean inflexibility and be a barrier towards sustainable policies (Höffe 2009:308). Arguments that more participation will lead to greener politics have to be examined closely. This includes the assumption that deliberation can overcome discounting.

"The vision of the democratic process [...] stretches human possibilities to their limits and perhaps beyond", but it at the same time, according to Dahl, is "the surest way [...] by which human beings can protect and advance interests and goods they share with others" (1989:311). Churchill famously described democracy as the best among bad forms of government. There are many scholars who believe in the possibility of combining democracy and environmentalism although "democratic majorities can and frequently do favour decisions and policies that degrade or destroy the natural environment" (Ball 2006:131f.).[422]

Many bold claims are made in regard to democracy's sustainability.[423] The causal mechanisms for good environmental governance are still insufficiently understood (Karapin 2014). It is not clear how structures can support better outcomes, thence claims need further investigation. [424] Consequentially, a serious engagement with the question of democracy's sustainability means further elaborating the varying accounts of sustainable democracy. It is important to look at all factors that determine environmental politics; especially in regard to the discrepancy between theory and practice (Ward 2008, Burnell 2009). Helfrich sees a relationship between responsibility and co-determination (2011:139). Herein, less co-determination is understood as directly connected to less responsibility taking. The people are perceived as having collectively more saying in their lives as citizens in a participative democracy. In the case of strong democracy this form of self-determination takes place through participation in collective decision making. In contrast in a liberal democracy, citizens are understood to have more space of individualised self-determination with a widened private sphere and limited state interference. Both camps may agree with many arguments presented earlier and object to either a call for "more engagement" or "more freedom". Whereas both camps claim democracy as a foundation for society, their suggestions for greening it lead into different directions. Simplified, liberal democracy puts the burden of achieving sustainability on the citizen as individual, while participative democracy puts the burden on society as a community of participants. While the last chapter showed cognitive challenges and an enlarged private sphere as barriers to sustainability, this chapter will examine if unsustainability can be overcome by moving the

---

[422] "We have tried to craft a way of looking at environmental and social problems consistent with the notion of democracy" (Buell and De Luca 1996:138).

[423] "Pluralist governments more successfully than other regimes met the challenges of regulating production and consumption, without adopting the heavy-handedness of authoritarian regimes or threatening the sanctity of private property or civic rights" (Josephson 2005:30).

[424] Levy accentuates that "green democracy theories usually assume that conflicts and disagreements regarding the shape of the environmental conduct of society should be resolved through non-coercive argument and deliberation. This fundamental demand, grounded in the reality of moral pluralism, is, I believe, the trademark of contemporary green political thought" (2004:50; Connelly et al. 2012:63).

environment into the public sphere. Attested shortcomings might be solved within public discourses.

Given the plurality of democratic theory and the criticism of different approaches by democracy theorists themselves, one must ask whether and how participation and deliberation can bring greener outcomes. First this chapter looks at the idea of democracy as postdemocracy – a form of management of pluralistic values, which can be interpreted as an extension of the discussion on green liberalism. This includes a continued critique of liberal democracy. It will lay the foundation for a critical reflection on the calls for more democratic participation. Noteworthy, strong democracy may be 'overrepresented' in the field in general. It is typically argued that the lack of substantial green politics is not due to problems of democracy as such, but due to a lack of participation and citizen engagement. Agency as chances for participation is popular within green political theory as a facilitator for greener politics. So called 'new modes of governance' are seen a possible solution to overcome unsustainable practices.

> "Environmental policy that may well require sacrifice on the part of citizens is more likely to be seen as legitimate if it has been created in a context of dialogue involving those who are to be subject to its requirements" (Smith 2004:Loc. 3807-11).[425]

Involvement is often described to be a main driver of legitimacy. The idea is also that once more people are more involved, better decisions for the commons would be made possible. New forms of governance are presented as "increased opportunities" for more direct input (Baker and Eckerberg 2014:194). Examples regarding the environment show grave limitations on deliberation's possibilities.[426] Findings indicate that there are significant problems with involvement itself beyond 'the tyranny of participation' (Crooke and Kothari 2001). Overall this chapter will deepen the question whether sustainability can be achieved via democracy; hence whether democracy cannot only be understood as an end (by itself), but also as a means to sustainability. Herein, it will further look into the consequences for life support systems. Correspondingly it ends with the way democracies cope with the future and their ability to adjust to the environment as an external circumstance(s). To understand democracy's potential for sustainability the results in regard to nature in particular its prospects for sustainable governance for and in the future need close examination. Here the examination turns back to

---

[425] Given plurality of worldview, there "raises the danger that one person's conception of ennobling sacrifice may be regarded by another person as a brutal, totalitarian imposition. Consequently, while there may be a general, prima facie obligation to sacrifice, the time and nature of the sacrifice ought to be determined through democratic consent, rather than authoritarian coercion" (Cannavo 2010:221).

[426] "Despite the win-win promise of new modes of environmental governance, actors involved in environmental policy practice have trouble meeting the multiple expectations embedded in the deliberative turn. In line with critics of deliberative models of democracy, this finding suggests that there is no guarantee that deliberative governance arrangements will deliver green outcomes. The long-standing tension in green political theory between process and outcomes, input and output legitimacy, remains valid" (Bäckstrand et al. 2010b:225; see also Dryzek 2005:100ff.).

democracy in general in order to assess its adaptability and capacity to mitigate successively unfolding environmental destruction. At the end, facing environmental destruction as truth is central to democracy's sustainability.

2.3.1. POSTDEMOCRACY AND THE END OF TRUTH

There is a vivid discussion around the term 'postdemocracy' and its usefulness (Merkel 2011). Theorists who employ the idea criticise the latest developments in many democracies as 'postdemocratic' (e.g. Crouch 2008). They see democracy as having been hollowed out.[427] In their view today's democracy rather manages different interests and therefore could not be classified as democracy. Crouch accentuates that a liberal understanding of democracy can lead to low expectations in its performance, which means that problems can be overlooked easily (2008:10). Postdemocracy is characterised as a democracy that does not see politics as a field of struggle about values but instead as a field of managing values. The label is eurocentric, since most scholars using the term are concerned with Western democracy and democratic practice outside a Western context does not appear deprived of value conflict.[428] Crouch, who coined the term with his book *Postdemocracy*, focused on the US, the UK and Italy (2008). Arguing for an application of the term, he writes that the seemingly greater publicity and transparency of politics could be nothing more than appearances (2008:23ff.). This is reminiscent of a classification as simulation. Wider participation by civil society according to Crouch may not necessarily be a sign of a functioning democracy, but a symptom of declining political institutions. Citizens may get active outside of the normal channels because they lost trust. While Crouch defines democracy as a government that challenges privileges and social hierarchy, postdemocracy for him is defined by their denial (2008:71). He admits however that capitalist societies have failed to separate between justice, democratic and economic rights, since rich citizens have always been able to afford better lawyers and lobbyists (Crouch 2008:105). As mentioned earlier, there is no agreement on the meaning of democracy, which certainly complicates the question of whether the 21st century is postdemocratic.

Any classification as 'postdemocratic' inevitably comprises the idea that democracy in a pure version existed. Latour's reservations against the concept 'postmodern' are equally valid for the term 'postdemocratic'. Just like the claim that "We have never been modern" the claim that "We have never been democratic" needs to be critically assessed. Latour's claim hints at the very

---

[427] "Conflictual politics is deemed to belong to the past; the favoured type of democracy is consensual and depoliticized" (Mouffe 2002:12). The idea of favouring a middle ground between more radical politics is sometimes presented as the Third Way.

[428] Though some of the arguments could be labelled as overwhelmingly 'Western', a discussion is nonetheless important. Not only a majority of the big polluters fall under this label, international institutions such as the UN as well as academia are still dominated by the language provided by Western discourses.

problem of pure forms. Simply that they never existed in the first place.[429] Despite this objection, it may be still useful to speak of 'apolitics' to demark a line, where a majority of the Western publics do not take an interest in politics and political institutions or at least political actors have limited agency in contrast to other institutions that are not political in a narrow sense.[430] If called 'postdemocracy' or not, the critique, scholars on both sides are raising, is important for the subject of this work. Traditionally, politicians in a metaphorical sense fought for the truth Aristotle saw politics as the specific place for ethical considerations (1986). Politics deprived of ethics by this definition are not politics. 'Postpolitical' could be signified as the agreement to disagree, which is a commonly used concept.[431] When green liberalism declares ethics and convictions as private, they follow the same rationale (Wissenburg 2001a; 2001b; 2004; 2006).[432] But politics in its essence is partisan and cannot stop there (Mouffe 2011). When Mouffe calls for an agonistic democracy, she calls for politics that revive struggle and accept conflict as inevitable (2002). In her elaboration deliberative democracy theorists fail to acknowledge that conflicts will not vanish and miss to recognise that it is a genuine part of democracy.

A particularly strong case against liberal pluralism is made by Estlund, who highlights its relativism and problematic relation to truth (2009).[433] Treating all claims as equally valid can be a consequence of such a pluralism (Dryzek 2005:119; Dobner 2010). The normative rationale behind says that

> "no person can legitimately be coerced to abide by legal rules and arrangements unless sufficient reasons can be given that do not violate that person's reasonable moral and philosophical convictions, true or false, right or wrong" (Estlund 2009:Loc. 664-67).

This effectively narrows the realm of politics extremely. The application of the harm principle even in a thin version becomes difficult. In his book Estlund asks a particularly important question for environmental politics: "Why should objections based on false doctrines be thought

---

[429] While ideal types are useful tools of scientific inquiry too often their existence is implicated.

[430] "Post-politics marked by managerial logic" is blind and "ignores inherent antagonism and heterogeneity" (Swyngedeouw 2011:75).

[431] Dahrendorf notably describes the behaviour of the public intellectuals within fascism as conformism without engagement but also without resistance (2006:110). The contrast between the statement in general and Dahrendorf's observation of most liberal intellectuals appears stark, yet, the difference is smaller than it appears. The term 'Environmental Holocaust' is used occasionally.

[432] More generally, Graham comments: "Almost everyone assumes that the arguments about religion and politics can be transferred without significant loss to a similar debate about politics and morality. But can they?" (2013:Loc. 1320-22).

[433] Interestingly, there is no rational argument why rationality should have priority over irrationality prioritizing and it is therefore irrationality itself (Dahrendorf 2006:74).

to defeat justifications that employ true premises and sound reasoning?" (2009:Loc. 756-59)[434]
Most critically, while false assumptions are politically acceptable under Rawls' doctrine,

> "we do count people as unreasonable for failing to hold certain views, such as, perhaps, that all people are morally free and equal, that even reasonable people can disagree, and so on. Here is one more thing they must accept: a certain view of who counts as reasonable or qualified. We assert its moral significance simply by saying that if you don't accept this view of who is qualified, then you are not qualified" (Estlund 2009:Loc. 919).

Anyone who objects to this for being overly inclusive is excluded. Meanwhile, De-Shalit argues that since liberalism and liberal society in essence means "respect for others", it is fertile for respecting nature (2001:388).[435] He thereby overlooks the fact that this respect often means the toleration of destructive practices. Repeatedly, overinclusion needs to be addressed. Pluralism of norms and values mean collective unaccountability (Heintel 2011; cf. Elling 2008:18ff.).[436] Overinclusion does not only diminish chances for effective and encompassing policy making, the individualisation in society also outsources green issues. Hausknost punctuates the avoidance of politics:

> "Choice, finally, does not require any political justification at all, as it operates on the individual level and produces aggregate results outside the political system (governments readily support voluntary labelling schemes by providing the legal frameworks, but do not openly impose choices on individuals)" (2014:367).

An insistence on choice frees governments of the need to provide justifications for their actions and diverts attention from the common good, while also disarming governments. The capacity for solving environmental issues is said to be further shrunken within 'postdemocratic' structures (Blühdorn 2011). Respectively, the 'posts'-debates can be found in green thought as well. 'Hollow democracies' are said to be incapable of handling the ecological crisis. However, the development of environmental movements and green parties overlapped with the general 'depolitisation' of the environment as an issue and their delegation to the private realm. The attested depolitisation is characterised by the absence of actual political programs and politics which do "not revolve around choosing one trajectory rather than another" (Swyngedeouw 2011:70). Politics are tamed more generally, seemingly freed of big issues. Here, environmentalism has become "inherently reactionary" and a part of 'the liberal order' (2011:73). Swyngedeouw describes this governing as an operation

> "with the generally accepted consensus of a global and largely (neo-)liberal capitalism, the right of individual choice, an ecological awareness and the necessity to continue this, to

---

[434] E.g. "We too, like Hobbes, have made the discovery that the business of politics is peace, and that those who think that politics is for enforcing the truth will achieve neither truth nor peace" (Minogue 1966:65; cf. Kenis and Lievens 2014).

[435] Shearman and Smith think that it is the opposite: "Liberalism fails to provide a philosophy of life. If one has no philosophy of life then one cannot accept the value of nature" (2007:115).

[436] "Given the lack of an authority that could decide about conflicting validity claims, a consensual and co-ordinated approach does not seem possible" (Blühdorn 2012:134).

sustain the state of the situation (that is allegedly in serious danger).Discussions and dispute are tolerated, even encouraged, in so far the general frame is not contested" (2011:77).

This form of hollowed-out politics that are essentially deprived of important value conflicts consequentially can be made without dividing people (Swyngedeouw 2011:76; Kenis and Lievens 2014).

> "[E]nvironmentalism has a normative and moral dimension determining the way in which the whole environmental issue makes sense to us — if at all. It is with regard to this dimension that we ask whether environmentalism has come to an end" (Levy and Wissenburg 2004a:Loc. 361-63).[437]

Green issues might be integrated into politics as management.[438] Ecological integrity, on the other hand, demands prioritisation.

Allowing for extensive pluralism in regard to nature is pernicious. It is an obstacle to environmental politics, because "[p]luralism of culture destroyed the belief in ecological categorical imperatives existence" (Blühdorn 2011:22f.).[439] Whence 'postpolitics' has no truth but celebrates appearances and multiplicity, while the ecological crisis is real.[440] A celebration of diversity in the name of liberal tolerance is in direct conflict with the reality of environmental destruction.[441] As mentioned earlier, scientific facts cannot be matters of public opinion and

> "environmental problems are actual problems — irreversible ecological damages, health problems and depletion of natural resources that are real and dangerous — not merely a matter for representation, interpretation or discussion (apart from scientific disputes and 'selling' the story to the media). Environmental problems are out there in the world, not just in our world view" (Talshir 2004:Loc. 623-26).

Sound ecological politics, then, cannot allow for pluralism and tolerance towards other worldviews in environmental matters. Such relativism risks chances for sustainability. While liberalism warns against trading freedoms, the consequences of the inaction such a philosophy produces, should be clear (Harris 2013; Oreskes and Conway 2014). Liberalism and naïve social

---

[437] Writing about the possible end of environmentalism Levy observes that "[o]ne of the central objectives of rethinking green politics is to see that it is not geared towards the discovery of some scientific or metaphysical truth regarding social-environmental relations, but rather is concerned with the creation of agreement in respect to those relations" (2004:50). Though problematic by its name a theory of postecologist politics' "aim is to capture and explain a political reality, that is a factually happening politics of nature, which is clearly no longer – if actual politics ever has been – determined by ecologist principles and which can therefore not adequately be described by ecologist theories" (Blühdorn 2012:152). It helps to explain a disengagement of scientific facts and political action. A position arguing for the importance of agonism in regard to climate change politics is presented by Swyngedeouw (2011).

[438] "The post-political environmental consensus is radically reactionary forestalls articulation of divergent, conflicting and alternative trajectories for the future" (Swyngedeouw 2011:78).

[439] Blühdorn describes Habermas' idea to replace truth with agreement as dangerous (2012:107). Notably, "concrete environmental politics [...] responds first and foremost to concerns and anxieties which are quite evidently social constructs" (2012:48).

[440] Elling states that "objective certainty has lost its meaning" (2008:18).

[441] "The diversification of social values and individual lifestyles constantly increases the number of legitimate viewpoints and interests, and renders the resulting social conflicts ever more complex and irresolvable (democratic sclerosis)" (Blühdorn 2012:28).

constructivism can be equally destructive. What Hannigan jokingly writes about the latter, could be said for the former as well: "Even less charitable critics from other disciplines have depicted the social constructionist as a sort of Darth Vader, perverting the force of sociological understanding and ignoring the 'reality' of the environmental crisis" (2006:29).[442] Some scholars therefore believe that only a realist account of nature "provides the basis for identifying or imposing limits upon the public, without which environmental arguments for social and political change are left floating as mere preferences in a sea of pluralistic interests" (Meyer 2006:784). One side underlines the importance of truth claims against "relativism, developers, and the demands of a democratic public", while another side fears a reification that might justify "illegitimate exercises of political authority" (2006:784).[443] Latour shows the general flaw in the old distinction between politics and science (2004; see also Hache and Latour 2009 and Harris 2013:Loc. 116). At the beginning of *The Politics of Nature. How to Bring the Sciences into Democracy*, Latour writes:

> "We have no choice: politics does not fall neatly on one side of a divide and nature on the other. From the time the term "politics" was invented, every type of politics has been defined by its relation to nature, whose every feature, property, and function depends on the polemical will to limit, reform, establish, short-circuit, or enlighten public life" (2004:1).

Nature cannot be understood outside of politics, as something independent. Instead the cognition of nature has to be understood within a political context. Any conception of nature then is political. A motif for silence by scientists, according to Latour, is that environmental destruction is actually a moral issue. It is less about knowledge which is novel for scientists. Here, the division between science and politics ceases to exist. When too many people are affected by the results such a separation cannot be maintained. Moreover, the distinction is not useful, when matters of fact are also matters of concern. Climate science therefore needs to be understood as politics. Building on his extensive work in the sociology of science, Latour advocates a strategic positivism.[444] Above all, there cannot be an end of environmentalism, ecology or nature.

---

[442] Hannigan explains that social constructivism does not deny the powers of nature, but reiterates "that the magnitude and manner of this impact is open to human construction" (2006:31). The importance actors attribute to a problem does not necessarily match an actual need.

[443] Estlund concerned with truth in democracy claims that "the existence of normative political truths needn't lead in any despotic direction. If political truth led inexorably to the legitimacy of dictatorship by experts (roughly Plato's view), then we should suspect that something in the argument has gone wrong, possibly the idea that there are political truths at all. I want to argue that there are philosophical costs to denying political truth, and, anyway, they do not justify dictatorship" (2009:Loc. 396-99).

[444] Again, Rawls' perpetuation of public reason creates difficulties. Since the idea of public reason specifies at the deepest level the basic political values and specifies how the political relation is to be understood, those who believe that fundamental political questions should be decided by what they regard as the best reasons according to their own idea of the whole truth—including their religious or secular comprehensive doctrine—and not by reasons that might be shared by all citizens as free and equal, will of course reject the idea of public reason" (2011:Loc. 6829-38). Clearly science is seeking an "idea of the whole truth". Strategic positivism cannot be as liberal as Rawls' public reason. Strategic positivism will be elaborated in a later chapter.

Elling criticises that "ecology insists that *nature* tells us what to do" and that its "thinking is based on precisely this unattainable modernistic ideal about truth in total harmony with an extra-discursive reality" (2008:30). Ecologist thinking often embraces a principle of unity instead of plurality and follows a modernist reasoning (2012). Blühdorn affirms this

> "there is only one nature, one global ecological equilibrium, one human interest of survival, one intrinsic value of nature and one human rationality which has to be – and eventually will be – able to convince everybody that it is in humankind's best interest to act rationally, that is to respect the integrity of nature and organise society in accordance with ecological principles. Irrespective of the fact that ecologists are talking a lot about pluralisation and democracy, ecological thought has so far been firmly based on this principle of unity, which is actually the core principle of all modernist thinking" (2012:35).

A strategic positivist or postpositivist position has the advantage that it acknowledges its premise. It may openly declare the importance of scientific truths in contrast to pluralism that allows for their denial. While taking precaution against scientific error, political theory needs to nonetheless take nature seriously and openly stand against an 'End of Truth'.[445] Whether such a position can be integrated into a democratic framework remains questionable (see Levy 2004). Currently "the overwhelming majority of empirical instances of politics have nothing to do with truth. They organise a mixture of power and opinions" (Badiou 2004:97).[446]

Discussing Luhmann's systems theory, Blühdorn emphasizes that the major obstacle which sustainability faces is that "unless the eco-movements can legitimately claim some superior kind of rationality, the question arises why society should take the problems they raise (construct) any more seriously than those raised by any other system" (2012:137).[447] Bringing back 'the political' is not only a call by Mouffe and the likes, but also by green theorists such as Eckersley (2004). She attests

> "a palpable shift in the dominant understanding of the very role and rationale of the state in ways that appear to make it even more difficult to uphold the values of environmental protection and environmental justice through the state. Social aspirations and expectations of the state have changed in ways that make it harder to revive or reinvent an ethical ideal of the state as embodying any substantive social and ecological purpose" (2004:Loc. 812-15).[448]

---

[445] "Environmental political thought should free itself from the suffocating embrace of tolerance and re-engage in uncompromising truth-talk. Strengthened by a reasonable commitment to seek the right answers to our environmental problems, environmentalists should set out to criticize contemporary political culture as well as to reconsider their own positions and commitments with regard to the shape of society in general" (Levy 2004:59).

[446] In his critique, Crouch also mentions the inclusion of expert commissions in the British government as problematic since some are dependent on funding by corporations (2008:61)

[447] "Deep ecology recognized that morality is rooted in our sentiments. Consequently, the search for a rational, objective basis for ethical rules was itself highly problematic" (Radcliffe 2002:65).

[448] Note that Rawls for example did not intend to deprive all substance from politics. "What is important in [Rawls'] perspective is that if we consider impartially what society ought to provide for individuals [...] we must conclude that it ought to furnish them with procedural as well as more substantive liberties and rights" (Pettit 2012:185).

Barry describes the green state that scholars like Eckersley envision as 'postliberal' and not 'antiliberal' (2001:59).[449] Ultimately, sound environmental politics need to be not only guided by a facts, but also by normative claims regarding a 'should'.[450]

> "By whatever name, however, we live in paradoxical and perilous times rendered more so by a deficit of vision. If our future were made into a movie and fast-forwarded a few decades, it would have no good ending [...]. The challenge to those intending to lead is to help create a vision of a decent human future within the bounds of ecological possibility" (Orr 2009:9).

Orr specifically uses the indefinite article singular. It implies that if sustainability is to be achieved, unsustainable visions need to be excluded and cannot be managed as equally valid among others. The preservation of life support systems has to become most relevant. "Under democracy it is not pregiven interests that determine political outcomes. Rather, democracy itself, deliberatively and heuristically, defines the content of interests" (Dunn 1999:138). Thence, if sustainability via democracy is possible, participation needs to green this interests and enforce the implementation.

2.3.2. PARTICIPATION AS PANACEA

Most green theorists do not question democracy's potential for sustainability. The fact that sustainability is not achieved anywhere is not attributed to democracy, to the contrary. Participation, not exclusion, is meant to give the environment more relevance. The green mainstream position is to call for more democracy.

> "Above all else, the green theory treats individual human beings as agents who naturally are, and morally ought to be, autonomous and self-governing entities. Politically, that pretty directly implies the central theme of the green political theory of agency: the importance of the full, free, active participation by everyone in democratically shaping their personal and social circumstances" (Goodin 2013:Loc. 2945-48).

Participation is seen as a key to better environmental governance. It is seen not only as an end in itself, but also as a means to overcome destructive practices. Leggewie and Welzer understand the current crisis as a metacrisis that needs radical change (2009:13f.).[451] In accordance with the majority of greens, they claim that this crisis asks for more, not less democracy. In particular the willingness of the individual to take responsibility and collective engagement are highlighted as necessities.

---

[449] Eckersley states it herself: "Ecological freedom for all can only be realized under a form of governance that enables and enforces ecological responsibility. Ecological democracy is a postliberal rather than antiliberal democracy" (2004:Loc. 1328-29)

[450] In their article "Searching for 'the political' in environmental politics", Kenis and Lievens recall Zizek's description of postpolitics, where "the conflict of global ideological visions embodied in different parties which compete for power is replaced by the collaboration of enlightened technocrats (economists, public opinion specialists...) and liberal multiculturalists; via the process of negotiation of interests, a compromise is reached in the guise of a more or less universal consensus" (2014:536). Even the political protesters remain in the same discourse by buying Starbucks etc., they maintain the system.

[451] They describe the 'climate crisis' as a metacrisis, since it threatens the system itself.

Here and again expectation of such willingness may be unrealistic. Green theorists themselves have to acknowledge this. The call for more democratic participation for a sustainable democracy in fact includes two claims. The first claim is often taken as a given. It is assumed that people want to engage politically or at least should want to be engaged. The question whether people are actually interested in participating does demand more attention. Just as liberalism insists on autonomy and self-determination as premises for flourishing, most popular green political theory presupposes active participation. Both are agency-centred but do not acknowledge the possibility of non-engagement or non-determination as an agency option. Active involvement in politics is generally low. Despite the celebration of participation as a means of attaining freedom and self-determination, many people might not be interested in participation. People neither theoretically nor practically attribute the same importance to participation as popular democratic theory suggests. Instead they typically do not define freedom in regard to political participation (see for example Alford 2003:158). In Alford's study only a couple interviewees talked about freedom in terms of political participation. Though the study is based on people's perceptions in the US, it should not be taken lightly, since participative democracy itself advocates taking people's ideas seriously. Furthermore, citizens may be much less likely to participate in politics than theory suggests. For instance the participation rate in Swiss referenda in the last 40 years is around 42.5% (Merkel 2011:51). In ancient Athens 90% of the citizens, who were paid for appearing, were absent for the majority of debates (Latouche 2005). Even Germany, sometimes taken as the closest approximation to a green state (Jahn 2014:94; Sommerer 2014), does not have the desired participation. Despite a substantial variety of channels for political participation, most Germans remain unengaged (Böhnke 2011:18f.). Citizens rarely get active beyond voting and signing petitions. In spite of campaigns for voluntary engagement, regular and long-term engagement actually decreases.[452] Even in countries with high environmental consciousness, citizens barely participate in environmental groups. Environmental protection clubs make up only 1% of all German club memberships (Leggewie and Welzer 2011:194).[453] The above data shows that it is not a given that people want to be

---

[452] Engagement cannot be assessed precisely. Some organizations offer free memberships that only take a couple clicks. A membership in the World Environmental Organization for example requires solely name and email address (world.org).

[453] If participation is what really matters, and material goods provide a language to facilitate that, then richer societies ought to show more evidence of better environmental governance including performance (see Jackson 2012:Loc. 2682-84).

involved and determine politics.[454] The second and vocal claim is the green mainstream assumption that participation will bring greener outcomes, meaning that wider open procedures eventuate better substance, is hard to assess.[455] Still the belief pervades green thought. "Participatory modes are framed as a means to achieve better outputs, decrease implementation barriers and thus improve environmental quality" (Hogl et al. 2012b:282). So far, both claims remain unsubstantiated. Newig accentuates the lack of proof regarding the positive effects of political participation on the environment and highlights that "studies provide only sporadic evidence to support theoretical claims from various strands of the literature" (2012:58; see also Hogl et al. 2012b).[456] Examples of participation in water management imply that effectiveness of institutions determines the quality of participation and not the opposite (Hagberg 2010:139ff.). This is similar to the findings by anthropologists in regard to the preservation of common pools. Newig and Fritsch find furthermore that the outcome of participative processes is better if a government agency is included in the process (2011). In his comparison of the developments of wind energy in Germany and the United States, Karapin draws the conclusion that government support is a premise for progress (2014:119; see also Bäckstrand et al. 2010). The institutional settings, this entails the political structure and its derivative agency, need to be heeded accordingly.[457]

Besides, it seems self-evident that the results of participative decision making are highly dependent on the stances of the active participants. So far, studies show that the substance is largely determined by "the preferences of the actors involved, context variables crucially influenced the impact of participation on environmental outcomes" (Newig 2012:58; see also Duit 2014a). Successful resource management is extremely context dependent and "seemingly small differences in institutional rules and actor incentive structures" change the outcome (Duit and Hall 2014:295). Thus, praising participation without any reservation blatantly ignores the obvious. Newig underlines that

> "in societal contexts characterized by a highly committed environmental administration and a less environmentally friendly citizenship, participatory decision-making is likely to weaken ecological goals. Whether participation will improve or deteriorate environmental standards

---

[454] Invoking this disinterest as a form of false consciousness is a paternalism as well. I see Young's discussion about the possibility to understand monkey wrenching as a means of a widening democracy in this light (1997; see also Carter 2013). Instead of understanding such a practice as anti-democratic, he makes the case that it could be seen as enhancing democracy beyond parliamentary representation, especially when it fails to protect the environment and since equal participation has not been achieved.

[455] Newig and Kvarda state that there are "doubts about the universal validity" (2012:36).

[456] Studies tend to focus on small and medium scale (Duit and Hall 2014:295).

[457] Jahn sees a particular need for further research here: "The gap between institution building and policy on the one hand, and the outcomes on the other, indicates that more research is necessary to reveal the causal mechanisms between environmental policy and institution building and environmental performance" (2014:103).

most likely depends on the kind of actors involved and the respective interests they pursue" (Newig 2012:52f.).[458]

Environmentalism and its agenda are not excluded from the mechanisms inherent in participative decision making, just because greens promote the mechanisms as positive. In fact, a green political theory that fully relies on the belief in the positive effect of more participation underestimates the conditionality of participation and, as pointed out earlier, confuses procedure and substance. Some of the conditions have been acknowledged and debated within green political theory (see Carter 2007).

Beyond the claim that democracies are not sufficiently democratic lies a different but connected problem that most greens tend to ignore. There is a tradeoff between a commitment to small-scale or grassroots democracy and the need for effective coordination (Goodin 2013:Loc. 3480-82; Radcliffe 2002:21-45). Goodin phrases this paradox as follows:

> "This is just to say that greens simply cannot have it both ways. It cannot be true, at one and the same time, that (a) green issues ought to be of pressing concern because only concerted global action is capable of solving them, but that (b) the best way of responding to those issues is to devolve all decision-making powers down to very small political units who lack any way of acting in concert with one another" (2013:Loc. 3714-17).

It is hard to imagine how greens and green theorists can overcome this contradiction between decentralisation and centralisation in order to effectively ensure life support systems. So far, the few attempts are not convincing. Decentralisation and centralisation have different justifications and inevitably influence democracy's environmental performance. The potential clash between these two diametrically opposed processes is an important part of a wider discussion within democratic theory and practice.

Decentralisation of decision making is of importance, since units would need to be small enough to ensure that participants can have an influence.[459] Discussions need to be possible and participants need to be able to have the proper information, which includes knowledge about the issue as well the possible impact of decisions. Participation is premised on many conditions and if such are not met participation can hinder positive outcomes (Newig and Fritsch 2011). Hence, the claims that participation is a panacea for nature have to be scrutinised. In order to be a proper corollary, the assumption that participation generally produces better outcomes would

---

[458] "Contrary to the argument that participation improves the output of decisions [...] environmental standards of decisions are largely determined by the preferences of participating actors. This implies that in the case of a participatory process in which participants predominantly favor development interests, environmental standards will likely be decreased in the course of a participatory (as opposed to a non-participatory) decision process" (Newig and Kvarda 2012:37).

[459] Twenty years ago, Buell and De Luca suggested that seeing small communities as the only legitimate source of decision making can lead environmentalism to political irrelevance (1996:74).

have to be proven. So far, both remain propositions. The assumption that participation in democratic governance will impact nature positively is also inspired by the idea that not only does more government responsiveness and accountability stimulate greener politics, but also that they are to be achieved through localisation and grassroots democratisation (Carter 2007:56).[460] This would include diverse interests in decision making and the integration of the local level would mean that communities could have improved knowledge and therefore agency to protect their environment. Not only is localisation said to lay the foundation for better problem recognition and action, it is also argued that "forcing the institutions of civil society to respond to popular demands, participatory democracy is more likely to produce, if not morally perfect outcomes, then at least morally better ones" (2007:57; Goodin 2013; see also Dahl 2000:55).[461]

Romanticising city states, greens tend to believe that small-scale democracies give birth to more sustainability by making the inhabitant of a community closer to nature (2007:56ff.). Decentralisation is said to enable participatory democracy with a citizenry that is at the same time autonomous and other-regarding, so it voluntarily engages in a sustainable lifestyle. Such participatory approaches see a chance for stronger democratisation in smaller communities with local knowledge. Local decision making is meant to generate greener decisions. Still, as Newig points out, "contrary to sustainability goals, the interests of local actors tend to focus on shorter time horizons" (2012:53). Ball's description of the contrast between American environmentalists' rejection of oil drilling and the local population's favouring position is an example of how abstract environmentalism could fail in reality (2006). But it also shows that decentralised democracy is not per se environmentally friendly and that locals may often prefer economic use with direct returns (Newig 2012:55f.).[462] For example,

> "survey after survey shows that if the decision were made locally and democratically by Alaskans themselves, roads, oil rigs and pipelines would quickly cover Alaska's North Slope, the very real threat of oil spills would be ever present, and little or no heed would be given to the destruction of wildlife habitat or of the starkly beautiful scenery of that remote place. An overwhelming majority of Alaskans are more interested in jobs and in boosting the state and local economy than in protecting the natural environment" (Ball 2006:134).

Such preferences cannot be renounced when advocating smaller decision-making units. Decentralisation could mean that many local communities in charge of their own environmental politics could defect from the aim of sustainability. Carter however promotes eco-anarchy and

---

[460] General reservations against responsiveness and accountability to feedback have been raised in previous chapters.

[461] Baker and Eckerberg present evidence that "supports recent work on the centrality of the state in governing environmental problems. In practice, neither network nor market governance operates without state engagement nor can the pursuit of sustainable development be effective without the firm hand of the state steering it" (2014:197).

[462] Andersson et al., comparing three South American countries, find only some evidence that "de fact decentralization" could actually have a positive effect (2014:257).

supposes that locally self-sufficient governing is likely to make greener decisions (Carter 2013:31). The case of Alaska shows that this is not inevitable and that local priorities in fact may cause the opposite. Carter also suggests that green communities would not trade with those who do not follow the same standards (2013:249). This speculation is problematic, since trade between countries is hardly affected by sustainability or even (other) human rights' considerations (see for example Westra 1998a:118ff.). On the national level, countries with higher environmental standards trade with highly polluting countries. The individual level shows that most people are not willing to give up their lifestyle for such a consideration. Green communities would have to differ from both levels. The evidence on cooperation among people in stateless societies is inconclusive (Carter 2013:265).[463]

Research on the acceptance of the output diverges. Whereas it is typically suggested that deliberation will impel higher acceptance, the opposite can also be the case (Newig 2012:57). One major difficulty is to establish who will be affected by a policy (Shapiro 1999:38). Yet, not only may people disagree on the question of affectedness, learning can include enhanced awareness of the disadvantages.

> "Participation is expected to increase acceptance of and identification with decisions as well as improved trust relationships between state and non-state actors. This anticipated effectiveness is expected to lead to better acceptance and implementation of sustainable governance" (Newig and Kvarda 2012:35).

Formulated in this manner, participation has a strong instrumental dimension. Yet, if the reason for a participative approach is the assumed effectiveness, participation would have to be judged by its output. A motivated and active civil society can have an impact on politics. Through the democratic process it is possible for the citizen to bring an issue onto the agenda. All calls for green democracy are based on liberal ideas of some sort. One common argument assumes that an open society leads to less environmental destruction.

> "Where the state allows a full discussion both of what is and of what ought to be, where the state openly considers the balance between the costs of regulation to business, the costs of unfettered development, and the costs of postponing difficult decisions about resource use, there is less likely to be extensive, irreversible environmental devastation. In open systems, the technologies and approaches employed to manage and develop resources are less likely to contribute to social and environmental disruption" (Josephson 2005:25).

Democracy then might have the advantage of additional input by members of society. In practice, however, many democracies lag behind in implementation of environmental policies, since multiple channels for vetoing provide the opportunity to delay or even prevent action by actors who do not accept a given policy (Newig 2012:53). NIMBY means "Not in my backyard"

---

[463] Carter's suggestions are not just radical, but too radical. They presuppose an entirely different citizen.

and signifies self-interest in environmental matters as well as the gap between abstract and concrete demands as a common drawback. The NIMBY-mentality may motivate protest against concrete measures and good environmental politics may fail against the interests of the affected. Here again, individual preferences and the public good are in tension.

Moreover, NIMBY-mentality can occur on larger scales. Democratic citizens will probably try to oppose polluting industries locally and even lobby for higher standards. Yet, this can be interpreted as part of the NIMBY culture, since foreign products are still purchased. Discussing nationalism within the context of environmental politics, Scruton values *Heimatliebe*, love for one's home, as the single most powerful cause for nature's protection (2006:17; De-Shalit 2006a). Here, the *demos* does vote to get pollution out of their sight, but uses its pocket book to keep such industries running in the distance. Thereafter "national democratic structures become instrument of legitimation for externalization of ecological and social costs" (Blühdorn 2011:23). Democratic publics may decide collectively to regulate national industries. Much of the pollution is outsourced to other countries. Citizens may benefit from a cleaner local environment while at the same time allowing for the same level of consumption. Buchanan and Tullock point at democratic integration as instrumental in minimising external costs, while maximising decision costs (2001). In the context here, it is necessary to differentiate between different external costs. The external costs that are likely to be minimised are those that would be immediately felt by members of a society. The external costs that are not part of this logic are those that are further externalised. These constitute substantial costs for the environment. The costs affect those that are distant either in time, space or species.[464] At the same time, maximisation of decision-making costs also means that decisions will take longer, while overall environmentally relevant costs are not inevitably minimised.

Some Western European democracies seem to show significant reductions in overall emission, just as ecological modernisation theory promises. Some democracies have in fact shown reductions in pollution such as CO_2 emissions. Yet, even if the Kyoto Protocol involved sufficient reductions that were implemented locally, Europeans would still live largely unsustainably. At the first sight they seem to have a comparatively good environmental record, but typically this is not due to a series of solid environmental policies. In many cases improvements could be seen

---

[464] Proximity is an important aspect and the green citizen needs "to consider the impacts of global warming on people who are culturally and geographically distant from themselves (Pralle 2009:792). The relocation of pollution shows that this in practice poses a significant problem. "The important question which arises for cosmopolitans is whether universal emotions such as shame or guilt can become the grounds on which a stronger sense of moral obligation to the human race, future generations, nonhuman species and the natural habitat can be established" (Linklater 2006:114).

metaphorically as 'make up'. Environmental journalist Monbiot describes the phenomenon clearly. Writing about the British case he judges that "[w]hen our consumption emissions, rather than territorial emissions, are taken into account, our proud record turns into a story of dismal failure" (2013). General improvement of the environment is an illusion based on habituation, outsourcing and the success of some environmental politics in Central Europe that led to more norms, cleaner rivers and air (Leggewie and Welzer 2011:42). While pollution in many democracies is less visible than decades ago, lifestyles have become less sustainable in spite of eminent green rhetoric. Many reductions look substantial, yet are insignificant. The reductions are only a matter of interpretation, since the very important distinction needs to be made between territorially based emissions and consumption-based emissions. It often appears that decoupling of economic growth and pollution has been achieved, but pollution just occurs at a distance (Connelly et al. 2012:77). Consumption actually rose further and the demand for cheap products causes an ever greater environmental destruction. While European countries have agreed to cut emissions within their territory, as symbolised by the Kyoto Protocol, consumption-based emissions have been politically neglected. The transfer of carbon dioxide emissions from one country to another due to efforts in climate change or pollution mitigation is typically referred to as 'carbon leakage'. Since CO_2 is not the only pollutant it is more precise to be talk about 'pollution leakage'. Pollution leakage means that the harm is only relocated.

Even if statistics showed an indisputable gap between the pollution of democracies and autocracies fully accounting would change the whole picture (see for example Binder and Neumayer 2005).[465] The emission reductions within the countries themselves and the vast part of the reduction overall are not the outcome of good practices and decoupling, but simply outsourcing.[466] Many comparisons between countries do not include the environmental costs of consumption of imported products (e.g. Knill, Shikano and Tosun 2014). Instead of real change, pollution-intensive production is now based in 'developing' countries. A majority of the polluting industries has 'resettled'. Noteworthy, this means that while consumption within European countries rises, pollution does not. Such a development is problematic in multiple ways. The costs for the environment are not only transferred to other countries and thereupon out of sight, but additional costs can be generated by transportation, looser rules and older technology.

---

[465] Even authors who are especially concerned with criticizing autocracy do not deny pollution leakage: "It is true that democratic regimes—mainly the countries of North America and Europe—pushed by various economic and political pressures and pulled by consumer demand—often attempt to export the costs of resource use and waste disposal to postcolonial Regimes" (Josephson 2005:20).
[466] The 1990 emissions used as a benchmark for the Kyoto Protocol are problematic anyway, since they include the heavy polluting industry emissions of Eastern Europe, including the German Democratic Republic, which would have fallen anyway due to economic inefficiency.

Thence outsourcing contributes to the worsening of the global destruction instead of its mitigation. The population of powerful countries meanwhile perceives the environment as improving locally and therefore has a different perception of global pollution.[467] While rivers and air quality in many postindustrialist countries improve, the opposite is the case in other regions of the world. This also enables their citizens to reduce cognitive dissonance that is connected with their lifestyles. The effects of dangerous consumption habits are felt in a far distance, hence easily ignored. Green consumerism may advocate buycotting, but is largely ineffective, whilst further reinforcing a consumerist culture.

Furthermore pollution is brought to 'the poor' who typically already suffer from the effects of climate change disproportionally. Pollution leakage could be understood as a form of neocolonialism, in which, in a perverse way, rich nations transfer the costs of their lifestyles to the global poor. Once the origin of pollution is outsourced the responsibility of consumption is shifted in a way as well (the idea of responsibility literally contains response). The consumer as the person responsible lives far away from the affected person who seldom benefits but merely bears the costs. Trading with nations that do not implement sustainable practices means supporting exploitation of people and the natural environment (Buell and De Luca 1996:109). This includes that pollution is 'displaced', though formerly recorded it might now not even appear in records (Dryzek 2005:69). Global capitalism with its free trade agreements facilitates such developments.

> "Environmental laws are seen as surmountable by transferring manufacturing to developing countries, national environmental regulations are denounced as hindrances to free trade by the World Trade Organization" (Shearman and Smith 2007:91).

In order to avoid such leakages, governments would have to restrict the consumption of related products. This would be possible via import regulations, but regulations typically conflict with trade agreements and may also lead to higher prices for the consumer. The willingness (and/or ability) of the consumer to pay higher prices is limited and such policies are therefore unpopular as discussed earlier. Citizens and consumers choose in accordance with their preference.

---

[467] Lane summarizes different forms of pollution (visible, invisible, direct and indirect) which are prominent in different places (2011a:30f.): "1. Littering or petty pollution: it occurs massively in poor third world countries, like e.g. India or Fiji; 2. Toxic waste, metals and sewage: they are to be found on a large scale in the emerging economies where high levels of growth are combined with weak environmental protection; 3. CO2 pollution: it takes place in industrial and post-industrial economies requiring massive input of energy in various forms: transportation, heating, cooling, etc.".

Here, the discussion needs to come back to preference changes, since a democracy which outsources pollution cannot be understood as green. The relationship of participative democracy to preferences is ambiguous, too:

> "If participatory democracy takes preferences as given and simply provides a more effective way of aggregating them, then governments may be less likely to introduce progressive environmental policies" (Carter 2007:57).

This argument can be made against green liberalism, but not against the majority of green theorists who do not claim non-interference as a priority. Most greens have a different approach to autonomy, self-determination and preference.

> "Instead, greens want to alter human preferences because the radical transformation to a sustainable society will be easier to achieve if people can be persuaded by the force of argument that it is right for them to change their beliefs, attitudes and behaviour, rather than being told to do so" (2007:57).

Here the cognitive challenge and more importantly the value-action gap come into play. Carter discusses what could be either called a contradiction or 'theoretically naiveté'. While contemporary green thought is dominated by a defence of the right to self-determination and choice and therefore stance against nondemocratic solutions, participation is also praised for its assumed ability to change preferences.[468] One argument is that participatory democracy's

> "communicative and deliberative procedures provide the best *means* of changing individual preferences and facilitating the ecological citizenship necessary for the good society. Hence participatory democracy is a core green principle because it contributes to the *common good*, not because moral priority should reside with individual autonomy" (2007:57).

The tension between assumed autonomy (and respect for individual agency), on one hand, and the active influence of preferences on the other weakens the argument: In which way can the individual have legitimate autonomous preferences before entering the process, but then be influenced? If the preferences are not autonomous in the first place why should they matter? Lastly, if they are 'to be changed' anyway, they in fact do not matter. This again touches a philosophical question about the boundaries of freedom and paternalism, between choice and interest-oriented politics and their commensurability. The green idea of this process resembles the Socratic style in education. In one Platonic dialogue, Thrasymachus calls Socrates out on it (Plato 1982). The accusation is that Socrates pretends to ask questions, but in fact manipulates a conversation, spinning arguments to his conclusion. This implicitly includes dishonesty, but

---

[468] One further objection to decentralized small group decision making could be that they are often, rather than enhancing individual liberty, characterized by a high degree of social control and conformity (see Carter 2007:59). While such control helps against free riders etc., it can similarly suppress individuality and creativity, which greens try to protect in the first place.

Socrates never fully refutes it. The reader at the same does not typically question Socrates' superior intellect and good will (and may not view it as paternalism).[469]

Meanwhile, participation neither enhances choice- nor interest-protection automatically. Non-participation can have two reasons. People may be unable due to other obligations or people may not be interested. Participation in a dual way disadvantages the disadvantaged. Firstly, they may not have the means to participate. Secondly, despite the idea of undermining power structures, participatory politics repeatedly uphold the status quo. Power structures can be reproduced in the process (Bäckstrand et al. 2010b:229). Participatory governance therefore often upholds hierarchies. Examples from the developing aid sector show that if help is coupled with participation, it disproportionately excludes marginal groups which lack the resources to get engaged (Crooke and Kothari 2001).[470] There is no reason to assume that these mechanisms do not apply to environmental issues (Bäckstrand et al. 2010; Hogl et at. 2012). For instance a participative process in Denmark (regarding a national park) showed that this is likely to be the case as participants were 'the usual subjects' from civil society as well as strong interest groups (Boon, Nathan and Lund 2012). The better-educated have higher social status and since that can give them an increased feeling of agency, they are more likely to get engaged (Goodin 2013:Loc. 3029-36). Educated white men (Socrates as well as Thrasymachus) do not only have the rhetorical advantage. Przeworski warns accordingly: "Too often the calls for increased participation privilege those who have more resources to participate. Participation just cannot be equal and effective" (2010:169; see Dahl 2000:111).[471] But wishful green thinking brings about the "attempt to put onto future society the social cooperation exhibited by participants in some protest movements" (Radcliffe 2002:43). Having located the malaises (of unsustainability) in the lack of participation its promotion tends to overlook reality.

> "The case for participatory democracy starts from a critique of liberal democracy. Greens argue that liberal democracy is unable to produce the best decisions because it is characterised by hierarchy, bureaucracy, individualism and material inequalities. It offers limited opportunities to participate in the public sphere" (Carter 2007:55).

---

[469] Others may judge his technique as 'corruptive'.

[470] Crooke and Kothari collected interesting examples of failed participatory approaches in the context of development aid work under the title *Participation. The New Tyranny?* (2001).

[471] "[F]ace-to-face assemblies have shown that they are not necessarily democratic panaceas and are easily manipulated by powerful and experienced citizens" (Smith 2004:Loc. 3850-51). Governance networks do not inevitably abolish hierarchies. One natural resources management study found that "government actors used their privileged position to promote their own interests within these networks, enhancing traditional hierarchical patterns" (Baker and Eckerberg 2014:193). This might be a reason why in general projects with governmental support were more successful. Enhancing traditional hierarchy (while probably unintended), thus, could be an advantage for greener governance. Such a claim needs further research.

Participative democracy commonly has the same characteristics. Instead of overcoming them, it can give them another playground.[472] His namesake Carter stresses that even theorists of participative democracy acknowledge people are not prepared and lack the necessary qualities (2013:227). He also regards it as improbable that they will in the future, since status quo players will defend their privileges and current structures undermine such qualities.

NGOs are another way in which citizens can participate and have a voice in politics. In this way some of the barriers for participative processes at the individual level might be overcome. NGOs and other groups are normally understood as a sign of an open and 'vibrant civil society'. On the one hand, NGOs have multiplied and participation is typically celebrated. On the other hand, a large number of NGOs could be interpreted as a sign of state failure (Crouch 2008). Still, democracies do not have exclusivity on NGOs in general and the effect of these groups could be widely misjudged. Duit and Hall point out that the political right to freely form associations should have a greening effect on politics (2014:299ff.; see Geall 2013).[473] However, Binder and Neumayer found that environmental NGOs could not prove a positive impact on several forms of pollution (2005:537; see also Short 2009). The literature did not clearly show whether they actually trigger an improved "level of environmental quality" (Binder and Neumayer 2005:531). Frediksson et al.'s study claims the effectiveness of democratic participation (2005), but this is problematic. Their study is a good showcase for the complexities involved in shaping good environmental governance. It proposes that democratic participation paired with greater political competition instigates stricter environmental policies and that lobbying has a positive effect. Yet, such claims optimistically overlook important correlations. Frediksson et al. tried to substantiate their theory by studying different countries' regulations on lead. Although they assume that competitive participation is causal for lower lead contents other factors played a huge role. Countries which introduced better standards were at the same time countries with modern cars. Lead is in fact bad for these cars. In "The Secret History of Lead", Kitman further explains:

> "When safer alternatives are available, as they always have been, leaded gasoline's benefits are nil. It is not good for cars, and it prevents the use of modern emissions reduction

---

[472] Additionally, group dynamics can bring about decisions that are not in the "interests of those the group is supposed to represent" (Newig 2012:53). Group psychology cannot be left out of the consideration.

[473] Duit and Hall understand political rights as conditional "for collective action to challenge unsustainable resource use" and therefore understand corruption as problematic (2014:300). Yet, they could not find that corruption has a negative effect. Neither corruption nor protection of political rights led to differences in participation in decision-making processes. Furthermore, their full-sample model showed that local participation in implementation and levels of political rights were negatively correlated. NGOs and local involvement had a different effect depending on the average income of the country (2014:310f.) Any non-local stakeholder seemingly has no positive effect on management outcomes. Political rights also failed to be statistically significant for the effectiveness. The authors speculate that corruption, while possibly enabling illegal exploitation might also be a barrier to more efficient exploitation.

equipment, like catalytic converters, which, owing to the greenhouse effect, the world needs more desperately now than ever [...] It isn't even cheap" (2000).

As discussed by Wurster, the empirical literature often misevaluates environmental policies (2013). Too many factors play a role to confirm a specific theory of causation. Furthermore, clear differences between different classes of environmental policies are not drawn. Measures of 'weak sustainability' are regularly counted as if they actually meant sustainability, while they might only present politics of simulation. Here, a surprising observation made by Ward is that in a country "if anything, footprint goes up with membership of environmental groups, other things being equal" (2008:396). If members in those groups also have a high footprint or the same as the country average this could support the rational choice claim that these groups are used as indulgence only. It is in accord with prior observations in regard to the green consumption and low costs. Participation then would have to be viewed critically.[474] Ball concludes that decentralisation and grassroots participation are not preordained to produce a better environment and that "environmentalists have good grounds for fearing at least some democratically decided outcomes" (2006:134). Many assumptions are undermined by other fields of research such as social psychology.

2.3.2.1. DELIBERATION AND THE POWER OF THE GREENER ARGUMENT

The call for deliberative democracy is common in green thought. Decentralisation and grassroots democracy facilitate deliberative procedures. Deliberation is a highly valued form of participation. As famously advanced by Dryzek, hopes for more sustainable democracies are also put into the idea of deliberation (2005; Martin 2013). Deliberative democrats believe in epistemic democracy. This means that rather than believing that democracy is an aggregation of preferences, democracy itself is considered to have epistemic value. Deliberation and deliberative democracy are the dream of some political scientists (Bäckstrand et al. 2010a; see also Carter 2007 and Fishkin 2009). The belief is that "[t]hrough open and reasoned argument, free from manipulation and the exercise of power, better and more legitimate decisions will arise" (Bäckstrand el al. 2010a:5). Deliberative democracy is thought to enhance knowledge and understanding and therefore leads to better outcomes. Since deliberative democracy, like liberalism, is popular among many political theorists, it is difficult to mark distinctive traits. Deliberations can stand in contrast to elections as a different form of input into a democratic system. The language of deliberative democrats sounds promising (e.g. Dryzek et al. 2013:212).[475] Despite its dependence on an ecologically enlightened citizenship deliberative democracy has

---

[474] As pointed out earlier, increased participation is likely to have a negative effect on the time horizon.
[475] Eckersley raises the concern about missing guarantees in regard to the outcome of a deliberative process as well (1990). She argues that Dryzek failed to point at the problem believing that sustainability is a commonly recognizable collective good.

been presented as a solution to environmental degradation. Critical voices accordingly emphasize the lack of evidence as well as the additional conditions of the process.

> "'Deliberative democracy' has become an ecological buzz-word. However, so far ecologists have not produced any evidence for an intrinsic link between ecology and democracy. Practical experience suggests that public deliberation and participation are more likely to obstruct than promote ecological progress. They introduce even more interests and beliefs into the political arena and further dilute the ecological content and efficiency of any compromise that may be achieved. From a theoretical point of view, it may be added that the belief in deliberative democracy actually presupposes much of the consensus it only wants to establish" (Blühdorn 2012:21).

Many barriers have been touched upon earlier, but the particulars of deliberation should be subject to further investigation given its centrality within green political theory.[476] It is important to understand that deliberative democracy aims to overcome the gap between the green theory of value and the green theory of agency.[477] This is thought to be possible by the force of the better argument. It is assumed that once the framework for agency is set, the better argument will 'automatically' succeed and green values are the outcome. Some do not even see any meaningful consideration of environmental protection outside of democratic structures (Brulle 2006). Lövbrand and Khan summarise the trust in deliberative democracy as follows:

> "Resting upon an optimistic belief in the cognitive capacity and moral potential of the rational citizen, scholars in this field hope that inclusive and unconstrained reason-giving will help to transform personal preferences in favour of cooperative and collective solutions to environmental problems" (2010:60, Höffe 2009:295).

The trust in reason – the common precondition – is the foundation for the positive expectations. Arias-Maldonado for example believes that deliberations "allow the emergence of green values because of their objective rational appeal" (2007:235).[478] Yet, Blühdorn emphasizes that not only is there no evidence for the link between democracy and ecology, in fact deliberative and participative practices may even further hamper ecologically sound decision making (2012; see also Hobson 2013).[479]

---

[476] "Key questions are to what extent the deliberative process is open to competing discourses and arguments from citizens as well as elites, and how the process is conducted. Deliberative theorists suggest that reciprocity assures that arguments of different participants are included and treated in an impartial and respectful manner" (Kronsell and Bäckstrand 2010:41).

[477] It can be argued that deliberative democracy within a green paradigm needs to be persuasive using green reasoning and not employ arguments for more democracy (Arias-Maldonado 2007:234f.).

[478] While deliberative approaches normally celebrate pluralism, this idea at the same time shows a privileging. Enlightened reason is an aim. Note that global warming may also undermine level-headedness. As noted earlier heat leads to more desperate and violent behaviour, which is in conflict with rational decision making. (Bell et al. 2001).

[479] However, deliberative democratic practices in environmental politics might be hindered by the presence of older structures (Bäckstrand et al. 2010). This is open to speculation. The integration of existing institutions was shown to lead to positive results as mentioned earlier. Hildingsson, studying Sweden, suggests that new modes of governance do not bring the promised green outcomes and assumes that a "reason for this might be that the ideal conditions presumed in green political theory are largely incompatible with the realities of policy-making in advanced welfare states and, even more importantly, tend to ignore the key role of state institutions in the governance for sustainability" (2010:61f.).

Eckersley sees sustainability as a normative issue first and describes deliberative democracy "as the best model for reaching mutual understandings about common norms" (2004:Loc. 1459-6). Moreover, she defends the idea as a benchmark against those who deem it unrealistic (Eckersley 2004). Citizens might need training, but this does not preclude deliberative practices. Discussing Habermasian deliberations, Eckersley points out that

> "[h]is reassurance that pragmatic reasoning is nonetheless grounded in rules of fair bargaining that ensure equal consideration of the interests of all parties is unlikely to satisfy those who are concerned about unequal communicative power in the real world and "unrepresentative representation" in government in terms of discourses and social actors. Nor is it likely to reassure social and environmental justice advocates who find it desirable that political opinion and will-formation aspire toward higher rather than lower levels of intersubjectivity. Ecological democracy aspires toward moral rather than pragmatic reasoning, since moral reasoning directs deliberations toward the widest possible constituency of affected parties" (2004:Loc. 2015-18, 1990; see also Dryzek 1996).

Her green state includes comprehensive deliberations. This inclusion is meant to ensure greener outcomes. Here again reservations against an overinclusion cannot be avoided. Arias-Maldonado comments on the critique levelled against green deliberative democracy theory that "stressing the absence of any guarantee of success is somewhat superfluous, given the uncertainty and contingency which characterise political processes. The politics of nature cannot escape the nature of politics" (2007:247; Eckersley 2004:Loc. 2052-54). It is undeniable that the causality assumption between deliberative democracy and environmentally sound politics depends on a high degree of wishful thinking. Wissenburg accentuates the uncertainty, namely the possibility that participants of deliberative democratic processes choose self-interest over the preservation of a liveable planet and the conditionality of deliberative democracy given that "in real life, debates are usually won by the clever, not the right" (2001b:41).[480] So far, the discourse around the green state as a deliberative democracy includes several interconnected suppositions. De-Shalit differentiates between two types of arguments in favour of deliberative processes (2006b:97; Humphrey and Stears 2007:Loc. 2452): Firstly, participants are understood to be subjected to more information, hence gain a deeper understanding of environmental issues and therefore produce more rational and better decisions. Secondly, participation means that people will hear differing opinions, maybe even ecocentric arguments, and may develop empathy effectively looking beyond their own narrow self-interests.[481] Some advocates of deliberation actually think that it produces a 'correct answer'. Finding procedures that are more inclined to produce substantively good outcome, hence produce greener politics is an essential task of green

---

[480] "Exclusion of or any deliberative attempt to downplay scepticism might contradict the requirement of democratic inclusion to the extent that it is premised upon defensible moral considerations" (Lo 2014:565).
[481] "Deliberation particularly aims to transform individual preferences by widening the horizons of each citizen so that a policy can be endorsed by as many people as possible" (Gilley 2009:71).

political thought. Highlighting the fact that political processes seem not to be determined in general, does not weaken the argument against uncertainty.

"If there is one thing that stands out when one reads philosophical descriptions of deliberative democracy, it is how far these descriptions fall from reality" (Huemer 2013:Loc. 2008; Smith 2004; e.g. Eckersley 2004:Loc. 541-43). The success of deliberation is highly circumstantial. Effectively, the substance of "environmental assessment arrangements" cannot be predicted, since they depend on the context (Elling 2008:259f.). Too many factors influence the process and that is why – although it can be successful at times – it might as well be counterproductive (Newig 2012; e.g. Elling 2008:259ff.).[482] Deliberative politics cannot guarantee greener policies, despite the high expectation that it will lead to such. Deliberative politics face many prerequisite conundrums. Above all, as many scholars clearly state, deliberative democracy has too many requirements (Roemer 1999:58; Estlund 2009:Loc. 39067; see Lövbrand and Khan 2010).[483] Deliberations also bear high transaction costs. They are generally demanding. Elling locates important parts of the responsibility to the citizens (2008).[484] Resources need to be put aside for the process by all sides.[485] A positive result cannot be guaranteed, while the procedure itself is especially time-consuming. The possibility of failure to produce an outcome does not automatically have to be understood as negative. Ward writes that even if differences are too big to overcome, such processes have the advantage of pointing at the incommensurability and therefore still serve a function (2006:283). Though this is true, sustainability is less about the recognition of difference and more about the implementation of sustainable politics.

[482] Duit and Hall write that the "main message from [case study] literature is that decentralization and local democracy must be combined with actual transfers of competencies and accountability to local political actors if the benefits of stakeholder participation are to be realized" (2014:299f.). As discussed earlier, this does not inevitably mean a greener overall impact (see for example Lemos and Agawal 2009). Federal systems showed stronger commitment to environmental values on higher levels of government (Dryzek 2005:109).

[483] Some ecological thought stretches the idea of more democracy further. Additional requirements are introduced that, because possibly seeming utopian to many, have the potential to shed light on deliberative democracy in general. "Since all those potentially affected by environmental degradation (present and future generations, human and non-human subjects) cannot participate in practical discourse at the same time, green deliberative theorists are thus faced with the challenge to develop legitimate and effective means of representation" (Lövbrand and Khan 2010:48). Usually the minimum requirement to participate is the line between human and non-human animal. Animals are excluded at the very least for their lack of speech. It seems clear that animals are incapable of participation. Deliberative democracy may ask for too much from the citizen in theory, but in practice cannot in fact ask for more than the capability of speech and an age minimum. "An inclusive democracy or biocracy requires not only or literally listening to those who can speak – i.e. human beings – but to entities that are dumb but not mute" (Ball 2006:142, see also Dryzek 1996). The contrast between the ideal in theory and the necessity of pragmatic practice is manifested in the human chauvinism that clearly differentiates between human and non-human without giving actual criteria.

[484] Rostboll writes that "any argument for institutions and laws that make people take part in deliberation before they vote – or encourage them to do so – should not be justified with reference to their own good but be justified with reference to the idea that they are not merely exercising power over themselves, rather also over others" (2005:387). Deliberations then are a joint challenge in which power over others has to be acknowledged. Power normatively carries responsibility.

[485] The question of unachievable conditions is central, especially when "in a society dominated by the pursuit of economic growth and consumption, there is little time for active citizen participation in the democratic activities" (Carter 2007:49). In all likelihood, a sustainable culture is rather than an outcome the precondition.

One of the preconditions of deliberation is the availability of information. A connected main objection to more participative forms of democracy is the necessary expertise environmental decision making presupposes. This includes government and citizens. Newig criticises that

> "competing approaches deny that public authorities suffer from an information deficit, especially because many decisions in environmental governance are highly technical in nature and thus call for expert knowledge instead of lay contributions" (2012:52).

Ignoring this and demanding the incorporation of citizens is not only romantic, but also naïve. As touched upon earlier, in order to sway the public high certainty might be an unachievable premise. Full disclosure of science is then likely to mislead the public and hence could hinder action. A short examination of any scientific work shows the common practice of disclaiming, which to the layman is likely to undermine the information and the call to action. Moreover, there are other cases where transparency can be counterproductive to the protection of nature. Oksanen and Kampula discuss transparency of environmental information and stress that there are cases in which giving out information can in fact be in conflict with protection (2013). In some countries protection of species limits "environmentalist claims for transparency, the right to know, and the creation of the 'green public sphere'" (2013:975). Oksanen and Kampula see different ideals of sustainable democracy in tension. A comparison between liberal democracies shows differing approaches in practice. In Finland for example information access depends on the effect on the subject/object of the information and is based on considerations of security and privacy (2013:983). A commitment to transparency is restricted by the fact that

> "if files are thoroughly public, then there is a high risk of organised environmental vandalism, poaching, illegal gathering of plants and eggs, and even inadvertent disturbance" (2013:988).

Full transparency is frequently understood to be a condition for participation. A praise of full transparency overlooks the fact that not all participants may have good intentions or stick to the decisions made.

Trust is a further condition for successful deliberation. This is particularly difficult if personal as well as corporate interests are involved. High stakes may direct participants to caution.[486] Most environmental issues additionally aggravate the problem by not only having dispersed benefits and costs, but also by significant power asymmetries.[487] On the one hand, "communicative rationality requires that social interaction is free from domination, manipulation and strategic

---

[486] "Paranoia and distrust are particularly damaging to democratic forms of deliberation and action, to the operation of a tolerant civil society, which requires a considerable measure of trust and interdependence" (Glass 2006:738).
[487] "A program that [...] allows citizen to consider environmental and equity issues with their peers puts them in a position to choose the risks for the sake of generally recognized and widely distributed benefits" (Buell and De Luca 1996:133).

behaviour" (Lövbrand and Khan 2010:50).[488] On the other hand, the expectation that people overcome their own preferences is hindered by the immediacy of self-interest, while successful rhetoric counts more than content (Graham 2013). While seen as an important part of deliberative democracy, being affected and engaged in the problem-solving process at the same time is a hindrance. The recognition that something should happen, but without one's own sacrifice, is so common that there is the already mentioned abbreviation NIMBY for this practice. NIMBY is symbolic. Deliberations have shown that even when all sides work on the conditions for deliberation, positive outcomes may not occur. Especially when the consequences are severe, it is difficult to cope with arguments based on judgments such as "Wind mills are ugly" (see Carter 2007:317). Such arguments show the fallacy of trusting in enlightened citizenship. Arias-Maldonado points out that

> "the belief that citizens in a deliberative context will spontaneously acquire ecological enlightenment, and will push for greener decisions, relies too much on an optimistic, naive view of human nature, so frequently found in utopian political movements" (2007:248; Taylor 2013).

Unfortunately, the more at stake for the participants, the harder it gets to find solutions and the less willing people become to compromise. While seemingly self-evident, it is important to point this out. One example of this problem in deliberative practice is given by Johnson's discussion in "The Discourse of Democracy in Canadian Nuclear Waste Management policy" (2007). While good conditions for deliberation were set in place, the outcome of the process itself remained sobering and the author comes to the conclusion that

> "[t]he process also suggests that unaffiliated participants are generally more willing to reason in the shared interest and to seek agreement on that basis. Participants with a history of activism or with direct stakes in a given policy area have more difficultly reasoning in the collective interest and seeking agreement" (2007:95).

If it comes to sacrifices regarding the environment, most people who actually have a voice also have something at stake or have affiliation with some form of interest group in the broad sense. This is a critical observation not only for local governance, but especially for environmental politics overall. Coming back to the characterisation of politics, deliberative democratic theory underestimates this conflictual nature and maintains a theoretical claim regardless of facts (see Leist 2011). Estlund harshly questions the idealism of deliberative democratic theory:

> "[P]olitics is not, and probably could never be, mainly a matter of the impartial exchanging of reasons. How are these two things compatible? How can deliberation belong at the center of normative democratic theory even though it is by no means the predominant form of political activity even in favorable conditions?" (2009:Loc. 2639-41).

---

[488] For an important elaboration on manipulation by the powerful as well as the powerless see Scott (1990).

While impartiality is difficult to achieve, it is even more difficult in case of affectedness (see Commoner 1992).

> "It is unrealistic to expect that the virtues of deliberation and an orientation toward the common good will be the natural starting point for most of the people who come to democratic community meetings and who keep coming and stay involved. By and large, the consumerist orientation is going to be very strong – if not dominant – at the grassroots level, at least at the outset. People will invest their time in such process only if they feel that they will benefit from it and that it will serve their interest" (Jennings 2010:230f.; Arias-Maldonado 2007:249).

As argued in regard to participation, rhetoric may play a momentous role. The impartiality assumption is in tension with the focus on affectedness.[489] Eckersley convincingly criticises affectedness as a standard for its exclusivist logic that "dispenses with the whole idea of community" (2006:107). Such a standard only reproduces ideas of self-interest against the common good. Most crucially, cutting back on consumption can be understood by many as a huge sacrifice and therefore is a direct stake. The affected who are not likely to oppose, because they will not have to cut back from their current levels, are the so called 'subalterns', who, while sharing the burden of pollution, have by definition no voice (Spivak 1988). In other words, if deliberation is only successful among non-involved participants, fruitful deliberation in environmental politics becomes nearly impossible. Accordingly, the editor's note of an issue of *Environmental Values* states that "even in a purely political setting, faith in convergence on environmental ideals may be misplaced" (Spash 2007:145).

There is not only a power asymmetry concerning the communicative process and educational advantages, some interests may also be neglected because they are organisationally weak. The disproportional bargaining power of some interest groups remains a problem. The underrepresentation of animal interests is an obvious example, once one assumes that animals can have legitimate interest (see Eckersley 2004). An advantage of new styles of democratic governance may lie in the potential to include new voices, in particular, since traditional ones seemed to have failed to integrate ecological concerns (Humphrey and Stears 2007). However, even if deliberative democracies provide a wider platform to different interests "[t]he inclusion of formerly excluded arguments does not necessarily lead to acceptance" (Arias-Maldonado 2007:237). Some interests may be disqualified as 'utopian' and therefore excluded from serious discussions (see Hausknost 2014; Humphrey and Stears 2007:Loc. 2906). Advocates of vegan lifestyles are obvious subjects of many of these disadvantages.[490]

---

[489] For instance, "local councils tend to put the interests of their local constituency above the willingness to deliberative and negotiate agreements with external actors in a network" (Baker and Eckerberg 2014:195).
[490] That is even though many people might attribute a moral high ground to such a stance.

Critical theory suggests a procedure that involves the participation of all affected, but does not suggest a specific moral guideline.[491] It does not provide any solutions, but leaves decisions open (Brulle 2006:55). This importantly means that it

> "cannot adequately integrate concern for non-human nature, since it only considers the development of norms between mutual participants in a discourse. This omits consideration of the fate of other species that are not capable of participating in this dialogue" (Brulle 2006:56).

Hence, critical theory in itself is anthropocentric. With the insistence on human emancipation it cannot lead to a holistic protection of nature (see Blühdorn 2012). Here, those concerned with justice ordinarily follow the idea of deliberative democracy, while others see sustainability elsewhere. Brulle openly dislikes the idea of limits to political acceptability. He, in particular, directs his attention to the primacy of arguments based on science, since he interprets this as a limitation for a broader consensus on environmental protection shaped by multiple worldviews.[492] While giving the example of Evangelical Christians, ethical duty to protect nature, he fails to acknowledge that exactly this kind of cherry-picking is unacceptable in an inclusive democracy. An inclusive democracy does not only include pro-environmental beliefs, but equally needs to deal with anti-ecological morals. While science may serve as a delegitimation of some pro-ecological worldviews, it may equally delegitimise destructive ones. Discourse theory in general opposes the idea of the primacy of the better argument. While deliberations are not only exhausting and influenced by special interests, science is usually the space where the better argument actually succeeds (Höffe 2009:289ff.). This may appear tragic given that many deliberative democrats argue against science as authority.[493]

Green political scientists tend to understand democratic practice as a means to bridge externally (by natural science) and socially constructed concepts of nature whereby their "implicit democratic faith, here – both in the movements and in the possibilities for democratizing the practice of political theory – is striking" (Meyer 2006:786). Ward proposes that citizens' jury as

---

[491] Stakeholder management is the alternative to the traditional idea of conservation of access restriction by experts (Duit and Hall 2014:294).

[492] Estlund discusses the irony of the neutrality assumption in the context of deliberative democracy: "The idea of procedure-independent standards of political decisions may seem to lead inexorably, then, to the legitimacy of rule by the genuine experts, whomever they may be. The choice can seem to be between epistocracy, or rule by the wise, on the one hand, and deep proceduralism, the denial that such independent standards exist, on the other. If only it can be established that there is no genuine substance in the first place, then the proceduralist flight from substance is complete. Deliberative democracies are then existentially free and self-determining. The value of democratic deliberation is vindicated by making democratic deliberation itself the final political value" (2009:Loc. 472-75).

[493] "Participatory science can be conceived as an instrument to dethrone science or to deprive scientific knowledge of its authority and legitimacy conferred by modern society. If the democratization of science is conceived as a project of overthrowing science, sceptics are quick to rally and argue that this will endanger the quality of scientific knowledge and, finally, environmental policy process that relies on 'sound' science" (Bäckstrand 2004:110; see also Bäckstrand 2003). Scepticism could be based on the assumption that participatory science is a prioritization of quantity (of participants) over quality.

an unconventional approach could be less likely to underappreciate the environment (Ward 2006:286). He meanwhile suggests that the literature describes different techniques. If these are used in a determined direction, the charge of manipulation or at least influencing the decision-making processes from outside via the specific selection of a procedure cannot be avoided. Moreover, it also stands to debate why an externally constructed concept of nature is inferior. The problem of autonomy is recurring here, since deliberation builds on some form of autonomy, albeit its acknowledgement of social construction. In his article "Preferences and Paternalism. On Freedom and Deliberative Democracy", Rostboll tries to circumvent many concerns by redefining autonomy (2005). He problematises any non-fluent understanding of autonomy as well as an external imposition of autonomy (2005:273ff.). Whereas he values critical theory for studying barriers to free preference formation, he at the same time warns that "we should never from an external perspective take some preferences as not worthy of respect, and we should not see the state as an instrument to changing these preferences from without" (2005:379). Curiously, autonomy for him is also dependent "on whether people still hold [preferences] after they have seen them in light of the reasons given and the information imparted by public deliberation" (2005:379). He understands deliberation as a process that supports reflection.[494] Rostboll writes that

> "[d]eliberation triggers self-reflection not only regarding one's first-order preferences but also regarding one's reflexive preferences. It does so because one must be willing to defend one's opinions and give reasons for them to others and because one must be willing to listen to the reasons others have for their views. The deliberative process also imparts information about the world because this inevitably will be part of the arguments given for different points of view" (2005:376).

He establishes "must be willing" as a requirement and proceeds to claim that the preferences are still autonomous, given one has considered and heard the "relevant information" (2005:377).[495] Various biases that might hinder any such process have been discussed. Rostboll sees an advantage in deliberative democracy in the acknowledgement of "the possibility that preferences can be non-autonomously formed and that they can be unjustifiable to others in public deliberation" (2005:371). Deliberative democratic theory generally acknowledges that preference formation takes place within a social context. Paternalism is difficult to 'locate' and Rostboll

---

[494] According to Estlund, hypothetical participant's interests are usually personal and follow "the self-service conception of participation", meaning that reasons need to be personal to be accounted for (2009:Loc. 3538-39). Yet, he points out that contractual approaches do aspire to enlightened citizenry i.e. they ask for the considerations of others (e.g. Rousseau 2002).

[495] "The ideal [of public reason] also expresses a willingness to listen to what others have to say and being ready to accept reasonable accommodations or alterations in one's own view. Public reason further asks of us that the balance of those values we hold to be reasonable in a particular case is a balance we sincerely think can be seen to be reasonable by others. Or failing this, we think the balance can be seen as at least not unreasonable in this sense: that those who oppose it can nevertheless understand how reasonable persons can affirm it" (Rawls 2011:Loc. 4137-50).

argues that the line could run between treating people as objects or subjects.[496] The former involves calculation of behaviour and providing direction. Though people might not understand their own interests, giving only healthy options in a canteen could be classified as paternalism (Rostboll 2005; see also Thaler and Sunstein 2009 and Conly 2013). Such actions from the side of states sometimes lead to the accusation of a 'nanny state' and are in stark contrast to the agency that most deliberative approaches suggest. The introduction of a Veggieday in public canteens in Germany is a practical example of the difficulty that goes along with environmental politics. A belief in human flourishing via autonomy restricts environmental government, while the value-action gap shows non-interference as handicap. In comparison to paternalism, deliberation seeks not to replace one's choice with somebody else's choice, but instead aims to metamorphose participants' choices into what in a sense resembles Rousseau's general will (see Rostboll 2005).[497]

Theorists who advocate deliberative approaches believe in "fostering social learning to address ecological degradation through the development and instantiation of binding ecological norms" as the key to sustainability (Brulle 2006:53).[498] Some advocates of deliberation believe that the process activates environmental values (Dryzek 2005:112f.). Discourse ethics assumes that norms need to be developed intersubjectively in an inclusive and non-coercive setting, where free discussions can take place (Humphrey 2007). Yet, fertile grounds for such social learning are indispensible. Currently, societal practice seems to, rather than enable such learning in regard to environment, disable any attempts. Psychological research shows that even if participants deliberate about the environment, positive effects of such deliberations are lost within a short time span (Bell et al. 2001; Hobson 2013:67ff.).[499] Environmental education "is quite ineffective" in many cases (Bell et al. 2001:479; Newig and Fritsch 2011).[500] Theory and practice may be largely divergent.

---

[496] Interestingly, Rostboll thinks that freedom of opinion is an all-or-nobody issue in the sense that either everyone forms their opinion freely or nobody does (2005).

[497] For a discussion of sustainable citizenship as neocolonial see Micheletti, Stolle and Berlin (2014).

[498] "Citizens learn and profit from conflict and argument, and when their arguments follow public reason, they instruct and deepen society's public culture" (Rawls 2011:Loc. 704-7). In one sense "deliberative democracy is not so much a search for ethically or empirically defensible solutions as it is a process of personal development for citizens" (Baber and Bartlett 2005:Loc. 2134).

[499] Hobson's study for example showed that "(post-deliberatively), participants did not go on to make notable contributions to enlivening the ailing public sphere or to adopting pro-environmental practices" (2013:68). He cautions against claims made in favour of deliberative democratic processes, but also points out that that does not mean that citizen's behaviour cannot be positively influenced. Learning might be possible in other context. See for example Mazur (2013).

[500] Hannigan criticizes the set up in many environmental hearings where people insufficiently listen, too many graphs are used and experts sit on a stage (2006:118).

Although Arias-Maldonado for example believes that deliberation has more legitimacy, he also writes that

> "[c]laims in favour of participatory science frequently express an exaggerated optimism over the will and ability of citizens to understand complex subjects in differentiated societies where expert knowledge is not easily accessible for the majority" (2007:245; see also Duit 2014).

Participants, as stated above, need to be willing to invest a considerable amount of time and energy in order to understand science. Most intriguingly,

> "the deliberative citizen who has frequent crosscutting political discussion, who can intelligently articulate arguments both on behalf of her own views and on behalf of contrary views, and who has a high level of objective political knowledge tends not to participate in politics, and the active political citizen tends not to deliberate much" (Bell 2015:Loc. 620).[501]

Participatory democracy stands on the opposite side of a meritocracy (Radcliffe 2002:31).[502] The political equality assumption equalises the knowledge of layman and expert theoretically. It must assume that the layman has a valuable contribution to the process and the decisions. However, Hogl et al. studying effectiveness and legitimacy in environmental governance conclude that

> "not only the idea of using science to make policy-making more effective could often not be achieved but also the second of the aforementioned expectations, namely, to make it more democratically legitimate and more accountable, frequently falls short of its promises. Public discussion and confrontation between experts and counter experts over the interpretation of scientific knowledge and its consequences indicate a lack of social and political trust in scientific knowledge" (2012b:294).

Fundamental for sustainable citizenship are "high trust in institutions" and "strong faith in the capacity of people and corporations to change society" (Micheletti, Stolle and Berlin 2014:225).

If one puts sustainability before the justice concerns of deliberative democrats one is unlikely to believe in the effectiveness of participative processes. This probably stems from the general lack of sustainability achieved anywhere. Radical environmentalist McBay summarises his experience: "Persuasion has not worked and persuasion is not going to work" (2012). Given past experiences, the triumph of the greener argument seems implausible. Humphrey and Stears judge changing citizens' mind, in particular in regard to their worldviews, as extremely rare, and problematise the deliberative process as the belief in citizens "somehow persuading their fellow citizens to change their minds and thus change their actions by the force of their arguments, or the power of their reasons" (2007:Loc. 256; Orr 2013:Loc. 6197-99). Discussing Fishkins' approach and claims for deliberative polls' values as "recommending force", Althaus accentuates

---

[501] In spite of this, forcing people to participate might be understood as undesirable by many (such mechanisms exist in the form of jury duty for instance).
[502] "Many deliberative democrats have had surprisingly little to say on the subject of experts and their role in the process of collective decision making" (Baber and Bartlett 2005:Loc. 2353).

that these are focused on individual level interests and not collective preferences, and that the defining criteria for the evaluation of an interest as enlightened are not self-evident (Althaus 2003:139). Eckersley especially blames sectarian logic and bargaining power of interest groups for the failure of liberal democracies to make environmentally sound decisions (2004:Loc. 1215-18). Yet also a citizens' jury, supposed to find inclusive answers, does not tend to employ universal arguments. Actually declaring biases is "normatively sanctioned in democratic deliberation" (Ward 2006:278). Meanwhile views may be maintained and strengthened, which is often in conflict with Rostboll's requirement for autonomy (Dryzek, Norgaard and Schlosberg 2013:Loc.581). But if

> "public reason fails to overcome the sectarianism of comprehensive doctrines [...], and public reasons are merely sectarian expressions of liberalism masquerading as non-ideological terms, then the whole edifice of deliberative democracy would be in danger of crumbling. As a central tenet of deliberative democracy public reasons are intended to operate as reasons that are accessible across ideological and religious boundaries, available to all who adhere to reasonable doctrines in a reasonable manner" (Humphrey 2007:Loc. 3166).[503]

Green citizenship in theory and practice "requires citizens to put their private life in a more political context by relating processes of sustainable development at home and abroad" (Micheletti, Stolle and Berlin 2014:218; see Bäckstrand 2004). One form of particularism that is present in deliberations and in conflict with sustainability is their tendency to be guided by short-term thinking (Höffe 2009:298). "[E]cological citizenship does possess an additional dimension which turns out to be more difficult to fit into deliberative politics: its emphasis on duties and responsibilities" (Arias-Maldonado 2007:241). Ecological citizenship must include "practices concerning nonreciprocal responsibility in both public and private life" (Micheletti, Stolle and Berlin 2014:210). The power of the greener argument is clear neither in practice nor in theory.

Besides, a decisive part of the deliberative democratic approach is its open-endedness. This applies not only to its lack of implicit moral guidelines; its decisions are also understood as temporary rather than final. It is assumed that decisions can be revoked, changed and further improved. This idea is a good counterbalance to the idealism of discourse ethical approaches and it is in a sense a disclaimer for the validity of decisions made. Yet, especially environmental politics not only work in a different timeframe, but also challenge the idea of reversibility i.e. the process being open-ended (Humphrey 2007:Loc. 2010). Climate change is an irreversible process that – set off by decisions in the past – ultimately disregards the reversibility axiom.

---

[503] Brulle writes that "no one ethics or argument will fit all situations or cultural beliefs. Decisions regarding protection of the natural environment will always be partial, temporary and contingent. So a universal morality guiding our treatment of nature is most probably an impossibility" (2006:64).

2.3.2.2. CONSENSUS TOWARDS SUSTAINABILITY AND THE IPCC AS AN EXAMPLE

Environmental politics needs decision making, which in regard to deliberations ideally involves consensus. Consensus is a frequently used term that is generally understood as positive, although in itself only descriptive, signifying agreement. A perfect consensus is hardly possible and "genuine unforced lasting unanimity is rare in human affairs" (Dahl 2000:54). Yet, if the superiority of the rational argument was true a consensus based on the rational argument should last as long as circumstances do not change (which is similar to Plato's ideas). There is a similarity between the idea of laws of nature represented in the natural sciences and Plato's pure forms.[504] Scientific debates have an advantage (in contrast to debates about morals) in that their setting follows most rules of an idealised discourse. Climate change has reached consensus status within the realm of science. The IPCC, although not outside the realm of international politics, provides most favourable conditions for deliberation. Thus, the IPCC is a good case for understanding some problems of deliberation in environmental politics.

The aim of deliberative democracy "is the creation of a rational consensus. This consensus would be reached by using deliberative procedures with the aim of producing outcomes that were impartial and met everyone's interests equally" (Mouffe 2002:2). The underlying assumption is that political decisions can be made rationally, which ignores differences in morality as a barrier. It not only dismisses passions, but also neglects conflict.[505] Humphrey and Stears understand agreement as a necessity for governing, stating that

> "it is precisely because states must govern that we need to be able to reach agreement on the questions that trouble us. In this regard, at least, environmental activists appear closer to deliberative democrats than to their agonistic critics" (2007:Loc. 2875).

There are two objections to this. First, the agreement in a democracy does not have to include all parts of society. The exit problem may force those who disagree to live under such an agreement. Second, the agreement often means agreement on the lowest common denominator and is therefore catastrophic for the prospects of sustainability (see Giddens 2009:115).[506] Consensus on environmental protection could only arise if all parties had similar objectives. Since this is not the case, deliberative democrats have to vow for compromises as a form of consensus. Where irreversibility reigns, compromise itself needs to be questioned (see Young 1996). Compromises

---

[504] Once more it is important to mention that though this work acknowledges different truth claims in the realm of ethics, it does not allow for relativism in regard to the application of science.

[505] "For agonists, deliberative democrats' primary error lies in their apparent claim that the processes of deliberation could result in a substantial 'agreement' between citizens on matters of fundamental moral importance" (Humphrey and Stears 2007:Loc. 2858).

[506] Experience from referenda shows that, instead of risking the chance for consensus, proposals often contain only 'weak sustainability' suggestions (Stadelmann-Steffen 2011:500). The lack of long-term policies is endemic to democracy and "standard democratic mechanisms provide an explanation for sub-optimal outcomes (Sprinz 2009:3).

regularly lead to weak solutions which in fact cannot be understood as solutions, whereas decision making without participation, in contrast, allows for stronger policies (Newig and Fritsch 2011).

According to Elling, seeing the "environment as a public good, in the context of a political distribution struggle, will bring the conflict between economy and environment" to the individual level, and "citizens will not find it easier to gather around shared views and actions" (2008:257). Yet, if deliberation cannot cope with such a conflict, can it be understood as a useful mechanism? Elling raises an objection that is symbolic for the general rejection of many deliberative democrats to acknowledge conflict. Newig and Fritsch show that while participation can school actors' environmental consciousness, local economic interests make up for the gain (2011:210). Value-pluralism can leave a blind spot for conflict. It cannot be ignored that pluralism includes mutually exclusive wolrdviews. Attfield lists "anthropocentrism, zoocentrism, biocentrism, and ecocentrism" as examples (2014:49).[507] One of the most prominent examples of a conflict of interest is forest protection. The interests of environmentalists and loggers are typically diametrically opposed. This portends that consensus building measures are destined to fail (Dryzek 2005:7). The drawback can be simplified in one sentence: "Each call for compromise between loggers and environmentalists means more forest is felled" (Shearman and Smith 2007:146). Green political theory needs to acknowledge conflict, asymmetry of power and difference in vulnerability. Schrecker highlights these shortcomings:

> "The most pernicious claims in sustainable development discourse are (1) that we are all in this together, or that we will all win from environmental sustainability, and (2) that there are no necessary conflicts between legitimate economic aspirations and the goal of environmental sustainability"(1998:218).

The requirement of unanimity is particularly dangerous, since it makes each person a possible veto player. Inequalities play their role in consensus building. Goodin accentuates the threat of self-interest that such a form of consensus brings, since

> "a consensus rule gives each member the power of veto over all group decisions. That veto will naturally be used as a bargaining lever. What it is one is bargaining for, with it, is variable. In politics-as-usual, the lever is characteristically employed by those with most to win or least to lose to feather their own nest" (2013:Loc. 3490-93).

The logger can effectively block the chance for sustainability by standing firm on 'his right' to cut trees. If any form of compromise preserves unsustainable policies, the advocates of nature

---

[507] "Because cost-benefit analysis is likely to end up striking compromises between conflicting values, some deep Greens who do not like such trade-offs might reject anything that legitimates them" (Ward 2006:284).

cannot possibly gain from mechanisms that are fixed on consensus.[508] Deliberative democrats often fail to acknowledge this, not only because of their trust in the rational argument, but also since they do not recognise the existence of a disharmony of interests and real-life tradeoffs.[509] Those who do not profit from sustainability can veto and the whole project is doomed to fail. Poloni-Staudinger points at two effects of consensus democracy (2008:412ff.). On one hand, it can ensure formal representation of green issues in government, while on the other hand is also has more veto player. Though consensus democracies appear to have greener politics, they in fact only succeed at 'weak sustainability'.[510] Poloni-Staudinger describes the process as a matter of image. Many actors will try to appear environmentally friendly, i.e. support measures that from a sustainability standpoint can be labelled as 'simulation' (see Edelman 2005). The summary of different studies shows that results are inconclusive:

> "Consensus democracies (executive-parties dimension) appear to do better when environmental effectiveness is measured in the mundane form. Majoritarian (executive-parties dimension) systems do better when environmentalism is measured in terms of conservation. In addition, consensus democratic characteristics related to the federal-unitary dimension are in both instances positively related to environmental effectiveness" (Poloni-Staudinger 2008:425).

There are reasons to suggest that consensus democracies score high on effectiveness, since once consensus is reached, all parties support the policies.

As described above, consensus-building almost inevitably instigates conservative decisions. Environmental politics are an example where conservatism is precarious, since it means that changes to the status quo remain minimal. Yet, there is a further dimension that played a role even prior to decision making. Science can be particularly conservative. The thought that a paradigm shift occurs when a generation of intellectuals dies is not easily dismissed (see Kuhn 2012). If one understands scientific discourse as following a deliberative model – with much of their practice including peer-review and revision of theories – the International Panel on

---

[508] Explaining the failure of American environmental politics, Harris writes that "US policymaking process requires major consensus or a large majority in favor of action in Congress to pass legislation, but this is impossible due to the increasingly partisan politics between those who want the United States to address climate change (many Democratic lawmakers, excepting those from coal-mining and automobile-manufacturing states) and those who view action on climate change as a threat to economic growth or do not believe in the problem at all (most Republicans, particularly those on the radical right)" (2013:Loc. 1130).

[509] "An earlier generation of environmental thought at least acknowledged the threat of "job blackmail" by corporate managers, reflecting the fact that in a market economy such conflicts are real when, and because, the owners of the plant or the logging rights say they are. The new trend is instead to deny the significance of such tradeoffs" (Schrecker 1998:219; see also Brulle 2006). Here again the field of those who claim to be green is vast. Some more marginal environmentalists still use slogans such as "There are no jobs on a dead planet".

[510] "Many elected officials are less willing to 'rock the boat' with a large change to the status quo. As more layers of political institutions are added, major policy usage suffers due to increased difficulty in achieving consensus. Consequently, the usage of minor policies increases concomitant to the number of [veto players]. Minor climate policies may be used to appease or quell advocates of broad and expansive climate-change policy regimes, or simply because public policy tends towards incrementalism" (Madden 2014:583).

Climate Change can be understood as a close approximation to a rational discourse. While Bäckstrand calls for a "de-monopolization and democratization of science", it appears that science already has inherently deliberative qualities (2004:109). Claims against an objective reality of environmental destruction have been established as dangerous in previous chapters.

The IPCC as a core institution both in international and national climate change debates appears particularly powerful. At the same time, the IPCC regularly underestimates the actual impact of environmental destruction. Hobson writes about the IPCC that "it is worth noting that the negotiated nature of these findings makes them strongly conservative, thus they likely underplay the true level of threat" (2012:978; Baber and Bartlett 2005, Hamilton 2013). While the IPCC is occasionally accused of alarmism, the opposite is the case (Hartmann 2013:Loc. 378-83). The IPCC reports include lower estimates. Correspondingly, Beeson describes the chapter on human security as

> "extremely cautious, the claims modest and hedged with caveats, and the conclusions provisional. It is noteworthy that there is no sustained discussion of the possible impact of key issues such as rising sea levels and melting glaciers" (2014:2; see also Grantham 2012).

He argues that this is particularly striking given the potential misery. Just as many scientific journals, the IPCC favours caution and reservation in its publications. The official statements therefore have historically downplayed the risks. Instead of presenting a worst case scenario that might spark stronger action, they have assisted further delay. Numbers have to be corrected with every new report. Those who claim 'alarmism' underestimate the actual threat and overestimate the reports' effect on actual politics (Hogl et al. 2012b:294). Environmental dangers "may be transformed into less threatening political issues" on the surface (Hannigan 2006:73; Neumayer 2002). While environmentalists can be comparatively effective in impacting abstract demands, the implementation of environmental politics that suggest sustainability is rare. Climate scientist Anderson accentuates the discrepancies between science and politics (2012:19f.). Whether staying within 2°C degrees is achievable or not, the actual impact has been underestimated. Furthermore the 2°C degrees are a political concept which is not supported by science (see Andrew et al. 2013). There is no specific reason for such a goal. Long-term goals are more politically convenient. Moreover, opponents often postpone decisions by postponing the problem and asking for further research. If consensus on an issue is made necessary, calling for more research is likely. Yet even the downplaying consensus of the IPCC reports is not taken seriously. Here, defending a precautionary principle means to recognise the uncertainty resulting in stronger demands rather than weaker claims (Bäckstrand 2004). If Bäckstrand criticises science for its conservatism, she equally needs to caution against more democratic approaches. Demanding consensus, for instance, can also lead to a restraint/precaution on precaution.

One central question in the pursuit of making democracy sustainable is whether it is possible to exclude some (geographically included) voices from participation.[511] Studying climate change denial in Australia, Lo points out that a person with strong rights-based beliefs is more likely to deny climate change (2014:562). While seeing the rejection of science as "regrettable", he allows for "legitimate" "cultural reasons" and concludes that it is morally necessary to engage individuals and their concerns (2014:564). If one follows the principle of value pluralism, sceptics have to be involved. Yet such an inclusion is dangerous, since it endangers substantively good outcomes. While arguing for broader inclusion and participation, Lo in fact provides an argument against participation. In his study it shows that

> "[a]sserted absolute rights to private property (or land generally) can provide moral energy for rejecting or neglecting proven science when the alternative would be seen as compromising these rights. This reluctance to believe may be socially pathological and a problem to tackle, but the cultural or ethical motives behind it can be reasonable and eligible for inclusion. Given the correlation between these two, characterising climate scepticism as a troubling problem to tackle is at odds with the pledge to respect dissidents in participatory processes" (2014:565).

The respect for dissenting voices can in fact halt all decision making.[512] Exclusion, on the other hand, is inconsistent with the inclusive logic of participatory processes. This indicates that either the political equality axiom or the chance for a greener outcome has to be sacrificed. Wider inclusion in decision making can mean inclusion of people that are interested in the exploitation of nature (Newig 2012:52). This consequentially hinders effective resource protection. Overinclusion can make consensus on the lowest common denominator at best leading to 'weak sustainability'. At the same time, those excluded and their potential need for 'strong sustainability' lack attention.

2.3.2.3. Exclusion and Inclusion as a Conundrum

A prevalent problem in democratic theory is that of the excluded. Dahl notes that for collective decisions the good of all affected should be taken into consideration (1989:306). Typically, the discussion involves two kinds of 'contemporary' exclusion. The legal right to participate in democratic elections is not given to those who are not part of 'the people' i.e. foreigners and those who are not qualified i.e. children and people classified as lacking sufficient mental

---

[511] This opens the door for excluding all those perceived as unwilling or unreasonable.
[512] Dahl at the same time judges: "The opportunity to disagree about specific choices is the very reason for valuing the arrangements that make the opportunity possible" (1989:307).

capacity permanently (see Graham 2013:Loc. 720-22).[513] The former are excluded on the basis of an abstract idea of belonging. Democratic politics are for the most part tied to the nation-state and nationality. The latter are excluded because they are not seen as fit to participate. They are seen as not having the capacity to understand politics. Animals are categorically excluded. Though one can make an argument that they have interests, they cannot utter any preferences. The limited capacity to participate effectively means that future generations, animals and nature do not vote and do not "contribute money to political campaigns either" (Ball 2006:131). The Anthroposcene is marked by a mass extinction with unprecedented scope. Flora and fauna are already suffering from human actions and the excluded groups are among the most affected victims of environmental destruction.[514] If animals are understood as having intrinsic value, they also bear rights. At the very least the fact that they can suffer pain must signal that they have interests. Though an ecocentric worldview might not be shared by the majority, most people nonetheless assign intrinsic value to animals. Humans typically think that animals have more than instrumental value and that inflicting unnecessary pain onto them, for example, is immoral. Accordingly, animals are seen as holding at least a minimum of rights. Democracy does not include such considerations. Singer concentrates on the consideration of animals on the basis of their ability to suffer (1975, 2006). He argues that there are large differences of capabilities within mankind, which makes them an unsuitable point of reference. His ethical approach means that the "relevant moral community comprises all those able to feel pain and pleasure" (Connelly et al. 2012:24). It does not entail that they need to be treated equally but that their suffering should be counted. Much environmental destruction occurs in their habitats and animals are often sensitive to changes in their environment. While small changes can destroy whole ecosystems, they do not have a guaranteed voice in democracies.

Exclusion constitutes a legitimacy problem in democratic theory. Those excluded are excluded from self-determination, which is the core of the legitimation of democracy as a system. Flora and fauna are overtly excluded from democratic representation. The question is what representation means if the majority of sentient beings remain unrepresented. A minority rules over a majority that is affected by its decision making to the extent that decisions can be life-threatening and deadly. Though this work tries to avoid going beyond an anthropocentric ethical

---

[513] Though different factors play a role, it is interesting that a mock EU Parliament election in Germany which included 33.000 students below the age of 18 actually showed significant support for green issues (Menzel 2014). Though Christian Democrats won most votes with 24.3 %, the Greens landed second place with 19 %. Combined with 6 % that voted for the animal protection party, green issues proved most important for those currently excluded. It is unclear what kind of role Merkel's prominence played.

[514] Those who have most access to political power and decision-making power are typically those most remote from environmental degradation and this is true for powerless human beings as well as animals (see Plumwood 2001). Pets are closer to power and less vulnerable to climate change than wildlife.

point of view, the concern with animal rights sheds further light on the discussion. A brief reflection therefore broadens an understanding of possible concerns. On the one hand, Latour comments against authoritarianism that "[t]he last thing we need is for someone to compose in our stead the world to come" (2004:225). Yet, if the "we" is a factual minority such claims are less relevant. Self-determination becomes a minority right. Here, Humphrey points out that ecoauthoritarian literature questions traditional interpretations of not only democracy and liberalism, but justice as well, and in "their place are offered a value or set of values that is/are taken to be more in keeping with our newly discovered obligations to the non-human world or future generations" (2007:Loc. 543). The lack of mechanisms that ensure the protection of nature, in liberalism, on the other hand, is overt. De-Shalit formulates this shortfall of liberal democracies bluntly: "Since trees cannot be parties to a contract, liberalism excludes them thoroughly" (2001:387; e.g. Wissenburg 2006). Rawls admits that the environment poses a problem to justice as fairness (2011:Loc. 1035). It is not clear which responsibility exists. Wissenburg even calls anthropocentrism "one genetic defect that liberalism inherited from the Enlightenment that cannot so easily be discarded" (2006:21).[515] Liberal democracy thoroughly empowers the representatives of destruction, while underrepresenting victims.[516] The excluded are purely subject to the mercy and passions of the demos. In other words, though they do not hold democratic rights, they are subject to democratic decisions.[517] Wissenburg points out that, while some argue that the fact that one does not choose to be born into a certain generation means that natural resources should be shared equally, others say that if procreation is a choice, one can neither be "held responsible for the fate of other people's children", nor even one's own grandchildren (2006:27). Similar arguments could be made for animals. One is normally not responsible for their existence.

In contrast, those who believe in the inadequacy of the liberal model, but still believe in a green democracy try to find safeguards and integrate the excluded.

> "Green political theory's unique addition [...] is to draw out the links between democracy and environmental justice and to extend our understanding of the category of subjects excluded from any meaningful representation or participation in the liberal state, even though they may be harmed by decisions and actions made in the name of the state" (Eckersley 2004:1080)

---

[515] "Liberalism then is flawed for being a "human chauvinist" moral theory, a theory with an unjustified bias in favor of humans" (Shearman and Smith 2007:108f.).

[516] Wissenburg writes about the problem of these excluded: "There is, of course, a long series of epistemological problems [...] that face a potential representative of the non-represented — it is unclear exactly what to represent. In addition, democratic representation, no matter how much we like to think of it in terms of being ethically desirable or even obligatory, is based on considerations of power. Representatives have little incentive to represent or to wish to represent politically inconsequential entities. Second, there is reason to suspect that liberal democratic institutions are unfit to represent the actual interests they would want to see represented" (2004:64).

[517] I deliberately use the word 'subject' instead of 'object' in this context given the appeal to rights and interests.

Saward argues for some form of representation of the excluded as well, stating that they have "interests that ought to be represented within our political structures" (2006:188). Eckersley suggests that a green democracy needs to find a way in which those currently excluded have a voice (2004; see also Tremmel 2011). For many green theorists and activists alike, a green state needs to have mechanisms that, though not equally nevertheless, consider non-human animals' wellbeing and ensure their chance for survival. Anthropocentric as well as intrinsic value arguments can converge here. It does not mean to consider every single animal, but it does include a consideration of the needs of species as a whole. When Spivak asks whether the subaltern can speak, she famously showed important grievances of those who do not have an active voice (1988). The answer that once the subaltern speak they cease to be subaltern hints at a possible insurmountability for animal representation. Animals can never speak and, therefore figuratively always remain subaltern. Though pets may live better than many humans, most animals do not enjoy decisive concern. Many are endangered. Though some democracies have animal protection parties, animals are dependent on humans to vote in favour of them. Their survival is dependent on the constituency's preferences and is therefore only one issue among others. In non-anthropocentric ethical systems animal welfare can take a position of importance. In purely anthropocentric systems animals are only considered in so far as they have instrumental value for humans. If one assumes that human beings assign actual intrinsic value to pets, at least when they are visible and not behind closed doors in breeding farms, the arbitrariness of the distinction, between pets and other animals, remains an ethical problem. This was explicitly pointed out by Singer in his works on animal liberation (1975).[518] Instead of an inconsistent differentiation that is often based on cultural norms, he applies the concept of sentience stringently. While Singer's concept follows a clear rationality and reason, most people's behaviour towards animals is directed by passion and lack of passion (see also Bentham 2000). Given earlier objections, it is hard to imagine an enlightened green citizen, who acknowledges his passions as arbitrary, allows for, and follows a more inclusive consideration. It therefore is also hard to imagine a green democracy that fully acknowledges that all kinds of sentient beings have rights on their own. Orr turns the issue upside down when he discusses humanity's value from an animal perspective (2009). He puts humanity on an imaginary trial. While he considers whether humanity is worth saving from the perspective of the animal kingdom, he furthers the discussion on the value of animals. Whereas his thought experiment is meant to elaborate on human actions, it indirectly characterises human actions as crimes and animals as worth saving – after all they remain innocent.

---

[518] Singer argues for moral extentionalism and against arbitrary exclusion. A moral sensibilisation is necessary for animals to be considered (Hache and Latour 2009).

Ball, like Eckersley and Saward, advocates for the protection of the interests of the excluded, which he says "along with our own is best accomplished by the kind of transgenerational and trans-species representative democracy" called 'biocracy' (Ball 2006:144).[519] Eckersley conceptualises green democracy as one not only of, but also for, the affected (2004). She and other green theorists discuss the problem of representation, which arises by the simple fact that, future generations and in that sense also animals, cannot be included in the decision-making processes. Against some critical voices, they believe that the excluded have interests which can be discovered and that nature "has interests that ought to be represented" (2006:189). They, therefore, mention the idea of putting someone into place as a spokesman of the excluded. While such idealism can be admirable, the practical implementation needs elaboration. However agreeable Eckersley and Ball's ethical assumptions are, the modalities that protect the excluded in the final decision making from annihilation are unclear. Eckersley and Ball think about the possibility of environmental organisations getting more weight in order to fulfil this role.[520] Many difficulties arise from the idea of representatives. De-Shalit comments that

> "if we allow environmental NGOs to form an extra constituency, why not allow other vulnerable groups, such as ethnic minorities, the working class, or what have you, to do the same? If we do this we might depart too far from the principle of equal representation" (2006b:96).

Finding adequate criteria for representation is a difficult task that necessarily involves new forms of exclusion. An easier case of representation seems to be the representation of direct descendants by their immediate relatives. At first sight, children appear as a valid reason for the consideration of future generations, at least for parents. It then follows that in fact future generations are represented by the current generation in so far as parents represent their children. Such bonds and the potential for sacrifices, accordingly, could be taken as a durable incentive to support sustainable politics. This hypothesis sounds plausible, but so far such supposed effect has no empirical support. As mentioned earlier cognitive processes can lead to denial and avoidance. Research in some Anglo-Saxon countries not only shows that people with children are less likely to believe in climate change and be concerned about it, but also that having children has no influence on attitudes (Marshall 2014:Loc. 3184; see also Micheletti,

---

[519] Leist thinks that arguments about future generations long ahead are only rationally not emotionally accessible (2011:39). This means that they can hardly be part of 'passionate' politics mobilizing emotions.
[520] Noteworthy, it has not been proven that environmental NGOs have a positive effect on environmental performance as mentioned above.

Stolle and Berlin 2014:222).[521] While Höffe takes the decline of families with children as a reason for additional discounting of the future (Höffe 2009:35), these studies indicate otherwise. In order to discuss intergenerational justice, it is possible to enlarge Rawls's veil of ignorance to include the future, which makes clear that some principle of saving is required (2011; Connelly et al. 2012:43). But if Rawls understands these obligations to be "tied to affection", as Connelly et al. point out (2012:44), his argument also rests on an imagined community. Two objections in case of the environment apply immediately. First, as mentioned above, altruism and a sense of community rarely extend beyond a certain degree of separation. Second, affection seems to have the opposite effect in regard to climate change given the optimism of people with children. Again, Rawls' theoretical constructs are in discord with empirical findings.[522] But even if future people are included in Rawlsian justice, it is difficult to determine what such procedures mean in terms of actual substance. Horstkötter sees the problem in "how to decide about these issues given not only uncertainty about many of the future generations' interests, but also reasonable pluralism in the present time" (2004:Loc. 4040-43). He criticises Rawls for the failure to be concrete.[523] Precaution needs benchmarks such as ecological health, but the concept derives from a distinct worldview.

The democratic process is said to serve contemporary society, but intergenerational justice includes "the transformation of present values by the application of some normative criteria of distributive justice" and the difficult task of characterising these criteria (Wallack 2004:Loc. 4314-18). So far, democracies could not even account for the poor living amidst today, which begs the question whether the inclusion of other sentient beings and future generations does not have to be disqualified as unfeasible. Ball sees the openness of democracy as enabling the possibility that those who claim to protect nature, but in fact do not, can be exposed (2006:139). Here again, one is reminded of the ideal vs. actual political practice and the additional level of cognitive dissonance that allows everybody to overlook inflicted harm. Stretton compares care for intergenerational sharing to giving to foreign aid with an even more remote recipient (1976:7). Degrees of separation play an important role for the capacity to empathise and therefore to give up something. One of the biggest parts of the problem is that externalities are to

---

[521] If set into a different framework, parents might feel "anticipation, fear, responsibility, guilt, and shame" (Marshall 2014:Loc. 1173). Marshall suggests that this could be done by simply asking them how much improvement to their living standards would be necessary to agree on causing irreversible damage to the world their children will inhabit. He sees framing as effective tool for overcoming the innocent bystander effect. Though such framing can alter people's perception, chances for lasting change are minimal as discussed above.

[522] Wissenburg discusses Rawls' revision in regard to intergenerational justice (detaching it from affection) and emphasizes that since a savings principle can be seen as "mutually beneficial" it is rational (2002:196; Rawls 2011).

[523] Yet, of these two, uncertainty might serve as an excuse. Norton writes that "[t]he problem at hand is not to predict what people in the future will want, but to articulate those values that are sufficiently important to present people that they are willing to make an effort to project these values into the future" (2002:Loc. 1197).

a certain degree invisible. Costs transferred to the future are externalities that are especially invisible and seem only potential. They are easily discounted. If the accounts proposed in this book so far are accurate, it is cardinal to conclude the discussion of democracy's sustainability with an account of democracy's adaptability and the means of coping with climate change mitigation and/or chaos (as consequences become more visible and pervasive).

2.3.3. ADAPTABILITY TO CHANGE AND EMERGENCIES[524]

Climate scientists cannot predict the exact scope of the coming changes, but since preventive measures are currently insufficient, it is necessary to include worst case scenarios.[525] Time is not a renewable resource. Societal institutions will have to adapt measures for impact mitigation. Since the publication of the *Limits to Growth* (LTG) (Meadows et al. 1972), many chances to alter the course have already been missed. Its core insights have been widely ignored.

> "During the first twenty-five years after its publication, no one seemed to pick up the real message of the study, which is that overshoot is a likely consequence of slow societal decision making, and that once in overshoot, there is only one way out, namely, decline back down into sustainable territory. The general view was that LTG had been proven wrong, because oil had not in fact run out" (Randers 2012:Loc. 6181-85).

Societies have yet to make a real step towards a sustainable future.[526] Today the way towards sustainability implies decline (e.g. Anderson 2012; Jackson 2012; Peach 2012). Sustainable growth equals 'degrowth'. Overshoot has become the norm signified by Earth Overshoot Day routinely moving down the calendar.[527] Most mitigation measures have failed to achieve even 'weak sustainability'. Accordingly, the question of adaptation involves an evaluation of democracy's efficiency in regard to change in a timely manner, its flexibility and its ability to react to urgent events. How well democracies will be able to adapt in case of rapid change of environmental conditions and in light of extreme weather events that call for immediate responses is a crucial question.

Humans tend to have an aversion towards change (Harmon-Jones and Mills 2009a:4). The longer environmental policies are delayed, the stricter the change necessary. Delay accordingly will make coping harder. Drastic change means substantial psychological pressure. In the worst

---

[524] Questions of adaptability are essential to the whole book. Other chapters cover specific problems. To avoid redundancy they will not further presented here.

[525] The actual worst case of a runaway greenhouse effect would transform Earth into a Venus-like planet, but this is highly unlikely (Hansen 2009).

[526] International climate conferences are symbolic for this lack of action: "U.N. Secretary-General Ban Ki-moon welcomed the Copenhagen conference as an "essential beginning." The climate negotiations are always beginning, or in their favorite cliché, "setting the stage" for the drama to come" (Marshall 2014:Loc. 2723).

[527] "August 19 is Earth Overshoot Day 2014, marking the date when humanity has exhausted nature's budget for the year. For the rest of the year, we will maintain our ecological deficit by drawing down local resource stocks and accumulating carbon dioxide in the atmosphere" (Global Footprint Network 2014). Earth Overshoot Day 2015 was August 13th (Overshootday.org).

case, they can cause trauma. Change aversion is already a factor, although the aversion could be used to convey sound policies as well. Clearly, emphasizing possible threats could contribute to higher willingness to make sacrifices. The earlier transformation of societies takes place the easier the change. Yet, democracies suffer from structural barriers as touched upon earlier. Multiplied veto players reduce chances for radical transformation (Lauth 2010a:113). It follows that "[t]he degree to which a climate policy disrupts the status quo may also be a determinant of adoption rates" (Madden 2014:576; Stadelmann-Steffen 2011:490). Democracies suffer in general from a status quo bias (see Gilens and Page 2014). This entails that adjustment is less likely than business as usual until substantial change affects a critical mass. Though the peaceful transition of government is a ledge of democracy, most governments stay in office. Schmidt sees temporary mandates with the chance of change as an advantage of democratic systems (2010:59ff.). But Przeworski calculated that between the years 1788 and 2000 incumbents only lost in about 20% of the cases (2010:167).[528] *Ergo*, democracy is rather marked by continuity of government than change. Continuity is a weakness as long as it means that unsustainable lifestyles are sustained as long as possible.[529] The conjecture that democracy fosters the status quo leads to the conjecture that democracy is part of the problem of unsustainability (Blühdorn 2011:21). Presumably, change aversion including the status quo bias contributed greatly to the steady support of ecological modernisation theory. Ecological modernisation theory rationalises a status quo of a growth directed economy that is based on mass consumption, since it "leaves capitalist economy and industrial production unchallenged" (Connelly et al. 2012:74). Thus sustainability remains the subject of the free market rather than politics. Including the rhetoric of corporate responsibility, systematic change, then, is ruled (out) by the market logic.

> "Experience shows that it is hard for democratic, free-market economies to make proactive decisions to increase voluntary investments before they are unavoidable. It is much simpler after crisis has struck and there is an externally imposed threat of destroyed infrastructure and livelihoods. The situation is a little better in more socialist, higher-tax regimes, where the pattern of investment is more heavily influenced by the state. More authoritarian, state-capitalist societies are capable of the most rapid response—but run the risk of moving in the wrong direction. This picture won't change fast, because there is an important ideological difference between private and public activity. In the eyes of the free-market liberal, government spending is inferior to private spending, simply because a big government is less attractive than a small government. And the ideal of the free market is well established in the ruling belief system in the current West. Like any other deeply held value, this ideal won't fade away easily. For many, the distinction between private and public investment will remain important, even in the face of crisis, and worth fighting for" (Randers 2012:Loc. 1973-82).

---

[528] Whereas this might be interpreted as a reason for long-term policy making or at least an incentive for an incumbent government for longer strategies, winning could also be an outcome of positively perceived short-term policies. The chance of getting voted out of office exists, so this statistic is unlikely to affect political strategies of ruling parties.
[529] Nondemocratic China in contrast has shown a wide variety of approaches (Bell 2015).

Randers summarises essential problems of the status quo clearly. He pinpoints the free market and connected values as a barrier to rapid responses. Limits on the interference of the state mark the limits of available instruments. The values and behaviour of consumer and citizen and the line marking private and public therefore have to be thought as determinants of adaptability and transformation. Here, democracies in a sense depend on the flexibility of their citizens and their ability to recognise and act in accordance with material necessities. Again values and behaviour do not change quickly.

Green citizenship needs education (e.g. Ball 2006). Whereas green theorists are not reluctant to point at this fact, they avoid discussing time frames. In the meantime, climate change mitigation is an urgent matter. Although at the core of good environmental governance, it is often ignored in the discussion. Litfin comments as follows:

> "Sensing the urgency of the mounting environmental megacrisis, one might ask a valid question: do we have enough time for such a developmental unfolding, or should we perhaps act with greater urgency in the direction of a more coercive politics of sacrifice?" (2010:138).

Climate models show that it is not possible to wait until a new eco-conscious generation has been raised (e.g. Meadows, Meadows and Randers 2004; Anderson 2012; Randers 2012). The projections show that there is no time left. Education needs time. This is one reason for ecoauthoritarians to be pessimistic about democracy. Shearman and Smith for example "doubt if any transformation of the mass is possible, at least to the extent needed for a radical democratic transformation of the present system" (2007:165). Schmidt understands the predictability of political institutions, processes, and results within democratic frameworks as positive (2010:59ff.). This predictability allows for claims about future climate policies. Regardless of predictability being positive or negative this means that the likelihood of sound environmental politics can also be determined. A huge factor for prediction is the mentioned status quo affinity. An unsustainable status quo points at a potentially grim future. So far, democracy has not shown to be effective in tweaking people's behaviour into a greener direction. On the contrary, democracy has shown ineffective in coping with modification of people's behaviour (de Geus 2001:22). Especially a tendency of liberal democracy to see preference as black boxes and in a sense prior to politics is a barrier to governments inducing changes. Policies aiming at transforming behaviour may be judged as intrusive and paternalistic and therefore illegitimate interference into the private sphere.

Given the time lag with which CO_2 affects the global climate, it is probable that only reactive measures will be possible (Anderson 2012). The emergence of permanent crisis management is not unlikely (Beeson 2010).[530] Who is in control over life-supporting infrastructure is essential to the question of means for coping (see Gurr 1985). For instance the impact of scarcity differs if water is privately owned or if it is publicly owned. In the former case, it is likely that it will be allocated to the highest bidder following the logic of the free market. This comprises that while some people are still able to water the lawn, others might not be able to afford water at all. If water is publicly owned, democratic publics will have to decide over the rationale of distribution indirectly or directly. It is hard to argue against the desirability of the inclusion of expertise in such a decision making. Especially when fast responses are paramount, public decision making could handicap effective and 'fair' governance. Those democracies which are orientated around consensus are incapable of coping with urgent events (Leggewie 2011:29). Hence, Shearman and Smith write: "We should not be blind to the possibility that an authoritarian meritocracy might have advantages in world crisis management compared to the present democratic mediocrity" (2007:13). Conversely, political theorist Dahl writes: "In the face of risks or choices, people commonly make logically inconsistent judgments, and the performance of experts, it appears, is not better than that of ordinary people" (1989:75). While he is defending democracies, his assessment can only be understood as partially true. In the policy management experiment mentioned earlier, managers did clearly do better than students (Diekmann and Preisendörfer 2001:46).[531]

Crisis management requires decisive politics. The drought in California in 2014 for example showed that despite pleas by state officials to preserve water, some citizens and municipalities were unwilling to follow (e.g. Chaussee 2014). Emergencies make compliance essential. They need ardent leadership and unequivocal rules. If the case is urgent stronger governments evidently have more leverage to make adjustments, while weaker governments have less means of implementing restrictions. Subsequently, not only might democracy be incapable of implementing the needed climate change policy, it might also be threatened by climate change itself. Adjacent to Shearman and Smith's observation, Lovelock speculates:

> "But what if at some time in the next few years we realized as we did in the 1940s that democracy had temporarily to be suspended and we had to accept a disciplined regime that

---

[530] "Water supplies will be falling due to reduction in river flows, falling groundwater tables, and saltwater intrusion into groundwater. Heavy precipitation events will cause extensive flooding and landslides, leading to disruption of public water, electricity, sanitation, and transportation systems. Sea-level rise will increase coastal erosion and subsidence, causing substantial damage to residential and commercial structures. Temperature, precipitation, and humidity will boost the range, life cycle, and rate of transmission of infectious diseases. Higher temperatures and extended heat waves will greatly boost heat-related mortality. Hundreds of millions from the countryside, where adverse effects of climate change will be even more horrific, will nonetheless be streaming into these climate-troubled cities. At the same time, employers, jobs, and wealthier residents will be fleeing these same cities in search of more secure places to live and to do business, often in newly developed cities or distant places. The adverse effects of climate change will thus fall disproportionately on those without the resources to move" (Randers 2012:Loc. 2730-39).

[531] Expert decision making is a main issue of the latter two parts of this book.

saw our nation as a legitimate but limited safe haven for civilization. It could be forced upon us by a weather event like a series of hurricanes as severe as Katrina. Perhaps this would be enough to bring to the fore a leader whose rhetoric would fire the nation to make the effort needed to adapt properly to change instead of just patching its problems in an incoherent way. Orderly survival requires an unusual degree of human understanding and leadership and may require, as in war, the suspension of democratic government for the duration of the survival emergency" (2009:1023).

Independent of the question whether democratic institutions can produce sustainability or not a second question remains. If dramatic weather events occur and become more frequent including heat waves, droughts and subsequent famine can democracy manage these forms of crisis?[532] In order to fulfil its functions properly and to maintain itself any system needs to be open to its environment (Easton 1965). The system itself is at risk if it does not react to changes. In this case the alterations of the environment are literally alterations of the environment. Climate change as a crisis may produce crises for democracy (Ophuls 1977; Burnell 2009; Beeson 2010; see also Leeson 1979). Actual states of emergency are not unknown within the history of many democracies. Permanent states of emergency cannot be excluded with certainty.

Resilience of institutions depends on their strengths. The probability for abandonment of democratic institutions in times of crisis is relatively high. Shearman and Smith name the Patriot Act as an example (2007:123). It was passed as measures taken after the terrorist attacks of September 11th, although it included unconstitutional parts. Such legislation is often too extensive in scope for politicians to read. Vulnerability and sensitivity to climate change are extremely dependent not only on the physical conditions of a country, but also on the stability, flexibility and adaptability of its institutions. Generally "[i]nstitutionalization means that problems and solutions are defined within the prevailing political and administrative arrangements" (Connelly et al. 2012:155). Consequentially institutions will play a positive or negative role in bringing about necessary changes or coping with new challenges.[533] Especially democracies with weak institution, hence limited agency, might collapse under the pressure of severe environmental conditions. An opportunistic power might take over the government. In this case it can be up to chance who will take over. Food crises are known to produce political instability and heat is associated with greater violence (Bell et al. 2001:168-203). Both are typical consequences of climate changes. Overexploitation of resources is common practice, which

---

[532] In their look back from the future Oreskes and Conway's describe the failure: "As the devastating effects of the Great Collapse began to appear, the nation-states with democratic governments—both parliamentary and republican— were at first unwilling and then unable to deal with the unfolding crisis. As food shortages and disease outbreaks spread and sea level rose, these governments found themselves without the infrastructure and organizational ability to quarantine and relocate people" (2014:647).

[533] Carpenter writes about a common misconception about agency in the future: "Coping implies choice and, therefore, applies mostly to the behavior of the industrialzed world and the elites within the developing countries; i.e. those whom actual choices are available" (1998:291).

makes food crises almost inevitable. Depletion of resources paired with harsher and less stable weather conditions could bring the world to the edge to environmental and economic collapse (Brown 2011b). 'Climate wars' become more likely. Developments in North Africa and the Middle East are an excellent example for the connection between political instability and environmental conditions (Lagi, Bertrand and Bar-Yam 2011). Historically, civilisations collapse due to resource scarcity (Ophuls 2012; e.g. Wang et al. 2010). The Easter Islands are the simplest example of self-induced collapse. Long-term resilience is essential since climate change does not have an end. States of emergency then could become a permanent condition rather than intermediate and passing phases. Marshall writes that due to wrong metaphors climate change is perceived as "a finite challenge that can be cured, overcome, or won rather than as an open-ended and irreversible condition that can only be managed" (2014:Loc. 1949). Permanence makes adaptation a necessity. In *The Green State – Rethinking Democracy and Sovereignty*, Eckersley concludes that "the future of democracy looks rather grim" (2004:Loc. 1842; see also Gurr 1985).[534]

---

[534] Possible technological interventions do not improve such a judgment. "Space mirrors, stratospheric sulfur schemes, and the like all require concentration of materials and political authority. By this measure, many geoengineering schemes have a distinctly anti-democratic flavor" (Nicholson 2013:Loc. 7132-34).

2.4. Part Conclusion: If the People 'Decide'

"Democracy, an emerging argument holds, is both an inappropriate and ineffective political system to meet the challenges of the consequences of climate change in politics and society, particularly in the area of necessary emission reductions. Democratically organized societies are too cumbersome to avoid climate change; they act neither in a timely fashion nor are they responsive in the necessary comprehensive manner" (Stehr 2013:58).

The preceding discussions cast serious doubt on democracy's sustainability. In an article published in 1979, Holsworth suggested that ecoauthoritarians fail to see the real potential of existing systems in coping with environmental destruction (1979). Although this work cannot provide conclusive evidence, the claims by green democracy advocates find limited support in practice.[535] Democracies engage in green rhetoric, but they are far from being sustainable in any meaningful sense. Only a few democracies succeed initiating and implementing moderately greener policies. Hence, 'simulation' is a label that has to be given to the majority of current efforts (see Baudrillard 2010 and Edelman 2005). Reasons for the failure involve multiple dimensions. At core, there are two fundamental objections to the democratic process: "(1) It may do harm. (2) It may fail to achieve the common good" (Dahl 1989:163). If sustainability is taken as a litmus test for democracy, it fails.[536]

Estlund asks whether outcomes are to be understood as good "because they are democratically chosen, or are they democratically chosen because they are good?" (2009:Loc. 969-70). Some scholars will assign to the former or the latter, while many surmise that both are related. Mill discussed the issue of understanding something as good by pointing out that

"[q]uestions of ultimate ends are not amenable to direct proof. Whatever can be proved to be good, must be so by being shown to be a means to something admitted to be good without proof" (1879:6).

Democratic theorists regularly ignore that they have not yet shown that democracy passes this test in practice. If democracy is the ultimate good above all others, the lack of sustainability is mainly a dilemma for democracies in practice, but not in theory. However, many democracy theorists tie the value of democracy to human flourishing being grounded in an abstract form of self-determination. Shapiro writes: "Democracy has intrinsic value as a subordinate good, but this value is only realised in conjunction with superordinate goods" (1999:23). He sees

---

[535] Many studies come to this conclusion. Scruggs for example states that their results "raise doubts about the environmental efficacy of democracy. The limited evidence that we do find to support a positive democratic effect is accounted for more by economic change (specifically the collapse of the Eastern bloc), not political liberalization" (2009:2).

[536] "On one hand, if most people actually prefer socially and environmentally destructive behavior — if they want to drive everywhere, to buy cheap plastic packaging, to use dangerous pesticides — then we face a crisis of democracy. If the people can be trusted only to pursue awful destruction, then benevolent dictators may offer the only hope for social and environmental change. On the other hand, if forces beyond popular control strongly encourage destructive behaviors, then democracy might guide us through social challenges" (Williams 2010:266).

democracy's role in serving as an instrument rather than being the end. But, what if democracy rather than being a means is an obstacle to a higher good? If one is committed to democracy normatively, the consequentialist answers are hard to accept. The gap between the claims in democratic theory and practice are grave. Furthermore, where democracy fulfils the criteria set by democratic theory in practice (in varying forms), mechanisms do not necessarily lead to positive outcomes for the environment, but are often counterforces. Burnell discusses the issue of democracies' environmental performance in an article that asks "Is Democratisation Bad for Global Warming?" (2009). He points out that the theoretical argument is that

> "democracies value human life and so will address threats to life, unlike autocracies, which prioritise power and ideology; democratic institutions are accountable to the public; democracies have greater openness and learning and educative capabilities compared to autocracies; the dispersion and decentralisation of power in democracies allows for a plurality of local and grass-roots initiatives (as in the US, where state-level and municipal initiatives can take place even if central government is negligent); the implementation of government solutions to complex problems requires willing obedience and cooperation from those who are affected, and this is more likely to be forthcoming in democracies; elected governments (know they) can be held to account for how they respond to current prognoses of future problems, which means democracies are more likely to show sensitivity to the needs and entitlements of future generations; civil society, environmental non-governmental organisation (ENGO) pressure groups specifically can organise freely and help build influential multi- and trans-national movements" (2009:3).

Each of his claims has been fully discussed.[537] In sum, political freedom and sustainability have not even been proven to be positively correlated. Newer studies about pollution for example clearly indicate this:

> "Most coefficients are in the wrong direction, suggesting that, if anything, more political freedom implies more pollution, directly contradicting the majority of existing results. For several high profile pollutants, sulfur dioxide and carbon dioxide, democracies have significantly higher levels of pollution" (Scruggs 2009:15; Shearman and Smith 2007:107).

A closer examination of theory and empirical research show that none of the optimistic claims are as straightforward as they appear.

A general observation is that democracy is a technique of government that is neither reliable nor necessarily trustworthy (Agamben 2012:9). This is specially the case when it comes to the environment as a common good. Democracy relies on input and feedback, thus the effective

---

[537] They can be listed as seven claims: 1. Democracies value human life and therefore will address threats to life. 2. Democratic institutions are accountable to the public. 3. Democracies have greater openness and more learning capabilities compared to autocracies. 4. Its decentralization of power allows for a plurality of local and grass-roots initiatives. 5. Democratic are more likely to gain the willingness and cooperation of the affected. 6. Elected government can be held accountable for their response to prognosis for future problems, so they are more likely to be sensitive to the need of future generations. 7. Pressure groups can organize freely.

operation of human intellect and morals.[538] Democracies are more responsive (Leggewie and Welzer 2011:173). This can be an advantage but could also be a disadvantage depending on the demand of the stakeholders and the process. Human nature and nurture can equally play a negative role for the preservation of life support systems. While democracy scores high if one values inclusiveness (of citizen today), it fails to prove that it produces greener outcomes. More democracy automatically means less expert influence (see Höffe 2009). As Graham highlights putting wants over truth can give democracy a ledge over expert decision making and if the ends

> "are not a matter of what is known, but of what is wanted. If this is correct, we do seem to have an argument in favour of democracy, because the expert (whether Platonic philosopher or contemporary social scientist), whose advice may be essential in deciding upon political means, has no special role to play in settling upon political ends. Who has the 'expertise' to tell people what they want?" (2013:Loc. 454-58).

The irony of such a statement, when put into the context of catastrophe, should be clear at this point. On the one hand, developments, in particular in the US, suggest that "in the popular mind, one person, one vote somehow came to mean that any political judgment is as good as any other" (Bell 2013:16). On the other hand, the discussion of cognition showed reoccurring handicaps for basic understanding. There is the widespread belief that "[i]f voters and politicians are perfectly informed, then politicians offer and voters vote for platforms that maximize their welfare" (Przeworski 1999:34). The phrasing of this if-clause already shows the impossibility by using the superlative "perfectly". Any commitment to public reason is problematic and "the wisdom of collective preferences" has not been proven (Althaus 2003:31). Green theorists argued that democracies are more likely to realise 'long-term' sustainability

> "because the success of ecologically sustainable development policies is dependent on an informed citizenry which understands and supports the need for such policies and freely cooperates with a government which the majority accepts as legitimate" (Eckersley 2001:322; cf. Ophuls 1977).

But this is based on assumptions.[539] Free cooperation has not proven to be effective, if costs are involved. Moreover, the correlation between consciousness and actual environmental behaviour is weak at best. Understanding the necessity and supporting it does not implicate actually supporting concrete policies. Individualism, as an ideology that seems deeply intertwined with democracy is not only hardly capable of environmentalism it has also been shown as counterproductive.

Stehr comments:

---

[538] "But the people and crowds can make bad decisions, including ones that would paradoxically destroy democracy. Foolish people, in other words, can wreck even the best possible political system, while people with more foresight and public spirit can make a lesser system work well" (Orr 2009:60)

[539] Among other issues, a government does not necessarily need to be democratically elected for the majority to accept it.

> "Is democracy and are societal institutions that are governed by principles of liberty such as the market place capable of dealing with harms and risks to society that are located in the future? Political theory has been noticeably silent on the second theme" (2013:57).

Market mechanisms have failed to show sustainability and due to the inherent logic of externalising costs seem problematic. Market mechanisms need to be considered carefully in regard to the proliferated values, since these cannot be regarded as environmentally sound or even value-free. The protection of nature is not ensured in any democracy, nor is it clear whether it can protect nature as a common good, since these ideas premise accepting a specific worldview. Where the emphasis is on inclusiveness and acceptance of pluralism, it cannot be on green ends.[540] The IPCC not only as an institution concerned with the climate but also as one that utilises consensus building shows difficulties of deliberative democrats' expectations. While the IPCC's results themselves are conservative estimations based on compromise, they show that it is too late to rely on "the evolution of true democracy through bottom-up reform" (Shearman and Smith 2007:166).[541] The hopes put in participation and deliberation for elevating the protection of nature to an end and implementing green policies could not be substantiated by practice.[542]

Carter describes the reform-oriented environmentalism that stays within the current systems as too radical for the institutions, while at the same time not radical enough given the threat of current destruction (2013:294; see also Leonard 2013:Loc. 5338-42). However, since democracy as an 'ultimate form of government' is to be seen as normative and far from evidently inferred from (human) nature, the process of naturalisation, critically spoken, can always be called 'indoctrination'. Green democracy theorists may admit weaknesses of democracy one by one, but it is a widely spread taboo to draw the conclusion that democracy is not suitable to reach the goals which are used to justify its existence. Levy asks for intellectual honesty suggesting "that if our aim is the good and green society, it would be better to argue for that directly, rather than to

---

[540] "Insofar as the give-and-take politics of liberal democracy requires compromise, the green programme will be enacted (if at all) in dribs and drabs and pieces. And this will not do, inasmuch as the green programme is of a piece and must be taken whole" (Ball 2006:43).

[541] Fiala "explains how even conscientious environmentalists may be tempted to take up Nero's fiddle. [...] First, short-term self-interest is reasonable and it is even more reasonable in the midst of a severe crisis. Second, voluntary action is insufficient to solve the global environmental crisis when voters and consumers base their behavior on short-term self-interest. Given our quite reasonable commitment to democratic government and our reasonable fear of the power of Leviathan, it is unlikely that voters will choose leaders who advocate radical coercive action. Third, perception is the key to voluntary action. In order to stimulate people to act voluntarily to solve the crisis, they need to perceive the severity of the crisis. Fourth, perception of a crisis can lead to despair and retreat to self-interest. If we believe the crisis is unsolvable, then short-term self-interest is rational. One obvious solution is thus to find some way to stimulate hope that the crisis can be averted through individual action and collective reform" (2010:64).

[542] "Democracy American style places a heavy premium on the right to deliberate, the dignity of the individual, and the hope that political disputes can be resolved democratically" (Buell and De Luca 1996:137). While the inevitability of the dependence of "the dignity of the individual" on democracy is disputable, the United States' bad environmental record is a fact.

hope that it will come to us as a by-product of democracy" (2004:49). Once democracy shows to destroy its own foundations, it is difficult to argue for its practice. The outcome of democratic practice stands in contradiction to its own ends. If democracy cannot produce sustainability, it cannot reach human flourishing. Basic goods such as clean air and food are a precondition for such a flourishing. Thence, democracy scholars must not only admit its inner tensions, but critically discuss priorities and its consequences. While this work focuses on sustainability, it is linked to this wider discussion of means and ends. Meanwhile, "[i]f there is no effective agency, then the agent of change is the rest of nature" (McLaughlin 1995:268). This will make all politics reactionary. Not only will this further reduce political agency, but liberty in general. The inertia of democracy paired with the inertia of climate systems could amount to an uninhabitable planet.

The question of good governance might be as old as human society itself. The political science canon encompasses an incredibly rich collection of theorists. The first part of this book has shown that it is critical to rethink good governance when it comes to environmental protection. It has in particular highlighted difficulties of democracy to be green. Increasingly scholars understand the prevalent political institutions as unable to cope with ecological challenges (Tremmel 2011:153).[543] There is much to discover in the politics of nature. Whereas it is possible to understand who takes the environment seriously, "we do not have a very good grasp of the underlying causes of [observed] performance differences and similarities" (Meadowcraft 2014:45).[544] Duit highlights Meadowcraft's conclusion that green thought is far from apprehending factors for good environmental government (2014b:328). Maybe parts of the lack of understanding can be explained by the concentration on democracy instead of openness to all factors. An impartial discussion of green democracy unmasks that many ends of green political theory are in fact in conflict with each other. "To endorse green ends without supporting the means necessary to achieve them is incoherent or, worse, hypocritical" (Ball 2006:143). Accordingly, Westra claims that

> "although democracy is taken to be the form of government that is the best supporter and defender of human rights, it is precisely the unquestioned acceptance of the primacy of democratic institutions that presents the major obstacle to the prevention of public harms, particularly environmentally induced risk to public health" (1998a:58). [545]

While many theorists have attempted to tie environmentally friendly politics to democracy, an honest inquiry reveals that the evidence is insufficient at best. Given the catastrophic consequences of environmental destruction good governance needs to change focus and prioritize greener performance.[546]

Currently not a single state is approaching sustainability given other priorities. Duit describes this as follows:

---

[543] Randers tells his readers: "I advise you choose as your new homeland a country that is capable of acting proactively in the decades ahead. This means a country that is capable of convincing its population to choose the narrow path. Or to be blunt, a country that does not rely solely on democracy and free markets. China certainly has the ability to act in a farsighted manner" (2012:Loc. 6810-15).

[544] So far, "despite a growing volume of work, a sophisticated theoretical understanding of comparative environmental performance remains elusive" (Meadowcraft 2014:46). The difficulty of comparing environmental performances starts at the basis. The EPI report 2012, for example, notes the lack of data in regard to various aspects listing "toxic chemical exposures; heavy metals (lead, cadmium, mercury); municipal and toxic waste management; nuclear safety; pesticide safety; wetlands loss; species loss; freshwater ecosystems health; water quality (sedimentation, organic and industrial pollutants); recycling; agricultural soil quality and erosion; desertification; comprehensive greenhouse gas emissions; and climate adaptation" (2012:5; see also Forsyth 2003). Accumulative effects of chemicals are a danger even, when they individually stay below a legal level.

[545] "Even the harshest contemporary philosophical critic of the right to vote in the Western world affirms (without any empirical evidence)" the superiority of democracy (Bell 2015:Loc. 405).

[546] This condition means that good governance and good green governance can be used synonymously throughout the remainder of this work.

"There are no examples of strong ecostates in the contemporary political landscape, as even countries with the most ambitious green agendas are not close to favouring the environment over economic growth consistently. The strong ecostate, therefore, should be thought of as an ideal type, which is mainly useful for providing a contrast" (2014b:323).

Yet, talking about a "strong ecostate" as an ideal conveys that other forms exist in practice and that they can be labelled 'ecostate'. As argued earlier in terms of sustainability, it does not make sense to call weak forms 'sustainability', since they are not sustainable. Consequently, it is equally misleading to call anything that is not sustainable an 'ecostate'. If the prefix 'eco' even marks unsustainable forms of governance, the charge of concept-stretching cannot be dismissed.[547] Following the conclusion of the first part, that democracy is unlikely to produce an ecostate, the second and third part will discuss how alternatively an ecostate could be constructed. This part's focus is devising an alternative ethical framework for ecologically sound governance, hence revising what is typically meant by good governance.[548] Hereby, this part will include an elaboration of normative foundations for nondemocratic governance stressing the importance of the commons protection and the role of the state. Given material realities, it attempts to formulate guidelines using principles that adhere to the unique qualities and characteristics of ecological integrity as benchmark. Because consequentialism is outcome-orientated it will be facilitated throughout this part. Its advantages and implications need to be assessed. Furthermore an ethic for the governance of nature that accepts material necessities inevitably has to give science a central role. Accordingly this part conceptualises the philosophical justification for Hypothesis 2 i.e. a meritocracy with focus on ecologically sound governance is feasible.

Ecoauthoritarianism consists of the prefix 'eco' and authoritarianism. The prefix here indicates the authority/authorship of the rule, namely the environment. Ecocracy is also sometimes used as a rule 'for the environment'. To understand ecocracy as necessarily democratic is green washing democracy and lacks theoretical and practical foundation. Despite the fact that the *demos* of any democracy could theoretically set ecological integrity as the highest standard, the sovereignty remains in the *demos*. Ecocracy and ecoauthoritarianism, on the other hand, signify

---

[547] Some authors make similar arguments for democracy, but this is not subject of inquiry here.
[548] Following Aristotle, this discussion takes the orientation of the government towards the common good as the main benchmark for good governance (2009).

a specific rationale of rule.[549] It is a common practice among green democratic theorists to condemn less participatory approaches as 'ecoauthoritarian' and sometimes even 'ecofascist'.[550] This comes in handy, since authoritarianism in general is perceived negatively by the majority of scholars as well as many publics and therefore provokes negative feelings. Ecoauthoritarianism serves as the green bogey-man that can be employed against serious criticism. At the same time ecoauthoritarianism is seldom discussed comprehensively. In his book, Carter for example divides approaches towards the environment into three political perspectives: "eco-authoritarianism", "eco-reformism" and "eco-Marxism" (2013). However his discussion of ecoauthoritarianism is restricted to right-wing ecoauthoritarianism and takes up only 1.5 pages, while eco-reformism is discussed on about 9 pages and eco-Marxism on about 27 pages.[551] Meanwhile, "[p]olitically, there has never been enough imagination as to how the agenda might be pursued, and the discourse never really got past the simplistic draconian authoritarianism of the 1970s survivalists" (Dryzek 2005:50).

What differentiates ecoauthoritarianism from the majority of green thought is its insistence on the necessity of a strong state. Radcliffe states that the beliefs that an "authoritarian state can cope with bigger size and complexity", that it will be environmentally literate, that it will be sustainable indefinitely and that it will be ruled by a benevolent elite are common among ecoauthoritarians (2002:28). Comparatively extensive means are thought to enable truly

---

[549] The term 'ecocracy' can be criticized on the basis that human beings cannot be taken as distinct from nature. Since everybody is subject to the laws of nature, ecocracy has no meaning. Holland highlights that "it may turn out to be unwise to rely exclusively on the moral and instrumental case. It may be worth holding out for the point that what is important is precisely the fact that nature goes its own way—not which way it goes—and that this is important even if, and probably because, it makes things uncomfortable for humans" (2013:Loc. 1014). Here, the idea of an ecocracy also has the potential to revive mistakes of modern positivism. Similar arguments can be made for the term 'biocracy'. Noteworthy, 'economy' also contains the prefix 'eco' originating from the Greek term for household. Today, the common origin appears cynical to many concerned with sustainability.

[550] Such a label is bitter for those who recognize the comprehensiveness of environmental destruction. Whilst degrading all life support systems, critiques of environmental policies employ this kind of rhetoric. Westra highlights: "Respect for eco-systems is ipso facto respect for all natural entities" (1998a:137). An unsustainable lifestyle on the other hand, itself could be seen as ecofascist, since it could ultimately condemn the great majority of lives to impoverished conditions.

[551] Though one can argue that an eco-Marxism discussion overlaps with ecoauthoritarianism, such imbalance is representative for many works in the field. Anyhow, most popular Marxists did not assign to the ideas further developed in this part: "Political meritocracy was valued neither by Marx nor by Mao, and Lenin's idea of the vanguard party was also different" (Bell 2015:Loc. 3845).

sustainable policies.[552] Study after study indicates that states are central to good environmental governance. "The state initiates and coordinates policy networks" whereas "the absence of state leadership is shown to have a detrimental effect on the implementation of sustainable development strategies and plans" (Duit 2014b:334). Ecoauthoritarianism also acknowledges the flexibility of democracy to produce sustainable and unsustainable outcomes. Ecoauthoritarianism can be non-ecocentric, but as noted in the introduction always overlaps in some of its ends with ecocentrism. In a sense ecoauthoritarians are the realists of green theory. They take some components as unchangeable or at least not changeable within a short timeframe. Differences aside two premises signify ecoauthoritarianism:

1. The necessity and urgency of environmental sound politics[553]

2. The necessity of taking (a) human nature into account[554]

In his book on antidemocratic thought Spitz divides the critiques of democracy into two camps; those who believe in the undesirability and those who believe in the impossibility of democracy (1965). It is fair to place the majority of ecoauthoritarianism, including parts of this work, into the second category. Most ecoauthoritarians appreciate democracy as an ideal, but assume good environmental governance is implausible within democratic regimes. Though they too wish for an ecological citizenship, they point at the utopic quality of enlightened citizens to be in the majority.[555] Heilbroner for example emphasized that the prospects of humanity lead him to draw conclusion which are contrary to his inclinations (1976:18). Humphrey suggests that Heilbroner and Ophuls, both as advocates of cultural change, would have vowed for less stringent forms of government, if environmental destruction was less urgent (Humphrey 2007:Loc. 825; Ophuls 1977:204). A 'realistic' vision of the future acknowledges cultural contexts and looks for capable

---

[552] "A strong government, for instance, would be able to shift a nation from cheap and dirty fossil energy to more expensive solar energy—before the latter is competitive. It is a government that would act in the long-term interest of the people, even if they do not agree in the short term. It is a government that is capable of withstanding not only the opposition from the existing energy business, but also the opposition from the voting majority who will want the cheapest possible energy in the short run. A strong government would also be capable of convincing the people to wait for a better solution and pay for its development while waiting. I agree that there is always the risk that the government may choose the wrong solution (and that the market might not have made the same mistake). But the risk can be reduced, for example, by letting the government define the goal and put up the money while allowing the market to choose the technique through a bidding process. Will strong government come in time to solve the climate problem? As you have seen from my forecast, I think not. But by 2052 the acceptance and belief in strong government will far exceed that of today, and some of the obvious solutions will be well on their way" (Randers 2012:Loc. 5068-78).

[553] "Authoritarian environmentalism is a non-participatory approach to public policy-making and implementation in the face of severe environmental challenges" (Gilley 2012:287).

[554] "In addition to the judgement that individuals are unlikely to make a democratic choice for outcomes that curtail the freedoms and material benefits that they currently enjoy, there are other assumptions about human psychology that play a part in eco-authoritarian arguments" (Humphrey 2007:Loc. 522).

[555] Shearman and Smith still believe that democracy has a future (2007:125). Humphrey states this tendency as follows: "Democracy, however, remains merely a contingently bad form of political organisation for these writers, and if a form of democracy can be found that addresses the depletion/population/pollution problems that they are concerned with, it would be considered a viable political system" (2007:Loc. 3558).

means. Most decisively, it does not await a new better human being (Höffe 2009:193).[556] In the book *What is radical politics today?*, Heartfield states that "what counts as radicalism is more likely to take the people as a problem than the solution" (2009:45). By definition the people are the roots of democracy. Any concept that diverts from democracy is in that sense radical.

Although it looks as if ecoauthoritarianism must not be exclusively left-wing, the writings with rare exceptions tend to emphasize social justice (e.g. Goodland and Daly 1996 and Westra 1998a).[557] The focus on social justice for a green state is a moral decision that can be justified to a certain extent by citing that inequality causes worse environmental records (Wilkinson and Pikett 2011; see also Cox 2013).[558] The likelihood of a sufficient protection of the commons, hence sound environmental governance within democratic frameworks, has been proven to be low. In particular, focusing on the environment as the commons that need the protection of a strong state speaks in favour of a more authoritarian solution. This strong state protects what is public from private and therefore particular interest. The realm of the state depends on the line between public and private. *Res publica*, the Latin term for state, can be used to explain huge differences in political philosophy. The term's interpretation in regard to life support system protection will be the subject of an examination. The strong state stands in contrast to much of green theory which, as pointed out earlier, influenced by liberalism resembles its focus on the individual as an actor and often the protection of the private. In environmental matters, such a focus might prove as a fatal mistake, since barely any decision by 'citizens or consumers' today can be understood as a decision that does not go beyond even a widely defined private sphere (Singer 1994; Hamilton 2010). Importantly, as acknowledged by Dahl, if there is a difference between the general good and an aggregation of individual interests, "the case for guardianship is strengthened" (1989:72).[559] The convoluted relationship between public reason and the

---

[556] "[I]f human nature and nature are less holistic and more unpredictable than environmentalist commonly assume, then respect for such uncertainties needs to be drawn into analytical framework and policy prescriptions" (Buell and DeLuca 1996:60).

[557] Notably, Kassiola argues that sustainability depends on justice: "Sound environmental policymaking and implementation must include considerations of social justice for both moral and environmental reasons" (2002:Loc. 905). Justice considerations need to go beyond the fact that natural disasters hit the poor the hardest and that absolute poverty can lead to environmentally damaging practices.

[558] Stretton warns that "equality a first condition of the contentment [with living standards], and of any general environmental self-restraint" (1976:181).

[559] Hobbes asserts that private reason has to be subordinated to public reason (2007; Minogue 1966:63). His often rejected solution is authoritarian. Baxter argues that the chance that a non-democratic states is eco-friendly exists, however "the standard liberal arguments against 'benevolent dictatorships' apply as strongly as ever" (2005:178). He equally rejects early republican democracy and believes in "strong liberal arguments against republican democracy, and the communitarianism on which it rests, such as that, in the absence of a vibrant civil society, the critical role of the informed, virtuous citizen is highly problematic and that republican democracy really only provides us with a recipe for simple oppression by the guardians of the state-sponsored 'good life'" (2005:178). Here he appears to see no difference in practice. Such liberal arguments lose force with the absence of a significant enlightened citizenry even under comparatively good condition, in addition to a functioning ecosystem being a premise to any flourishing.

common good was established earlier. First and foremost protecting the environment means protecting society from physical harm (Westra 1998a). Being consistent, when claiming that the state's responsibility is protecting the citizen's from harming each other physically, then, is to extend the public sphere if necessary. Consequently, ecological integrity as a public good falls under the state's authority.[560] Thereupon, the realm of the state is extended.

While any form of autocracy risks to go astray and become a full grown totalitarian system, the most important issue to note here is that nothing is more totalitarian, in the sense of penetrating all areas of life, than 'a state of nature', where breathing causes diseases, food is scarce and life becomes a constant struggle to fulfil even the most basic needs (see Hobbes 2009).[561] Once it is accepted that this worst case scenario does not allow for the very foundation of human flourishing and that the current course leads there, the next logical step is to avoid this development by setting priorities. Not just the chance of dictatorships being an eminent threat in case of environmental chaos has to be taken serious. The totalitarian quality of environmental destruction itself cannot be denied and will to be understood as outweighing the consideration of the risks of a stronger state.[562] Again, functioning life support systems are a precondition for anything else. Scientists clearly classify current levels of pollution as threatening and call for drastic reductions (see Stehr 2013). Anderson, for example, counters the political argument that the proposed reductions are impossible with the question whether a drastic rise in global average temperature is "less impossible" (2012:35).[563] Similarly democrats generally call curtailing political freedoms 'impossible' failing to acknowledge climate scientists' reservation.[564] The differentiation between 'hollowed out'/empty rights and actual rights is highly consequential. Generally categorised as ecoauthoritarian, Westra accentuates that 'ecoviolence' is already worse than the lack of civil rights before emancipation in the sense that one formally possesses all the rights, "freedom of choice and the right to life", yet one supports and maintains a system that

---

[560] Even if privatization of public goods was sustainable and excluding considerations of fairness, some environmental goods such as air or even bees can hardly be commoditized. There are attempts to sell canned air and producing biotech bees.

[561] "Though few today embrace either Hobbes' radical egoism or his totalitarianism, many accept his basic argument in favor of government. It is commonly held that the more pessimistic one is about human nature, the more absolute the form of government one should endorse – so that Hobbes, with the most cynical view of human nature, naturally endorses totalitarian government. In contrast, it is often thought, anarchists must hold radically optimistic views about human nature" (Huemer 2013:Loc.4820).

[562] "Among the reasons why people turn to democracy in the quest for justice is that injustice is so often experienced as arbitrary domination" (Shapiro 1999:20). Yet, natural catastrophes in a sense are arbitrary dominance, although people (so far) rather ascribe caused affliction to chance than injustice. In order to be understood as unjust, they need to be recognized as 'avoidable'. Climate change is not bad luck.

[563] Goodland and Daly "believe that in conflicts between political feasibility and biophysical realities, the former must eventually give way to the latter, although we cannot specify exactly how long "eventually" will be" (1996:1012f.).

[564] Consequentially an important question is "how can we even begin to retrench and start to view freedom as a possible enemy of the common good instead?" (Westra 1998a:179).

suppresses oneself (1998a:54).[565] She sees ecoviolence as institutionalised by powerful corporations manipulating the public (Pauly 2013). Notably, "policy choices and preferences, even in democratic nations, are manipulated by economic interests that promote their own goals against the wider public interest" (Westra et al. 2013:Loc. 7949). Westra highlights that environmental destruction as violence does not get the same attention as other kinds of violence (2013). Moreover, she believes that recognising a destructive activity as violence is a step towards improving the environment. According to her, anchoring life support systems within a human rights framework could counter ecoviolence and its deleterious consequences on human health (see also Hayward 2003 and McMichael 2013). Westra, who follows a biocentrist ethics herself, points out that many anthropocentric ethical systems are not restrictive enough within their framework (Pauly 2013:Loc. 4658).

Reframing the environment as *res publica,* the looming catastrophe as totalitarian and environmental destruction as violence demonstrates the need for the discussion to reflect realities. Thereafter interrelatedness should become central to policy making. Subsequently political science needs to acknowledge tensions between different freedoms and rights while refraining from categorising the world into binary oppositions along the lines of liberal and illiberal or even free and 'unfree'. Meyer suggests dividing liberalism into economic, social and political liberalism (2006:781). There is no reason why an ecoauthoritarian state cannot be socially liberal to the extent that it allows all lifestyles as long as they do not lead to further environmental degradation.[566] A green state can still be liberal in the sense that it allows for all lifestyles that do not harm others – however difficult a definition of harm and its boundaries might be.[567] It does not need to provide guidelines on all moral questions.

> "The crucial moral questions of our day are not about homosexuality or abortion. Instead moralists should be asking: what are the obligations of all of us in the affluent world when

---

[565] "Often, our inherited political vocabulary rests on notions of human agency that implicitly deny the moral seriousness of the very problems environmentalists wish to decry" (Whiteside 2006:93). Ecoviolence is a concept put forward to articulate the violent character of ecological destruction. The concept does not only entail the existence of victims, but also points at the structural violence perpetuated in environmental conflicts. 'Ecoviolence' is a compelling term with ramifications.

[566] Furthermore, a "liberal order is conceptually consistent, at least, with pure meritocracy. Imagine a meritocracy in which the ruling class is selected on a self-perpetuating basis by open examination with no discrimination by class, gender, race, etc. It nonetheless runs a liberal state" (Skoruspki 2013:119). Bell asserts this asking "what if classical liberals lose their case, and what if nondemocratic liberal societies (such as Hong Kong) do a better job at promoting an ideal of moral and aesthetic self-development? Perhaps classical liberals need to be more open to the possibility of nondemocratic liberal institutions" (2013:12). Shahar accentuates that "the early Eco-Authoritarians were eager to stress the importance of finding ways to preserve as much liberty as possible within such authoritarian regimes" (2015:350; e.g. Ophuls 1977:204ff.). Baber and Bartlett also point at this stating that "ecological rationality does not fully preempt or supplant other forms of rationality: rarely is it completely determinative, and it has little relevance to many dimensions of human activity" (2005:Loc. 241).

[567] Mill pointed out that "liberty is often granted where it should be withheld, as well as withheld where it should be granted" and "[t]he State, while it respects the liberty of each in what specially regards himself, is bound to maintain a vigilant control over his exercise of any power which it allows him to possess over others" (1901:74).

people are slowly starving in Somalia? [...] Are we entitled to continue to confine billions of non-human animals in factory farms, treating them as mere things to serve the pleasures of our palate? And how can we change our behaviors as to preserve the ecological system on which the entire planet depends?" (Singer 1994:19).

Singer's crucial questions regard those parts of life that affect others. Life involves multiple dimensions and it is useful to understand it as such, not all actions have an impact on other lives. Thus, a green state does not necessarily regulate the whole life. Dasgupta and Maskin highlight that "authoritarian governments can leave citizens alone to pursue their lives" (1999:80). In order to classify regimes it is useful to ask for the boundaries of rule (Merkel and Thiery 2010:190f.). Whereas democracies typically divide between private and public sphere and base them in constitutions and laws, autocracies may not have clear divisions and lines are said to be drawn rather arbitrarily by the regime itself. Nonetheless, the state usually does not penetrate all aspects of life. Admittedly, duties and responsibility become a focal part of a green society. But individual life choices do not inevitably become subject of a green state. Hence, in some areas 'the private sphere' may even be extended. Here, it is fruitful to deeply integrate science. Nevertheless, since science does not provide guidelines for many questions ecoauthoritarianism needs to confront the problem. Neutrality was discussed as a catch 22 earlier. Green is not neutral (Light and De-Shalit 2003a:13), neither is the harm principle.[568]

Empirically, a state's legitimacy depends on the protection and implementation of (human) rights (Gilley 2009:36). As advanced by Petersen, democracies do not necessarily have a monopoly on the rule of law (2009:31).[569] The protection of the rule of law and human rights are autonomous institution (independent from democracy). Thus, a nondemocratic regime type with rule of law and the protection of human rights is possible. It is reasonable to assume a nondemocratic state without the 'arbitrariness' suggested by many definitions. Here, governance along the lines of sustainability needs a consistent framework. Consistency could be an advantage of expert rule. Ecoauthoritarianism poses the unavoidable question: what liberties are ecologically unsustainable (Barry 2001)? Prominently, sound environmental governance needs to offer answers to moral questions. Meadowcraft importantly states that judgements about environmental performance have "an irreducibly *normative* character" (2014:29). While good environmental governance employs science to present complex issues, it has to be substantiated

---

[568] In his discussion of Rawls' and other value pluralistic approaches, Kassiola assures that "in our value-skeptical— some would say nihilist—modern culture, any explicit normative position is likely to be criticized merely for being deontological" (2002:Loc. 808).

[569] Moreover, it is not unknown that democracies suspend the rule of law (if not made a definitional precondition of the term 'democracy'). Nonconstitutional democracy for example has a weakness for popular governments who 'emancipate' themselves from such bindings as laws (Schmidt 2010:464).

by a vision (see Carr 2001; Höffe 2009). In other words: "Meaningful foresight is evaluative – not merely predictive" (Caldwell 1998:5). In this regard Humphrey remarks that

> "seeking to challenge what they see as widely accepted and deeply held values in contemporary societies, the eco-authoritarians seek to both promote a new set of values and recontest or downgrade existing ones on the grounds that they are harmful to the prospects of ecological survival" (2007:Loc. 556).

Recontesting values where negative effects on the environment could in fact lead to stronger substantive human rights and be more consistent than contemporary liberalism's prioritizing neutrality.[570]

However, a further factor comes into play. For the implementation of ecologically sound politics a robust power basis is essential.[571] For a sustainable politics one needs to capture the conditions, know how to change it and at the same time have the power as the chance to implement such changes (Höffe 2009:31).[572] This part of the book will argue that these three criteria offer support to a strong rule by an elite consisting of experts, who have proven to be of extraordinary understanding. Hence the form of government that is suitable to solve environmental crises is a meritocracy.[573] Since such a meritocracy would be directed towards achieving sustainability, it is more precise to call it 'ecomeritocracy'.[574] Of course the idea of meritocracy is not novel and has been reoccurring in the history of political thought. A century ago Schmitt notes that

> "elements of a genuine elite in the sociological sense of the word, an elite that is capable of producing authority and legitimacy, could be borne through a professional cadre that creates stability and is entrusted with the guarantee of the public interest. Such an elite would have qualities like incorruptibility, separation from the world of striving for money and profit, education, sense of duty and loyalty, plus certain obviously diminishing tendencies toward co-optation" (2004:Loc. 772-80; see also Plato 1982).

Like many descriptions of democracy, such an interpretation too has to be carefully contested. Unfortunately, contemporary political theory is relatively silent on the issue; books in favour or

---

[570] "Classical liberals were liberal individualists, but they were not ethical neutralists about the state" (Skoruspski 2013:121).

[571] Despite his critique of autocracy Josephson admits that "state power is the key—that is, how well it fosters protection of private and public property through laws and regulations and how well it gives access by the public to legal proceedings" (2005:121).

[572] "While technological innovation is no doubt essential for a sustainability transition, it might require courageous political decisions to change the trajectory of development and [...] to impose certain environmental innovations onto the polity and to take the unsustainable alternatives off the market (e.g. SUVs, non-organic meat, and short-haul flights)" (Hausknost 2014:369).

[573] In contrast, "it seems peculiar to take an almost unquestioned stance in favor of a system that does not require experience (and expertise) for leadership" (Bell 2015:Loc. 362). Again, questioning democracy has not been part of the *Zeitgeist* of the past two decades; this has not always been the case. Macintyre wrote in 1966: "What is interesting is that no single theme has engaged western political theory as the attempt that this ideal [equal opportunity and participation] is never realized, that people *cannot* rule themselves, that ruling in politics and management in industry are necessarily the specialized function of minority *élite*, and that inequality is a political and social necessity" (1966:185; e.g. Cicero 2001).

[574] Most ecoauthoritarians suggest a rule of experts. Ecomeritocracy in that sense describes most ecoauthoritarianism more precisely, while avoiding the charged term 'authoritarianism' that is frequently used as vituperation.

even focusing on meritocracy are extremely rare.[575] Notably though, critics of meritocracy often find arguments that could be equally used against democracy theorists.[576] Here, the interest is to see how such a nondemocratic system can function in regard to the environment. An ecomeritocracy by definition is ecologically sustainable. "If we construe aristocracy in its proper sense – rule by the best – then presumably it inevitably produces good government" which does not "require the consent of the governed, whereas the whole point of democracy is that it is consent-based government" (Graham 2013:Loc. 766-69).[577] Philosophical as well as practical considerations of this revised version of good governance are central to an understanding of its potential to protect the common environment. Before turning to an ethical conceptualisation of a green political theory beyond democracy, this part begins with a brief introduction of ecoauthoritarianism.

---

[575] Bell writes that "[t]here are hundreds if not thousands of books on the theory and practice of democracy, but it is hard to think of a single recent (and decent) English-language book on the idea of political meritocracy" (2013:5). He himself published two books on the topic in the last couple years (Bell and Li 2013; Bell 2015).

[576] Chan lists two arguments raised against meritocracy (2013). He writes: "The first is that there is no objective basis to differentiate people according to merit. The second is the weaker claim that there is no reliable institutional mechanism to identify and select those of merit. The first reason, I believe, is too strong to be tenable. The virtues and competence we expect of political leaders are neither mysterious nor highly contestable. We want leaders to be knowledgeable about their tasks, to have the ability to think and express clearly and to understand complex arguments, and to possess such virtues as public spiritedness, a sense of responsibility, integrity, trustworthiness, civility, benevolence, and so forth. These virtues are human virtues that can be known and experienced in many social contexts. It is possible to judge whether people do or do not possess these abilities and character traits. In fact, we feel that we are able to make this sort of judgment about the people with whom we closely work or interact – our colleagues, fellow members of a committee or group, or friends" (2013:42).

[577] "On a question which is the best worth having of two pleasures, or which of two modes of existence is the most grateful to the feelings, apart from its moral attributes and from its consequences, the judgment of those who are qualified by knowledge of both, or, if they differ, that of the majority among them, must be admitted as final" (Mill 1879:16; see also Estlund 2009:Loc. 2420-21).

3.1. THE LIMITS TO GROWTH AND ECOAUTHORITARIANISM

The Limits to Growth discourse prominently produced an early generation of ecoauthoritarians (Meadows et al. 1972). Based on computer modelling, the book's projections drew a dire future. As the title signals the core of the publication was the 'discovery' that growth cannot continue *ad infinitum* (1972; see also Dryzek 2006:31ff.). Any discussion of the book, its content and its reception should start with comparing its assumption with reality. Different simulations were part of the modelling.[578] While often represented as completely wrong, only some models mismatch reality. To be precise, the authors miscalculated and misjudged the amount of resources.

> "Back in the 1970s, the Meadows expected to see significant resource scarcities before the new Millennium. That didn't happen. Remember this was almost 40 years ago when basic data on natural resources were even scarcer than they are today. But the prospect of scarcity wasn't far behind their expectations" (Jackson 2012:Loc. 464-68).

Unfortunately, it looks as if its negative scenario, which represented business as usual, i.e. ignoring the book's findings, is closest to the actual developments. Accordingly, the 1992 report stated that little had changed in regard to humans' interaction with nature, yet the problem had become more urgent after 20 years of inaction (Dryzek 2005:33; see also Meadows, Meadows, Randers 2004 and Randers 2012).[579] The data of the simulations compared with real-world data "provides considerable but not complete confirmation of the "overshoot and collapse" dynamics" (Turner 2008:35). The concentration of carbon dioxide in the atmosphere has surpassed 400 ppm and is therefore significantly higher than the 350ppm threshold suggested as safe by scientists (see 350.org).[580] Yet, from the beginning it has been claimed that limits to growth are such nonsense "that nobody could possibly take it serious" (Beckerman 1972:327).[581] Such claims mostly assumed that technology will lead to substitution and fix the pollution. The book itself contained technological progress as a positive scenario with significant reductions. It is clear by now however that one cannot only trust in scientific innovations to handle climate change and resource scarcity. Technological progress is not likely to solve all problems created by

---

[578] Many contemporary scholars judge it fair to think in apocalyptic proportions. Orr for example writes that "it is a mistake, I think, to regard the possible suicide of humankind as an anomaly rather than the logical outcome of a wrong turn that now must be quickly undone. For all of its complexity, the essence of the issue of sustainability was put by the writer of Deuteronomy long ago: "I have set before you life and death, blessing and cursing: therefore choose life, that thou and thy seed may live" (2009:127).

[579] Hardin had indirectly pointed at how democracy can be used to veto change, warning that "worshippers of the status quo sometimes imply that no reform is possible without unanimous agreement, an implication contrary to historical fact" (1968).

[580] The concentration of CO2 in the atmosphere is much more meaningful than the average temperature.

[581] "By comparison with the real problems, the problems of raw material exhaustion or pollution are minor diversions, and they present relatively few difficulties, as far as devising the correct solutions is concerned, and provided one does not aim at perfection. So you can now all go home and sleep peacefully in your beds tonight secure in the knowledge that in the sober and considered opinion of the latest occupant of the second oldest Chair in Political Economy in this country, although life on this Earth is very far from perfect there is no reason to think that continued economic growth will make it any worse" (Beckerman 1972:344).

environmental destruction as mentioned earlier (and it can equally allow for more destruction). A stable climate cannot be substituted. Instead sustainability will not be solved via technology but "is fundamentally a matter of politics" (Leach 2013:Loc. 5107-8). Dryzek warns that while there is wishful thinking "[m]issing in many analysis and associated public debates is sustained attention to the politics, economics, and – crucially – political economy of survival" (2005:35). The trajectory in the meantime increases the probability of geoengineering as mitigation effort in the future. Geoengineering in its nature relies on centralised power. Additionally, prominent climate scientists discuss nuclear power as a necessity and point at environmental movements as a hindrance to this 'carbon-neutral' solution. By highlighting that the PRC can build a plant within 5 years whereas the US needs 15 years (Hansen 2015), they unconsciously imply that less inclusive governance proves more effective in regard to an essential part of environmental politics, namely energy production.[582]

For Dryzek the limits discourse is straightforward because the solutions lie in "greater control of the existing systems by administrators, scientists and other responsible elites" (2005:15). He classifies survivalism as the part of the limits discourse that, while radical in its emphasis on survival, does not fundamentally question society or industrialism. Here, he remarks that most survivalists do not know how to approach global capitalism, since "some of their financial sponsors are global capitalists" (2005:50). He lists the writings of Brown, Ehrlich, Myer and Hardin as survivalist.[583] In the 70s most survivalists advocated authoritarianism and centralisation, because the problem was seen as "largely a matter of individuals and other actors pursuing material interests in decentralized systems" which have "no cohesive leadership directing them: examples include markets, liberal democratic systems, and the international system" (Dryzek 2005:36). Dryzek finds the survivalists' thought lacking discussions about individual problem-solving, the capability to cooperatively find solutions, markets, social movements, gender aspects, resilience of ecosystems, states and interest groups. Instead he interprets it as focused on finite resources, carrying capacity and elites while making assumptions about human interaction to be shaped by conflict, hierarchy and control (2005:39ff.).[584] He judges 'the politics of scarcity' as elitist, viewing "most people as 'a

---

[582] I had the chance to ask a couple of leading nuclear and climate scientists at COP21 in Paris, if they were aware that they indirectly suggest that an autocratic government has better capacity to handle climate change. They negated. Davis writes that originally only few people actually criticised the Club of Rome's assumption that "governmental planning and direction were the best answer, a method labelled by critics as dirigisme" (2007:34).
[583] In contrast, ecology takes primacy in Ophuls and others, according to Dryzek (2005:37).
[584] One might argue that this is a wide range to be covered by only a handful of scholars. Some aspects are incorporated into ecoauthoritarianism today.

population', effectively denying them agency, the capacity to act" (Dryzek 2005:42). Radcliffe uses harsh words writing that

> "some green thinking has rejected human interest altogether, in that the non-human nature begins to take precedence. This was explicit within the writings of some early environmental writing such as Ehrlich and their belief in the need to substantially reduce the global population" (2002:204).

While those who oppose nondemocratic solutions may agree with Radcliffe's assessment, many ecoauthoritarians claim that they take human interests more seriously, when emphasizing the indispensability of functioning ecosystems. Acknowledging environmental destruction and limits to growth, ecoauthoritarianism infers that expertise rule and control over the common pool is made imperative. This chapter will review some ecoauthoritarian positions briefly. While repeating some arguments, it serves as a bridge between the first part and the following two parts.

3.1.1. EARLY ECOAUTHORITARIANISM

Many works are closely clustered around the publishing of *The Limits to Growth* (Meadows et al. 1972; e.g. Hardin 1968; Ehrlich 1971; Heilbroner 1976). In spite the recognition of cultural construction as a factor, the 70s ecoauthoritarianism was mostly positivist in its tone. Reading the urgency with which the authors like Ehrlich described the threat can be surprising (1971). On the one hand, their alarming language had hardly any impact and processes have only accelerated and are more pronounced. On the other hand, their alarming language is used to discredit all environmentalism, since the doom is yet to come. Instead of letting destruction unfold, ecoauthoritarians standardly envisioned strong institutions that would be able to plan according to the physical limits of Earth. Commoner famously put forward four "Laws of Ecology" emphasizing a closed interconnected system with clear limits, hence illustrating insuperable necessities (1979).[585]

The attempt of unlimited accumulation within a limited system is standardly presented as catastrophic. Accordingly, critique of capitalism on behalf of the life support systems, which is still a central part of environmentalist thought, is a major contribution of the earlier works.[586] Prominent ecoauthoritarians Commoner and Heilbroner put an emphasis on the economic system. For Commoner, the challenge would not be economic development itself or population, but "how to create a system of production [...] in harmony with the environment" (1992:148). In

---

[585] "Everything Is Connected to Everything Else" (1979:16ff.). "Everything Must Go Somewhere" (1979:19f.). "Nature Knows Best" (1979:20f.). "There Is No Such Thing as a Free Lunch" (1979:22ff.).
[586] Accordingly Stretton writes in 1979 about environmentalists that they "want another economic revolution" (1976:3).

accord with the idea that environmental degradation would need to become a social fact, Ophuls writes that "a genuine cure would require a revolution in human thought greater than the one that created the modern world" (2012:Loc. 78). However, like many other green theorists he doubts its possibility.

> "Moreover, my analysis suggests that there is very little that we can do. Most of the trends I identify are inexorable, and complex adaptive systems are ultimately unmanageable. To the extent that we can do something, the required measures are far outside the bounds of what is feasible or even thinkable today" (2012:Loc. 77).

Ophuls' books have a pessimistic undertone. In his early writings, he considered a Hobbesian solution given the return to scarcity (1977; Radcliffe 2002:23), while his later work is much more ambiguous (e.g. Ophuls 2012). The above statement is particularly fatalistic. Baber and Bartlett, while acknowledging the partiality in all approaches (2005:Loc. 2196), use Ophuls as an example of an author, who is critical of consensus as a standard of decision making. Decades ago Ophuls already problematised the underlying status quo bias (1977).

In line with this, scepticism towards the chance for existential changes is thorough. Commoner writes

> "a social mandate for ecologically sound production decisions would need to be implemented through some sort of planning – which has clearly been unable to successfully govern the Soviet's Union's system of production. Given this record, the view that social governance of production – environmental democracy – could ever become a reality takes on the cast of illusion" (1992:227).

Seeing the chief cause for environmental destruction in capitalism, control over companies and the planning of economic development appeared as the obvious solution. Where the economy is governed by profit seeking, "environmental constraints ought to determine the choice of production technology. And that choice should govern economic investment policy" (1992:101).[587] The government should use its purchasing power as means of interference (1992:194). Governments should also ban pollutants, since controls have proven to be less effective.[588] Ophuls' writings equally recommended planning and controlled decline. Because he does not believe in a technological solution, he proffers controlling exponential growth (2012:Loc. 425). A deep appreciation for planning and expertise marks writings arguing for top-down interference. In comparison to policy making, Commoner underlines that

> "relevant attributes of science are, first, its demand for rigorous, validated methods that are independent of the results, and second, its objectivity, or independence of the data and analysis used to reach results from the interests of those affected by them" (1992:76f.).

---

[587] The gaps between profitable and indispensable for survival as well as profitable and 'the greener solution' with the connected mechanisms have been discussed in Chapter 2.2.3. extensively.
[588] "In task of restoring environmental quality, prevention works; control does not" (Commoner 1992:44).

Heilbroner concurrently assumes the need for economic planning. A total reorganisation of production would be inevitable (Heilbroner 1976:102). Instead of competition for individual success, collectively organised and assigned functions are likely to be implemented (1976:103). Ophuls' suggestion, to go back to a system that "resembled the natural economy" (2012:Loc. 627), appears nostalgic. It is assumed that post-industrial societies would be rather like static preindustrial societies and lack significant privileges of the 20th century. In his critique of ecoauthoritarianism, Shahar highlights that for example Heilbroner himself "admitted" that a centralised planned economy is difficult (Shahar 2013:351). Although planned economies failed in the past, this does not need to portend that they will in the future. Barring that capitalism fails in regard to the environment anyway, modern infrastructure makes planning plausible again.

Whereas peak fossil fuels appears central, the trend or "terminal decline" towards low footprint societies is more critical (Ophuls 2012:Loc. 587). Tipping points are not the only danger ahead. In contrast to Beckerman, Heilbroner understood that while the planet does have plenty of each element, they vary greatly in concentration, which means that ever growing exploitation requires better technology and involves higher costs (1976:33).[589] He further already wrote about diminishing returns on wealth in correlation to happiness and problematised mass consumption and mass production on this dimension, besides the obvious negative effects on nature. Here, relative deprivation and unwillingness are obstacles to lowering living standards (1976:48). Since socialism and communism were equally marked by quantitative thinking, they also would not be able to create satisfaction, even though they tried to abolish consumption as a standard (1976:53f.). Meanwhile, he saw little prospects in expecting people to take future generations into account. As aforementioned, the degree of separation is too great in particular since even much contemporary suffering is tolerated globally (1976:105). Radcliffe asserts that Heilbroner questioned the potential of capitalism for social responsibility in a limited world (Radcliffe 2002:9). Heilbroner's critique is a clear critique of capitalism, whose compatibility with political equality he questioned in general. He underlines Sahlin's suggestion that "[p]overty is a social status. As such it is the invention of civilization" (1995:28; Sahlin 1972; see also Gorz 1980).[590] Heilbroner speculated that the adaptability of capitalism would not be sufficient to overcome social tensions arising from the demand of redistribution by the poor in a post-growth scenario (1976:61ff. see also Skoruspski 2013:122). Less resource availability has catastrophic

---

[589] Though still true today, Heilbroner was wrong in assuming that this will in fact reduce destruction and economic growth before irreversible climate change has been triggered (1976:38). As with the misjudgment in the case of the *Limits to Growth,* natural resources, for better or worse, have proven less scarce than assumed. Rather than the lack of fossil fuel etc. the limited capacity of sinks, in particular the oceans and the atmosphere are the key problem. Irreversible climate change has been triggered, but mitigation still demands modesty.

[590] See Polanyi for an understanding of economics as a 'socio-political' act (1977).

consequences if it undermines the very fabrics of societies. Ophuls fears that civil wars caused by food shortages could become the norm. He wishes that individual desires would be restrained by "powerful negative feedback, just as in natural ecosystems" (Ophuls 2012:Loc. 635).

In accordance with the last chapter of this book's first part, Heilbroner assumed that the developments would rather lead to more authoritarian forms of government (1976:77; Buell and De Luca 1996:143; Radcliffe 2002:22). Democratic capitalism (and democratic socialism) is likely to lead to a Hobbesian scenario when faced with non-growth. While authoritarian socialism is probably to coerce some kind of solution, it could become indistinguishable from authoritarian capitalism according to Heilbroner (1976:67; see Stretton 1976). Here, Heilbroner sees political obedience as a precondition for political power and national identification as a precondition for regime strength. Meanwhile, the danger of nationalism is a serious problem for the future of humanity, since people are able to create categories such as those who do (relevant) and those who do not count (irrelevant) and competition for resources as a counterforce to international solidarity (1976:81; cf. Scruton 2006). Heilbroner also speculates that the threatening potential of identification might be the key to survival in the future (see De-Shalit. 2006a). He asked about three decades ago, whether another society (where such a high level of consumption would be inacceptable, where self-interest could not be defended as rational) could create transcending solidarity (Heilbroner 1976:83ff.; 1988). He has no answer to the question and also remains unsure, whether freedoms and pleasures of the individual could survive the pressures such a society would have to create. In line with other ecoauthoritarians, Ophuls is openly essentialist calling human nature as a core problem. Whilst

> "mastering the historical process would require human beings to master themselves, something they are very far from achieving. (This is why democracy, considered by some to be an asset in the struggle against the forces that challenge industrial civilization, is in fact a liability) (2012:Loc. 81).[591]

Discussing different claims about human nature, Heilbroner writes that "[at] this point of history our attention should rather be directed to what humans probably are instead of what they could be" (1976:87; my translation). According to him, the weakest point of humanism is not to fully consider unchangeable characteristics of human nature, whether for incompetence or lack of acceptance (1976:89ff.). He asks for more courage to explore human nature, to view potential dangers and therefore to be able to develop policies to divert destruction. Instead of building on hope and false beliefs, limitations need to be recognised (see Hobbes 2009). As described earlier

---

[591] "Homo sapiens's bold attempt to rise above the natural state in which the species lived for almost all of its two hundred thousand years on Earth. Unfortunately, by its very nature, this effort to become greater encounters four implacable biophysical limits. It also sets in motion a seemingly inexorable moral and practical progression from original vigor and virtue to terminal lethargy and decadence" (Ophuls 2012:Loc. 119; [sic!]).

ecoauthoritarianism is typically a realist position. Heilbroner does not only assert characteristics about the environment, he also sees political obedience as a part of human nature. In his opinion, a purely functional analysis of political authority and objective aims often misses the latent functions of stability. Hierarchy leads to psychological stability by reproducing childhood conditions according to Heilbroner (1976:75; see Dahl 1989). Humphrey recites such a position writing that especially in emergencies,

> "politics is pushed in the direction of authoritarianism, and because people feel a need for leadership in crisis situations, they revert to childhood attitudes and look for a parental figure to guide them through difficult times" (2007:Loc. 524).

For Heilbroner, human nature is marked by the proclivity to "power and submissiveness" (1995:118). Here, Saretzki suggests however that as long as genes for longing for authority and hierarchy cannot be proven, 'diversion' from human nature is not a justified critique (2011:54). As remarked, diversion from nature cannot serve as an objection anyway, since naturalness should not be taken as a measure of adjudication. On the other hand, ignoring human nature can have negative consequences, when it makes policies ineffective. The central question of one of Heilbroner's earlier books, whether there is still hope for humanity, is answered negatively. Instead he is sure that humanity will pay a terrible price (1976:100ff.). In this situation he suggests intellectuals to function as guardians who have to prepare people for sacrifices, takeover leadership and redefine a framework of legitimate power and freedom for a future where more control and less freedom (than 'back then') is a necessity. Heilbroner accentuates that in particular those who win from the freedoms of an open society complain about authoritarian tendencies, but that intellectual rigor demands to admit that the ecological challenges might only be overcome with the help of governments who can secure obedience better than democracies. He states this clearly writing that "when the survival of humanity is at stake, those governments might be inevitable, even necessary" (1976:78f; my translation).

In sum, early ecoauthoritarians argued that

> "[a]n adequate response to the ecological crisis requires new limits and new values, which are most expeditiously established by some form of authoritarian government, as well as immediate strict controls if massive social and political upheavals are to be avoided" (Leeson 1979:313). [592]

This conclusion remains the same for contemporary ecoauthoritarianism. One difference however is signalled by the emphasis on the unknown as a central factor in particular in regard to climate change. Clearly climate change has progressively become more threatening. After all,

---

[592] In the article "On the political consequences of scarcity and economic decline", Gurr proposes "that bureaucratic-authoritarian states should be better able than democracies to tolerate the stresses of future ecological crises" (1985:70).

if early warnings were taken seriously, it could have been avoided, while today only mitigation and adaption are possible. Though in newer writings, the tragedy might not fully unravel for 'a while', the threat has the similar, and in a sense more, immediacy.

3.1.2. 21ST CENTURY ECOAUTHORITARIANISM

Goodin described a shift in green concerns from individual animals to whole species and so on arguing that through this lens problems culminating in climate change appear "more compelling" (2006:12). While it used to be the protection of a specific animal, causes are broadened and cover attempting to save whole species from extinction. Yet, majorities overtly show insufficient interest in avoiding catastrophe. Green causes still do not attract majorities. Contemporary works supporting ecoauthoritarian governments are rare nonetheless. Green thought appears to crudely ignore the fact that democracies are unsustainable. Besides the 70s generation, there are only a couple other names typically connected with such an approach. Often the work they published on the topic remains limited. Much of the writing has been incorporated into earlier elaborations within this work. Beeson, Gilley, Shearman and Smith and Westra are among the few scholars who openly suggested that alternative forms of government could be or will become inevitable (Beeson 2010; Gilley 2012; Shearman and Smith 2007; Westra 1998a). Beeson's relatively short article on the "The coming of environmental authoritarianism" is enough to get him regularly cited by critics. The most intensive discussion can be found in Westra's support of ecological integrity and empirically supported works on nature, rights and justice (1998a; 1998b; 2013; Westra et al. 2013). Her work is vital to the argumentation of this and the following parts and therefore will be cited throughout. Some of the earlier ecoauthoritarians continue to write in similar vein, yet extensive works on green nondemocratic political theory are absent from the environmental discourse.

Here, Shearman and Smith's openly ecoauthoritarian stance is refreshing. They argue: "We are stuck with the elites, so let us have the right sort of elites" (2007:90). The disillusionment with the means of democratic governance and the prospects of opportunistic power grabbing leads them to suggest expert rule as the only chance.[593] Shearman and Smith do not only judge the historical context as troubling, they also imply that human nature is not inclined to lead to successful democracy. As mentioned above, classifying human nature as part of the problem is typical for ecoauthoritarian positions, attesting the threat of power grabbing is as well. Concurrently, instead of democracy, they rather "advocate a form of governance by

---

[593] The book contains countless clear statements such as "It is clear that the hard environmental choices cannot be made in liberal democratic societies, for the elites and the citizens of market economies have become too selfish to make sacrifices" (Shearman and Smith 2007:140) and "We doubt if any transformation of the mass is possible, at least to the extent needed for a radical democratic transformation of the present system" (2007:165).

authoritarianism abhorrent to liberal thinkers" (Shearman and Smith 2007:131).[594] Such a government would be led by platonic philosophers who do not attain knowledge for itself, "but knowledge in the service of life on earth" (2007:141; see Jiang 2013 and Bell 2015). Resembling Rousseau's critique of rationalism and loss of compassion, Shearman and Smith advocate for an education that proliferates wisdom because knowledge alone "may allow people to become greater and greater destroyers of ecological services" (2007:145; Rousseau 2002). If the fears are justified, ecoauthoritarian thought needs more attention and its possibilities should be further explored. When democratic participation is not a factor for good governance, meritocracy should be subject of closer investigation. In a sense it shifts the discussion from government of the people to government for the people, since the main purpose of the state becomes protecting the commons (see Cicero 2001).

---

[594] Shearman and Smith, for instance, judge a nationalized banking system as essential (2007:159).

3.2. *Res Publica* or the Commons

The main concern of this work – environmental destruction – can be interpreted as the ultimate common good problem (see Ophuls 1977:196ff.).[595] The following chapter approaches the politics of nature from this perspective. The elaboration builds on a definition of the common good and proceeds by describing theoretical and empirical means of its protection. Adding to the previous discussions, it is fruitful to analyse functioning life support systems as a common good.[596] Of great importance is the position or priority attributed to the commons by particular forms of governance, as well as the way governing the commons is or is not integrated into an institutional setting. Certainly, ecoauthoritarians understand the protection of the commons to be best secured in the hands of the state.

The relationship between the Latin term for 'the state' and the commons is thought-provoking. *Res publica* literally means 'the thing public', which makes it in a sense conterminous with the commons (PONS 1999:897). The state is an institution whose very legitimation is to overcome collective action problems.

> "What makes dealing with collective-action problems central to the pursuit of governance is the fact that all members of the group stand to benefit from the creation of governance systems but that individual members are unable to bring about this change on their own" (Young 2009:16; see Dahl 1989).

The aim of governing, then, is to ensure a collective good that individuals are unable to ensure by themselves. A definition of the common good, however, can be subject to debate and disagreement. It is regularly claimed that there is

> "no such thing as a uniquely determined common good that all people could agree on or be made to agree on by the force of rational argument. This is due not primarily to the fact that some people may want things other than the common good but to the much more fundamental fact that to different individuals and groups the common good is bound to mean different things" (Schumpeter 2003:251).

Schumpeter points at the lack of consensus and the difficulty of finding a common ground, since he assumes a plurality of opinion and interests. His interpretation implies that the common good is what people 'want', hence their preferences.

It is possible to divide positions towards the common good into at least three groups. The first position assumes an objective common good. The other two positions both believe in

---

[595] "Humphrey claims that we can appeal to the objective value of certain environmental goods. Preserved and protected nature may form part of a good human life, regardless of whether people subjectively believe so. If this is true, Humphrey claims, then we should give policies such as nature preservation more weight in calculations about justice than we would if we considered individuals' preferences only" (De-Shalit 2006b:92).
[596] One problem identified by Westra is the lack of an "overarching conception of "the good" for all that can be contrasted with the corporations' perception of the good" (1998a:55).

subjectivity. While the second emphasizes the common good as a matter of worldview, the third denies the existence of a common good more generally. Supporters of an objective common good may remark that the subjective positions fail to differentiate between preferences and needs (see Nussbaum 1992), thus objectivity can still be recovered despite subjectivity. Dahl's description of the contemporary understanding of the common good expresses the difficulty that arises from a pluralist interpretation (1989). He states that

> "the notion of common good is stretched much more thinly in order to encompass the heterogeneous attachments, loyalties, and beliefs formed among the body of diverse citizens with a multiplicity of cleavages and conflicts. It is stretched so thinly, in fact that we are compelled to ask whether a concept of the common good can now be much more than a poignant reminder of an ancient vision that irreversible change has made irrelevant to the conditions of modern and postmodern life" (1989:218).

Yet, for the purposes of this work, as suggested earlier, environmental integrity is prioritised as a prerequisite common good. It is thus openly assumed that there are objective common goods and that it can be known at least in some cases.[597] In fact, a healthy environment is the common good par excellence. Despite many attempts to privatize commons, in nature, commons still exist.[598] Air, water and the climate can hardly be privatized. Notwithstanding possible disagreements on the scope of the common good, a majority of people would agree that at a stable environment qualifies as a common good.[599] There are many reasons to count a healthy environment also as merit good. Other goods depend on it, whereas the opposite, environmental destruction is an obvious bad. Pollution can have serious externalities. For instance, air pollution causes depression and depression makes people less social and cooperative (Bell et al. 2001:243). The Schumpeterian objection, hereupon, can only count for a minority who views

---

[597] In the article "Are Environmental Values All Instrumental?", Sagoff lists what he calls "two crucial scientific postulates": "The first asserts that the individual is the best judge of what will benefit him or her, that is, how well off he or she is in a given situation. The second holds that the satisfaction of the preferences of individuals, insofar as resources allow, constitutes the chief aim or goal of environmental policy" (2002:Loc. 1323). He, at the same time, points at the difficulty of the idea of preferences and choice and furthermore claims that surveys suggesting that the individual decides on the basis of a perceived common good instead of self-interests are not reliable. Respondents of such surveys often do not have the time to include enough information into their judgment. Even more answering in general terms does not necessarily reflect actual behaviour.

[598] Notably, the environmental commons include "commons already divested to private ownership" (Shearman and Smith 2007:164).

[599] This part employs a narrow interpretation of the common good. Though there are many reasons to consider broader definitions in other contexts, the common good taken as a priority here, is materialist for purposes of simplification and generalisability. Many public goods may not directly affect individuals. While it can be argued that public libraries contribute to the general improvement of a society, not everyone likes to visit them. Jacobs points out that "[m]any social goods do not make us better off as individuals; rather, they help to create a better society in which we as individuals then live" (1997b:57). Granted that in many cases opinion vary on the necessity of a public good and its overall impact, it is hard to argue against a clean environment as merit good for all. Even people who prefer a shopping mall to a forest will agree on the importance of clean air. While quality of life arguments remain difficult, arguing for preconditions is not. Plato argued for health as such an "indisputable good" (Westra 1998a:155; Plato 1982).

catastrophe as something positive.[600] Anybody else should see value in the protection of common goods such as clean air or a liveable climate.

Still, individual and collective actions, so far, have failed to protect the natural commons. Causes are manifold. The effects of this failure are monumental, which makes their causes hard to grasp. Despite the widespread knowledge about their decay, the common goods are largely neglected. Given the disastrous course of environmental destruction, it is fair to say that the environment as a common good does not attract enough attention. Shapiro's description of the different approaches towards collective action between liberals and democrats explains how the environment can take a position of irrelevance in liberalism as well as in democracy:

> "Liberals, who typically regard individual freedom as the greatest good, usually focus on devices to protect the individual from the realm of collective action. Democrats, by contrast, try to structure collective action appropriately to embody the preferences of the governed" (1999:31).

Neither is therefore concerned with the protection of the collective good from the individual and the preferences of the governed. In fact, it is rather the opposite. As long as the common good is not in conflict with the individual and the perceived preferences of the governed, there is no conflict. Representative government was born under an ideology that postulated a basic harmony of interests in society (Przeworski 2010:21; see also Bensaid 2012). Believing in congruence is naïve not just in theory, but also because reality disproves it.[601] If all individuals protected the environment, the state would not be needed for this. It would not be a collective action problem. In case of conflict, liberalism prioritizes negative freedom and democracy conforms to other interests, as elaborated in previous chapters. Democracy often does not prioritize society, but "is, first of, a system in which competing interest groups form parties to fight, according to the rules of the political game, for *their* interests" (Roemer 1999:59, my emphasis; see also Hume 2013:Book III). If the majority decided for environmental protection,

---

[600] Rawls states: "If a reasonably just society that subordinates power to its aims is not possible and people are largely amoral, if not incurably cynical and self-centered, one might ask with Kant whether it is worthwhile for human beings to live on the earth? We must start with the assumption that a reasonably just political society is possible, and for it to be possible, human beings must have a moral nature, not of course a perfect such nature, yet one that can understand, act on, and be sufficiently moved by a reasonable political conception of right and justice to support a society guided by its ideals and principles" (2011:Loc. 777-81). Moreover, Shapiro accentuates that the interest in the survival of a democracy, too, is presumed, although "[i]t might nonetheless be asked why people should be said to have an interest of any kind, let alone a basic interest, in engaging in [...] responsible behaviour" (1999:90).

[601] Graham summarises important assumptions: "It is democracy that ensures, or at least is the best way of ensuring, that the government which controls the State reflects the beliefs and opinions of society at large and thus pursues policies that are genuinely in accordance with the general interest and the will of the people. This is an attractive line of thought. Indeed, in my estimation it is belief in the cogency of this line of thought (a belief more often assumed than expressed) that sustains our faith in the democratic State. This faith has two elements. It holds, first that we need the State for the promotion and protection of justice and the general good, and second, that we need democracy to make sure its operation really is in accordance with that good and that those who run it are accountable to the people they govern" (2013:Loc. 326-34).

the state could be an institution for its implementation. The possible conflict between procedure and substance was pointed out by Schumpeter long ago:

> "If results that prove in the long run satisfactory to the people at large are made the test of government for the people, then government by the people, as conceived by the classical doctrine of democracy, would often fail to meet it" (2003:256).

Government by the people does not have to fulfil public needs. Correspondingly, Shearman and Smith see a huge potential for environmental destruction where a minority of 49%, who wants to protect nature, can easily lose against the tyranny of the majority (2007:11).[602] In regard to the substance, democracy is probably not a system that can effectively ensure the commons.

In any case, the modalities of successful common pool protection are still subject of an ongoing debate and core of this work.[603] Collective action problems and the common good are approached from different ideological standpoints. Various disciplines study collective goods. The famous 'nuts game' administered by psychologists exemplifies common pool problems (Bell et al. 2001:477ff.). Participants were put in front of a bowl of nuts with the goal of maximising their individual amount of nuts. While participants could take nuts from the bowl, the remaining nuts were doubled every ten seconds. Though the best strategy for everyone would have been to wait until the end, and then divide the nuts, groups typically failed to follow this strategy. Though identification with the group and social cohesion made a difference, the majority inopportunely depleted the pool even before the end of the game. Here, it is important to point out that there is a difference between random groups and actually established groups which identify as a collective. Hardin's elaboration of "The Tragedy of the Commons" resembles the nut game in a sense (1968). In his classic article on the environmental common pool problem, Hardin writes that

> "the rational herdsman concludes [...] to add another animal to his herd. And another; and another... But this is the conclusion reached by each and every rational herdsman sharing a commons. Therein is the tragedy. [...] to increase his herd without limit--in a world that is limited [...] Freedom in a commons brings ruin to all" (1968:1244; see Berkez 2005).

Notably, the herdsman is characterised as an individual rather than a member of a specific group. It is hard for humans to empathise beyond a certain level of separation, so social cohesion is absent on a global level. The identification with humanity as a whole and therefore as one

---

[602] Dahl warns that "the right to self-government entails no right to form an oppressive government" (1989:208). If environmental destruction is understood as oppressive, it then cannot be legitimate, even if it is the outcome of democratic processes.

[603] "Common property (common pool) resources shared two characteristics: (a) exclusion or the control of access of potential users was difficult, and (b) each user was capable of subtracting from the welfare of all other users" (Berkez 2005:14). Freeriding, that means benefiting from the public good without contributing, risks the good (Connelly et al. 2012:144). Put differently, the landowner might be able to water his garden during a draught only because others save water.

group is beyond the cognitive capacities of most people (Höffe 2009:168). This is why Hardin's example can be employed when seeing climate change as a collective action problem. According to Berkez, the commons can be divided into four property regimes, namely open-access, private property, national property and communal property (2005:15). Only the first is clearly inferior in regard to sustainable practices at first sight.[604] While Hardin's solution to common pool problem is understood to be privatisation, Nobel Prize winner Ostrom is famous for proving that common pool problems do not necessarily need private ownership (1990).[605] Many descriptions of common pool problems depend on the idea of *homo oeconomicus*.[606] In spite of its reductionist view of human nature, rational choice theory is self-reinforcing. When people believe others will act selfishly, they are more likely to act selfishly. For many common goods, it is sufficient if a decisive majority acts in accordance with such an axiom.

Generally, behavioural rules need to be institutionalised for the purpose of solving common pool problems (Diekmann and Preisendörfer 200178ff.). Although it is said that more democracy leads to better protection (Ostrom 1990), examples show that the existence of a culture that protects common resources is of major importance. Localised control typically does make a significant difference, if people have an actual understanding of the resource (e.g. Atran et al. 2002). What is routinely overlooked is that many successful common pool resource management projects only appear to be bottom-up in comparison to formerly unsuccessful national government policies. It is a matter of perspective.[607] While many small projects can make up successful management, they do not necessarily have to be democratic by themselves. Localised resource management in Oceania led to significant improvement, but this can hardly be understood as an outcome of grassroots democratisation. Oftentimes, the authority has been given back to traditional leaders (Johannes 2002). "In many local communities, some rudimentary forms of cooperation on the commons have been sustained and enforced over generations by traditional authority structures", while the introduction of participatory politics and social change can have a negative impact on formerly legitimate structure that fostered

---

[604] It should be noted that it is not typical for local commons to be 'open access' (Dasgupta and Maskin 1999:76).

[605] Ostrom stood against Hardin arguing that sustainability of common pools is possible given "free communication, a shared vision, a high level of trust, and a mobilization" (Marshall 2014:Loc. 3146). In sum, she objected that Hardin forgot about social capital (Connelly et al. 2012:149). Ostrom develops eight rules for successful resource management (1990; see also Diekmann and Preisendörfer 2001:92ff.). The following works led to the belief that "Hardin's model applied to the open-access, or free-for-all, exploitation of the commons, but it was not valid for many community-based resource use systems" (Berkez 2005:14).

[606] Considering the opposite side, Singer remarks that "institutions based on altruism to strangers can work, as long as they do not rely on a large proportion of the population to act altruistically – and the greater the sacrifice asked, the smaller the proportion of the population that we should expect to respond to it" (1999:58; see also Ophuls 1977).

[607] For many the label 'bottom-up' implies more inclusive (and democratic) structures. Notably, greens typically want democracy and justice as universal standards, but also the protection of indigenous groups, which leads to the question "what if those practices, which may be environmentally sustainable, are themselves based on the dominance of a particular social group?" (Connelly et al. 2012:62f.).

solidarity (Bradhan 1999:106). In Atran et al.'s fieldwork in South America, the group with a "highly interconnected network, with no dominant individual or subgroup" was the group which farmed least sustainably (2002:439). The matter is not one of democracy then.

Mellor also points at the importance of mechanisms but, in contrast to Hardin, sees the solution in collective ownership.

> "A commons is not just the existence of a common resource, but a collective social mechanism for its use. Commons cannot be secured unless people are certain they can have equal access and that others will not take more than their share. This can only be achieved within a political framework based on equality and mutuality: that is, socialism. For socialists and for many greens, provisioning structures would be based on social ownership and control" (Mellor 2006:47).[608]

While Mellor stands on the opposite side of Hardin, she emphasizes self-interest as well. Her solution is more inclusive, but runs into the difficulty of sizing the unit i.e. defining who to include in "people". Collective action problems are hard to solve. As argued earlier, there are many examples were the interest depends on the unit. Local communities may, in contrast to the overall pollution it causes, disproportionately benefit from mining coal. Similar to private ownership localised ownership may not be helpful. There is a power asymmetry, since the interest in the common good is always diffused in contrast to special interests (Raschauer 2011:224). Thus, whether local resource management improves overall sustainability depends on the resource and culture. Conditions for effective 'bottom-up resource management' may be utopian. Dryzek, Norgaard, and Schlosberg note for climate change that

> "on Ostrom's own account, the conditions for effective polycentric governance prove demanding [..]; reliable information on the condition of the resource, trust among key actors, social capital (i.e. dense social networks involving public-spirited behavior), good communication about the state of the resource, effective monitoring of one another's behavior by those who access the resource, long time horizons, and linkage to individual benefits (such as lower fuel bills if renewable energy proves successful). None of these can be taken for granted. In treating climate change as mainly a problem of collective action (i.e. coordination of actors toward a common end), Ostrom's polycentric approach also ignores the divisive politics concerning especially who should bear the burden of action, the existence of powerful interests such as fossil fuel corporations that want to block action, and the growth-maximizing imperatives of local and national governments" (2013:Loc. 2081; see also Berkez 2005).

The problem of powerful interest groups is a constant obstacle to better environmental politics. Democracy typically does not produce decisions and actions against their interests (see Gilens and Page 2014). However, discussing democracy and nature, Ball concludes that

---

[608] While "income inequalities are less where common-property resources are more prominent" (Dasgupta and Maskin 1999:76), the sustainability of common-property regimes have shown to be highly dependent on the institutional context. Note that traditional management may not grant equal access, but provides a rationale for the usage.

"democracy is by its very nature committed to diversity: authoritarian rule is, politically speaking, a monoculture, whilst democracy is a multiculture consisting of diverse and sometimes cacophonous voices, interests and agendas. Democracy, reconceptualised and retheorised as biocracy, widens the circle of those whose interests are included and whose 'voices' are heard and heeded" (Ball 2006:145).

Plurality and conflict hinder agreement on a common good and its enhancement, as observable with the multiplication of veto players. In his statement, Ball effectively ignores this dynamic. Social injustice is still a problem in many democracies, so chances for the successful inclusion of a wider group of other's interests need to be assessed critically.[609] Again, green democracy advocates like Eckersley find the internalisation of other's interests plausible (2004; Saward 2006).[610] Contrasting this idea with reality, Höffe gives examples of issues where citizens find common goods too costly in comparison to their own pleasures (2009:256). Whereas they are willing to pay for expensive movies and vacation, they are not willing to support all educational institutions.

Lippmann's observation that the sum of incapable individuals cannot lead to collective competence has value in the collective action problems (1998:193; Bensaid 2012). For the issue at hand, one should equally critically consider the idea that the sum of self-interests can lead to collective interest. This is parallels Rousseau's distinction between the general will and sum of all wills (2002).[611] If the incongruence is large, this could support guardianship (see Dahl 1989). Yet, democracy can only defend minimal grounds, meaning that it is "detached from the classical expectation that it can rationally represent a general will" (Shapiro and Hacker-Cordon 1999a:4).

---

[609] This can serve as an indication that classifying environmental goods as social goods and reinterpreting human rights in favour of environmental protection is important, but it is not sufficient. Human rights violations can be found almost anywhere. Democracy may not protect human rights (Westra 1998a). Griffith points at the problem of powerlessness in regard to current injustices and the representation of future generations. Either's interests may be "overridden" (2003:155). However, when discussing trusteeships over nature, he invokes the example of British 'court of equity', which functions as a protector of disadvantaged people (as nondemocratic institution).

[610] From ancient Athenian point of view "justice is what tends to promote the common interest, a good polis must also be just; and therefore it must aim at developing citizens who seek the common good. For one who merely pursues his own interest cannot be a good citizen: a good citizen is one who in public matters aims always at the common good" (Dahl 1989:15).

[611] Rousseau's romanticism seems to be an excellent starting point for any approach that focuses not just on nature, but also on commons (2002). Many arguments in his thoughts are useful in a modern context. It is hard to dispute today that it is the human capability to reason, his rationality that created the technology that might bring destruction and that mores and virtues do not develop simultaneously with technology (Pfetsch 2003; Jonas 1984). After all, Rousseau characterized rationality mixed with vanity, pride and egocentrism as dangerous traits. Non-anthropocentric discourses resemble his language and appeal to what Rousseau describes as one of the highest qualities: compassion. The whole idea of a general will that aims at the common good and is not just the sum of individual wills, could be easily facilitated as a moral justification for environmental politics. The total relinquishing of the individual member's rights to the community is part of his social contract. Though Rousseau believes that each member can understand the general will, he does not expect altruism (2002; Thompson 1966). He also acknowledges that his ideals need the virtuous citizen. His social contract needs virtuous citizen that practice modesty (Schmidt 2010). Rousseau clearly states that good laws might impose deprivation (2002). Despite the overt potential of Rousseau's writings for environmental politics, his approach is problematic. His idea of the general will as a benchmark demands too much.

Nonetheless, it is commonly assumed that democracies must deliver goods to a broader public than 'autocracies', which motivates larger expenditures on public goods (Schmidt 2010:464; Simmons 2011). Environmental protection may be among them, but if democratic governments cater to the public, they concentrate on measures of quick return, as discussed earlier. The result is that environmental protection is likely to be weak instead of including comprehensive measures (see Wurster 2013).

> "While environmental degradation is ultimately the result of aggregated individual choices, individual choices are responses to incentives and other forms of guidance from government and other institution via laws, taxes, and even normative pronouncement" (Keohane et al. 1995:7).

Accordingly, there is a deep responsibility on the side of the government to recognise and act upon environmental necessities. The protection of nature as the chief common good cannot be subject to negotiation. Revising governance along these lines means defining nature's protection as the purpose of the state. This has clear consequences.

3.3. NECESSITÀ AND THE NON-NEGOTIABILITY OF NATURE

"A livelihood that over time destroys, degrades or exhausts the resource base upon which it depends or upon which others might depend or which degrades our common environment is not physically or ecologically sustainable [...] is not ethically sustainable" (Miller 1998:139).

The fact that many contemporary lifestyles are unsustainable is regularly invoked. While destroying the common good, unsustainability is seldom raised as an ethical issue.[612] Society's morals need to match the reality of a limited world. This precludes a fundamental shift in focus of widespread 'ethics'.[613] The previous chapters demonstrated how democracy fails to acknowledge and implement sustainability as a critical necessity. Arguing for certain necessities is an intellectual honesty that many green thinkers are avoiding. They distance themselves from fundamentalism, although "any statement of ecological problems and imperatives is ultimately based on the non-negotiability of nature and the natural" (Blühdorn 2012:7f.).[614] This chapter explores the consequences and modalities of placing the necessity of nature at the centre of governance. It seeks to develop an ethical basis for nondemocratic rule, revise the position of science within governance and at the same time to integrate critiques of science. Herein, it analyses the meaning of imperatives and non-negotiability for the politics of nature. This examination intends to lay the groundwork for a potential alternative of ecologically sound governance.

---

[612] "For much of the twentieth century, when for the first time many professional moral philosophers were atheists, it was unfashionable for philosophers to grapple with questions about what we ought to do" which makes secular ethics a comparatively neglected field (Singer 1994:17). Environmental ethics have to be understood as lacking even more attention. They include "competing definitions of what is risky are ultimately moral judgments about the proper way to organise society" (Hannigan 2006:110).

[613] "The subject matter of environmental philosophy begs the question whether it should have an advocacy component distinct from other forms of philosophical activity" (Light and De-Shalit 2003a:9).

[614] "Our situation does not have to end in catastrophe, but it certainly will unless we act soon to recalibrate economies, political systems, and personal expectations to the realities of the biosphere" (Orr 2009:26).

While science can narrow down physical necessities for ecologically sound politics, it needs to be supplemented by moral guidelines.[615] Beyond the question of survival lies the question which kind of living can be judged acceptable. As emphasized earlier, politics cannot be separated from ethics. Climate change mitigation etc. cannot take place outside politics. Because it is utterly political in nature it must involve a decision over values, though postdemocratic tendencies disguise this. By the definition used throughout this book, politics avoiding value conflicts is not politics. Furthermore, a political theory that is unconcerned about material realities is incomplete. While seemingly ineffective, criticising liberal positions on such regards has a long tradition. About 40 years ago Stretton wrote:

> "Although it may strain some liberal hypocrisies, let us for once be honest about the environmental problem. It consists of too many people using and spoiling limited resources. We must therefore reduce the number of people or the allowance of resources to each, or preferably both. If we don't nature will. Environmentalists believe that managed transition would be better than the mass killing by war and famine and poisoning, followed by survival in stripped and polluted wasteland, which are likely alternatives to it" (1976:16; see for example Ehrlich 1971).[616]

Stretton's quote contains both aspects: physical and moral necessities. He points at physical limits as well as a moral judgment. Whereas mass killings appear to be overtly morally wrong, this is the current course of politics globally (Anderson 2012; Randers 2012; Oreskes and Conway 2013). Utilising the term 'mass killing' is justified once destruction is identified as violence. Arguably then the ethical aspect needs to gain prominence in the discourse judging environmental governance (Westra 1998a). Ethics is fundamentally about the question which desires are good and which are bad. One of the possible reasons why nominally procedural legitimacy is sometimes judged as superior to substantive moral principles might be the missing

---

[615] "The prospects for science and ethics are greatly intertwined in dealing with environmental conservation and ecosystem sustainability" (Carpenter 1998:308). Holland comments that "the amount of integrity required is radically conditional upon the kind of conception people have of a worthwhile human life. Of course, policymakers would dearly love their decisions to be made for them by scientists. But what makes life worthwhile is an ethical and political question, not a scientific one. A wiser strategy is to engage in the normative debate about what makes human life worthwhile" (2013:Loc. 1136). Criticism against rather instrumental approaches is widespread among green theorists: "It would be no exaggeration to suggest that the logic of efficiency, which is the hallmark of capitalist organization of production, is also coming to colonize the goal of environmental conservation and sustainable development" (Lemos and Agawal 2009:80). The Habermasian camp writes against a pragmatic reduction of instrumental rationality and the rule by technocratic elites (Eckersley 1990; Elling 2008; see also Luke 1999). Their critique in general can only make sense if one assumes democracy is necessary for human flourishing and omits the fact that the current unsustainable course may hollow out all basis for life and therefore democratic life as well. Further separating science and technocratic elites from the political context is in fact impossible. Pollution can never be a purely scientific problem as their solutions cannot be either. Much of the critique against technocratic elites consequentially has to be understood as a critique against neoliberalism, as for example in form of the postdemocracy debate, and not the rule of technocrats per se. Here again, this work sees instrumental rationality as well as rule by an elite as neutral; what counts are the effects on the (green) common good (see Sagoff 2002).

[616] In a recent work Rees formulates the problem as follows: "Regaining long-term global biological health will require a massive effort at ecosystems restoration (we are using 30 percent more planet than we have right now). Whatever its goals and strategies, conservation policy cannot succeed in a vacuum. Establishing conservation reserves will ultimately be to no avail if population trends are not reversed and material demands moderated. When push comes to shove, set-asides will be reclaimed by desperate people to satisfy their immediate needs" (2013:Loc. 2965).

certainty about "what is substantively morally correct, whereas we do know what a desirable procedure is" (Huemer 2013:Loc. 4240).[617] However, climate change appears to be an easier case for a moral compass. Either way, most ethical systems can be narrowed down to some kind of consequentialism, since they must have a guideline, even when aims are not clearly formulated.[618] Though happiness is relative, it is dependent on the absence of primary evils (Marcuse 2006). The physical necessities have been largely ignored albeit they should clearly lead to moral necessities. A majority will see environmental degradation and a possible catastrophe as substantively morally incorrect or bad.[619] Though unsure about the details, most people will agree that destroying the planet is irresponsible. However expressed in positive terms, this conveys that humanity has 'some kind of responsibility' to protect the planet. Hence, the avoidance of degeneration is not only desirable. Avoidance is also widely accepted as morally right.[620] The current course then is not just irresponsible but also morally wrong. Yet, such a classification has consequences.

> "We do not call anything wrong, unless we mean to imply that a person ought to be punished in some way or other for doing it; if not by law, by the opinion of his fellow creatures; if not by opinion, by the reproaches of his own conscience. This seems the real turning point of the distinction between morality and simple expediency. It is a part of the notion of Duty in every one of its forms, that a person may rightfully be compelled to fulfil it. Duty is a thing which may be exacted from a person, as one exacts a debt. Unless we think that it might be exacted from him, we do not call it his duty. Reasons of prudence, or the interest of other people, may militate against actually exacting it; but the person himself, it is clearly understood, would not be entitled to complain" (Mill 1879:76).

What is more, taking more than a fair share from the world's resources could be understood as theft (see Westra 1998a). Acknowledging realities leads to a reinterpretation of destructive behaviour as a crime, thence state interference is justified. States are said to protect citizens against crimes (see Dobner 2010). Criminal prosecution for harmful actions is already ubiquitous and could be broadened to include indirect harm through environmental destruction (Westra 1998a:184f.). Penal codes typically punish those who expose other human beings to bodily harm and states understand freedom from bodily harm as fundamental right. Meanwhile, promoting pluralism of values often means that neither responsibility and duty nor immorality is

---

[617] Again, procedures also derive from ideas of fairness etc. In China, on the other hand, "arguments for democracy appealing to the intrinsic value of voting will not be very effective because political surveys show that citizens in East Asian societies typically understand democracy in substantive rather than procedural terms: that is, they tend to value democracy because of its positive consequences rather than valuing democratic procedures per se" (Bell 2015:Loc. 397).

[618] "Recommendations to virtue are all very well, but how are we to decide in any given case which of the actions open to us is the brave, kind, or prudent thing to do unless we pay some attention to the consequences of what we do? Or when our principles finally land us in an impasse, how are we to extricate ourselves other than by resort to consequentialist considerations?" (Holland 2014:109).

[619] "What would it mean for our conceptions of our cities and ourselves if we were to dare to leave the cave, facing the challenge of making our conveniences and competitions conform to the implacable demands of external reality?" (Lane 2011b:4).

[620] Why such actuality fails to be met with proper political response has been subject of earlier discussions.

emphasized. The limitedness of the discourse seems to be reflected in the green language. Whereas the positively connoted term 'eco-friendly' is widespread, negatively connoted terms have been less popular at least in English (see Cohen 2011).[621] This could be a reflection of a mind-set that forgoes duty and care as a central part of human interaction (and interrelation) and denies any necessities.

Dahl problematises the question which interests are "so fundamental that they should be inviolable by the democratic process" (1989:180). In regard to the public good, Shapiro writes that "that the imposition of a public good is justified only when the good in question is essential to the operation of a democratic order and cannot be attained in any other way" (1999:56). If environmental integrity is understood to be fundamental to all other rights and as a premise and if people are not willing to voluntarily ensure this premise, both conditions are met. The destructive majority decisions thereafter are in fact illegitimate. Environmental policies accordingly could be imposed. When it comes to the point of necessity even eco-anarchists like Carter argue for interference against the majority's expressed will (2013). It is ironic that there are scholars and activists who argue for direct action albeit their commitment to more democracy.[622] Humphrey asserts:

> "It is a fundamental part of the legitimation of the democratic way of doing business that there is policy reversibility. The lack of reversibility over an important range of environmental outcomes adds weight to the justification for environmental direct action" (2007:Loc. 1784).[623]

Whereas this quotation hints at a 'procedural problem' that occurs with environmental destruction, Carter widens legitimate instances to involving question of justice. A conceivable interpretation is that direct action is justified when the substance of the decision is judged wrong by the perpetrators of the direct action. He writes that one consideration following Singer about civil disobedience is that if the community's

> "sense of justice is imperfect, surely civil disobedience could be untaken not merely to introduce the majority to reconsider whether or not its decision satisfy the principles of justice it currently values but also to reconsider whether or not the conception of justice is adequate" (Carter 2013:281; e.g. Singer 2006).

Such a justification of disobedience is important, because if one justifies actions by a minority as such it may as well be the ruling green minority that confronts a mainstream culture of

---

[621] The limits discourse itself uses powerful metaphors of overshoot and collapse, Earth as a spaceship, the lily pond, cancer and viruses (Dryzek 2005).
[622] Similarly, NGOs are often praised as a participative element of civil society, despite their lack of procedural legitimacy by themselves (Leist 2011:39).
[623] "It is difficult to see why, if you oppose policy x now and believe that this policy will have bad non-reversible consequences, you should nonetheless accept the democratic outcome on the grounds that further argument may lead to 'different choices later'" (Humphrey and Stears 2007:Loc. 2815).

consumerism. Advocates rationalise direct action with the urgency and supposed 'false' consciousness of the population.

> "Put more simply: anthropogenic environmental decline in the light of life-affirming values and political inaction demands analysis of the obstacles to effective action, including laws and mores that might constrain it. Given the urgency of the situation, extralegal tactics should be on the table, as they were in earlier causes where great moral urgency was properly felt. This does not, however, answer the question of whether the time for resistance has come" (Taylor 2013:Loc. 6685-88).

It is particularly interesting when such arguments are employed by democracy advocates. Here again the idea of a possible enlightenment that is yet to come serves as a bridge between arguments for action outside the system and the pledge to improve the system itself. In the meantime a minority is thought to take up active resistance in order to act upon the emergency. Any argumentation that justifies such an action can also justify minority rule as long as it is for the purpose of a greater good. Protest is a legitimate action within any democracy, extra legal action is obviously not. It is unclear where the line is drawn for the stakes being high enough, thus it appears unclear if time "has come".[624] The question whether or not disobedience is justified in democratic as in undemocratic states as considered by Singer has consequences.

> "Justifications of political obligation which provide no reason for being more obedient to a democratic than to an undemocratic regime would seem to oblige one to any effective regime, no matter how unsavoury – a conclusion few rational people would accept" (Carter 2013:282).

Though here Carter argues that some scholars see participation in the procedures as providing greater legitimacy to democratic laws, this would only be true if one accept these procedures and had the possibility of exit (see Estlund 2009). Disobedience is often pronounced legitimate, if voices remain unheard. Those excluded by time, space, and species largely remain unheard. Those advocating disobedience and direct action outside the democratic framework should have trouble arguing against any paternalism directed towards a greener good.[625] The justifications for such an interference are not just utilitarian, they also implicate that a group or a person claims to be wiser than the majority therefore it is legitimate to at least temporarily disregard democratic principles for the sake of a 'greater good'.[626] Westra asserts that

> "the use of force in our defense is not only permissible but morally obligatory. The extensive legal and philosophical framework supporting self-defense provides a strong basis for coercive laws aimed at protecting not only humans but also all life that is both intrinsically and instrumentally valuable and indirectly necessary for all" (1998a:178).

---

[624] The uncertainty of threshold events should lead to precaution.

[625] "Since current laws and political activities have failed to redress the situation and appear unlikely to do so, it is incumbent to ask what strategies and tactics might be successful. Such an assessment should include determining whether strategies and tactics must be constrained by existing laws and prevailing assumptions about what constitutes acceptable political action" (Taylor 2013:6681-85).

[626] "If you happen to have the power to implement [the] correct assessment, you should do so, despite the fact that your assessment will not attract the unanimous assent of those affected" (Arneson 2004:54).

Ecoauthoritarianism follows this motif of protection, but does not stop here.

Connelly et al. divide the ethical discourses about the environment into three moral traditions: stewardship, utilitarianism and deep ecology (2012:18-53).[627] The idea of stewardship is part of the Christian tradition and has a strong anthropocentric component. Given that animals are God's creation, it can be argued that animals do have intrinsic value nonetheless. Though occasionally presented as an ideological cause of environmental harms, because God gave dominion, stewardship also implies a role as a care taker. Utilitarianism can be anthropocentric as well as non-anthropocentric depending on the inclusiveness of the relevant community. Singer prominently includes all sentient beings, by using the criterion of suffering and not reason (2012:24f.; see also Bentham 2000). Deep ecology, on the other hand, always follows an ecocentric perspective. "Deep green politics presents a radical challenge to existing mores, which has the disturbing effect of undermining the philosophical basis of human civilisation" (Kingsnorth 2009:38). This includes asking about duties towards more than just fellow humans, but animals and nature in general (Connelly et al. 2012:21). So far, this form of critical engagement with environmental ethics is limited. The field especially lacks holistic approaches.

> "The largest number of articles pursue the entirely justifiable goal of exploring a relatively narrow environmental issue from a single philosophical perspective, with an emphasis on clarifying the grounds upon which an individual might build his or her own view of the subject. On only rare occasions (perhaps 5 percent of all articles) have the authors directly examined what political philosophy or a particular political philosopher might contribute to a practical environmental ethics that would advance the cause of reconciling democratic politics and environmental protection" (Baber and Bartlett 2005:Loc. 41).

The question of democracy and the environment was examined earlier therefore the discussion here revolves around alternative ethical frameworks that provide sustainability. The preceding arguments led to the assumption that environmental ethics and environmental protection in fact need a philosophy beyond democracy, since sustainable democratic politics are rather contingent. Political philosophy has a vast literature, which could inspire a revised green theory.[628] Here, Machiavelli and Mill are particularly useful, since they judged the consequences of uttermost importance and recognised context dependency as well as boundaries. Importantly, both understood the conflictual nature of politics and that good governance also means

---

[627] The principle of utility/greatest happiness principle here is only discussed as a moral not economic theory. Other applications are irrelevant in this context (see Carter 2013). Liberalism is only represented to a certain extent within this division.

[628] Hood sees huge potential in environmental ethics following the practice of biomedical ethics, which actively engages in the practice of medicine (2003).

prioritizing between different goals.[629] The first part of this book established that a green theory of agency is hardly compatible with a green consequentialist view. It indicated that green theory of agency and green theory of value are in tension. Scholars often focus on either one of them. Using green outcomes as the benchmark is an openly consequentialist approach.[630] It is utilitarian in that it counts working ecosystems as the most useful criterion of good governance.[631] Given the devastating consequences of alternatives, the constant throughout this book is that what ultimately counts as good governance needs to enhance sustainability. If the circumstances demand a dismissal of the green theory of agency in favour of green values, this should be acknowledged stringently.

3.3.1. THE PRINCE IN GREEN

In *The Prince* Machiavelli declares that following *necessità* is the core of good governance (2009).[632] *Necessità* can be partly coped with through the comprehension of the context and an idea about the future (Pfetsch 2003:105ff.). Consequentialism's actual potential, once humans are understood as social beings for green ethics, is commonly overlooked. Utilitarianism allows for revising governance with green priorities.[633] Albeit, Connelly et al. remark that in "utilitarianism, actions should be judged by their consequences, not their intrinsic rightness" and that its ambiguity makes it unsuitable for new environmental ethics (2012:24). Such a judgment is simplistic. There is no reason to view the utilitarian agent as purely instrumental. Rather, one can assume aspired congruence between means and ends, in that the utility of the agent as well as of others is part of the equation. If the agent experiences altruistic goals as more fulfilling than others and/or his interests are in accord with the interests of society, the critique of instrumental rationality seems meaningless anyway. Mill hoped for this identification of the individual with society (1901; Höntzsch 2010). This would constitute the melting together of

---

[629] A clear definition of what constitutes good governance is the core problem for political theory. Mill claimed that "the test of good and bad government, so complex an object as the aggregate interests of society, we would willingly attempt some kind of classification of those interests, which, bringing them before the mind in definite groups, might give indication of the qualities by which a form of government is fitted to promote those various interests respectively. It would be a great facility if we could say the good of society consists of such and such elements; one of these elements requires such conditions, another such others; the government, then, which unites in the greatest degree all these conditions, must be the best. The theory of government would thus be built up from the separate theorems of the elements which compose a good state of society. Unfortunately, to enumerate and classify the constituents of social well-being, so as to admit of the formation of such theorems is no easy task" (1862:27). Aforementioned, the classification of sustainability as ultimate precondition advanced here, simplifies the judgment.

[630] As explained in the case of offsetting, it does not make sense to calculate one good against one bad in order to arrive at a morally neutral consequence (see Hale 2014:162). Saving another person does not erase the former wrong such as killing one person. The implementation of reparations does not annul the action of destruction.

[631] "The legitimacy problem is perhaps the most serious threat to the meritocratic system" (Bell 2015:Loc. 256). The chapter lays ground for solving the legitimacy problem.

[632] Pfetsch uses the term "*Sachzwang*" which can be translated as either 'inherent necessity' or 'practical constraint' (2003:105ff.). Though typically not translated as such, it literally also means 'matter's coercion', which has a far stronger emphasis on inevitability.

[633] Hiller highlights that utilitarianism in ethics was developed during a time in which individualism dominated (2014:62). For him, this could be a reason why it is not widely used in environmental ethics.

means and ends on a large scale and satisfy even the Kantian condition of people never purely being means. The objection that such an intended morality restrains the freedom of the individual is dependent on a specific interpretation of freedom. Moreover, utilitarianism as a guideline does include an ultimate good, it therefore includes intrinsic rightness.[634] Connelly et al. underestimate utilitarianism's potential resulting from the environment being a precondition for most goods and the ramifications of environmental destruction (2012).[635] As quoted earlier, following Mill here means that "[q]uestions of ultimate ends are not amenable to direct proof. Whatever can be proven to be good, must be so by being shown to be a means to something admitted to be good without proof" (1879:6). The ends are intrinsically right. Good environmental governance is uncontroversial in the sense that few people will reject sustainability of life support systems as its aim. Advocates of state neutrality fail to acknowledge that this, even within their moral pluralism, legitimises substantial interference. Falsely accused of ecofascism, consequentialism can be "consistent with there being a large plurality of values" and include individual humans and non-humans as having intrinsic value and causing them harm as negative (Hiller 2014:66).[636] Stressing the importance of natural systems does not mean to negate cultural beliefs.

Customarily described as a realist Machiavelli looked at actual practice, which is likely to heighten awareness for necessities. Dressing Machiavelli's prince in green means making the environment the necessity to be considered at all times. Most crucially, a green prince recognises and includes conflict in his calculation. In the long run, successful governance also requires

---

[634] Nevertheless, "there are still important distinctions between consequentialism and non-consequentialism; in particular, consequentialists are those who claim that an evaluation of the rightness or wrongness of an act cannot be determined without considering the full range of consequences of the action, even if the action itself has value or disvalue" (Hiller and Kahn 2014:4).

[635] Arguing that even beyond the harm principle Mill advocated for sustainability can be judged as anachronistic, however he clearly valued prudence and permanence among other qualities of governance. He also regarded order as a prerequisite for further development and the social good. The following passage shows such a position clearly: "If we intend to comprise in the idea of Order all that society requires from its government which is not included in the idea of Progress, we must define Order as the preservation of all kinds and amounts of good which already exist, and Progress as consisting in the increase of them. This distinction does comprehend in one or the other section every thing which a government can be required to promote. But, thus understood, it affords no basis for a philosophy of government. We can not say that, in constituting a polity, certain provisions ought to be made for Order and certain others for Progress, since the conditions of Order, in the sense now indicated, and those of Progress, are not opposite, but the same. The agencies which tend to preserve the social good which already exists are the very same which promote the increase of it, and vice versâ, the sole difference being, that a greater degree of those agencies is required for the latter purpose than for the former. What, for example, are the qualities in the citizens individually which conduce most to keep up the amount of good conduct, of good management, of success and prosperity, which already exist in society? Every body will agree that those qualities are industry, integrity, justice, and prudence. But are not these, of all qualities, the most conducive to improvement? and is not any growth of these virtues in the community in itself the greatest of improvements? If so, whatever qualities in the government are promotive of industry, integrity, justice, and prudence, conduce alike to permanence and to progression, only there is needed more of those qualities to make the society decidedly progressive than merely to keep it permanent" (1862:29-31 [sic!]).

[636] Hiller draws the contrast to deep ecology in its prioritization: different living beings do not have to have the same value (2014). As suggested in the Introduction for the purposes of wider accessibility the intrinsic value of animals will not be central to considerations of necessity here.

constant adaptation to the changing context. Consequentialism should be openly supported.[637] The statesman who recognises bads only when they are happening is a bad statesman (Machiavelli 2009:23). Democratic politics have displayed this very flaw in being reactive instead of proactive. Here, Carter sees one problem for the politics of nature in the unknown (2014).[638] To decide retrospectively about an outcome can involve an act of randomness.[639] Yet, any policy is based (on the probability of) an effect. Policies as means to an end usually follow instrumental rationality. A carbon tax for example is introduced to reduce emissions and not because one assumes that taxes are inherently good. The earlier qualification that judged such a tax as immoral shows that consequentialism can in effect judge an action while differentiating between multiple outcomes: a carbon tax is immoral, because it means that the rich get to pollute with the poor possibly having difficulty to pay for heating. Thence such tax sets up a system in which polluting is morally neutral and only depends on wealth. As a consequentialist, it is possible to oppose such a tax despite its potential to have a positive effect on overall pollution for setting up a moral framework that runs contrary to an overall good. This is made possible by the fact that consequentialism is flexible. Thinking about foregone alternatives would run contrary to a consequentialist ethic in so far as it leads to less satisfaction. A consequentialist ethic that looks retrospectively must be inconsistent, in that such an attention is only able to promote the good, if it is possible to learn from the alternatives for the future. If it is not possible coherent consequentialism has to use potential outcomes as its directive, which always includes the unknown as a factor. Consequentialism as such is progressive and proactive. It can in fact have the very Popperian quality which Dryzek suggested as a necessity for a sustainable future (2005:111f.). The multiplicity of factors cannot be a hindrance to an action, since such a limitation does not only apply to consequentialism, but to all frameworks (see Carter 2014). A good ruler has to adjust to the context and include possible bad fortune into his strategy (Machiavelli 2009). In Machiavelli, the rightfulness of the action stands in relation to the

---

[637] There is an interpretation of consequentialism as "committed to a view about the kinds of metaphysical entities that can be bearers of intrinsic value; it is also committed to a view about what one ought to do about intrinsic value: one ought to bring it about. The consequentialist agent isn't just supposed to sit around admiring good consequences, she is supposed to produce them. Furthermore, she is supposed to produce them not just once, but as much as possible" (McShane 2014:19).

[638] "As things are, our ignorance of the possible consequences of our actions is so great that useful predictions of the future are almost ruled out" (Lovelock 2000:Loc. 2331). This statement is both true and false at the same time. It is extremely difficult and nearly impossible to include all potential chain events, tipping points and interaction. To calculate the effect of clouds for example is still a new field. However, as science and technology advances more factors can be included. Predictions are useful even though certainty is not possible.

[639] This is acknowledged in the convention that no law is applied retrospectively.

expected consequence. Including the unknown fortunes as a factor of disruption is part of being a green prince.[640]

Notably personal affectedness, though often seen as a reason for democratic inclusion, reduces chances for rational solutions – prominently sought after in consequentialism. Research has

> "shown that in reasoning about personal moral dilemmas (dilemmas where one is contemplating doing something that will directly harm another particular individual), areas of the brain associated with emotion and social cognition are activated. In reasoning about impersonal moral dilemmas (where harm will result from one's choice, but not direct harm to another identifiable individual), areas of the brain associated with abstract reasoning and problem" (McShane 2014:25).

Asking for a wider good is a common characteristic of environmental policy and consequentialism. The latter follows the logic that: "If we cannot possibly do right by all of the legitimate claims made on us, then perhaps the next best option is to minimize the total amount of harm that our actions produce in the world" (McShane 2014:29). Machiavelli advises choosing the smaller misery since some form of misery is inevitable (2009).[641] In the short run, good governance can mean foregoing principles for the cause of a greater good.

> "A wedge issue in distinguishing consequentialist from non-consequentialist theories is whether it is acceptable to directly cause some harm in the service of a greater good. This question arises prominently in environmental ethics since so many of our actions cause some harm to the environment and to people in a way that is hard if not impossible to avoid. Is it possible for such harm ever to be justified? If not, is there a way to remedy the harm?" (Hiller and Kahn 2014:10).

Smaller miseries – such as possibly abolishing universal suffrage – have to be accepted for the sake of sustaining a liveable planet. A consequentialism informed by an understanding of ecological integrity, hence by this logic should produce the most sustainable outcome. Such governance accordingly could score high on substantial legitimacy. In contrast to political equality, equal consideration, as a basic moral axiom, can appear as an argument for guardianship.[642] McShane's description of consequentialist decision making is reminiscent of a green prince.

> "The ideal consequentialist agent will make choices as a wise ruler does: by considering which course of action will produce the best consequences for everyone, all things considered, over the long run. A wise ruler shouldn't be swayed by the fact that some courses of action will be

---

[640] Machiavelli directs particular attention to including *fortuna*, as the unknown, into the discussion of good governance (2009). *Fortuna* can be balanced by *virtù* that is prominently the courage and understanding of necessities (Pfetsch 2003:104). Good Governance includes anticipation.

[641] "We often decide whether to adopt a course of action by asking simply whether the action is good or bad. But the more appropriate question is whether the action is better or worse than the alternatives" (Huemer 2013:Loc. 4481).

[642] Holland accentuates that while nature does not care about the individual (of any species) morality demands the considerability of each individual, which could be causal for extensive demands made towards nature (2014). The environment needs to be addressed globally, democracy addresses local issues. Though the reasoning of an authoritarian system does not necessarily go beyond national borders, the unit for which an elite feels responsible is easier to be expanded than within a democracy (see Bell 2015).

better for her or for her friends and family. The job of a wise ruler is to determine what is best for everyone. Such an agent is in the business of trying to bring about the best state of the world possible in the future. Because of this approach, some have argued that consequentialism cannot account for what have been called "agent-relative reasons" or "personal values"" (McShane 2014:21).[643]

Hereafter, the wise ruler is guided by the common good, which by all means builds on working ecosystems. While critics oppose the "impersonal even alienating quality of consequentialist thinking" as it does not take individual situations into account (Holland 2014:109), exactly the dissolution of agent and matter leads to decisions that are more rational in achieving a common good.[644] In Dahl's dialogues the aristocrat advances his argument similarly, stating that "highly qualified people [...] can reasonably be counted on to possess both the knowledge and virtue to serve the good for everyone subject to the laws" (1989:53).[645] Crucially, revised green governance escapes the accusation of arbitrariness. It follows the laws of physics looking for the best consequence for the collective. The logic of rule and boundary setting of ecomeritocracy for instance seek consistency. Studies show that natural resource protection above all needs trust in reciprocity, therefore the governed must believe that the government will keep its promises (Sjöstedt 2014:270ff.).[646] Even if the rule of law was not upheld by its principles in general, rule of law would be necessary for practical reasons. Seeking consistency also means that destructive uncertainty of environmental governance would be diminished. The idea of freedom as nondomination excludes "the capacity to interfere in their affairs on an arbitrary basis" (Pettit 1999:165). It does not mean self-mastery or non-interference, but absence of the mastery of others (Shapiro and Hacker-Cordon 1999:14).[647] While some scholars doubt the power of a nondemocratic state to bring their citizens to act green, legitimacy, hence one of central incentives for compliance does not depend on democracy (see Mill 1862; Gilley 2009:84; Weber 2014). It is not political rights but consent, fairness, a feeling of natural duty and common aims

---

[643] "Choices based on preference-satisfaction are often blind to other individual rights and to justice considerations. They can also be "culturally relative" (for example, for some culture female genital mutilation is part of a "moral" family-oriented ideal), hence many such preferences may not be universally defensible from a moral standpoint" (Westra 1998b:278).

[644] If Leist is right in classifying arguments about future generations as only rationally (but not emotionally) accessible (2011:39) and it is supposed that they have at least some kind of right to be considered, it further speaks for a consequentialist approach.

[645] In "The Right to a Competent Electorate", Brennan argues that because one has the right to be governed by competent people, universal suffrage actually means a violation of this right (2011; see also Bell 2015:Loc. 646). Bell lists the qualities politicians of democracies need as "a very thick skin, the ability to think quickly on one's feet, the need to exaggerate differences with political opponents and to give the same partisan stump speech with the same apparent degree of enthusiasm repeatedly during the campaign season, as well as the ability to switch to a more inclusive political discourse that seeks to explain and justify policies to the public after election victory" (2015:Loc. 1561). Understanding of the actual matters of politics is not on his list.

[646] The example of African fisheries illustrates that the strict enforcement of rules plays a key role (Sjöstedt 2014). Forest management suggests stable funding as a premise for success (Andersson et al. 2014:244). Many eco-friendly innovations need long-term guarantees.

[647] Note that "[s]eeing freedom as a quality of agency is different, conceptually, from seeing it as an absence of something, no matter how robust one's conception of that "something" turns out to be" (Christman 2005:80).

that lead to compliance (Gilley 2009:147ff.). If an ecostate can communicate its reasons it gains in additional effectiveness. Understanding the importance of passion and affection an ecomeritocracy can use them as tools to further climate change as a social fact. Notably, Ekardt stresses that rational explanations are the opposite of coercion and degradation (2011:41). A nondemocratic rule which follows ecological necessities can provide rational explanations.[648] By Ekardt's account such a rule would not be coercive. However, such a judgment is only relevant, if manifold reservations such an omnipresence of power and structural violence etc. are declared trivial. Once social reality is understood as a web of relations, coercion might be redefined as a matter of degree just like oppression and freedom; tradeoffs will be recognised. Ophuls highlighted that the matter of the state is the control of power and not its abolishment (1977:200ff.). Coercion is consequentially a normal part to all politics.

Meanwhile, Machiavelli discusses the issue of legitimacy while advancing the idea that it is practically better to be feared than loved (2009). The latter is understood less resilient. Despite the latter being a possible outcome of output legitimacy, a consistent green political theory might have to admit that green political practice might have to follow Machiavelli's recommendation. One central reason is that effective environmental governance is preventive, which also means that it becomes harder to prove empirically. The effects of restoration may be visible and easily measurable (such as improved water quality), but the effects of prevention cannot always be proven. This is especially the case, since climate systems are subject to time lags.[649] If short-term outputs and refraining from imposing costs on voters have been understood as a barrier to sustaining green aims in the first part of this work, the remainder has to suggest alternatives. Hence, a green prince could gain support by bread and games, but has to set restrictive laws into place. Since this is unlikely to lead to love, good environmental governance will have to ensure that the people fear breaking such laws. Ideally, people follow laws because they believe in them. Machiavelli's political psychology can be applied to the issue itself. People do not have to love living sustainably (as mainstream greens hope), but simply fear the consequences of destruction. However loss aversion (short-term) and consumption understood as freedom will remain major obstacles to such voluntary change. Questions about the meaning of oppression are reoccurring. A green prince can be charged with paternalism, but so can the doctor who ensures that the drug addict is rehabilitated. As with the meaning of democracy it is unlikely that scholars will agree on one interpretation of oppression. Here, besides Machiavelli, Hobbes' works are a "reminder that

---

[648] The prefix 'auto' can be interpreted as falsely applied, when speaking of a form of ecologically sound governance, since it is not so much a self-rule, but rather a rule under the demand of respect for nature. In any case it is misleading.
[649] Some further complications arise from distortions produced by aerosols currently accumulated in the atmosphere (see Lovelock 2009).

not everyone regards civic freedom or political tolerance as absolute goods" (Glass 2006:734; Hobbes 2009).[650] Important for the following elaboration is that Machiavelli insisted that the prince and more so private persons should act in accordance with moral standards, whenever the situation allows so. Respectively, civic freedom and political tolerance are not crossed out as goods in general. These typically liberal ideals are merely ranked behind ecological integrity.[651] Looking at the overall context it should be easy to argue that

> "[t]he old type of environmentalism which used to be directed at goal setting, technical planning and general policy design will be replaced by new forms which will have to balance ecological considerations against arguments in favour of freedom of action, individual longing for pleasure and craving for luxury (Levy and Wissenburg 2004a:Loc. 439-42).

An honest balancing of different goods is the strength of a green consequentialist approach. Instead of an end of environmentalism such consequentialism brings back 'the political' into the centre of politics and reformulates values drawing attention to interrelatedness and the necessity to minimise harm.

3.3.2. INTERRELATIONS: A CONSISTENT APPLICATION OF THE HARM PRINCIPLE AND CAPPED CAPABILITIES

A revision of good governance mandates a creation of guiding principles. The broader framework of consequentialism implies the harm principle as is an obvious choice. Interrelations are essential to a consistent application of the harm principle. Crucially, acknowledging the interrelations of human and non-human animals included in global life support systems should result in recognising that conflict and harm are omnipresent. In the meantime, a capability approach can narrow the spectrum of what is considered acceptable 'harming' (see Westra 1998a:160f.). The tendency of social injustice to lead to worse environmental records gives additional support to seeking a guideline that focuses on equalising conditions. Since harm is ubiquitous it should be a central component of any discussion, about good environmental governance.[652] This part attempts to avoid grounding anything on tastes and instead tries to base

---

[650] Hardin's famous essay appears to be compatible with Hobbes's social contract: "Coercion is a dirty word to most liberals now, but it need not forever be so. As with the four-letter words, its dirtiness can be cleansed away by exposure to the light, by saying it over and over without apology or embarrassment. To many, the word coercion implies arbitrary decisions of distant and irresponsible bureaucrats; but this is not a necessary part of its meaning. The only kind of coercion I recommend is mutual coercion, mutually agreed upon by the majority of the people affected" (Hardin 1968:1247). Dagger adds that "it will be easier to agree to this mutual coercion if we see our rights not as inviolable barriers against others but as forms of relations that entail responsibilities to others" (2006:201). Hardin's and other social contract solutions inherit the problems from the original contractarians, namely the utopian quality of such contract, questions of maintaining consent and exit. The irreversibility and the inclusion of "the majority of people affected" further add to such problems.

[651] Carter establishes a multidimensional axiology: equality, average utility, worthwhile lives, freedom and ecocentric contributory value (2014; see also Humphrey 2007:Loc. 576). In a consequentialist manner he advocates a pragmatism that opts for practicability instead of strictness pointing out that it might prompt better overall compliance (Carter 2014:83).

[652] Non-consequentialism fails to fully accept interrelationship and is therefore in a sense dishonest, since not harming is seldom an actual choice.

arguments purely on the question of physical harm. The full spectrum of human interaction involves many cases that are in grey areas and those that cannot be decided by scientific research (yet). In any case, this examination will work with the premise that prevention of harm trumps pleasure. From hereupon freedom should be set into a new context i.e. be freedom revised not abolished.[653]

First and foremost, freedom and/or liberty may be widely 'advertised' values but cannot be fundamental or ultimate values, since without a 'minimum' of ecological integrity, freedom and autonomy are meaningless. The latter depends on other goods to be fulfilled; hence they have a secondary position. Put more tangibly: "If one is not living, one cannot be free" (Shearman and Smith 2007:85; Ekardt 2011). In spite of it being seemingly self-evident, this is often ignored. It is for example absurd to ask whether the right to food is more important than the right to vote, since clearly voting is not possible, if one starved.[654]

> "Significantly from both practical and moral perspectives, climate change is not about violating just any rights; it is about violating the most basic ones, those that precede and are prerequisites for all others, such as physical security, subsistence, health, and life itself" (Harris 2013:Loc. 1945).

As stated above, environmental destruction is incompatible with the harm principle as a guideline.[655] With its severe impact on people's basic needs, harming the environment inevitably means harm to others. The harm principle is not only famously employed by Mill. Indeed, harming others is usually seen as negative across cultures. The golden rule, as it appears in the Bible, is a prevalent ethical formula for human interactions. At the same time, the more one assumes its penetration into global society, the more perplexing the damaging behaviour towards nature and fellow humans. Reasons for its failure have been employed.

It is indispensable to discuss not only the harm principle's reasoning but also its legitimacy for morality as well as usefulness for an alternative. Its application undoubtedly embarks on a constant reflection of tradeoffs and consequences.[656] The consequences of interdependency and the fact that a common world is shared are seldom thought through as described above. Above and beyond, "even if we believe that liberty presents the highest good, liberty from harm for all

---

[653] Though not directly relevant here, this should be applied to animals as well. This is certainly a controversial stand, but logically consistent. The majority would agree that it is wrong to shot a cat or dog for fun. But hunting, on the other hand, still remains a respected hobby in many parts of societies.

[654] Less extreme forms of poverty still impair political freedom as mentioned earlier.

[655] Though Wissenburg claimed compatibility of liberalism and green values via harm principle (2001a), it is questionable if a consistent application would lead to a system that can still be called 'liberal' in its common-sense interpretation.

[656] "If the priority is to avoid harm, it is plausible to argue that this must be relatively open-ended commitment, especially in the case of irreversible, non-remediable damage, such as the extinction of species or the poisoning of the planet through nuclear radiation" (Connelly et al. 2012:41).

demands restraints for many, so justice might prevail" (Westra 1998a:58; see also Hayward 2003).[657] Though liberal theorists draw a line where one person's freedom encroaches on others, the exact position of this line remains unclear. Theoretically liberals would not defend that one has the freedom to physically harm others, but what they defend as freedom in most cases indirectly harms others and effectively limits the agency of a great part of humanity.[658] Hence, freedom, autonomy and the connected self-actualisation are ideals, whose costs are not properly calculated. If the harm principle was taken more seriously, contemporary liberal theory would end up having to redefine freedom and rights completely.[659] The most essential 'liberal hypocrisy' is the blind eye to the effects of their idea of liberty and freedom and the fact that any form of freedom and rights involves a necessary tradeoff as touched upon earlier (Stretton 1976). Most prominently, the costs of defending certain forms of personal freedoms are externalised through space and time.[660] "Harm rarely occurs at the exact moment that the harmful action is performed" (Carter 2013:288). Correspondingly, the line between consequentialism and non-consequentialism could be cynically viewed as the line between acknowledging and disregarding interrelations. Environmental integrity as an absolute necessity remains unnoticed, exactly because concepts are not applied fully. To again express it more clearly: today's freedom could lead to tomorrow's totalitarianism. Following Dahl, Fishkins says that "tyranny occurs when there is an avoidable severe deprivation, and let us mean by severe deprivation the denial of a person or group's most basic rights or fundamental interests" (1997:53).[661] Nothing can be more totalitarian than a world where one cannot breathe air without getting sick. Hereafter, a radical reinterpretation of what constitutes freedom that allows for the comprehensive accommodation of a necessity is crucial for ensuring a minimum of meaningfulness of the concept itself. Worthwhile concepts of freedom cannot ignore the necessity of a finite world.[662] Human rights need to be rethought. Thinking of the protection of the common good as a human rights problem

---

[657] According to Höntzsch, justice as an equal claim/right to freedom and security is a condition for the development of social empathy and equality in Millian utilitarianism (2010:56).

[658] "Each person has the right not to be wrongfully harmed by others in ways that would violate her Lockean rights, these rights being understood to include rights against coercion, physical assault, theft of one's property, fraud, the suffering of physical damage in consequence of the actions of others without one's consent, and the threat of any of the above. One's right to act as one chooses in concert with others so long as one does not wrongfully harm others who do not consent to bear these costs includes the right to suffer any purported injury to which one voluntarily consents" (Arneson 2000:40).

[659] This goes beyond questions of structure and agency and/or questions of free will (e.g. Bourdieu and Wacquant 2006).

[660] Putting the costs of one's actions onto others can be interpreted as exploitation.

[661] "What concerns environmental ethicists and advocates is not straightforwardly that the world is being destroyed in every corner everywhere, but that so many of the actions that we take, individually and collectively, appear to be taken haphazardly and without good reason" (Hale 2014:161).

[662] "How individual activity that negatively affects the environment must be regulated, with what punishments, with preservation of what opportunities for alternatives, are questions that should always be encouraged within the political space rather than excluded by a rhetoric of harmonization, real selves, and the end of civilization" (Buell and De Luca 1996:91).

is another way to recognise its fundamentality. Though not a new approach, it still lacks mainstream recognition. Meanwhile,

> "the carbon-spewing nations are embarking on *the greatest violation of human rights the world has ever seen*. The consequences of global warming and widespread environmental degradation—flooding people from their homes, exposing them to new disease vectors, disrupting food supplies, contaminating or exhausting freshwater sources, uprooting the material bases of traditional cultures—are a systematic denial of human rights. By whom? By the wealthy nations and the wealthiest subpopulations of all nations, who cannot or will not stop releasing more than their fair share of carbon into the atmosphere. For what? For the continuing consumption of material goods and the accumulation of wealth" (Hohensee 2013:Loc. 4953-59; my emphasis).

Hohensee clearly classifies the degeneration of nature as human rights violation. A consistent human rights framework should incorporate the importance of nature as a basis for life.

3.3.2.1. THE DUTY TO CARE AND CHOICE VIOLATING NECESSITY

Calling for moderation has been met with vocal aversion, while green consumerism has not managed to produce sustainable results.[663] At the same time, Höffe asks an intriguing and provoking question. Does humanity have a right to carelessness? (2009:215). Many of the perceived entitlements imply a right to carelessness. First, as mentioned before, the damaging behaviour is neither equally shared, nor do the biggest destructors feel a proportional share of the damage.[664] Second, carelessness risks future prosperity. Even further, there needs to be a duty to care, unless the collective right to a viable ecosystem is made a duty of the citizen, chances for the avoidance of ecocide are infiniteseminal. If seen from an impersonal individual rights stand, today's humans and future humans are entitled to the same (Jonas 1984). There is no theoretical difference between sacrificing today for the future and sacrificing the future for today's happiness. However, Jonas points out that the latter means that there is no future (1984:35). Some argue that "giving future generation an equal moral standing with the present one could condemn us to intolerable levels of self-denial" (Whiteside 2006:48). However, "[o]ur moral responsibility is supported by the grave consequences of many of our choices" (Westra

---

[663] The global consumer even claims the right to certain goods, including a new computer and phone every other year. Here again environmental governance must be careful "when considering questions of resource depletion, to distinguish needs from wants" (Connelly et al. 2012:46). Yet, the distinction is often disregarded: "Individual well-being consists in the satisfaction of the wants agents either have, or would have if fully informed, and hence public policy which is concerned with the optimal realisation of welfare must be want-regarding" (O'Neill 2006:164). The car today is almost interpreted as much part of subsistence as bread in the French Revolution, since individual mobility is nearly perceived as a human right (Leggewie and Welzer 2011:89; see also Stretton 1976:21ff.). Politics centred on perceived needs or wants are impotent in regard to a large percentage of unsustainable consumption.
[664] People in developing countries are the most concerned about climate change (Giddens 2009:103). While they are often least responsible, the impact hits and will hit them harder than many developed countries in milder climates. This is in particular the case, since adaption will be costly. This discussion is part of a wider global justice discussion, but applies to situations within nation states as well.

1998a:103). Too often rights and duties do not stand in a reciprocal relationship. Instead there has been dissociation between the two.[665]

The question of rights reformulated as duties that means that "if current emissions levels in your everyday life are unjust, you have a responsibility to stop that infringement of another's rights" (Dryzek et al. 2013:Loc. 1271).[666] Duty in many contexts still implies choices. Whence, the protection of other's right would depend on the chance that one fulfils his duties voluntarily.[667] However, moral obligations cannot become dispersed and therefore be insignificant (see Hall 2010). Carter employs the example of drowning children at a lake (2013:290ff.). Even if 100 people were watching and inactive, one would have the moral obligation to save a drowning child. Even if one has saved one child, one has the moral obligation to save another child who would drown otherwise. In other words, society and individuals carry a moral responsibility despite what others do, "each of us is under moral obligation to 'wade in' and change the present situation" (2013:292). Carter applies the example to the contemporary regard to nature. It is a moral obligation to change the situation and act according to the necessities.[668] Though the example could be perceived as too extreme, it is appropriate, since climate change already causes a huge loss of lives annually (see EPI 2012). Consequently, for individual duty it is irrelevant, if others fail to act. Sen accurately points out that delving into the discussion of conditions and tradeoffs of freedoms opens Pandora's Box. He remarks "[...] *valuing* negative freedom *must* have some positive implications" (1998:313).[669] Human rights should also include a "right not to be exposed to risk of harm" and "democracy is insufficient to contain or eliminate the repeated threats to which we are exposed" (Westra 1998a:57; Höffe 2009:112). If one person sees that another person is about to get harmed, him having the right not to get harmed, implies that the

---

[665] Individualistic perspectives may be the cause of the process in which the two concepts got separated. Claiming rights can work via money which signifies the loss of social relationships to the wider society. Duties therefore can easily be forgotten and be substituted by monetary exchange. The question posed by Höffe could be ironically answered as follows: "if one has the financial means" (2009; see also Hamilton 2008; Westra 1998a:120). This is a dangerous trend that needs to be reversed, when attempting to preserve life support systems.

[666] There is a strong tendency in Asian societies to focus on a system of duties and the community than on rights (Petersen 2009:45).

[667] Defenders of 'free market environmentalism' argue for the existence of destructive choices in the name of freedom, while even invoking fairness: "Some might think that even those at low-income levels ought to choose spiritual, cultural, or environmental fulfilment, but freedom means accepting a person's choice to buy an iPod rather than protect endangered species" (Anderson and Huggins 2008:10).

[668] Such position is not uncontroversial. "The deeper problem, I argue, stems from the fact that we are invited to see our role as agents to be that of "promoters of the good," whether this good be maximal or merely sufficient" (Holland 2014:111). Holland warns that an agent inclined to perceive himself as such could engage in crusades. Again given the current course, crusading against the destruction of nature can hardly be described as negative. Much environmentalist writing sees in the current situation a war against nature. Correspondingly promoters of the green good are rather defenders than religious zealots. Assigning responsibility for others comes with risks, but so does diffusing responsibility.

[669] "Once trade-offs based on consequential evaluation are accepted, there is no obvious stopping place for a theory that was set up on a purely procedural approach" (Sen 1998:312).

first person has to inform the second person (Mill 1901). The drowning children example shows how each human being is responsible. Therein lays a collective failure.

> "The collaboration of the public, those who do not share the fanaticism of the hardline deniers, is the most worrying feature of this history. For if the citizens of each nation were to maintain an allegiance to the truth, that is, to Enlightenment rationality, they could demand that their governments respond fully and forcefully to these warnings. The drift into an irreversibly hostile climate does not reflect confusion about how to respond, but an abandonment of our duties — to protect the world's poorest, to protect future generations, and to protect the Earth itself" (Hamilton 2014:341).

In Epicurean philosophy of ascetics, which is commonly mistaken for hedonism, one finds not sacrifice of happiness, but of one thing for another thing (Marcuse 2006). Sacrificing is normally understood as giving up something valuable for something more valuable (see Hall 2010). Sacrificing can be interpreted as voluntary act, but occurs in a context of necessity (Hall 2010:66). For the drowning children's survival the motive does not play a role. The survivor may as well be coerced into helping. Wapner proposes that "sacrifice is fundamentally a matter of morality. It has to do with caring for others, especially a kind of care that entails limiting oneself so that others can have the ecological space to live out their lives" (2010:35). In this sense, greens attempt at being Epicurean. Still, they tend to employ the wrong argument when emphasizing quality of life. Carter's example is much closer to the pinpoint where priorities should be set: the duty to protect the inalienable human rights of everyone. Here, some countries already recognise the duty to protect other people and in some cases have criminal punishments for the failure to render assistance. Arneson understands Lockean thought as judging the legitimacy of state inference by "the quality of the voluntary consent each party gives to the transaction, not at all the character of objective goods and harms that may accrue to the parties" (2000:40).[670] While the first part is a matter for democratic theory, the latter for the environment, since the environment as an 'objective good' is pivotal.

The green democratic state that can only exist if citizens – voluntarily – recognised respect for ecosystems as in their interest and acted upon it, in an ironic way resembles Hegelian concept of freedom.[671] The citizens become free within the state via identifying their interests with the law of

---

[670] Such an account neglects power relations and other reservation towards the idea of 'voluntary consent' in general.
[671] Hegel questioned the concept more intensively than many scholars before him. Freedom became more conditioned, although to a certain extent easier attained. Locke would have questioned that somebody in a 'slave relation' could have enjoyed freedom, Hegel held it to be possible. The slave's freedom could be reached through fulfilling his functions. Hegel has an atypical understanding of freedom, which seeks for an equation of freedom being the pleasing of one's duties (see for example Hegel 2005). Hardin openly signed onto the Hegelian understanding of freedom as the recognition of necessity (1968). See also Jonas (1984:364ff.).

the state (of nature). This similarly holds true for Millian freedom.[672] The citizen is free if he identifies his own good with the greater collective good and they become identical (see Höntzsch 2010). In the green liberal case, it is the identification and practice with a green lifestyle that enables being free and green. In the latter two cases being free depends on the recognition of higher goals or purposes, hence following the demands for protection.[673]

> "While the finitude of life sets boundaries on human freedom, it does not eliminate it. One might argue here that our freedom is precisely our ability to make choices within the context of life's limitations. To make conscious choices to prioritize what we value most — to sacrifice things we care about, but care about less, for the sake of things we care about more — is to be free because it is to live in accordance with our own values. And in fact, this element of freedom exists even within humanly constructed limitations. Sacrifice is thus a product of, and mediates between, freedom and constraint, for to sacrifice is to choose freely how best to live within limits that circumscribe freedom" (Hall 2010:68).

The idea of sacrifice for Hall surmises constraint and sees freedom in making a choice. Without freedom, there cannot be sacrifice. Having options is commonly interpreted as freedom. Here, Arneson remarks:

> "If my choice set contains just one option, which I must take, I am worse off, other things being equal, then I would be if I had additional options, even if the singleton option is still the best option in the expanded set. In this way freedom can be seen to be intrinsically, not just instrumentally, valuable" (2000:61; see Rostboll 2005).

There is no need to reject such reasoning, since the concern is choices that affect others negatively.[674] Adjusting the example to this context, the additional choice would be one that harms somebody else now or in the future.[675] Carter puts the tension between freedoms into a nutshell by writing that

> "freedom to act so as to compromise ecological integrity is, in the long run, freedom-inhibiting. Hence, the freedom to act so as to destroy the planet and thereby restrict future freedom is, surely, not what anyone who truly valued freedom would demand. The highly selfish activities of the affluent of today are unlikely to be the sorts of things which anyone who genuinely valued freedom would applaud, never mind defend" (2013:301).

Not many see consumption as a human rights issue, but an adequate interpretation acknowledges that although direct interference by the state can endanger freedom, missing protection from fellow human beings undermines freedoms as well (Ekardt 2011; see also

---

[672] Happiness is the internalisation of the right morals and subjugation of individual happiness to collective happiness is unnecessary for Mill, since he thinks the educated will understand both as congruent (Höntzsch 2010). Here again, such optimism is typical for liberal trust in education, the belief in rationality and hence neglecting cognitive dissonance.

[673] "Well-being is realised not by satisfying given wants, but by educating our capacities of judgement and our desires, such that we come to prefer what is good" (O'Neill 2006:164).

[674] From a utilitarian standpoint having only one choice does not necessarily mean that one is worse off. One can imagine a scenario where an extra choice makes choosing more difficult and creates psychological pressure. The intrinsic value of freedom itself (or choice) is not at the centre of interest here. Empirically research has also shown that people tend to choose the default option (Conly 2013). In other words, they tend to not choose at all and are inactive even against their own interests.

[675] How much freedom will future people be able to enjoy?

Rousseau 2002). Whereas the additional choice would 'add freedom' to the agent, it has the potential to 'subtract freedom' from others. For that reason, Hardin broaches that laws against murder do not make people less, but more free (1968).[676] Similarly, laws against unsustainable production and consumption, though seen as serious infringements on one's liberty by many, could ensure a minimum of freedom not just for future generations, but for today as well (see Westra 1998a).[677] It is imperative to grasp the contingency of justification of contemporary practices via an individual rights discourse. One might argue after all, that letting the children drown should be a choice.

3.3.2.2. A (GREEN) PATERNALISM AS PROTECTION OF RIGHTS

Nonetheless, most people currently do not have worldviews and behaviour required for sustainability, or even those required for some form of equity today. The huge change towards sustainability demands a fundamental revision of morals and moral approach (Höffe 2009:177). On the other hand, with strict regulations, taxes and prohibitions on damaging activities as well as positive reinforcement of eco-friendly behaviour "we don't have to use our own willpower to resist" (Hall 2010:79). The difficulty of transitioning to sustainable values is the reason why "downgrading of rights and liberties has to be achieved through policy and institutional change, even while the question of a long-term change of values is also addressed" (Humphrey 2007:Loc. 641).[678] Similarly, Beeson writes that "efforts to mitigate the impact of, or respond to, environmental change may involve a decrease in individual liberty as governments seek to transform environmentally destructive behaviour" (2010:276; Randers 2012). It can easily be argued that they have to involve a decrease in individual liberty, if governments want to be most effective, whereas democratic governments are said to provide a maximum freedom of self-determination (Dahl 2000:53). Again, the maximum freedom of self-determination will also be rendered meaningless in case of environmental catastrophe. Ideally the agent had both options and would decide for the one option that does not seriously harm anyone. When hope in the agent has proven to be misplaced, interference can be justified. When faced with significant

---

[676] Clearly, when taking the choice to kill animals for entertainment, laws against hunting purely for sports free animals.

[677] While Hardin's solution differed, most of his critique applies here: "Every new enclosure of the commons involves the infringement of somebody's personal liberty. Infringements made in the distant past are accepted because no contemporary complains of a loss. It is the newly proposed infringements that we vigorously oppose; cries of "rights" and "freedom" fill the air. But what does "freedom" mean? When men mutually agreed to pass laws against robbing, mankind became more free, not less so. Individuals locked into the logic of the commons are free only to bring on universal ruin once they see the necessity of mutual coercion, they become free to pursue other goals. I believe it was Hegel who said, "Freedom is the recognition of necessity"" (Hardin 1968:1248).

[678] "But the problem is that the behaviors that hurt the environment are also richly rewarding, which is why people do them in the first place. [...] The key here would be to transform our understanding of how individuals should use their liberty, i.e., in ways that are not merely self-interested and focused on short-term gain" (Fiala 2010:56).

tradeoffs insistence on abstract liberty could not be worth bearing the costs (Conly 2013). The primacy of the harm principle obliges protection, thus

> "if by his vices or follies a person does no direct harm to others, he is nevertheless (it may be said) injurious by his example; and ought to be compelled to control himself, for the sake of those whom the sight or knowledge of his conduct might corrupt or mislead" (Mill 1901:56).[679]

This passage clearly illustrates Mill's consequentialism and the boundary of his conception of freedom. Though harm is only caused indirectly given its potentiality he "ought to be compelled to control himself". One crucial argument states

> "that, since human beings in society can act in ways that are individually rational but socially destructive, and thus highly detrimental to all, societies need an institution in which coercion can be used to advance and protect the general good, a general good that is in the longer-term interests of everyone" (Graham 2013:Loc. 309-12).

Laws to help others in case of medical emergency are an example of such ideas already in place. Arneson in due course concludes that "(if) paternalism succeeds in bringing about a greater human good that is fairly distributed, restriction of liberty is unobjectionable, call it illiberal if you like" (2000:63).[680] Paternalism can be justified on different grounds. People may not know what is good and/or best for them and/or they do not know the means to these goals (Rostboll 2005:384).[681] Dahl writes that in the case of guardianship the people "never outgrow their

---

[679] "Encroachment on their rights; infliction on them of any loss or damage not justified by his own rights; falsehood or duplicity in dealing with them; unfair or ungenerous use of advantages over them; even selfish abstinence from defending them against injury—these are fit objects of moral reprobation, and, in grave cases, of moral retribution and punishment. And not only these acts, but the dispositions which lead to them, are properly immoral, and fit subjects of disapprobation which may rise to abhorrence. Cruelty of disposition; malice and ill-nature; that most anti-social and odious of all passions, envy; dissimulation and insincerity; irascibility on insufficient cause, and resentment disproportioned to the provocation; the love of domineering over others; the desire to engross more than one's share of advantages (the πλεονεξία [Greek: pleonexia] of the Greeks); the pride which derives gratification from the abasement of others; the egotism which thinks self and its concerns more important than everything else, and decides all doubtful questions in its own favour;—these are moral vices, and constitute a bad and odious moral character: unlike the self-regarding faults previously mentioned, which are not properly immoralities, and to whatever pitch they may be carried, do not constitute wickedness" (Mill 1901:55; see also Bowersox 2002).

[680] De-Shalit in contrast describes extending rights and liberties, guaranteeing distributive justice and the protection of the environment as "(some might say) equally important missions for humanity", which (for them) means that "the project for environmental political theory is not to determine which is more important but to see how working for one goal sustains others" (2006:89). Once more such position downplays the incompatibility and tradeoffs. For instance, Rawls' discussion here appears deficient too. He seems to underestimate the inseparability of some public goods and basic liberties. "The priority of liberty implies in practice that a basic liberty can be limited or denied solely for the sake of one or more other basic liberties, and never, as I have said, for reasons of public good or of perfectionist values. This restriction holds even when those who benefit from the greater efficiency, or together share the greater sum of advantages, are the same persons whose liberties are limited or denied. Since the basic liberties may be limited when they clash with one another, none of these liberties is absolute; nor is it a requirement that, in the finally adjusted scheme, all the basic liberties are to be equally provided for (whatever that might mean) (Rawls 2011:Loc. 4700-4716). Functioning eco-systems are at the same time public goods as they are prerequisite to what Rawls calls "basic liberties". The need for equal provision furthermore appears to be meaningless, if one is understood as necessary for others. Rawls' vague language including the admission "whatever that might mean" disguises this.

[681] Even a perfectionism that is focused on autonomy can allow for paternalism. A "[r]estriction of choice now even to the extent of forcing a single choice upon the individual can pave the way to autonomous choice of that good or others later. This long-run fostering of autonomous choice of the good is easier to bring about if the coercion does not force upon the agent a single option thought to be good but instead prohibits some tempting bad options while leaving many other options open" (Arneson 2000:44; see also Barry and Smith 2008).

childhood" (Dahl 1989:105; see also Kant 1999). While such a statement in regard to politics needs to be substantiated by scientific studies, understanding dependency as negative is contingent. Ball judges: "Authoritarian regimes replace education with indoctrination, and rational persuasion with propaganda and coercion" (2006:145). He points at Mill problematising the absence of encouraged deliberation and education through participation. There are two dimensions in which such a judgment can be criticised. First, it is difficult to differentiate between education and indoctrination, rational persuasion and propaganda.[682] Lines are blurry and normally depend on a judgment about the content rather than the means. For example, even in an ideal case where children are taught along enlightened ideals, they are usually surrounded by advertisement, hence propaganda, indoctrinating them towards a consumerist lifestyle.[683] Second, perceiving rational persuasion as superior, again, is not a neutral claim. The commitment is more to the means than consequences. It is likely that greener ends can be achieved by employing a population's passions, instead of only trying to invoke reason. Several passages of Mill indicate a potential compatibility with paternalism depending on the interpretation (Bai 2013). He writes:

> "first, that laws and social arrangements should place the happiness, or (as speaking practically it may be called) the interest, of every individual, as nearly as possible in harmony with the interest of the whole; and secondly, that education and opinion, which have so vast a power over human character, should so use that power as to establish in the mind of every individual an indissoluble association between his own happiness and the good of the whole" (Mill 1879:26; Höntzsch 2010).[684]

Once critiques use the term 'coercion' however, approaches are automatically dismissed as authoritarianism. This is typical for a constant discounting of the plight of those who are subject to structural violence by democratic systems as well as discounting the tragedy ahead. Coercion while not to be understood as legitimate in general, is justifiable for some ends. "Well-organised states accomplish large-scale collective goals and enable individuals and groups to contribute resources and action to collective goals by facilitating social coordination" however they rely on "coercion in case of non-compliance" (Young 1999:159). There are obvious examples of coercion used to impede a person in harming others. Westra highlights the practice of putting people who

---

[682] Hardin implicitly sees responsible behaviour not as a result of social interaction, but as a result of coercion. He writes: "A Madison Avenue man might call this persuasion; I prefer the greater candor of the word coercion" (1968:1247). He "dismissed appeals to conscience as being based on hypocrisy and self-interest" (Radcliffe 2002:10). The destruction of nature can easily be understood as a collective action problem that springs from the lack of control and "the entire field of environmental governance can be conceived as a study in what happens when the conditions for "perfect coercion" fail [while perhaps] most important, there may not exist the political will to pass legislation creating the requisite coercive power" (Lyon 2009:46f.).

[683] Can allowing private actors to interfere in the formation of a citizen be understood as qualitatively different and furthermore less intrusive/problematic? Certainly most greens would oppose the idea, while at the same time citizens may oppose governments actually restricting non-governmental interference.

[684] "One can imagine a public reaction against government promotion of happiness, as people claim the right to be unhappy in their own way, insisting that government should limit itself to providing less controversial and demanding goods such as safety and basic welfare" (Lane 2011b:103).

are sick with highly contagious and deadly diseases into quarantines as a coercive practice that is meant to protect a larger public (Westra 1998a).[685] Some forms of coercion are understood to be legitimate nearly everywhere. If someone evades his taxes, he might be put in prison. If someone is *declared* suicidal, he might be temporarily institutionalised for his own safety.[686] The definition of coercion and legitimate evidently changes with its context.[687] Williams discusses the use of carrots and sticks in regard to the proliferation of cycling (2010:263f.). While highlighting that preferences are not shaped independently, he shows examples of choice editing.[688] Adjacent to earlier discussions, Arneson highlights that

> "[a]utonomy is a value, and it may well be a value that affects the value of any chosen activity, but it is still one value among others, and can be outweighed. The arguments that try to establish on conceptual grounds that coercion and manipulation of an agent cannot improve the perfectionist quality of her life do not succeed" (2000:44f.).

Paternalism in environmental matters can be justified by the fact that people are subject to gross errors and that it is empirically proven that human nature and nurture impede the individual's chance to act eco-friendly (see Jackson 2012:Loc. 2984-86 and Conly 2013). Most crucially, their 'choices' clearly infringe upon other's ability and capacity to live a healthy life. Coercion in environmental matters does not disrespect subjects, it merely focuses on protection. The accumulation of wealth within a limited world is a clear infringement.

Noteworthy, in "Freedom and Borderline Experience", Alford points out that an 'all or nothing' perspective, where material conditions take priority, seems to be the most widespread perception (2003). Along the line of consequentialism, this leads to intriguing questions. For instance, if people do not perceive themselves as free what then, is the value of the freedoms they objectively have? Further, if environmental destruction becomes more severe what effect will this have on people's perception of freedom? If material conditions play a more significant role in the perception of freedom, positive freedoms might be more likely to satisfy people's expectations. Thus, a polluted city environment, where people are unable to walk outside without masks in a democratic setting, may be perceived as less free by the inhabitants than a less polluted city environment within an autocracy. Elling asserts that "not all degrees of

---

[685] "For liberalism, the nemesis of agency is domination through physical coercion – the use of force to compel individuals to do what they otherwise would not do" (Bowles and Gintis 1986:13). Such cases are overt cases of domination however.

[686] Once more, it should be noted that 'collective suicide', 'homicide' and 'addiction' are terms regularly used for unsustainable behaviour globally (e.g. Busch 2011:93).

[687] Poor people are not coerced into eating inferior food or visiting a cheaper hospital, instead it is said that they or the circumstances force them. This kind of cognitive differentiating allows for ignoring the tension between the individual good and a public good.

[688] "Choice editing is a practice that ensures consumers do not get the opportunity to choose environmentally and socially damaging products and services" (Randers 2012:Loc. 4305-7). 'Choice editing', 'nudging', 'tweaking' are terms describing the directed interference into people's 'choices'.

freedom can be satisfied if one wishes to be free of the scourge of environmental problems" (Elling 2008:260). Yet, if Alfred's observations are generalisable, the subject could feel 'unfree' within most political arrangements. Though his research has to be discussed with caution, the perception of freedom as 'all or nothing' outwardly makes arguing for paternalism easier, since people would feel unfree either way.[689]

When more than 40 years of environmentalism and attempting to raise global awareness in order to initiate voluntary change of behaviour, have demonstrated that collective rights cannot be subject to trust in voluntary actions, the duty to care about the environment must be enforced.[690]

> "[Humanity] will have to trade its liberty to live as it wishes in favor of a system where survival is paramount. Perhaps this choice should not be put for democratic approval, or humanity will elect to live as it wishes" (Shearman and Smith 2007:4; see Saretzki 2011).

Strict restrictions are vital for climate mitigation (Höffe 2009:183). Arguing that one should have the choice to harm others is difficult, even when the existence of choices is valued by itself. A consistent understanding of the harm principle classifies overconsumption not only as neglected duty, but as crime. Once the harm principle is accepted as an ethical principle for environmental governance, it needs clear boundaries, in order to be employed for political decision making. The question what freedoms are indispensable is intimately connected to the question: what freedoms should one not have?[691] Hence the question: what liberties are ecologically unsustainable? The strength of using a capabilities approach is its focus on justice. Arneson lists Nussbaum's criteria as

> "living out a normal lifespan, having good health and its requisites, freedom of movement, freedom from assault, freedom of choice in sexual matters, the capacity and opportunity to engage in imagining, thinking, and reasoning" (Arneson 2000:48).[692]

None of these capabilities is intrinsically tied to democratic regimes. An advanced green version of such approach does not only employ the idea of a minimum, but also resorts to capping consumption. This will inevitably look to those used to a certain lifestyle as grief sacrifices.

---

[689] "In most contexts to say that you are free to choose between the options – that in that sense you have freedom of choice – is to imply that the option to be realized is up to you. And it can be up to you only if you have the resources and capacity to make such a choice: only if you are free of vitiation, not just free of invasion" (Pettit 2012:42).

[690] "If there are genuine biophysical limits to economic growth, if the uncertainties and potential consequences are such that acting as though there were such limits represents the only prudent course, the considerations of distributive justice arguably demand radical redistribution not only of income and wealth, but also of related access to the world's resources and environmental services. However the political realism easily derived from our routine experience of tax and social policy debates in the industrialized countries strongly suggests that even relatively modest proposals for intra-national redistribution of income and wealth will confront intense resistance" (Schrecker 1998:226).

[691] "The very meaning of constraint presupposes a range of normal (and perhaps morally valued) action types that humans are thought to pursue" (Christman 2005:84).

[692] These issues, although not random, should not be understood as criteria of degrees of humanness.

Holland develops a capability approach for environmental justice that includes a minimum and a maximum (2008). She argues that

> "capability ceilings can help us to identify and put limits on the capabilities of those who experience high levels of capability protection that make it unrealistic for society to achieve basic conditions of justice for others"

and states that "Nussbaum's capabilities approach is valuable in revealing capability conflicts that arise at the intersection of economic and ecological processes" (2008:421).[693] A limit on consumption in a limited world is inevitable. Yet, renunciation is the weak spot of the green movement (Ertner 2009:62). As witnessed in many instances, the green movement has tried to overcome this central problem. They have redressed messages with the intention of advancing an idea of a higher quality of life – without sacrificing and modesty. A capabilities cap in contrast removes the issue from a seemingly limbo and makes it a justice consideration. The amount of carelessness thence is capped in regard to contemporary as well as future generations enabling a fair usage and distributing of resources within a sustainable framework. Sacrifice as a concept "remains curiously unexamined in both activist and academic conversations about environmental politics" and the use of sacrifice as a concept often marks the boundary of acceptability (Meyer and Maniates 2010a:3). The consequence of Hall's definition is that without 'options' there technically cannot be any sacrifice (2010). Ertner underscores that legally spoken renunciation is a waiver of a right, but a right implies an existing legitimate claim (2009:63). Meaning that living sustainable can actually not be considered a sacrifice, thus choice. A capabilities approach can uncover ways to manage different claims. Prominently, a capabilities cap differentiates between legitimate claims and illegitimate claim i.e. those who harm others by their fulfilment. Utilitarianism already included a minimum and a maximum cap from its beginnings: "Everybody to count for one, nobody for more than one" (see Mill 1879). The slogan attributed to Bentham's utilitarianism in a sense symbolises the problem of today's consumerist world. Sen asks

> "if results such as starvation and famines were to occur, would the distribution of holdings still be morally acceptable despite their disastrous consequences? There is something deeply implausible in the affirmative answer. Why should it be the case that rules of ownership, etc. should have such absolute priority over life-and-death question?" (1998:312).

He answers the question raised in the first part of this book in regard to the sanctity of property. Confronted with a life-and-death question, property redistribution cannot be illegitimate. This is a restriction of economic freedom beyond that of restricting contamination of the environment. People should use the resources necessary for one person, they regularly use more. This is not

---

[693] For clarity of evaluation, it is possible to divide between primary rights, secondary rights and 'supposed rights' (see Nussbaum 1992).

only eminent in Western industrialised countries, but can also be observed in the rest of the world's growing middle and upper classes. Despite all efforts of environmentalists to school awareness of this problem, for example by calculating the Earth Overshot Day, destructive practices continue. The second part of Bentham's slogan is as crucial as the first part, thus nobody should count for more than one. "Comfortable living, convenience and luxury are not legitimate in circumstances when they inevitably lead to the damaging of the natural surroundings of others" (de Geus 2004:Loc. 2584-85). The capabilities approach narrows the field. It strengthens arguments for redistribution from top to bottom. There are various arguments for diminishing inequality of wealth for the purposes of greener governance beyond the social justice aspect. Aforementioned, income inequality is correlated to larger footprints (Whiteside 2006; Wilkinson and Pikett 2011; Cox 2013). High footprint lifestyle as status symbol becomes insignificant if anybody can afford the same lifestyle. Extreme poverty can lead to environmentally destructive behaviour and wealth gives opportunities for exorbitant pollution. Environmental sustainability can be imagined in a grossly unjust world, but this would include interference and coercion into the majorities' lives for the sake of a small minority.[694] Yet, this is incompatible with any notion of the common good advanced earlier and therefore categorically excluded as a green vision here. The former option explicitly advances respect for ecosystems while implicitly advancing social justice. Social justice should be pursued in a relatively egalitarian interpretation for greater sustainability. As noted, ensuring collective survival in a sense follows a theory of justice that is concerned with the least well-off (see Arneson 2000). For Holland a big problem in consequentialist thinking is posed by the setting of a framework (2014:113). According to Holland what needs to be included and what counts as best is not easily identifiable. A harm principle in combination with a capabilities approach within the framework of prioritizing sustainability and utilising science for assessment and decision making has great potential. Such considerations endorse the state's role as a protector of the common good (see also Aristotle 2009). Where 'society' fails, good governance needs to secure minimal living conditions.

3.3.3. SCIENTIFIC PROPHECIES: CASSANDRA VS. LATOUR

Since good governance is based on sound science, questions about the role of science are pivotal; in particular, which means can help bridge the gap between 'scientific prophecies' and environmental politics? The idea of climate change and the consequences of environmental

---

[694] "Where responsibilities and burdens are perceived to be shared widely, then they are also more likely to be embraced as one's own", whereas "[w]here the distribution of such burdens appears to fall disproportionately on the poor or disadvantaged, then they will carry the added weight of this hypocrisy and misdistribution" (Meyer 2010:25). Currently the burden is greatly disproportionate in regard to perpetuator and victim.

destruction have been described and explained in thousands of articles, books and documentaries.

> "Often, however, we dismiss bearers of bad news or inconvenient truths until the point of crisis, when reality can no longer be evaded. The mythical figure of Cassandra and the Old Testament prophet Jeremiah were fated to be ignored" (Orr 2009:Loc. 76-81).

How do experts on the environment resemble Cassandra and Jeremiah? Both are particularly tragic figures. Whilst Cassandra is able to foresee the future, she is cursed not to be believed. Although trusted to a certain extent, environmental scientists are largely ignored, which in consequence makes no difference for the environment. Drastic reductions in greenhouse gases within less than a decade are required in order to avoid tipping points that will make the planet uninhabitable for the next century. Hence, radical change is urgent.[695] Cassandra predicted the destruction of Troy. Many scientists fear the destruction of Earth's life support systems. God chose Jeremiah to tell the people about the consequences of their sins, nonetheless he was reluctant to do so. From an ecological standpoint today's consumption can clearly be described as sin. In both stories disaster was not diverted, but it could have been, if and only if the people listened, believed and acted. Predictions about the upcoming catastrophe are not made by a god or even by an overarching authority (Höffe 2009:167).[696] Scientists are relatively powerless. The man who leaves Plato's cave and returns equally tells a story about the unwillingness of humans to accept 'truth' and change (1982).[697]

The majority of scientific disciplines is quite separated from everyday life and functions relatively independent. Environmental science, however, has some unique qualities.

> "The controversy in question is not of the kind that is normal in scientific communities as investigators test and challenge findings and hypotheses. Rather, it puts scientists in a pitched battle fought on very public terrain, with powerful political interests financing attacks on the integrity, content, and process of climate science — along with personal attacks on its practitioners. There are people who have much to lose if the overwhelming consensus among climate scientists is right: their lifestyles, their profits, and, in some cases, their livelihoods" (Dryzek et al. 2013:Loc. 227; Lane 2011b).

So far scientists appear to be the tragic figures from these mythological stories. The comparisons reveal the seriousness as well as the dilemma most environmentalists face. Environmental destruction is irresponsible and irrational (Baber and Bartlett 2005). Scientists have sufficient

---

[695] Late action makes mitigation and adaptation more difficult: "Flying, driving, heating our homes, using our appliances, basically everything we do, would need to be zero carbon – and note, zero carbon means zero carbon. Carbon capture and storage could not, as we understand them today, get near to delivering this" (Anderson 2012:25).
[696] The incumbent pope talks about climate change as a problem. The actual impact is likely to be minor, but hard to estimate. At least a moderate (potentially only short-term) effect on the views of Christian Americans for example was observed by a joint study of George Mason University and Yale (Maibach et al. 2015).
[697] As discussed earlier, cognition plays a core role.

knowledge in many areas, yet lack the power to change the set course. The ways in which human beings destroy nature are known well enough.

What is more, even if it was true that human activities had no influence on the climate per se, politics would still have to react. If pollution did not lead to climate change, it still causes enough damage and suffering. Whether or not there will be an extreme transformation of global weather conditions, resources still need to be protected and used wisely. Of course, arguments regarding the future always contain an element of speculation.[698] Given the status quo of the environment and current tendencies, distressing predictions are not prophecy, but based on mathematical calculations. Höffe reminds his readers that there is a difference between utopia, vision and dystopia (2009:190ff.). He emphasizes that smart politics need a vision or it will lack the agency to create something and barely react. One could imagine Cassandra and Jeremiah being equipped with substantial power to make people revise their behaviour – the earlier discussions established that beliefs are not enough. Meriting such change in agency could transform them from being observers into active 'agents of change'.

By definition democratic politics do not follow the demands of scientists. In the end scientists have the same guaranteed decision-making power as a shopkeeper, a baker, or anybody else above the age of 18 or 21.[699] Deliberative democracy supports civic science as an important pillar. Representative democracy trusts in delegation for the understanding of scientific findings. Levelling playing fields means also indiscrimination between expertise and ignorance. Democracy advocates sustain their arguments by insisting on political equality.

> "One practical argument for democracy is that infallible green policies will not simply drop like apples from a theory of value, so the means of reaching decisions do matter. Those arguments that defend the use of non-democratic methods often contain an implicit technocratic assumption that a governing elite of politicians, scientists and professionals knows best" (Carter 2007:54; see also Mill 1862).

It is indisputable that Cassandra, Jeremiah and Plato's cave returnee know better. It is also indisputable that climate scientists have a better grasp of the climate than other citizens. If not science would be useless. On the other hand, Dahl writes that "[n]o intellectually defensible claim can be made that policy elites (actual and putative) possess superior moral knowledge or

---

[698] Scientists are unsure, if tipping points are already passed or if it can be avoided that change will be dictated out of necessity because of biophysical limits. At the end "all of the computer models, scientific predictions, and economic scenarios are constructed around the most important and uncertain variable of all: whether our collective choice will be to accept or to deny what the science is telling us" (Marshall 2014:Loc. 97).

[699] "The sad fact is that citizens in electoral democracies won't even question their right to choose their political rulers, no matter how intellectually incompetent or morally insensitive their political judgment may be" (Bell 2015:Loc. 3265).

more specifically superior knowledge of what constitutes the public good" (Dahl 1989:337).[700] There are two reservations to this claim. First, this work provides a clear idea of an indispensable public good. Natural scientists attain superior knowledge of this public good since they have a deeper understanding of sustainability (see also Bowersox 2002). Following Beck, Hannigan writes about contemporary risks that they are "largely invisible to lay people, identifiable only through sophisticated scientific instrumentation" (2006:23).[701] Scientists are better prepared to realise unavoidable measures so as to protect the commons. Since being affected is a clear barrier to abstract reasoning, scientists gain even further grounds in handling difficult situations.[702] The 'unaffected' scientist is more likely to engage in the required reasoning, since consequentialist thinking that considers the common good is "psychologically difficult for people in a number of predictable way" (McShane 2014:30).[703] Once the common good is identified some form of instrumental rationality (with precaution) needs to be applied. Scientists can adjudicate between different policies in regard to sustainability as a moral end. In view of that, many scholars wish for a greater role of science; including prediction and evaluation of policy goals (see for example Lemons 1998:94f.). Dahl himself admits that governments need the help of experts (2000:78). However, ensured expertise is typically found in those institutions that could be regarded as less democratic and constraining democracy such as a constitutional court (Bell and Li 2013, Pettit 2013).[704] Pralle makes the suggestions that "[d]ifferent indicators may have to be selected for different audiences, depending on the effects that most worry them, but clarity of communication and ease of understanding should be a priority" (2009:789). In spite of its prevalence in consumer culture, such a process could be presented as manipulation by

---

[700] Critiques against the concept of such meritocratic decision-making are common. Huxley jokes: "There seems to be a touching belief among certain PhD's in sociology that PhD's in sociology will never be corrupted by power. Like Sir Galahad's, their strength is as the strength of ten because their heart is pure — and their heart is pure because they are scientists and have taken six thousand hours of social studies" (2000:66). Heilbroner also warns that the social scientist morally involved and intertwined with his subject (1976:15). In his elaborations on happiness, Marcuse writes that even the purest philosophy is followed by a 'swamp of dirty disciples' (2006:69f.; my translation). Admittedly, power could be as corruptive as many sayings assume and the question if training can channel such tendencies needs to be studied. Still, one might assume that there is a difference in truth claims between scientists and entrepreneurs (cf. Radcliffe 2002:7f.).

[701] Hall stresses that "a large part of the reason why the consequences of our choices are unidentified is because they affect things that are not in our ordinary range of vision: people we don't know and never will, future generations not yet living, elements of ecosystems that we don't see or interact with in our daily lives" (2010:72). Baber and Bartlett comment: "It would seem that now is not the time for experts to go missing in action" (2005:Loc. 2345).

[702] "All that the mathematician requires [...] is at least one other mathematician to recognise the validity of his proof. In order to assure itself of the thought that it is, love needs only assume the two. The artist ultimately needs no one. Science, art and love are aristocratic truth procedures" (Badiou 2004:142).

[703] 'Unaffected' here is meant in opposition to 'the affected' of participative governance.

[704] The British government employs a Government Scientific Chief Advisor. Yet, following his advice is not mandatory.

liberals and conservatives alike, when employed by science and policy experts.[705] In this case, it is difficult to maintain a difference between the rule of scientists and the vote by people whose choices have been strategically shaped by comprehensive psychological research. Second, those trained in ethics may in fact be uniquely equipped to know what is good for everyone and to develop policies accordingly. While a consequentialist environmentalist utilises science to think about the good, the public typically has private preferences (De-Shalit 2001). Despite the wide consensus among scientists about anthropogenic climate change, political entrepreneurs cherry pick from the vast research (Dryzek et al. 2013:Loc. 435).[706] So far, "science is expected to fall in line with the policy priorities of the government of the day" (Dryzek 2005:82), instead of priorities being set by an understanding of reality. Pralle's suggestion could be feasible and might show effects. It does neither foster transparency nor represent a deeper trust in the people's capacity to comprehend the actual issue.

3.3.3.1. STRATEGIC POSITIVISM, *FORTUNA* AND THE PRECAUTIONARY PRINCIPLE

Meanwhile past examples of the application of scientific ideas should serve as a reminder of precaution. Science has been used for good and bad as it by itself is morally neutral. There are warnings against the 'colonialisation of life' by science: "The more scientific a history, the more oppressive it tends to be in the experimental laboratory called the third world" (Nandy 1993:48; see also Forsyth 2003). Yet, as mentioned earlier the alternatives are likely to be more oppressive and governance today needs to integrate social and natural science to develop feasible green policies. While Nandy cautions against the potentially oppressive character of science, overcaution is equally problematic. Pluralism of worldviews facilitates disagreement on the problem itself, finding solutions becomes even more problematic. In conclusion, a cooperative relationship between science and policy-making is a premise for sustainability.[707]

Elling accuses natural scientists of largely holding the view that "nature is universally good with a universal value of its own in need of no further legitimation" (2008:43; see also Talshir

---

[705] On the other hand, "[i]f scientists choose not to engage in the public debate, we leave a vacuum that will be filled by those whose agenda is one of short-term self-interest" (Mann 2014). Thus, scholars like Giddens find not all so called 'choice editing' objectionable saying that for example there are "no civil liberties issue in cases where our behaviour is already being significantly influenced, or manipulated, by companies, and where the object of government policy is to counter that influence" (2009:109).

[706] "Policy entrepreneurs should communicate that 'the debate is over' and should point out that the detailed climate models developed by scientists have helped them correctly predict climate change trends and impacts" (Pralle 2009:790).

[707] Note that this statement does not exclude the chances for indigenous knowledge and its application to qualify as sustainable. But its application for new challenges would have to be carefully evaluated and there sciences would be in the picture again. Scientific knowledge and indigenous knowledge are not mutually exclusive. Generally, indigenous does not necessarily mean sustainable, "although natives in the Amazon claim to be living harmoniously with nature (and they are indeed less disruptive to natural processes than commercially exploitive foreign practices in the area), their goals and those of conversation biology does do not necessarily mesh" (Westra 1998b:267). Species extinction is sometimes caused endogenously.

2004).[708] It is fallacy to derive morality from facts (Jonas 1984:146ff.; Singer 1999:11). Marxist ecologists typically oppose positivism as lacking comprehensive ethics (Radcliffe 2002:52). Yet, Elling's accusation is unfair. It might appear that natural scientists see intrinsic value in facts, but natural science does not need to lead to reductionism. Similar reservations against ecologists are problematic. Today's science is not purely positivist. Natural scientists and ecologists alike have different ideological backgrounds or worldviews. Science and ecology in particular as non-anthropocentric may actually lead to a widening of a moral framework and therefore a more critical view on binary ethics. Both are essentially occupied with interrelations. Nonetheless, Elling believes that ecology is not able of forming a consistent ethical framework (2008:39; Gillroy and Bowersox 2002; see Goodin 2013). Here postpositivism admits the critique by "conservatives and postmodernists, united in the belief that scientific neutrality is impossible, that all science is ideologically colored" (Dryzek 2005:78).[709] According to Bäckstrand, postpositivism

> "questions the boundary between scientific expert knowledge and lay knowledge, between global western knowledge and local indigenous knowledge. In this perspective, all expert knowledge is situated in a specific political and cultural context, inherently value-laden and imbued with worldviews. As a corollary, scientific and technological decision-making should rest on participation by and collaboration among scientists, citizens and civil society. In contrast, an objectivist epistemology emphasizes the uniqueness of scientific knowledge epitomized by its systematic features, its transformative effects and its global impacts" (2003:39).

In spite of this description other forms of postpositivism are possible. One does not necessarily have to accept her corollary. The scientific method can still be understood as taking priority for informing accounts of reality and scientific evaluation as authority. The acceptance of situatedness of all knowledge does not by logical necessity have to lead to participative decision making.[710] Because the urgency and severity of climate change demands action, politics need to use a specific interpretation of the world (see Gorz 1980:11ff.). Good governance needs to

---

[708] "If we mix facts and values, we go from bad to worse, for we are depriving ourselves of both autonomous knowledge and independent morality. We shall never know, for example, whether the apocalyptic predictions with which the militant ecologists threaten us mask the power scientists hold over politicians or the domination politicians exercise over poor scientists" (Latour 2004:4).

[709] "Although the world of truth differs absolutely, not relatively, from the social world, the Scientist can go *back and forth* from one world to the other no matter what: the passageway closed to all others is open to him alone. In him and through him, the tyranny of the social world is miraculously interrupted when he leaves, so that he will be able to contemplate the objective world at last; and it is likewise interrupted when he returns, so that like a latter-day Moses he will be able to substitute the legislation of scientific laws, which are not open to question, for the tyranny of ignorance. Without this double interruption there can be no Science, no epistemology, no paralyzed politics, no Western conception of public life" (Latour 2004:11).

[710] After elaborating on some problems with precaution and democratic deliberation Whiteside writes: "Given these deficiencies of popular opinion relative to risk assessment, how can so many authors argue that implementing the precautionary principle requires popular participation?" (2006:120). One of the reasons he gives is the need to include additional perspectives. Checks against pure 'armchair or ivory tower governance' can be found in other mechanisms as will be discussed in the third part. Bäckstrand's statement also neglects the fact that much of indigenous knowledge can be bound to elites and as such be restricted and anti-democratic.

acknowledge both the limitations of earlier positivism as well as confronting dangerous relativism applying what can be called 'strategic positivism' (Latour 2007).[711] So far, this work attempted to provide arguments that neutrality is not only impossible, but that climate mitigation advocacy has become a duty for those valuing life (see Lemons 1998).

As touched upon earlier, not just democracy, but also the mechanisms within the scientific community lead to structural conservatism (Leggewie and Welzer 2011:29f.). Given the restricted knowledge of today, judgments are only "provisional" and often measurements are inadequate (Meadowcraft 2014:32ff.; see also Jasanoff 1999).[712] Hannigan warns that scientific proof is "a slave to statistical levels of significance" with "pure science" needing a minimum confidence level of 95% for the recommendation of action (2006:114). In the meantime, uncertainty in climate politics is used as leverage against policies, but also "to assert that the situation is alarming" (Hannigan 2006:97). The investment specialist Grantham perceives scientists as not talking about the dangers connected to the melting of the permafrost and the possible impact of a sudden release of methane gas and alleges that instead of risking an overstatement (e.g. illustrating tipping point scenarios), they risk the planet (2012; Peltz 2014, see also Oreskes and Conway 2013). Investment and insurance companies' decisions in regard to climate change are relevant, since their business does not only depend on expert prediction, but also decision making.[713] A precautionary principle demands action.[714] Guided by strategic positivism it can be the basis for proactive guidelines. Strategic positivism, in contrast to a 'strict' science standard, could further be described as pragmatic positivism. Environmental politics needs to use the latest science to formulate politics towards the goal of sustainability. 'Normal science' can take long to produce claims (see Kuhn 2012). So called 'post-normal science' is concerned with science under the condition of limited certainty and urgency. Here, experts of different disciplines may be integrated to improve the output. Objectives should be formulated along the lines of environmental necessities. After determining the minimum conditions for the survival of life support systems as well as optimal conditions, it is possible to measure, monitor and evaluate policies (as well as possibly promoting excellence).[715]

---

[711] For strategic positivism and precaution speak the high stakes (Jonas 1984:77).

[712] "Ecosystems are complex, and our knowledge of them is limited, as the biological scientists who study them are the first to admit" (Dryzek 2005:9).

[713] Here, most action is also focused on short terms. Notably, many liabilities from climate change precipitated catastrophes have long been taken out of insurance policies (Whiteside 2006:32).

[714] "Precautions are taken in advance of damage, not after it has already begun. We have overwhelming evidence that we've already triggered a rapid rate of oceanic and atmospheric warming. We're currently reacting to climate change already in progress, not deploying precautions against warming that might or might not happen in the future" (Oreskes and Conway 2014:Loc. 905).

[715] Such approach has to be dynamic and be continuously evolving; including new developments.

Prominent green theorist Eckersley deems the precautionary principle as solid check in favour of protecting and representing ecological citizens and the new constituency (2004; Bührs 2012:418).[716] Precaution encompasses rethinking and questioning knowledge of nature including its interrelations. A precautionary principle "also means rethinking the very notion of public interest" (Whiteside 2006:27). With the aim of taking precaution, various experts from different fields may be consulted.[717] Repeatedly misunderstood, it cannot be contrasted with "science-based regulation", because it equally employs science (2006:30). The precautionary principle applies to badly understood risks. These are the situations where costs-benefit calculations are unreliable. It is therefore not comparable. Hereby, a fully functioning ecoauthoritarian state needs to take the worst cases into account to ensure the survival of basic life support systems. There are concerns that the precautionary principle can be used as a protectionism and hinder free trade (2006:83).[718] This argument loses force, not only because it narrows down concerns to an economic level, but also because free trade from an environmental point of view is rather destructive. Free trade arguments are part of the growth ideology, which has been shown to be theoretically and empirically incapable of producing ecological sound output. Moreover, under a precautionary principle economically discounting the future is not permissible. So far, "liberal arrangements seem incapable of actually preventing severe ecological problems" (2006:85).

Conspicuously, harm to the environment is not problematic in most moral codes (see Whiteside 2006:36ff.). Jonas' discussion of responsibility proves incredible foresight (1984). Many of the aspects are still presented by scholars today. He diagnosed the shrinking of a 'salubrious distance' between everyday activities and the planet.[719] Nature did not use to be subject to human responsibility and, except medicine's handling of nature, was not subject to ethical considerations (1984:22ff.; Hood 2003). He classified traditional ethics as anthropocentric, based on immediacy of action and consequence.[720] Hence, the other was limited to coevals.[721] The belief, that everyone can recognise what is morally right (e.g. Rousseau 2002), is connected to this limited framework or considerability. Erstwhile, people did not assume nature to be vulnerable and subject to mutation through human interference. People's actions were also unlikely to harm other sentient beings in the distance. This has changed. Consecutively,

---

[716] "No single decision rule is likely to do more to protect environmental victims" (Eckersley 2004:Loc. 1675).

[717] If a precautionary principle focuses on risks in isolation, it can be criticized on such reductionism (Whiteside 2006:44).

[718] The precautionary principle can restrict research (Whiteside 2006:41).

[719] Aristotle's understanding of politics as beyond the realm of necessity, which reigns within the household (2009), can be interpreted as derived from this old logic.

[720] It might seem obvious to many, but it should be noted that "[p]olitical thought is not shaped in the closed laboratory of our minds, but is a result of reflecting, in our various and strange ways, on experiences we have undergone, directly or vicariously" (Freeden 2003:33; see Hegel 2005).

[721] There are some cultures that did have considerations of future generations, but they have negligible influence.

knowledge about the impact becomes a responsibility, while the gap between knowledge and agency constitutes an ethical problem (Jonas 1984:26ff.). The precautionary principle "raises profound philosophical questions about the very nature of good governance" (Whiteside 2006:87). Part of it involves rethinking the idea that majorities understand when they are endangered. Man generally lacks the wisdom demanded by the situation and Jonas was already concerned that representative governments will be unable to deter destruction, since they are accountable to contemporary interests (1984:54f.).

In spite of this, it is possible to extend ethical considerations and expand older imperatives to include newer developments and ensure survival. A precautionary principle's rationale is consequentialist (Whiteside 2006:123ff.). It does set clear priorities. One of the strongest comparisons is that of Earth as a patient in intensive care. Crucially, Shearman and Smith employ the comparison between a physician in charge of a patient in emergency care and a crowd in charge throughout their book (2007). Lovelock uses the same idea seeing scientists as the doctors advising the government (2009; see also Conly 2013). In contrast to the sciences and politics, in medical practice, doctors act much earlier. Good governance should apply a strategic positivism similar to the practice in an emergency room. Such a principle overlaps with a significant part of earlier considerations. In accord with Höffe stressing the functional need for a vision (2009), science needs clear guidelines for accountability.

3.3.3.2. THE PRIORITY OF ECOLOGICAL INTEGRITY

Ecological integrity could be a used as a reference point for good governance. Since functioning life support systems are the *sine quo non* of all life itself, it is easy to argue for their priority. The concept of integrity has a more normative quality than sustainability, in that it includes an idea of health, pureness, wholeness. Sustainability is useful as a term for everyday language, but not as a guiding principle given its 'looseness'. The discussants of the role of science within democratic framework tend to object to comparatively fixed concepts and fear the potential of domination by science. However,

> "only if integrity is scientifically definable, quantifiable, and as predictive (in a limited sense) as other scientific concepts are can it be practically useful in guiding public policy. [...]

Integrity is also philosophically meaningful, heuristic, and applicable to ethics and useful in decision-making precisely because of its scientific characteristic" (Westra 1998a:9).[722]

At the same time, Thompson proffers reservations against Westra's ethics, calling her interpretation of ecological integrity "very teleological" (2003:194). Importantly, he points out that "[e]volutionary biology provides no basis for thinking that one succession has any moral or metaphysical superiority over any other" (2003:195).[723] It follows that each understanding of ecological integrity of a particular ecosystem is based on the decision to give significance to a certain stage of its existence. Hence, there is a decision to deem it valuable. Reservations against the reification of nature are worthwhile philosophically and overlap with reservations against positivism that need to be taken into account, when opting of a strategic positivism. In spite of the difficulty, defining integrity along clear guidelines gives it the quality necessary to measure good governance. It is a chief component in building an ecomeritocracy. Merit in such a rule can be defined relatively easy by a positive impact on the environment. Again, a functional understanding of ecological integrity avoids many value questions (see Holland 2013). However, ecological integrity has to be formulated quasi autonomous from needs produced by much of contemporary cultures, hence properly reflect upon the unsustainability of many lifestyle demands.[724] Humphrey summarises Westra's observations on ecological integrity as follows:

"Only such a principle can protect people from un-chosen harm, whereas democracy inflicts the preferences of the majority on the minority, which may include preferences for exposure to harms, or at least risk of harms. Such democratically imposed harms cannot fit an informed consent model, as they remain unchosen by the minority, and thus the usually accepted connections between primary human rights and democracy can be shown to be weaker than usually thought" (Humphrey 2006:315).

---

[722] Holland in contrast writes "that it is unwise to attempt to answer the question, How much integrity do we need? and that we should attempt instead to answer a different question. There are several reasons for refusing to answer the question as given. First, it would create the entirely misleading impression that it is possible to attain some measure of precision and accuracy about such things. The fact is that we live in a world increasingly characterized by radical uncertainty and indeterminacy, in which (1) the size, gravity, extent, and likelihood of impacts are difficult or impossible to predict or estimate; (2) even innocent and justifiable actions can conspire to produce devastating consequences that are slow to materialize, are cumulative in their effects, and combine in unpredictable ways; and (3) resulting harms become less and less specific, as do assignable agents of harm. Given this account of our current human predicament, the attempt to quantify the amount of integrity required to serve human needs is bound to be virtually meaningless. The second reason concerns the perils of quantification as such, both for environmentalists and for policymakers more generally" (2013:Loc. 1094).

[723] Discussing the concept of environmental crisis, Blühdorn accentuates nature's evolving character. He writes that "the natural environment has never been a stable system, but has always been subject to processes of constant transformation (2012:14). In the *Politics of Environmental Science*, Forsyth warns that many processes are still badly understood and that evaluations differ greatly (2003). Yet, this speaks for and not against a stricter and more cautious standard.

[724] "The great risk in espousing environmental sustainability as the touchstone for environmental policy is that it protects the natural world just insofar as, and in the form that, it has the capacity to sustain human economic systems—or more precisely, in whatever form makes the relation between ecological and economic systems sustainable. And without some stand being taken on the character of the economic system in question, this requirement contains no guarantee of the continuance of the wild world" (Holland 2013:Loc. 1117). Integrity is a more stringent concept that is focused rather on nature than on existing human practice. The problem here can also be understood as one of definition and be solved by using sustainability in a more limited way than it is commonly applied. Given its diverse usage attempting to redefine sustainability in general seems naïve.

As suggested by Humphrey, the prioritisation of ecological integrity as part of a human rights framework protecting others from harm is dominant in Westra's writing.

Generally, Humphrey doubts the ability of the liberal harm principle to include biodiversity protection (2007:Loc. 1965).[725] It is possible though to protect biodiversity under a harm principle with comprehensive precautionary principle taking potentiality into account (see Westra 1998a). If any harm principle when applied stringently can still be understood as liberal is a different question. Interestingly, Westra takes Kant's prohibition of physical harm as basis for her suggestions (Westra 1998a:60ff.). The second order principles Westra develops are not deductive from the first order, but construed by further research.[726] Her suggestions give valuable insights into the possible implications of making a concept of ecological integrity the benchmark. Westra's green ethics include eight of these second order principles (SOPs):

> "SOP 1 In order to protect and defend ecological integrity, we must start by designing policies that embrace complexity. SOP 2 We should not engage in activities that are potentially harmful to natural systems and to life in general. Judgments about potential harms should be based on the approach of "post-normal" science. SOP 3 Human activities ought to be limited by the requirements of the precautionary principle. SOP 4 We must accept an "ecological worldview" and thus reject our present "expansionist worldview" and reduce our ecological footprint. SOP 5 It is imperative to eliminate many of our present practices and choices as well as the current emphasis on "technical maximality" and on environmentally hazardous or wasteful individual rights. SOP 6 It is necessary for humanity to learn to live as in a "buffer." Zoning restraints are necessary to impose limits both on the quality of our activities, but also on their quantity. Two corollary principles follow: (a) we must respect and protect "core"/wild areas; (b) we must view all our activities as taking place within a "buffer" zone. This is the essential meaning of the ethics of integrity. SOP 7 We must respect the individual integrity of single organisms (or micro-integrity), in order to be consistent in our respect for integrity and also to respect and protect individual functions and their contribution to the systemic whole. SOP 8 Given the uncertainties embedded in SOPs 1, 2, and 3, the "Risk Thesis" must be accepted, for uncertainties referring to the near future. We must also accept the "Potency Thesis" for the protection of individuals and wholes in the long term" (Westra et al. 2013:Loc. 696; Westra 1998a).

Most of these second order principles have been advanced as necessary within the discussions earlier (in particular in the subchapters 3.3.2. and 3.3.3.). They do not need any further explanation. SOP 1 might be obvious to the natural scientists. Ecosystems are often complex, trying to sustain optimal capacity for the future means to allow for these complexity. SOP 2 integrates focal characteristics of the challenge of nature's distraction, in particular lack of knowledge. SOP 3 Provides the ethical guideline for action. SOP 4 demands a change in metaphysical outlook. SOP 5 problematises a widespread lifestyle and its endorsement. SOP 6

---

[725] "Biodiversity – plants, animals, microorganisms and the ecological processes that interconnect them – forms the planet's natural productivity. Protecting biodiversity ensures that a wide range of "ecosystem services" like flood control and soil renewal, the production of commodities such as food and new medicines, and finally, spiritual and aesthetic fulfillment, will remain available for current and future generations" (EPI 2012:42).
[726] She also notes the absence of strong environmental movements that have an actual effect on performance.

provides a more concrete requirement. Zoning and the emphasis on living in a buffer ensures the required stringency. Human health is dependent on the existence of wild space (Westra 1998a:31).[727] SOP 7 is derived from a more ecocentric worldview in general. It is not just a tribute to consistency, but also embedded in the recognition of interrelation. Importantly, in contrast to the criticism towards a stronger state and to the fear of 'total illiberalism', it puts in emphasis on all life. While Westra is a candidate for being accused of fascism, this position shows more consistency and respect than an individualistic one. Nonetheless governance in accord with these principles would mean a revolution. "This requirement demands the elimination of many accepted and institutionalised practices that ultimately rob us and nonhuman life of a normal future" (Westra et al. 2013:Loc. 714). SOP 8 is acknowledged in the application of the precautionary principle. The inclusion of risks is indispensible to good governance. A green ethics "need to include potential harm, that is, harm that may affect not only present but also future individuals" (Westra 1998a:47).[728]

Finally the rationale of instituting ecological integrity as a priority of governance is, as touched upon earlier, freedom inhibiting and maximising rather than minimising.

> "By rigorously forbidding actions that would diminish natural systems' capacities, in essence it does preserve maximum human choice without paternalistic attempts at defining or limiting those choices. [...] its primary focus is the respect for life in the most general form, yet its mandates are far more restrictive than mandates attempting to "balance" present preferences alone" (Westra 1998a:45; see also Conly 2013).

Though different in their outlook, republicanism and the demand of ecological integrity share two core goals: the minimisation of domination and the maximisation of potentiality (see Barry and Smith 2008). One main difference, it appears, is the weight given to interconnectedness. Whereas contemporary republicanism recognises interrelations and positive freedoms, it nonetheless is part of a liberal tradition and as such still undervalues interconnectedness and places great hopes in citizenry (see Bai 2013 and Fan 2013). The prioritisation of life support system can take place in a nondemocratic setting however. Following the established guideline of good governance, the harm principle, the capped capabilities approach, and the principle of ecological integrity, the next step is to look at the compatibility with nondemocratic governance.

---

[727] "There is an absolute imperative to protect wild areas if we hope to be able to preserve and restore enough of the planet's ecological integrity to ensure the continuation of critical life-support systems" (Westra et al. 2013:Loc. 752).
[728] "To date, however, no affluent democracy has seriously tried to enfranchise future people and there is no reason to expect much progress in the future" (Bell 2015:Loc. 1022).

Taking conditions for life as the absolute good appears self-explanatory. Here it is useful to recall Mill's remark: "Whatever can be proved to be good, must be so by being shown to be a means to something admitted to be good without proof" (1879:6). Anything that is considered valuable is dependent on survival. From there on sustainability is axiomatic to good governance.

> "Both justice and happiness are taken to be foundational in ethics. Integrity is arguably, an even more foundational concept, as it precedes the other two temporally and conceptually. One must be alive in order to be happy and to be treated justly" (Westra 1998a:9; cf. Rawls 2011).[729]

Life is a precondition for all things and a consistent green political theory must emphasize life support systems as such. Hereafter ecological integrity as an end is the first building block. What follows is a green ethics that is consistent with sustainability, thus actually means sustainable without stretching the concept.

> "The first moral principle is that nothing can be moral that is in conflict with the physical realties of our existence or cannot be seen to fit within the natural laws of our environment in order to support the primacy of integrity" (Westra 1998a:11).

Hence, ignoring realities is not only bad statesmanship but also immoral.[730] Foundations for accepting conscious destruction as immoral are inherent in many societies and reflected in the view that destroying the planet is at least 'somehow wrong'. In accordance, Westra et al.

> "assert that the reasons most often offered in support of the status quo (especially in affluent Northwest countries) do not stand up to scrutiny. First, the damage we wreak is potentially destabilizing to critical biophysical systems in the short term and interferes with slower natural evolutionary processes of change over the long term. Second, even democratic choices, if manipulated and uninformed, do not validate decisions that attack our life-support systems and our lives" (2013:Loc. 798).

Good governance needs to take the context into account and implement policies that take the future seriously. In *Visions of the Future. The Distant Past, Yesterday, Today, and Tomorrow*, Heilbroner made suggestions about the future by looking at the past in a Machiavellian fashion (1995). He concludes the book declaring:

> "Given the shortsideness of the wisest among us, perhaps a politics of caution is best suited for ordinary times. But in the face of strains and dysfunction, such politics may not be the best if we hope to alter that vision" (1995:111).

Precaution is focal, since threshold events are hard to locate policies need to be designed accordingly (Heilbroner 1976:32). Threshold events are non-linearities and in case of

---

[729] "Virtue as health is the precondition both for happiness and for agency. Without sufficient rational self-governance, and the courage, self-control, and justice which this requires and facilitates, we will not be the sort of agents which the public realm requires, and neither will we be best placed to achieve our own ends or to pursue happiness. Virtue is not an optional perfectionist pursuit. In this light, it is the basic parameter of health, without which soul and city risk crumbling into disorder, at worst dissolving into civil war. Health itself is the basis of agency, again not an optional perfectionist pursuit as one might take happiness to be, but rather the order without which one cannot coherently intend or act at all" (Lane 2011b:105).

[730] "Our primary moral responsibility is to the optimum capacity of natural life-support systems" (Westra 1998:45).

catastrophe more emergency governments will emerge. For decades, ecoauthoritarians have been warning that the limits to growth must be respected. When Hobbes condoned an authoritarian state, he did this on the basis of the recognition of the tradeoffs (2007). The consequence of unsustainable governance is a brutish life. If the state's purpose (and its Latin origins suggest this) is the protection of the common good, this has to be taken seriously. Here, arguments about the problem of subjectivity cannot hold. Nature is the ultimate common good. Good governance has to be in accordance with the necessities. Acknowledging life support systems as a precondition not only makes it a non-negotiable, it also legitimises a stronger role of science and the state. This part's elaboration suggested principles for coping with interrelatedness in a limited world and gave thereby guidelines for sound ecological governance. It showed the need to apply the harm principle consistently and proposed to supplement it with a capped capabilities approach as well as a strategic positivism. The first part and this second part make a clear case for guardianship. The protection of people from each other (and themselves) and the neglect of shared responsibility and duty justifies paternalism. Overall, the recognition of a limited and interconnected world demands reconceptualising good governance and further devising ecoauthoritarianism.

"If our leaders were all great and powerful, they could ban the keeping of pets and livestock, make a vegetarian diet compulsory, and fund a huge program of food synthesis by the chemical and biochemical industries—doing this might limit the loss of life to pets and livestock only. [...] Changes in lifestyle, agriculture, and eating habits are not a popular political option, and governments are more likely to take the easy way of using tax and subsidy to drive farms, industry, and the public in whatever direction their political ideology favors" (Lovelock 2009:Loc. 76).

Lovelock's proposals for powerful leaders will seem extreme to many. An autocracy with strong institutions would have certainly the means to become sustainable, if the leadership sets a green orientation. Once the sustenance of life support systems becomes the benchmark, other systems of governance can be evaluated for their sustainability. Building on earlier explorations, this part tries to supplement the environmental discourse by examining an alternative to democracy more intensively. After examining a philosophical and practical basis while integrating sciences, this part attends to advocacy of ecoauthoritarianism. First, this part presents arguments about autocracy and nature and before reviewing meritocracy with a reflection of China as an approximation to meritocracy and its potential for green governance. It then briefly sketches an ecomeritocracy attempting to provide one way of how it could be envisioned. Last, it will formulate policies accordingly and venture into the more practical aspects by proposing strategies such as population management programs and footprint budgeting. With such, this part assesses assumptions of ecoauthoritarianism and attempts to enrich green theory by openly engaging with unpopular ideas. It gives a nonconformist interpretation of governing and living in accordance with material necessities (and social justice).

Ecoauthoritarianism appears to be a way of governance to which people mostly subscribe behind closed doors. Unlike scholars defending democracy, who often perceive their advocacy as a self-evident matter – they either point it out or do not feel the need to point it out – ecoauthoritarians are harder to be classified as such.[731] Not only is it seemingly a taboo within Western academia, since it goes against many essential beliefs, it can also be easily used to dismiss any proposals as mentioned above. One is also more likely to find ecoauthoritarians in the natural sciences than the social sciences (Dryzek 2005).[732] Notably, the connection between green theory of agency and green theory of values seems to be rather a historical by-product than

---

[731] Usually claims are carefully phrased: "Democratic society will pursue short-term satisfaction and choose their leaders accordingly. Thus success in limiting consumption will require an element of benevolent authoritarianism" (Randers 2012:Loc. 847-50). Formulations are frequently soft statements such as "an element of benevolent authoritarianism".

[732] It can only be speculated that it is connected to the tendency of the former to be positivist and to the fact that the relevant community is bigger.

a rational outcome of commitments to the understanding and protection of nature (see Dobson 2007:105ff.).[733] Goodin questions the common green package deal stating that in his view

> "you would not have to practice holistic medicine or have some wild-eyed faith in the powers of grassroots democracy in order to be green to the core, in the public policy terms that matter most to the fate of the earth" (2006:15).

Hierarchies are preeminent in many areas. Whereas claiming that the lion is the head of the animal kingdom is anthropomorphism – after all he can kill other animals but does not have authority over them – assuming that humans can be separated from nature is equally disputable. Justifying the classification line between humans and animals has been an enduring task and many ecologists and ethicists use human animal and non-human animal to point at its arbitrariness (Singer 1975; Westra 1998a). Flourishing in green thought is generally defined as living in accordance to one's nature (Eckersley 2004; Humphrey 2007). Whence putting human animals into their own category apart from the partly hierarchical animal kingdom allows for a redefinition of human flourishing.[734] Otherwise there is no reason to assume that democracy is natural to humans and many reasons against the idea can be provided. By this definition, human animals attain a unique position to the point where each human theoretically gets to identify/actualise his individual-specific nature by following life's choices. Again, democracy is not the 'self-evident benchmark'. Perhaps the best way to judge an alternative to democracy is by first looking at autocracy, since it is commonly defined as the opposite.

---

[733] "Political commitments such as justice, democracy and liberty cannot be developed from purely ecological considerations, although ecological ideas can have implications for their preferred form" (Connelly et al. 2012:73).
[734] Discussing different forms of animal groups and their form of organization is beyond the point of this work. The label 'natural' does not carry moral significance for the arguments advanced anyway.

The first national environmental plans were established by a few pre-eminently authoritarian countries such as Madagascar and Ghana in 1987 (Freedom House 1998 and Muno 2010:353).[735] A year later the Kingdom of Denmark was the first democratic nation to introduce a plan. Though the existence of such a plan is not necessarily meaningful, it is nonetheless symbolic. Wurster's empirical study sees no evidence in support of the better capacity of autocratic states to ensure either weak or strong sustainability (2013). Comparing autocracies' and democracies' environmental performance as well, Ward notes that many oil-producing countries are autocracies, which can distort overall statistics (2008). Since oil production is positively correlated to high ecological footprints, the system itself might not be pivotal. The lack of evidence noted by Wurster has little significance though anyway. Ecoauthoritarian states do not exist. Consequently, an empirical study of the environmental performance of autocracies cannot falsify ecoauthoritarian assumptions. Humphrey notes that

> "although this literature tended to a naïve view of what authoritarian regimes would be able to achieve, the empirical rebuttal of the claim that green authoritarianism is needed, i.e. that no heretofore existing authoritarian regime has a good environmental record ('ecocide' in the USSR for example) is rather beside the point [...]. The only appropriate counter-example would be a failed authoritarian regime that had prioritized environmental goals. After all, authoritarian regimes do tend to achieve those things to which they accord highest priority, even if inefficiently and often with great cruelty" (2004:Loc. 3089-95).

What could be compared is the performance of different regime types, set aside the small-N problem, but as long as there is no autocracy that commits itself to green values beyond all others, ecoauthoritarianism cannot be falsified as a theory in general. The negative performance of democracies, on the other hand, does indicate a lack of capability in regard to sustainability. This is not to measure unfairly by different standards. Democratic theorists insist on democracy's core to be self-determination. Consequentially, the lack of evidence for a sustainable democracy weighs more. The fact that 'the people' did not decide to develop a green democracy and the weakness of green parties have repercussions on the viability of a green democratic state. Any discussion of ecoauthoritarianism needs to be understood as a discussion of potentiality at this point. In particular, as long as democracy theorists continue to discuss the ideal and thereby deny democratic reality extensive examination, they cannot reject the proposition of non-democracy "on the grounds of its anticipated failure" (Graham 2013:Loc. 920-25). Until a state declares itself an 'ecostate' i.e. makes environmental integrity a priority, claims can hardly be falsified. It is noteworthy though that Chinese family planning had a positive impact on the global population.

---

[735] The quality of the Freedom House Reports is disputed, but details are not relevant here.

Some scholars argue that ecoauthoritarianism would be likely to fail because history proved dictatorships too immobile and incompetent to react to dynamic processes (Leggewie and Welzer 2011:172). This reservation can be lifted. If one looks at recent Chinese history it is easy to demonstrate that the politburo has actually displayed the widest range of possible policies (Bell 2015; see also Colomer 2011).[736] While innovation in Western democracies depends on legislation periods, a politburo can also implement the measurements judged necessary with more continuity (Leggewie and Welzer 2011:65; Bell 2015). This is most certainly an advantage in environmental politics.

> "Ultimately, the most important lesson is that effective planning requires strong, sustained political leadership that can be institutionalised across policy sectors through legislation, institutional reform, target-setting and monitoring of progress" (Carter 2007:312).

A strong state with guaranteed continuity in leadership meets such a requirement. The often invoked 'dictator dilemma' can mean that

> "the more a dictator rules by repression, the less reliable information he can expect from the population. This can be a big disadvantage as far as the implementation of reasonable environmental protection measures is concerned. The use of repression in autocracies can even cover up – to a certain degree and for a limited period of time – weak legitimacy produced by poor ecological output performance" (Wurster 2013:79).

Such a consideration is important, but does not apply if the regime is focused on environmental protections and its evaluative instruments utilise science. It merely describes how destruction can be passed over in general. The focus on output legitimacy could also make a regime more likely to focus on effectiveness than on simulation. Shahar expresses Wurster's points similarly writing that a

> "fearful and uninvolved citizenry is also not likely to provide the sort of honest, informative, and critical feedback that would enable administrators to calibrate policies to the details of local circumstances, detect their own mistakes, and catch misbehaving officials who undermine the pursuit of public goals" (2015:360).[737]

Granted this was the inevitable effect of nondemocratic governance, democracy would have to prove that they successfully employ such feedback in order for it to weigh in as a comparative disadvantage. The existence of 'alternatives' and social norms play a role in the reporting of

---

[736] Variety within nondemocratic states regularly remains unnoticed. "Authoritarian states usually experience significant institutional changes without the outside world paying much attention" (Gilley 2009:170).

[737] "Command systems might seem to have a greater capacity to respond to a new type of threat because the people in command can simply direct people and resources to deal with it. But these systems have several inherent difficulties in actually doing this. Because relatively few people have an input into decisionmaking, there is lower capacity to recognize novel threats and to innovate against them. Subjects—those who are expected to follow orders—are typically less than enthusiastic in obeying. Finally, change can be threatening to those with power and privilege, so maintaining the relations of power" (Martin 2013:Loc. 5857-61). However, "experiments defy common assumptions about authoritarian rule, such as exploring ways of harnessing nonstate actors to provide health care for the elderly and rights for migrant workers, using transparency as a governance tool to curb corruption, and improving accountability by allowing citizens to request information. Different Chinese cities are also experimenting with different ways of evaluating the performance of public officials" (Bell 2015:Loc. 3583).

errors and in the mechanisms to fix them across all political systems (Gilley 2009:86). Whereas there might be less feedback, there are also fewer veto players, which is a huge advantage given that the status quo is unsustainable and a shift is needed. A further possible reservation to this being a problem is that environmental advocates in contrast to other critical groups may actually not be perceived as threatening to the regime and hence their input is treated as more 'acceptable' and could even be a niche for engagement. Doyle and Simpson note for their research that

"[g]reen groups that deal with issues of ecology are permitted, even encouraged, but only within a tightly apolitical discourse and while green activism is interpreted by some scholars as questioning of the system and roots for democracy evidence from Iran contradicts"

the assumption (2006:759; see also Hilton 2013 and Zhang et al. 2013). Again, typical assumptions of democratic theory do not necessarily hold true in regard to the politics of nature.

So far, it appears that autocracies are not better in altering people's environmental consciousness and "that authoritarian environmentalism is more effective introducing policy outputs than outcomes" (Gilley 2012:287).[738] Again, this might be due to the fact that none of them actually prioritises ecosystem health, thus governments may follow the same pattern of simulation and weak commitments described earlier. Gilley describes emissions in the case of China as "seen by the leadership largely as a matter of international diplomacy rather than environmental sustainability" (2012:295). Hamilton compares Beijing's attitude with the Bush government that has

"a number of policies designed to cut the emissions intensity of electricity and transport, but the sheer expansion of the economy is swamping all attempts at constraining the growth of carbon pollution" (2010:4).

Dryzek et al. are pessimistic about prospects of a green PRC stating that while they are in an advantageous position, they have not shown such tendencies. They explain that China is "attractive to climate change authoritarians (for example Beeson, 2010) because its government seems capable of acting quickly and decisively, having accepted the reality of climate change", but for them

"China perhaps illustrates the inability of authoritarian systems to cope with multifaceted, complex problems associated with greenhouse gas emissions from multiple sources— introducing new technologies is by far the simplest part of the puzzle, and that is all China has been able to do so far (though in 2012 it began experimenting with a localized emissions trading scheme)" (Dryzek et al. 2013:Loc. 1484).

---

[738] China for Gilley demonstrates "the basic tenets of environmental authoritarianism with two amendments. First, even with executive authority concentrated, implementation becomes highly dispersed in a large, decentralised system; in modern governance, much policy will be made at these downstream stages. Secondly, even when public participation is narrowly defined in official frameworks, there may be considerable mid-level activism within those narrow boundaries. Society does not become dormant even in an authoritarian model, but merely shifts its involvements towards acceptable areas" (2012:293).

Gilley mentions that on the one hand policies can be established fast, but on the other hand the integration of civil society actors and local administration could have led to greater legitimacy (2012:298). Protest over compensation and exclusion from the decision-making process could possibly be avoided. Assessments of the PRC's environmental politics differ greatly, but before going into detail, this chapter has to look at autocracy and its environmental practice in general.

Ward approached the topic by facilitating commonly used indicators such as footprint and therefore asked the question if "liberal democracies perform better than autocracies on sustainability indicators?" and taking a closer look he points out that "[t]heory strongly suggests that they should, but the empirical evidence is ambiguous" (2008:386). This statement needs to be divided into two separate claims. To study dynamics of environmental politics it is vital to directly confront the assumptions against 'autocracies'. It is necessary to examine which theory "strongly suggests". Concentrating on a rational choice perspective mainly, Ward claims the theoretical basis that democracies should behave more sustainably is clear (2008). He lists arguments from rational choice perspectives against sustainability in autocracy, which are roughly dividable into four separate, but non-exclusive arguments here:

1. Authoritarian regimes had no incentive to implement sustainable policies and focused on gaining legitimacy through rapid economic growth.

2. Since they control a large amount of resources, they were prone to use these resources to ensure followers and see less gain from providing public goods such as a functioning ecosystem. Plus, environmental regulations would affect the ruling elite disproportionately.

3. Authoritarian regimes were more likely to neglect future generations.

4. Democracies fight each other less and authoritarian regimes are said to be more likely to lapse into civil wars and war always involves exploitation of resources.

All four claims can be contended.[739] Herein, a distinction between different forms of authoritarian regimes is not only theoretically desirable; their performance in practice logically depends on its form (Wurster 2013; Lauth 2010a:96).[740] Either way the four assumptions represent a distorted picture. They should be discussed in general before focusing on ecomeritocracy as a specific regime type.

---

[739] This points are partly in line with Burnell's claims listed in the conclusion of the first part (2009:3), but deserve a separate analysis focusing on autocracy.

[740] Studying actual performance reveals that "results are rather mixed within the autocratic spectrum. Monarchies and civilian dictatorships are superior to military regimes with regard to 'weak sustainability'. With regard to 'strong sustainability', however, the story is different. Here, monarchies perform worse than their autocratic counterparts, while civilian autocracies achieve significantly better results than the mean of the democratic states. Considering the findings, the variance between subtypes of democratic and autocratic regimes implies that comparative averages alone are not sufficient for explaining performance results" (Wurster 2013:86).

The first argument totally negates the possibility of any kind of benevolence by a ruling class and further denies alternative sources of legitimation. It neither allows for the chance that the ruling elite actually cares for the subjects, nor does it take into account that not all authoritarian regimes are short-lived (see Bell and Li 2013).[741] Arguments for any regime being short-sighted can be easily found. Arguing that autocratic governments do not last as long as democratic ones, also fails to acknowledge that democratic governments are subject to election circles (Gilley 2009:170).[742] Sustainable policies will provide legitimation in the future. Reversely, failure to implement policies today is more likely to become relevant and cannot be blamed on the opposition as easily in an ecomeritocracy. The deterioration of the environment is already a factor of instability, but is likely to be the main threat to any government in the future (see Beeson 2010; Lekakis and Kousis 2013:20). In fact, many protests in the PRC are directed towards grievances over the effects of pollution (Veauthier 2012; Zhang et al. 2013). The first argument therefore also fails to take actuality into account. Since environmental problems are already a great source of discontent, it is wrong to focus on economic performance as the only legitimation today. It is naïve to believe that a cleaner environment will not lead to higher approval rates and that nondemocratic governments must be blind to this possibility. While economic growth may be a source of legitimacy, there are not only other forms of outputs, but also other orientation of legitimacy.[743] For instance, at first sight Weber's typology into charismatic, legalistic and traditional does not need any kind of output orientation (2014). Rational choice literature typically underestimates other sources of legitimation and legitimacy, but the limited explanatory value of such approaches is well known. If political science denies any form of legitimacy to regimes that lasts over decades, the concept becomes meaningless (Tong 2011). There may be grounds for arguing that despite taking away people's freedom, a state can claim the authority that goes with legitimacy on distinct grounds and that legitimacy does not have to be interpreted in freedom-centred terms.[744] "Perhaps the state is successful in epistemic terms, letting people reliably identify the requirements of justice without subjecting them to the rule of others" (Pettit 2012:148). Looking at this particular matter, Tong argues regarding the Chinese government that

> "the current regime legitimacy is maintained because of the historically rooted moral bond between the state and society and the societal expectation that the state would be responsible for the wellbeing of the population" (2011:141).

---

[741] Shearman and Smith write that the Catholic Church proves the potential longevity of authoritarian structures (2007:135).

[742] Bührs actually proposes empowering democratic governments by making them less democratic in a sense (2012). He proposes that extending electoral circles would be a possible measure against short-termism, but at the same time doubts its effectiveness given the priority of economics.

[743] Regime support in China does not depend on income (Gilley 2009:172).

[744] "A legitimate state is less dominating over its citizens because legitimate use of power minimizes the negative consequences of power" (Gilley 2009:140).

Describing how the regime sustains legitimacy, he uses concepts such a as morality, benevolence, compassion, responsibility and welfare. These concepts imply that the regime should have a rather long-term and holistic approach to governing. Such form of legitimacy is highly desirable for an ecomeritocracy. It would not only help compliance, but in the future possibly mean sustainability by itself.

Focusing on the economy, Josephson describes the environmental degradation by autocracies in the name of progress (2005). He is right about the devastation, but the interpretation of it could be different. The aim was economic growth above all and this aim had been achieved (see Humphrey 2004). The target was not an improved environment. However, if it was not possible to set economic growth as the only target in the past, it is certainly not possible now (e.g. Bell 2015). If the Chinese government relied purely on economic performance, the inevitable slowdown of the economy "would have to shift some of the burden of legitimation to political and procedural bases, such as more competitive elections and more political incorporations" (Tong 2011:142). It is questionable, whether this would be in the interest of the central government. In fact "the promotion of cadres in experimental low-carbon-emission cities such as Hangzhou is based on criteria that incorporate environmental, energy, and climate-change-related performance criteria" (2015:Loc. 1081). GDP has stopped to be a measurement of officials' performances in many smaller cities and instead poverty and environmental quality have become part of the evaluation (Bell 2015:Loc. 3592, see also Gilley 2009). Whereas a major factor in the bad environmental record of autocracy was their concentration on economic growth, such a shift can mean a major step towards the advancement of environmental governance. Bell asserts that the

> "reason for China's pollution problem is that in the past cadres tended to be promoted almost exclusively based on standards that measured economic growth, but wider assessment criteria are being used now: targets for pollution control are being linked to cadre evaluation processes" (2015:Loc. 1078).

If followed through further, arguments in favour of an ecomeritocracy could be evaluated empirically. Developments should be watched closely, especially since the environment has become a matter of concern for the elites.

Murphy and Morgan studied another example of a nondemocratic government, namely Cuba, and found that the country's greening is significant (2013). The authors understand Cuba as a model since "in the past two decades it has reduced its carbon dioxide (CO_2) emissions by 25 percent, from 3.2 tons per person in 1990 to 2.4 tons in 2009" (2013:Loc. 7229-32). Although factors other than the particular system of governance certainly play a role in this context such a development leads into the right direction. It shows success despite limited resources with a strategy that is not privileging economic growth, "material success as measured by energy consumption is secondary, while other quality-of-life issues are given priority" (2013:Loc. 7459-61).

The second argument is focused on the dangers of power, but disregards opportunities. If the government holds a significant amount of the country's natural resources, it holds huge power. From an outcome-oriented and instrumental perspective, this is again a mere description. The chance to implement extensive policies is a precondition to sustainable governance. In general the centralisation of power can have positive and negative effects (Connelly et al. 2012:315). It is true that structures of patronage can lead to the overexploitation of resources, but control over the natural resources also has huge potential. Burnell points out that

> "[t]here is an important analytical distinction between the political freedom of a regime to make political choices favouring climate mitigation over the economy with or without incurring political risk (the political opportunity structure) and the executive capability to implement and enforce the policy choice, which is a matter of governance" (2009:14).

Governments that are in charge of a vast part of the resources can implement strict environmental laws and therefore protect local ecosystems.[745] Additionally, research finds that "in certain cases, crude command-and-control regulations can perform better than sophisticated incentive regulations" (Lyon 2009:49). Governments are also more likely to take the whole society into account and maintain public goods for the benefits of society than private actors. This is independent of the regime type. Therefore a large amount of resources in government control is rather an opportunity than a risk theoretically. Government can play a huge role in providing services that are not profitable economically but which inhibit huge externalities such as protecting forests. It is equally questionable, whether authoritarian governments have less "political advantage" in providing public goods (Ward 2008:387; cf. Tullock and Buchanan 2001). One could even make a stronger case for the need for an autocracy to focus on public goods in contrast to any given democracy. Some scholars suggest that dictatorships "secure in their rule can take the long view and, in the manner of stationary bandits, have a greater incentive to invest in public goods" (Eaton and Kostka 2014:367). As touched upon above, rational choice theory classifies autocracies as performance-orientated. While a one-sided view only understands this in immediate economic terms, provision of public goods is a huge part of a

---

[745] "The combination of a higher degree of state autonomy and a society habituated to the exercise of coercive power may confer certain advantages on "eco-elites" in non-democracies. China's rapid advances in environmental protection have made it a focal point of debate over the relative merits of democratic and authoritarian environmentalism. Proponents of China's approach admire its state leaders' ability to compel businesses and citizens to comply with stringent environmental regulations. Chinese authoritarians' toolkits contain many more, and sharper, implements to elicit such compliance. For instance, many energy-inefficient companies that failed to comply with demanding energy efficiency regulations have found their electricity and water supply summarily cut off by local governments" (Eaton and Kostka 2014:360).

government's overall performance. Since a democracy has the advantage of bearing procedural legitimacy, i.e. the government has a mandate through elections, it is only logical to assume that the lack of this very source of legitimation leads to autocracies trying to make up for this leeway in other dimensions. To assume that legitimacy i.e. public support or at least silent consent of the public is unnecessary for a nondemocratic government would be delusional. If the argument is only aiming towards monetary as well as any other material benefits for the ruling elite, it still rests on weak logic, since it overestimates the value of materialist goods in regard to immeasurable goods such as power and status. Patronage is a possibility in democracy as well as autocracy.[746] The argument about self-interested elite rule sets up a trap for advocates of liberal democracy. It is self-defeating, since the same rationale could doubt that the current *demos* (quasi an elite by chance of birth) will support restrictions. Reasons to believe that today's *demos* could make decisions based on the expected interests of future generations have been dismantled earlier. Whereas the public is less likely to engage in the consequentialist thinking proposed as a basis for an ecomeritocracy, an expert chosen on this very basis is by definition motivated to expand the morally relevant community. "Meritocratically selected leaders can make long-term-oriented decisions that consider the interests of all relevant stakeholders, including future generations" (Bell 2015:Loc. 3377). Democratically selected ones are seen as bound to the voter's will even if most abstractly – and the future has no interest group power either.

The third argument has been partly discussed already. It holds that authoritarian regimes are likely to ignore future generations, because their power basis is often weak. Depending on the classification, a vast majority of the democracies in the world may also rest on weak foundations. One speculation assumes that autocracies have shorter time horizons than democracies, because the median voter is assumed to have less "incentives to maximize rents and exploitation of natural resources" than an autocrat (Shum 2009:289). Difficulties with this speculation were discussed extensively. Frequently changing governments, on the other hand, hinders stable environmental policies across systems. If future-oriented governing depended on the means of

---

[746] Democracies are not immune to corruption, instead corruption is a problem spread across different systems. Democratic theory cannot redefine democracy in a way that excludes corruption. "In a democracy, leaders get their legitimacy from being chosen by the people, and the people can change their leaders in the next election if they aren't satisfied. If the next batch of leaders is still corrupt, to a certain extent the people need to blame themselves. Corruption in a democracy doesn't mean that the political system is not democratic" (Bell 2015:Loc. 2234). What is understood as corruption also varies depending on culture and legal code. Here, Bell sees corruption, even when legalised, as a bigger legitimacy problem for nondemocratic states, since they do not have the kind of consent by the people that is provided by elections. Again, though undesirable in normative terms, Duit and Hall could not find a negative effect of corruption on environmental performance (2014). In some occasions, what is translated as corruption or nepotism in Western academia has shown to contribute to better implementation. For example, "Xiaoyi's leadership group has also used its guanxi ties to induce local businesses to share the burden of reducing Xiaoyi's economic dependence on coal" (Eaton and Kostka 2014:377).

controlling power, as put forward in this argument (see Ward 2008), the reverse may be expected. It could be hypothesized then that the more centralised control, the more likely is a future-orientation.

Last, the argument of democratic peace is only valid for wars of democracy against democracy. The number of democracies going to war against democracies is significantly lower (Heidelberger Institut für Internationale Konfliktforschung 2016). But the argument here also states that autocracies are more likely to engage in civil wars and therefore more prone to extreme exploitation of natural resources. Particularly because wars are commonly about control over resources as well as the choice of system it does not make sense to draw a line between peaceful democracies and non-peaceful authoritarian regimes. Bell highlights that standardly listed consequentialist arguments for democracy, democracies being peaceful and democracies avoiding famines, also apply to Singapore and China who "have consciously implemented meritocratic reforms designed to improve the quality of political leadership (starting from the mid-1960s in Singapore and the early 1980s in China)" (2015:Loc. 410). Prominently, states with weak institutions are likely to fail and turn into chaos, institutions are more important than the rationale of rule (Huntington 1969). For this reason, Burnell advises that

> "international actors committed to promoting democracy, [should consider] that in developing countries stable authoritarian rule might be better placed than regimes in political transition to mitigate climate change as well as adapt to its effects" (2009:1).

Frequently dangerous transitions are supported by foreign democracies under the banner of democracy promotion. Encouraged transitions, without adequate foundations, regularly lead to long-term resource depleting wars. If, on the other hand, the argument of democratic peacefulness is redirected from the level of official declarations of war to the question of environmental destruction and depleting by war, the picture changes even more. Dwarfing all other countries in military spending, the United States clearly also has the worst environmental impact in this area. This is particularly true, if the full extent of the extremely polluting military machinery is measured. Above all, the picture of democratic peace is likely to dissolve when weapon-manufacturing and exporting is excluded from the idea of peacefulness.

4.2. MERITOCRACY AND *THE CHINA MODEL* AS AN EXAMPLE

In contrast to what is known about democracy in theory and practice, little is known about meritocracy. Historically meritocracy is not a novel idea. Two of the most influential philosophers, namely Plato and Confucius, argued for a rule based on skills and virtue (Plato 1982 and Confucius 2015). In Platonic philosophy, ruling is a matter of obligation and position in the just order. Plato wanted the philosopher king to be someone who does not want to rule. Confucian philosophy also derives responsibility from superior skills and virtues. Both scholars appear to support a hierarchy in regard to power, but do not tie personal benefits to holding positions of power. The emphasis lies on duties rather than on rights. Plato and Confucius believed that human qualities can be independent heritage. Meritocracy demands equal opportunities and the selection of rulers on the basis of merit. Plato and Confucius believed that such merit can be understood. This chapter will discuss meritocracy as elaborated by Bell using China as an example (2015; Bell and Li 2013). The reason for this choice is rather obvious. Although meritocratic mechanisms can be found in many places, the selection of actual politicians by meritocratic means is rare. As with any other system ideal and real types diverge.

> "Chinese-style meritocracy is plagued with imperfections, but few would deny that the system has performed relatively well compared to democratic regimes of comparable size and level of economic development, not to mention family run dictatorships in the Middle East and elsewhere. And the world is watching China's experiment with meritocracy" (Bell 2015:Loc. 150).

Though not directed towards sustainable governance, the Chinese system provides valuable insights into setting 'measurable' competency and success as a benchmark for politicians and politics. Commonly, Bell finds that the political meritocratic mechanisms of the Chinese system lack systematic study. His discussions can enhance an understanding of meritocracy and lay the foundation for an evaluation of the PRC's sustainability i.e. the potential for green governance. [747]

As in democracy, perceived fairness of selection is a foundation for legitimacy and system survival, thus prerequisite for rule abidance (Gilley 2009; Doherty and Wolak 2012; Newig 2012). The Chinese examination system, despite its flaws, is viewed as fair enough to support the regime (Bell 2015:Loc. 1773). Whereas legitimacy is hard to measure both surveys and the fact that the regime persists indicate at least a minimum in legitimacy. In particular the legitimacy grounded in the success of meritocratic elements in advancing a common good is of interest for this elaboration. On the ideological dimension,

---

[747] "One would perhaps expect the rich world to lead the way. But the rich countries are the most democratic, and hence, as I see it, the most short-term. In fact they are so short-term that it may well be that more authoritarian states are the first to move. Current developments in China are interesting. The authorities are experimenting with the idea of a harmonious society (in other words, a society in harmony with nature) seeking adequate well-being for all, rather than maximum disposable income. A problem may be that the Chinese leadership is too far ahead of its people" (Randers 2012:Loc. 4223-27).

"the state or regime seeks to be seen as morally justified in the eyes of the people by virtue of certain ideas that it instantiates and expresses in its educational system, political speeches, and public policies" (2015:Loc. 2750; cf. Kagan 2008:69).

The idea of meritocracy is deeply ingrained in Chinese culture, represented in the various ways to describe the virtuousness of a ruler in Putonghua i.e. Standard Chinese. Confucian philosophy embraces a form of *noblesse oblige* (Confucius 2015*)*.[748] While accepting inequality, it assigns no special rights to those who possess greater abilities. The rationale for this is based on rather self-evident observation: "Being born with ability confers no moral right to wealth because what one is born with, or without, is not of one's own doing" (Bell 2015:Loc. 178). 'Equal ability' as in political equality then matters less. Being born with or without ability has different moral repercussions if seen as natural and a matter of chance. In fact, Confucian philosophy clearly recognised that people are unequal, but this is not seen as a reason to deserve more, but reason to have more responsibility.[749] Power conceivably carries responsibility (see Jonas 1984:174). In contrast to the primacy of autonomy, the

"Confucian-inspired ideal of harmony is that relations among family members, citizens, and countries, as well as between humans and nature, are key to human flourishing, both in the sense that they matter for well-being and in the moral sense that they generate social obligations. Those relations should all be characterized by peaceful order and respect for diversity" (Bell 2015:Loc. 1137).

Acknowledging interrelation can lead to an easier acceptance of responsibility towards each other, society and nature. As long as the government continues to take responsibility for the people's livelihood, the concept of "parental officials" will remain in the societal subconscience (Tong 2011:152; see Chu et al. 2010). Asked in surveys, the Chinese population supports political meritocracy and displays "strong attachment to "guardianship discourse," defined as the need to identify high-quality rulers who enact good policies on behalf of their people and society" (Bell 2015:Loc. 3180).[750] This leads Bell to suggest that in the Chinese context a combination of democracy and meritocracy at different levels is suitable.

4.2.1. THE SELECTION OF VIRTUOUS GUARDIANS

Corruption is currently one of the biggest problems, but Bell proposes instead of trying to abolish it by democratic votes, a reduction of corruption by establishing independent checks: "reducing dependence between the public and private sectors, increasing the salaries of public officials, and

---

[748] Buddhism and Daoism are less influential in Chinese political thought.
[749] Ignoring political inequality is also likely to preserve deficient mechanisms of support for the powerless. Taking responsibility may be intimately connected with the recognition of inequality.
[750] My own research in Changsha in 2012 is in accord with these findings.

implementing a more systematic program in Confucian moral education" (Bell 2015:Loc. 2468; see also Bai 2013 and Fan 2013).[751] Again, institutions are essential for functioning governments. The accountability in an autocracy is correlated to the degree of institutionalisation (Petersen 2009:19).[752] Accountability has to be taken seriously, as discussed earlier. Feedback is a part of such mechanisms. Notably,

> "research suggests that people behave badly when they are not held personally accountable, when nobody raises a critical voice, and when human beings over whom they have power are dehumanized and deindividualized" (Bell 2015:Loc. 1176).

This also means that the overall performance of governance is dependent on decision makers being accountable and the rule of law (see Cicero 2001). "Accountability mechanisms are particularly important in averting disasters; in their absence, major ecological damages in the Soviet Union and Eastern Europe went on unchecked for too long" (Bradhan 1999:102). Here, Bradhan underscores that India has not been able to succeed in poverty reduction at the level of the Chinese government. As discussed, diverse input is far from being a monopoly of democracy. Nonetheless, concerns over malfeasance need to be addressed.

Securing benevolence is a major obstacle for a political system.[753] Dahl asks the central question whether the guardians would be virtuous (1989:76; see also Stretton 1976).[754] Discussing ecoauthoritarianism, Carter similarly poses the questions

> "how can its [power] exercise be guaranteed to remain benevolent? Even if a particular leader does turn out to be genuinely benevolent, even if he or she is not corrupted by the exercise of power or the need to retain it, how can it be guaranteed that those who inherit his or her position will be equally benevolent?" (2013:26).

Yet, the same critique can be applied to democracies.[755] Rational choice theorists allude to this indirectly when regarding the motives of politicians as self-interest either way (see Simmons 2011). Notably, they often understand self-interest as less dangerous than altruistic motivation,

---

[751] "Imperial China may offer some lessons: Tang dynasty law prohibited merchants and artisans from social intercourse with officials, banned the upper echelons of the public service from entering urban markets, and forbade merchants and artisans from sitting for the public service exams and holding public office. Such drastic measures may be difficult to implement today, but imposing some limits on social interaction between public and private officials can help: for example, Zhang Lu suggests that China can learn from an anticorruption law in South Korea passed in 2001 that forbids public officials and business persons from playing golf together" (Bell 2015:Loc. 2349). Under a political philosophy focused on liberal rights such restrictions would be understood as invasive. Under a political philosophy that focuses on duty, on the other hand, this is possible (see Plato 1982) and could protect the powerless against nepotism.

[752] One proposal for ensuring accountability is to reintroduce formerly known institutions such as independent academies (see Bell 2015:Loc.5197).

[753] If a benevolent dictatorship was absurd, would not a benevolent public be at least equally absurd?

[754] A rational choice approach poses the general question why bureaucrats should work for the common good, since no punishment is expected (Simmons 2012). Such a question is based on an extremely reductionist view of society that is deprived of all social context. One may ask why not more people steal, since chances to get caught are very low.

[755] The "positive picture of democracy is only possible with certain demanding assumptions: not only that there are virtuous people willing to run for offices, but also that voters are themselves virtuous enough to want to put those people in office and have enough knowledge of the candidates to pick the right ones" (Chan 2013:40).

since *homo oeconomicus* appears more restricted, calculated and calculable.[756] Here, clear differences between political theories are drawn.

> "Contrary to the Western preference for political theory that is based on rational calculation and institutional logic, the Chinese have traditionally emphasized a normative order and the moral responsibilities of their leaders. The mutually (both the state and society) perceived state responsibility for the wellbeing of the population provides the foundation for regime legitimacy" (Tong 2011:156).[757]

Though Tong's description and a rational choice approach are in stark contrast, due to diversity theories and practice are more overlapping.[758] Gilley evokes Weber for whom "legitimacy was a citizen's willingness to comply with a system of rule, out of not selfishness, expedience, or habit but rather considered belief in the moral validity of the rule" (Gilley 2009:3; Weber 2014).[759] A core problem of political meritocracy is the assessment of virtue. While ability in form of knowledge and techniques can be tested in exams, virtues beyond persistence are hard to prove in such a form (Bell 2013:22). Bell writes that in comparison to 'before' when top students might have been uninterested in party membership, the Communist Party today takes "only high-performing students who have undergone thorough character checks are admitted" (2013:21). This form of selection hints at highly a selective system.[760]

Proving the integrity of people is problematic. Beginning with Plato those arguing in favour of actual meritocracy assume that a training in morals will make one a better leader (1982; see also Bai 2013). Bell describes the Chinese examination as such a means of training (2015). While he does not argue that such training makes immoral action impossible, his elaborations on the possible effects of such training are reasonable. Whereas moral training gives no guarantee, the likelihood for morally right behaviour increases. Believing purely in knowledge as the main driver would mean the same trap as discussed earlier in the value-action gap. Yet, a training of moral virtue could have practical parts to avoid such disconnect. Contemporary China sends their leaders into the villages in order to learn about rural people's lives and challenges (Bell

---

[756] In contrast, Heilbroner underlined in his book *Behind the Veil of Economics* that "the impetus to amass wealth is only a sublimation of deeper-lying nonrational drives and needs" (1988:46).

[757] As advanced in the context of procedural and substantive legitimacy, institutions can be valued for either or both (see Gilley 2009:67).

[758] The British House of Lords is a compelling case. Comparing its debates with those of the House of Commons in regard to environmental politics could be enlightening.

[759] "Willing acts of consent, then, redeem invisible power from the charge of being nefarious. Further, there is always a gnawing suspicion that habit and tradition may account for some of the legal and justificatory legitimacy of states" (Gilley 2009:7).

[760] My personal experience while teaching at Hunan International Economics University in Changsha in 2011/12 was different. Being friends with a 22 year old party member, I witnessed how people unknown to her called her a couple hours before the recruitment meeting and asked for her endorsement. They seemed to have considered her support as normal. I further observed a student asking the Spanish teacher for a D, since a failing grade would 'look bad' on his application. The expectations of the class were extremely low, so a passing grade did not mean anything. The student had simply failed to attend class. Although this is purely anecdotal, it still leads me to doubt that the party was applying high standards either on character or educational performance at least at the entrance level.

2015). Despite the program needing strong enforcement, it is evident that such experiences add to the skill set. The cognitive framework of the leadership is widened.[761] Machiavelli advised that the prince practices for war and thereby gains familiarity with his lands (2009). Meanwhile the prince would be in contact with his inferiors and possibly learn about their issues. Bringing different findings together, it is fair to assume that such comprehensive training, which can be understood as a training in morals, schools empathy and therefore the guardian's virtue.[762]

However, one problem with meritocratic selection is the comparative educational advantage of wealthy elites, but once economic inequality decreases, so does this advantage (Bell 2015:Loc. 2606). In spite of this advantage examinations are a relatively fair way of selection. The governance in the PRC is marked by "evaluations at each step of the way, to move further up the chain of political command" and though still flawed

> "has been substantially "meritocratized" over the past couple of decades and the political impact of "meritocratization" has been far more substantial than the widely reported and researched local-level elections. Yet somehow—until very recently—the "meritocratization" of the political system in China has fallen under the radar screen of major media outlets and academic researchers have not paid sufficient attention to it (Bell 2015:Loc. 3322).

Bell is an exemption in that he describes China in a more positive light than usual. Judging the country not by the standards of democratic but wider political theory, he summarises:

> "The advantages of "actually existing" meritocracy in the CCP are clear. Cadres are put through a grueling process of talent selection, and only those with an excellent record of past performance are likely to make it to the highest levels of government. The training process includes programs for public administration at various levels of government, consulting experts, learning from best practices abroad, rotational career postings though different sectors, as well as the cultivation of virtues such as compassion for the disadvantaged by means such as limited periods of work in poor rural areas" (2015:Loc. 3363).

Mistakes are not only reduced by the fact that for the purpose of becoming a member of the politburo extensive experiences and education is a condition, but also by power sharing mechanisms. Before becoming a member of the politburo one

> "must normally have served as governors or party secretaries of two provinces, each the size and population of most countries. In short, top leaders must pass through a battery of merit-based tests and accumulate decades of extensive and diverse administrative experience" (2015:Loc. 3637).

Bell sees one advantage of the Chinese context in the fact that the "system does not clearly distinguish between "bureaucrats" and "power-holders"" (2015:Loc. 3391). When career paths

---

[761] This is one way to minimize concerns about the risk of biases that are justifiably raised against the rule of the educated (see Estlund 2009).
[762] In a democracy, "political leaders are chosen by the people and need not have received training designed to extend class sympathies; no sort of political leadership training could be made compulsory in electoral democracies. Hence, a political meritocracy will find it easier to implement compulsory political training for leaders designed to make them understand and care for the interests of the less-well-off members of society" (Bell 2015:Loc. 941).

are not seen as mutually exclusive and mobility within the system can be expected, people are more willing to start at low levels, according to Bell. This can increase the likelihood of very skilled people at the bottom as well as on the top, since the latter have the advantage of experience. In spite of these tendencies, skilled bureaucrats are not exceptionally rare within advanced democracies. Of course, the quality of bureaucrats is closely linked to the education system.

4.2.2. MIXED SYSTEMS: MERITOCRATISING DEMOCRACY?

If skilled leadership is taken as an essence of good governance, it leads to the question of how to ensure a system's 'meritocraticness'.[763] While the first part of this work brought light to the lack of green literacy, the second and this part present competency as a key. In the face of the additions a brief examination of proffering a mixed system as a solution provides further insights without constituting a digression. Advocacy of mixed systems as well as criticism have a long tradition (see for example Aristotle 2009 vs. Plato 1982). A comprehensive discussion of the arguments is beyond the scope of this work, nonetheless some considerations should be presented.

There are different ideas to ensure competence though democracy. For instance an independent institution could be in charge of testing all public servants and politicians for their qualification (Bell 2015:Loc. 3108-3123). Yet, Bell underscores that a public will have difficulty to accept examinations if a popular politician does not pass. It is generally difficult to evaluate the viability of a restricting mechanism. It would certainly depend on the cultural context, the timing of the testing and above all the perceived legitimacy of the testing institution. Filtering politicians along established guidelines certainly could meritocratise governments. Another means is the establishment of a meritocratically chosen chamber. Bell reviews Jiang's proposal for a mixed system. Jiang has reservations against democracy as "the politics of desire" (Bell 2015:Loc. 3193). Jiang is especially interesting, because he is concerned about the disability of democracy for good environmental governance. Jiang, a Confucian scholar, proposes building a House of Exemplary Persons (2013), to whom reflecting upon "the long-term environmental consequences of policies" would be a central task (Bell 2015:Loc. 3246). For Jiang democracy undermines Confucianism and is wasteful and 'pretentious'. Accordingly, he gives the meritocratically composed house veto power, especially to protect the environment (2013). Bell understands this proposal, although far from China today, as within the imaginable given that large changes have occurred in the past (2015). Nonetheless, he sees a danger in Jiang's proposal

---

[763] Here, "the need for training of leaders over several electoral cycles means that meritocracy is incompatible with multiparty rule and the possibility that it would lead to the alternation of political power" (Bell 2015:Loc. 717).

including an elected house of government, since the electorate will see their choices as more legitimate and hence refuse to accept a House of Exemplary Persons as superior (2015:Loc. 3255). Accordingly he concludes: "Jiang Qing is typically criticized for being too anti-democratic, but the irony is that his proposal is too democratic" (Bell 2015:Loc. 3270). Moreover, he sees the same difficulty for other mixed systems including one of his own suggestions (Plato 1982; cf. Aristotle 2009).[764] Here, difficulties become more overt, when discussing concrete ideas. In an earlier publication by Bell and Li, Chan lists details about his proposal of a mixed system (2013). While limiting the power of an additional chamber that stands aside a democratically elected first chamber, it

> "should still be able to exert a healthy influence on society despite its limited power, for the most unique and valuable function of its members is to serve as role models in public deliberations for politicians and citizens. The number of seats would not be fixed; it depends entirely on how many qualified senior public servants are selected – the quality of deliberation is more important than rigid adherence to a "magic" number of members or votes. Members can serve a maximum of two terms. To fulfill the advisory and role-modeling functions, deliberative meetings would be fully broadcast through free public television and radio channels. Members of the second chamber would wield their influence mainly through their justly obtained reputation and prestige as virtuous and competent citizens, the force of their arguments, and their powers to criticize the government and the first chamber as well as delay bills" (Chan 2013:48).

Although desirable in theory, Chan's suggestion is grounded on the same assumption of deliberative democrats namely the power of the rational argument.[765] With some reservations including the note that it needs to be put on trial, Chan proposes setting up a list with candidates through (self-) nomination and then

> "eligible selectors from the three sources (senior public servants, senior secretariat staff, and experienced journalists) would be asked to evaluate the candidates' virtue (most notably in terms of public spiritedness, sense of responsibility, fairness, integrity, and civility) and competence (in terms of the ability to understand complex arguments from diverse points of view, open-mindedness, knowledge of certain fields of public service, etc.) by giving each candidate an overall mark for each of the two dimensions" (2013:48).

Granting that Chan's suggestions might sound promising, the potential falls with the acceptance of a second chamber as legitimate check on the first chamber as well as with the extent of their authority being binding. Supplementing an elected chamber with a meritocratically selected chamber is an attempt to meritocratise horizontally as far as neither chamber has authority over the other. Meritocratising vertically might be far more suitable.

---

[764] Bell for example writes that the Chinese "political system needs to be further "meritocratized" so that government officials are selected and promoted on the basis of ability and morality rather than political connections, wealth, and family background. And the right formula for judging improvement should be, more or less, the vertical model of democratic meritocracy: democracy at the bottom, with the system becoming progressively more meritocratic at higher levels of government" (2015:Loc. 3402).

[765] Prominently, "the expectation that everybody in a large, modern, and pluralistic political community can agree about what needs to be done is not realistic. Perhaps small, relatively homogenous communities can agree in a consensual way about what needs to be done, but the result of striving for a genuine, unforced consensus in a country like China is that nothing would get done" (Bell 2015:Loc. 1220).

Following a long tradition in political thought, Bell explains that the most productive ground for democracy is at the local level (2015:Loc. 3292).[766] He suggests three main reasons. First, people actually know their local leaders and therefore are more capable to judge competency and morality. When criticising examinations as a selection process (in contrast to voting), Chan also foregrounds the Confucian belief that one needs to observe the actions and behaviour of a person closely to understand his virtuousness (2013).[767] Second, issues at the local level tend to be simpler, thus can be understood by almost everyone.[768] Third, people are often affected at the local level, where they can also have more impact on the outcomes. While the affectedness has been discussed as problematic, the former reasons show that not all problems of democracy occur at all levels.[769] Complexity typically decreases with the size of the relevant community; hence it ceases to be a focal point of critique.

Bell sees climate change exactly as a possibly too costly outcome of the 'people's decisions'. One of his suggestions for better policies:

> "To deal with controversial cases in a more scientific way, the government can set up an advisory body of experts in the social sciences with the mandate to evaluate the advantages and disadvantages of ongoing experiments in different parts of the country. If experts are chosen at random from, say, the nation's twenty leading universities, the advisory body would be seen as disinterested and could make recommendations based on moral considerations and social scientific knowledge" (2015:Loc. 3759).

The difficulty of demarking the actual authority of such advice should not be underestimated as it weighs heavily.[770] Establishing advisory chambers may mean a meritocratisation of democratic regimes. With limited warrants such approach in practice may not lead to desired outcomes given all the reservations against a democratic system and the likely prioritisation of an elected chamber. Establishing different systems at different levels however, for example a meritocracy with democratic elements, could diminish such problems. Bell's examination of meritocratic

---

[766] At the village level the Chinese governance is already mixed with a leader chosen "from above who is often more educated than elected leaders and has the task of trying to ensure the implementation of center-driven policies that may be unpopular, such as birth control and land acquisition" (Bell 2015:Loc. 3648; see also Brown 2011a). In the province Zhejiang there has even been experimentation with "a form of deliberative polling: randomly chosen citizens were invited to review the proposed government budget and to recommend budget priorities" (Bell 2015:Loc. 3700).

[767] Chan demurs examinations, since he believes that "people will engage in crafty hypocrisy and as a result the righteous man of principle will seldom get promoted" (2013:45). Though if people were only 'faking it', internalisation could actually improve governance overall anyway (cf. Bai 2013).

[768] Bai sizes the unit of the community along the answer to the question "how much democratic participation depends upon how likely the participants are able to make sound decisions that are based on public interests" (2013:68). The stand of Alaskans on resource extraction demonstrated that this also varies with the issue at hand (see Ball 2006:134).

[769] In the Hang dynasty "[t]he rule of avoidance prohibited officials from serving in their home areas in order to avoid conflict between local ties and pursuit of the common good" (Bell 2015:Loc. 2258). Here, affectedness is openly seen as a barrier to consequentialist thinking (that was also described earlier).

[770] In regard to the central question of this work, Chan proffers that "the second chamber might have more power in policy areas (e.g., environmental and population issues) that affect nonvoters such as future generations" (2013:53). This suggestion does not solve the problem though, once the nature of environmental destruction is defined as all-encompassing.

mechanisms in China is a fruitful addition to ecoauthoritarian thought. Whereas it can inform a theory of ecomeritocracy, it also raises the question in how far China is green.

4.2.3. THE PEOPLE'S 'GREEN' REPUBLIC OF CHINA

Despite its current bad environmental record, many scholars are hopeful about the PRC.[771] In Oreskes and Conway's semi-fiction work, China leads the world in their depiction of the future (2014). When it comes to the environment Randers is also optimistic:

> "By 2052, China will have shown the world how a strong government is much better at solving the type of challenges humanity will face in the twenty-first century. China will easily redirect the 5% of their GDP that is required to solve the oncoming barrage of problems" (2012:Loc. 4369-74).

There is a basis on which upon a People's Green Republic could be built. In its founding period the Communist Party instituted guidelines on land reform that could be classified as progressive and advancing innovation.[772] Interestingly, these guidelines could also be understood as representing the Popperian attitude, which Dryzek saw necessary for sustainability and only possible within a liberal democracy (see Dryzek 2005 and Jasanoff 2012). Scholars see a particular advantage of the China model in the freedom the central government gives to the local government (Eaton and Kostka 2014; Bell 2015; cf. Betz 2013).[773] Directives are still setting a framework within which local leaders are allowed to design and try different strategies. Conversely, this is not the case if policies "prove to be particularly innovative and effective at dealing with social problems, in which case the central government seeks to generalise good policies elsewhere, to the extent conditions allow" (Bell 2015:Loc. 2670). Trying policies small-scale before applying them at a wider level is useful for the obvious reason that mistakes locally are far less costly. Here, Bell judges elections as the obstacle that the PRC avoids.

> "The practice of experimentation in between central and local levels of government is difficult to implement in democratic contexts because experiments can take decades to bear fruit and elected politicians worried about the next election tend to have shorter time horizons. Also, the same party may not control the different levels of government and the top may not have the power to launch pilot projects in the whole country, particularly with regard to experiments in political reform" (2015:Loc. 3812).

The advantage of time periods however is held off in some contexts. Eaton and Kostka see one problem in the development of sustainable governance at the local level, where leaders tend to change offices rather frequently, which makes them more inclined to enact policies with

---

[771] Betz writes: "Contrary to popular perceptions in the West, China has not only set goals for itself regarding the improvement of its environmental and energy policies but also made significant strides in achieving them" (2013:14).

[772] The guidelines include: "(1) train work team cadres and send them down to localities; (2) carry out model experiments; (3) accomplish breakthroughs in a key point; (4) broaden the campaign from point to surface; (5) integrate point and surface with regard to the applied measures; (6) unfold the campaign in steady steps" (Bell 2015:Loc. 3557).

[773] The downside of this flexibility is that it gives local leaders, at least partly, the chance to avoid unpopular directives (Eaton and Kostka 2014:366).

immediate rewards (Eaton and Kostka 2014). In spite of this, rotation also "helps implementation of successful projects by transferring leaders" (2014:371). Hence adjoining the system of personnel selection and recruitment is a system of policy implementation. Both combined fulfilled and further deepened could engender fertile ground for sustainability.

The PRC's environmental politics are far from satisfactory. Nonetheless many examples indicate the right direction.[774] Leggewie and Welzer see the Chinese acknowledgement of environmental destruction as a sensitive issue proven by the fact that their stimulus packages spared 34% to the environment (2011:156). Substantial improvements have been made in the energy field (Myllyvirta 2016).[775]

> "China's autocratic political system may be more of an advantage than a hindrance to a shift in energy policies at this stage of the country's development, which will make reorientation quite a bit more difficult in future" (Betz 2013:29).

An environmental tax is said to substitute particular resource taxes by 2017 and further a coal cap will be introduced to reduce today's emissions by 2020 (Chen and Patton 2015). Though not sufficient the politburo targets multiple sources of environmental destruction.

The potential of ecoauthoritarianism is visible in several plans. Harris also places some hope in China since they

> "could take on this leadership role by explicitly placing climate-related restrictions on its most affluent citizens. The Chinese government could start doing this by, for example, heavily taxing luxury goods and using the resulting funds to help its poorest citizens escape poverty and cope with the effects of climate change. It could outlaw polluting automobiles and all luxury and sports cars" (2013:Loc. 2503).

Luxury taxes in order to combat pollution are in discussion and bans on car usage for example, while not unknown in Western countries, have been employed as a means to reduce smog by Beijing in its recent past. Gilley writes that restricting liberties in one local case in 2008 meant the requirement that

---

[774] The energy shift in the PRC is far from achieved, but this is not necessarily caused by the system's lack of democracy: "The partial privatization of energy companies and the corporatization of state energy companies, together with their greater operational freedom and widespread corruption within the relevant agencies, are doing the rest to considerably undermine centralized energy governance" (Betz 2013:19).

[775] Energy politics is a core battleground for environmentalists. Support for renewables is often mobilized by classifying them as 'democratizing'. Nuclear power, necessitating centralized politics on the other hand, is typically denounced as non-renewable and too risky. Either way interference by states has proven to be most effective (see Karapin 2014).

"all drivers leave their cars at home at least one day a week; that elevators not be used to reach the first three floors of public buildings; and that public sector employees wear casual clothes to work in the summer" (2012:290).[776]

He also points out that "population control policies have been cited as a model for future limits on individual choices related to climate change" (Gilley 2012:290).[777] Cities have cut power to reach targets with good examples, but there are also some negative ones such as indiscriminately cutting off schools and medical facilities (see also Held, Roger and Nag 2013a:40ff.). Undisputedly, this needs to be avoided. Gilley sees the demand to levy the way into a sustainable future as putting local governments under pressure. As mentioned earlier, some promotions in fact depended on reaching energy targets (Betz 2013). This is something that is clearly in line with the concept of ecomeritocracy.

Held, Roger and Nag posit that the PRC's ambitious plans are hindered by "the rising number of stakeholders that will need to be coerced or co-opted" and that "potentially more costly or draconian – strategies will be required on the part of local governments" (2013a:47; cf. Geall 2013). Such a statement does not implicitly say that a strong state vital for reaching sustainability, but it clearly hints at such an assumption. As suggested in the first part a system of regulations, laws, incentives including clear punishments, is the most effective tool for greening. In spite of the Chinese potential for a meritocratic system that produces good green governance, generalisability is doubtful. For Bell, only Vietnam might have the right context to implement such a political regime (2015:Loc. 3808). Nonetheless, given the impact a green China could have on the global scale (Reuscher et al. 2011:11) and as a benchmark, it is fruitful to investigate the question of ecological integrity via meritocracy further.[778]

---

[776] Of course, even with technology to enforce such restrictions, people may work their way around (taking the lift to the fourth floor and then walk down). However policies should be tried despite the potential of laws to be avoided. Small nudging could also be sufficient, especially when supplemented by reasons (such as health and energy saving). Punishment is an additional option (in proportion to the crime and mean as a deterrent).

[777] Limits on pets (such as dogs) are also environmentally beneficial.

[778] Studying if meritocracy by itself can have a greening effect, hence if sustainability becomes intrinsic to a meritocratic system given its indispensability is an intriguing question. If China shows stronger commitments in the future to the environment it would be interesting to investigate, if this is caused by meritocratic elements. Similarly, studying meritocratic elements in other political communities (e.g. within the EC) can give more insides on possible greening effect of expert involvement.

"Political meritocracy is perhaps the most studied and the least studied topic in political theory. The idea that a political system should aim to select and promote leaders with superior ability and virtue is central to both Chinese and Western political theory and practice. The reason seems obvious: we demand trained and qualified persons in leadership positions in science, law, and corporations; why not also in the most important institution of all?" (Bell 2015:Loc. 116).

People do not wish to be ruled by incompetent leaders in any system and this might be an explanation why the belief in a system being meritocratic is usually even entertained against facts.[779] Democratic theory repeatedly assumes that the people will understand the competency of a candidate. Hence, the idea that democracies are meritocratic is often upheld against all odds.[780] A meritocracy is by its own nature a rule of "trained and qualified persons". Ecomeritocracy initially only describes two factors: rule by/for nature and rule by qualified persons. Given the unlikelihood of democracy fulfilling either or even both, nondemocratic can be added. The subsequent consideration is an expansion on ecological integrity as the highest end of governance and meritocracy as a means to achieve good governance. Here, the question between substance and procedure and a possible synergy can be reintroduced.[781] This chapter combines findings on political meritocracy and environmental politics exploring arguments for and modalities of ecomeritocracy.

In the first part Estlund's critique that "[p]rocedural fairness is about the retreat from substance, and the question is when to retreat and when to hold our ground" was presented as valid (2009:Loc. 1242). It was declared as valid in so far as democratic processes do not necessarily lead to good outcomes for the environment and thus a tradeoff persists. Yet, the connection between a fair selection process, i.e. procedural fairness, and good governance may exist if the focus is shifted towards meritocratic elements. The answer here is speculative. What is more: Can the critique of truth by definition be equally applied? If the system does not produce green outcomes, it is not meritocratic enough (just like green democracy is to be achieved by being more democratic according to a substantial number of democracy advocates). In spite of this seemingly similar logic, there is a crucial difference. With the focus on meritocracy, the selection process is based on the substance such as objective qualification including former achievement. There is likely to be a causal relation, while a "distinction between political meritocracy and

---

[779] Leeson criticizes early ecoauthoritarian on the ground that none of their "prescriptions for Leviathan includes measures to insure its wisdom or political skill" (1979:317).

[780] This could be another instance where people abstractly claim, what is not believed in the concrete, but it is not of concern here.

[781] It should be noted that meritocracy does not purely represent a means. Rather the attribute 'meritocratic' can be descriptive and merely describing a quality of a system. A common understanding of fairness often includes meritocratic elements.

meritorious rule" can be made (Chan 2013:31; see also Pettit 2013). It is reasonable to expect a leader chosen on the basis of education and achievement rather than on popular popularity to continue similarly. As a result, the selection process should increase the likelihood of a synergy of procedure and substance. By this logic defining ecomeritocracy as good green governance would be tautological (if theory can be put into practice). In a democracy, the selection process is determined by public vote and as such subjective. Thereby, hopes are that objective and subjective qualification can be equated (or the existence of objective qualification is categorically denied).[782] Meritocracy has to understand skill and virtue as somehow measurable, because otherwise there cannot be a system of evaluations. Consequentially, the idea is subject to criticism from many fields, who typically remark that measurements are subjective and can be manipulated by ruling elites to ensure power maintenance. Arguably, measurements of merit are never neutral nor can they be purely based on science as elaborated earlier. This still does not mean that they are as subjective as the perception of a *demos*. To put it concretely; a math test is likely to show if a person has an understanding of the subject. Whereas letting people vote on the question if someone is able to solve equations is less reliable.[783] Admittedly, not all areas of life can be judged by such testing. Judging the quality of a poem for example is not simple arithmetic. Such reservations like reservations in regard to tastes or belief systems are unlikely to ever vanish. They should be taken seriously, acknowledged and recognised. A great part of governance at the same time can be evaluated. Health, life expectations and ecosystem functionality can be presented in numbers.[784] As follows, it can be safely said that not only is governance regularly measured – just like measuring other things is omnipresent in the 21st century – the quality of governance can also be approximated along these lines. Monitoring policies and judging governance is common practice and seems self-explanatory. In spite of the fact that most jobs with high responsibility require the successful passing of examinations, politicians are normally excluded from these practices.[785] The logic of value pluralism strangely mirrors the reasoning that because the competency of a politician is said to be a subjective

---

[782] In accord, following his observations Bell summarizes: "My conclusion is that China can and should improve its meritocratic system, but it must do so within the system: a meritocratic system can be explicitly designed to increase the likelihood that political leaders have the motivation and ability to enact sound policies, and in that sense China has a clear advantage over electoral democracies that leave the whole thing up to the whims of the people unconstrained by the lessons of philosophy, history, and social science" (2015:Loc. 2159).

[783] Here too degrees of separation matter. Performance can be observed better from nearby.

[784] Literacy is a criterion often measured to calculate 'the development' of a country, although some groups only support literacy for the male population, hence do not see a higher rate as progress.

[785] While examinations are in discord with the idea that everyone is qualified to participate, they can still fulfil the standard of a right to politics for everyone. After all, one can study to succeed. The advantage is that the right to politics and to participate in politics would be directly connected to a duty to get informed ahead of the participation. Bai proffers that "at each higher level, each voter has to take a class and participate in discussions, or take a test specially designed for this level before he or she can be allowed to vote. Different weights may be given to their votes based upon their performances in class or in the test, or based upon their educational levels, social and political roles, and other relevant factors" (2013:68). They could be compensated with scholarships in order to not make it a privilege of the wealthy, but such system is contrary to the concept of political equality.

judgment, it makes sense that the selection is based purely on a subjective evaluation.[786] Allowing for perceptions to take priority may follow from the trust in enlightened rationalism, but is unlikely to lead to more than suboptimal outcomes for the environment (and in regard to social justice). Meritocracy, as characterised by Bell, recognises differences not only as of subjective judgment, but as of objective qualification (2015; Bell and Li 2013; see also Plato 1982 and More 1992).

Bell sees a substantial lack of research into political leadership. "Most books on leadership are written for the business world and few distinguish between the qualities required of business leaders and the qualities required of political leaders" (Bell 2015:Loc. 1396). This not only means that performance is measured in a reductionist fashion, economists may propagate that companies create value for the general public, yet this in particular in regard to the environment is highly questionable. As suggested earlier, good governance is about the protection of the common good, something that is contrary to the logic of the externalisation of costs. So, it needs to be determined what good leadership means in politics consistent with the red line drawn throughout this book. Discussing the argument for guardianship, Dahl writes that the guardians "must possess no interests of their own inconsistent with the good of the polis" (1989:53). The functionality of life support systems as the leading goal of governance and the recognition of such as 'collective self-interest' mean that the guardian's interest and the good of the polis will be congruent. Transparency of salary and monitoring of income of public servants, politicians and scientists included, is possible, once it is not understood as a private matter and the public servant aspect is emphasised. Performance evaluations based on ecological integrity as the only inlet of career advancement further lessen the chance for inconsistency.[787] There again, it can be argued that a restriction of those eligible by the means of measuring qualifications increases the likelihood of good governance. After all, outcomes in regard to a healthy ecosystem can and have in fact been measured objectively. Leaving this potential of evaluation untapped is lavish.

---

[786] Government can have the single biggest impact on everyone's life, yet politicians in many cases do not need any objective qualifications (with the exception of sometimes age). The irony of this can be demonstrated by giving examples of qualification sometimes judged subjective: What makes a good driver is subjective, yet in order to drive one has to get a license. What makes a good architect is subjective, but one has to get a degree. What makes a good doctor is subjective, yet one has to get a degree to practice. In none of these cases asking for a minimum of training, knowledge and skill is seen as problematic. It is rather the opposite.

[787] "Westra offers the overarching value of (ecological) 'integrity' as the embodiment of this politics of the common good" (Humphrey 2007:Loc. 579).

Standards should be set and processes of evaluation need to be developed.[788] For now, utilitarianism can justify exclusion. Dahl asserts that for Mill competency trumps other priorities (Dahl 1989:125). Höntzsch declares that in Mill's works, freedom therefore is to be only granted to adults with full faculties living in civilised societies (2010:103; e.g. Mill 1862).[789] This key disclaimer may be applied in the context of climate science in a way that excludes a majority of the population. In the emergency room, doctors have the decision-making power and that is normally understood to be for everyone's benefit.[790] There is a clear hierarchy along the idea of qualification and experience. Physicians have to earn their position through the process of learning and testing. Doctors swear the Hippocratic Oath and thereafter are trusted to mean well. Overall scientists try to abide by meritocratic standards, although with some reservations it is often possible to identify the brightest of a field (see Latour 2007).[791] Rawls allows for economic inequality if it is advantageous to the least advantaged (2012). This leads one, as Bai points out, to the idea that 'institutionalised' political inequality could be legitimate if it benefits the most disadvantaged (2013:81; see also Arneson 2004). Whereas CEOs are not typically judged by the standard of living of the worst-off employee, political theory may advance that a government should be judged on this very basis. The veil of ignorance and difference principle (with its justice concern) could reasonably lead to a meritocracy.

> "Hierarchies may be necessary in a modern, complex society, but theorists in the Western world generally agreed that we should regard all hierarchies as morally problematic and definitely not attempt to institutionalize them in the political system" (Bell 2015:Loc. 2193).

This appears a separating distinction between democracy and meritocracy. Democracy can often mean that neither hierarchies are exploited for better policies nor are derived injustices

---

[788] In the meantime, Bell also advances an argument for the targeted recruitment of women attributing "superior social skills" after pointing out that examinations cannot filter out people without social skills (2015:Loc. 2098). As with the argument that 'women are closer to nature', such claims need to be part of further research, which in this context should be more precisely targeted towards not only the question of general validity, but the effect on the government's green performance. Similarly to other questions of virtue, social skills may be not be guaranteed, but can be advanced via education and training. After all, Bell argues that training in moral thought schools empathy. Bell is as daring as to suggesting a "somewhat arbitrary" ratio of "a 60:20:20 ratio for assessment of moral character, with 60 percent of the weighting given to peers and 20 percent each given to superiors and subordinates" (2015:Loc. 2122). He also remarks that while "high-level political leaders in large, peaceful, and modernizing meritocratic states need to be strong in terms of intellectual ability, social skills, and virtue" they "need not be at the top of the scale on any one dimension" (2015:Loc. 2141). Factors for good performance are self-evidently highly contextual. They vary with specific branches of government and level.

[789] Mill asserts that the ideal form of government is context dependent and governance demands different qualifications according to the local culture (1862:13ff.). His idea of civilized translates into 'with civic virtue'. In that sense he might have (equally) disqualified a disinterested majority in a contemporary democracy as uncivilized.

[790] From the perspective of a future, Oreskes and Conway write about now: "A key attribute of the period was that power did not reside in the hands of those who understood the climate system, but rather in political, economic, and social institutions that had a strong interest in maintaining the use of fossil fuels"(2013:Loc. 487).

[791] Whiteside asks: "When we put science at the heart of decision making, are we effectively accepting not just a method of risk evaluation but a particular *ethic* of risk taking?" (2006:29). The answer is affirmative, however, such ethics is open for development as Whiteside shows throughout his book on the precautionary principle.

abolished. The acknowledgment of hierarchies is also one reason why nondemocratic green theory is sometimes despised as Realpolitik. The latter does not built on a utopia.

That accountability is strengthened by institutionalisation should be utilised. Setting up a system of checks and balances is not exclusive to democracy and "constraints, checks, and balances can reasonably be developed in light of a detailed account of how leaders should lead" (Fan 2013:91). Moreover, separate institutions could be organised in a way that represents a division of power (see Bell and Li 2013; Bell 2015). It is beyond the scope of this work to devise a set-up of an ecomeritocratic regime. Claims cannot be tested, but theoretically a separation of powers by the means of establishing distinct institutions with meritocratically selected civil servants could introduce checks and balances. For concreteness, imagine the first institution sets the standards according to the demands of sound environmental governance and the local context, while the second institution devises the policy with a third one being responsible for its implementation. The first institution then would be responsible for monitoring the results as they have to regularly check the resilience of life support systems in any case. At the same time another institution such as a constitutional court could constantly oversee the processes.[792] On one side Eckersley suggests that the

> "bureaucratic rationality of the administrative state is seen as too rigid, hierarchical, and limited to deal with the variability, nonreducability, and complexity of ecological problems. Bureaucratic rationality responds to complex problems by breaking them down, compartmentalizing them, and assigning them to different agencies that respond to a hierarchical chain of command. This often leads to the routine displacement of problems across bureaucratic system boundaries" (2004:Loc. 1112-15).

Such a displacement needs to be avoided, depending upward mobility (career success) on problem solving could be an effective mean of minimising such processes. Where Eckersley notes the concern against a rigid administrative state, Westra, like many others, does not believe that people will voluntarily reduce their consumption to a fair share, which exactly conditions the need for strict institutions. She clearly posits that the

> "only hope for real change now lies in the emergence of global regulatory institutions willing to act on our behalf [...] The top-down regulatory and public policy aspect will have to be prescribed by an interdisciplinary team of biologists, ecologists, political scientists, medical

---

[792] I do not claim to know a golden mean of meritocratic governance. Without testing it is impossible to know where a balance between division of labour, separation of responsibility, effective communication and performance may lie. Despite a meritocratic system, success may still depend on the chance of good chemistry between civil servants of different institutions (Eaton and Kostka 2014:377). Good governance would depend on effectiveness of interdisciplinary, interinstitutional work – not despite but because of the multiplication of input. Areas and authority would have to be clearly demarked. Arguably, such a setup could have still, when compared to democracy, fewer veto players and faster policy making.

specialists and philosophers with a strong traditional moral basis" (Westra 1998:198f.; see also Delmas and Young 2009:6).[793]

Regulations and bans in particular are the most effective way of reducing nature's destruction. Laws are for most corporations the main driver of environmental activities (Diekmann and Preisendörfer 2001:125ff.). In some cases, companies have a green identity or try greening, which could be more depending on the people's perception than on their actual practices. Much potential remains untapped up to now.

> "Demand-side opportunities dwarf supply-side opportunities, and we can change demand in the very short term. Toasters have a one-to-two year life span, cars only about eight years in reality. Refrigerators and white goods about three-to-eight years. Real change could be brought about very rapidly through a stringent regulatory framework setting minimum standards" (Anderson 2012:37).

Written regulations have the advantage of allowing for clear instructions, but for their effectiveness they need to go beyond and arbitrary minimum and their violation has to be sanctioned (Muno 2010:352).[794] Nepotism could be countered by means of examinations and by result-orientated monitoring as suggested by Bell (2015). Additionally, independent universities for example, supported by independent funds from taxes, could be reviewing results (see Jasanoff 1999). Meritocracy must not mean that citizen feedback is excluded from all processes. After all, their trust is essential for the functioning of any system (see Easton 1965). An ecomeritocratic government should be amenable, meaning open and responsive to suggestions, while at the same time not influenced by common sense beliefs. This quality is promoted in science as well.

The strength of an ecomeritocratic approach is also that such central scientific findings can be facilitated without having to consider whether it is unpopular or paternalistic.[795] Here, two anthropological findings could have a huge impact on environmental politics. First, as

---

[793] Here a "division of labour works only if the division has been made responsibly and thoroughly, and if it includes a role for continual assessment of how well it is meeting the ends of the whole. Without such a role or responsibility, the result is that no one is considering the whole. Worse, no one is required to consider the whole. Even worse, what people are required to consider can positively militate against their considering the whole, requiring them to blinker themselves even to the obvious long-term or overall impact of their actions" (Lane 2011:173f.).

[794] "Regulation has an obvious appeal to policymakers. It appears to offer precision, predictability and effectiveness: an exact standard is set, the regulator and regulated both know what is expected of them and enforcement is ensured by a regulatory agency backed up by the force of law. Regulations can be administratively efficient, especially when a substance or an activity is completely banned, as they do not require complete information about a problem" (Carter 2007:324).

[795] Harris suggests that, because of the difficulty to change people's mind-sets into those of environmental citizens "[i]nterventions might therefore include extensive education, historical stories, and propaganda akin to what has proved successful (some might say too successful) in developing powerful feelings of loyalty to specific nationalities and nation-states (even to the point where many people become willing, even eager, to die for those ideas). [...] It is the role of institutions to help and encourage people to move toward this realization as quickly as possible" (2013:Loc. 2627-2632). Harris' proposals could be described as paternalistic. He does not classify his position as ecoauthoritarian though, but he sees the government's role in an active interference in people's character formation.

mentioned there and again, a change in values is often a consequence of a change in behaviour. Changing people's practices and action is more effective than changing people's values. Values normally follow behaviour, but behaviour does not necessarily follow values. Mill pointed out that custom is a quasi-second nature. The description of virtue as a habit by Aristotle, at first appears to be profane or even strange, but it shows a deeper understanding of human nature. Research in internalisation shows how the process of habituation is extremely powerful (Bourdieu 1977). Rituals are a central part of the maintenance of culture. Applying this finding to environmental governance also means to accept that people should have to practice environmentally friendly behaviour regardless of the persuasion. If the outcome of imposed policies is a change of values, it means that extrinsically motivated behaviour leads to intrinsic motivation. Hence, in the long run there should be no difference even for those who judge intrinsically motivated action as superior to extrinsically motivated. Even more, wishes to preserve the environment may not occur without active interference. Thus whereas 'coercion' can produce such values, no nudging at all leaves the outcome to chance.[796] Once people get used to an action their understanding will change and the worldview can follow. Second, humans are social animals (see for example Aristotle 2009). Behaviour tends to mimicry and be subject to social norms and pressure. Social facts were introduced as guiding human behaviour within society without necessarily being written into law. An action is normally judged as right if it is "consistent with the moral expectations of a political community" (Gilley 2009:4). As long as the norms of unsustainability are hegemonic, social animals are more likely to conform than to develop deviant behaviour. Good environmental politics tries to establish the priority of ecological integrity as a social fact.[797] This may also mean that policies could become less stringent after behaviour becomes widespread, supporting the idea that an ecomeritocratic state does not necessarily need to be oppressive in the traditional sense at least not long-term. Whiteside writes about Jonas that

> "he seems to have in mind a regime in which a political elite consults scientific advisers about nature's objective limits and the technologies that threaten to succeed them. It would then be up to this elite to impose the necessary discipline" (Whiteside 2006:97).[798]

---

[796] This is not to say that nudging is never useful. In any case definitions of nudging may vary (see Cox 2013).

[797] "In spite of a growing desire for change, it's almost impossible for people to simply choose sustainable lifestyles, however much they'd like to. Even highly-motivated individuals experience conflict as they attempt to escape consumerism. And the chances of extending this behaviour across society are negligible without changes in the social structure. Conversely, of course, social structures can and do shift people's values and behaviours" (Jackson 2012:Loc. 2850-55).

[798] In general, "the problem requires governments to commit to a series of policy measures, with the probability that progressively more stringent targets will have to be enacted and enforced over time. In short, the climate change crisis requires that the issue remains a priority item that is not displaced by economic downturns and other political, economic and social developments" (Pralle 2009:783).

Such a system would need surveillance as Whiteside points out. Yet, a system that utilises tendencies in human nature is likely to be able to significantly reduce the level of interference and surveillance. To improve public policy performance, Singer for example suggests that it could

> "appeal to the widespread need to feel wanted, or useful, or to belong to a community – all things that are more likely to come from cooperating with others than from competing with them" (1999:Loc. 460-62).

Following a similar logic Randers sees an advantage in the supposed collectivism of Asian societies. He writes:

> "[Asian countries] must stress that public interest takes precedence over individual rights, although this conflicts fundamentally with the core arguments of consumption-driven capitalism. They must stand up against the claim that allowing everyone to pursue their individual self-interest eventually will lead to benefits for all" (2012:Loc. 816-18).

Here, a meritocratic leadership has the comparative advantage that it does not have to wager for votes. Hence, it has neither to split the public nor appeal to self-interest to mobilise electoral support.

> "A strong authoritarian government, unhampered by the need to win elections or protect liberal rights, might coerce self-interested individuals into acting in the collective interest by, say, producing fewer children and living more frugal lifestyles" (Carter 2007:53).

Fewer children and more frugal lifestyles are the most effective means of reducing the destruction of life support systems. Realism does not degrade people by honestly assessing people's abilities, whereas pretending someone has a quality in fact is disrespectful (see Conly 2013 and Arneson 2004:52).

When strong states solve the collective action problems and demand compliance from all citizens alike, they can also ensure compliance easier. What Conly describes as 'coercive paternalism', which implicates directly forbidding harmful actions, is forthright (2013). Notably, preserving ecosystems because of their complexity means above all humans managing themselves not trying to manage the environment (Rees 2013; Pimentel, Westra and Noss 2013). After sketching an ecomeritocracy the following chapter will investigate what effective policies could look like in the more concrete. Ecomeritocracy was described as rule by qualified experts, who determine limits, propose policies to stay within these limits and lead the implementation. Making science the benchmark would mean to subordinate the majority of people. At the same time empowering scientists could be a crucial element in changing the narrative (of Cassandra and Jeremiah). Given that experts already put forward their evaluations, in particular in regard to the limits, a conjecture on which policies and ecomeritocracy is not baseless and can show how such a system could fructify. If nothing less, the elaborations below can also inspire democratic politics directed towards sustainability by especially demarking their limits.

4.4. Earth First: Policies Based on the Acknowledgement of Physical Limits

The *Blueprint for Survival* discusses one comprehensive strategy under the title "Orchestration" calling for "most careful synchronization and integration" (Goldsmith et al. 1972:45).[799] The following part is a consideration of core goals and instruments for achieving good governance that could be part of a careful orchestration i.e. harmonic interplay (not simulation). By exploring desirable policies, more theoretical thoughts on the desirability and practicability of an ecomeritocracy can be furthered. In an imagined ecomeritocracy, interdisciplinary committees lengthy could discuss and evaluated needs before implementing policies. There is a huge potential for stronger government though coming with seemingly invasive implications. Resource reductions regimes will need to consider and cover all parts of life (Randers 2012:Loc. 829-30).[800]. Entering a policy debate also sheds light on potential solutions.[801] Sophisticated research into concrete environmental policies beyond the widespread cry for 'putting a price on carbon' can expose shortcomings of current governance. This last chapter attempts to stipulate future research by venturing into and proposing practices that are commonly accepted as

---

[799] Their proposal includes:
"a. establishment of national population service
b. introduction of raw materials, amortization and power taxes; antidisamenity legislation; air, land, and water quality targets; recycling grants; revised social accounting systems
c. developed countries end commitment to persistent pesticides and subsidize similar move by undeveloped countries
d. end of subsidies on inorganic fertilizers
e. grants for use of organics and introduction of diversity
f. emergency food programs for undeveloped countries
g. progressive substitution of nonpersistent for persistent pesticides
h. integrated-control research program
i. integrated-control training program
j. substitution of integrated control for chemical control
k. progressive introduction of diversified farming practices
l. end of road building
m. clearance of derelict land and beginning of renewal programs
n. restrictions of private transport
o. development of rapid transit
p. research into material substitution
q. development of alternative technologies
r. decentralization of industry: part one (redirection)
s. decentralization of industry: part two (development of community types)
t. redistribution of government
u. educational research
v. teacher training
w. education
x. experimental community
y. domestic sewage to land
z. target date for the basic establishment of network of self-sufficient, self-regulating communities" (1972:47). Their proposal is outside the frame advanced here with its ultimate stage, where the world would consist of small self-sufficient and stable communities. Yet, many of the items on the list are not only desirable, but indispensable for good governance. The authors further acknowledged that small-scale societies are unlikely to be governed democratically. Meanwhile, some of the rather optimistic assumptions could spring from their scientific positivism as well as romanticism (e.g. 1972:86).
[800] "Decreases in both human population size and its impact (as much an outcome of how we consume as our total numbers) may raise some uncomfortable questions, such as, Can we have a sustainable civilization while fully respecting people's freedom to reproduce or consume without limits? However, not wrestling with these limits may prove much more perilous" (Assadourian 2013:Loc. 6443-48 [sic!]).
[801] A more comprehensive discussion can be found in Stretton (1976:207-308).

enhancing sustainability. While this list is not comprehensive and whereas not exclusively possible in nondemocratic regimes, it should be evident by now that such practices face greater opposition and are harder to implement in democracies. Action cannot be longer deferred if the devastation is to be kept at a minimum.[802]

The discussion here is in so far restricted as the ethical elaboration of the harm principle and ecological integrity are used as guidelines for desirable politics. In order to be applied by a meritocracy the policies needs to satisfy two conditions. 1. It needs to show that it allows for a maximum extension of the harm principle under the banner of a capped capabilities approach. 2. It needs to show to clearly seek ecological integrity as an absolute end. The application of the principles suggested in the previous discussions can be described as "putting Earth First".[803] From early on the ecological footprint was seen as a function of population, consumption and technology. Means for curtailing destruction have regularly been (although not followed through) described as obvious.

> "Reducing impacts of human activities upon the environment can be achieved only by change in the three variables in the equation. Reducing impact (I) means either (1) limiting population growth; or (2) limiting affluence; or (3) improving technology, thereby reducing throughput intensity of production" (Goodland and Daly 1996:1011).

The most effective governance will include all three factors.[804] While technology is one of these three factors and the continuous improvement should be fostered by supporting research, development and implementation, technology alone cannot solve the problem. In any case, consumption cannot outstrip supply. Advocating reshaping population growth and infrastructure, Randers warns that "resource trends have an enormous inertia" and that exploitations are "driven by population size and the infrastructure already in place—cities, power stations, roads, and airports" (2012:Loc. 3072-75). The reduction and control of affluence and

---

[802] When challenging current resource distribution, one should take into account that history is driven by conflicts over resource distribution and interests more than by ideology (Mitchell 2011).

[803] Note that although the group Earth First! is often criticized, much of their practice is in accord with the justifications for direct action discussed by Carter and alike (2013).

[804] Forsyth warns that the equation (population affluence and technology) forgets culture (2003), but this is only the case if one reifies all three. Reiterating common suggestions, Harris writes that adjusting to a limited world "could involve policies such as redistribution of carbon through personal carbon trading; redistribution of work and time, in part to "break the habit of working to earn to consume" but also to allow people to have a better balance between work and other activities; redistributing income and wealth to ensure that changes in the economy do not harm the less well-off and, in the process, to discourage conspicuous material consumption among the most affluent people in society (which has perverse consequences, including driving consumption trends up among the less well-off); and, very likely, family planning geared toward reducing population" (2013:Loc. 2579).

population are presumably most effective for designing sustainable politics in order to divert and mitigate disastrous consequences.[805]

4.4.1. POPULATION PLANNING: LIMITED CHILDREN IN A LIMITED WORLD

While many factors regarding the future remain unknown and scientific inquiries are particularly difficult due to complex interrelations, demography is a field that still allows some form of prognosis. Since its factors are relatively stable, it is possible to make valuable estimations.[806] The medium-variant projection derived from current trends assumes a world population of a staggering rise to 11.2 billion in 2100 (UN 2015:1). History shows that "excessive growth of the population and the continually increasing population densities" are typically main causes for land losing its capacity to even provide for a basic level of subsistence (Yan and Wang 2004:614).[807]

> "[W]ith rapid increases in population, demands for food, fuel and material jump sharply, upsetting the balance of the carrying capacity, leading to a manner of development and management akin to plundering" (2004:620).

Countless studies show the outcome of overpopulation and the connected overexploitation of resources is not only environmental migration, but typically civilisations collapse under these pressures (Ophuls 2012).[808] The current projection of population development paired with the fact that resources are already overexploited point at a dangerous development. Though the global population might have passed 'peak child', demographic time lags reach far into the future.[809] "The difficulties of changing demographic trajectories mean that the problem should have been addressed sooner, rather than later" (Ehrlich and Ehrlich 2013). Addressing population as a major factor in environmental destruction is so urgent, that politics cannot wait for demographic transmissions.

---

[805] Directing resources towards the research and development of sustainable technology is essential. Technological advances will be excluded from the discussion here in so far as they are not a subject of social science. The need to advance so called 'clean technology" should be uncontroversial. Admittedly, a stronger government, as has been discussed above, has the chance of more effective interference into research by setting specific agendas and funding.

[806] Better educated people tend to have fewer children than those who could not enjoy an education. Huge population growth typically happens in the transition phase from an agriculturally based society. While this period is signified by drastic improvements in health care, reproductive practices do not keep up with the changes. The higher survival rate leads to bigger family sizes. The declining trend in population size in postindustrialist societies could be understood as a consequence or adjustment to the conditions of a 'modern' world. Still, this trend is restricted to a couple of countries and most countries despite experiencing a drop in birth rate still grow in numbers.

[807] 40-60% of the global increase of emissions is attributed to growing populations (UNFPA 2009:21).

[808] Note that the idea of overpopulation itself is subject to dispute. It is highly contextual. *The Population Bomb* was wrong in its predictions (Ehrlich 1972), but that does not mean that the books assumptions were wrong in general. Ehrlich and Ehrlich "tended to exaggerate, but their insight about the dangers of overpopulation was right. In theory, we could eat less and save energy, but in practice we never will, unless made to do so" (Lovelock 2009:Loc. 79).

[809] Peak child is an analogy to peak oil etc. and marks the point where the global average child per women is the highest.

Though world population is assumed to peak without active interference, effective population management could mean a significant relief for global life support systems.[810] However, "many scientists still tend to treat population growth as an exogenous variable, when it should be considered an endogenous one" (Ehrlich and Ehrlich 2013). Depending on the view, population is understood as endogenous or exogenous variable, which reflects the attitude to interference (Tremmel 2011).[811] Population is not the only factor in resource consumption but it is a decisive factor in the equation. Hence a drop in population will almost certainly amount to improved chances for sustainability. Biologists speak of carrying capacity as "the maximal population size of a given species that an area can support without reducing its ability to support the same species in the future" (Daily and Ehrlich 1992:762). Depending on the perspective of the carrying capacity has either already been surpassed or will be soon. Numbers for the actual carrying capacity vary due to different levels of consumption, yet, this should not provoke optimism. Even, if the planet could carry more than the current 7.3 billion in theory, questions of equity and social justice would be major obstacles in practice (UN 2015:1). It is true that some Western nations have declining populations and that modern affluence leads to smaller family sizes. But the difference in consumption needs to be accounted for in such a manner that numbers actually match resources.

When a population as a whole lives beyond its means, it is misleading to argue that the country's birth rate is below replacement rate.[812] Effective resource management is easier to be met by shrinking the population than by lowering living standards and changing to sustainable lifestyles. As discussed earlier loss aversion marks people's attitude towards restrictions. The desirability of living a comparatively good life (which could be defined by a capabilities approach) is hardly disputed (Nussbaum 1992; Sen 1993; Holland 2008), but inequality in

---

[810] Potts promotes family planning under the slogan "The elephant in the room could be our friend" (2013).

[811] Hardin describes the right to multiply, which he sees as a choice put forward by the Universal Declaration of Human Rights, as 'unfortunate' (1968). China falls into the category of "coordinated population control efforts" (Dryzek 2005:43). Trying to influence population has been attempted in Western countries as well, but largely remained an 'individual choice' (Goodin 2013:Loc. 187-92).

[812] The problem with reproduction choices in prosperous societies is not only the higher consumption by the children themselves, but the fact that they can father whole lineages of overconsumers (Hamilton 2010:41f.; see also Ehrlich 1971). The responsibility or impact of one child more is disproportionate. The estimated "carbon legacy of the average female in the United States is 18,500 tonnes of CO2 while that of a Bangladeshi woman is only 136 tonnes. In other words, the future stream of carbon emissions following a decision by an American couple to have an extra child is 130 times greater than that of a decision by a Bangladeshi couple. Put another way, to have the same impact on future global carbon emissions, a decision by one American couple not to have a child would have to be matched by 130 Bangladeshi couples. So population policies should be targeted now at the United States and the larger European countries (including Russia) rather than poor but populous nations like Bangladesh, India and Nigeria" (Hamilton 2010:42). Hamilton also writes that "the situation we face has arisen not from the old working-class vice of excessive copulation but the modern middle-class vice of excessive consumption" (2010:44).

global distribution is unlikely to vanish (Stretton 1976).[813] Huge numbers of people remain without food and access to other basic resources, despite the fact that it might be possible to ensure 'decent' living conditions for all. The standards of postindustrialist countries cannot be supported by the planet's natural resources and voluntary changes in behaviour are not to be expected in the near future as mentioned above (e.g. Maniates and Meyer 2010). Meanwhile, technological advances and innovations are not sufficient to raise the living standards in developing countries to match the standards in the West. Even if it was possible and likely, the demographic effects would be delayed by decades. Thus, the induced decrease in the world's population would be one of the most effective measures against environmental depletion. Thence, the argument can be made that population control should be considered by all governments. An examination of the probably most effective 'greening' measure must include normative as well as practical considerations. The successes and failures of policies implemented by the Chinese government must be included and therefore will be part of the discussion of the usefulness of population size management. This elaboration will start by reviewing key discourses before concentrating on concrete measures, practice, and a calibration of the criticism.

4.4.1.2. POWERFUL DISCOURSES OF PERSONAL RIGHTS AND NATURALNESS

The preceding arguments ascertain that

> "some form of action is needed to prevent human population numbers from reaching the point where the impact on both the natural environment and human misery becomes irreversible, that action is likely to clash with our cherished notions of human rights, social justice and individual freedom of choice" (Kingsnorth 2009:41).

Stabilising the population requires "the courage to implement important changes coercively" (Heilbroner 1976:25). Population control is a 'thorny territory', but even Mill already considered its legitimacy (1901). To restrict the number of children is an extreme measure, but given the danger of an ever growing population such means might be labelled inevitable, and worthwhile especially if social justice is part of the consideration. Following Malthus, there are two types of checks on the population (1979; see also Townsend 1786).[814] Roughly applying Berlin's distinction between different forms of liberty they can be classified as 'positive' meaning the provision of something via interference and 'negative' as non-interference (1969). The first one is positive since it is preventative – limiting births through moral constraint and birth control. The

---

[813] Leggewie and Welzer see the asymmetry of distribution of resources and chances between rich and poor as major problems (2009:48).

[814] Malthus believed in an automatic balancing of population. "It is an obvious truth, which has been taken notice of by many writers, that population must always be kept down to the level of the means of subsistence" (1789:Loc. 16). This "obvious truth" is also understood as iron law.

second one is negative and its consequence involves famine, destitution, plague and war.[815] Notwithstanding its effectiveness interference is highly unpopular. Not only politicians but also mainstream environmental organisations will not touch the topic (Kingsnorth 2009:41). Only a few of the authors in *Political Theory and the Ecological Challenge* for example, mention population pressure as a challenge (Dobson and Eckersley 2006), while the chapter on feminism boldly ignores the issue (Plumwood 2006). Social scientists feel already uncomfortable with the term 'control', thus the term 'family management' or 'planning' is used in many cases.[816] Most importantly, as reproduction is one of the essential parts of life, it is often considered as 'natural' and, hence, as an inalienable right. In spite of people using the word 'overpopulation', solutions are seldom discussed. While many people are eager to hire professionals to 'exterminate' overpopulations of rabbits and insects, discussing measures against human overpopulation leaves a bitter aftertaste. In many people's minds the boundary between 'taming' overpopulation by lowering birthrates and actively killing people is blurry. Consequently, a widely acknowledged problem in academic circles is not part of a wider discussion within civil societies (Ehrlich 1971; Meadows et al. 1972; Ehrlich and Ehrlich 1990; Daily and Ehrlich 1992; Ehrlich, Ehrlich and Daily 1993; Potts 2013).

Although with many problems of its own, it can be argued that family planning should be the government's business. Discussing justice, Shapiro asserts that protecting the basic interests of children is "a duty that all the states fail to discharge for some of their citizens and many with respect to most of their citizens" (1999:88). Furthermore, the state needs to be concerned with the extensive costs of an ever growing population on the environment and therefore the population as the whole; future generations included. Children may create benefits and costs within the family, but there are also external costs and ecological footprints. For an overpopulated space, negative externalities outweigh the positive externalities and thus new children create a burden for society as a whole.[817] The result is an ever-growing pressure on resources. The protection of children then should involve protection from overpopulation. Hence it is imperative to discuss the issue as a policy measurement despite its notoriety deriving from undesirable practices, such as gender selection bias, forced abortion, forced sterilisation, and

---

[815] Convinced of the inevitability Ehrlich and Ehrlich write that "[t]he only remaining question is whether it will be halted through the humane method of birth control, or by nature wiping out the surplus" (1990:17).

[816] The fear of being perceived as supporting population control means that the UNFPA failed to mention it as a possible measure in the climate debate (Tremmel 2011). It is a widespread phenomenon. Davis for example writes: "Within the United States, the dangers of domestic overpopulation have been too controversial for official commissions. Even in terms of overpopulation abroad, the issue has been controversial" (2007:134).

[817] Mill writes bringing a "child into existence without a fair prospect of being able, not only to provide food for its body, but instruction and training for its mind, is a moral crime, both against the unfortunate offspring and against society; and that if the parent does not fulfil this obligation, the State ought to see it fulfilled, at the charge, as far as possible, of the parent" (1901:75).

even infanticide. Governments need to stop population pressure when people are unwilling to adopt changes on their own. Interference is justified if the state is to protect its citizens in accordance with the consistent application of the harm principle.

> "Logic demands that coercive population control be considered in relation to the UN's medium variant prediction of attempting to reach 10.9 billion by the year 2100 due to the fact that is highly likely that a major die off will occur prior to that year, caused by the growing population and the ever increasing usage of non-renewable and renewable resources. Simply put, only a lunatic and madman, would gamble the survival of the human species on voluntary population control without considering coercive population control. Every human right, except the right to produce children, which when exercised harms another human being is in some manner controlled and limited by society. Since the right to produce children not only could, but would, cause the deaths of billions there isn't any logical or moral reason why that right should not be controlled. Therefore, that right must be treated as every other right and controlled and limited by society" (Brent 2014).

The lack of regulation is not only inconsistent. It also means missed opportunities for environmental protection with a great scope of positive externalities not only for the ecosystem but also for humans as an inherent part. The premise of the argument was termed 'survival'. The reduction or at least stabilisation of the population is a crucial measure.[818] Heilbroner pointed out that population control, since governments will have to have the courage to use coercion, will only be possible in revolutionary systems (1976:25). He, meanwhile, was carefully optimistic towards China's population control policy. The People's Republic stands out in particular in that they have already set an example in establishing the one-child policy more than three decades ago. The control of population is a sensitive topic that touches not only what is perceived by many as the most private decision. Children may also be an essential part to people's concepts of womanhood (manhood, or marriage) as well as a natural drive. Additionally the size of the population is also subject to concepts of national strength and therefore nationalist discourses. Although in a variety of forms, this is apparent in many countries. These are different reasons for the unpopularity of restricting reproduction.

Defenders of reproductive rights on the basis of personal freedom disregard religious or national reasons as ignorant or even backward, while failing to realise that personal freedom itself is also a construction. When liberals defend the right to procreate as a personal freedom, they fail to take the freedoms of the unborn and the already born and their interest not to suffer into account.[819] Whereas it is popular to point at the personal freedoms of the parents to have children, the freedoms of the children themselves are easily forgotten. It is not hard to argue that living humans should have priority before the unborn in a sense that they have a claim to

---

[818] This can be justified by utilizing ecological integrity, capped capabilities and the harm principle presented earlier.
[819] Carter questions individual rights pointing out that the "rights of individual babies be upheld against the good of the larger biotic community" (2007:23).

sufficient resources to live a decent, however difficult to define, life. With pressures on all life supporting resources each newborn adds to the pressure. Under the mottos like "my body, my choice", many feminists and supporters ignore this real issue – when supporting abortion. Under the guise of 'private choice', they classify children as a personal matter. They therefore deny the wider consequences of their choice on not only the children, but the whole population. Democracy is often particularly repellent of any restrictions on family size. Especially democracy paired with an individualist culture does not allow for policies involving the downsizing of the population. Reproductive rights continue to be a matter of personal freedom protected by the state, and the severity of the issue remains unrecognised instead of allowing for state-governed population planning. People focusing on personal freedoms typically think within personal vs. state/private vs. public sphere dichotomies. To classify child-bearing as personal sets it diametrically opposed to the state. The narrow practice of placing children within the private realm only, allows for few regulations. The impact of a child on a wider scale remains muted.

> "We parents also prefer not to acknowledge that having children also involves making a huge contribution to climate change. A child in an industrialized economy will triple its parents' footprint; adding 9,441 metric tons of CO2" (Marshall 2014:Loc. 3199).

Despite the likelihood of environmental disaster, people oppose regulation and do not practice effective self-control. The discourse revolves around rights and seldom around duties. It seems impossible to establish a discourse where the very rights of future generations are taken seriously in this context. The discourse on a personal freedom to reproduce and have as many children as one wishes, remains one-sided. People eagerly defend their rights, while their children's future rights are barely a part of their cognitive scheme. Ecofeminists, for example, tend to understand interference in fertility rates by the states as an affirmation of patriarchy (Dryzek 2005:48).[820] They, thereby actively, avoid constructive engagement with the implications of a right to multiply. The responsibility of a family for the ecological footprint of their offspring remains unaccounted. One finds many scholars and probably the majority of academia defending reproductive rights on the basis of its claim as a personal freedom (Freedman and Isaacs 1993). Although crude speculation, this may be the case, because it is an issue that concerns almost everyone and easily shows disparities between theory and practice. One could explain it in terms of the dichotomy between rationality and nature or reason and drives – assuming that scholars could look beyond their own cultural embeddedness. It is therefore not just a simple conflict between values and the question of prioritizing different personal (or) human rights. To acknowledge population pressures and act in accordance is a

---

[820] Dryzek points out that the argument that such measures "serve established political power" is false, since the denial of limits serves global capitalism (2005:48).

'bitter pill' for many. Mill, on the other hand, highlighted reproduction as, not only, involving responsibility towards the child, but to society as well.

> "The fact itself, of causing the existence of a human being, is one of the most responsible actions in the range of human life. To undertake this responsibility—to bestow a life which may be either a curse or a blessing—unless the being on whom it is to be bestowed will have at least the ordinary chances of a desirable existence, is a crime against that being. And in a country either over-peopled, or threatened with being so, to produce children, beyond a very small number, with the effect of reducing the reward of labour by their competition, is a serious offence against all who live by the remuneration of their labour. The laws which, in many countries on the Continent, forbid marriage unless the parties can show that they have the means of supporting a family, do not exceed the legitimate powers of the state: and whether such laws be expedient or not (a question mainly dependent on local circumstances and feelings), they are not objectionable as violations of liberty" (1901:77).

The harm principle applies to the field of reproduction as well as other areas. Here individual freedom is not only inseparable from others; it is also conditioned by duty. The Millian state should also protect unborn children (Höntzsch 2012:108). Pointing at this passage in Mill, Lane clarifies the argument for the legitimacy of population control.

> "One solution would be to say that having children imposes a serious harm on others, because it creates a new source of carbon emissions (as well as other potential burdens, for example for the care for such children should the parents fail), which in the case of well-off children in the rich world will also be disproportionately larger than the footprint of the contemporary children who are poor" (Lane 2011b:73).

Such application of the harm principle involves an honesty that is seldom found in particular in politics. A capabilities approach that sets a maximum and minimum cap in regard to living standards needs to accompany a population planning to guard against moral relativism (see Holland 2008).

Additionally the cultural dimension of population control cannot be excluded. Even in the 21st century there are places where being a woman is inherently connected to producing children. Those women who do not bear children can be discriminated by society and not recognised as 'full women'. A study by medical anthropologist Schmidt Stiedenroth on infertile women in Pakistan for example shows this (2010). Women who do not have children can be stigmatized by their social environment. The fact that infertile women in some societies experience feelings of inferiority shows a strong cognitive scheme. Children in such a context are not only a right, but a necessity for an identity – self-actualisation and recognition. Consequently, a change in reproductive behaviour is not likely to occur voluntarily. It is questionable, if a drastic transformation in the perception is possible to take place. Many health organisations focus on the accessibility of reproductive care services. Instead of understanding the fertility and infertility as one of mind-set, most NGOs see it merely as a health care issue.[821] They too understand reproduction as a basic right and play a role in the same discourse. Besides other cultural factors, religions which forbid abortions and even birth control equally need to be understood as a major obstacle to population control. Especially Catholicism, but also other branches of Christianity restrain people from making full use of birth control. The nationalist side focuses on the effect of numbers. Some politicians publicly equate the demography of the population with global power and propagate higher birthrates. This can be seen especially in countries with median population size. The former Turkish Prime Minister Erdogan repetitively called for Turkish families to have at least three children in order to keep a young population. Russian President Putin even claims that it is a necessary standard for Russia. He says that "if a nation is unable to preserve and reproduce itself, if it loses its life guidelines and ideals, there's no need even for an external enemy. Everything will fall apart" (Hürriyet Daily News Online 2012). He equates a decreasing population with decline of a nation in general. His metaphorical usage shows that he understands it as self-destructive. Since nationalism is based on emotions such arguments cannot be disputed scientifically (Aydurmus 2009). While a young population can certainly have positive effects on a country's economy, a large number of unemployed youth might also lead to instability (Huntington 1998). Most certainly a young population has a higher consumption rate, thus a nation with a younger population is inclined to have a larger ecological footprint. Once recognized as means to relieve stress on life support system policies need to be put into place.

4.4.1.2. ONE-CHILD 'CONTROL'

Population growth is influenced by multiple factors. Negative factors, such as disaster and disease, will not be accounted for, since the basis of the moral arguments advanced earlier does not allow for human catastrophe as 'useful'.[822] Needless to say, the propagandisation and active support of multiplication by the state has ramifications. The state, however, can interfere positively. For instance, the state can provide and invest in universal education, including secondary education. Making education, especially sex education, mandatory can decrease the likelihood of teenage pregnancies. Education for various reasons lays the foundation for smaller

---

[821] In some contexts, it can be a form of orientalism, when Western NGOs do not allow themselves to interfere in the same way they do in their 'own' cultures.

[822] "The direct health effects of climate change would include altered rates of mortality and morbidity due to heatwaves and thermal stresses in general, the respiratory consequences of a change in patterns of exposure to aeroallergens (spores, molds, etc.), and the direct, often physical, hazards of any increases in extreme weather events—including storms, floods, and drought. The indirect health effects of climate change include alterations in the range and activity of vector-borne infectious diseases (such as malaria, leishmaniasis, and dengue); changes in the transmission of person-to-person infections (including food poisoning and waterborne pathogens); the nutritional and health consequences of local and regional changes in agricultural productivity; and the various consequences of rising sea levels" (McMichael 2013:Loc. 4710).

family sizes. Governments can further invest in the emancipation of women and attempt the modification of social norms.[823] Here, it should not be forgotten that norms and values often follow behaviour. Thus, the introduction of regulations on family size may induce a change in attitudes towards small families. Spacing is an effective means of decreasing a population. The time span between children and the age of first child birth can be actively increased. Mandatory education, in particular, can have such effect. The stronger integration of mothers into society might prove effective to prolong the time between births. Raising costs for children in form of artificially increasing the prices of child products might prove effective, but can have negative impacts on social justice and is therefore problematic as a tool. Societies that value marriage and only sanctify sex within such an institution can increase the minimum legal marriage age (Commoner 1992:161ff.). Accessibility of birth control of all forms plays a significant role and can serve as a form of empowerment. Publicly funded birth control advances its proliferation. The wider variety of means of birth control, the deeper will its usage penetrate society (UN 2015).

Government population control in practice can be highly problematic.[824] At a moral level, it is important to point out that the absence of such a practice is not only equally problematic but likely to have dire effects. The externalities cannot be disregarded easily. Practices varied and vary between forced sterilisation to voluntary educational programs.[825] The official rationale of the Chinese politburo pointed at infrastructural difficulties and pressures on resources, including environmental pollution (Greenhalgh 2003). China's effective population control program was built upon the realisation of limited resources, an extremely fast growing population, and the understanding that wealth and population growth are connected (2003:164). Overpopulation is seen "as a key factor in environmental pollution, urban congestion, low GDP per capita, and a host of other problems", even in the contemporary PRC (Yi 2007:217). Notably, policies were strongly influenced by natural science and the approach contained quantitative goals

> "in a rhetoric of numbers and national progress through science, their quantitative research showed that "the only solution" was a policy to encourage all couples to have only one child, regardless of the costs to individuals and society" (Greenhalgh 2003:178).

---

[823] The Chinese government employs the slogan "One is good, two is all right, and three is too many" (Davis 2007:122). Today's China appears to have developed a widespread small family culture, according to Cox (2013). Tremmel asserts that not all population policies have to be deemed immoral – in particular antinationalist behaviour can be incentivised by the state (2011).

[824] "Chinese population science like all population sciences is not detached from, but linked to and in varying degrees shaped by politics. A sharp distinction between the two domains is hard to sustain" (Greenhalgh 2003:165).

[825] A discussion of the legitimacy of involuntary sterilisation as an extreme measure is beyond the scope of this text. Such a medical procedure is invasive and typically only debated in case of mentally ill people's right to procreate. Hence, sterilisation is framed as a violation of reproductive rights, which leads back to the former arguments about priority setting. Atrocities committed hinder an honest engagement with the question of best interest and conflicting rights (the mother, the father, the child, society, nature). Bok asserts that the distinction for the legitimacy of methods runs along the lines of voluntary and involuntary (2010).

Natural science positivism therefore guided a giant social project.[826] While *The Limits to Growth* discussion seems to have been inconsequential within Western countries, the Chinese government took significant steps to control population growth.

> "For population specialists in the West, China provides a sobering case study of how Western scientific ideas of population crises warranting drastic solutions can be transported to a third world context, transformed from an academic proposal into a concrete policy, and then imposed on a rural population with the political will and force of a late communist party-state, at great cost to human health, well-being, and even life" (Greenhalgh 2003:188).

Population control did mean massive sterilisation campaigns including coercive measures such as forced sterilisations. Here, it should be mentioned that targets were set by the central government and local governments adjusted their practices differences, hence measures varied between regions (Cox 2013).

Aside from regional variations, measures and standards went through different phases. Economic conditions, in combination with low per capita resources, led to a stricter enforcement of the policy in 1980 (Yi 2007:216f.). Then in the project's second phase the policy was loosened to a 1.5 child policy. The implementation had led to popular resistance that amounted in a looser rule in 1984, which made the rule gender dependent. If the first child was a girl, a second child became 'legal'. This was decided despite the fact that such a rate would produce an 'ideal size' only by 2080 (Shen 1998:33). Population management can be a slow process. Regardless of its efforts, the actual fertility rate did not fall below two before 1990, which could be understood either as a failure of the programs or as a sign of its importance. Without the policy, population growth would certainly have been much higher. Shen calculates that, between 1970 and 1995 alone, 200 million more infants would have been born, probably leading to further exponential growth and malnutrition (1998:36). The disproportional growth of population, in comparison to grain in a country with comparatively scarce fertile land, could have led to more human misery. The possible costs of overpopulation can only be subject to speculation.[827] In spite of coercive politics causing enormous human suffering, the effects of their absence cannot be measured, hence discounted.

---

[826] "Whether the leadership had already committed itself to a one-child policy and simply sought scientific expertise to legitimate that fundamentally political decision, or it was wavering or internally divided and the scientists pushed them decisively in that direction, is a critical question. My research has produced no evidence that the central leadership was internally divided on the population question. To the contrary, a whole pantheon of top leaders was on record stating that excessive population growth was a serious problem" (Greenhalgh 2003:185).

[827] Comparison is often made between the ideal performance of one type of government and the actual performance of another type. Since China and India were at comparatively similar stages of development when the one-child policy was put into place, carefully studying its influence in comparison could be rewarding.

Criticism towards the one-child policy, or other population control regimes, goes beyond a rejection of its coerciveness. Scholars point at the cultural value of children in rural communities and the societal consequence of an ageing population, including a shortage of labour and soldiers (Greenhalgh 2003:183; see Höffe 2009). Though cultural values should not be disregarded in their entirety, there are important reservations to such criticism. First, the ongoing debate about protection of culture, within anthropology for example, shows that these reservations need to be put under scrutiny. Culture undoubtedly is emergent, negotiated and dynamic. This means that conservatism misunderstands traditions and authenticity, and overestimates continuity. The constant flux of culture and, the fact, that cultures are never isolated mean that cultural practices can hardly be understood as pristine.[828] Moreover, protection of culture for its own sake would cover protecting practices such as female genital mutilation. Therefore, the argument that a practice of population control undermines culture needs to be dismissed. A second important point is the fact that natural forces will not halt for cultural practices. The environment reacts to human behaviour, but ecosystems operate independent of cultural predilections. Hence, a further general argument that cannot be simply dismissed by classifying it as 'Neo-Malthusian' – and therefore positivist – can be made against these reservations.

In addition, shortage of labour is a relative concept that needs to be rejected as an argument as well (apart from the possibly utopian idea of full employment today). Major inventions have been made as a consequence of labour shortages. The technological advances after the Black Death are some among many. Findings also indicate that the fear that an ageing society is less innovative, less open to risks and has less output are not empirically substantiated (Ehrlich and Ehrlich 1990; Höffe 2009:292; Randers 2012:Loc. 1523-25). The reservation that an increasing group of elderly cannot be supported by those working, misses the fact that another group that needs support will decrease (Ehrlich and Ehrlich 1990:158ff.).[829] Fewer children will need care and education, so human capital will be freed to provide for the ageing population. Arguments about the funding of transfer schemes have to be disregarded, either way, because such schemes cannot build on unsustainable politics in the long run and payment would be insecure in world hit by environmental catastrophes, too. Besides, better health care means that people can actively participate in public life for a much longer time span. Furthermore, today's technological advances make human capital less important and can actually replace labour. Many jobs that used to require human labour can be handled by computers. Degrowth has already been discussed as a means of reducing environmental destruction. Less material consumption,

---

[828] See for a discussion of authenticity Duerr (1987).
[829] Xenophobia disregarded, immigration remains an option, if a country actually faces a labour shortage.

necessitated by the aim of sustainability, additionally makes a large amount of labour unnecessary. In its consequence, fewer working hours would be sufficient. The argument about the necessity of young people for the military has no place in a world of scarce resources. As discussed earlier, the military industrial complex has an unjustifiable ecological footprint. The waste cannot be justified by any threat since climate change and pollution surpass any other threat to national security. Despite, large militaries are likely to produce conflicts instead of solving them. The fact that modern military operations use advanced technology and therefore need less man power is beyond the point.

The Chinese case shows that population planning comes with negative and positive effects. Yet, valued against other rights, introducing comprehensive planning can be understood as consistent with the harm principle. Collective rights are not just taken as priority. The rights of the existing populations and individual claims to resources can be used as a justification. Curtailing a right to multiplication ensures resources for the existing population. The tradeoff, in fact, can be seen as one ensuring freedom in its positive sense as claims to something and not freedom from interference by the state (see Westra 1998a). Such measures are likely to prevent possibly catastrophic events, such as famine, as an external and less humane way of coping with overpopulation. Admittedly, most countries do not have the chance to implement such measures, due to limited means to interfere into people's lives. Even if it can be explained in terms of an ethic of ecological integrity, restrictions would face significant opposition. The advantage of an ecomeritocracy in comparison to a democracy, here, lies in the fact that issues will not be used to catch voter's attention and polarisation is less likely to be used as an instrument of mobilisation. Misinformation campaigns such as the regular attacks against Planned Parenthood are far less likely under such circumstances. Population policies could be framed as a necessity. An ecomeritocracy must not only establish a carrying capacity, but also carefully evaluate suitable means in accordance to social and ecological necessity.[830] Experts of different fields can contribute to policies that aim at minimum suffering by taking multiple factors into account. Here again, though science can provide information about the potential of different policies and their effects, science cannot solve moral dilemmas. Which means are considered acceptable depends on the prioritisation and needs to involve serious reflections on the tension between private and public goods as well as their interplay. Policy aims should take

---

[830] A friend, who is an expert in the field, suggested tutelage/joint parenting as a substitute for some people. Such a possibility and its means of implementation could be studied by an expert commission. The potential of a democratic state, in contrast to an ecomeritocratic state, to develop such an option is too speculative to be part of the discussion here. Given that values often follow behaviour, the popularity of a program based on the idea could increase after its introduction.

all human costs into account (Westra 1998a).[831] There are no securities that an ecomeritocracy would solve the problem of coercion. Nonetheless, if the alternative is existential harm to others, a certain degree of coerciveness can be justifiably applied. Details and limits would have to be set by experts from all fields. A smaller population ameliorates resource pressures. Population decline eases food security and pressures on other essentials and simplifies the distribution of fair shares.

4.4.2. RATIONING EARTH: "EVERYBODY TO COUNT FOR ONE, NOBODY FOR MORE THAN ONE."

Rationing is essential in a scarce world.[832] Among many, Leggewie and Welzer asserted that if emissions do not decline soon, unrealistic and strict reduction become necessary (2011:168).[833] Exactly because methods of sharing are probably not going to develop by themselves, Cox argues, it is paramount to understand and further develop such mechanisms (2013). Even personal carbon trading has been subject to only a few political discussions so far. Since carbon dioxide is not the only factor, the elaboration here will utilise the idea of footprint budgeting instead.[834] Moreover, tradability and monetisation of nature have been discussed as problematic in the first part in the context of market mechanisms. For instance, this gives little incentive to rich people to significantly reduce their footprint, even if the budget was reduced on an annual basis continuously. Frequently rationing has proven to be an effective instrument of price control, hence means sharing the burden of scarcity more equally (see Cox 2013). Aside from the ethical questionability, typically acceptability and compliance stand in relation to the perceived fairness of a government program (Meyer 2010; Bristow et al. 2010; see also Roodhouse 2007).[835] Historical cases of rationing show that success is dependent on "the capacity to compel universal participation and the ability to cut down on illegal transactions" (Cohen 2011:213).[836]

---

[831] Social justice demands that discrimination on the basis of (group) identity needs to be addressed, abolished and prevented.

[832] Note that people are already subject to rationing. 'Modern man' is so used to money that the fact that money is a rationale of rationing – even a rather arbitrary one – often escapes his cognition. Rationing by head count is as Cohen's article suggests rather meliorating inequality (2011).

[833] Despite the IPCC using carbon capture and storage in their calculations it seems unlikely that it will be operational comprehensively before 2030 (Hamilton 2010:162).

[834] 'Allowances', 'rationing', 'budgeting', 'quota' and 'entitlements' are among the many possible terms available. Each term carries different connotations and policy makers should be advised to include that in their proposals.

[835] This is likely to be part of the success of the two main examples achieved by strong state policies presented in this chapter: 1. "Although wealthy Chinese often pay fines so that they can have more than one child, few if any top political leaders have violated the one-child rule. (How many politicians in the West would be willing to sacrifice their personal interests in this way?)" (Bell 2015:Loc. 2078; Cox 2013). 2. "Public acceptance of rationing during the Second World War was based on trust in the government administration of fair scheme suitable for purpose, evasion being swiftly punished. The promotion of wartime rationing based on the strict fairness of shares for all helped to foster support for the scheme" (Seyfang, Lorenzoni and Nye 2007:7).

[836] A successful programs needs to show that "evaders are few in number, likely to be detected and liable to stiff penalties if found guilty" (Roodhouse 2007; Sjöstedt 2014). There will always be a black market and the total eradiation of related crimes is utopian (see also Cohen 2011).

Rationing has proven an impressive tool of mitigating scarcity and in this case, rationing would be guided by ecological limits.

Currently, the ecological footprint of citizens within countries and the footprint of the average citizen in different countries vary immensely.

> "When considering food and energy supplies, we have to keep in mind that the immediate needs of human consumers is only one part of the problem. We need also to sustain the infrastructure of the cities, the housing, health, and other services, including schools, waste disposal, and transport" (Lovelock 2009:Loc. 78; Randers 2012).

This means that budgets have to be regionalised taking infrastructure, but also other parts of the context such as climatic particularities into account.[837] Obviously, budgeting would have an impact on the economies. From the ethical perspective introduced in this part, economic decline is good as long as poverty does not increase. Ignoring this fact, the idea that mankind can live the American dream remains comforting. Correspondingly,

> "most politicians and most citizens have not yet accepted the unrealistic nature of this goal. Most people would accept that it is desirable for low-income countries to be as rich as the North – and then leap to the false conclusion that it must therefore be possible!" (Goodland and Daly 1996:1004; see Jacobs 1997; cf. Beckerman 1972).

That fairness involves richer societies or wealthier people within a society to cut back appears unacceptable for people living in relative abundance. Stopping overconsumption and sharing the burden of living on a planet with limited resources is not taken as a serious issue.

> "There is no debate as to the reasons for more luxuries in North America, Europe and Australasia, because the cake can grow regardless of who gets to eat it of how. There is no stark contrast between deciding whether millions of people suffer and die rather than airplane, car, oil, coal and energy supply companies having to adjust their operations and rich consumers their consumption habits. There is no question as to precaution in the face of strong uncertainty. There is no moral storm" (Spash 2007:144).

At the same time, the idea of every Chinese purchasing a car is scary to many as well. This tends to be thought of one-sided. While the authors of the *Blueprint for Survival* misjudged the potential of technological progress they classified the Westerner of the early 70s as consuming "disproportionate amounts of protein, raw materials, and fuel that unless they considerably reduce their consumption there is no hope of the undeveloped nations markedly improving their standard of living" (Goldsmith et al. 1972:12). In World War II, Americans showed that without rationing, rampant consumption continued simply because no one was willing enough to sacrifice without binding obligations (Cox 2013; see also Ophuls 1977). The wealthy kept taking

---

[837] However, fair management of resources is likely to raise the question, whether people should live in the desert or under other extreme conditions. If they cannot live within their footprint allowance the answer within a fair share doctrine is negative. Adjusting for context is not elastic indefinitely and needs to be assessed by experts. "If we take for granted the importance of material commodities for social functioning, there is never any point at which we will be able to claim that enough is enough" (Jackson 2012:Loc. 2735-38).

more than their fair share and while others were deprived. Rationing on the other hand, was seen as an attack on democracy and individual freedom (with others interpreting democracy as equal shares of duty). Cox' recapitulation of the problem narrows it down to the market principle as the highest value of all. Plato already criticised oligarchy for its unwillingness to restrain the freedom to use property freely (1982). Noteworthy, he underlined that material wealth and prudence cannot be appreciated at the same time. Income disparities are currently too huge to make tradable budgets not simply a means of maintaining the gap between rich and poor. This is where the capped capabilities approach (Holland 2008), which was discussed earlier as normatively desirable, could be manifested into actual practice. In line with this thought, Cox follows Kalecki suggesting a system were leftover credits can be sold back to the government, since such system would reward saving, while not allowing the rich to buy extra credit (2013; Kalecki 1941:103f.; see also Harris 2013:Loc. 3337). Such a system would support the poor without enabling the rich to directly profit from the poor's 'underconsumption'. Instead everyone's consumption would be capped by rationing at the same level.[838] Eventually all discretionary material consumption could decrease.[839]

Notably, a degrowth society does not have to be poor, but the way a society would be built is substantially different (see Gorz 1980). Goldsmith et al. assume that a stable society, would refocus and therefore "literature, art, music, painting, sculpture, and architecture would play a greater part" would flourish (1972:126; see also More 1992). Correspondingly, Druckman et al. suggest approaching emissions reduction by considering changing ways people spend time instead of "changing the basket of goods and service" (2012). Self-evidently, emissions vary greatly depending on the specific leisure activity. Though change in activity is likely to be accompanied by a change in emissions, factors are too numerous, as they admit, to promote one activity over another as an effective instrument of mitigation at this point. Further research could lead to valuable insights and the promotion of less emission-intense behaviour in general is necessary. However, footprint budgeting is more transparent than attempts in nudging, which could built on such research. It will exclude the chance for a behaviour shift that in fact does not cut emissions by setting an absolute cap. Besides, it is actually more open in regard to the liberal conception of autonomous choice (see Conly 2013), even if within a fair share doctrine. Needless to say, a combination of a budget as a more concrete instrument and the promotion of a more sustainable lifestyle as an ideology, are desirable in regard to a greener outcome.

---

[838] Taxes in contrast to money-independent personal budgets maintain social injustices.
[839] Given the enormous footprint of luxury goods, such as private jets, they do not even have to be forbidden as such, but would simply become impossible within a person's budget.

Though the budget would have to integrate current practices, its clear priority should be on ecological soundness. Footprint budgeting would mean that at least every adult would be supplied with a budget. Policy measures directed to the consumer are particularly useful, since they have shown effective all the way from demand to supply (Reuscher et al. 2011:8ff.). Given interrelation, budgeting will not only have an immediate but also a long-term effect. Budgeting needs to internalise all costs, from material over production to transportation and storage. The technical aspects such as the question whether one would be able to use a cell phone or a card or even both are of less importance (see for example Harris 2013).[840] The most reasonable idea would be to establish an institution or ministry that would be responsible for the budgeting. This is most reasonable, because budgeting needs to be adjusted with the help of different experts from various fields according to changing circumstances. Budgeting does not only have to be flexible, it would also have to be monitored. There are a couple historical examples of such institutions. Most academic contributions to the subject are concerned with the budgeting of health care.[841] Cohen described the latest case of food rationing in an affluent country dating back to the British government's efforts after World War II and highlights that this "consumption control regime" was based on calculations by an experienced and established agency that needed "an acute understanding of the relationship between sufficient household provisions and civilian morale" (2011:210). There are different ways of rationing. The straightforward approach specifies a good and a time schedule, while points can also be given for free spending (Cox 2013). Food commonly fell into the first category and (other) commodities historically have been rationed with the second rationale. The sheer diversity of modern products and the general conditions of today make the latter more plausible. However, Kalecki exposed the unfairness of an open rationing system given prior inequalities of wealth (1941). For example, people with huge wardrobes will need less clothing and hence could spend all their points on food. Such free choice system therefore would have to be evaluated in regard to equity in addition to sustainability. Different goods would have to belong to different categories.

Seyfang, Lorenzoni and Nye are especially concerned with fairness and individual agency within the context of different measures (2007). They point at the helplessness of the individual when not supported in achieving and educated on the matter of emissions reduction. It is clear that humans are differently skilled in budgeting. Subsistence goods need to be ensured. Given that a

---

[840] There should also be evaluations on the specific means. Imaginable is employing iris scans in order to avoid the flexible interchange of budgets between people. It is questionable if this would be desirable. For sure, it would make it harder for one person to run an errand for another person. This must not be interpreted negatively, since making shopping more difficult might be desirable for a society that does not have widespread sustainable values yet.
[841] The necessity of budgeting within health care is probably discussed more often, since the issue is more immediate. The subject makes the difference between death and survival and the need for rational calculation more tangible.

money economy already involves rationing for many people, if well-developed, rationing probably improves the situation for the poor. Here various scenarios are possible. For this, the industrial and agricultural context of each country influences the workable models. In general, it makes sense to group goods according to their necessity, footprint and renewability/replaceability. Local seasonal vegetables are the most prominent among the possibly excluded items. Produced locally, their footprint might often be insignificant. Imported products would be equally subject to the credit point system. A budgeting institution may further decide to leave certain items such as medicine outside the system. Most countries already have systems in place that regulate the flux of biomedicine. On the other side could be goods that would be phased out or even forbidden. Fossil-fuel based cars should be a candidate to be indirectly phased out for example. Setting high footprint credit prices for oil is bound to achieve a serious decline in its consumption.

Seyfang, Lorenzoni and Nye also problematise the calculations of allowances for children (2007:18). The fact that they are concerned that different schemes could mean that allowances for individuals without children could be less, shows that they do not apply a concept of ecological integrity. Their concern still appears to reflect an individualist instead of a common good perspective.[842] In sum, calculating the overall budget needs to take current running costs and the physical limits into consideration. It needs to balance the budget in a way that impels significant cuts securing living essentials for all. In this it needs to emphasize that it is meant to secure living 'indefinitely', thus instigate fundamental changes: "The cap must be environmentally robust and allocated emission levels must go beyond business as usual to avoid oversupply, market power, perverse windfalls, and poor demand for permits" (2007:9). While conditions for each product would have to be calculated by itself and vary from location, the budget for each individual should be seen in a global context.

> "Even if such a scheme or schemes were to be implemented only at the national or the subnational level, obligations should be based on global calculations of environmental sustainability – how much greenhouse gas pollution that each person can safely produce without bringing about dangerous climate change – and on individuals' rights to assistance for adaptation to climate change" (Harris 2013:Loc. 2596).

---

[842] In the British experience bigger households had more opportunities under a rationing regime than smaller ones. "In the case of food, the primary means of consumption regulation was based on flat-rate rationing. This system required consumers to register with a specific retailer and to acquire each week all of their rationed provisions through this channel. Such an arrangement was the foundation for the concept of "fair shares for all" and everyone was entitled to the same allowance regardless of age, occupation, or other considerations. To ensure adequate supplies, retailers received stock in proportion to their number of registered customers and were then required to collect coupons in exchange for the distributed goods. The government carefully controlled the prices of rationed products to keep inflation in check and to ensure that consumers could afford to purchase their weekly share" (Cohen 2011:211). Since the same applies within a money economy, rationing cannot be subject to a separate critique for benefitting larger households. The same is true for social needs that can be easier fulfilled. Additionally, sharing many non-food goods and services among a larger group is more sustainable for the environment anyhow.

In general, Leggewie and Welzer identify three big parts of resource exhaustion: too many calories, too much heating and too many cars (2011:29). These could be reduced with budgeting. They will be classified and discussed under essentials, which includes food and energy and non-essential. Though planning economies are said to have failed in the past and footprint crediting has to take various factors into account, advances in modern technology should make the operation of a budgeting institution feasible. Unless the population is under the impression of a serious and immediate threat, they are unlikely to cut their discretionary consumption. Exploitation and emissions would stay above dangerous levels.[843]

4.4.2.1. CONSUMING ESSENTIALS

The three steps necessary to cut carbon emissions are well known: reducing energy consumption, increasing energy efficiency and shifting from non-renewable to renewable sources of energy.[844] Energy, water and food consumption are interdependent variables and essential to life. Apart from energy for food consumption, the needed energy for heating and other activities varies greatly, which means that an energy reduction plan would need an extensive discussion of needs and set clear limits.[845] Food and water in this regard may be comparatively easy. A brief description of the possibility of food rationing provides valuable insights for a much needed debate.

Rationing food appears undesirable. Nonetheless, it could be the unpalatable consequence of current irresponsible behaviour.[846] Contrary to reservations that rationing will spur malnutrition, Britain's poor have profited from the system, which had controlled prices for basic goods during times of crisis (Cohen 2011:212). Rationing has produced more nutritional equity than other mechanisms (Cox 2013). In order to ensure a minimum living standard for the poor, some basic goods could also be excluded from budgeting. This would satisfy concerns over bad budgeting and subsequent starvation. Goodland and Pimentel discuss diets and "by applying good economics and good environmental management to food and agriculture" come to the conclusion that "conversion efficiency and "polluter pays" principles should be used" (2013:Loc. 2657). Although putting prices on the footprint is not part of the analysis here, their equity considerations can be used as an example by simply substituting the idea of taxes with (footprint) credits. Under their scheme, no taxes "would be paid on grains (rice, maize, wheat,

---

[843] One of the examples is the substantial drop in electricity consumed after the earthquake of 2011 in Japan.

[844] "Globally, the energy sector generates the largest share of anthropogenic GHG emissions, but individual countries' emissions profiles vary widely" (EPI 2012:53).

[845] Nonetheless there are already means of rationing in practice. Central heating distributes a certain amount of heat per living unit.

[846] In *World on the Edge: How to Prevent Environmental and Economic Collapse*, Brown worries about a food bubble, created by the extensive use of aquifers in at least 18 countries, which could burst any time (2011a).

buckwheat), starches (potatoes, cassava), and legumes (soy, pulses, beans, peas, peanuts)" while some goods could receive modest subsidies in order to "alleviate hunger" (Goodland and Pimentel 2013:Loc. 2668). Given the properties of such goods they judge the probability for abuse unlikely. Such distinctions add to the question of footprint a broad understanding of value for nourishment. Nutritional qualities and ecological footprint do not stand in direct relation. Food programs therefore have to adjust their accounting in such a way that it is possible to cover all essentials. Nutritional qualities were included in policies in the past, when governments had to cope with scarcity of food (Cox 2013) and they will have to be included in sound food management in a future, when governments do not only have to cope with scarcity, but environmental impact too. Choices between vegetables and meat would reflect the actual costs of the product. This could reverse the nudge(s) from meat consumption that is not only subsidies, but also the fact that costs are externalised and therefore widely shared. Meat consumption is field were reductions could be enormous. Livestock alone makes up for a significant part of environmental destruction.

> "Globally, the sector contributes 18 percent (7.1 billion tonnes CO2 equivalent) of global greenhouse gas emissions. Although it accounts for only nine percent of global CO2, it generates 65 percent of human-related nitrous oxide (N_2O) and 35 percent of methane (CH_4), which have 296 times and 23 times the Global Warming Potential (GWP) of CO2 respectively" (FAO 2016).

Soil erosion and water consumption are a crucial part of the overall impact of livestock. Different foods vary greatly in their impact on human health and the environment. The reduction of meat, dairy and other animal products, thus is central to a decrease in emissions. Differences in footprint and the necessity of reducing high energy production have been pointed out for decades.[847] Although not news in science they are seldom translated into policies due to opposition.

The ethical arguments for an adjustment of consumption patterns are overt.

> "Diet is one of the urgently needed measures to approach environmental sustainability in the agricultural sector, and to help resolve food/population balance. Improving diets by notching down the food chain, eating less meat and more grains, would vastly improve food efficiency and reduce waste. Improving diets also improves health. Ethicists promote diet shifts because equity is more likely to be improved, while pain and animal killing is reduced. These are compelling arguments to notch down the food chain. The only reason to eat high up are vastly weaker, namely fashion, taste and status" (Goodland 1998:262).

---

[847] "Corn grown by small farmers in Mexico, for example, produces 83 calories of energy for every calorie of fossil fuel energy used. Beef produced in an American feedlot reverses the equation: it uses 33 calories of fossil fuel energy for every calorie of food energy it produces. We have developed a pattern of agriculture that relies on using up stored energy instead of capturing solar energy" (Singer 1994:52).

Seeing meat consumption purely as a matter of taste and status is reductionist. Reasons for eating environmentally damaging foods are important for policies that try to nudge people additionally to rationing. A policy cannot totally ignore the cultural context.[848] Movements to buy local often attempt to reduce footprints. Such behaviour is well-intended but can be misguided. Local food does not always have the lower footprint, in particular if it has to be stored for a long time. Laymen even when interested can hardly access which product is produced sustainably. This is exactly why experts are necessary to calculate the full costs and internalising them into the footprint price of a product. Goodland and Pimentel summarise people's inclination and the need for a shift.

> "Ethicists try to interpret people's behavior, but people often are neither strictly logical nor consistent in their diets. Nor need they be. Flexibility and opportunism in diet are valuable, especially for the poor. The issue is to produce food more sustainably, and at lower environmental, social, and economic costs. People should always be allowed to choose the diet that they want, but the full costs of their choices should be reflected in the price that they pay for their diet. Richer people eat higher on the food chain than poor people do. When people get richer, they tend to move up the food chain and eat more meat. This partly explains why the world is hurtling away from sustainability. For sustainability to increase, and to help reduce hunger in poorer societies, incentives are needed to encourage people to descend the food chain, eat less meat, and move toward plant-based" (2013:Loc. 2618).

Footprint budgets would mean that people would have to bear not only the market costs, but must additionally the footprint cost. Food grown privately (and within a limit) could be allowed outside a budget. Since water given its centrality and hence its need for protection would not be excluded from rationing, it becomes unlikely that people would sell large quantities of privately produced harvest on a black market. At the same time leaving private gardening and conceivably community gardening excluded, could encourage food sovereignty, social learning and therefore resilience. Redistribution or allocation of land for the purposes of self-sufficiency, are imaginable as a supplements to food rations.

At the meantime, budgeting can fight wasteful practices on multiple dimensions. Food waste takes up a significant part of landfills and much of the production is spoilt even before it is available to the consumer (Reuscher et al. 2011). Reducing waste thusly is a priority and a first step to ensuring food security. Here, it is possible to make companies subject to budgeting, too. One option could be to punish companies for unsold food or other products by regulating their production on the basis of goods actually purchased by a consumer. The annual footprint credits spent by the consumer on a specific product could be used to calculate production allowances for each year. At the same time companies could be charged an extra fee for leftovers or products

---

[848] "While current taboos on cannibalism or eating dead relatives are understandable, the question is one of timing. Few balk at eating mangoes form the tree planted on Grandmother's grave; yet many would balk at feeding dead relatives to the family pig" (Goodland 1998:252).

spoilt before arriving at a supermarket. Companies who sell all their products could be rewarded with a greater allowance for the following year. Fees and allowances would have to be adjusted in such a way that overproduction on a regular basis is not economically viable. The argument that this would bring some companies to bankruptcy, has no standing here, since ecological viability is the ultimate measure and companies which can only survive in a manner that is wasteful are harmful for society. Evidence from the past also shows that staying within limits is easier when products are less diverse, but more durable (Cox 2013). Hence, a smaller variety of products is likely to enhance sustainability. It might even improve happiness given the 'paradoxes of choice' and the importance of relative consumption that is consumption in comparison and not as in absolute terms (see also Jackson 2012).

4.4.2.2. CONSUMING NON-ESSENTIALS

The line between essential goods and non-essential goods is blurry. Quantity and quality are divisive. Frequently essentialness and footprint correlate. Water will be very cheap in credit terms and at the same time is easily understood as the most essential good. On the other side of this spectrum could be a resource exhausting medicine. The latter could be still considered an essential good. A budgeting institution has to evaluate which goods are pivotal regardless of their footprint. Yet, many goods' consumption would decline if the costs are merely integrated. Declaring certain goods as non-essential and then internalising the full costs cannot be seen as interference into preference shaping. It would not violate negative liberty. Declaring something as essential and supporting its production or artificially reducing its price constitutes interference, but there is no coercion into buying one product over the other. The latter category of non-essential simply consists of all goods that are not under particular consideration due to their necessity. A budget system in contrast to giving a specific good in a quantity allows for the liberty to choose within the frame of the biophysical limits of the planet. Citizens after all can freely spend their footprint budget according to their preferences.[849]

The consumption of such discretionary goods could be significantly reduced depending on the good. Some popular foods such as chocolate and coffee might become extremely expensive in terms of the footprint budget. Restrictions on car usage are not unknown and are inevitable (Diekmann and Preisendörfer 2001:177). At the beginning rationing in UK war rationing for

---

[849] Stretton emphasized that 'actual' life needs to be considered and warned against simplistic assumptions. "A good test of any ideology is to insist that it answer that question *in detail* – minute by minute, hour by day by year, what should ordinary people be able to do with their time, and what are they likely to want to do with it? Most of them do not wish to divide most of their time between cocktail parties and *avant-garde* theatre; nor between watching television in a landless apartment and socializing in strictly public spaces. They want much more complicated pattern of diverse activities, private and familial and social and public, including a great many active, productive, creative activities" (Stretton 1976:202f. [sic!]).

example differentiated between three categories of private users "essential users (e.g., doctors) had an annual allocation of approximately 9,000 miles, semi essential users (e.g., commercial travellers) had an annual allocation of approximately 4,800 miles, and non-essential (or basic) users" (Cohen 2011:215). So far, driving cars for pleasure is a hobby that externalises most costs. Strict budgeting would decrease the amount of time people took their cars for leisure, convenience or simply habituation. Notably, car-sharing is an obvious way of enabling greater consumption if it is not affordable otherwise. Transportation is an obvious category for reduction and private car usage is often evoked in the budgeting discourse. However, entertainment is a huge category that beyond the obvious activities, vacationing and shopping, seems to have remained largely uncontested (see Druckman et al. 2012). For instance, though it is easy to find discussions of the carbon footprint of the Burning Man Festival, greens are typically silent on the issue of large blockbusters' footprints as one of the most common means of entertainment.[850] This example in fact is symbolic for the difficulty of footprint budgeting.

Resource control regimes have to take all aspects of life that cause environmental destruction into account. There and again, while the charge of regulating many parts of life is legitimate, these aspects of life are already regulated by economic terms, hence are not exactly free either way. Here too a budgeting matrix would give choice to the consumer. In contrast products could be altered in order to reduce the consumption. Cox writes that the US government during the World War II had considered forcing manufactures to produce ugly shoes, but ultimately set a limit to three pairs a year (2013). Such idea shows the line between essential and non-essential. Ugly shoes, it was assumed, would reduce consumption, since people only bought such if needed. While the shoe example may be judged by many as overstepping of authority, governments sometimes forbid addictive substances in food. Shopping for too many shoes is bad for society. On the other hand, consuming unhealthy foods is mainly bad for the individual. This example shows the limits of a budgeting approach and also that government interference is judged contextually. Its success is dependent on many factors, which need to be carefully considered. In case of a serious addiction doctor's supervision is typically advised.

---

[850] While DiCaprio was celebrated for his comments at the Oscars, the footprint of his movie was mostly ignored.

4.5. PART CONCLUSION: ECOMERITOCRACY AND IF EXPERTS DECIDED

"If we plan remedial action with our eyes on political rather than ecological reality, then very reasonably, very practically, and very surely we shall muddle our way to extinction" (Goldsmith et al. 1972:15). For most cases, implementing widespread expert rule is outside the imaginable. Nonetheless, the advanced discussions attempted to focus on ecological reality following Goldsmith et al.'s warning. Herein, the examination shed a light on the realm beyond mainstream green thought and what is possible once the accusations of fascism are ignored and even reversed.[851]

> "Oppression is ultimately a matter of definition, and its perception is the product of a worldview. Change the worldview, and what once seemed natural and legitimate becomes an instance of cruelty and sadism" (Nandy 1993:22).[852]

While the absence of some political and economic rights appears as oppression to many, the absence of breathable air, or soil to grow food, has a different and more totalitarian quality. Life itself is dependent on nature, but strong sustainability demands ecologically sound government. The fact that there are clear tradeoffs and that these necessitate prioritisation cannot be emphasized enough (see More 1992). An ecomeritocracy implies an overt hierarchy of needs and rights. There are different forms imaginable and the preceding elaborations constitute an alternative.[853] There is consensus on the needs.

> "Conserve integrity and live sustainably by constraining and redesigning methods, patterns, and rates of resource extraction, processing, consumption, and waste disposal" (Miller and Rees 2013:Loc.328).

Meritocratic elites have a greater chance fulfilling such needs. Chan writes that those chosen to govern via examination are

> "in a politically more secure position [than an elected body] to tackle long-term policy issues that require short-term sacrifices on the part of voters. They are also in a better position to care about the interests of nonvoters, whether foreign workers, future generations, or animals" (2013:44).

Such position reiterates the qualities of a consequentialist leader and stresses the greater potential for inclusiveness, which is central to ecological thought. Ecomeritocracy also implies that environmentally literate people take responsibility and are put into government. If ecomeritocracy can be shown to ensure conditions for life, it passes the Millian test by demonstrating "to be a means to something admitted to be good without proof" (Mill 1879:6).

---

[851] Radical green group raise the question of who is the ecoterrorist: Are ecoterrorists the ones that destroy the lumber mill or the lumber companies that destroy the forest?

[852] Many who have heard a vegan talking about meat consumption will immediately understand the meaning of this quote.

[853] As pointed out earlier, this part is an elaboration along utilitarian lines. For various reasons presented, I judged utilitarianism as most suitable. Nevertheless, other lines of reasoning could have been explored.

This part started with a consideration of the relationship between the autocracy and the environment in general. Building on the framework established in the second part, it was central to deepen the analysis by engaging with meritocracy in a more practice oriented manner. *The China Model* illustrates potential as well as pitfalls, but is still promising in regard to the general Hypothesis 2: A meritocracy with focus on ecologically sound governance is feasible. Whether an ecomeritocracy could succeed, cannot be said conclusively. Population planning can achieve substantial decline in numbers and institutionalised rationing can insure nutrition under conditions of scarcity. Factors for good environmental governments can be summarized as "providing information, dealing with conflict, inducing rule compliance, providing infrastructure, and being prepared for change" (Lyon 2009:65). There is a solid case to be made that an ecomeritocracy's greater ability and guaranteed competency as well as its concentration on ecological integrity as a common good give it a comparative advantage.

"They're not going to care how you or I lived our lives. They're not going to care how hard we tried. They're not going to care whether we were nice people. They're not going to care whether we were nonviolent or violent. They're not going to care whether we grieved the murder of the planet. They're not going to care whether we were enlightened or not. They're not going to care what sort of excuses we had to not act (e.g., "I'm too stressed to think about it," or "It's too big and scary," or "I'm too busy," or "But those in power will kill us if we effectively act against them," or "If we fight back, we run the risk of becoming like they are," or "But I recycled," or any of a thousand other excuses we've all heard too many times). They're not going to care how simply we lived. They're not going to care how pure we were in thought or action. They're not going to care if we became the change we wished to see. They're not going to care whether we voted Democrat, Republican, Green, Libertarian, or not at all" (Jensen, McBay and Keith 2011:Loc. 81-89).

Future generations will care about the condition of the planet they inherit.[854] They will care about the consequences not the modalities of today's politics. Unless there is human extinction – a risk that cannot be disregarded. In that case, they obviously will not exist. Enough wake-up-calls have been made. If radical change does not come soon, not just imaginary future people, but many or even most people currently living on this planet will experience rapidly deteriorating conditions. An honest engagement with green political theory must put green in its pure form as a premise and central aspect of good governance. It cannot follow the perception of those who proclaim to be green, but must focus on ecological responsibility as the ultimate aim (without any distortions). In this context, it is possible to adjudicate on the potential of a specific regime type for ecological integrity. The dangers ahead in mind, this work attempted to make a step beyond the democracy and autocracy dichotomy, where one is represented as good and the other as evil. Here, attention was paid to democracy not as an undesirable regime, but as a system that fails to protect the common good. Democracy was not questioned as a normative regime in an ideal world. Some scientists in support of nuclear power declare that it is a necessity and that they have 'done the maths' (Hansen 2015).[855] Though in an ideal world, they would prefer to exclude nuclear power their calculations say that it is improbable to succeed without. This book's conclusion reflects such statements. In a similar vein, it has 'done the maths'.[856] When democracy is unlikely to produce green outcomes, and given the magnitude of environmental destruction, good green governance needs to be revised.

---

[854] In 1972, the editors of *The Ecologist* stated at the beginning of *A Blueprint for Survival* that "if current trends are *allowed* to persist, the breakdown of society and the irreversible disruption of life-support systems on this planet, possibly by the end of the century, certainly within the lifetimes of our children, are inevitable" (Goldsmith et al. 1972:vii; my emphasis).

[855] Many IPCC projections rely on technologies that are not available today (see Hamilton 2010).

[856] "Many types of evidence support the conclusion that constitutional democracies produce morally best results on the whole and over the long run, but this judgement is contingent, somewhat uncertain, and should be held tentatively rather than dogmatically. In some possible worlds, probably some past states of the actual world, and possibly in some future actual scenarios, autocracy wins by the best results test and should be installed. Democracy is extrinsically not intrinsically just" (Arneson 2004:41).

While democracy advocacy is hegemonic, green democracy does not exist and is improbable. Whereas a green democracy could have already existed, a green meritocracy has not had a chance. Overall, nature's protection is endorsed abstractly, but concrete policies tend to be forestalled. Despite the activity of various actors, manifold grassroots movements and engaged environmentalists worldwide, life support systems are closer to collapse than ever. To expect a sudden greening from below means disregarding the experience from more than 30 years, since the first establishment of green parties.[857] The prospects do not leave space for optimism that substantial change is going to occur before major thresholds have been overtly passed at which point many governments may collapse. Henceforth, Hypothesis 1 stands valid: Democracy is incapable of ecologically sound governance or in other words, the "fundamental nature of democracy is unsustainable" (Shearman and Smith 2007:96).[858] Though monetising nature and asking for fast returns is unsustainable, capitalism alone cannot be blamed. Unsustainability can also be related to political systems. Since democracies are said to first and foremost value the citizen's self-determination, advocates of green democracy have to admit that their ideas have failed at least to a certain extent. It cannot be argued that lack of knowledge is the main issue, but the fact that citizens have different priorities. Greening a democracy from above, on the other hand, is contrary to mainstream green ideals. Declaring that citizens are holding false beliefs and act wrongly, and wanting to actively modify them is a form of paternalism that is largely inconsistent with green theory of agency. However, artificially separating the world into a public and private sphere cripples politics and in environmental matters leaves much power to the fittest. Though not necessarily theoretically, in an interconnected world the private/public division ultimately supports Thrasymachus' judgment that the practice of justice is determined by the strongest.[859] It leaves the state with limited means to secure commons and limits the effective agency of many disadvantaged.

---

[857] The comparison to a Climate Holocaust and the inaction of many liberals during the Holocaust casts serious doubts on the suitability of various liberalisms to be a counterforce. Jensen, McBay and Keith judge: "The vast majority of the population will do nothing unless they are led, cajoled, or forced" (2011:Loc. 256-257).

[858] "Let us examine at what point in the descending series representative government ceases altogether to be admissible, either through its own unfitness or the superior fitness of some other regimen. First, then, representative, like any other government, must be unsuitable in any case in which it can not permanently subsist – i.e., in which it does not fulfill the three fundamental conditions enumerated. These were, 1. That the people should be willing to receive it. 2. That they should be willing and able to do what is necessary for its preservation. 3. That they should be willing and able to fulfill the duties and discharge the functions which it imposes on them. The willingness of the people to accept representative government only becomes a practical question when an enlightened ruler, or a foreign nation or nations who have gained power over the country, are disposed to offer it the boon" (Mill 1862:81f.).

[859] Discussing paternalism Stretton notes that "[t]here are good and bad fathers and good and bad decisions for fathering. The bad ones don't justify abolishing the rest. (The most numerous of all classes of disadvantaged children are those without fathers when they need them.) The literary Left who made 'paternal' a politically abusive word were doubtless thinking of some misuses of authority or benevolence. But they made a weapon for the enemy – 'paternalistic' is now any winner's convenient, dismissive swearword for any love, help, care, compunction or responsibility towards losers" (1976:210).

At the same time, it is a widely spread perception that dignity is inseparably tied to freedom (Breit 2003:86ff.). Freedom is regularly misunderstood as the basis for human dignity. It looks as if, when facing the choice between fewer liberties or oblivion, many implicate choosing the latter.

> "Do we want to feel better or do we want to be effective? Are we sentimentalists or are we warriors? For "sustainable" to mean anything, we must embrace and then defend the bare truth: the planet is primary. The life-producing work of a million species is literally the earth, air, and water that we depend on. No human activity—not the vacuous, not the sublime—is worth more than that matrix" (Jensen, McBay and Keith 2011:Loc. 248-51).

Even if one accepted dignity as tied to freedom, one person's freedom cannot legitimately severely harm others. There is nothing dignified about overconsumption or underconsumption and the fight for resources.[860] There is no right to ecological irresponsibility. There are many human rights that are violated by unsustainable behaviour and its consequences. Once unsustainable behaviour is reformulated as taking someone else's share, it becomes theft. Once identified as contributing to the total collapse of life support systems, hence cause of death of other living beings, humans and non-humans alike, it becomes taking part in killing. The question of participation or relative innocence is meaningless for a majority who will be the victim.[861] Harming others by taking more than one's fair share can hardly be understood as dignified action. In a world of chaos, still a huge probability with the current course of action, dignity might have to be rendered a useless concept.

Sound environmental governance is axiomatic to anything currently valued in societies.[862] Discussing sustainability means discussing the causes and possible remedies of environmental destruction. It means accepting *necessità* i.e. the consequences of the physical limitedness of Earth in combination with tendencies from human nature. Fully disclosing the scope of the consequences of contemporary politics should lead to a reinterpretation of environmental pollution as tyranny. Thereafter current politics could be classified as tyrannical as it is manifested in ecoviolence, which will only be aggravated. From a moral standpoint that includes all sentient beings, the majority of positions fail to actually acknowledge not only the severe structural violence environmental degradation inflicts on the poor, which they simultaneously insist to recognise more fully, but also seem to ignore the voices of non-humans. Repeatedly democracy advocates disregard realities and tradeoffs. As a prominent theorist of democracy,

---

[860] Ophuls highlights that "there is general agreement among [famous historians and philosophers] that the decline is intimately related to the decay of the civilization's moral core or guiding ideal" (2012:Loc. 922).

[861] Where there is a victim here, there is a crime.

[862] "If there was a way of saving democracy then we should save it, but it is unlikely that there is any such way because the ordinary person or "mass man" is not made of the right heroic stuff necessary to meet the challenge of our age" (Shearman and Smith 2007:165).

Dahl's contestation and reservations have been taken into account. With a warning he admits that cases for guardianship can be made.

> "A heavy burden of proof should [...] be required before the democratic process is displaced by quasi guardianship. It should be necessary to demonstrate that the democratic process fails to give equal consideration to the interests of some who are subject to its laws; that the quasi guardians will do so; and that the injury inflicted on the right to equal consideration outweighs the injury done to the right of a people to govern itself" (Dahl 1989:192).

Human rights law does not know a human right to democracy (Petersen 2009:59). The majority of humans as well as non-humans throughout time and space do not enjoy equal consideration and are even seriously harmed by democratic decisions. The current situation cannot be sustained, since it is too late for avoiding climate change. It is already unfolding. Nature as the primary common good has not been protected. This is of major significance. Green thought has to admit such widespread findings. They make a case for guardianship.

Generally, all authoritarianism is treated as the same. Buell and De Luca write that

> "some radicals believe we have already done such irreversible damage to the planet that we must impose substantial reductions in our access to such demands. Some doubt the willingness of society to accede to such demands. They worry that scarcities and environmental damage will lead to disorganization, war, and the rise of dictatorship. They then may be forced into making a Hobbesian choice: a benevolent, ecologically attentive aristocracy [...] or a severe authoritarian regime that engages in unjust triage to avoid thorough ecosuicide" (1996:xv).

20 years of further destructions later, such assumptions appear far less radical. Those who criticise the idea of ecoauthoritarianism from the left fail to suggest concrete solutions. Their ideas might be noble but while rightfully pointing at the dangers of power centralisation and control, they concentrate on deconstruction instead of constructing viable alternatives (see Luke 1999 and Zizek 2012). Thus they cannot withstand the very critique about Carr expressed nearly a century ago (2001). For him, sound political thinking needs to take reality into account and be guided by a vision. By circular logic, authoritarianism is 'unecological', if ecologism is defined as democratic (e.g. Macauley 1996a:6). Yet, this does not have to be the case. Authoritarian regimes are sometimes admired for their effective way of mobilising all resources towards an aim. Theoretically, they have many advantages for achieving sustainability.

Since survival hangs on curbing nature's degradation, the idea of ecomeritocracy could be advanced as an alternative system, which aims at the protection of basic life support systems. Some conclusions derived from actual practice support the argument that an ecomeritocracy could be a viable system that succeeds in achieving the – by now seemingly impossible – establishment of an ecological society. Wise leadership is more urgent than ever. An ecomeritocracy can be understood as wishful thinking on behalf of the author of this text; however such judgment applies to democracy advocates as shown throughout the first part.[863] In regard to democracy Saretzki points out that the potential for abuse cannot be taken as a reservation against a particular system in every context (2011:46). This is equally true for a nondemocratic government. Though it is not an argument for meritocracy that democracy cannot ensure the benevolence of leadership either, tying leadership positions to competence means that meritocracy has the advantage in a higher chance for competent leaders. Evidence supports that experts are more likely to engage in the kind of abstract consequentialist thinking that is needed. It is reasonable to assume that education in morals at least increases the likelihood for benevolence. Admittedly, searching for virtuous leaders is difficult, when in many places strong morals are barriers to careers rather than seen as an asset (e.g. McNamee and Miller 2009). Benevolence is not necessary, however, if positions in power are located in accordance with successful environmental performance. Independent monitoring institutions can make use of the relative measurability of such performance. An ideology that emphasises joint affectedness and fair sharing of the burden can help compliance. This is not to say that an ecomeritocracy can function anywhere, but that there lies a chance. Hypothesis 2 is plausible for countries like China: A meritocracy with focus on ecologically sound governance is feasible. It is yet to see if meritocratic elements itself could lead to more ecologically sound politics.

One final question that I have not answered in detail and that the literature mostly ignores is how an eco-friendly society could actually look. It is fair to say that if planned, a sustainable society would look radically different from current societies and at the same time is unlikely to resemble societies of the past given the use of technology.[864]

> "Constructing an ecologically sustainable society has never been accomplished before, and so we do not know in advance what will or will not work, including ethics, institutions or individual personality characteristics. Thus any efforts to create this society should proceed through a practice of trial and error in a 'logic of justified hope and controlled experiment'" (Brulle 2006:64f.).

Sustainable democracy is utopian, defending ecomeritocracy appears foolish. However, when reading climate reports the sacrifice of some rights for ecological integrity seems 'more possible' or more tenable than risking all (see Anderson 2012). In the discussion at the very end of the book *The Moral Austerity of Environmental Decision: Sustainability, Democracy, and Normative Argument in Policy and Law*, Bowersox admits: "One of the other conclusions that

---

[863] After discussing the idea of a confederation of Europe, Rousseau comments that "[i]f in spite of all this, the project remains unrealized, that is not because it is utopian; it is because men are crazy, and because to be sane in a world of madmen is in itself a kind of madness" (2009:156). If Rousseau saw Europe at its peak of cooperation, he might have judged such confederation realised.

[864] In Atran et al.'s research the group where political leaders were also forest experts lived most sustainable (2002).

we must accept is that if we are going to espouse democracy, we have to be willing to lose. Oftentimes as environmentalists, [I think we have] ... a real fear of losing" (2002:Loc. 5968; see also Dahl 1989:192).[865] Yet, this means exactly what Jonas rejected as unethical: Gambling with something that does not belong to us (1984:77ff.).[866] Survival cannot be subject to negotiations and luck. The possibility of losing everything demands exceptional means and efforts in Jonas' view. One can live without the highest good, but not with the biggest evil.[867] Finally, it is sensible to assume and hope that the future will refute some of the suggestions made in throughout this work. If nothing less this book should provide enough material to stimulate and provoke further debates. The grass is always greener on the other side.[868]

---

[865] "All voting is a sort of gaming, like checkers or backgammon, with a slight moral tinge to it, a playing with right and wrong, with moral questions; and betting naturally accompanies it. The character of the voters is not staked. I cast my vote, perchance, as I think right; but I am not vitally concerned that that right should prevail. I am willing to leave it to the majority. Its obligation, therefore, never exceeds that of expediency. Even voting for the right is doing nothing for it. It is only expressing to men feebly your desire that it should prevail. A wise man will not leave the right to the mercy of chance, nor wish it to prevail through the power of the majority. There is but little virtue in the action of masses of men" (Thoreau 1849:Loc. 85-90; see also Ophuls 1977:204ff.).

[866] Again, seen through time, space, and species democracy is a minority government by chance of birth.

[867] As quoted above: "The issue is whether in the long run a democratic process is likely to do less harm to the fundamental rights and interests of its citizens than any nondemocratic alternative" (Dahl 2000:48).

[868] In any case: "The human species has no clear function within a system: it is affected by any serious alteration in the collective functions and processes within the system it inhabits, but their possible alteration or extinction is not equally hazardous to other species or to the evolution of the system as a whole" (Westra 1998a:213). Human survival as valuable is a matter of opinion (see Jonas 1984:88ff.).

REFERENCES

Agamben, G. 2012. Einleitende Bemerkung zum Begriff der Demokratie. In G. Agamben et al. (eds.), *Demokratie? Eine Debatte. Mit Beiträgen von G. Agamben, A. Badiou, D. Bensaid, W. Brown, J.-L. Nancy, J. Ranciere, K. Ross und S. Zizek*. Berlin: Suhrkamp, pp. 9-12.

Agamben, G. et al. (eds.) 2012. *Demokratie? Eine Debatte. Mit Beiträgen von G. Agamben, A. Badiou, D. Bensaid, W. Brown, J.-L. Nancy, J. Ranciere, K. Ross und S. Zizek*. Berlin: Suhrkamp.

Aklin, M. and J. Urpelainen 2014. Perceptions of scientific dissent undermine public support for environmental policy. *Environmental Science & Policy 38*:173-177.

Alemann, U. v., J. Klewes and C. Rauh 2011. Die Bürger sollen es richten. *APuZ 44-45*:25-32.

Alford, C. F. 2003. Freedom and Borderline Experience. *Political Psychology 24 (1)*:151-173.

Althaus, S. 2003. *Collective Preferences in Democratic Politics. Opinion Surveys and the Will of the People*. Cambridge: Cambridge University Press.

Alvarez-Rivera, M. 2015. *Election Resources on the Internet*. http://www.electionresources.org

Anderson, K. 2012. Climate change going beyond dangerous – Brutal numbers and tenuous hope. *Climate, Development and Equity 12(15)*:16-40.

Anderson, T. and L. E. Huggins 2008. *Greener Than Thou: Are You Really an Environmentalist?* Stanford: Hoover Institution Press.

Andersson, K. et al. 2014. Decentralization and Deforestation: Comparing Local Forest Governance Regimes in Latin America. In A. Duit (ed.), *State and Environment. The Comparative Study of Environmental Governance*. Cambridge and London: MIT Press, pp. 239-263.

Andrew J. et al. 2013. Going beyond two degrees? The risks and opportunities of alternative options. *Climate Policy 13(6)*:751-769.

Arias-Maldonado, M. 2007. An imaginary solution? The green defense of deliberative democracy. *Environmental Values 16(2)*:233-252.

Aristoteles [Aristotle] 1986. *Nikomachische Ethik*. Stuttgart: Reclam.

Aristoteles [Aristotle] 2009. *Politik*. Stuttgart: Reclam.

Arneson, R. J. 2000. Perfectionism and Politics. *Ethics 111(1)*:37-63.

Arneson, R. J. 2004. Democracy is not intrinsically just. In K. Dowding, R. E. Gooding and C. Pateman (eds.), *Justice and Democracy. Essays for Brian Barry*. New York: Cambridge University Press, pp. 40-58.

Arrow, K. J. 1970. *Social Choice and Individual Values*. 2nd ed. New York: John Wiley & Sons.

Arrow, K. J. et al. 2004. Are We Consuming Too Much? *The Journal of Economic Perspectives 18(3)*:147-172.

Asafu-Adjaye, J. et al. 2015. *An Ecomodernist Manifesto*. http://www.ecomodernism.org/manifesto-english/

Assadourian, E. 2013. Building an Enduring Environmental Movement. In The Worldwatch Institute (ed.), *State of the World 2013: Is Sustainability Still Possible?* Kindle Edition: Island Press.

Atran, S. et al. 2002. Folkecology, Cultural Epidemiology, and the Spirit of the Commons. A Garden Experiment in the Maya Lowlands, 1991-2001. *Current Anthropology 43(3)*:421-448.

Attfield, R. 2014. Can Biocentric Consequentialism Meet Pluralist Challenges? In A. Hiller, R. Ilea and L. Kahn (eds.), *Consequentialism and Environmental Ethics*. New York and London: Routledge, pp. 35-53.

Aydurmus, D. 2009. *Identität(en) – Die Problematik von Klassifikationsschemata anhand von Rasse, Nation oder Ethnie*. Ebook: Grin Verlag.

Baber, W. F. and R. V. Bartlett 2005. *Deliberative environmental politics*. Cambridge: MIT Press.

Badiou, A. 2004. *Metapolitics*. London and New York: Verso.

Badiou, A. 2012. Das demokratische Wahrzeichen. In G. Agamben et al. (eds.), *Demokratie? Eine Debatte. Mit Beiträgen von G. Agamben, A. Badiou, D. Bensaid, W. Brown, J.-L. Nancy, J. Ranciere, K. Ross und S. Zizek*. Berlin: Suhrkamp, pp. 13-22.

Bai, T. 2013. A Confucian Version of Hybrid Regime. How Does It Work, and Why is It Superior? In D. A. Bell and C. Li (eds.), *The East Asian Challenge for Democracy. Political Meritocracy in Comparative Perspective*. Kindle Edition: Cambridge University Press, pp. 55-87.

Bainchini, L. and F. Revelli 2013. Green Politics: Urban Environmental Performance and Government Popularity. *Economics & Politics 25(1)*:72-90.

Baker, S. and K. Eckerberg 2014. The Role of the State in the Governance of Sustainable Development: Subnational Practices in European States. In A. Duit (ed.), *State and Environment. The Comparative Study of Environmental Governance*. Cambridge and London: MIT Press, pp. 179-202.

Ball, T. 2006. Democracy. In A. Dobson and R. Eckersley (eds.), *Political Theory and the Ecological Challenge*. New York: Cambridge University Press, pp. 131-147.

Barber, B. 1984. *Strong Democracy. Participatory Politics for a New Age*. Berkeley: University of California Press.

Barnard, A. and J. Spencer (eds.) 2006. *Encyclopedia of Social and Cultural Anthropology*. London and New York: Routledge.

Barr, S. 2006. Environmental Action in the Home: Investigating the 'Value-Action' Gap. *Geography 91(1)*:43-64.

Barry, J. 2001. Greening Liberal Democracy: Practice, Theory and Political Economy. In J. Barry and M. Wissenburg (eds.) 2001. *Sustaining Liberal Democracy. Ecological Challenges and Opportunities*. New York: Palgrave, pp. 59-80.

Barry. J. 2004. From environmental politics of the politics of the environment. The pacification and normalization of environmentalism? In Y. Levy and M. Wissenburg (eds.), *Liberal Democracy and Environmentalism: The End of Environmentalism?* Kindle Edition: Routledge, pp. 179-192.

Barry, J. and K. Smith 2008. Civic Republicanism and Green Politics. In D. Leighton and S. White (eds.), *Building a Citizen Society: The Emerging Politics of Republican Democracy*. London: Lawrence and Wishart.

Barry, J. and M. Wissenburg (eds.) 2001. *Sustaining Liberal Democracy. Ecological Challenges and Opportunities*. New York: Palgrave.

Barth, F. 1997. Economy, Agency and Ordinary Lives. *Social Anthropology 5(3)*:233-242.

Bassi, A. 2013. *Weather, Mood, and Voting: An Experimental Analysis of the Effect of Weather Beyond Turnout.*
http://papers.ssrn.com/sol3/papers.cfm?abstract_id=2301470

Baudrillard, J. 2010. *Simulacra and Simulation.* Ann Arbor: The University of Michigan Press.

Baxter, B. 1999. *Ecologism: An Introduction.* Washington: Georgetown University Press.

Baxter, B. 2005. *A Theory of Ecological Justice.* Oxon: Routledge.

Bäckstrand, K. 2003. Civic science for sustainability: reframing the role of experts, policy-makers and citizens in environmental governance. *Global Environmental Politics 3(4):*24-41.

Bäckstrand, K. 2004. Precaution, szientization or deliberation? Prospects of greening and democratizing science. In Y. Levy and M. Wissenburg (eds.), *Liberal Democracy and Environmentalism: The End of Environmentalism?* Kindle Edition: Routledge, pp. 101-112.

Bäckstrand, K. et al. (eds.) 2010. *Environmental Politics and Deliberative Democracy. Examining the Promise of New Modes of Governance.* Cheltenham: Edward Elgar.

Bäckstrand, K. et al. 2010a. The promise of new modes of governance. In K. Bäckstrand et al. (eds.), *Environmental Politics and Deliberative Democracy. Examining the Promise of New Modes of Governance.* Cheltenham: Edward Elgar, pp. 1-27.

Bäckstrand, K. et al. 2010b. Environmental politics after the deliberative turn. In K. Bäckstrand et al. (eds.), *Environmental Politics and Deliberative Democracy. Examining the Promise of New Modes of Governance.* Cheltenham: Edward Elgar, pp. 217-234.

Beck, U. 1997. Global Risk Politics. In M. Jacobs (ed.), *Greening the Millennium? The New Politics of the Environment.* Malden: The Political Quarterly, pp. 18-33.

Beckerman, W. 1972. Economists, scientists, and environmental catastrophe. *Oxford Economic Papers 24 (3):*327-344.

Beeson, M. 2010. The coming of environmental authoritarianism. *Environmental Politics 19(2):*276-294.

Beeson, M. 2014. *The end is nigh – don't read all about it.*
http://theconversation.com/the-end-is-nigh-dont-read-all-about-it-25146

Beeson, M. 2015. *Environmental Authoritarianism and China.*
https://www.academia.edu/14542093/Environmental_authoritarianism_and_China

Bell, P. et al. 2001. *Environmental Psychology.* 5th ed. Croydon: Routledge.

Bell, D. A. 2015. *The China Model. Political Meritocracy and the Limits of Democracy.* Kindle Edition: Princeton University Press.

Bell, D. A. 2013. Introduction. The Theory, History, and Practice of Political Meritocracy. In D. A. Bell and C. Li (eds.), *The East Asian Challenge for Democracy. Political Meritocracy in Comparative Perspective.* Kindle Edition: Cambridge University Press, pp. 1-27.

Bell, D. A. and C. Li (eds.) 2013. *The East Asian Challenge for Democracy. Political Meritocracy in Comparative Perspective.* Kindle Edition: Cambridge University Press.

Bender, C. and E. Wiesendahl 2011. „Ehernes Gesetz der Oligarchie": Ist Demokratie möglich? *APuZ 44-45:*19-24.

Bensaid, D. 2012. Der permanente Skandal. In G. Agamben et al. (eds.), *Demokratie? Eine Debatte. Mit Beiträgen von G. Agamben, A. Badiou, D. Bensaid, W. Brown, J.-L. Nancy, J. Ranciere, K. Ross und S. Zizek.* Berlin: Suhrkamp, pp. 23-54.

Bentham, J. 2000. *An Introduction to the Principles of Morals and Legislation.* Ebook: Batoche Books.

Berkez, F. 2005. Commons Theory for Marine Resource Management in a Complex World. In N. Kishigami and J. M. Savelle (eds.), *Indigenous Use and Management of Marine Resources.* Osaka: National Museum of Ethnology, pp. 13-31.

Berlin, I. 1969. *Four Essays on Liberty.* Oxford: Oxford University Press.

Betz, J. 2013. The Reform of China's Energy Policies. *GIGA Working Papers No. 216.* https://www.giga-hamburg.de/de/system/files/publications/wp216_betz.pdf

Binder, S. and E. Neumayer 2005. Environmental pressure group strength and air pollution: An empirical analysis. *Ecological Economics 55(4):527-538.*

Blühdorn, I. 2011. Zur Zukunftsfähigkeit der Demokratie. Nachdenken über die Grenzen des demokratischen Optimismus. In Forum Wissenschaft & Umwelt (ed.), *Demokratie und Umweltkrise. Brauchen wir mehr Mitbestimmung?* München: oekom, pp. 19-27.

Blühdorn, I. 2012. *Post-Ecologist Politics: Social Theory and the Abdication of the Ecologist Paradigm.* Kindle Edition: Routledge.

Bok, S. 2010. Population and Ethics: Expanding the Moral Space. In J. S. Fishkin and R. E. Goodin (eds.) 2010. *Population and Political Theory.* Ebook: Wiley-Blackwell, pp. 5-20.

Bookchin, M. 1980. *Toward an Ecological Society.* Quebec: Black Rose Books.

Boon, T. E., I. Nathan and D. H. Lund 2012. The national park process in Denmark: a network governance approach to democratize nature policy-making? In K. Hogl et al. (eds.), *Environmental Governance: The Challenge of Legitimacy and Effectiveness.* Cheltenham: Edward Elgar, pp. 89-108.

Booth, W. J. B.; P. James and H. Madwell (eds.) 1993. *Politics and rationality.* New York: Cambridge University Press.

Bourdieu, P. 1977. *Outline of the Theory of Practice.* Cambridge: Cambridge University Press.

Bourdieu, P. and L. Wacquant 2006. *Reflexive Anthropologie.* Frankfurt: Suhrkamp.

Bowersox, J. 2002. Environmental Justice: Private Preference or Public Necessity? In J. M. Gillroy and J. Bowersox (eds.), *The Moral Austerity of Environmental Decision: Sustainability, Democracy, and Normative Argument in Policy and Law.* Kindle Edition: Duke University Press.

Bowles, S. and H. Gintis 1986. *Democracy and Capitalism. Property, Community, and the Contradiction of Modern Social Thought.* New York: Basic Books.

Böhnke, P. 2011. Ungleiche Verteilung politischer und zivilgesellschaftlicher Partizipation. *APuZ 1-2:18-25.*

Bradhan, P. 1999. Democracy and Development: A complex relationship. In I. Shapiro and C. Hacker-Cordon (eds.), *Democracy's Value.* Cambridge: Cambridge University Press, pp. 93-111.

Brand, U. and M. Wissen 2011. Clean Capitalism? Die Inwertsetzung von Natur als Krisenstrategie. In Forum Wissenschaft & Umwelt (ed.), *Demokratie und Umweltkrise. Brauchen wir mehr Mitbestimmung?* München: oekom, pp. 99-105.

Breit, G. 2003. Picco della Mirandola. In P. Massing and G. Breit (eds.), *Demokratietheorien. Von der Antike bis zur Gegenwart. Texte und Interpretationshilfen.* Schwalbach: Wochenschau Verlag, pp. 83-93.

Brennan, J. 2011. The Right to a Competent Electorate. *Philosophical Quarterly 61(245)*:700-724.

Brent, J. 2014. *Choice.*
http://mahb.stanford.edu/blog/choice/

Bristow, A. L. et al. 2010. Public acceptability of personal carbon trading and carbon tax. *Ecological Economics 69*:1824-1837.

Brown, K. 2011a. *Ballot Box China: Grassroots Democracy in the Final Major One-Party State.* Zed Books: London.

Brown, L. R. 2011b. *World on the Edge: How to Prevent Environmental and Economic Collapse.* Kindle Edition: The Earth Policy Institute.

Brown, W. 2012. Wir sind jetzt alle Demokraten... In G. Agamben et al. (eds.), *Demokratie? Eine Debatte. Mit Beiträgen von G. Agamben, A. Badiou, D. Bensaid, W. Brown, J.-L. Nancy, J. Ranciere, K. Ross und S. Zizek.* Berlin: Suhrkamp, pp. 55-71.

Brulle, R. J. 2006. Habermas and green political thought: two roads converging In P. H. G. Stephens, J. Barry and A. Dobson (eds.), *Contemporary Environmental Politics. From margins to mainstream.* London and New York: Routledge, pp. 52-69.

Buck, C. D. 2013. Post-environmentalism: an internal critique. *Environmental Politics 22(6)*:883-900.

Buchanan, J. M. and G. Tullock 2001 (1965). *The Calculus of Consent. Logical Foundations of Constitutional Democracy.* Ebook: Michigan University Press.

Budescu, D. V. et al. 2014. The interpretation of IPCC probabilistic statements around the world. *Nature climate change 4*:508-512.

Buell, J. 1995. Ecopopulism, democracy, and individuality. *Capitalism Nature Socialism 6(1)*:56-66.

Buell, J. and T. DeLuca 1996. *Sustainable Democracy. Individuality in the Politics of the Environment.* Thousand Oaks: Sage.

Buhr, M. and A. Kosing 1974. *Kleines Wörterbuch der Marxistischen-Leninistischen Philosophie.* Berlin: Dietz Verlag.

Bundesamt für Statistik 2015. [election results].
http://www.politik-stat.ch

Bundeswahlleiter 2015. [election results].
http://www.bundeswahlleiter.de/de/bundestagswahlen

Bundesministerium für Ernährung und Landwirtschaft 2013. *Ergebnisse der Waldzustandserhebung 2013.*
http://www.bmel.de/SharedDocs/Downloads/Landwirtschaft/Wald-Jagd/ErgebnisseWaldzustandserhebung2013.pdf?__blob=publicationFile

Bundesministerium für Inneres 2015. [election results].
http://wahl13.bmi.gv.at

Burchell, J. 2002. *The Evolution of Green Politics: Development & Change within European Green Parties.* London: Earthscan.

Burnell, P. 2009. *Is Democratisation Bad for Global Warming?* Working Papers. Coventry: University of Warwick.

Burnell, P. 2010. Is there a new autocracy promotion? *Fride Working Paper 96.*

Busch, H.-J. 2011. Das Unbehagen des Prothesengotts. Sozialpsychologische Anmerkungen zur umweltschädlichen Destruktivität in der spätmodernen Gesellschaft. In S. S. Schüttemeyer (ed.), *Politik im Klimawandel. Keine Macht für gerechte Lösungen?* Baden-Baden: Nomos, pp. 81-95.

Butler, W. F. and T. G. Acott 2007. An Inquiry Concerning the Acceptance of Intrinsic Value Theories of Nature. *Environmental Values 16*:149-168.

Bührs, T. 2012. Democracy's Myopia: The Search for Correction Aids. *Australian Journal of Political Science 47(3)*:413-425.

Cahn, M. A. and R. O'Brien (eds.) 1996. *Thinking about the environment: Readings on politics, property, and the physical world.* New York: ME Sharpe.

Caldwell, L. K. 1998. The Concept of Sustainability: A Critical Approach. In J. Lemons, L. Westra and R. Goodland (eds.), *Ecological Sustainability and Integrity: Concepts and Approaches.* Dordrecht: Springer, pp. 1-15.

Callaghan, J. 2000. Environmental Politics, the New Left and the New Social Democracy. *The Political Quarterly 71(3)*:300-308.

Callero, O. 2009. *The Myth of Individualism: How Social Forces Shape Out Lives.* Plymouth: Rowman and Littlefield Publishing.

Campbell, A. et al. 1980. *The American Voter.* Chicago: University of Chicago.

Cannavo, P. F. 2010. Civic Virtue and Sacrifice in a Suburban Nation. In M. Maniates and J. M. Meyer (eds.), *Environmental Politics of Sacrifices.* Cambridge: MIT Press, pp. 217-246.

Caplan, B. 2006. *The Myth of the Rational Voter. Why Democracies Choose Bad Policies.* Princeton: Princeton University Press.

Caradonna, J. et al. 2015. *A Degrowth Response to an Ecomodernist Manifesto.* http://mahb.stanford.edu/blog/degrowth-response-ecomodernist-manifesto/

Carlsen, F. 2000. Unemployment, inflation and government popularity – are there partisan effects? *Electoral Studies 19(2-3)*:141-150.

Carpenter, R. A. 1998. Coping with 2050. In J. Lemons, L. Westra and R. Goodland (eds.), *Ecological Sustainability and Integrity: Concepts and Approaches.* Dordrecht: Springer, pp. 290-311.

Carr, E. H. 2001. *The Twenty Years' Crisis. With a new introduction by Michael Cox.* Chippenham: Palgrave.

Carrington, D. 2013. Amazon deforestation increased by one-third in past year. *The Guardian November 15, 2013.* http://www.theguardian.com/environment/2013/nov/15/amazon-deforestation-increased-one-third

Carter, A. 2013. *A Radical Green Political Theory.* New York: Routledge.

Carter, A. 2014. Indirect, Multidimensional Consequentialism. In A. Hiller, R. Ilea and L. Kahn (eds.), *Consequentialism and Environmental Ethics.* New York and London: Routledge, pp. 70-91.

Carter, J. R. 2006. An empirical note on economic freedom and income inequality. *Public Choice 130*:163-177.

Carter, N. 2007. *The politics of the environment: Ideas, activism, policy.* 2nd ed. Cambridge: Cambridge University Press.

Casalegno, S. 2011 (ed.). *Global Warming Impacts – Case Studies on the Economy, Human Health, and on Urban and Natural Environments*. Rijeka: InTech.

Chan, J. 2013. Political Meritocracy and Meritorious Rule: A Confucian Perspective. In D. A. Bell and C. Li (eds.), *The East Asian Challenge for Democracy. Political Meritocracy in Comparative Perspective*. Kindle Edition: Cambridge University Press, pp. 31-54.

Chen, K. and D. Patton 2015. China should stop adding new coal-fired power plants -state researchers. *Reuters November 6, 2015*.
http://www.reuters.com/article/china-coal-electricity-idUSL3N1311O920151106

Confucius 2015. *The Analects. Translated by Roberto Eco*. Ebook.
http://www.indiana.edu/~p374/Analects_of_Confucius_%28En0-2015%29.pdf

Conly, S. 2013. *Against Autonomy. Justifying coercive paternalism*. Kindle Edition: Cambridge University Press.

Cook, J. et al. 2013. Quantifying the consensus on anthropogenic global warming in the scientific literature. *Environmental Research Letters 8(2)*:1-7.

Cox, S. 2013. *Any Way You Slice It: The Past, Present, and Future of Rationing*. London and New York: The New Press.

Chaussee, J. 2014. *California couple conserving water amid drought could face fine for brown lawn*.
http://www.reuters.com/article/2014/07/17/us-usa-california-drought-idUSKBN0FM2OA20140717

Christman, J. 2005. Saving Positive Freedom. *Political Theory 33(1)*:79-88.

Chu, Y.-H. et al. (eds.) 2010. *How East Asians View Democracy*. New York: Columbia University Press.

Cicero, M. T. 2001. *De Res Publica /Vom Gemeinwesen* I. *Latein /Deutsch. Übersetzt u. herausgegeben von Karl Büchner*. Stuttgart: Reclam.

Clayton, S. and S. Opotov (eds.) 2003. *Identity and the Environment. The Psychological Significance of Nature*. Cambridge and London: MIT Press.

Cohen, M. J. 2011 "Is the UK preparing for "war"? Military metaphors, personal carbon allowances, and consumption rationing in historical perspective." *Climatic Change 104(2)*:199-222.

Colomer, J. M. 2011. The More Parties, the Greater Policy Stability. *European Political Science*
http://works.bepress.com/cgi/viewcontent.cgi?article=1041&context=josep_colomer

Colomer, J. M. 2012. Firing the Coach: How Governments Are Losing Elections in Europe. *Democracy & Society 10(1)*:1-6.

Commoner, B. 1979. *The Closing Circle. Nature, Man, and Technology*. New York: Bantham Books.

Commoner, B. 1992. *Making peace with the planet*. [U.S.]: The New Press.

Connelly, J. et al. 2012. *Politics of the Environment. From Theory to Practice*. 3rd ed. Abingdon: Routledge.

Cotgrove, S. 1976. Environmentalism and utopia. *The Sociological Review 24(1)*:23-42.

Crepaz, M. M. L. 2006. Explaining national variations of air pollution levels. Political institutions and their impact on environmental policy-making. In P. H. G. Stephens, J. Barry and A. Dobson (eds.), *Contemporary Environmental Politics. For margins to mainstream*. London and New York Routledge, pp. 254-275.

Croissant, A. 2010. Regierungssysteme und Demokratietypen. In H.-J. Lauth (ed.), *Vergleichende Regierungslehre. Eine Einführung. 3. ed.* Heidelberg: VS Verlag, pp. 117-139.

Crooke, B. and U. Kothari (eds.) 2001. *Participation. The New Tyranny?* London and New York: Zed Books.

Crouch, C. 2008. *Postdemokratie*. Frankfurt: Suhrkamp.

Dahl, R. A. 1989. *Democracy and its critics*. New Haven and London: Yale University Press.

Dahl, R. A. 1990. *After the Revolution? Authority in a Good Society, Revised Edition*. New Haven and London: Yale University Press.

Dahl, R. A. 2000. *On democracy*. New Haven and London: Yale University Press.

Dahrendorf, R. 2006. *Versuchungen der Unfreiheit. Die Intellektuellen in Zeiten der Prüfung*. Lizenzausgabe für die Bundeszentrale für politische Bildung. München: C. H. Beck.

Daily, C. G. and P. R. Ehrlich 1992. Population, Sustainability, and Earth's Carrying Capacity. *BioScience 42(10)*:761-771.

Darnall, N. and S. Sides 2008. Assessing the Performance of Voluntary Environmental Programs: Does Certification Matter? *Policy Studies Journal. 36(1)*:95-117.

Dasgupta, P. and E. Maskin 1999. Democracy and other goods. In I. Shapiro and C. Hacker-Cordon (eds.), *Democracy's Value*. Cambridge: Cambridge University Press, pp. 69-90.

Davis, D. H. 2007. *Ignoring the Apocalypse: Why Planning to Prevent Environmental Catastrophe Goes Astray*. Westport: Praeger.

Delmas, M. A. 2009. Research opportunities in the area of governance for sustainable development. In M. A. Delmas and O. R. Young. (eds.), *Governance for the Environment*. Kindle Edition: Cambridge University Press, pp. 221-238.

Delmas, M. A. and O. R. Young (eds.) 2009. *Governance for the Environment*. Kindle Edition: Cambridge University Press.

De-Shalit, A. 2001. Is Liberalism Environment-Friendly? In M. Zimmerman et al. (eds.), *Environmental Philosophy: From Animal Rights to Radical Ecology*. Upper Saddle River: Prentice Hall, pp. 386-406.

De-Shalit, A. 2006a. Nationalism. In A. Dobson and R. Eckersley (eds.), *Political Theory and the Ecological Challenge*. New York: Cambridge University Press, pp. 75-91.

De-Shalit, A. 2006b. Thirty Years of Environmental Theory: From Value Theory and Meta-Ethics to Political Theory. *Critical Review of International Social and Political Philosophy 9(1)*:85-105.

Die Grünen 2014. [welcome page].
http://www.gruene.de

Diekmann, A. and P. Preisendörfer 2001. *Umweltsoziologie. Eine Einführung*. Reinbek: Rowohlt Taschenbuch Verlag.

Dobner, P. 2010. *Bald Phoenix-bald Asche. Ambivalenzen des Staates*. Lizenzausgabe für die Bundeszentrale für politische Bildung. Berlin: Verlag Klaus Wagenbach.

Dobson, A. 2002 (ed.). *Fairness and Futurity. Essays on Environmental Sustainability and Social Justice*. New York: Oxford University Press.

Dobson, A. 2007. *Green Political Thought. 4th edition*. London and New York: Routledge.

Dobson, A. and R. Eckersley (eds.) 2006. *Political Theory and the Ecological Challenge*. New York: Cambridge University Press

Doherty, D. and J. Wolak 2012. When Do the Ends Justify the Means? Evaluating Procedural Fairness. *Political Behavior 34*:301-323.

Donner, S. D. and J. McDaniels 2013. The influence of national temperature fluctuations on opinions about climate change in the U.S. since 1990. *Climate Change 118(3-4)*:537-550.

Dowding, K., R. E. Gooding and C. Pateman (eds.) 2004. *Justice and Democracy. Essays for Brian Barry*. New York: Cambridge University Press.

Downs, A. 1985. *An Economic Theory of Democracy*. New York: Harper.

Doyle, T. and A. Simpson 2006. Traversing more than speed bumps: Green politics under authoritarian regimes in Burma and Iran. *Environmental Politics 15(5)*:750-767.

Drengson, A and Y. Inoue (eds.) 1995. *The Deep Ecology Movement: An Introductory Anthology*. Berkeley: North Atlantic Publishers.

Driver, J. 2014. Moral Bookkeeping, Consequentialism, and Carbon Offsets. In A. Hiller, R. Ilea and L. Kahn (eds.), *Consequentialism and Environmental Ethics*. New York and London: Routledge, pp. 164-173.

Dryzek. J. S. 1996. Political and Ecological Communication. In F. Mathews (ed.), *Ecology and Democracy*. London: Frank Cass, pp. 13-29.

Dryzek, J. S. 2005. *The politics of the earth: environmental discourse*. New York: Oxford University Press.

Dryzek J. S., B. Honig and A. Phillips (eds.) 2006. *The Oxford Handbook of Political Theory*. Norfolk: Oxford University Press.

Dryzek, J. S., R. B. Norgaard and D. Schlosberg 2013. *Climate-Challenged Society*. Kindle Edition: Oxford University Press.

Dryzek, J. S. et al 2003. *Green States and Social Movements. Environmentalism in the United States, United Kingdom, Germany, & Norway*. Oxford: Oxford University Press.

Duerr, H. P. 1987 (ed.). *Authentizität und Betrug in der Ethnologie*. Frankfurt: Suhrkamp.

Duit, A. (ed.) 2014. *State and Environment. The Comparative Study of Environmental Governance*. Cambridge and London: MIT Press.

Duit, A. 2014a. Introduction: The Comparative Study of Environmental Governance. In A. Duit (ed.), *State and Environment. The Comparative Study of Environmental Governance*. Cambridge and London: MIT Press, pp. 1-23.

Duit, A. 2014b. Conclusion: An Emerging Ecostate? In A. Duit (ed.), *State and Environment. The Comparative Study of Environmental Governance*. Cambridge and London: MIT Press, pp. 321-342.

Duit, A. and O. Hall 2014. Causes and Consequences of Stakeholder Participation in Natural Resource Management: Evidence from 143 Biosphere Reserves in Fifty-Five Countries. In A. Duit (ed.), *State and Environment. The Comparative Study of Environmental Governance*. Cambridge and London: MIT Press, pp. 293-319.

Dumont, L. 1992. *Essays on Individualism: Modern Ideology in Anthropological Perspective*. Chicago: University of Chicago Press.

Dunlap, R. et al. (eds.) 2002. *Sociological Theory and the Environment*. Lanham: Rowman & Littlefield.

Dunn, J. 1999. Democracy and Development? In I. Shapiro and C. Hacker-Cordon (eds.), *Democracy's Value*. Cambridge: Cambridge University Press, pp. 132-140.

Durkheim, E. 1982. *The Rules of the Sociological Method*. ed. S. Lukes. New York: Free Press.

Easton, D. 1965. *A Framework for Political Analysis*. New York: Prentice-Hall.

Eaton, S. and G. Kostka 2014. Authoritarian Environmentalism Undermined? Local Leaders' Time Horizons and Environmental Policy Implementation. *The China Quarterly 218*:359-380.

Eckersley, R. 1990. Habermas and Green Political Thought: Two Roads Diverging. *Theory and Society 19(6)*:739-776.

Eckersley, R. 1999. The Failed Promise of Critical Theory. In C. Merchant (ed.), *Ecology: Key Concepts in Critical Theory*. New York: Humanity Books, pp. 65-77.

Eckersley, R. 2001. Politics. In D. Jamieson (ed.), *A Companion to Environmental Philosophy*. Oxford: Blackwell, pp. 316-330.

Eckersley, R. 2004. *The Green State – Rethinking Democracy and Sovereignty*. Kindle Edition: MIT Press.

Eckersley, R. 2006. Communitarism. In A. Dobson and R. Eckersley (eds.), *Political Theory and the Ecological Challenge*. New York: Cambridge University Press, pp. 91-108.

Edelman, M. 2005. *Politik als Ritual: Die symbolische Funktion staatlicher Institutionen und politischen Handelns*. Frankfurt: Campus Verlag.

Ehrlich, P. R. 1971. *The Population Bomb*. Cutchogue: Buccaneer Books Inc.

Ehrlich, P. R. and A. H. Ehrlich 1990. *The Population Explosion*. New York: Simon and Schuster.

Ehrlich, P. R., A. H. Ehrlich and G. C. Daily 1993. Food security, population and environment. *Population and development review*:1-32.

Ehrlich, P. R. and A. H. Ehrlich 2013. Can a collapse of global civilization be avoided? *Proc. R. Soc. B 7 280(1754)*.
http://rspb.royalsocietypublishing.org/content/280/1754/20122845.full.pdf+html

Ehrlich, P. R. and A. H. Ehrlich 2014. *Humanity's Gamble*.
http://mahb.stanford.edu/blog/humanitys-gamble/

Ekardt, F. 2011. Umwelt und Menschenrechte. Ein Replik auf Anton Leist. In Forum Wissenschaft & Umwelt (ed.), *Demokratie und Umweltkrise. Brauchen wir mehr Mitbestimmung?* München: oekom, pp. 41-42.

Elinder, M. 2010. Local economies and general elections: The influence of municipal and regional economic conditions on voting in Sweden 1985-2002. *The European Journal of Political Economy 26(2)*:279-292.

Elling, B. 2008. *Rationality and the Environment. Decision-making in Environmental Politics and Assessment*. London and Sterling: Earthscan.

Elliot, L. 2014. Climate change will 'lead to battles for food', says head of World Bank. *The Guardian April 3, 2014*.
http://www.theguardian.com/environment/2014/apr/03/climate-change-battle-food-head-world-bank

Ertner, S. 2009. Verzicht. *Polar. Zeitschrift für politische Philosophie und Kultur 6*:62-63.

Escobar, A. 1998. Whose Knowledge, Whose nature? Biodiversity, Conservation, and the Political Ecology of Social Movements. *Journal of Political Ecology 5*:53-82.

Estlund, D. A. 2009. *Democratic Authority: A Philosophical Framework*. Kindle Edition: Princeton University Press.

Etzioni, A. 1998. A Communitarian Perspective in Sustainable Communities. In D. Warburton (ed.), *Community and Sustainable Development: Participation in the Future*. London: Earthscan, pp. 40-52.

Fan, R. 2013. Confucian Meritocracy for Contemporary China. In D. A. Bell and C. Li (eds.), *The East Asian Challenge for Democracy. Political Meritocracy in Comparative Perspective*. Kindle Edition: Cambridge University Press, pp. 88-115.

Ferguson, J. 1992. The Cultural Topography of Wealth: Commodity Paths and Structure of Property in Rural Lesotho. *American Anthropologist 94(1)*:55-73.

Fiala, A. 2010. Nero's Fiddle: On Hope, Despair, and the Ecological Crisis. *Ethics & the Environment 15(1)*:51-68.

Fishkin, J. S. 2009. *When the People Speak. Deliberative Democracy and Public Consultation*. Ebook: Oxford University Press.

Fishkin, J. S. 1997. *The Voice of the People. Public Opinion and Democracy*. London and New Haven: Yale University.

Fishkin, J. S. and R. E. Goodin (eds.) 2010. *Population and Political Theory*. Ebook: Wiley-Blackwell.

Food and Agriculture Organisation of the United Nations 2016. http://www.fao.org/agriculture/lead/themes0/climate/en/

Forsyth, M. G., H. M. A. Keens-Soper and P. Savigear (eds.) 2009. *The Theory of International Relations. Selected Texts from Gentili to Treitschke*. New Brunswick and London: AldineTransaction

Forsyth, T. 2003. *Critical Political Ecology. The politics of environmental science*. London and New York: Routledge.

Forum Wissenschaft & Umwelt (ed.) 2011. *Demokratie und Umweltkrise. Brauchen wir mehr Mitbestimmung?* München: oekom.

Fredriksson, P. G. et al. 2005. Environmentalism, democracy, and pollution control. *Journal of Environmental Economics and Management 49*:343-365.

Freeden, M. 2003. Political Theory and the Environment: Nurturing a Sustainable Relationship. In A. Light and A. De-Shalit (eds.), *Moral and Political Reasoning in Environmental Practice*. Cambridge and London: MIT Press, pp. 31-44.

Freedman, L. P. and S. L. Isaacs 1993. Human Rights and Reproductive Choice. *Studies in Family Planning 24(1)*:18-30.

Freedom House 1998. *Freedom in the World 1998*. https://www.freedomhouse.org/report/freedom-world/1998

Firth, R. 2013. *Primitive Polynesian Economy*. Kindle Edition: Routledge.

Geall, S. (ed.) 2013. *China and the Environment. The Green Revolution*. Kindle Edition: Zed Books.

Geertz, C. 1994. *Dichte Beschreibung. Beiträge zum Verstehen kultureller Systeme*. Frankfurt: Suhrkamp.

Geus, M. de 2001. Sustainability, Liberal Democracy, Liberalism. In J. Barry and M. Wissenburg (eds.), *Sustaining Liberal Democracy. Ecological Challenges and Opportunities*. New York: Palgrave, pp. 19-36.

Geus, M. de 2004. The environment versus individual freedom and convenience. In Y. Levy and M. Wissenburg (eds.), *Liberal Democracy and Environmentalism: The End of Environmentalism?* Kindle Edition: Routledge, p. 87-99.

Giddens, A. 2009. *The politics of climate change*. Cambridge: Polity Press.

Gifford, R. and Y. Heath 2006. Free-market ideology and environmental degradation: The case of belief in global climate change. *Environment and Behavior 38*:48-71.

Gilbert, J. and J. Littler 2009. Beyond Gesture, Beyond Pragmatism. In J. Pugh (ed.), *What is radical politics today?* Basingstoke: Palgrave Macmillan, pp. 127-135.

Gilens, M and B. Page 2014. Testing Theories of American Politics: Elites, Interest Groups and Average Citizen. *Perspectives of Politics 12(3)*:564-581.

Gilley, B 2009. *The Right to Rule. How States Win and Lose Legitimacy*. Chichester: Columbia University.

Gilley, B. 2012. Authoritarian Environmentalism and China's Response to Climate Change. *Environmental Politics 21*:287-307.

Gillroy, J. M. and J. Bowersox (eds.) 2002. *The Moral Austerity of Environmental Decision: Sustainability, Democracy, and Normative Argument in Policy and Law*. Kindle Edition: Duke University Press.

Gimenez, M. E. 2000. Does Ecology Need Marx. *Organization & Environment 13(3)*:292-304.

Glass, J. M. 2006. Paranoia and Political Philosophy. In J. S. Dryzek, B. Honig and A. Phillips (eds.), *The Oxford Handbook of Political Theory*. Norfolk: Oxford University Press, pp. 729-748.

Global Footprint Network 2014. http://www.footprintnetwork.org/en/index.php/GFN/page/earth_overshoot_day/

Goldsmith, E. et al. 1972. *A blueprint for survival*. Boston: Houghton Mifflin.

Goodland, R. 1998. Environmental Sustainability in Agriculture. In J. Lemons, L. Westra and R. Goodland (eds.), *Ecological Sustainability and Integrity: Concepts and Approaches*. Dordrecht: Springer, pp. 234-265.

Goodland, R. and H. Daly 1996. Environmental sustainability: universal and non-negotiable. *Ecological Applications*:1002-1017.

Goodin, R. E. 2006. The high ground is green. In P. H. G. Stephens, J. Barry and A. Dobson (eds.), *Contemporary Environmental Politics. For margins to mainstream*. London and New York Routledge, pp. 11-17.

Goodin, R. E. 2013 (1992). *Green Political Theory*. Kindle Edition: Polity.

Gorz, A. 1980. *Ecology as Politics*. Boston: South End Press.

Graham, G. 2013. *The Case Against the Democratic State: An Essay in Cultural Criticism*. Kindle Edition: Imprint Academic.

Granados, J. A. and O. Carpintero 2009. *Dispelling the smoke: CO2 emissions and economic growth from a global perspective*. Working Paper. University of Michigan. [No longer available online].

Grantham, J. 2012. Be persuasive. Be brave. Be arrested (if necessary). *Nature News & Comment. November, 14 2012*.

http://www.nature.com/news/be-persuasive-be-brave-be-arrested-if-necessary-1.11796#/javascript:0

Greenhalgh, S. 2003. Science, Modernity, and the Making of China's One-Child Policy. *Population and Development Review 29(2)*:163-196.

Gruber, P. C. (ed.) 2008. *Nachhaltige Entwicklung und Global Governance. Verantwortung. Macht. Politik.* Opladen and Farmington Hills: Verlag Barbara Budrich.

Gunster, S. 2010. Self-Interest, Sacrifice and Climate Change: (Re-)Framing the British Columbia Carbon Tax. In M. Maniates and J. M. Meyer (eds.), *Environmental Politics of Sacrifices*. Cambridge: MIT Press, pp. 187-216.

Gurr, T. R. 1985. On the political consequences of scarcity and economic decline. *International Studies Quarterly 29*:51-75.

Habib, A. 2014. Future Generations and Resource Shares. In A. Hiller, R. Ilea and L. Kahn (eds.), *Consequentialism and Environmental Ethics*. New York and London: Routledge, pp. 136-146.

Hache, E. and B. Latour 2009. Die Natur ruft. Wem gegenüber sind wir verantwortlich? Eine Sensibilisierungsübung. *Polar. Zeitschrift für politische Philosophie und Kultur 6*:73-78.

Hadler, M. and M. Haller 2011. Wie viel „Umwelt" wollen die Menschen? Über Umwelteinstellungen und die Chancen der demokratischen Umweltpolitik. In Forum Wissenschaft & Umwelt (ed.), *Demokratie und Umweltkrise. Brauchen wir mehr Mitbestimmung?* München: oekom, pp. 198-201.

Hagberg, L. 2010. Participation under administrative rationality: implementing the EU Water Framework Directive in forestry. In K. Bäckstrand et al. (eds.), *Environmental Politics and Deliberative Democracy. Examining the Promise of New Modes of Governance.* Cheltenham: Edward Elgar, pp. 123-141.

Hale, J. R. 1966. Machiavelli and the Self-sufficient State. In D. Thompson (ed.), *Political Ideas. The study of the most significant and fundamental ideas of eminent European political thinkers of the last five hundred years.* Bungay: Penguin Books, pp. 22-32.

Hale, B. 2014. Can We Remediate Wrongs? In A. Hiller, R. Ilea and l. Kahn (eds.), *Consequentialism and Environmental Ethics*. New York and London: Routledge, pp. 147-163.

Hall, C. 2010. Freedom, Values, and Sacrifice: Overcoming Obstacles to Environmentally Sustainable Behaviour. In M. Maniates and J. M. Meyer (eds.), *Environmental Politics of Sacrifices*. Cambridge: MIT Press, pp. 61-86.

Hamilton, C. 2008. *The freedom paradox. Towards a post-secular ethics.* Crows Nest: Allen & Unwin.

Hamilton, C. 2010. *Requiem for a Species. Why We Resist the Truth about Climate Change.* Crows Nest: Allen & Unwin.

Hamilton, C. 2014. Moral Collapse in a Warming World. *Ethics & International Affairs 28(3)*:335-342.

Hannigan, J. 2006. *Environmental Sociology.* 2nd Edition. New York: Routledge.

Hansen, J. 2009. *Storms of my Grandchildren. The Truth About the Coming Climate Catastrophe and Our Last Chance to Save Humanity.* Kindle Edition: Bloomsbury.

Hansen, J. 2015. *Energy for Humanity Press Conference at COP21*
https://www.youtube.com/watch?v=KnN328eD-sA

Hanson, M. 2004. A precautionary approach. In Y. Levy and M. Wissenburg (eds.), *Liberal Democracy and Environmentalism: The End of Environmentalism?* Kindle Edition: Routledge, pp. 127-138.

Hardin, G. 1968. The Tragedy of the Commons. *Science 162*:1243-1248.

Harmon-Jones, E. and J. Mills (eds.) 2009. *Cognitive dissonance. Progress on a pivotal theory in social psychology*. Washington: American Psychological Association.

Harmon-Jones, E. and J. Mills 2009a. An Introduction to Cognitive Dissonance Theory and an Overview of the Current Perspectives on the Theory. In E. Harmon-Jones, E. and J. Mills (eds.), *Cognitive dissonance. Progress on a pivotal theory in social psychology*. Washington: American Psychological Association, pp.3-21.

Harris, P. G. 2013. *What's Wrong with Climate Politics and How to Fix It*. Cambridge and Maiden: Polity Press.

Hartmann, T. 2013. *The Last Hours of Humanity. Warming the World to Extinction*. Kindle Edition: Waterfront Digital Press.

Harvey, D. 2014. *Seventeen Contradictions and the End of Capitalism*. Kindle Edition: Oxford University Press.

Hausknost, D. 2014. Decision, choice, solution: 'agentic deadlock' in environmental politics. *Environmental Politics 23(3):*357-375.

Hayward, T. 2001. Environmental Constitutional Rights. In J. Barry and M. Wissenburg (eds.), *Sustaining Liberal Democracy. Ecological Challenges and Opportunities*. New York: Palgrave, pp. 117-135.

Hayward, T. 2003. Constitutional Environmental Rights: A Case for Political Analysis. In A. Light and A. De-Shalit (eds.), *Moral and Political Reasoning in Environmental Practice*. Cambridge and London: MIT Press, pp. 109-129.

Hegel, F. 2005. *Die Philosophie des Rechts*. Frankfurt: Suhrkamp.

Heidelberger Institut für Internationale Konfliktforschung 2016. http://hiik.de/

Heilbroner, R. L. 1976. *Die Zukunft der Menschheit*. Frankfurt: Suhrkamp.

Heilbroner, R. L. 1988. *Behind the Veil of Economics. Essays in the Worldly Philosophy*. New York and London: W. W. Norton.

Heilbroner, R. L. 1995. *Visions of the Future. The Distant Past, Yesterday, Today, and Tomorrow*. Oxford and New York: Oxford University Press.

Heintel, P. 2011. Öko-Moral gegen (Neo-) Liberalismus? Über den demokratischen Umgang mit der Macht des Faktischen. In Forum Wissenschaft & Umwelt (ed.), *Demokratie und Umweltkrise. Brauchen wir mehr Mitbestimmung?* München: oekom, pp. 29-34.

Held, D., C. Roger and E.-M. Nag (eds.) 2013. *Climate Governance in the Developing World*. Cambridge and Malden: Polity Press.

Held, D., C. Roger and E.-M. Nag 2013a. China's Governance of Energy and Climate Change. In D. Held, C. Roger and E.-M. Nag (eds.), *Climate Governance in the Developing World*. Cambridge and Malden: Polity Press, pp. 29-52.

Helfrich, S. 2011. Tragödie, abgesetzt. Warum der demokratische Spielplan eine Neufassung der „Tragik der Allmende" braucht. In Forum Wissenschaft & Umwelt (ed.), *Demokratie und Umweltkrise. Brauchen wir mehr Mitbestimmung?* München: oekom, pp. 135-143.

Henderson, J. A. and J. Brooks 2014. *Rain and Representation: The Effect of Margin of Victory on Incumbent Legislative Behavior.*
http://ssrn.com/abstract=2409078 or http://dx.doi.org/10.2139/ssrn.2409078

Hildingsson, R. 2010. The deliberative turn in Swedish sustainability governance: participation from below or governing from above? In K. Bäckstrand et al. (eds.), *Environmental Politics and Deliberative Democracy. Examining the Promise of New Modes of Governance.* Cheltenham: Edward Elgar, pp. 145-164.

Hiller, A. 2014. System Consequentialism. In A. Hiller, R. Ilea and L. Kahn (eds.), *Consequentialism and Environmental Ethics.* New York and London: Routledge, pp. 54-69.

Hiller, A., R. Ilea and L. Kahn (eds.) 2014. *Consequentialism and Environmental Ethics.* New York and London: Routledge.

Hiller, A. and L. Kahn 2014. Introduction: Consequentialism and environmental Ethics. In A. Hiller, R. Ilea and L. Kahn (eds.), *Consequentialism and Environmental Ethics.* New York and London: Routledge, pp. 1-14.

Hilton, I. 2013. Introduction. The return of Chinese civil society. In S. Geall (ed.) 2013. *China and the Environment. The Green Revolution.* Kindle Edition: Zed Books.

Hobbes, T. 2007. *Leviathan.* Stuttgart: Reclam.

Hobsbawm, E. J. 2004. *Nationen und Nationalismus. Mythos und Realität seit 1780.* London and New York: Campus Verlag.

Hobson, C. 2012. Addressing Climate Change and Promoting Democracy Abroad: Compatible Agendas? *Democratization 19:974-992.*

Hobson, K. 2013. On the making of the environmental citizen. *Environmental Politics 22(1):56-72.*

Hogl, K. et al. (eds.) 2012. *Environmental Governance: The Challenge of Legitimacy and Effectiveness.* Cheltenham: Edward Elgar.

Hogl, K. et al. 2012a. Legitimacy and effectiveness of environmental governance – concepts and perspectives. In K. Hogl et al. (eds.), *Environmental Governance: The Challenge of Legitimacy and Effectiveness.* Cheltenham: Edward Elgar, pp. 1-26.

Hogl, K. et al. 2012b. Effectiveness and legitimacy of environmental governance – synopsis of key insights. In K. Hogl et al. (eds.), *Environmental Governance: The Challenge of Legitimacy and Effectiveness.* Cheltenham: Edward Elgar, pp. 280-304.

Hohensee, J. 2013. Corporate Reporting and Externalities. In The Worldwatch Institute (ed.), *State of the World 2013: Is Sustainability Still Possible?* Kindle Edition: Island Press.

Holland, A. 2002. Sustainability: Should We Start From Here? In A. Dobson (ed.), *Fairness and Futurity. Essays on Environmental Sustainability and Social Justice.* New York: Oxford University Press, pp. 46-82.

Holland, A. 2013 Ecological Integrity and the Darwinian Paradigm. In D. Pimentel, L. Westra and R. F. Noss (eds.), *Ecological Integrity: Integrating Environment, Conversation and Health.* Kindle Edition: Island Press.

Holland, A. 2014. On Some Limitations of Consequentialism in the Sphere of Environmental Ethics. In A. Hiller, R. Ilea and L. Kahn (eds.), *Consequentialism and Environmental Ethics.* New York and London: Routledge, pp. 107-121.

Holland, B. 2008. Ecology and the Limits of Justice: Establishing Capability Ceilings in Nussbaum's Capabilities Approach. *Journal of Human Development 9(3):401-425.*

Holsworth, R. D. 1979. Recycling Hobbes: The Limits to Political Ecology. *The Massachusetts Review 20*:9-40.

Horstkötter, D. 2004. Sustainability and plurality. From the moderate end of the liberal equilibrium to the open end of a situated liberal neutrality. In Y. Levy and M. Wissenburg (eds.), *Liberal Democracy and Environmentalism: The End of Environmentalism?* Kindle Edition: Routledge, pp. 155-166.

House of Commons Library 2015. *General Elections 2015.* http://researchbriefings.parliament.uk/ResearchBriefing/Summary/CBP-7186

Höffe, O. 2009. *Ist die Demokratie zukunftsfähig? Über moderne Politik.* Lizenzausgabe für die Bundeszentrale für politische Bildung. Nördlingen: C. H. Beck.

Höntzsch, F. 2010. *Individuelle Freiheit zum Wohle Aller. Die soziale Dimension des Freiheitsbegriffs im Werk des John Stuart Mill.* Wiesbaden: VS Verlag für Sozialwissenschaften.

Huemer, M. 2013. *The Problem of Political Authority. An Examination of the Right to Coerce and the Duty to Obey.* Kindle Edition: Palgrave Macmillian.

Hume, D. 2013. *Traktat über die menschliche Natur: Band II: Zweites und Drittes Buch. Über die Affekte. Über die Moral.* Hamburg: Meiner.

Humphrey, M. 2004. Ecology, democracy and autonomy. A problem of wishful thinking. In Y. Levy and M. Wissenburg (eds.), *Liberal Democracy and Environmentalism: The End of Environmentalism?* Kindle Edition: Routledge, pp. 115-126.

Humphrey, M. 2006. Democratic Legitimacy, Public Justification and Environmental Direct Action. *Political Studies 54*:310-327.

Humphrey, M. 2007. *Ecological Politics and Democratic Theory. The challenge to the deliberative ideal.* Kindle Edition: Routledge.

Humphrey, M. 2009. Rational Irrationality and Simulation in Environmental Politics: The Example of Climate Change. *Government and Opposition 44(2)*:146-166.

Humphrey, M. and M. Stears 2007. Deliberative democracy and the challenge of radical environmentalism. In M. Humphrey, *Ecological Politics and Democratic Theory. The challenge to the deliberative ideal.* Kindle Edition: Routledge.

Huntington S. P. 1969. *Political order in changing societies.* New Haven and London: Yale University Press.

Huntington, S. P. 1998. *Kampf der Kulturen. Die Neugestaltung der Weltpolitik im 21. Jahrhundert.* München and Wien: Europa Verlag.

Hurrell, A. 2006. The state. In A. Dobson and R. Eckersley (eds.), *Political Theory and the Ecological Challenge.* New York: Cambridge University Press, pp. 165-182.

Huxley, A. 2000. *Brave New World Revisited.* Ebook: Rosetta Books.

Hürriyet Daily News 2012. Putin echoes Erdogan's call for three children. *Hürriyet Daily News December 12, 2012.* http://www.hurriyetdailynews.com/putin-echoes-erdogans-call-for-three-children.aspx?pageID=238&nid=36684&NewsCatID=353%29

Ingolfur, B. 2004. Post-ecologism and the politics of simulation. In Y. Levy and M. Wissenburg (eds.), *Liberal Democracy and Environmentalism: The End of Environmentalism?* Kindle Edition: Routledge, pp. 32-47.

International Energy Agency 2012. *World Energy Outlook 2012.* Paris: IEA/OECD.

Jacob, K. 2008. Industrie im Spannungsfeld von Ökonomie und Ökologie. *Informationen zur politischen Bildung 287*:31-35.

Jacobs, M. (ed.) 1997. *Greening the Millennium? The New Politics of the Environment*. Malden: The Political Quarterly.

Jacobs, M. 1997a. Introduction: The New Politics of the Environment. In M. Jacobs (ed.), *Greening the Millennium? The New Politics of the Environment*. Malden: The Political Quarterly, pp. 1-17.

Jacobs, M. 1997b. The Quality of Life: Social Goods and the Politics of Consumption. In M. Jacobs (ed.), *Greening the Millennium? The New Politics of the Environment*. Malden: The Political Quarterly, pp. 47-61.

Jackson, T. 2012. *Prosperity without growth: Economics for a finite planet*. Kindle Edition: Routledge.

Jackson, T and P. A. Victor 2015. Does credit create a 'growth imperative'? A quasi-stationary economy with interest-bearing debt. *Ecological Economics 120*:32-48.

Jahn, D. 2014. Three World of Environmental Politics. In A. Duit (ed.), *State and Environment. The Comparative Study of Environmental Governance*. Cambridge and London: MIT Press, pp. 81-109.

Jamieson, D. (ed.) 2001. *A Companion to Environmental Philosophy*. Oxford: Blackwell.

Jasanoff, S. 1999. The Fifth Branch: Science Advisers as Policymakers. Kindle Edition: Harvard University Press.

Jasanoff, S. 2012. Science and Public Reason. Kindle Edition: Earthscan.

Jenkins, R. 2008 (1997). *Rethinking Ethnicity. Arguments and Exploration*. London: Sage.

Jenkins, T. N. 1998. Economics and the environment: a case of ethical neglect. *Ecological Economics 26(2)*:151-164.

Jennings, B. 2010. Beyond the social contract of consumption: democratic governance in the post-carbon era. *Critical policy studies 4(3)*:222-233.

Jensen, D., A. McBay and L. Keith 2011. *Deep Green Resistance: Strategy to Save the Planet*. Kindle Edition: Seven Stories Press.

Jiang, Q. 2013. *A Confucian Constitutional Order: How China's Ancient Past Can Shape Its Political Future. Translated by Edmund Ryden. Edited by Daniel A. Bell and Ruiping Fan*. Princeton and Oxford: Princeton University Press.

Johannes, R. E. 2002. The Renaissance of Community-based Marine Resource Management in Oceana. *Annual Review of Ecology and Systematics 33*:317-40.

Johnson, G. F. 2007. The Discourse of Democracy in Canadian Nuclear Waste Management Policy. *Policy Sciences 40(2)*:79-99.

Johnson, J. 2010. What Rationality Assumption? Or, How 'Positive Political Theory' Rests on a Mistake. *Political Studies 58*:282-299.

Jonas, H. 1984. *Das Prinzip Verantwortung. Versuch einer Ethik für die technologische Zivilisation*. Frankfurt: Suhrkamp.

Josephson, P. R. 2005. *Resources under Regimes. Technology, Environment, and the State*. Cambridge: Harvard University Press.

Kagan, R. 2008. *Die Demokratie und ihre Feinde. Wer gestaltet die neue Weltordnung?* Lizenzausgabe für die Bundeszentrale für politische Bildung. München: Siedler Verlag.

Kalecki, M. 1941. Notes on General Rationing. *Bulletin of the Oxford University Institute of Economics & Statistics 3(5)*:103-105.

Kant, I. 1999. *Was ist Aufklärung? Ausgewählte Schriften. Mit einer Einleitung von E Cassier.* Hamburg: Felix Meiner Verlag.

Karapin, R. 2014. Wind-Power Development in Germany and the United States. In A. Duit (ed.), *State and Environment. The Comparative Study of Environmental Governance.* Cambridge and London: MIT Press, pp. 111-145.

Kareklas, I., D. D. Muehling and T. J. Weber 2015. Reexamining Health Messages in the Digital Age: A Fresh Look at Source Credibility Effects. *Journal of Advertising 44(2)*:88-104.

Karmasin, M. 2011. „Ökologisierung" der Öffentlichkeit? Umweltberichterstattung und mediale Verantwortung im Zeitalter der ökologischen Krise. In Forum Wissenschaft & Umwelt (ed.), *Demokratie und Umweltkrise. Brauchen wir mehr Mitbestimmung?* München: oekom, pp. 185-190.

Kassiola, J. J. 2002. Issue 2: Environmental Justice without Social Justice? Why Environmental Thought and Action Must Include Considerations of Social Justice. In J. M. Gillroy and J. Bowersox (eds.), *The Moral Austerity of Environmental Decision: Sustainability, Democracy, and Normative Argument in Policy and Law.* Kindle Edition: Duke University Press.

Kelly, M. J. 2013. Why a collapse of global civilization will be avoided: a comment on Ehrlich & Ehrlich. *Proc. R. Soc. B 280.*
http://rspb.royalsocietypublishing.org/content/280/1767/20131193

Kenis, A. and M. Lievens 2014. Searching for 'the political' in environmental politics. *Environmental Politics 23(4)*:531-548.

Kennedy, M. 2012. *Geld geht auch anders. Gute Gründe Geld neu zu gestalten.*
http://www.erziehungskunst.de/artikel/januar-2012-die-rollen-des-geldes/geld-geht-auch-anders-gute-gruende-geld-neu-zu-gestalten/

King, A. and M. W. Toffel 2009. Self-regulatory institutions for solving environmental problems: perspectives and contributions from the management literature. In M. A. Delmas and O. R. Young. (eds.), *Governance for the Environment.* Kindle Edition: Cambridge University Press, pp. 98-116.

Kingsnorth, P. 2009. Victim of success: politics today. In J. Pugh (ed.), *What is radical politics today?* Basingstoke: Palgrave Macmillan, pp. 36-44.

Kishigami, N. and J. M. Savelle (eds.) 2005. *Indigenous Use and Management of Marine Resources.* Osaka: National Museum of Ethnology.

Kitman, J. K. 2000. The Secret History of Lead. *The Nation. March 2, 2000.*
http://www.thenation.com/article/secret-history-lead?page=0,0

Knapton, S. 2014. BBC staff told to stop inviting cranks on to science programmes. *The Telegraph July 4, 2014.*
http://www.telegraph.co.uk/culture/tvandradio/bbc/10944629/BBC-staff-told-to-stop-inviting-cranks-on-to-science-programmes.html

Knill, C., S. Shikano and J. Tosun 2014. Explaining Environmental Policy Adaption: A Comparative Analysis of Policy Developments in Twenty-Four OECD Countries. In A. Duit (ed.), *State and Environment. The Comparative Study of Environmental Governance.* Cambridge and London: MIT Press, pp. 53-79.

Kollmuss, A. and J. Agyeman 2002. Mind the Gap: Why do people act environmentally and what are the barriers to pro-environmental behavior? *Environmental Education Research 8(3)*:239-260.

Kronsell, A. and K. Bäckstrand 2010. Rationalities and forms of governance: a framework for analyzing the legitimacy of new modes of governance. In K. Bäckstrand et al. (eds.), *Environmental Politics and Deliberative Democracy. Examining the Promise of New Modes of Governance*. Cheltenham: Edward Elgar, pp. 28-46.

Krysmanski, H.-J. 2011. Geldmacht gegen Demokratie. Naomi Kleins Katastrophenkapitalismus und die Privatisierung der Macht. In Forum Wissenschaft & Umwelt (ed.), *Demokratie und Umweltkrise. Brauchen wir mehr Mitbestimmung?* München: oekom, pp. 65-81.

Kuhn, T. S. 2012. *The Structure of Scientific Revolutions: 50th edition*. Kindle Edition: The University of Chicago Press.

Kurian, G. T. et al. (eds.) 2011. *The Encyclopedia of Political Science. Vol. 1-5*. Washington: CQ Press.

Kurtz, M. J. and A. Schrank 2007. Growth and Governance: A Defense. *The Journal of Politics 69(2)*:563-569.

Laclau, E. 2005. Populism: What's in a Name? In F. Panizza (ed.), *Populism and the Mirror of Democracy*. London and New York: Verso.

Lagi, M., K. Z. Bertrand and Y. Bar-Yam 2011. *The Food Crises and Political Instability in North Africa and the Middle East*.
http://necsi.edu/research/social/food_crises.pdf

Lam, K.-C. and G. Shi 2008. Factors Affecting Ethical Attitudes in Mainland China and Hong Kong. *Journal of Business Ethics 77*:463-479.

Lamparter, D. H. 2011. Im dritten Anlauf. *Zeit Online September 7, 2011*.
http://www.zeit.de/2011/36/VW-Kleinwagen

Lane, J.-E. 2011a. The CO2 Equivalent Emissions and Total Economic Output. In S. Casalegno (ed.), *Global Warming Impacts – Case Studies on the Economy, Human Health, and on Urban and Natural Environments*. Rijeka: InTech, pp.29-36.

Lane, M. 2011b. *The Eco-Republic: What the Ancients Can Teach Us about Ethics, Virtue, and Sustainable Living*. Kindle Edition: Princeton University Press.

Latinis, D. K. 2000. The development of subsistence system models for Island Southeast Asia and Near Oceana: the nature and role of arboriculture and aboreal-based economics. *World Archeology 32(1)*:41-67.

Latouche, S. 2005. Can democracy solve all problems? *The International Journal of Inclusive Democracy (1)3*.
http://www.inclusivedemocracy.org/journal/vol1/vol1_no3_latouche.htm

Latour, B. 2004. *The Politics of Nature. How to Bring the Sciences into Democracy*. Cambridge: Harvard University Press.

Latour, B. 2007. *Elend der Kritik. Vom Krieg um Fakten zu Dingen von Belang*. Zürich: Diaphanes.

Latour, B. 2013. *Facing Gaia. A new enquiry into Natural Religion*. [Gifford Lecture series talks] The University of Edinburgh.
http://www.giffordlectures.org/lectures/facing-gaia-new-enquiry-natural-religion

Laurance, W. et al. 2014. Apparent Environmental Synergism Drives the Dynamics of Amazonian Forest Fragments. *Ecology 95(11)*:3018-3026.

Lauth, H.-J. 2010 (ed.). *Vergleichende Regierungslehre. Eine Einführung. 3. ed.* Heidelberg: VS Verlag.

Lauth, H.-J. 2010a. Regierungstypen: Totalitarismus – Autoritarismus – Demokratie. In H.-J. Lauth (ed.), *Vergleichende Regierungslehre. Eine Einführung. 3. ed.* Heidelberg: VS Verlag, pp. 95-116.

Lawlor, R. 2014. Delaying Obsolescence. *Science and Engineering Ethics 21(2)*:401-427.

Leach, M. 2013. Pathways to Sustainability: Building Political Strategies. In The Worldwatch Institute (ed.), *State of the World 2013: Is Sustainability Still Possible?* Kindle Edition: Island Press.

Leahy, M. P. T. 2005. *Against Liberation. Putting Animals in Perspective.* Ebook: Taylor & Francis

Lee, J.-S. 2013. Climate Governance in South Korea. In D. Held, C. Roger and E.-M. Nag (eds.), *Climate Governance in the Developing World.* Cambridge and Malden: Polity Press, pp. 91-109.

Leeson, S. M. 1979. Philosophic Implications of the Ecological Crisis: The Authoritarian Challenge to Liberalism. *Polity 11*:303-318.

Leggewie, C. 2011. 2050: Die demokratische Frage heute*. In S. S. Schüttemeyer (ed.), *Politik im Klimawandel. Keine Macht für gerechte Lösungen?* Baden-Baden: Nomos, pp. 25-39.

Leggewie, C. and H. Welzer 2009. Anpassung an das Unvermeidliche? Klimawandel als kulturelles Problem. *Polar. Zeitschrift für politische Philosophie und Kultur* 6:9-13.

Leggewie, C. and H. Welzer 2011. *Das Ende der Welt, wie wir sie kannten. Klima, Zukunft und die Chancen der Demokratie.* Frankfurt: Fischer.

Leif, T. 2011. Herdentrieb und Tempospirale. Umweltjournalismus in der PR- und Nachrichtenfabrik. In Forum Wissenschaft & Umwelt (ed.), *Demokratie und Umweltkrise. Brauchen wir mehr Mitbestimmung?* München: oekom, pp. 191-197.

Leighton, D. and S. White (eds.) 2008. *Building a Citizen Society: The Emerging Politics of Republican Democracy.* London: Lawrence and Wishart.

Leiserowitz, A. et al. 2014. *What's In A Name? Global Warming vs. Climate Change.* New Haven: Yale Project on Climate Change Communication.

Leist, A. 2009. Konflikt statt Konsens. Zur vergeblichen Demokratisierung der Umwelt. *Polar. Zeitschrift für politische Philosophie und Kultur* 6:35-39.

Leist, A. 2011. Moralische oder politische Demokratie? Worauf kann die globale Umweltvorsorge bauen? In Forum Wissenschaft & Umwelt (ed.), *Demokratie und Umweltkrise. Brauchen wir mehr Mitbestimmung?* München: oekom, pp. 35-40.

Lekakis, J. N. and M. Kousis 2013. Economic Crisis, Troika and the Environment in Greece. *South European Society and Politics 18(3)*:1-17.

Lemos, M. C. and A. Agawal 2009. Environmental governance and political science. In M. A. Delmas and O. R. Young. (eds.), *Governance for the Environment.* Kindle Edition: Cambridge University Press, pp. 69-97.

Lemons, J., L. Westra and R. Goodland (eds.) 1998. *Ecological Sustainability and Integrity: Concepts and Approaches.* Dordrecht: Springer.

Lemons, J. 1998. Burden of Proof Requirements and Environmental Sustainability: Science, Public Policy, and Ethics. In J. Lemons, L. Westra and R. Goodland (eds.), *Ecological Sustainability and Integrity: Concepts and Approaches*. Dordrecht: Springer, pp. 75-103.

Leonard, A. 2013. Moving from Individual Change to Societal Change. In The Worldwatch Institute (ed.), *State of the World 2013: Is Sustainability Still Possible?* Kindle Edition: Island Press.

Lerner, M. 1980. *The Belief in a Just World. A Fundamental Delusion*. New York: Plenum Press.

Levitt, A. 2013. *Should You Invest In Weapon Stocks?*
http://www.investopedia.com/stock-analysis/2013/should-you-invest-in-weapon-stocks-lmt-gd-avav-swhc0117.aspx

Levy, Y. 2004. The end of environmentalism (as we know it). In Y. Levy and M. Wissenburg (eds.), *Liberal Democracy and Environmentalism: The End of Environmentalism?* Kindle Edition: Routledge, pp. 48-59.

Levy, Y. and M. Wissenburg (eds.) 2004. *Liberal Democracy and Environmentalism: The End of Environmentalism?* Kindle Edition: Routledge.

Levy, Y and M. Wissenburg 2004a. Introduction, In Y. Levy and M. Wissenburg (eds.), *Liberal Democracy and Environmentalism: The End of Environmentalism?* Kindle Edition: Routledge, pp. 1-9.

Levy, Y. and M. Wissenburg 2004b. Conclusion. In Y. Levy and M. Wissenburg (eds.), *Liberal Democracy and Environmentalism: The End of Environmentalism?* Kindle Edition: Routledge, pp. 193-196.

Lewandowsky, S. et al. 2012. Misinformation and its correction continued influence and successful debiasing. *Psychological Science in the Public Interest 13(3)*:106-131.

Light, A. and A. De-Shalit (eds.) 2003. *Moral and Political Reasoning in Environmental Practice*. Cambridge and London: MIT Press.

Light, A and A. De-Shalit 2003a. Introduction: Environmental Ethics – Whose Philosophy? Which Practice? In A. Light and A. De-Shalit (eds.), *Moral and Political Reasoning in Environmental Practice*. Cambridge and London: MIT Press, pp. 1-27.

Linklater, A. 2006. Cosmopolitanism. In A. Dobson and R. Eckersley (eds.), *Political Theory and the Ecological Challenge*. New York: Cambridge University Press, pp. 109-129.

Lippmann, W. 1998. *Public Opinion. With a New Introduction by Michael Curtis*. New Brunswick and London: Transaction Publishers.

Litfin, K. 2010. The Sacred and the Profane in the Ecological Politics of Sacrifice. In M. Maniates and J. M. Meyer (eds.), *Environmental Politics of Sacrifices*. Cambridge: MIT Press, pp. 117-144.

Lo, A. Y. 2014. The right to doubt: climate-change scepticism and asserted rights to private property. *Environmental Politics 23(4)*:549-569.

Locke, J. 2008. *Über die Regierung*. Stuttgart: Reclam.

Lomborg, B.
http://www.lomborg.com

Lopez, F (dir.) 2011. *End:CIV* [documentary]. Canada and United States: SubMedia.

Lovelock, J. 2009. *The Vanishing Face of Gaia: A Final Warning*. Kindle Edition: Basic Books.

Lövbrand, E. and J. Khan 2010. The deliberative turn in green political theory. In K. Bäckstrand et al. (eds.), *Environmental Politics and Deliberative Democracy. Examining the Promise of New Modes of Governance*. Cheltenham: Edward Elgar, pp. 47-64.

Luhmann, N. 1986. *Ökologische Kommunikation. Kann die moderne Gesellschaft sich auf ökologische Gefährdungen einstellen?* Opladen: Westdeutscher Verlag.

Luke, T. W. 1999. *Capitalism, Democracy, and Ecology. Departing from Marx*. Urbana and Chicago: University of Illinois Press.

Lukes, S. 1998. *Power: A Radical View*. Basingstoke: Palgrave Macmillan.

Lyon, T. P. 2009. Environmental governance: an economic perspective. In M. A. Delmas and O. R. Young. (eds.), *Governance for the Environment*. Kindle Edition: Cambridge University Press, pp. 43-68.

Macauley, D. (ed.) 1996. *Minding Nature: The Philosophers of Ecology*. New York: Guilford Press.

Macauley, D. 1996a. Greening Philosophy and Democratizing Ecology. In D. Macauley (ed.), *Minding Nature: The Philosophers of Ecology*. New York: Guilford Press, pp. 1-23.

MacCracken, M. C. 2011. *The Real Truth about Greenhouse Gases and Climate Change: Paragraph-by- Paragraph Comments on an Article by Dr. William Happer*. Washington: Climate Institute. http://www.climatesciencewatch.org/wp-content/uploads/2011/09/The-Real-Truth-About-Greenhouse-Gases-and-Climate-Change.pdf

Macedo, S. 2013. Meritocratic Democracy. Learning from the American Constitution. In D. A. Bell and C. Li (eds.), *The East Asian Challenge for Democracy. Political Meritocracy in Comparative Perspective*. Kindle Edition: Cambridge University Press, pp. 231-256.

Machiavelli, N. 2009. *Il Principe/Der Fürst. Italienisch/Deutsch*. Philipp Rippel (ed.). Ditzingen: Reclam.

Macintyre, A. C. 1966. Recent Political Thought. In D. Thompson (ed.), *Political Ideas. The study of the most significant and fundamental ideas of eminent European political thinkers of the last five hundred years*. Bungay: Penguin Books, pp. 180-190.

Madden, N. J. 2014. Green means stop: veto players and their impact on climate-change policy outputs, *Environmental Politics 23(4)*:570-589.

Maibach, E. et al. 2015. *The Francis Effect: How Pope Francis Changed the Conversation about Global Warming*. Fairfax: George Mason University Center for Climate Change Communication. http://environment.yale.edu/climate-communication-OFF/files/The_Francis_Effect.pdf

Maier, F. 2008. Rhetorik und Realität. Artenschutz und Biodiversität im „reichen" Österreich. In P.C. Gruber (ed.), *Nachhaltige Entwicklung und Global Governance. Verantwortung. Macht. Politik*. Opladen and Farmington Hills: Verlag Barbara Budrich, pp.125-139.

Malthus, T. R. 1979. *An Essay on the Principle of Population*. Kindle Edition: A Public Domain Book / J. Johnson St. Paul's Church-Yard.

Maniates, M. and J. M. Meyer 2010 (eds.). *Environmental Politics of Sacrifices*. Cambridge: MIT Press.

Mann, M. E. 2014. If You See Something, Say Something. *New York Times January 17, 2014*. http://www.nytimes.com/2014/01/19/opinion/sunday/if-you-see-something-say-something.html

Manno, J. 2013. Commodity Potential: An Approach to Understanding the Ecological Consequences of Markets. In D. Pimentel, L. Westra and R. F. Noss (eds.), *Ecological Integrity: Integrating Environment, Conversation and Health*. Kindle Edition: Island Press.

Marcuse, L. 2006. *Philosophie des Glücks von Hiob bis Freud*. Zürich: Diogenes.

Markandya, A. et al. 2002. *Dictionary of Environmental Economics*. Sterling: Earthscan.

Marshall, G. 2014. *Don't Even Think About It: Why Our Brains Are Wired to Ignore Climate Change*. Kindle Edition: Bloomsbury.

Martin, J. 2009. A Politics of Commitment. In J. Pugh (ed.), *What is radical politics today?* Basingstoke: Palgrave Macmillan, pp. 120-126.

Martin, B. 2013. Effective Crisis Governance. In The Worldwatch Institute (eds.), *State of the World 2013: Is Sustainability Still Possible?* Kindle Edition: Island Press.

Martin, T. 2015. *Economic Growth is a meme – a learned idea that we can change and mature.* http://mahb.stanford.edu/blog/economic-growth-meme/

Massing, P. and G. Breit 2003. (eds.), *Demokratietheorien. Von der Antike bis zur Gegenwart. Texte und Interpretationshilfen*. Schwalbach: Wochenschau Verlag.

Mathews, F. (ed.) 1996. *Ecology and Democracy*. London: Frank Cass.

Mauss, M. 1990. *Die Gabe. Form und Funktion des Austauschs in archaischen Gesellschaften*. Frankfurt: Suhrkamp.

Mayr, C. 2009. Erklärungshilfen zur Entwicklung der internationalen Klimapolitik: Spieltheorie und Public Choice Theorie. Hamburg: Igel Verlag.

Mazur, L. 2013. Cultivating Resilience in a Dangerous World. . In The Worldwatch Institute (ed.), *State of the World 2013: Is Sustainability Still Possible?* Kindle Edition: Island Press.

McBay, A. 2012. Commentary. In F. Lopez (dir.) 2011. *End:CIV* [documentary]. Canada and United States: SubMedia.

McComick, J. P. 2004. Introduction. In J. Seitzer (ed.), *Carl Schmitt. Legality and Legitimacy. Translated and edited by J. Seitzer with an introduction by J.P. McCormick*. Kindle Edition: Duke University Press.

McGarr, A. 2016. *Fracking, wastewater disposal, and earthquakes* https://absuploads.aps.org/presentation.cfm?pid=11803

McLaughlin, A. 1995. For a radical ecocentrism. In A. Drengson and Y. Inoue (eds.), *The Deep Ecology Movement: An Introductory Anthology*. Berkeley: North Atlantic Publishers.

McMichael, A. J. 2013. Global Environmental Change in the Coming Century: How Sustainable Are Recent Health Gains? In D. Pimentel, L. Westra and R. F. Noss (eds.), *Ecological Integrity: Integrating Environment, Conversation and Health*. Kindle Edition: Island Press.

McNamee, S. J. and R. K. Miller 2009. *The Meritocracy Myth*. Lanham: Rowman and Littlefield Publisher.

McShane, K. 2007. Anthropocentrism vs. Nonanthropocentrism: Why Should We Care? *Environmental Values 16(1):169-186*.

McShane, K. 2014. The Bearer of Value in Environmental Ethics. In A. Hiller, R. Ilea and L. Kahn (eds.), *Consequentialism and Environmental Ethics*. New York and London: Routledge, pp. 17-34.

Meadowcraft, J. 2014. Comparing Environmental Performance. In A. Duit (ed.), *State and Environment. The Comparative Study of Environmental Governance*. Cambridge and London: MIT Press, pp. 27-51.

Meadows, D. et al 1972. *The Limits to Growth: A Report for the Club of Rome's Project on the Predicament of Mankind*. New York: Universe Book.

Meadows, D., D. Meadows and J. Randers 2004. *Limits to growth: The 30-year update*. White River Junction: Chelsea Green Publishing.

Mellor, M. 2006. Marxism. In A. Dobson and R. Eckersley (eds.), *Political Theory and the Ecological Challenge*. New York: Cambridge University Press, pp. 35-50.

Menzel, M. 2014. Junge Deutsche wollen ein anderes, grüneres Europa. *Die Welt May 17, 2014*. http://www.welt.de/politik/deutschland/article128117846/Junge-Deutsche-wollen-ein-anderes-grueneres-Europa.html

Merchant, C. (ed.) 1999. *Ecology: Key Concepts in Critical Theory*. New York: Humanity Books.

Merkel, W. 1999. Defekte Demokratien. In W. Merkel and A. Busch (eds.), *Demokratie in Ost und West*. Frankfurt: Suhrkamp, pp. 361-381.

Merkel, W. 2011. Volksabstimmungen: Illusion und Realität. *APuZ 44-45*:47-55.

Merkel, W. and A. Busch (eds.) 1999. *Demokratie in Ost und West*. Frankfurt: Suhrkamp.

Merkel, W. and P. Thiery 2010. Systemwechsel. In H.-J. Lauth (ed.), *Vergleichende Regierungslehre. Eine Einführung*. 3rd ed. Heidelberg: VS Verlag, pp. 186-212.

Meyer, J. M. 2006. Political Theory and the Environment. In J. S. Dryzek, B. Honig and A. Phillips (eds.), *The Oxford Handbook of Political Theory*. Norfolk: Oxford University Press, pp. 773-791.

Meyer, J. M. 2010. A Democratic Politics of Sacrifice? In M. Maniates and J. M. Meyer (eds.), *Environmental Politics of Sacrifices*. Cambridge: MIT Press, pp. 13-32.

Meyer, J. M. 2011.We have never been liberal: the environmentalist turn to liberalism and the possibilities for social criticism. *Environmental Politics 20(3)*:356-373.

Meyer, J. M. and M. Maniates 2010a. Must We Sacrifice? Confronting Politics of Sacrifice in an Ecologically Full World. In M. Maniates and J. M. Meyer (eds.), *Environmental Politics of Sacrifices*. Cambridge: MIT Press, pp. 1-8.

Meyer, J. M. and M. Maniates 2010b. Seeing Sacrifices in Everyday Life. In M. Maniates, M. and J. M. Meyer (eds.), *Environmental Politics of Sacrifices*. Cambridge: MIT Press, pp.87-90.

Micheletti, M., D. Stolle and D. Berlin 2014. Sustainable Citizenship: The Role of Citizens and Consumers as Agents of the Environmental State. In A. Duit (ed.), *State and Environment. The Comparative Study of Environmental Governance*. Cambridge and London: MIT Press, pp 203-236.

Milic, T. and B. Rosselot 2011. Grün, wenn die Parole stimmt. Umweltpolitik in der schweizerischen direkten Demokratie. In Forum Wissenschaft & Umwelt (ed.), *Demokratie und Umweltkrise. Brauchen wir mehr Mitbestimmung?* München: oekom, pp. 168-177.

Mill, J. S. (1862). *Considerations on Representative Government*. Kindle Edition: A Public Domain Book / Harper & Brothers Publishers.

Mill, J. S. (1879). *Utilitarianism*. Kindle Edition: A Public Domain Book / Longmans, Green, and Co.

Mill, J. S. (1901). *On Liberty*. Kindle Edition: A Public Domain Book / The Walter Scott Publishing.

Miller, P. and W. E. Rees 2013. Introduction. In D. Pimentel, L. Westra and R. F. Noss (eds.), *Ecological Integrity: Integrating Environment, Conversation and Health*. Kindle Edition: Island Press.

Mills, M. and F. Kind 2004. The end of deep ecology? – Not quite. In Y. Levy and M. Wissenburg (eds.), *Liberal Democracy and Environmentalism: The End of Environmentalism?* Kindle Edition: Routledge, pp. 75-86.

Minogue, K. R. 1966. Thomas Hobbes and the Philosophy of Absolutism. In D. Thompson (ed.), *Political Ideas. The study of the most significant and fundamental ideas of eminent European political thinkers of the last five hundred years*. Bungay: Penguin Books, pp. 53-66.

Mitchell, T. 2011. *Carbon Democracy: Political Power in the Age of Oil*. Kindle Edition: Verso.

Moloney, G., et al. 2014. Using social representations theory to make sense of climate change: what scientists and nonscientists in Australia think. *Ecology and Society 19(3)*:19. http://www.ecologyandsociety.org/vol19/iss3/art19/

Monbiot, G. 2013. Let's stop hiding behind recycling and be honest about consumption. *The Guardian April 12, 2013*. http://www.theguardian.com/environment/georgemonbiot/2013/apr/12/escalating-consumption

Morus, [More] T. 1992. *Utopia*. Vor- und Nachwort Horst Günther (ed.). Frankfurt and Leipzig: insel taschenbuch.

Mosca, G. 1950. *Die herrschende Klasse. Grundlagen der politischen Wissenschaft*. Bern: Francke.

Mouffe, C. 2002. *Politics and passions. The stakes of democracy*. London: Center for the Study of Democracy.

Mouffe, C. 2011. Postdemokratie und die zunehmende "Entpolitisierung". *ApuZ 1-2*:3-5.

Muno, W. 2010. Umweltpolitik. In H.-J. Lauth (ed.), *Vergleichende Regierungslehre. Eine Einführung. 3rd ed.* Heidelberg: VS Verlag, pp. 349-372.

Murphy, P. and F. Morgan 2013. Cuba: Lessons from a Forced Decline. In The Worldwatch Institute (ed.), *State of the World 2013: Is Sustainability Still Possible?* Kindle Edition: Island Press.

Müller-Jung, J. 2014. Grüne Weltbürger nisten in jungen Bäumen. *Frankfurter Allgemeine September 24, 2014*. http://www.faz.net/aktuell/wissen/klima/waldschutz-fuer-das-weltklima-gruene-weltbuerger-nisten-in-jungen-baeumen-13167804.html

Myllyvirta, L. 2016. China's renewables drive down CO2 emissions. *The Ecologist January 21, 2016*. *http://www.theecologist.org/News/news_round_up/2986943/chinas_renewables_drive_down_CO2_emissions.html*

Nandy, A. 1993. *Traditions, Tyranny and Utopias: Essays in the Politics of Awareness*. New Delhi: Oxford University Press.

Neslen, A. 2014. UK opposition could doom EU efforts to curb plastic bag use. *The Guardian November 13, 2014*. http://www.theguardian.com/environment/2014/nov/13/uk-opposition-could-doom-eu-efforts-to-curb-plastic-bag-use

Nelson, C. and L. Grossberg (eds.) 1988. *Marxism and the Interpretation of Culture*. University of Illinois Press: Chicago.

Neumayer, E. 2002. Do Democracies Exhibit Stronger International Environmental Commitment? A Cross-country Analysis. *Journal of Peace Research 39(2)*:139-164.

Newig, J. 2012. More effective natural resource management through participatory governance? Taking stock of the conceptual and empirical literature – and moving forward. In K. Hogl et al. (eds.), *Environmental Governance: The Challenge of Legitimacy and Effectiveness.* Cheltenham: Edward Elgar, pp. 46-68.

Newig, J. and O. Fritsch 2011. Anspruch und Wirklichkeit. Befördert Partizipation umweltpolitisch „gute" Entscheidungen? In Forum Wissenschaft & Umwelt (ed.), *Demokratie und Umweltkrise. Brauchen wir mehr Mitbestimmung?* München: oekom, pp. 206-211.

Newig, J. and E. Kvarda 2012. Participation in environmental governance: legitimate and effective? In K. Hogl et al. (eds.), *Environmental Governance: The Challenge of Legitimacy and Effectiveness.* Cheltenham: Edward Elgar, pp. 29-45.

Nicholson, S. 2013. The Promises and Perils of Geoengineering. In The Worldwatch Institute (ed.), *State of the World 2013: Is Sustainability Still Possible?* Kindle Edition: Island Press.

Nohlen, D. 2004. Legitimität. In D. Nohlen and R.-O. Schultze (eds.), *Lexikon der Politikwissenschaft. Theorien, Methoden, Begriffe. Band 1 A-M.* Nördlingen: C. H. Beck, pp. 487-488.

Nohlen, D. and R.-O. Schultze (eds.) 2004. *Lexikon der Politikwissenschaft. Theorien, Methoden, Begriffe. Band 1 A-M.* Nördlingen: C. H. Beck.

Norgaard, K. M. 2006. We Don't Really Want to Know Environmental Justice and Socially Organized Denial of Global Warming in Norway. *Organization & Environment September 19*:347-370.

Norton, B. 2002. Issue 3: Nature Has Only an Instrumental Value Sustainability: Descriptive or Performative? In J. M. Gillroy and J. Bowersox (eds.), *The Moral Austerity of Environmental Decision: Sustainability, Democracy, and Normative Argument in Policy and Law.* Kindle Edition: Duke University Press.

Nussbaum, M. C. 1992. Human Functioning and Social Justice. In Defense of Aristotelian Essentialism. *Political Theory 20(2)*:202-246.

O'Connor, J. 1988. Capitalism, Nature, Socialism: A Theoretical Introduction. *Capitalism, Nature, Socialism 1 (1)*:11-38.

Oksanen, M. and A. Kumpula 2013. Transparency in conservation: rare species, secret files, and democracy. *Environmental Politics 22(6)*:975-991.

Olivier, J. G. J. et al. 2013. *Trends in global CO2 emissions: 2013 Report*. The Hague: PBL Netherlands Environmental Assessment Agency.

O'Neill, J. 2006. Public choice, institutional economics, environmental goods. . In P. H .G. Stephens, J. Barry and A. Dobson (eds.), *Contemporary Environmental Politics. For margins to mainstream.* London and New York Routledge, pp. 160-178.

Ophuls, W. 1977. *Ecology and the Politics of Scarcity*. New York: W.H. Freeman & Company.

Ophuls, W. 2012. *Immoderate Greatness: Why Civilizations Fail*. Kindle Edition: CreateSpace.

Oreskes, N. and E. M. Conway 2014. *The Collapse of Western Civilization: A View from the Future*. New York: Columbia University Press.

Orr, D. W. 2009. *Down to the Wire: Confronting Climate Collapse.* New York: Oxford University Press.

Orr, D. W. 2013. Governance in the Long Emergency. In The Worldwatch Institute (ed.), *State of the World 2013: Is Sustainability Still Possible?* Kindle Edition: Island Press.

Osborn, D. 1997. Making Environmental Policy. In M. Jacobs (ed.), *Greening the Millennium? The New Politics of the Environment.* Malden: The Political Quarterly, pp. 130-137.

Ostrom, E. 1990. *Governing the commons: The evolution of institutions for collective action.* Cambridge: Cambridge University Press.

Overshootday.org
http://www.overshootday.org/

Paech, N. 2012. Einleitung. In B. Woynowski et al. (eds.), *Wirtschaft ohne Wachstum?! Notwendigkeit und Ansätze einer Wachstumswende.* Freiburg: Institut für Forstökonomie, pp. 1-12.

Panizza, F. 2005 (ed.). *Populism and the Mirror of Democracy.* London and New York: Verso.

Pauly, D. 2013. Global Change, Fisheries, and the Integrity of Marine Ecosystems: The Future Has Already Begun. In D. Pimentel, L. Westra and R. F. Noss (eds.), *Ecological Integrity: Integrating Environment, Conversation and Health.* Kindle Edition: Island Press.

Peltz, M. 2014. Climate Change and the Year of Investing Dangerously. *Institutional Investor April 7, 2014.* http://www.institutionalinvestor.com/Article/3327752/Investors-Endowments-and-Foundations/Climate-Change-and-the-Years-of-Investing-Dangerously.html#.Vwr1oPgaT4Y

Pepper, D. 1996. *Modern Environmentalism: An Introduction.* Abingdon: Routledge.

Petersen, N. 2009. *Demokratie als teleologisches Prinzip: Zur Legitimität von Staatsgewalt im Völkerrecht.* Heidelberg: Springer.

Peterson, A. 2010. Ordinary and Extraordinary Sacrifices: Religion, Everyday Life, and Environmental Practice. In M. Maniates and J. M. Meyer (eds.), *Environmental Politics of Sacrifices.* Cambridge: MIT Press, pp. 91-116.

Pettit, P. 1999. Republican freedom and contestatory democratization. In I. Shapiro and C. Hacker-Cordon (eds.), *Democracy's Value.* Cambridge: Cambridge University Press, pp. 163-190.

Pettit, P. 2012. *On the People's Terms. A Republican theory and Model of Democracy.* Kindle Edition: Cambridge University Press.

Pettit, P. 2013. Meritocratic Representation. In D. A. Bell and C. Li (eds.), *The East Asian Challenge for Democracy. Political Meritocracy in Comparative Perspective.* Kindle Edition: Cambridge University Press, pp. 138-157.

Pfetsch, F. 2003. *Theoretiker der Politik.* Von Platon bis Habermas. Paderborn: Wilhelm Fink Verlag.

Pimentel, D., L. Westra and R. F. Noss (eds.) 2013. *Ecological Integrity: Integrating Environment, Conversation and Health.* Kindle Edition: Island Press.

Platon [Plato] 1982. *Der Staat.* Stuttgart: Reclam.

Platon [Plato] 2009. *Georgias oder Über die Beredsamkeit.* Stuttgart: Reclam.

Plehwe, D. 2011. Die bedrängte Demokratie. Von der doppelten Entgrenzung des Lobbyismus. In Forum Wissenschaft & Umwelt (ed.), *Demokratie und Umweltkrise. Brauchen wir mehr Mitbestimmung?* München: oekom, pp. 56-64.

Plumwood, V. 2006. Feminism. In A. Dobson and R. Eckersley (eds.), *Political Theory and the Ecological Challenge*. New York: Cambridge University Press, pp. 51-74.

Polanyi, K. 1977. *The Great Transformation*. Wien: Europa Verlag.

Poloni-Staudinger, L. M. 2008. Are consensus democracies more environmentally effective? *Environmental Politics 17(3)*:410-430.

PONS 1999. *Wörterbuch für Schule und Studium. Lateinisch-Deutsch*. Stuttgart, Düsseldorf and Leipzig: Ernst Klett Verlag.

Porrit, J. 1985. *Seeing Green: The Politics of Ecology Explained*. New York: Basil Blackwell.

Potts, M. 2013. *Water, Climate and Society: the Elephant in the Room Could be Our Friend*. http://mahb.stanford.edu/wp-content/uploads/2014/01/Philomath-handout-Nov-1.pdf

Pralle, S. B. 2009. Agenda-setting and climate change. *Environmental Politics 18 (5)*:781-799.

Princen, T. 2010. Consumer Sovereignty, Heroic Sacrifice: Two Insidious Concepts in an Endlessly Expansionist Economy. In M. Maniates and J. M. Meyer (eds.), *Environmental Politics of Sacrifices*. Cambridge: MIT Press, pp. 145-164.

Przeworski, A. 1993. *Capitalism and Social Democracy*. Cambridge: Cambridge University Press.

Przeworski, A. 1999. Minimalist conception of democracy: a defense. In I. Shapiro and C. Hacker-Cordon (eds.), *Democracy's Value*. Cambridge: Cambridge University Press, pp. 23-55.

Przeworski, A. 2010. *Democracy and the Limits of Self-Government*. New York: Cambridge University Press.

Pugh, J. (ed.) 2009. *What is radical politics today?* Basingstoke: Palgrave Macmillan.

Radcliffe, J. 2002. Green Politics. Dictatorship or Democracy? Basingstoke: Palgrave.

Randers, J. 2012. *2052: A Global Forecast for the Next Forty Years*. Kindle Edition: Chelsea Green Publishing.

Rapport, N. 2006. Individualism. In A. Barnard and J. Spencer (eds.) 2006. *Encyclopedia of Social and Cultural Anthropology*. London and New York: Routledge, pp. 298-301.

Raschauer, B. 2011. Es gibt keine gallischen Dörfer. Umweltkonflikte in der repräsentativen Demokratie. In Forum Wissenschaft & Umwelt (ed.), *Demokratie und Umweltkrise. Brauchen wir mehr Mitbestimmung?* München: oekom, pp. 221-228.

Ratter, B. M. W., K. H. I. Philipp and von Storch 2012. Between hype and decline: recent trends in public perception of climate change. *Environmental Science & Policy 18*:3-8.

Rawls, J. 2011. *Political Liberalism. Expanded Edition*. 2nd ed. Kindle Edition: Columbia University Press.

Rees, W. E. 2013. Patch Disturbance, Ecofootprints, and Biological Integrity: Revisiting the Limits to Growth (or Why Industrial Society is Inherently Unsustainable). In D. Pimentel, Westra, R. F. Noss (eds.), *Ecological Integrity: Integrating Environment, Conversation and Health*. Kindle Edition: Island Press.

Reiber, T. and F. Zelli 2011. Klimawandel in der Perspektive verschiedener Sicherheitsdiskurse In S. S. Schüttemeyer (ed.), *Politik im Klimawandel. Keine Macht für gerechte Lösungen?* Baden-Baden: Nomos, pp. 205-237.

Reisch, N. and S. Kretzmann 2008. A Climate of War. The war in Iraq and global warming. *Oil Change International March 2008.*

Renner, M. 2013. Climate Change and Displacements. In The Worldwatch Institute (ed.), *State of the World 2013: Is Sustainability Still Possible?* Kindle Edition: Island Press.

Reuscher, G. et al. 2011. *Mehr Wohlstand – weniger Ressourcen. Instrumente für mehr Ressourceneffizienz in Wirtschaft und Gesellschaft.* Düsseldorf: Zukünftige Technologien Consulting der VDI Technologiezentrum GmbH.

Roemer, J. E. 1999. Does democracy engender justice? In I. Shapiro and C. Hacker-Cordon (eds.), *Democracy's Value.* Cambridge: Cambridge University Press, pp. 56-68.

Roodhouse, M. 2007. Rationing returns: a solution to global warming? History and Policy Journal.
http://www.historyandpolicy.org/policy-papers/papers/rationing-returns-a-solution-to-global-warming

Rosar, U., M. Klein and T. Beckers 2008. The frog pond beauty contest: Physical attractiveness and electoral success of constituency candidates at the North Rhine-Westphalia state elections of 2005. *European Journal of Political Research* 47:64-79.

Rostboll, C. F. 2005. Preferences and Paternalism on Freedom and Deliberative Democracy. *Political Theory* 33(3):370-396.

Rousseau, J.-J. 2002. *The Social Contract and The First and Second Discourses Edited and with an Introduction by Susan Dunn with essays by Gita May, Robert N. Bellah, David Bromwich, Conor Cruise O'Brien.* New Haven and London: Yale University Press.

Rousseau, J.-J. 2008. *Vom Gesellschaftsvertrag oder Grundsätze des Staatsrechts.* Stuttgart: Reclam.

Rousseau, J.-J. 2009. Extract 3: The State of War. In M. G. Forsyth, H. M. A. Keens-Soper and P. Savigear (eds.), *The Theory of International Relations. Selected Texts from Gentili to Treitschke.* New Brunswick and London: AldineTransaction, pp. 167-177.

Sagoff, M. 2002. Are Environmental Values All Instrumental? In J. M. Gillroy and J. Bowersox (eds.), *The Moral Austerity of Environmental Decision: Sustainability, Democracy, and Normative Argument in Policy and Law.* Kindle Edition: Duke University Press.

Sahlins, M. 1972. *Stone Age Economics.* New York: Aldine de Guyter.

Sakrar, S. 2012. Öko-Sozialismus. Ergebnis meiner Suche nach einer Alternative. In B. Woynowski et al. (eds.), *Wirtschaft ohne Wachstum?! Notwendigkeit und Ansätze einer Wachstumswende.* Freiburg: Institut für Forstökonomie, pp. 273-280.

Sandbag.
http://www.sandbag.org.uk

Sanders, B. 2009. *The Green Zone: The Environmental Costs of Militarism. With a foreword by Mike Davis.* Oakland, Edinburgh and Baltimore: AK Press.

Saretzki, T. 2011. Der Klimawandel und die Problemlösungsfähigkeit der Demokratie. In S. S. Schüttemeyer (ed.), *Politik im Klimawandel. Keine Macht für gerechte Lösungen?* Baden-Baden: Nomos, pp. 41-63.

Saward, M. 2006. Representation. In A. Dobson and R. Eckersley (eds.), *Political Theory and the Ecological Challenge.* New York: Cambridge University Press, pp. 183-199.

Schlosberg, D. 2003. The Justice of Environmental Justice: Reconciling Equity, Recognition, and Participation in a Political Movement. In A. Light and A. De-Shalit (eds.), *Moral and Political Reasoning in Environmental Practice*. Cambridge and London: MIT Press, pp. 77-107.

Schmidt, M. G. 2010. *Demokratietheorien. Eine Einführung*. Berlin: Bundeszentrale für politische Bildung.

Schmidt Stiedenroth, K. 2010. *Infertility in Pakistan: Experience and Health Seeking Behavior among Baloch Women in a Karachi Slum*. Heidelberg: Bibliothek des Südasien-Instituts der Universität Heidelberg.

Schmitt, C. 2004 (1932). *Legality and Legitimacy. Translated and edited by J. Seitzer with an introduction by J.P. McCormick*. Kindle Edition: Duke University Press.

Scholtes, F. 2010. Whose Sustainability? Environmental Domination and Sen's Capability Approach. *Oxford Development Studies 38(3)*:289-307.

Schrecker, T. 1998. Sustainability, Growth and Distributive Justice: Questioning Environmental Absolutism. In J. Lemons, L. Westra and R. Goodland (eds.), *Ecological Sustainability and Integrity: Concepts and Approaches*. Dordrecht: Springer, pp. 218-234.

Schultze, R.-O. 2004. Demokratie. In D. Nohlen and R.-O. Schultze (eds.), *Lexikon der Politikwissenschaft. Theorien, Methoden, Begriffe. Band 1 A-M*. Nördlingen: C. H. Beck, pp. 124-127.

Schumpeter, J. 2003. *Capitalism, Socialism and Democracy. With a new introduction by Richard Swedberg*. London and New York: Routledge.

Schüttemeyer, S. S. (ed.) 2011. *Politik im Klimawandel. Keine Macht für gerechte Lösungen?* Baden-Baden: Nomos.

Schüttemeyer, S. S. 2011a. Politik im Klimawandel. Keine Macht für gerechte Lösungen? Eröffnungsvortrag zum 24. Kongress der Deutschen Vereinigung für Politische Wissenschaft. In S. S. Schüttemeyer (ed.), *Politik im Klimawandel. Keine Macht für gerechte Lösungen?* Baden-Baden: Nomos, pp. 11-22.

Scott, J. C. 1990. *Domination and the Arts of Resistance. Hidden Transcripts*. New Haven and London: Yale University Press.

Scruggs, L. 2009. *Democracy and environmental protection: an empirical analysis.* http://www.sp.uconn.edu/~scruggs/mpsa09e.pdf

Scruggs, L. and S. Benegal 2012. Declining public concern about climate change: Can we blame the great recession? *Global Environmental Change 22(2)*:505-515.

Scruton, R. 2006. Conservatism. In A. Dobson and R. Eckersley (eds.), *Political Theory and the Ecological Challenge*. New York: Cambridge University Press, pp. 7-19.

Sears, D. O., L. Huddy and R. Jervis (eds.) 2003. *Oxford Handbook of Political Psychology*. New York: Oxford University Press.

Seidl, I. and A. Zahrnt 2012. Wirtschaftswachstum: Hindernis für eine Politik in den „Limits to Growth". *GAIA 21(2)*:108-115.

Seitzer, J. (ed.) 2004. *Carl Schmitt. Legality and Legitimacy. Translated and edited by J. Seitzer with an introduction by J. P. McCormick*. Kindle Edition: Duke University Press.

Sen, A. 1998. *Resources, Values, and Development*. Cambridge and London: Harvard University Press.

Sen, A. 1993. Liberty and social choice. In W. J. B. Booth, P. James and H. Madwell (eds.), *Politics and rationality*. New York: Cambridge University Press, pp. 11-32.

Seyfang, G., I. Lorenzoni and M. Nye 2007. Personal carbon trading: Notional concept or workable proposition? Exploring theoretical, ideological and practical underpinnings. *CSERGE Working Paper EDM 7-3.*

Shahar, D. C. 2015. Rejecting Eco-Authoritarianism, Again. *Environmental Values 24(3)*:345-366.

Shapiro, I. 1999. *Democratic Justice.* New Haven and London: Yale University Press.

Shapiro, I. and C. Hacker-Cordon (eds.) 1999. *Democracy's Value.* Cambridge: Cambridge University Press.

Shapiro, I and C. Hacker-Cordon 1999a. Promises and disappointments: reconsidering democracy's value. In I. Shapiro and C. Hacker-Cordon (eds.), *Democracy's Value.* Cambridge: Cambridge University Press, pp. 1-19.

Shearman, D. and J. W. Smith 2007. *The Climate Challenge and the Failure of Democracy.* Westport: Praeger.

Shen, J. 1998. China's Future Population and Development Challenges. *The Geographical Journal 164(1)*:32-40.

Shin, S. 2013. China's failure of policy innovation: the case of sulphur dioxide emission trading. *Environmental Politics 22(6)*:918-934.

Short, C. 2009. The Forces Shaping Radical Politics Today. In J. Pugh (ed.), *What is radical politics today?* Basingstoke: Palgrave Macmillan, pp. 59-68.

Shum, R. Y. 2009. Can Attitudes Predict Outcomes? Public Opinion, Democratic Institutions and Environmental Polity. *Environmental Policy and Governance 19*:281-295.

Simmons, R. T. 2011. *Beyond Politics. The Roots of Government Failure. With a Foreword by Gordon Tullock.* Kindle Edition: Independent Institute.

Simon, J. 1983. *The Ultimate Resource.* Princeton: Princeton University Press.

Singer, P. 1975. *Animal Liberation.* New York: Harper Collins Publishing.

Singer, P. 1994. *How are We to live. Ethics in an age of Self-Interest.* Milsons Point: Random House.

Singer, P. 1999. *A Darwinian Left. Politics, Evolution and Cooperation.* Kindle Edition: Yale University Press.

Singer, P. (ed.) 2006. *In Defense of Animals. Second Wave.* Padstow: Blackwell Publishing.

Singer, P. 2013. *The Ethics of Big Food.*
http://www.project-syndicate.org/commentary/the-top-ten-food-companies--ethical-performance-by-peter-singer#ZouorzeP5eEJoeGr.99

Sjöstedt, M. 2014. Enforcement and Compliance in African Fisheries: The Dynamic Interaction between Ruler and Ruled, In A. Duit (ed.), *State and Environment. The Comparative Study of Environmental Governance.* Cambridge and London: MIT Press, pp. 265-292.

Skoruspski, J. 2013. The Liberal Critique of Democracy. In D. A. Bell and C. Li (eds.), *The East Asian Challenge for Democracy. Political Meritocracy in Comparative Perspective.* Kindle Edition: Cambridge University Press, pp. 115-137.

Smith, G. 2004. Liberal democracy and the shaping of environmentally enlightened citizens. In Y. Levy and M. Wissenburg (eds.), *Liberal Democracy and Environmentalism: The End of Environmentalism?* Kindle Edition: Routledge, p. 139-153.

Spash, C. L. 1998. Investigating Individual Motives for Environmental Action: Lexigrapraphic Preferences, Beliefs and Attitudes. In J. Lemons, L. Westra and R. Goodland (eds.), *Ecological Sustainability and Integrity: Concepts and Approaches*. Dordrecht: Springer, pp. 46-62.

Spash, C. L. 2007. Changing Climates, Changing Values, Changing Editors: 'All Change'. *Environmental Values 16(2):*143-147.

Spiegel Online 2012. *'Politicians Haven't Listened': Merkel Climate Advisor Blasts Global Inaction* http://www.spiegel.de/international/world/merkel-climate-advisor-blasts-politicians-for-doing-too-little-a-868024.html

Spitz, D. 1965. *Patterns of Anti-Democratic Thought. Revised Edition*. London: Collier-Macmillan.

Spivak, G. 1988. Can the Subalterns speak? In C. Nelson and L. Grossberg (eds.), *Marxism and the Interpretation of Culture*. Chicago: University of Illinois Press, pp. 271-313.

Sprinz, D. F. 2009. Long-term environmental policy: definition, knowledge, future research. *Global Environmental Politics 9(3):*1-8.

Sommerer, T. 2014. Early Bird or Copycat, Leader or Laggard? A Comparison of Cross-National Patterns of Environmental Policy Change. In A. Duit (ed.), *State and Environment. The Comparative Study of Environmental Governance*. Cambridge and London: MIT Press, pp. 149-177.

Stadelmann-Steffen, I. 2011. Citizens as veto players: climate change policy and the constraints of direct democracy. *Environmental Politics 20(4):*485-507.

Stehr, N. 2013. An Inconvenient Democracy: Knowledge and Climate Change. *Society 50(1):*55-60.

Stephens, P. H. G. 2001a. Green Liberalisms: Nature, Agency and the Good. *Environmental Politics 10(3):*1-22.

Stephens, P. H. G. 2001b. The Green Only Blooms amid the Millian Flowers: A Reply to Marcel Wissenburg. *Environmental Politics 10 (3):*43-47.

Stephens, P. H. G., J. Barry and A. Dobson (eds.) 2006. *Contemporary Environmental Politics. From margins to mainstream*. London and New York: Routledge.

Stern, N. H. et al. 2006. *Stern Review: The economics of climate change*. London: HM treasury.

Stretton, H. 1976. *Capitalism, Socialism, and the Environment*. Cambridge: Cambridge University Press.

Sustainable World Initiative 2014. *The challenge for humanity in the 21st century – adapting and sizing ourselves to fit within the capacity of one planet.* http://mahb.stanford.edu/blog/the-challenge-for-humanity/

Swyngedeouw, E. 2011. Climate Change as Post-Political and the Post-Democratic Populism. In S. S. Schüttemeyer (ed.), *Politik im Klimawandel. Keine Macht für gerechte Lösungen?* Baden-Baden: Nomos, pp. 65-80.

Taber, C. S. 2003. Information Processing and Public Opinion. In D. O. Sears, L. Huddy and R. Jervis (eds.), *Oxford Handbook of Political Psychology*. New York: Oxford University Press, pp. 376-433.

Talshir, G. 2004. The role of environmentalism. From The Silent Spring to The Silent Revolution. In Y. Levy and M. Wissenburg (eds.), *Liberal Democracy and Environmentalism: The End of Environmentalism?* Kindle Edition: Routledge, pp. 10-31.

Taylor, B. 2013. Resistance: Do the Ends Justify the Means? In The Worldwatch Institute (ed.), *State of the World 2013: Is Sustainability Still Possible?* Kindle Edition: Island Press.

Thaler, R. H. and C. R. Sunstein 2009. *Nudge: Improving Decisions About Health, Wealth, and Happiness.* Kindle Edition: Penguin Books.

The Worldwatch Institute 2013 (ed.). *State of the World 2013: Is Sustainability Still Possible?* Kindle Edition: Island Press.

Thoreau, H. D. (1849). *Civil Disobedience.* Kindle Edition: A Public Domain Book.

Thompson, D. (ed.) 1966. *Political Ideas. The study of the most significant and fundamental ideas of eminent European political thinkers of the last five hundred years.* Bungay: Penguin Books.

Thompson, D. 1966a. Rousseau and the General Will. In D. Thompson (ed.), *Political Ideas. The study of the most significant and fundamental ideas of eminent European political thinkers of the last five hundred years.* Bungay: Penguin Books, pp. 95-106.

Thompson, M. 2014. The Politics Philippine Presidents make. Presidential-style, Patronage-based, or Regime Relational. *Critical Asian Studies 46(3):*433-460.

Tilly, C. 2003. Inequality, Democratization, and De-Democratization. *Sociological Theory 21(1):*37-43.

Tomasi, J. 2013. *Free market fairness.* Kindle Edition: Princeton University Press.

Tong, Y. 2011. Morality, Benevolence, and Responsibility: Regime Legitimacy in China from Past to the Present. *Journal of Chinese Political Science 16(2):*141-159.

Townsend, J. 1786. *Dissertation on the Poor Laws.* http://socserv.socsci.mcmaster.ca/~econ/ugcm/3ll3/townsend/poorlaw.html

TransFair e.V. 2015. *Gemeinsam Mehr Erreichen. Jahres- und Wirkungsbericht* www.fairtrade-deutschland.de/jahresbericht-2014-2015/pdf/2015_transfair_jahresbericht_web.pdf

Tremmel, J. 2011. Klimawandel und Gerechtigkeit. In S. S. Schüttemeyer (ed.), *Politik im Klimawandel. Keine Macht für gerechte Lösungen?* Baden-Baden: Nomos, pp. 127-158.

Turner, G. M. 2008. A comparison of the limits to growth with thirty years of reality. Global *Environmental Change 18(3):*397-411.

United Nations. http://www.un.org/

United Nations 2014. *Objective information on military matters, including transparency of military expenditures. Report of the Secretary-General.* http://www.un.org/ga/search/view_doc.asp?symbol=A/69/135

United Nations 2015. *World Population Prospects. The 2015 Revision* http://esa.un.org/unpd/wpp/Publications/Files/Key_Findings_WPP_2015.pdf

United Nations Population Fund 2009. *State of the World 2009. Facing a changing world: women, pollution, climate.* http://www.unfpa.org/sites/default/files/pub-pdf/state_of_world_population_2009.pdf

Veauthier, S. 2012. Umweltproteste in China. Alles BANANA? *GIGA Focus 8.* https://www.giga-hamburg.de/de/system/files/publications/gf_asien_1208.pdf

Verhulst, B., M. Lodge and H. Lavine 2010. The Attractiveness Halo: Why Some Candidates are Perceived More Favorably than Others. *Journal of Nonverbal Behavior 23(2):*111-117.

Vincent, A. 1998. *Liberalism and the Environment. Environmental Values 7*:443-459.

Wallack, M. 2004. The minimum irreversible harm principle. Green inter-generational liberalism. In Y. Levy and M. Wissenburg (eds.), *Liberal Democracy and Environmentalism: The End of Environmentalism?* Kindle Edition: Routledge, pp. 167-178.

Wang, X. et al. 2010. Climate, Desertification, and the Rise and Collapse of China's Historical Dynasties. *Human Ecology 38*:157-172.

Wapner, P. 2010. Sacrifice in an Age of Comfort. In M. Maniates and J. M. Meyer (eds.), *Environmental Politics of Sacrifices*. Cambridge: MIT Press, pp. 33-60.

Warburton, D. (ed.) 1998. *Community and Sustainable Development: Participation in the Future*. London: Earthscan.

Ward, H. 2006. Citizens' juries and valuing the environment. In P. H. G. Stephens, J. Barry and A. Dobson (eds.), *Contemporary Environmental Politics. For margins to mainstream*. London and New York: Routledge, pp. 276-295.

Ward, H. 2008. Liberal democracy and sustainability. *Environmental Politics 17(3)*:386-409.

Wasky, A. J. 2011. Autocracy. In G. T. Kurian et al. (eds.), *The Encyclopedia of Political Science. Vol. 1-5*. Washington: CQ Press, pp.106-107.

Watkins, J. W. N. 1966. John Stuart Mill and the Liberty of the Individual. In D. Thompson (ed.), *Political Ideas. The study of the most significant and fundamental ideas of eminent European political thinkers of the last five hundred years*. Bungay: Penguin Books, pp. 154-167.

Weber, M. 2009. *Die protestantische Ethik*. Köln: Anaconda.

Weber, M. 2014. *Wirtschaft und Gesellschaft. Grundriß der verstehenden Soziologie*. Kindle Edition: Saga-Verlag.

Wehling, P. 2002. Dynamic Constellations of the Individual, Society, and Nature: Critical Theory and Environmental Sociology. In R. Dunlap et al. (eds.), *Sociological Theory and the Environment*. Lanham: Rowman & Littlefield, pp. 144-166.

Welzer, H. 2011. *Mentale Infrastrukturen: Wie das Wachstum in die Welt und in die Seelen kam. Schriften zur Ökologie Band 14*. Berlin: Heinrich Böll Stiftung.

Westra, L. 1998a. *Living in Integrity. A Global Ethic to Restore a Fragmented Earth*. Lanham: Rowman and Littlefield Publishers.

Westra, L. 1998b. Why We Need a Non-Anthropocentric Environmental Evaluation of Technology for Public Policy. In J. Lemons, L. Westra and R. Goodland (eds.), *Ecological Sustainability and Integrity: Concepts and Approaches*. Dordrecht: Springer, pp. 266-289.

Westra, L. 2013. Institutionalized Environmental Violence and Human Rights. In D. Pimentel, L. Westra and R. F. Noss (eds.), *Ecological Integrity: Integrating Environment, Conversation and Health*. Kindle Edition: Island Press.

Westra, L. et al. 2013. Ecological Integrity and the Aims of the Global Integrity Project. In D. Pimentel, L. Westra and R. F. Noss (eds.), *Ecological Integrity: Integrating Environment, Conversation and Health*. Kindle Edition: Island Press.

Whiteside, K. 2006. *Precautionary Politics: Principle and Practice in Confronting Environmental Risk*. Cambridge and London: MIT Press

Whitford, A. and K. Wong 2009. Political and Social Foundations for Environmental Sustainability. *Political Research Quarterly 62(1)*:190-204.

Wilkinson, R. and K. Pickett 2011. Nachhaltigkeit braucht Gleichheit. In Forum Wissenschaft & Umwelt (ed.), *Demokratie und Umweltkrise. Brauchen wir mehr Mitbestimmung?* München: oekom, pp. 81-82.

Williams, J. 2010. Bikes, Sticks, Carrots. In M. Maniates and J. M. Meyer (eds.), *Environmental Politics of Sacrifices*. Cambridge: MIT Press, pp. 247-270.

Wissenburg, M. 2001a. Sustainability and the Limits of Liberalism. In J. Barry and M. Wissenburg (eds.), *Sustaining Liberal Democracy. Ecological Challenges and Opportunities*. New York: Palgrave, pp. 192-204.

Wissenburg, M. 2001b. Liberalism is Always Greener on the Other Side of Mill: A Reply to Piers Stephens. *Environmental Politics 10(3)*:23-42.

Wissenburg, M. 2002. An Extension of the Rawlsian Savings Principle to Liberal Theories of Justice in General. In A. Dobson (ed.), *Fairness and Futurity. Essays on Environmental Sustainability and Social Justice*. New York: Oxford University Press, pp.pp. 173-198.

Wissenburg, M. 2004. Little green lies. On the redundancy of 'environment'. In Y. Levy and M. Wissenburg (eds.), *Liberal Democracy and Environmentalism: The End of Environmentalism?* Kindle Edition: Routledge, p. 60-71.

Wissenburg, M. 2006. Liberalism. In A. Dobson and R. Eckersley (eds.), *Political Theory and the Ecological Challenge*. New York: Cambridge University Press, pp. 20-34.

Worcester, R. 1997. Public Opinion and the Environment. In M. Jacobs (ed.), *Greening the Millennium? The New Politics of the Environment*. Malden: The Political Quarterly, pp. 160-173.

World Bank.
http://www.worldbank.org

World Environmental Organization 2015.
http://www.world.org

Woynowski, B. et al. (eds.) 2012. *Wirtschaft ohne Wachstum?! Notwendigkeit und Ansätze einer Wachstumswende*. Freiburg: Institut für Forstökonomie.

Wright, J. R. 2012. Unemployment and the Democratic Electoral Advantage. *American Political Science Review 106(2)*:685-702.

Wu, X. and B. Cutter 2011. Who votes for public environmental goods in California?:Evidence from a spatial analysis of voting for environmental ballot measures. *Ecological Economics 70(3)*:554-563.

Wurster, S. 2013. Comparing ecological sustainability in autocracies and democracies. *Contemporary Politics 19(1)*:76-93.

Yan, T. and Q. Wang 2004. Environmental migration and sustainable development in the upper reaches of the Yangtze River. *Population and Environment 25(6)*:613-636.

Young, O. R. 1996. 'Monkeywrenching' and the Process of Democracy. In F. Mathews (ed.), *Ecology and Democracy*. London: Frank Cass, pp. 195-209.

Young, O. R. 2009. Governance for sustainable development in a world of rising interdependencies. In M. A. Delmas and O. R. Young. (eds.), *Governance for the Environment*. Kindle Edition: Cambridge University Press, pp. 12-39.

Yi, Z. 2007. Options for Fertility Policy Transition in China. *Population and Development Review 33(2)*:215-246.

Zamir, T. 2007. *Ethics and the Beast: A Specieist Argument for Animal Liberation*. Princeton and Woodstock: Princeton University Press.

Zavestoski, S. 2003. Constructing and Maintaining Ecological Identities: The Strategies of Deep Ecologists. In S. Clayton and S. Opotov (eds.), *Identity and the Environment. The Psychological Significance of Nature.* Cambridge and London: MIT Press, pp. 299-315.

Zeller, C. 2011. Warum der Kapitalismus nicht „clean" wird. Eine Replik zu Ulrich Brand und Markus Wissen. In Forum Wissenschaft & Umwelt (ed.), *Demokratie und Umweltkrise. Brauchen wir mehr Mitbestimmung?* München: oekom, pp. 106-109.

Zhang, L. et al. 2013. Power politics in the revision of China's Environmental Protection Law. *Environmental Politics* 22(6):1029-1035.

Zilberman, D. et al. 2013. *Lessons from the California GM Labelling Proposition on the State of Crop Biotechnology.*
http://ageconsearch.umn.edu/bitstream/149851/2/Final%20Labeling%20Paper%20for%20AAEA%20Conference.pdf

Zimmerman, M. et al. (eds.) 2001. *Environmental Philosophy: From Animal Rights to Radical Ecology.* Upper Saddle River: Prentice Hall.

Zizek, S. 2012. Das >>unendliche Urteil<< der Demokratie. In G. Agamben et al., *Demokratie? Eine Debatte. Mit Beiträgen von G. Agamben, A. Badiou, D. Bensaid, W. Brown, J.-L. Nancy, J. Ranciere, K. Ross und S. Zizek.* Berlin: Suhrkamp, pp. 116-136.

350.org.
http://www.350.org/about/science/

LIST OF ABBREVIATIONS

BMEL Bundesministerium für Ernährung und Landwirtschaft [German Ministry of Food and Agriculture]

CCP Chinese Communist Party

CO2 Carbon Dioxide

EC European Commission

EU European Union

EPI Environmental Performance Index

FAO Food and Agriculture Organisation of the United Nations

GMO Genetically Modified Organism

IPCC International Panel on Climate Change

LTG Limits to Growth

NGO Nongovernmental Organisation

Ppm Parts per million

PRC People's Republic of China

UN United Nations

UNFPA United Nations Population Fund

US United States

WMO World Metrological Organization